INDUSTRIAL COMPETITIVENESS

Benchmarking Business Environments in the Global Economy

ORGANISATION FOR ECONOMIC CO-OPERATION AND DEVELOPMENT

ORGANISATION FOR ECONOMIC CO-OPERATION AND DEVELOPMENT

Pursuant to Article 1 of the Convention signed in Paris on 14th December 1960, and which came into force on 30th September 1961, the Organisation for Economic Co-operation and Development (OECD) shall promote policies designed:

- to achieve the highest sustainable economic growth and employment and a rising standard of living in Member countries, while maintaining financial stability, and thus to contribute to the development of the world economy;
- to contribute to sound economic expansion in Member as well as non-member countries in the process of economic development; and
- to contribute to the expansion of world trade on a multilateral, non-discriminatory basis in accordance with international obligations.

The original Member countries of the OECD are Austria, Belgium, Canada, Denmark, France, Germany, Greece, Iceland, Ireland, Italy, Luxembourg, the Netherlands, Norway, Portugal, Spain, Sweden, Switzerland, Turkey, the United Kingdom and the United States. The following countries became Members subsequently through accession at the dates indicated hereafter: Japan (28th April 1964), Finland (28th January 1969), Australia (7th June 1971), New Zealand (29th May 1973), Mexico (18th May 1994), the Czech Republic (21st December 1995), Hungary (7th May 1996), Poland (22nd November 1996) and the Republic of Korea (12th December 1996). The Commission of the European Communities takes part in the work of the OECD (Article 13 of the OECD Convention).

Publié en français sous le titre :

LA COMPÉTITIVITÉ INDUSTRIELLE
Comparaison internationale de l'environnement des entreprises

FOREWORD

Globalisation of industry is increasing international competition, which influences the industrial competitiveness of countries. Governments have a role in optimising the framework conditions for industry, or their business environment, through appropriate policies. In order to gauge the competitiveness of one country against that of other countries, an international benchmark, or a comparison relative to international standards in these framework parameters, is necessary.

After carrying out several studies on the globalisation of industry, the OECD Industry Committee initiated a project in 1994 on developing indicators for these framework conditions for industry. This publication represents the outcome of part of this project, and compiles a summary of benchmarking indicators on the following eight parameters: research and development infrastructure; education and the labour force; corporate governance environments; employment regulations; labour costs; corporate taxation; energy costs; telecommunication costs and infrastructure.

This report represents a first attempt to produce international comparisons of such parameters in a single volume as this information is generally dispersed in various reports and publications. Not all OECD Member countries could be covered, and other parameters, important for industrial competitiveness, have not yet been addressed. Each parameter is represented as a stand-alone chapter, and no linking of parameters or ranking in order of importance has been made, as this could give rise to differing interpretations.

Areas selected concentrate on parameters representing inputs to corporate processes. The publication does not analyse these parameters, but provides, in standardized formats, comparable information for a number of OECD countries. The figures thus speak for themselves, enabling the reader to use the information provided for his/her own analysis.

Co-operation with other OECD Directorates, and especially with the Directorate for Education, Employment, Labour and Social Affairs and the Directorate for Financial, Fiscal and Enterprise Affairs, has given access to data and expertise on the various parameters and is appreciated. The project was co-ordinated by Mr. Rauf Gönenç of the Industry Division of the Directorate for Science, Technology and Industry, assisted by Mr. Osman Erogan, consultant. The Industry Committee recommended the derestriction of the report, which is published on the responsibility of the Secretary-General of the OECD.

TABLE OF CONTENTS

Chapter 3

Chapter 7

Chapter 8

Chapter 9

INTRODUCTION: THE CHALLENGE OF GLOBALISATION

OECD area enterprises operate in a rapidly globalising economy, in which product markets are becoming integrated, a world-wide stock of technical and managerial knowledge is accessible, and financial resources are available from global capital markets. While changes due to this evolution have not fully occurred in all countries, sectors and companies, globalisation is the new paradigm for business strategy, economic growth and public policy. At the same time, enterprises remain rooted in the national business environment where most of their key operations are based. This environment constitutes the firm's "citizenship" and is the source of distinctive framework parameters for its operations and performance.

In the light of the framework conditions available in different national and regional environments, globalised firms tend to locate their activities where they can be carried out in the most cost-effective and productive way. In the global economy, such environments have become a major determinant of location and investment decisions by both local and multinational firms, and they affect both employment and income generation.

The Framework Conditions for Industry project was developed in response to the interest of OECD governments in comparing the characteristics, strengths and weaknesses of their domestic business environments in a dynamic perspective. This report provides country-specific snapshots in matrix form and *benchmarks* in eight areas: research and development infrastructure; educational profile of the labour force; corporate governance environments; employment regulations; labour costs; corporate taxation; energy costs; and telecommunication costs and infrastructure. It does not aim to rank countries on a unidimensional scale of competitiveness. Rather, its objective is an overall review of the main distinctive characteristics of national business environments.

National business environments are more or less supportive of different types of business activity, depending on the latter's cost structure, production factor needs, infrastructure and input requirements, organisational and labour relation prerequisites, etc. Assessing the impact of these diverse factors on the competitiveness of firms in various areas would require extensive analysis of industry and firm surveys. Establishing the general (macro level) attractiveness and supportiveness of national business environments for private investment – while taking into account the uneven growth of different industries and the specific framework needs of the most rapidly growing ones – would be the next step in this line of inquiry.

The information presented below is of a summary nature and does not address the details and complexities of the parameters discussed. Its goal is to provide Member countries with the information necessary to compare the basic elements of their domestic business environment to that of other OECD countries. The parameters selected are not ranked in any particular order, and the data should be not be interpreted in isolation and out of context.

Research and development infrastructure

The profile of R&D infrastructures depends on government policies and on the sectoral orientations of economies. When R&D infrastructures are purposefully and efficiently governed, firms located in environments with a strong infrastructure gain an edge over their competitors in product and process innovations and in productivity.

Certain OECD Member countries devote far more resources to R&D than others: *the share of R&D in GDP* ranges from 0.32 per cent in Mexico to 3.26 per cent in Sweden, with an OECD average of 1.7 per cent. In some countries, most R&D activities take place in government laboratories and universities, while in others most are carried out by private enterprises. The *proportion of researchers in private enterprises* in the total research population ranges from about 20 per cent in New Zealand and Iceland to around 70 per cent in Switzerland and Japan, with an OECD average of some 40 per cent. In addition, there are major differences in the *sectoral orientation* of R&D: New Zealand and Iceland focus 25 per cent of their R&D efforts on agro-technologies, while Japan and Germany devote more than 60 per cent of R&D to industrial machinery.

The quality of the R&D infrastructure has become more important for two reasons. One is changing research priorities. Until the early 1980s, more weight was given to energy and environment issues in national research expenditures; there has since been a shift towards activities that promote firms' competitiveness. This trend has been supportive of private R&D efforts and is echoed in an increase in the share of private expenditures on R&D. The second is the cost of R&D. R&D costs have been rising because ever more sophisticated human and material resources are needed for leading-edge R&D. As a result, the minimum efficient scale of research facilities has increased, as has the demand for research co-operation and consortia between enterprises and public research facilities, on the one hand, and among enterprises on the other. The responsiveness of national R&D institutions to these arrangements becomes a major component of their contribution to industrial competitiveness.

Education and the labour force

The quality of the labour force is a major contributor to business sector performance. The educational and skills profile of the labour force affects how well or how poorly firms can carry out the full range of management, research, engineering, manufacturing, marketing, finance, etc. The supply of various skills in the labour pool partly determines their availability and cost on the domestic labour market.

Resources dedicated to education and training vary widely across OECD countries. They are not, however, a satisfactory indicator of a nation's educational efforts, because expenditure needs are very sensitive to the population's age structure. *Educational attainment* (*i.e.* number of years of schooling) is a more valuable indicator of the basic skills present in labour force entrants, even if it does not capture the quality of the educational system. On the basis of this indicator, there are important differences among OECD countries: in some, most of the working population has below secondary-level education; in others, the bulk of the workforce has received upper secondary education. The proportion of college-educated workers in the active population nowhere exceeds 25 per cent, and is generally around 10 per cent.

Educational attainment is also an important factor in participation in the labour force and in employability. Countries display large differences in unemployment rates by level of education, a reflection of mismatches in labour force supply and demand. Individuals with high-level vocational education have the lowest unemployment rates in all countries.

Countries differ significantly in terms of the *professional specialisation* of the highly skilled segments of the labour force. Graduates in the physical sciences and engineering account for between 30 and 40 per cent of degrees granted in Switzerland and Germany, while most university degrees in other OECD countries are obtained in law and in liberal arts and the social sciences.

Corporate governance environments

The rules and practices that influence the allocation and monitoring of firms' capital resources – including the legal and practical procedures that influence key investment and management decisions – constitute a country's corporate governance environment. Countries differ significantly in this respect, as well as in the respective *rights*, *duties* and *responsibilities* of the main participants in the corporate process, i.e. investors, creditors, management, employees, board of directors, etc.

National corporate governance environments are compared in this report in three main respects: *i) laws and regulations*; *ii) standard business practices*; and *iii) implicit social rules.* All influence significantly the corporate governance process. They affect, in particular, the concentration of ownership in listed corporations (the average holdings of the five largest owners is around 25 per cent in the United States, 33 per cent in Japan, and 42 per cent in Germany); the influence and control of the principal banks over large enterprises; the composition and role of independent corporate boards; the types and sources of information used in governance decisions; and the use of restructuring mechanisms such as take-overs and bankruptcies.

Investors' expectation of profitability is a clear quantitative indicator of differences in corporate governance mechanisms. Despite the globalisation of capital markets, expected rates of return from investments remain uneven. While accounting differences influence the results, the reported annual return on equity of the top 20 largest firms over the past three years varied from around 5 per cent in Japan and Italy to over 20 per cent in the United States and the United Kingdom.

Owing to two recent developments, the importance of corporate governance in firm performance is increasing. First, owing to *structural changes*, corporate investments involve more intangible, riskier and often larger fixed investments. Investors often have to make investment decisions more flexibly and quicker; they therefore need better information, monitoring and control tools. Second, *liberalisation and globalisation in financial markets* make investors more sensitive, and much more demanding, with respect to the return to their investments. National corporate governance environments must respond to both challenges.

Employment regulations

Employment regulations determine the options available to firms for managing labour relations and establishing and maintaining contracts with employees. Today, incentive-enhancing (productivity-maximising) and cost-efficient contracts are a major element of firms' competitiveness. National environments differ greatly in terms of the institutional infrastructures they provide as they relate to *i) employment laws and regulations*; *ii) prevailing patterns of employment contracts*; and *iii) implicit societal expectations.*

Features of employment contracts affected by these differences, which are reviewed below, are: *working time rules*, *employment protection*, *wage bargaining procedures*, *employee representation*, and *firms' training responsibilities* for employees. A particularly notable difference concerns the respective roles of public legislation and free collective agreements.

In response to recent developments in technology, firm organisation and competition, all national jurisdictions are moving towards more flexible, less uniform, and more *ad hoc* employment rules across sectors, regions and companies. National regulatory environments are, however, not equally open to decentralisation of the regulation of employment contracts.

Labour costs

Labour costs are a key factor in firms' competitiveness. At the same time, productivity determines the wages that firms can afford to pay without losing competitive ground. Comparisons of labour costs should take both these dimensions into account.

Even within the OECD, there are wide differences in the *absolute levels of hourly compensation costs* for manufacturing workers. In 1993, they varied from US$2.56 in Mexico to US$25.70 in Germany, with an OECD average of US$16.07.

On the other hand, differences in productivity are reflected in *unit labour shares.* These are the ratio of labour compensation for all employees to value added. Calculated for 1993, they ranged from 0.27 in Mexico to 0.52 in Austria and 0.75 in Sweden, with an OECD average of 0.61.

Beyond these averages, *wage dispersion indicators* monitor the wage levels paid in different industries, and in this respect, the skills composition of the labour force appears to play a significant role. High-technology industries generally pay higher wages, followed by the medium- and low-technology industries. Japan, Spain and New Zealand, where the highest wages are observed in the medium-technology group, are the exception to this pattern.

Corporate taxation

Business enterprises pay taxes in order to operate in a given country and have access to its public services (national security, market institutions, enforcement of property rights, operation of basic infrastructures, etc.).

Corporate tax regimes directly affect firms' operating costs and influence the net profitability of their investments. Because the corporate tax system determines the minimum gross returns that must be earned before other (capital and labour) inputs are paid at market prices, taxation is an important consideration in firms' decisions on investment, location and capital structure.

The *corporate income tax rate* is the most visible and best-known element, but its net impact depends on incentives such as tax relief, credits and allowances. The *corporate income tax base* is influenced by the generosity of the depreciation system, the deductibility of various categories of expenses, and the provisions for R&D and other intangible investments. National corporate tax regimes differ in both respects. It is essential to cover both *tax rate* and *tax base* properly in international comparisons.

The complexity and intricacies of provisions in both areas are a striking feature of corporate tax regimes. In the past, these differences may have mattered less because of the relatively closed nature of savings-investment cycles in domestic financial markets. Today, the liberalisation of international capital movements and the international mobility of business investments tend to make international capital flows much more responsive to differences in tax regimes.

Energy costs

Maintaining an energy infrastructure that meets international standards of quality and cost is an important policy objective of OECD governments. Countries pursue these objectives through a range of regulations and market structures for *energy generation* and *distribution*. This report identifies a broad range of regulations and ownership institutions in energy utilities.

For industries that are heavy users of energy (*e.g.* steel, chemicals, pulp and paper), availability of energy with high capacity and at low price is a key framework factor and a significant decision parameter for localisation and investment decisions.

In 1994, electricity end-use prices for industry were high in Japan (0.173 US$/kWh) and Portugal (0.116 US$/kWh) and low in Sweden (0.037 US$/kWh) and New Zealand (0.036 US$/kWh). For indigenous production as a share of total primary energy supply, Norway had a very high 650 per cent, followed by Australia with some 200 per cent; Portugal and Luxembourg, instead, had shares of under 20 per cent.

Telecommunication costs and infrastructure

As providers of the infrastructure of the information economy, telecommunication services are becoming a key framework factor for OECD corporate sectors. The range and quality of services available and their prices influence users' technical choices and operating costs. The quality of the telecommunication system affects firms' ability to adopt leading-edge information technology applications.

The telecommunications infrastructure differs markedly among OECD countries, owing to uneven capital investment and a variety of institutional and regulatory arrangements. Despite active investment, competition and market access policies designed to promote the establishment of dynamic and cost-effective environments in many countries in recent years, completeness, quality and cost of these services continue to vary.

The number of *main telephone lines per 100 inhabitants* appears highest in Sweden, with nearly 70 main lines per 100 inhabitants in 1994, and lowest in Mexico, with less than 10. The OECD average is around 48. An indicator of recent progress is the number of *mobile telecommunication subscribers*. The Scandinavian countries lead the way: in 1994, Sweden had over nine cellular mobile subscribers per 100 inhabitants, with the OECD average above three. Another major indicator for corporate sector users, *business telephone charges* (both local and international), were highest in Turkey and lowest in the Scandinavian countries.

Chapter 1

GENERAL COUNTRY PROFILES

The data presented in the following country tables are compiled from various OECD sources. These are: *National Accounts*, *Foreign Trade by Commodities*, *Main Economic Indicators*, *OECD Economic Outlook*, *Historical Statistics*, *OECD Economic Surveys*, *Economic Structure at a Glance*: *OECD Indicators*, *Indicators of Industrial Activity* and *Main Science and Technology Indicators*.

Regional data is taken from *OECD Rural Indicators* of the OECD Rural Development Programme. Regional typology presented here is according to the methodology and definitions of this database.

UNITED STATES

Population (thousands) – 1995	263 090
Land area (thousand sq. kms.)	9 167
Employment (thousands) – 1995	124 900
Agriculture (percentage of total) – 1995	2.8
Industry (percentage of total) – 1995	19.4
Services (percentage of total) – 1995	74.4
Unemployment rate (standardised OECD rate) – 1995	5.6
Share of government in employment (percentage) – 1995	15.4
Government financial balance (percentage of GDP) – 1995	-2.0
GDP in US$ (current price and current exchange rate, bill.) – 1995	7 254
GDP growth (average annual volume growth over previous 5 years, %) – 1995	1.9
GDP per capita in US$ (current price and current exchange rate) – 1995	27 572
GDP per capita in US$ (in purchasing power parities) – 1995	27 572
Total industrial production (1990=100) – 1995	115.0
Gross national savings average (percentage of GDP) – 1991-95	15.1
Gross fixed capital formation (percentage of GDP) – 1995	16.7
Total exports of goods (million US$, 1995)	584 742.0
Food and beverages – 1995	50 226.7
Crude materials – 1995	37 360.7
Mineral fuels – 1995	10 478.1
Chemicals and miscellaneous products – 1995	203 815.6
Machinery and transport equipment – 1995	282 860.8
Total imports of goods (million US$, 1995)	743 445.0
Food and beverages – 1995	32 533.2
Crude materials – 1995	22 117.7
Mineral fuels – 1995	59 109.2
Chemicals and miscellaneous products – 1995	279 040.9
Machinery and transport equipment – 1995	350 643.8
Export of services (billion US$) – 1995	210.6
Import of services (billion US$) – 1995	142.2
Stock of Foreign Direct Investment (million US$)	
Inward investments – 1995	560 088
Outward investments – 1995	711 621
Technology balance of payments (export-import coverage ratio in percentage) – 1993	4.21
Gross public debt (percentage of GDP) – 1995	64.3
Consumer prices (all items, 1990=100) – 1995	116.6
Producer prices (wholesale, manufacturing industries, 1990=100) – 1995	107.4
Exchange rate (nominal, local currency per US$)	1.000

REGIONAL	National total or average	Predominantly rural regions	Significantly rural regions	Predominantly urbanised regions
Distribution of population (percentage, 1991)	100	36	34	30
GDP per capita (percentage, 1990)	100	..	..	..
Unemployment rate (percentage, 1990)	5.5	6.1	4.9	5.5

JAPAN

Population (thousands) – 1994	124 960
Land area (thousands sq. kms.)	378
Employment (thousands) – 1994	64 530
Agriculture (percentage of total) – 1994	5.8
Industry (percentage of total) – 1994	34.0
Services (percentage of total) – 1994	60.2
Unemployment rate (standardised OECD rate) – 1995	3.1
Share of government in employment (percentage) – 1993	8.2
Government financial balance (percentage of GDP) – 1995	-3.9
GDP in US$ (current price and current exchange rate, bill.) – 1995	5 108
GDP growth (average annual volume growth over previous 5 years, %) – 1994	2.1
GDP per capita in US$ (current price and current exchange rate) – 1994	36 732
GDP per capita in US$ (in purchasing power parities) – 1994	20 756
Total industrial production (1990=100) – 1995	96.2
Gross national savings average (percentage of GDP) – 1990-94	33.5
Gross fixed capital formation (percentage of GDP) – 1994	28.6
Total exports of goods (million US$, 1995)	443 047.2
Food and beverages – 1995	2 130
Crude materials – 1995	3 090
Mineral fuels – 1995	2 504.4
Chemicals and miscellaneous products – 1995	125 124
Machinery and transport equipment – 1995	310 198.8
Total imports of goods (million US$, 1995)	335 961.6
Food and beverages – 1995	51 087.6
Crude materials – 1995	32 952
Mineral fuels – 1995	53 344.8
Chemicals and miscellaneous products – 1995	120 655.2
Machinery and transport equipment – 1995	77 922
Export of services (billion US$) – 1995	258.0
Import of services (billion US$) – 1995	271.1
Stock of Foreign Direct Investment (million US$)	
Inward investments – 1993	16 884
Outward investments – 1993	259 795
Technology balance of payments (export-import coverage ratio in percentage) – 1993	1.1
Gross public debt (percentage of GDP) – 1994	73.2
Consumer prices (all items, 1990=100) – 1995	107.0
Producer prices (wholesale, manufacturing industries, 1990=100) – 1995	96.1
Exchange rate (nominal, local currency per US$) – 1995	94.1

REGIONAL	National total or average	Predominantly rural regions	Significantly rural regions	Predominantly urbanised regions
Distribution of population (percentage, 1991)	100	23	34	43
GDP per capita (percentage, 1990)	100	84	93	116
Unemployment rate (percentage, 1990)	3.0	2.9	2.9	3.2

GERMANY

Population (thousands) – 1994	81 407
Land area (thousands sq. kms.)	357
Employment (thousands) – 1994	35 894
Agriculture (percentage of total) – 1994	3.3
Industry (percentage of total) – 1994	37.6
Services (percentage of total) – 1994	59.1
Unemployment rate (standardised OECD rate) – 1995	8.2
Share of government in employment (percentage) – 1994	15.5
Government financial balance (percentage of GDP) – 1995	-3.5
GDP in US$ (current price and current exchange rate, bill.) – 1995	2 414.5
GDP growth (average annual volume growth over previous 5 years, %) – 1994	2.6
GDP per capita in US$ (current price and current exchange rate) – 1994	25 133
GDP per capita in US$ (in purchasing power parities) – 1994	19 675
Total industrial production (1990=100) – 1995	97.7
Gross national savings average (percentage of GDP) – 1990-94	22.2
Gross fixed capital formation (percentage of GDP) – 1994	18.5
Total exports of goods (million US$, 1995)	508 612.8
Food and beverages – 1995	23 880
Crude materials – 1995	11 040
Mineral fuels – 1995	4 700.4
Chemicals and miscellaneous products – 1995	216 793.2
Machinery and transport equipment – 1995	252 199.2
Total imports of goods (million US$, 1995)	443 348.4
Food and beverages – 1995	40 971.6
Crude materials – 1995	21 192
Mineral fuels – 1995	28 315.2
Chemicals and miscellaneous products – 1995	200 559.6
Machinery and transport equipment – 1995	152 310
Export of services (billion US$) – 1995	174.2
Import of services (billion US$) – 1995	219.5
Stock of Foreign Direct Investment (million US$)	
Inward investments – 1993	61 591
Outward investments – 1993	138 039
Technology balance of payments (export-import coverage ratio in percentage) – 1993	0.71
Gross public debt (percentage of GDP) – 1994	51.6
Consumer prices (all items, 1990=100) – 1995	119.0
Producer prices (wholesale, manufacturing industries, 1990=100) – 1995	106.9
Exchange rate (nominal, local currency per US$) – 1995	1.433

REGIONAL	National total or average	Predominantly rural regions	Significantly rural regions	Predominantly urbanised regions
Distribution of population (percentage, 1990)	100	8	26	66
GDP per capita (percentage, 1988)	100	81	88	106
Unemployment rate (percentage, 1991)	6.9	7.3	7.1	6.7

FRANCE

Population (thousands) – 1994	57 960
Land area (thousands sq. kms.)	552
Employment (thousands) – 1993	21 781
Agriculture (percentage of total) – 1993	5.1
Industry (percentage of total) – 1993	27.7
Services (percentage of total) – 1993	67.2
Unemployment rate (standardised OECD rate) – 1995	11.6
Share of government in employment (percentage) – 1993	24.3
Government financial balance (percentage of GDP) – 1995	-5.0
GDP in US$ (current price and current exchange rate, bill.) – 1995	1 538.6
GDP growth (average annual volume growth over previous 5 years, %) – 1994	1.1
GDP per capita in US$ (current price and current exchange rate) – 1994	22 944
GDP per capita in US$ (in purchasing power parities) – 1994	19 201
Total industrial production (1990=100) – 1995	99.0
Gross national savings average (percentage of GDP) – 1990-94	19.9
Gross fixed capital formation (percentage of GDP) – 1994	18.1
Total exports of goods (million US$, 1995)	280 568.4
Food and beverages – 1995	38 541.6
Crude materials – 1995	7 605.6
Mineral fuels – 1995	6 522
Chemicals and miscellaneous products – 1995	115 952.4
Machinery and transport equipment – 1995	111 945.6
Total imports of goods (million US$, 1995)	267 615.6
Food and beverages – 1995	27 073.2
Crude materials – 1995	10 894.8
Mineral fuels – 1995	18 308.4
Chemicals and miscellaneous products – 1995	116 334
Machinery and transport equipment – 1995	95 005.2
Export of services (billion US$) – 1995	256.6
Import of services (billion US$) – 1995	244.6
Stock of Foreign Direct Investment (million US$)	
Inward investments – 1993	107 461
Outward investments – 1993	147 262
Technology balance of payments (export-import coverage ratio in percentage) – 1993	0.72
Gross public debt (percentage of GDP) – 1994	54.7
Consumer prices (all items, 1990=100) – 1995	111.6
Producer prices (wholesale, manufacturing industries, 1990=100)	..
Exchange rate (nominal, local currency per US$) – 1995	4.991

REGIONAL	National total or average	Predominantly rural regions	Significantly rural regions	Predominantly urbanised regions
Distribution of population (percentage, 1990)	100	30	41	29
GDP per capita (percentage, 1988)	100	83	90	133
Unemployment rate (percentage, 1990)	10.9	11.1	11.1	10.5

UNITED KINGDOM

Population (thousands) – 1994	58 375
Land area (thousands sq. kms.)	254
Employment (thousands) – 1993	25 044
Agriculture (percentage of total) – 1993	2.2
Industry (percentage of total) – 1993	26.2
Services (percentage of total) – 1993	71.6
Unemployment rate (standardised OECD rate) – 1995	8.7
Share of government in employment (percentage) – 1993	16.8
Government financial balance (percentage of GDP) – 1995	-5.7
GDP in US$ (current price and current exchange rate, bill.) – 1995	1 103.5
GDP growth (average annual volume growth over previous 5 years, %) – 1994	0.8
GDP per capita in US$ (current price and current exchange rate) – 1994	17 468
GDP per capita in US$ (in purchasing power parities) – 1994	17 650
Total industrial production (1990=100) – 1995	105.5
Gross national savings average (percentage of GDP) – 1990-94	13.3
Gross fixed capital formation (percentage of GDP) – 1994	15.0
Total exports of goods (million US$, 1995)	242 490
Food and beverages – 1995	17 709.6
Crude materials – 1995	4 654.8
Mineral fuels – 1995	14 667.6
Chemicals and miscellaneous products – 1995	101 660.4
Machinery and transport equipment – 1995	103 807.2
Total imports of goods (million US$, 1995)	265 465.2
Food and beverages – 1995	25 254
Crude materials – 1995	10 969.2
Mineral fuels – 1995	9 274.8
Chemicals and miscellaneous products – 1995	111 051.6
Machinery and transport equipment – 1995	108 924
Export of services (billion US$) – 1995	210.8
Import of services (billion US$) – 1995	191.4
Stock of Foreign Direct Investment (million US$)	
Inward investments – 1993	196 810
Outward investments – 1993	253 210
Technology balance of payments (export-import coverage ratio in percentage) – 1993	1.14
Gross public debt (percentage of GDP) – 1994	54.6
Consumer prices (all items, 1990=100) – 1995	118.2
Producer prices (wholesale, manufacturing industries, 1990=100) – 1995	120.4
Exchange rate (nominal, local currency per US$) – 1995	0.634

REGIONAL	National total or average	Predominantly rural regions	Significantly rural regions	Predominantly urbanised regions
Distribution of population (percentage, 1991)	100	15	17	68
GDP per capita (percentage, 1989)	100	92	89	104
Unemployment rate (percentage, 1989)	7.3	5.7	6.8	7.4

CANADA

Population (thousands) – 1995	29 606
Land area (thousands sq. kms.)	9 976
Employment (thousands) – 1994	13 292
Agriculture (percentage of total) – 1994	4.1
Industry (percentage of total) – 1994	22.6
Services (percentage of total) – 1994	73.3
Unemployment rate (standardised OECD rate) – 1995	9.5
Share of government in employment (percentage) – 1993	21.7
Government financial balance (percentage of GDP) – 1995	-4.2
GDP in US$ (current price and current exchange rate, bill.) – 1995	565.4
GDP growth (average annual volume growth over previous 5 years, %) – 1994	1.1
GDP per capita in US$ (current price and current exchange rate) – 1994	18 598
GDP per capita in US$ (in purchasing power parities) – 1994	20 401
Total industrial production (1990=100) – 1995	112.0
Gross national savings average (percentage of GDP) – 1990-94	14.7
Gross fixed capital formation (percentage of GDP) – 1994	18.7
Total exports of goods (million US$, 1995)	192 105.6
Food and beverages – 1995	12 405.6
Crude materials – 1995	24 182.4
Mineral fuels – 1995	17 259.6
Chemicals and miscellaneous products – 1995	63 288
Machinery and transport equipment – 1995	74 970
Total imports of goods (million US$, 1995)	164 320.8
Food and beverages – 1995	8 997.6
Crude materials – 1995	6 098.4
Mineral fuels – 1995	5 943.6
Chemicals and miscellaneous products – 1995	58 633.2
Machinery and transport equipment – 1995	84 649.2
Export of services (billion US$) – 1995	34.2
Import of services (billion US$) – 1995	64.9
Stock of Foreign Direct Investment (million US$)	
Inward investments – 1993	110 188
Outward investments – 1993	87 142
Technology balance of payments (export-import coverage ratio in percentage) – 1993	1.01
Gross public debt (percentage of GDP) – 1995	99.1
Consumer prices (all items, 1990=100) – 1995	111.8
Producer prices (wholesale, manufacturing industries, 1990=100) – 1995	117.4
Exchange rate (nominal, local currency per US$) – 1995	1.373

REGIONAL	National total or average	Predominantly rural regions	Significantly rural regions	Predominantly urbanised regions
Distribution of population (percentage, 1991)	100	33	23	44
GDP per capita (percentage, 1985)	100	..	..	..
Unemployment rate (percentage, 1991)	10.2	11.9	9.3	9.5

ITALY

Population (thousands) – 1994	57 190
Land area (thousands sq. kms.)	301
Employment (thousands) – 1993	20 152
Agriculture (percentage of total) – 1993	7.5
Industry (percentage of total) – 1993	33.0
Services (percentage of total) – 1993	59.6
Unemployment rate (standardised OECD rate) – 1994	11.1
Share of government in employment (percentage) – 1993	17.9
Government financial balance (percentage of GDP) – 1995	-7.2
GDP in US$ (current price and current exchange rate, bill.) – 1994	1 017.3
GDP growth (average annual volume growth over previous 5 years, %) – 1994	1.0
GDP per capita in US$ (current price and current exchange rate) – 1994	17 796
GDP per capita in US$ (in purchasing power parities) – 1994	18 681
Total industrial production (1990=100) – 1995	107.8
Gross national savings average (percentage of GDP) – 1990-94	18.4
Gross fixed capital formation (percentage of GDP) – 1994	16.4
Total exports of goods (million US$, 1994)	189 802
Food and beverages	..
Crude materials	..
Mineral fuels	..
Chemicals and miscellaneous products	..
Machinery and transport equipment	..
Total imports of goods (million US$, 1994)	167 690
Food and beverages	..
Crude materials	..
Mineral fuels	..
Chemicals and miscellaneous products	..
Machinery and transport equipment	..
Export of services (billion US$) – 1995	103.4
Import of services (billion US$) – 1995	117.2
Stock of Foreign Direct Investment (million US$)	
Inward investments – 1993	52 510
Outward investments – 1993	76 420
Technology balance of payments (export-import coverage ratio in percentage) – 1993	0.57
Gross public debt (percentage of GDP) – 1994	123.9
Consumer prices (all items, 1990=100) – 1995	127.9
Producer prices (wholesale, manufacturing industries, 1990=100) – 1995	122.2
Exchange rate (nominal, local currency per US$) – 1995	1629

REGIONAL	National total or average	Predominantly rural regions	Significantly rural regions	Predominantly urbanised regions
Distribution of population (percentage, 1991)	100	9	44	47
GDP per capita (percentage, 1990)	100	..	..	..
Unemployment rate (percentage, 1989)	11.1	12.9	11.6	8.9

AUSTRALIA

Population (thousands) – 1994	17 840
Land area (thousands sq. kms.)	7 687
Employment (thousands) – 1993	7 680
Agriculture (percentage of total) – 1993	5.3
Industry (percentage of total) – 1994	23.7
Services (percentage of total) – 1994	71.0
Unemployment rate (standardised OECD rate) – 1995	8.5
Share of government in employment (percentage) – 1993	16.4
Government financial balance (percentage of GDP) – 1995	-2.4
GDP in US$ (current price and current exchange rate, bill.) – 1995	347.0
GDP growth (average annual volume growth over previous 5 years, %) – 1994	2.2
GDP per capita in US$ (current price and current exchange rate) – 1994	18 072
GDP per capita in US$ (in purchasing power parities) – 1994	18 382
Total industrial production (1990=100) – 1995	112.9
Gross national savings average (percentage of GDP) – 1990-94	16.3
Gross fixed capital formation (percentage of GDP) – 1994	21.4
Total exports of goods (million US$, 1994)	47 474.4
Food and beverages – 1994	10 184.4
Crude materials – 1994	9 741.6
Mineral fuels – 1994	7 903.2
Chemicals and miscellaneous products – 1994	14 094
Machinery and transport equipment – 1994	5 551.2
Total imports of goods (million US$, 1994)	49 923.6
Food and beverages – 1994	2 259.6
Crude materials – 1994	1 362
Mineral fuels – 1994	2 391.6
Chemicals and miscellaneous products – 1994	20 860.8
Machinery and transport equipment – 1994	23 049.6
Export of services (billion US$) – 1994	18.3
Import of services (billion US$) – 1994	30.7
Stock of Foreign Direct Investment (million US$)	
Inward investments – 1993	75 450
Outward investments – 1993	30 380
Technology balance of payments (export-import coverage ratio in percentage) – 1993	0.56
Gross public debt (percentage of GDP) – 1993	32.0
Consumer prices (all items, 1990=100) – 1995	113.2
Producer prices (wholesale, manufacturing industries, 1990=100) – 1995	109.7
Exchange rate (nominal, local currency per US$) – 1995	1.350

REGIONAL	National total or average	Predominantly rural regions	Significantly rural regions	Predominantly urbanised regions
Distribution of population (percentage, 1991)	100	23	22	55
GDP per capita (percentage, 1991)	100	..	..	..
Unemployment rate (percentage, 1991)	11.6	12.2	12.6	11.0

AUSTRIA

Population (thousands) – 1994	8 031
Land area (thousands sq. kms.)	84
Employment (thousands) – 1994	3 737
Agriculture (percentage of total) – 1994	7.2
Industry (percentage of total) – 1994	33.2
Services (percentage of total) – 1994	59.7
Unemployment rate (standardised OECD rate)	..
Share of government in employment (percentage) – 1993	21.1
Government financial balance (percentage of GDP) – 1995	-6.2
GDP in US$ (current price and current exchange rate, bill.) – 1995	233.3
GDP growth (average annual volume growth over previous 5 years, %) – 1994	2.5
GDP per capita in US$ (current price and current exchange rate) – 1994	24 670
GDP per capita in US$ (in purchasing power parities) – 1994	20 210
Total industrial production (1990=100) – 1995	107.9
Gross national savings average (percentage of GDP) – 1990-94	25.4
Gross fixed capital formation (percentage of GDP) – 1994	24.8
Total exports of goods (million US$, 1994)	45 027.6
Food and beverages – 1994	1 627.2
Crude materials – 1994	1 964.4
Mineral fuels – 1994	583.2
Chemicals and miscellaneous products – 1994	23 294.4
Machinery and transport equipment – 1994	17 557.2
Total imports of goods (million US$, 1994)	55 334.4
Food and beverages – 1994	2 889.6
Crude materials – 1994	2 428.8
Mineral fuels – 1994	2 433.6
Chemicals and miscellaneous products – 1994	26 581.2
Machinery and transport equipment – 1994	21 001.2
Export of services (billion US$) – 1995	36.5
Import of services (billion US$) – 1995	34.1
Stock of Foreign Direct Investment (million US$)	
Inward investments – 1993	11 400
Outward investments – 1993	8 110
Technology balance of payments (export-import coverage ratio in percentage) – 1993	0.28
Gross public debt (percentage of GDP) – 1995	69.4
Consumer prices (all items, 1990=100) – 1995	117.3
Producer prices (wholesale, manufacturing industries, 1990=100) – 1995	101.9
Exchange rate (nominal, local currency per US$) – 1995	10.08

REGIONAL	National total or average	Predominantly rural regions	Significantly rural regions	Predominantly urbanised regions
Distribution of population (percentage, 1991)	100	40	39	22
GDP per capita (percentage, 1991)	100	..	..	..
Unemployment rate (percentage, 1991)	5.3	4.7	4.9	7.1

BELGIUM

Population (thousands) – 1994	10 116
Land area (thousands sq. kms.)	31
Employment (thousands) – 1992	3 724
Agriculture (percentage of total) – 1992	2.6
Industry (percentage of total) – 1992	27.7
Services (percentage of total) – 1992	69.7
Unemployment rate (standardised OECD rate) – 1995	9.4
Share of government in employment (percentage)	..
Government financial balance (percentage of GDP) – 1995	-4.4
GDP in US$ (current price and current exchange rate, bill.) – 1994	258.5
GDP growth (average annual volume growth over previous 5 years, %) – 1994	1.6
GDP per capita in US$ (current price and current exchange rate) – 1994	22 515
GDP per capita in US$ (in purchasing power parities) – 1994	20 166
Total industrial production (1990=100) – 1995	98.6
Gross national savings average (percentage of GDP) – 1990-94	21.3
Gross fixed capital formation (percentage of GDP) – 1994	17.4
Total exports of goods (million US$, 1994) (Belgium and Luxembourg)	137 509.2
Food and beverages – 1994	13 794
Crude materials – 1994	3 740.4
Mineral fuels – 1994	4 161.6
Chemicals and miscellaneous products – 1994	77 113.2
Machinery and transport equipment – 1994	38 701.2
Total imports of goods (million US$, 1994) (Belgium and Luxembourg)	126 038.4
Food and beverages – 1994	12 840
Crude materials – 1994	7 084.8
Mineral fuels – 1994	8 702.4
Chemicals and miscellaneous products – 1994	65 226
Machinery and transport equipment – 1994	32 184
Export of services (billion US$) – 1995	146.9
Import of services (billion US$) – 1995	137.4
Stock of Foreign Direct Investment (million US$)	
Inward investments	..
Outward investments	..
Technology balance of payments (export-import coverage ratio in percentage) – 1993	0.90
Gross public debt (percentage of GDP) – 1995	133.5
Consumer prices (all items, 1990=100) – 1995	112.8
Producer prices (wholesale, manufacturing industries, 1990=100) – 1995	101.4
Exchange rate (nominal, local currency per US$) – 1995	29.50

REGIONAL	National total or average	Predominantly rural regions	Significantly rural regions	Predominantly urbanised regions
Distribution of population (percentage, 1991)	100	2	17	81
GDP per capita (percentage, 1989)	100	81	88	103
Unemployment rate (percentage, 1989)	8.1	6.8	10.9	7.6

CZECH REPUBLIC

Population (thousands) – 1993	10 328
Land area (thousands sq. kms.)	79
Employment (thousands) – 1993	4853
Agriculture (percentage of total) – 1993	6.9
Industry (percentage of total) – 1993	44.5
Services (percentage of total) – 1993	48.6
Unemployment rate (standard OECD) – 1993	3.5
Share of government in employment (percentage) – 1993	2.9
Government financial balance (percentage of GDP) – 1993	..
GDP in US$ (current price and current exchange rate, bill.) – 1993	31.24
GDP growth (average annual volume growth over previous 5 years, %)	..
GDP per capita in US$ (current price and current exchange rate) – 1993	3023
GDP per capita in US$ (in purchasing power parities) – 1993	8422
Total industrial production (1990=100) – 1993	68.0
Gross national savings average (percentage of GDP)	..
Gross fixed capital formation (percentage of GDP) – 1993	26.6
Total exports of goods (million US$)	..
Food and beverages	..
Crude materials	..
Mineral fuels	..
Chemicals and miscellaneous products	..
Machinery and transport equipment	..
Total imports of goods (million US$)	..
Food and beverages	..
Crude materials	..
Mineral fuels	..
Chemicals and miscellaneous products	..
Machinery and transport equipment	..
Export of services (percentage of GDP) – 1993	15.1
Import of services (percentage of GDP) – 1993	11.8
Stock of Foreign Direct Investment (million US$)	..
Inward investments – 1993	2.2
Outward investments – 1993	-0.3
Technology balance of payments (export-import coverage ratio in percentage)	..
Gross public debt (percentage of GDP) – 1993	17.4
Consumer prices (all items, 1990=100) – 1993	231.1
Producer prices (wholesale, manufacturing industries, 1990=100) – 1993	217.1
Exchange rate (nominal, local currency per US$) – 1993	29.15

REGIONAL	National total or average	Predominantly rural regions	Significantly rural regions	Predominantly urbanised regions
Distribution of population (percentage)	..	..	..	..
GDP per capita (percentage)	..	..	..	..
Unemployment rate (percentage)	..	..	..	..

Source: Czech government statistics.

DENMARK

Population (thousands) – 1994	5 206
Land area (thousands sq. kms.)	43
Employment (thousands) – 1994	2 508
Agriculture (percentage of total) – 1994	5.1
Industry (percentage of total) – 1994	26.8
Services (percentage of total) – 1994	68.1
Unemployment rate (standardised OECD rate)	..
Share of government in employment (percentage) – 1993	30.7
Government financial balance (percentage of GDP) – 1995	-1.8
GDP in US$ (current price and current exchange rate, bill.) – 1994	165.8
GDP growth (average annual volume growth over previous 5 years, %) – 1994	1.9
GDP per capita in US$ (current price and current exchange rate) – 1994	28 182
GDP per capita in US$ (in purchasing power parities) – 1994	20 546
Total industrial production (1990=100) – 1993	101
Gross national savings average (percentage of GDP) – 1990-94	17.5
Gross fixed capital formation (percentage of GDP) – 1994	14.8
Total exports of goods (million US$, 1995)	47 739.6
Food and beverages – 1995	11 665.2
Crude materials – 1995	2 365.2
Mineral fuels – 1995	1 585.2
Chemicals and miscellaneous products – 1995	19 386
Machinery and transport equipment – 1995	12 738
Total imports of goods (million US$, 1995)	42 160.8
Food and beverages – 1995	4 887.6
Crude materials – 1995	1 886.4
Mineral fuels – 1995	1 952.4
Chemicals and miscellaneous products – 1995	19 238.4
Machinery and transport equipment – 1995	14 196
Export of services (billion US$) – 1995	43.8
Import of services (billion US$) – 1995	48.2
Stock of Foreign Direct Investment (million US$)	
Inward investments	..
Outward investments	..
Technology balance of payments (export-import coverage ratio in percentage)	..
Gross public debt (percentage of GDP) – 1994	80.2
Consumer prices (all items, 1990=100) – 1995	110.2
Producer prices (wholesale, manufacturing industries, 1990=100) – 1995	103.0
Exchange rate (nominal, local currency per US$) – 1995	5.604

REGIONAL	National total or average	Predominantly rural regions	Significantly rural regions	Predominantly urbanised regions
Distribution of population (percentage, 1991)	100	39	38	23
GDP per capita (percentage, 1990)	100	..	..	..
Unemployment rate (percentage, 1989)	7.7	8.4	7.4	6.8

FINLAND

Population (thousands) – 1994	5 088
Land area (thousands sq. kms.)	338
Employment (thousands) – 1994	2 015
Agriculture (percentage of total) – 1994	8.3
Industry (percentage of total) – 1994	26.8
Services (percentage of total) – 1994	64.9
Unemployment rate (standardised OECD rate) – 1995	17.1
Share of government in employment (percentage) – 1993	23.3
Government financial balance (percentage of GDP) – 1995	-5.6
GDP in US$ (current price and current exchange rate, bill.) – 1995	126.0
GDP growth (average annual volume growth over previous 5 years, %) – 1994	-1.6
GDP per capita in US$ (current price and current exchange rate) – 1994	19 106
GDP per capita in US$ (in purchasing power parities) – 1994	16 208
Total industrial production (1990=100) – 1995	115.8
Gross national savings average (percentage of GDP) – 1990-94	15.9
Gross fixed capital formation (percentage of GDP) – 1994	14.6
Total exports of goods (million US$, 1995)	40 088.4
Food and beverages – 1995	931.2
Crude materials – 1995	3 598.8
Mineral fuels – 1995	775.2
Chemicals and miscellaneous products – 1995	20 684.4
Machinery and transport equipment – 1995	14 098.8
Total imports of goods (million US$, 1995)	29 004
Food and beverages – 1995	1 575.6
Crude materials – 1995	2 187.6
Mineral fuels – 1995	2 510.4
Chemicals and miscellaneous products – 1995	11 476.8
Machinery and transport equipment – 1995	11 253.6
Export of services (billion US$) – 1995	10.6
Import of services (billion US$) – 1995	16.4
Stock of Foreign Direct Investment (million US$)	
Inward investments – 1993	3 916
Outward investments – 1993	12 588
Technology balance of payments (export-import coverage ratio in percentage) – 1993	0.14
Gross public debt (percentage of GDP) – 1994	61.7
Consumer prices (all items, 1990=100) – 1995	112.0
Producer prices (wholesale, manufacturing industries, 1990=100) – 1995	110.8
Exchange rate (nominal, local currency per US$) – 1995	4.367

REGIONAL	National total or average	Predominantly rural regions	Significantly rural regions	Predominantly urbanised regions
Distribution of population (percentage, 1991)	100	47	32	21
GDP per capita (percentage, 1991)	100	..	..	..
Unemployment rate (percentage, 1990)	4.2	5.4	4.7	1.2

MEXICO

Population (thousands) – 1994	88 402
Land area (thousands sq. kms.)	1 967 183
Employment (thousands) – 1994	32 439
Agriculture (percentage of total) – 1994	25.8
Industry (percentage of total) – 1994	22.2
Services (percentage of total) – 1994	52.1
Unemployment rate (standard OECD) – 1995	6.3
Share of government in employment (percentage) – 1994	11.5
Government financial balance (percentage of GDP) – 1995	..
GDP in US$ (current price and current exchange rate, bill.) – 1995	1 580.0
GDP growth (average annual volume growth over previous 5 years, %) – 1994	3.0
GDP per capita in US$ (current price and current exchange rate) – 1994	3 991.2
GDP per capita in US$ (in purchasing power parities) – 1994	7 238.6
Total industrial production (1990=100) – 1995	103.5
Gross national savings average (percentage of GDP) – 1990-94	16.8
Gross fixed capital formation (percentage of GDP) – 1995	16.6
Total exports of goods (million US$, 1994)	60 882
Food and beverages	..
Crude materials	..
Mineral fuels	..
Chemicals and miscellaneous products	..
Machinery and transport equipment	..
Total imports of goods (million US$, 1994)	79 346
Food and beverages	..
Crude materials	..
Mineral fuels	..
Chemicals and miscellaneous products	..
Machinery and transport equipment	..
Export of services (percentage of GDP) – 1994	2.66
Import of services (percentage of GDP)	..
Stock of Foreign Direct Investment (million US$)	..
Inward investments	..
Outward investments	..
Technology balance of payments (export-import coverage ratio in percentage)	..
Gross public debt (percentage of GDP)	..
Consumer prices (all items, 1990=100)	..
Producer prices (wholesale, manufacturing industries, 1990=100)	..
Exchange rate (nominal, local currency per US$) – 1995	6.421

REGIONAL	National total or average	Predominantly rural regions	Significantly rural regions	Predominantly urbanised regions
Distribution of population (percentage, 1991)	..	..	..	..
GDP per capita (percentage, 1990)	..	..	..	..
Unemployment rate (percentage, 1990)	..	..	..	..

NETHERLANDS

Population (thousands) – 1994	15 382
Land area (thousands sq. kms.)	37
Employment (thousands) – 1994	6 631
Agriculture (percentage of total) – 1994	4.0
Industry (percentage of total) – 1994	23.0
Services (percentage of total) – 1994	73.0
Unemployment rate (standardised OECD rate) – 1994	6.8
Share of government in employment (percentage) – 1993	11.0
Government financial balance (percentage of GDP) – 1995	-3.3
GDP in US$ (current price and current exchange rate, bill.) – 1995	395.5
GDP growth (average annual volume growth over previous 5 years, %) – 1994	2.3
GDP per capita in US$ (current price and current exchange rate) – 1994	21 733
GDP per capita in US$ (in purchasing power parities) – 1994	18 589
Total industrial production (1990=100) – 1995	105.6
Gross national savings average (percentage of GDP) – 1990-94	24.4
Gross fixed capital formation (percentage of GDP) – 1994	19.3
Total exports of goods (million US$, 1995)	159 236.4
Food and beverages – 1995	30 288
Crude materials – 1995	10 130.4
Mineral fuels – 1995	11 767.2
Chemicals and miscellaneous products – 1995	64 005.6
Machinery and transport equipment – 1995	43 045.2
Total imports of goods (million US$, 1995)	140 106
Food and beverages – 1995	16 350
Crude materials – 1995	8 647.2
Mineral fuels – 1995	11 966.4
Chemicals and miscellaneous products – 1995	56 850
Machinery and transport equipment – 1995	46 292.4
Export of services (billion US$) – 1995	76.9
Import of services (billion US$) – 1995	74.4
Stock of Foreign Direct Investment (million US$)	
Inward investments – 1993	85 837
Outward investments – 1993	132 633
Technology balance of payments (export-import coverage ratio in percentage) – 1993	1.01
Gross public debt (percentage of GDP) – 1995	79.1
Consumer prices (all items, 1990=100) – 1995	114.4
Producer prices (wholesale, manufacturing industries, 1990=100) – 1995	100.7
Exchange rate (nominal, local currency per US$) – 1995	1.605

REGIONAL	National total or average	Predominantly rural regions	Significantly rural regions	Predominantly urbanised regions
Distribution of population (percentage, 1991)	100	..	15	85
GDP per capita (percentage, 1988)	100	..	97	101
Unemployment rate (percentage, 1989)	8.5	..	..	..

NEW ZEALAND

Population (thousands) – 1994	3 526
Land area (thousands sq. kms.)	270
Employment (thousands) – 1994	1 560
Agriculture (percentage of total) – 1994	10.4
Industry (percentage of total) – 1994	25.0
Services (percentage of total) – 1994	64.6
Unemployment rate (standardised OECD rate) – 1995	6.3
Share of government in employment (percentage) – 1993	15.6
Government financial balance (percentage of GDP) – 1995	..
GDP in US$ (current price and current exchange rate, bill.) – 1995	57.7
GDP growth (average annual volume growth over previous 5 years, %) – 1994	2.5
GDP per capita in US$ (current price and current exchange rate) – 1994	14 513
GDP per capita in US$ (in purchasing power parities) – 1994	16 248
Total industrial production (1990=100)	..
Gross national savings average (percentage of GDP) – 1990-94	17.3
Gross fixed capital formation (percentage of GDP) – 1994	20.0
Total exports of goods (million US$, 1995)	13 833.6
Food and beverages – 1995	5 721.6
Crude materials – 1995	2 646
Mineral fuels – 1995	217.2
Chemicals and miscellaneous products – 1995	4 074
Machinery and transport equipment – 1995	1 176
Total imports of goods (million US$, 1995)	13 958.4
Food and beverages – 1995	956.4
Crude materials – 1995	506.4
Mineral fuels – 1995	745.2
Chemicals and miscellaneous products – 1995	5 881.2
Machinery and transport equipment – 1995	5 870.4
Export of services (billion US$) – 1995	5.1
Import of services (billion US$) – 1995	9.8
Stock of Foreign Direct Investment (million US$)	
Inward investments	..
Outward investments	..
Technology balance of payments (export-import coverage ratio in percentage) – 1993	1.33
Gross public debt (percentage of GDP)	..
Consumer prices (all items, 1990=100) – 1995	110.8
Producer prices (wholesale, manufacturing industries, 1990=100) – 1995	109.2
Exchange rate (nominal, local currency per US$) – 1995	1.524

REGIONAL	National total or average	Predominantly rural regions	Significantly rural regions	Predominantly urbanised regions
Distribution of population (percentage, 1991)	100	..	61	39
GDP per capita (percentage, 1989)	100	..	..	..
Unemployment rate (percentage, 1989)	7.1	..	..	..

NORWAY

Population (thousands) – 1994	4 337
Land area (thousands sq. kms.)	324
Employment (thousands) – 1993	1 970
Agriculture (percentage of total) – 1993	5.6
Industry (percentage of total) – 1993	23.1
Services (percentage of total) – 1993	71.3
Unemployment rate (standardised OECD rate) – 1995	4.9
Share of government in employment (percentage) – 1993	30.8
Government financial balance (percentage of GDP) – 1995	3.1
GDP in US$ (current price and current exchange rate, bill.) – 1995	145.6
GDP growth (average annual volume growth over previous 5 years, %) – 1993	2.1
GDP per capita in US$ (current price and current exchange rate) – 1994	28 434
GDP per capita in US$ (in purchasing power parities) – 1994	21 968
Total industrial production (1990=100) – 1995	127.1
Gross national savings average (percentage of GDP) – 1990-94	22.7
Gross fixed capital formation (percentage of GDP) – 1993	21.9
Total exports of goods (million US$, 1995)	41 700
Food and beverages – 1995	3 422.4
Crude materials – 1995	1 380
Mineral fuels – 1995	20 018.4
Chemicals and miscellaneous products – 1995	11 496
Machinery and transport equipment – 1995	5 384.4
Total imports of goods (million US$, 1995)	32 904
Food and beverages – 1995	2 032.8
Crude materials – 1995	2 580
Mineral fuels – 1995	1 033.2
Chemicals and miscellaneous products – 1995	14 671.2
Machinery and transport equipment – 1995	12 586.8
Export of services (billion US$) – 1995	17.4
Import of services (billion US$) – 1995	19.0
Stock of Foreign Direct Investment (million US$)	
Inward investments – 1993	14 463
Outward investments – 1993	13 482
Technology balance of payments (export-import coverage ratio in percentage) – 1993	0.67
Gross public debt (percentage of GDP) – 1993	43.3
Consumer prices (all items, 1990=100) – 1995	112.5
Producer prices (wholesale, manufacturing industries, 1990=100) – 1995	106.0
Exchange rate (nominal, local currency per US$) – 1995	6.337

REGIONAL	National total or average	Predominantly rural regions	Significantly rural regions	Predominantly urbanised regions
Distribution of population (percentage, 1991)	100	51	38	11
GDP per capita (percentage, 1986)	100	84	94	194
Unemployment rate (percentage, 1990)	2.7	2.8	2.7	2.7

PORTUGAL

Population (thousands) – 1994	9 900
Land area (thousands sq. kms.)	92
Employment (thousands) – 1994	4 372
Agriculture (percentage of total) – 1994	11.5
Industry (percentage of total) – 1994	32.8
Services (percentage of total) – 1994	55.7
Unemployment rate (standardised OECD rate) – 1995	7.1
Share of government in employment (percentage) – 1993	17.1
Government ginancial balance (percentage of GDP) – 1995	-5.1
GDP in US$ (current price and current exchange rate, bill.) – 1994	87.0
GDP growth (average annual volume growth over previous 5 years, %) – 1994	1.4
GDP per capita in US$ (current price and current exchange rate) – 1994	8 792
GDP per capita in US$ (in purchasing power parities) – 1994	12 335
Total industrial production (1990=100) – 1995	99.4
Gross national savings average (percentage of GDP) – 1990-94	25.2
Gross fixed capital formation (percentage of GDP) – 1994	25.7
Total exports of goods (million US$, 1995)	22 094.4
Food and beverages – 1995	1 425.6
Crude materials – 1995	1 588.8
Mineral fuels – 1995	729.6
Chemicals and miscellaneous products – 1995	12 488.4
Machinery and transport equipment – 1995	5 862
Total imports of goods (million US$, 1995)	31 890
Food and beverages – 1995	3 739.2
Crude materials – 1995	1 818
Mineral fuels – 1995	2 710.8
Chemicals and miscellaneous products – 1995	12 817.2
Machinery and transport equipment – 1995	10 804.8
Export of services (billion US$) – 1995	11.8
Import of services (billion US$) – 1995	10.7
Stock of Foreign Direct Investment (million US$)	
Inward investments	..
Outward investments	..
Technology balance of payments (export-import coverage ratio in percentage)	..
Gross public debt (percentage of GDP) – 1995	70.7
Consumer prices (all items, 1990=100) – 1995	141.5
Producer prices (wholesale, manufacturing industries, 1990=100)	..
Exchange rate (nominal, local currency per US$) – 1995	149.9

REGIONAL	National total or average	Predominantly rural regions	Significantly rural regions	Predominantly urbanised regions
Distribution of population (percentage, 1991)	100	35	24	41
GDP per capita (percentage, 1990)	100	..	..	..
Unemployment rate (percentage, 1989)	4.9	..	..	..

SPAIN

Population (thousands) – 1994	39 150
Land area (thousands sq. kms.)	505
Employment (thousands) – 1994	11 760
Agriculture (percentage of total) – 1994	9.8
Industry (percentage of total) – 1994	30.1
Services (percentage of total) – 1994	60.2
Unemployment rate (standardised OECD rate) – 1995	22.7
Share of government in employment (percentage) – 1993	14.5
Government financial balance (percentage of GDP) – 1995	-6.2
GDP in US$ (current price and current exchange rate, bill.) – 1995	559.1
GDP growth (average annual volume growth over previous 5 years, %) – 1994	1.5
GDP per capita in US$ (current price and current exchange rate) – 1994	12 321
GDP per capita in US$ (in purchasing power parities) – 1994	13 581
Total industrial production (1990=100) – 1995	103.2
Gross national savings average (percentage of GDP) – 1990-94	19.9
Gross fixed capital formation (percentage of GDP) – 1994	19.8
Total exports of goods (million US$, 1995)	91 716
Food and beverages – 1995	13 018.8
Crude materials – 1995	3 356.4
Mineral fuels – 1995	1 502.4
Chemicals and miscellaneous products – 1995	35 138.4
Machinery and transport equipment – 1995	38 698.8
Total imports of goods (million US$, 1995)	115 018.8
Food and beverages – 1995	13 902
Crude materials – 1995	7 719.6
Mineral fuels – 1995	9 561.6
Chemicals and miscellaneous products – 1995	43 311.6
Machinery and transport equipment – 1995	40 524
Export of services (billion US$) – 1995	53.3
Import of services (billion US$) – 1995	39.5
Stock of Foreign Direct Investment (million US$)	
Inward investments – 1993	53 780
Outward investments – 1993	21 020
Technology balance of payments (export-import coverage ratio in percentage) – 1993	0.46
Gross public debt (percentage of GDP) – 1995	68.4
Consumer prices (all items, 1990=100) – 1995	128.6
Producer prices (wholesale, manufacturing industries, 1990=100) – 1995	116.8
Exchange rate (nominal, local currency per US$) – 1995	124.72

REGIONAL	National total or average	Predominantly rural regions	Significantly rural regions	Predominantly urbanised regions
Distribution of population (percentage, 1991)	100	19	46	35
GDP per capita (percentage, 1989)	100	80	97	115
Unemployment rate (percentage, 1989)	16.9	17.0	18.6	14.8

SWEDEN

Population (thousands) – 1994	8 781
Land area (thousands sq. kms.)	450
Employment (thousands) – 1994	3 926
Agriculture (percentage of total) – 1994	3.4
Industry (percentage of total) – 1994	25.0
Services (percentage of total) – 1994	71.6
Unemployment rate (standard OECD) – 1995	9.2
Share of government in employment (percentage) – 1993	33.2
Government financial balance (percentage of GDP) – 1995	-6.2
GDP in US$ (current price and current exchange rate, bill.) – 1995	229.2
GDP growth (average annual volume growth over previous 5 years, %) – 1994	-0.3
GDP per capita in US$ (current price and current exchange rate) – 1994	22 389
GDP per capita in US$ (in purchasing power parities) – 1994	17 422
Total industrial production (1990=100) – 1995	114.0
Gross national savings average (percentage of GDP) – 1990-94	14.6
Gross fixed capital formation (percentage of GDP) – 1994	13.6
Total exports of goods (million US$, 1994)	61 262.4
Food and beverages – 1994	1 231.2
Crude materials – 1994	4 920
Mineral fuels – 1994	1 537.2
Chemicals and miscellaneous products – 1994	25 947.6
Machinery and transport equipment – 1994	27 626.4
Total imports of goods (million US$, 1994)	51 537.6
Food and beverages – 1994	3 852
Crude materials – 1994	1 978.8
Mineral fuels – 1994	3 896.4
Chemicals and miscellaneous products – 1994	22 324.8
Machinery and transport equipment – 1994	19 485.6
Export of services (billion US$) – 1995	29.8
Import of services (billion US$) – 1995	38.2
Stock of Foreign Direct Investment (million US$)	
Inward investments – 1993	12 890
Outward investments – 1993	44 560
Technology balance of payments (export-import coverage ratio in percentage) – 1993	8.89
Gross public debt (percentage of GDP) – 1994	81.5
Consumer prices (all items, 1990=100) – 1995	124.2
Producer prices (wholesale, manufacturing industries, 1990=100) – 1995	121.7
Exchange rate (nominal, local currency per US$) – 1995	7.134

REGIONAL	National total or average	Predominantly rural regions	Significantly rural regions	Predominantly urbanised regions
Distribution of population (percentage, 1991)	100	49	32	19
GDP per capita (percentage, 1990)	100	..	..	..
Unemployment rate (percentage, 1990)	1.8	2.1	1.9	1.2

Chapter 2

RESEARCH AND DEVELOPMENT INFRASTRUCTURE

The data provided are drawn from the Science Technology Indicators Unit database (STIU) of the Directorate for Science, Technology and Industry (DSTI).

Introduction

Scientific and technological achievements and their dissemination are having an increasing impact on the restructuring of OECD economies, on the growth of new activities, and on employment and income generation performance of national business sectors. Firms located in environments with a strong research and development (R&D) infrastructure, or having access to or interaction with such environments, gain an edge over their rivals in their product and process innovations and ensuing productivity performance. The quality of R&D infrastructure is increasingly recognised as a key framework factor for firms' competitiveness in an increasing number of sectors.

The scientific and technological process is not confined to one dimension, *i.e.* leading from basic research to new products and processes. It is often characterised by loops and complementarities where industrial applications require further scientific exploration and contributions. This has resulted in the emergence of a new and closer, symbiotic relationship between science, technology and industry, rendering all the more vital the continuous contribution of research and development infrastructure to industry.

These arguments partly help to explain why the frontier between basic research and applied research has become blurred by the gradual involvement of enterprises in basic research. Furthermore, they point to the inherent long-term character of most of today's applied research. It is becoming increasingly important for OECD economies to extend the frontier of innovation by bridging the gap between "basic" and "applied" research. The best way to accomplish this objective is to carry out not simply more, but also better co-ordinated and focused, research-development activities in the government, business, higher education and private non-profit sectors, and through their co-operation with the enterprise sector.

Two new developments are making the quality of research-development infrastructure more important for business sector performance:

- The first is the changing pattern of research priorities, as well as the changing priorities of the public for research and development activities, as indicated in government budgets. Although government's share in the national research-development effort varies markedly across countries, a significant shift in its composition has occurred. Until the early 1980s, growing weight was given to research on energy sources and environmental issues; this has been followed more recently by a fairly widespread move towards greater emphasis on R&D programmes for industrial competitiveness. This trend has been supportive of private R&D expenditures, and echoed by a structural increase in private business expenditures for research and development.

- Second, the costs of many components of research-development have tended to rise as a result of the growing sophistication of human and material resources necessary to undertake state-of-the-art research and development. This has contributed to raising the minimum efficient scale of scientific facilities, and has created demand for research co-operation and consortia between, on the one hand, enterprises and public research facilities, and on the other, among enterprises themselves. Research cost optimisation and technology specialisation of laboratories' and enterprises' research activities are transforming research-development infrastructure into a complex network of complementarities and co-operation.

In each country, the pattern of the funding and execution of basic R&D, applied R&D and experimental development is conditioned by the broad institutional framework of the R&D system, which changes only slowly. In particular, as illustrated in the following country matrices and comparative graphs, there are still major variations across countries in the relative importance of government, industry and higher education sectors in the funding and actual performance of research and development work. These differences also extend to the institutions and mechanisms governing the transfer of research results between public R&D facilities and enterprises, and among enterprises themselves, at both the domestic and international levels.

This chapter presents "basic" comparative information on resources devoted to R&D, the institutional structure for carrying out the national R&D effort and the sectoral distribution of R&D resources in ten OECD Member countries. The information is drawn from OECD's DSTI/EAS databases on research and development, and is organised as follows.

Table 1. Gross domestic expenditure on R&D as a percentage of GDP

This summary indicator measures the size of the national research and development effort in comparison with the size of the economy. Data are provided for the period 1990-94.

Table 2. Gross domestic expenditure on R&D by sector of performance and type of activity

This table provides a breakdown of the performance of the main types of R&D activities (basic research, applied research and experimental development) among the government, higher education, private non-profit and business enterprise sectors. The latest data available for most countries is for 1991. The type of activity data is generally less internationally comparable than the data in the other tables.

Table 3. Industrial breakdown of business enterprise sector expenditures on R&D

A detailed industrial breakdown of R&D expenditure in the business enterprise sector is provided in this table. The data cover the period 1990-94, and distinguish agriculture, mining, manufacturing, public utility, construction and service sectors. Manufacturing is disaggregated into ten industries.

Table 4. R&D personnel by sector of employment

The distribution of national human capital devoted to research and development, among government, higher education, non-profit and enterprise sectors is provided. Three main categories of personnel (scientists and engineers, technicians and other support personnel) are distinguished. The latest available data by occupation categories for most countries are for 1991.

Table 5. Structure of the R&D system (funding and distribution of gross domestic expenditures on R&D)

This diagram summarises the contributions of the main sectors (government, higher education, private non-profit and business enterprise) to the financing and performance of the national R&D effort. A flow of funds approach is used which includes funds from abroad. **The data are shown in US dollars (converted using current GDP purchasing power parities) for the latest year available (1993 or 1994 for most countries).**

At the end of these summary country matrices, an Annex containing background notes is provided. These notes have two objectives: *i)* to provide additional technical explanations on each table; and *ii)* to provide cross-country comparative graphs on all or part of the country tables. Although the "benchmarking" graphs in the Annex do reveal interesting differences across countries, they should not be used for detailed comparisons because of differences in national methodologies.

RESEARCH & DEVELOPMENT INFRASTRUCTURE: COUNTRY TABLES

UNITED STATES

Table 1. GERD (Gross domestic expenditure on R&D) as a percentage of GDP

	1990	1991	1992	1993	1994
Percentage of GDP	2.82	2.84	2.78	2.66	2.54

Source: OECD, STIU database.

Table 2. GERD by sector of performance and type of activity, 1992

Percentage

	Government	Higher education	Private non-profit	Enterprises	Total	%
Basic research	11.08	59.40	8.18	21.35	100.00	15.78
Applied research	11.86	16.22	4.61	67.32	100.00	23.31
Experimental development	10.95	3.55	1.75	83.75	100.00	60.91
Not specified	..	..	..	..	..	0.00
Total	11.18	15.31	3.43	70.08	100.00	100.00

Source: OECD, STIU database.

Table 3. Industrial breakdown of BERD (Expenditure on R&D in the business enterprise sector)

Percentage

ISIC	1990	1991	1992	1993	1994
Agriculture	..	..	..	..	..
Mining	..	..	..	..	..
Manufacturing	81.05	75.66	75.71	73.62	..
Food, beverages & tobacco	..	1.09	1.16	1.13	..
Textiles, fur & leather	..	..	..	..	..
Wood, paper, print. & publ.	0.97	..	..	..	..
Coke, petrol, nucl. fuel, chem. prod. & plast	..	..	..	..	..
Non-metallic mineral products	..	..	..	..	..
Basic metals	0.67	0.61	0.44	0.57	..
Fabric. metal products	0.86	0.83	0.85	..	..
Machin., instruments & transport equip.	60.39	55.00	54.85	49.64	..
Furnit. & other manufact., nec	..	..	..	..	..
Recycling	..	..	..	..	..
Electricity, gas & water supply	0.22	0.24	0.25	0.29	..
Construction	..	..	..	..	..
Service sector	18.73	24.10	24.05	26.10	..
Total	100.00	100.00	100.00	100.00	..

Source: OECD, STIU database.

Table 4. R&D personnel by sector of employment

Percentage

Occupation	Government	Higher education	Private non-profit	Enterprises	Total	%
Scientists and engineers	6.07	12.19	0.91	80.83	100.00	..
Technicians	..	..	..	..	..	..
Other personnel	..	..	..	..	..	..
Total	..	..	..	..	..	..

Source: OECD, STIU database.

Table 5. Structure of the R&D system (Funding and performance of GERD)

In million US$

1994

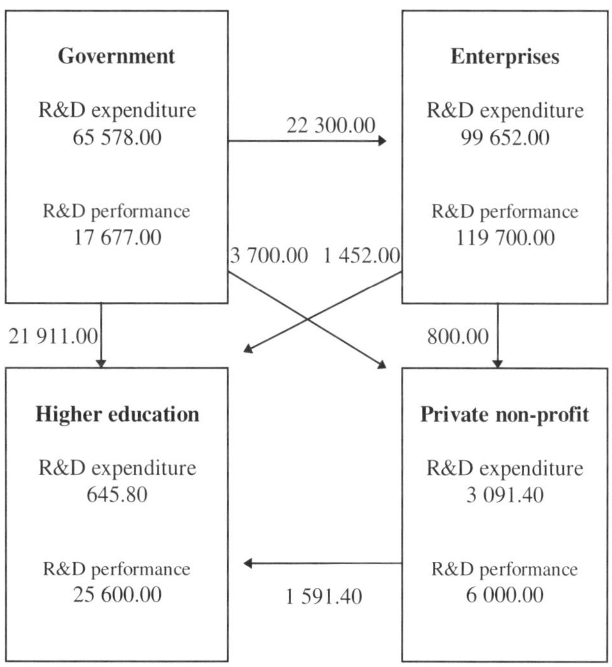

R&D expenditure: All R&D funded by the sector performed in this and other sectors.

R&D performance: R&D performed in this sector.

JAPAN

Table 1. GERD (Gross domestic expenditure on R&D) as a percentage of GDP

	1990	1991	1992	1993	1994
Percentage of GDP	2.89	2.86	2.81	2.73	..

Source: OECD, STIU database.

Table 2. GERD by sector of performance and type of activity, 1989

Percentage

	Government	Higher education	Private non-profit	Enterprises	Total	%
Basic research	8.36	49.56	5.99	36.09	100.00	12.30
Applied research	9.60	18.55	3.96	67.88	100.00	22.04
Experimental development	7.95	1.59	3.84	86.62	100.00	58.05
Not specified	4.10	90.89	5.02	0.00	100.00	7.61
Total	8.07	18.02	4.22	69.69	100.00	100.00

Source: OECD, STIU database.

Table 3. Industrial breakdown of BERD (Expenditure on R&D in the business enterprise sector)

Percentage

ISIC	1990	1991	1992	1993	1994
Agriculture	0.12	0.06	0.08	0.09	..
Mining	0.32	0.41	0.30	0.31	..
Manufacturing	93.45	94.38	93.83	93.38	..
Food, beverages & tobacco	2.54	2.31	2.42	2.77	..
Textiles, fur & leather	0.95	0.94	1.24	1.03	..
Wood, paper, print. & publ.	1.20	1.26	1.07	1.14	..
Coke, petrol, nucl. fuel, chem. prod. & plast	18.76	19.42	20.33	20.78	..
Non-metallic mineral products	2.32	2.67	2.24	2.19	..
Basic metals	4.80	5.22	4.79	4.80	..
Fabric. metal products	1.40	1.41	1.33	1.33	..
Machin., instruments & transport equip.	60.74	60.35	59.60	58.53	..
Furnit. & other manufact., nec	0.75	0.80	0.81	0.80	..
Recycling	..	..	..	..	..
Electricity, gas & water supply	1.05	0.93	1.15	1.21	..
Construction	2.29	2.10	2.55	2.74	..
Service sector	2.77	2.12	2.09	2.26	..
Total	100.00	100.00	100.00	100.00	..

Source: OECD, STIU database.

Table 4. R&D personnel by sector of employment, 1993

Percentage

Occupation	Government	Higher education	Private non-profit	Enterprises	Total	%
Scientists and engineers	5.68	21.76	2.80	69.76	100.00	63.22
Technicians	2.86	10.37	4.96	81.81	100.00	11.90
Other personnel	11.23	19.11	4.47	65.19	100.00	24.88
Total	6.73	19.75	3.47	70.06	100.00	100.00

Source: OECD, STIU database.

Table 5. Structure of the R&D system (Funding and performance of GERD)

In million US$

1993

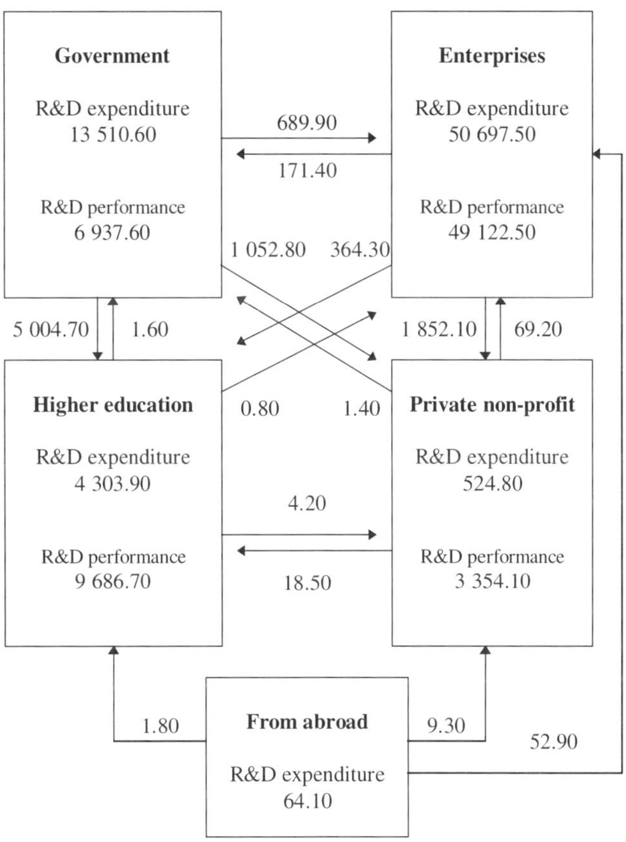

R&D expenditure: All R&D funded by the sector performed in this and other sectors.

R&D performance: R&D performed in this sector.

GERMANY

Table 1. GERD (Gross domestic expenditure on R&D) as a percentage of GDP

	1990	1991	1992	1993	1994
Percentage of GDP	2.76	2.61	2.49	2.48	2.37

Source: OECD, STIU database.

Table 2. GERD by sector of performance and type of activity, 1991

Percentage

	Government	Higher education	Private non-profit	Enterprises	Total	%
Basic research	24.35	56.12	0.34	19.20	100.00	21.04
Applied research	..	..	..	..	..	0.00
Experimental development	..	..	..	..	..	0.00
Not specified	10.08	5.41	0.43	84.07	100.00	78.96
Total	13.08	16.08	0.41	70.42	100.00	100.00

Source: OECD, STIU database.

Table 3. Industrial breakdown of BERD (Expenditure on R&D in the business enterprise sector)

Percentage

ISIC	1990	1991	1992	1993	1994
Agriculture	..	0.16	..	..	..
Mining	..	0.59	..	..	..
Manufacturing	..	95.39	..	..	..
Food, beverages & tobacco	..	0.68	..	..	..
Textiles, fur & leather	..	0.53	..	..	..
Wood, paper, print. & publ.	..	0.62	..	..	..
Coke, petrol, nucl. fuel, chem. prod. & plast	..	21.40	..	..	..
Non-metallic mineral products	..	0.99	..	..	..
Basic metals	..	1.19	..	..	..
Fabric. metal products	..	2.24	..	..	..
Machin., instruments & transport equip.	..	67.64	..	..	..
Furnit. & other manufact., nec	..	0.11	..	..	..
Recycling	..	..	..	..	..
Electricity, gas & water supply	..	0.51	..	..	..
Construction	..	0.32	..	..	..
Service sector	..	2.36	..	..	..
Total	100.00	100.00	100.00	100.00	..

Source: OECD, STIU database.

Table 4. R&D personnel by sector of employment, 1991

Percentage

Occupation	Government	Higher education	Private non-profit	Enterprises	Total	%
Scientists and engineers	15.08	25.82	0.52	58.59	100.00	46.73
Technicians	18.25	13.86	0.48	67.40	100.00	24.90
Other personnel	18.82	16.36	0.37	64.45	100.00	28.36
Total	16.93	20.16	0.47	62.45	100.00	100.00

Source: OECD, STIU database.

Table 5. Structure of the R&D system (Funding and performance of GERD)

In million US$

1994

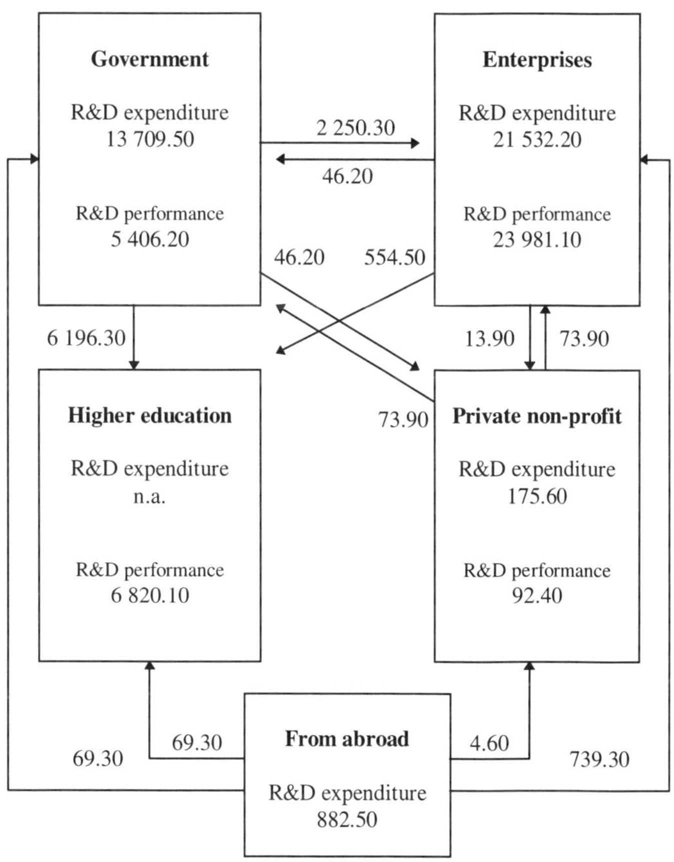

R&D expenditure: All R&D funded by the sector performed in this and other sectors.

R&D performance: R&D performed in this sector.

FRANCE

Table 1. GERD (Gross domestic expenditure on R&D) as a percentage of GDP

	1990	1991	1992	1993	1994
Percentage of GDP	2.41	2.41	2.42	2.45	..

Source: OECD, STIU database.

Table 2. GERD by sector of performance and type of activity, 1992

Percentage

	Government	Higher education	Private non-profit	Enterprises	Total	%
Basic research	18.74	65.58	2.52	13.16	100.00	21.03
Applied research	36.23	5.41	2.04	56.32	100.00	31.49
Experimental development	10.28	0.10	0.34	89.28	100.00	47.48
Not specified	..	..	..	..	..	0.00
Total	20.23	15.54	1.34	62.89	100.00	100.00

Source: OECD, STIU database.

Table 3. Industrial breakdown of BERD (Expenditure on R&D in the business enterprise sector)

Percentage

ISIC	1990	1991	1992	1993	1994
Agriculture	0.97	0.92	1.12	1.14	..
Mining	0.28	0.10	0.85	0.67	..
Manufacturing	92.35	92.10	88.84	88.67	..
Food, beverages & tobacco	1.76	1.76	1.68	1.93	..
Textiles, fur & leather	0.37	0.47	0.48	0.57	..
Wood, paper, print. & publ.	0.38	0.42	0.38	0.42	..
Coke, petrol, nucl. fuel, chem. prod. & plast	21.13	20.63	19.75	20.26	..
Non-metallic mineral products	0.96	1.07	1.16	1.20	..
Basic metals	1.87	1.99	1.95	1.84	..
Fabric. metal products	0.88	0.96	1.09	1.37	..
Machin., instruments & transport equip.	64.77	64.61	62.04	60.64	..
Furnit. & other manufact., nec	0.22	0.21	0.32	0.44	..
Recycling	..	..	..	..	..
Electricity, gas & water supply	1.85	1.87	1.96	1.94	..
Construction	0.67	0.79	0.77	0.78	..
Service sector	3.87	4.23	6.46	6.81	..
Total	100.00	100.00	100.00	100.00	..

Source: OECD, STIU database.

Table 4. R&D personnel by sector of employment, 1991

Percentage

Occupation	Government	Higher education	Private non-profit	Enterprises	Total	%
Scientists and engineers	20.00	32.47	1.61	45.92	100.00	..
Technicians	..	..	..	..	..	..
Other personnel	..	..	..	..	..	..
Total	23.90	22.09	1.78	52.24	100.00	..

Source: OECD, STIU database.

Table 5. Structure of the R&D system (Funding and performance of GERD)

In million US$

1993

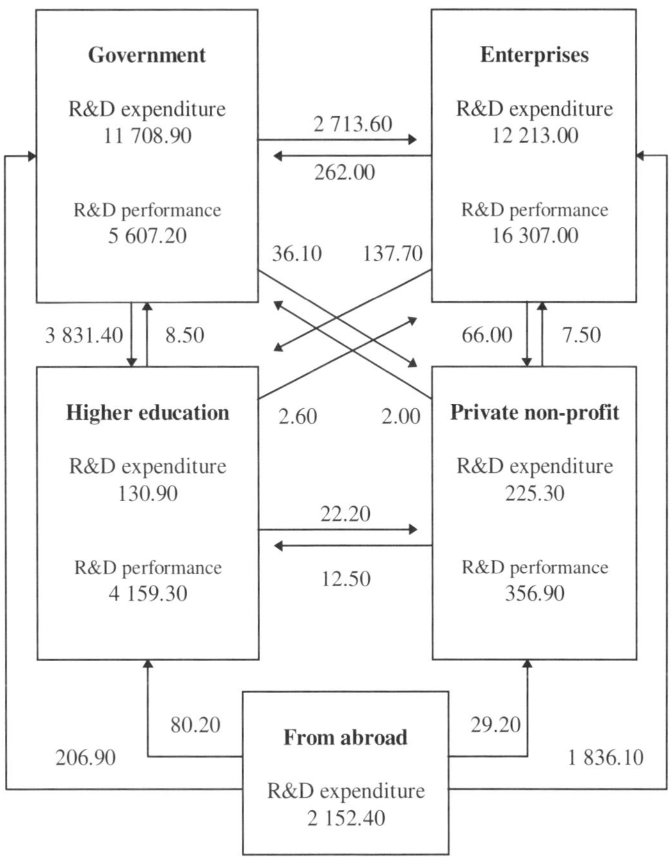

R&D expenditure: All R&D funded by the sector performed in this and other sectors.

R&D performance: R&D performed in this sector.

UNITED KINGDOM

Table 1. GERD (Gross domestic expenditure on R&D) as a percentage of GDP

	1990	1991	1992	1993	1994
Percentage of GDP	2.23	2.16	2.18	2.19	..

Source: OECD, STIU database.

Table 2. GERD by sector of performance and type of activity, 1991

Percentage

	Government	Higher education	Private non-profit	Enterprises	Total	%
Basic research	..	..	..	..	..	..
Applied research	..	..	..	..	..	..
Experimental development	..	..	..	..	..	..
Not specified	..	..	..	..	..	..
Total	..	..	..	..	..	..

Source: OECD, STIU database.

Table 3. Industrial breakdown of BERD (Expenditure on R&D in the business enterprise sector)

Percentage

ISIC	1990	1991	1992	1993	1994
Agriculture	0.81	0.93	0.94	0.98	..
Mining	1.38	1.59	1.48	0.68	..
Manufacturing	79.25	78.35	78.80	77.63	..
Food, beverages & tobacco	2.22	2.27	2.52	1.95	..
Textiles, fur & leather	0.23	0.28	0.29	0.49	..
Wood, paper, print. & publ.	0.52	0.47	0.45	0.45	..
Coke, petrol, nucl. fuel, chem. prod. & plast	26.18	26.31	28.21	28.76	..
Non-metallic mineral products	0.58	0.48	0.44	0.30	..
Basic metals	0.97	0.79	0.77	0.73	..
Fabric. metal products	0.63	0.59	0.74	0.79	..
Machin., instruments & transport equip.	47.67	46.91	45.11	43.93	..
Furnit. & other manufact., nec	0.25	0.26	0.27	0.23	..
Recycling	..	..	..	..	..
Electricity, gas & water supply	2.26	2.36	2.20	2.36	..
Construction	0.23	0.23	0.18	0.12	..
Service sector	16.04	16.52	16.37	18.23	..
Total	100.00	100.00	100.00	100.00	..

Source: OECD, STIU database.

Table 4. R&D personnel by sector of employment, 1993

Percentage

Occupation	Government	Higher education	Private non-profit	Enterprises	Total	%
Scientists and engineers	10.07	23.02	5.04	61.87	100.00	50.18
Technicians	11.86	16.95	3.39	67.80	100.00	21.30
Other personnel	17.72	29.11	6.33	46.84	100.00	28.52
Total	12.64	23.47	5.05	58.84	100.00	100.00

Source: OECD, STIU database.

Table 5. Structure of the R&D system (Funding and performance of GERD)

In million US$

1993

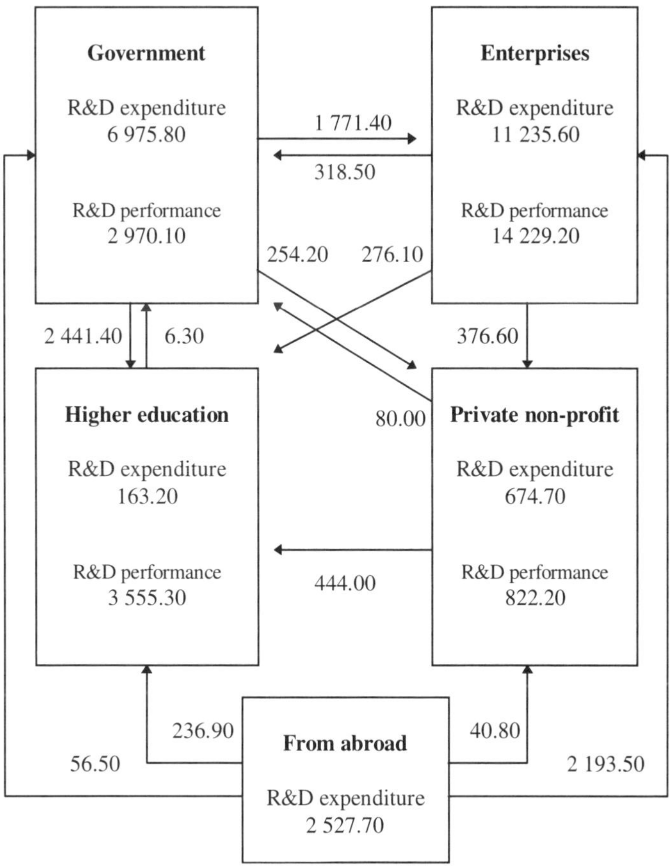

R&D expenditure: All R&D funded by the sector performed in this and other sectors.

R&D performance: R&D performed in this sector.

CANADA

Table 1. GERD (Gross domestic expenditure on R&D) as a percentage of GDP

	1990	1991	1992	1993	1994
Percentage of GDP	1.46	1.51	1.51	1.50	1.47

Source: OECD, STIU database.

Table 2. GERD by sector of performance and type of activity, 1992

Percentage

	Government	Higher education	Private non-profit	Enterprises	Total	%
Basic research	..	..	..	..	..	..
Applied research	..	..	..	..	..	..
Experimental development	..	..	..	..	..	..
Not specified	..	..	..	..	..	..
Total	..	..	..	..	..	..

Source: OECD, STIU database.

Table 3. Industrial breakdown of BERD (Expenditure on R&D in the business enterprise sector)

Percentage

ISIC	1990	1991	1992	1993	1994
Agriculture	0.48	0.61	0.41	0.42	..
Mining	2.36	2.28	2.30	1.88	..
Manufacturing	67.26	65.75	63.95	64.35	..
Food, beverages & tobacco	1.37	1.23	1.06	1.04	..
Textiles, fur & leather	0.78	0.97	0.74	0.73	..
Wood, paper, print. & publ.	3.15	2.35	2.37	2.33	..
Coke, petrol, nucl. fuel, chem. prod. & plast	11.94	11.56	11.48	11.71	..
Non-metallic mineral products	0.32	0.28	0.22	0.21	..
Basic metals	3.53	3.42	3.32	3.34	..
Fabric. metal products	0.72	0.79	0.68	0.68	..
Machin., instruments & transport equip.	44.89	44.55	43.44	43.66	..
Furnit. & other manufact., nec	0.59	0.63	0.63	0.64	..
Recycling	..	..	..	..	..
Electricity, gas & water supply	4.29	4.34	5.17	5.28	..
Construction	0.29	0.20	0.09	0.09	..
Service sector	25.32	26.81	27.01	26.55	..
Total	100.00	100.00	100.00	100.00	..

Source: OECD, STIU database.

Table 4. R&D personnel by sector of employment, 1991

Percentage

Occupation	Government	Higher education	Private non-profit	Enterprises	Total	%
Scientists and engineers	11.49	41.18	0.89	46.45	100.00	57.07
Technicians	19.12	20.14	2.91	57.82	100.00	24.03
Other personnel	28.56	35.00	1.39	35.05	100.00	18.90
Total	16.55	34.96	1.47	47.02	100.00	100.00

Source: OECD, STIU database.

Table 5. Structure of the R&D system (Funding and performance of GERD)

In million US$

1993

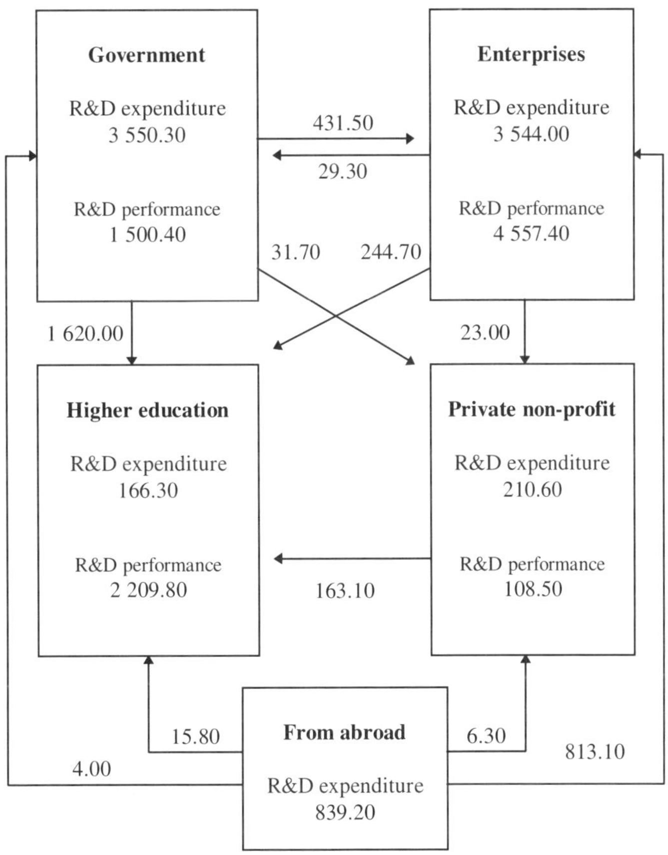

R&D expenditure: All R&D funded by the sector performed in this and other sectors.

R&D performance : R&D performed in this sector.

ITALY

Table 1. GERD (Gross domestic expenditure on R&D) as a percentage of GDP

	1990	1991	1992	1993	1994
Percentage of GDP	1.30	1.32	1.31	1.31	1.21

Source: OECD, STIU database.

Table 2. GERD by sector of performance and type of activity, 1991

Percentage

	Government	Higher education	Private non-profit	Enterprises	Total	%
Basic research	44.18	51.84	0.00	3.99	100.00	17.73
Applied research	27.85	15.94	0.00	56.21	100.00	46.57
Experimental development	7.94	2.97	0.00	89.09	100.00	35.70
Not specified	..	..	..	..	..	0.00
Total	23.64	17.67	0.00	58.69	100.00	100.00

Source: OECD, STIU database.

Table 3. Industrial breakdown of BERD (Expenditure on R&D in the business enterprise sector)

Percentage

ISIC	1990	1991	1992	1993	1994
Agriculture	0.00	0.00	0.00	0.00	..
Mining	..	..	..	..	..
Manufacturing	89.60	87.63	85.63	84.37	..
Food, beverages & tobacco	0.81	0.82	0.94	1.26	1.28
Textiles, fur & leather	0.19	0.18	0.15	0.16	0.16
Wood, paper, print. & publ.	0.09	0.06	0.04	0.03	0.03
Coke, petrol, nucl. fuel, chem. prod. & plast	22.29	21.47	21.43	20.89	21.34
Non-metallic mineral products	0.53	0.53	0.46	0.36	0.39
Basic metals	1.98	1.68	1.38	1.14	0.96
Fabric. metal products	1.61	1.39	1.15	1.32	1.47
Machin., instruments & transport equip.	62.02	61.32	59.93	58.99	59.24
Furnit. & other manufact., nec	0.09	0.16	0.17	0.21	0.23
Recycling	..	..	..	..	..
Electricity, gas & water supply	2.91	3.45	4.54	4.41	..
Construction	0.11	0.04	0.03	0.04	..
Service sector	7.38	8.96	9.79	11.18	..
Total	100.00	100.00	100.00	100.00	..

Source: OECD, STIU database.

Table 4. R&D personnel by sector of employment, 1992

Percentage

Occupation	Government	Higher education	Private non-profit	Enterprises	Total	%
Scientists and engineers	17.63	44.11	0.00	38.27	100.00	52.10
Technicians	29.97	20.65	0.00	49.38	100.00	31.07
Other personnel	26.82	18.87	0.00	54.31	100.00	16.83
Total	23.01	32.57	0.00	44.42	100.00	100.00

Source: OECD, STIU database.

Table 5. Structure of the R&D system (Funding and performance of GERD)

In million US$

1994

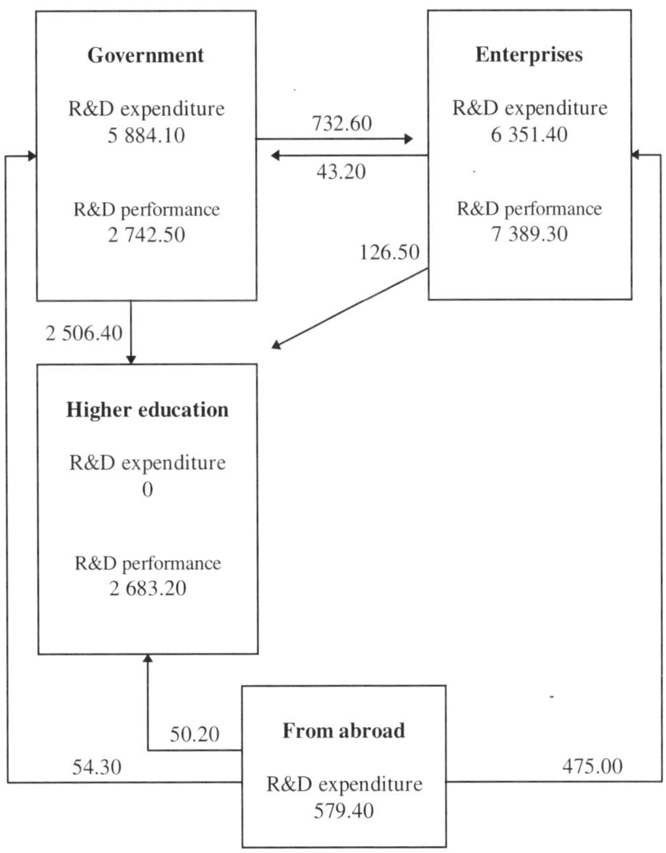

R&D expenditure: All R&D funded by the sector performed in this and other sectors.

R&D performance: R&D performed in this sector.

AUSTRALIA

Table 1. GERD (Gross domestic expenditure on R&D) as a percentage of GDP

	1990	1991	1992	1993	1994
Percentage of GDP	1.36	..	1.58	..	..

Source: OECD, STIU database.

Table 2. GERD by sector of performance and type of activity, 1988

Percentage

	Government	Higher education	Private non-profit	Enterprises	Total	%
Basic research	29.45	58.42	3.13	9.00	100.00	27.36
Applied research	43.08	19.95	1.06	35.91	100.00	39.91
Experimental development	18.82	5.13	0.23	75.81	100.00	32.72
Not specified	..	..	..	..	..	0.00
Total	31.42	25.63	1.35	41.60	100.00	100.00

Source: OECD, STIU database.

Table 3. Industrial breakdown of BERD (Expenditure on R&D in the business enterprise sector)

Percentage

ISIC	1990	1991	1992	1993	1994
Agriculture	..	..	..	..	..
Mining	4.90	6.67	6.03	10.21	..
Manufacturing	54.64	56.97	59.36	55.70	..
Food, beverages & tobacco	4.15	4.70	4.79	4.62	..
Textiles, fur & leather	0.75	0.76	1.01	1.21	..
Wood, paper, print. & publ.	1.96	2.99	2.10	3.80	..
Coke, petrol, nucl. fuel, chem. prod. & plast	10.81	10.41	9.83	8.33	..
Non-metallic mineral products	0.85	1.05	1.09	1.02	..
Basic metals	8.35	7.63	10.25	8.33	..
Fabric. metal products	1.27	1.15	1.56	1.33	..
Machin., instruments & transport equip.	25.80	27.51	28.35	26.57	..
Furnit. & other manufact., nec	0.68	0.76	0.38	0.48	..
Recycling	..	..	..	..	..
Electricity, gas & water supply	2.72	2.21	2.32	1.89	..
Construction	0.26	0.26	0.53	0.46	..
Service sector	37.48	33.88	31.76	31.73	..
Total	100.00	100.00	100.00	100.00	..

Source: OECD, STIU database.

Table 4. R&D personnel by sector of employment, 1992

Percentage

Occupation	Government	Higher education	Private non-profit	Enterprises	Total	%
Scientists and engineers	17.93	54.11	1.04	26.92	100.00	65.66
Technicians	36.57	27.98	1.98	33.48	100.00	22.10
Other personnel	37.31	27.52	2.51	32.67	100.00	12.24
Total	24.42	45.08	1.43	29.07	100.00	100.00

Source: OECD, STIU database.

Table 5. Structure of the R&D system (Funding and performance of GERD)

In million US$

1992

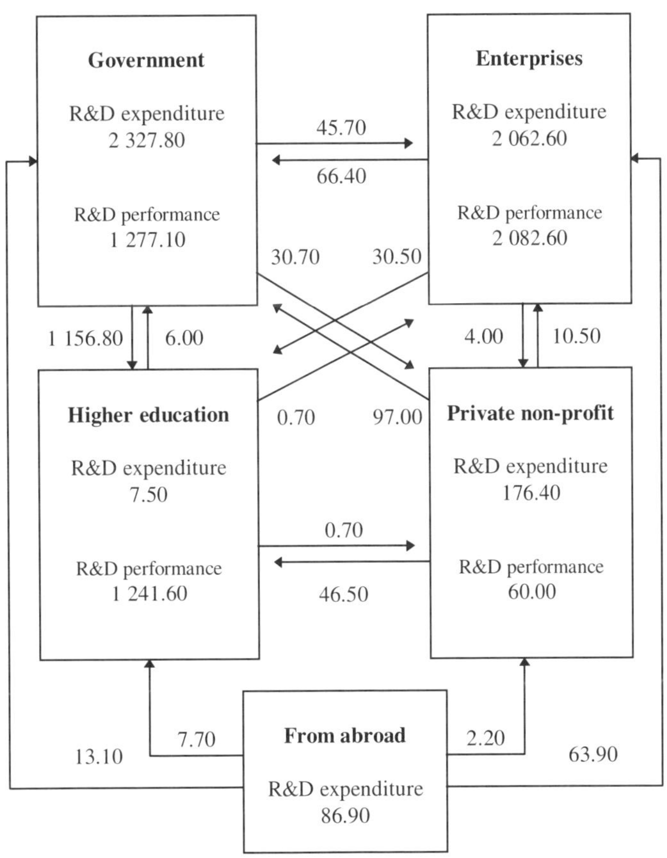

R&D expenditure: All R&D funded by the sector performed in this and other sectors.

R&D performance: R&D performed in this sector.

BELGIUM

Table 1. GERD (Gross domestic expenditure on R&D) as a percentage of GDP

	1990	1991	1992	1993	1994
Percentage of GDP	..	1.66	..	..	..

Source: OECD, STIU database.

Table 2. GERD by sector of performance and type of activity

Percentage

	Government	Higher education	Private non-profit	Enterprises	Total	%
Basic research	..	..	..	..	..	..
Applied research	..	..	..	..	..	..
Experimental development	..	..	..	..	..	..
Not specified	..	..	..	..	..	..
Total	..	..	..	..	..	..

Source: OECD, STIU database.

Table 3. Industrial breakdown of BERD (Expenditure on R&D in the business enterprise sector)

Percentage

ISIC	1990	1991	1992	1993	1994
Agriculture	..	0.46	..	..	..
Mining	..	0.20	..	..	..
Manufacturing	..	93.09	..	..	..
Food, beverages & tobacco	..	2.71	..	..	..
Textiles, fur & leather	..	1.65	..	..	..
Wood, paper, print. & publ.	..	1.07	..	..	..
Coke, petrol, nucl. fuel, chem. prod. & plast	..	40.44	..	..	..
Non-metallic mineral products	..	2.21	..	..	..
Basic metals	..	5.34	..	..	..
Fabric. metal products	..	2.51	..	..	..
Machin., instruments & transport equip.	..	36.95	..	..	..
Furnit. & other manufact., nec	..	0.19	..	..	..
Recycling	..	..	..	..	..
Electricity, gas & water supply	..	0.06	..	..	..
Construction	..	0.38	..	..	..
Service sector	..	5.81	..	..	..
Total	..	100.00	..	..	..

Source: OECD, STIU database.

Table 4. R&D personnel by sector of employment, 1991

Percentage

Occupation	Government	Higher education	Private non-profit	Enterprises	Total	%
Scientists and engineers	8.39	89.84	1.77	0.00	100.00	23.35
Technicians	..	..	..	..	..	..
Other personnel	..	..	..	..	..	..
Total	6.52	36.94	0.85	55.69	100.00	..

Source: OECD, STIU database.

Table 5. Structure of the R&D system (Funding and performance of GERD)

In million US$

1991

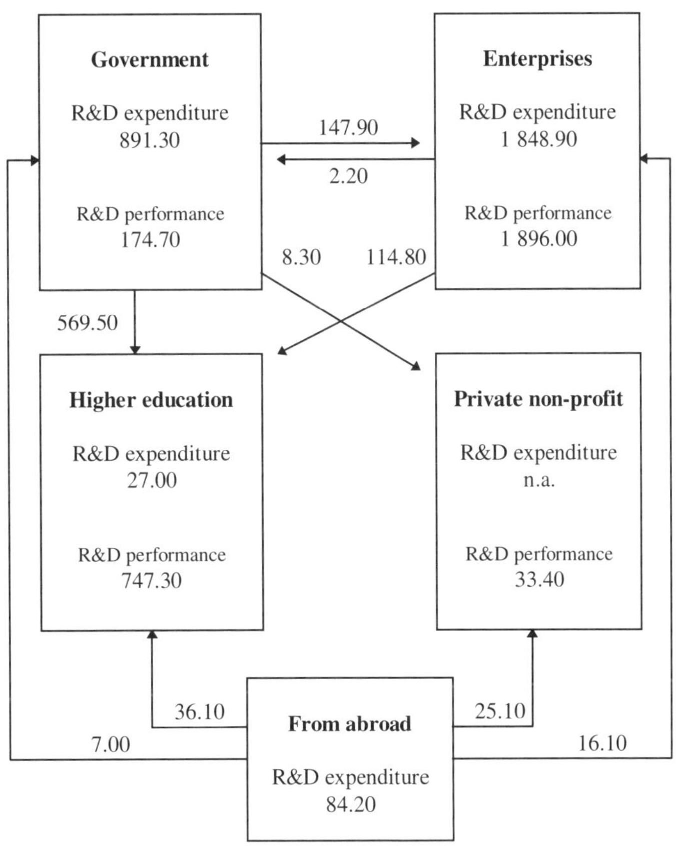

R&D expenditure : All R&D funded by the sector performed in this and other sectors.

R&D performance : R&D performed in this sector.

CZECH REPUBLIC

Table 1. GERD (Gross domestic expenditure on R&D) as a percentage of GDP

	1990	1991	1992	1993	1994
Percentage of GDP	2.19	2.12	1.83	1.35	1.25

Source: Statistical Yearbook of the Czech Republic, 1995.

Table 2. GERD by sector of performance and type of activity

Percentage

	Government	Higher education	Private non-profit	Enterprises	Total	%
Basic research	..	..	..	..	..	..
Applied research	..	..	..	..	..	..
Experimental development	..	..	..	..	..	..
Not specified	..	..	..	..	..	..
Total	..	..	..	..	..	..

Source: OECD, STIU database.

Table 3. Industrial breakdown of BERD (Expenditure on R&D in the business enterprise sector)

Percentage

ISIC	1990	1991	1992	1993	1994
Agriculture	..	..	0	0	0
Mining	..	..	1.32	0.75	0.43
Manufacturing	..	..	59.32	60.63	64.55
Food, beverages & tobacco	..	..	0.96	0.69	0.30
Textiles, fur & leather	..	..	6.61	1.51	0.91
Wood, paper, print. & publ.	..	..	0.57	0.20	0.26
Coke, petrol, nucl. fuel, chem. prod. & plast	..	..	7.71	9.51	11.43
Non-metallic mineral products	..	..	1.01	0.98	1.56
Basic metals	..	..	3.57	5.16	6.08
Fabric. metal products	..	..	4.44	1.77	1.72
Machin., instruments & transport equip.	..	..	33.17	39.17	41.11
Furnit. & other manufact., nec	..	..	1.28	1.64	1.17
Recycling	..	..	0.01	0	0
Electricity, gas & water supply	..	..	0.06	0.01	0.10
Construction	..	..	0.49	0.41	0.47
Service sector	..	..	38.81	38.20	34.45
Total	..	..	100.00	100.00	100.00

Source: Czech statistical office.

Table 4. R&D personnel by sector of employment, 1994

Percentage

Occupation	Government	Higher education	Private non-profit	Enterprises	Total	%
Scientists and engineers	37.27	12.99	0.00	49.74	100.00	35.27
Technicians	26.62	1.91	0.00	71.47	100.00	25.86
Other personnel	25.21	10.07	0.00	64.72	100.00	38.87
Total	29.83	8.99	0.00	61.18	100.00	100.00

Source: Czech statistical office.

Table 5. Structure of the R&D system (Funding and performance of GERD)

(not available)

DENMARK

Table 1. GERD (Gross domestic expenditure on R&D) as a percentage of GDP

	1990	1991	1992	1993	1994
Percentage of GDP	1.63	1.70	1.75	1.80	..

Source: OECD, STIU database.

Table 2. GERD by sector of performance and type of activity, 1993

Percentage

	Government	Higher education	Private non-profit	Enterprises	Total	%
Basic research	23.43	73.23	3.33	0.00	100.00	19.10
Applied research	59.16	38.95	1.89	0.00	100.00	17.66
Experimental development	63.25	34.94	1.82	0.00	100.00	5.90
Not specified	0.00	0.00	0.00	100.00	100.00	57.33
Total	18.66	22.93	1.08	57.33	100.00	100.00

Source: OECD, STIU database.

Table 3. Industrial breakdown of BERD (Expenditure on R&D in the business enterprise sector)

Percentage

ISIC	1990	1991	1992	1993	1994
Agriculture	0.00	0.00	..	0.60	..
Mining	0.00	0.00	..	..	..
Manufacturing	72.11	70.38	68.04	65.93	..
Food, beverages & tobacco	5.04	4.58	4.23	3.92	..
Textiles, fur & leather	0.35	0.40	0.33	0.27	..
Wood, paper, print. & publ.	0.70	0.67	0.48	0.32	..
Coke, petrol, nucl. fuel, chem. prod. & plast	21.17	21.48	21.22	20.99	..
Non-metallic mineral products	1.51	1.45	0.92	0.44	..
Basic metals	2.47	1.18	..	1.10	..
Fabric. metal products	..	1.38	..	..	..
Machin., instruments & transport equip.	34.87	34.00	33.08	32.26	..
Furnit. & other manufact., nec	5.99	5.25	5.98	6.63	..
Recycling	..	..	..	..	..
Electricity, gas & water supply	0.18	0.31	0.35	0.38	..
Construction	0.87	0.82	0.68	0.55	..
Service sector	26.85	28.46	30.60	32.53	..
Total	100.00	100.00	100.00	100.00	..

Source: OECD, STIU database.

Table 4. R&D personnel by sector of employment, 1993

Percentage

Occupation	Government	Higher education	Private non-profit	Enterprises	Total	%
Scientists and engineers	22.01	33.85	1.11	43.03	100.00	49.91
Technicians	..	..	..	..	..	..
Other personnel	..	..	..	..	..	..
Total	17.95	22.70	1.04	58.31	100.00	..

Source: OECD, STIU database.

Table 5. Structure of the R&D system (Funding and performance of GERD)

In million US$

1993

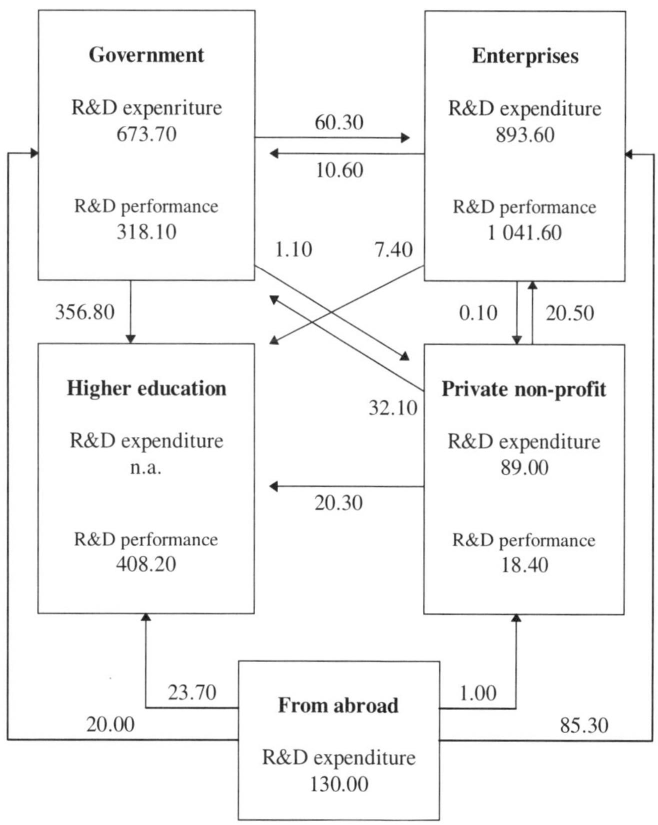

R&D expenditure : All R&D funded by the sector performed in this and other sectors.

R&D performance : R&D performed in this sector.

FINLAND

Table 1. GERD (Gross domestic expenditure on R&D) as a percentage of GDP

	1990	1991	1992	1993	1994
Percentage of GDP	1.91	2.07	2.18	2.22	..

Source: OECD, STIU database.

Table 2. GERD by sector of performance and type of activity

Percentage

	Government	Higher education	Private non-profit	Enterprises	Total	%
Basic research	..	..	..	..	..	..
Applied research	..	..	..	..	..	..
Experimental development	..	..	..	..	..	..
Not specified	..	..	..	..	..	..
Total	..	..	..	..	..	..

Source: OECD, STIU database.

Table 3. Industrial breakdown of BERD (Expenditure on R&D in the business enterprise sector)

Percentage

ISIC	1990	1991	1992	1993	1994
Agriculture	..	0.03	..	0.08	..
Mining	..	0.27	..	0.36	..
Manufacturing	..	83.13	..	84.53	..
Food, beverages & tobacco	..	8.09	..	4.89	..
Textiles, fur & leather	..	1.06	..	0.50	..
Wood, paper, print. & publ.	..	7.45	..	5.41	..
Coke, petrol, nucl. fuel, chem. prod. & plast	..	15.28	..	15.55	..
Non-metallic mineral products	..	1.65	..	2.31	..
Basic metals	..	6.16	..	5.26	..
Fabric. metal products	..	3.68	..	1.60	..
Machin., instruments & transport equip.	..	38.74	..	48.47	..
Furnit. & other manufact., nec	..	1.03	..	0.54	..
Recycling	..	..	..	..	..
Electricity, gas & water supply	..	2.95	..	2.10	..
Construction	..	0.85	..	0.65	..
Service sector	..	12.77	..	12.29	..
Total	100.00	100.00	100.00	100.00	..

Source: OECD, STIU database.

Table 4. R&D personnel by sector of employment, 1993

Percentage

Occupation	Government	Higher education	Private non-profit	Enterprises	Total	%
Scientists and engineers	..	..	..	..	..	..
Technicians	..	..	..	..	..	..
Other personnel	..	..	..	..	..	..
Total	21.80	27.59	0.88	49.73	100.00	..

Source: OECD, STIU database.

Table 5. Structure of the R&D system (Funding and performance of GERD)

In million US$

1993

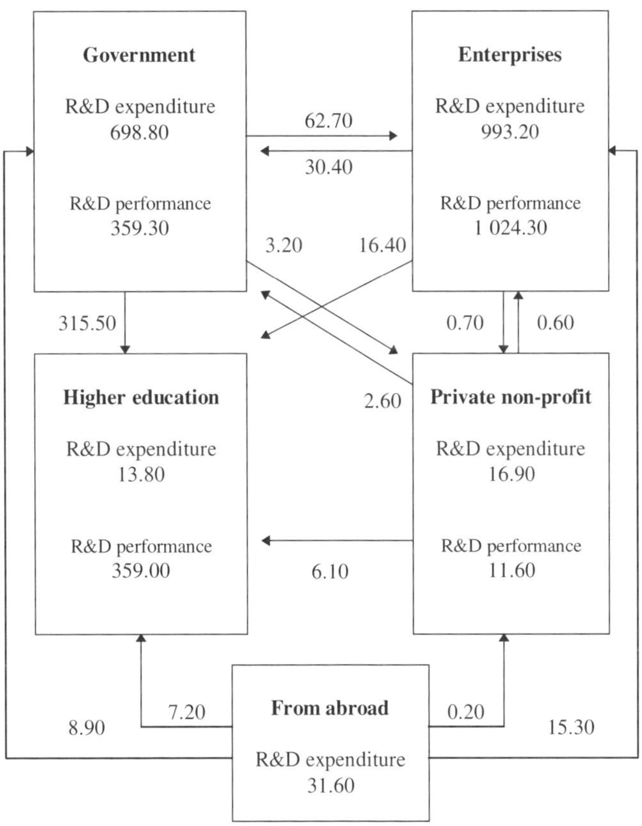

R&D expenditure: All R&D funded by the sector performed in this and other sectors.

R&D performance: R&D performed in this sector.

GREECE

Table 1. GERD (Gross domestic expenditure on R&D) as a percentage of GDP

	1990	1991	1992	1993	1994
Percentage of GDP	..	0.46	..	0.60	..

Source: OECD, STIU database.

Table 2. GERD by sector of performance and type of activity

Percentage

	Government	Higher education	Private non-profit	Enterprises	Total	%
Basic research	..	..	..	..	..	..
Applied research	..	..	..	..	..	..
Experimental development	..	..	..	..	..	..
Not specified	..	..	..	..	..	..
Total	..	..	..	..	..	..

Source: OECD, STIU database.

Table 3. Industrial breakdown of BERD (Expenditure on R&D in the business enterprise sector)

Percentage

ISIC	1990	1991	1992	1993	1994
Agriculture	..	0.28	..	..	..
Mining	..	5.86	..	..	..
Manufacturing	..	61.42	..	..	..
Food, beverages & tobacco	..	5.47	..	..	..
Textiles, fur & leather	..	0.49	..	..	..
Wood, paper, print. & publ.	..	1.07	..	..	..
Coke, petrol, nucl. fuel, chem. prod. & plast	..	15.38	..	..	..
Non-metallic mineral products	..	4.18	..	..	..
Basic metals	..	0.86	..	..	..
Fabric. metal products	..	5.69	..	..	..
Machin., instruments & transport equip.	..	26.76	..	..	..
Furnit. & other manufact., nec	..	1.54	..	..	..
Recycling	..	..	..	..	..
Electricity, gas & water supply	..	2.16	..	..	..
Construction	..	0.31	..	..	..
Service sector	..	29.98	..	..	..
Total	..	100.00	..	..	..

Source: OECD, STIU database.

Table 4. R&D personnel by sector of employment, 1993

Percentage

Occupation	Government	Higher education	Private non-profit	Enterprises	Total	%
Scientists and engineers	23.66	59.29	0.42	16.62	100.00	55.14
Technicians	29.66	41.23	0.37	28.74	100.00	22.42
Other personnel	59.58	19.66	0.85	19.90	100.00	22.44
Total	33.07	46.35	0.51	20.08	100.00	100.00

Source: OECD, STIU database.

Table 5. Structure of the R&D system (Funding and performance of GERD)

In million US$

1993

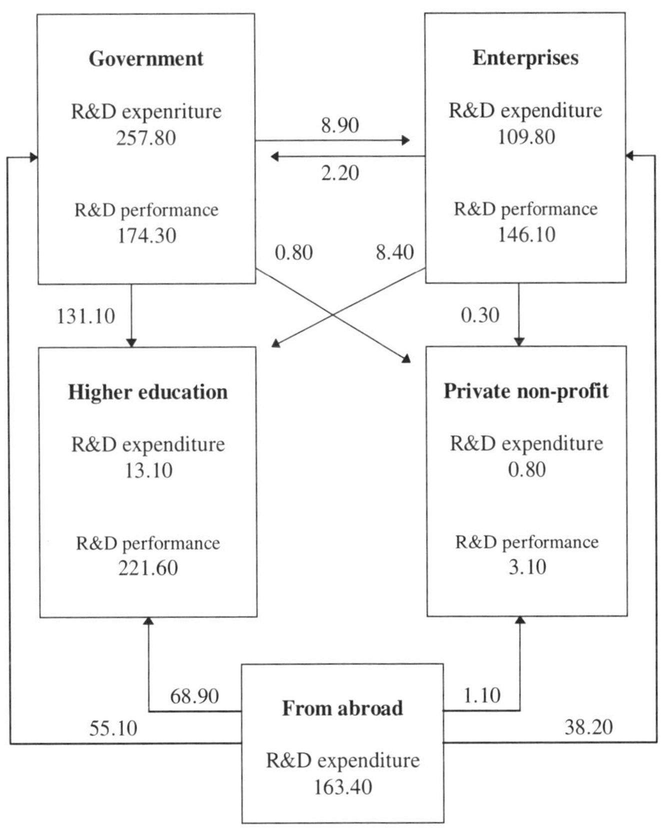

R&D expenditure : All R&D funded by the sector performed in this and other sectors.

R&D performance : R&D performed in this sector.

HUNGARY

Table 1. GERD (Gross domestic expenditure on R&D) as a percentage of GDP

	1990	1991	1992	1993	1994
Percentage of GDP	1.60	1.07	1.06	0.98	0.89

Source: Central Statistical Office of Hungary.

Table 2. GERD by sector of performance and type of activity

Percentage

	Government	Higher education	Private non-profit	Enterprises	Total	%
Basic research	55.6	37.4	..	7.0	100.0	25.0
Applied research	24.4	27.0	..	48.6	100.0	32.9
Experimental development	13.6	13.6	..	72.8	100.0	23.2
Not specified	..	..	..	..	100.0	18.9
Total	25.1	21.4	..	34.6	100.0[1]	100.0

1. Including those amounts which are not detailed by type of activity and sector of performance.

Source: Central Statistical Office of Hungary.

Table 3. Industrial breakdown of BERD (Expenditure on R&D in the business enterprise sector)

Percentage

ISIC	1990	1991	1992	1993	1994
Agriculture	..	..	28.9	22.6	19.6
Mining	..	..	0.1	0.0	0.1
Manufacturing	..	..	61.2	64.1	71.6
Food, beverages & tobacco	..	..	0.5	0.3	1.7
Textiles, fur & leather	..	..	..	0.0	0.2
Wood, paper, print. & publ.	..	..	..	0.0	0.3
Coke, petrol, nucl. fuel, chem. prod. & plast	..	..	47.9	45.8	53.2
Non-metallic mineral products	..	..	0.2	0.0	0.4
Basic metals	..	..	2.1	1.7	0.9
Fabric. metal products	..	..	0.7	0.4	1.2
Machin., instruments & transport equip.	..	..	9.8	15.9	13.7
Furnit. & other manufact., nec	..	..	0.0	0.0	0.0
Recycling	..	..	..	..	..
Electricity, gas & water supply	..	..	0.4	0.2	3.0
Construction	..	..	0.0	0.1	0.5
Service sector	..	..	9.4	13.0	5.2
Total	..	..	100.0	100.0	100.0

Source: Central Statistical Office of Hungary.

Table 4. R&D personnel by sector of employment, 1992

Percentage

Occupation	Government	Higher education	Private non-profit	Enterprises	Total	%
Scientists and engineers	31.1	38.6	..	30.3	100.0	50.9
Technicians	28.4	21.9	..	49.7	100.0	29.6
Other personnel	30.2	33.2	..	36.0	100.0	19.5
Total	30.2	32.7	..	37.1	100.0	100.0

Source: Central Statistical Office of Hungary.

ICELAND

Table 1. GERD (Gross domestic expenditure on R&D) as a percentage of GDP

	1990	1991	1992	1993	1994
Percentage of GDP	0.99	1.16	1.33	..	..

Source: OECD, STIU database.

Table 2. GERD by sector of performance and type of activity, 1992

Percentage

	Government	Higher education	Private non-profit	Enterprises	Total	%
Basic research	34.78	57.14	8.07	0.00	100.00	25.08
Applied research	56.21	25.82	4.25	13.73	100.00	47.66
Experimental development	29.14	14.29	0.00	56.57	100.00	27.26
Not specified	..	..	..	..	..	0.00
Total	43.46	30.53	4.05	21.96	100.00	100.00

Source: OECD, STIU database.

Table 3. Industrial breakdown of BERD
(Expenditure on R&D in the business enterprise sector)

Percentage

ISIC	1990	1991	1992	1993	1994
Agriculture	7.98	5.90	5.59	..	..
Mining	..	0.14	0.39	..	..
Manufacturing	71.89	65.54	66.90	..	..
Food, beverages & tobacco	25.35	18.45	17.41	..	..
Textiles, fur & leather	1.81	1.84	1.84	..	..
Wood, paper, print. & publ.	0.50	0.35	0.33	..	..
Coke, petrol, nucl. fuel, chem. prod. & plast	13.35	13.74	13.10	..	..
Non-metallic mineral products	..	..	..	..	..
Basic metals	5.42	4.47	4.43	..	..
Fabric. metal products	0.88	..	..	..	..
Machin., instruments & transport equip.	23.27	25.71	28.87	..	..
Furnit. & other manufact., nec	1.30	0.98	0.93	..	..
Recycling	..	..	..	..	..
Electricity, gas & water supply	5.71	4.28	4.06	..	..
Construction	6.26	5.85	5.79	..	..
Service sector	8.17	18.30	17.27	..	..
Total	100.00	100.00	100.00	..	..

Source: OECD, STIU database.

Table 4. R&D personnel by sector of employment, 1992

Percentage

Occupation	Government	Higher education	Private non-profit	Enterprises	Total	%
Scientists and engineers	40.34	31.73	2.82	25.11	100.00	56.99
Technicians	26.15	40.00	5.23	28.62	100.00	26.13
Other personnel	50.00	30.95	9.52	9.52	100.00	16.88
Total	38.26	33.76	4.58	23.39	100.00	100.00

Source: OECD, STIU database.

Table 5. Structure of the R&D system (Funding and performance of GERD)

In million US$

1992

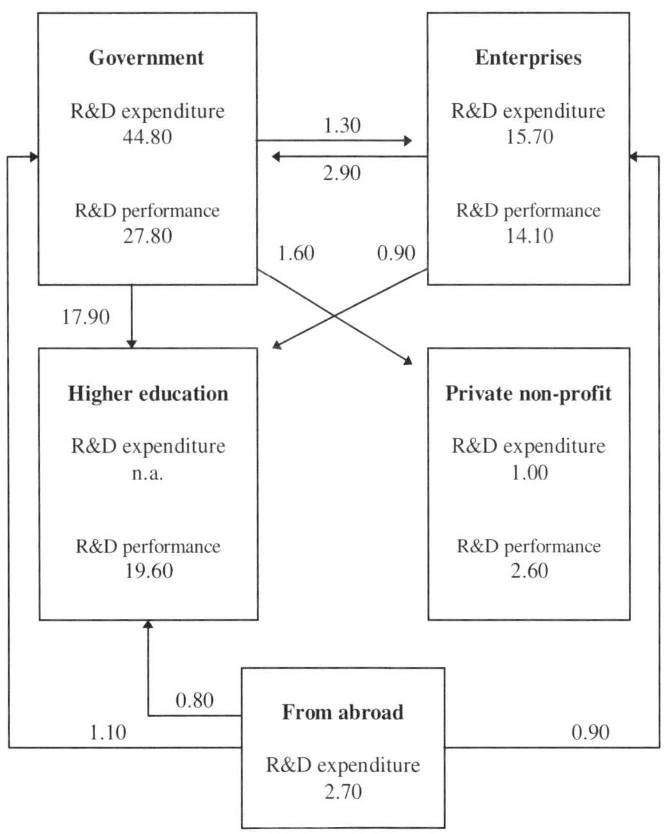

R&D expenditure : All R&D funded by the sector performed in this and other sectors.

R&D performance : R&D performed in this sector.

IRELAND

Table 1. GERD (Gross domestic expenditure on R&D) as a percentage of GDP

	1990	1991	1992	1993	1994
Percentage of GDP	0.87	1.01	1.10	1.22	..

Source: OECD, STIU database.

Table 2. GERD by sector of performance and type of activity, 1992

Percentage

	Government	Higher education	Private non-profit	Enterprises	Total	%
Basic research	..	..	..	..	..	..
Applied research	..	..	..	..	..	..
Experimental development	..	..	..	..	..	..
Not specified	..	..	..	..	..	..
Total	..	..	..	..	..	..

Source: OECD, STIU database.

Table 3. Industrial breakdown of BERD (Expenditure on R&D in the business enterprise sector)

Percentage

ISIC	1990	1991	1992	1993	1994
Agriculture	2.40	1.16	..	..	..
Mining	0.52	1.00	..	..	..
Manufacturing	93.51	94.36	..	..	..
Food, beverages & tobacco	8.96	12.29	..	..	..
Textiles, fur & leather	1.31	2.87	..	..	..
Wood, paper, print. & publ.	1.25	1.28	..	..	..
Coke, petrol, nucl. fuel, chem. prod. & plast	23.20	20.10	..	..	..
Non-metallic mineral products	1.45	1.60	..	..	..
Basic metals	0.28	0.95	..	..	..
Fabric. metal products	2.22	2.49	..	..	..
Machin., instruments & transport equip.	54.58	52.43	..	..	..
Furnit. & other manufact., nec	0.26	0.35	..	..	..
Recycling	..	..	..	..	..
Electricity, gas & water supply	0.15	0.00	..	..	..
Construction	0.06	0.11	..	..	..
Service sector	3.36	3.37	..	..	..
Total	100.00	100.00	..	..	..

Source : OECD, STIU database.

Table 4. R&D personnel by sector of employment, 1992

Percentage

Occupation	Government	Higher education	Private non-profit	Enterprises	Total	%
Scientists and engineers	9.14	46.70	3.81	40.35	100.00	66.86
Technicians	..	..	..	..	..	..
Other personnel	..	..	..	..	..	..
Total	13.27	34.53	3.62	48.58	100.00	..

Source: OECD, STIU database.

Table 5. Structure of the R&D system (Funding and performance of GERD)

In million US$

1993

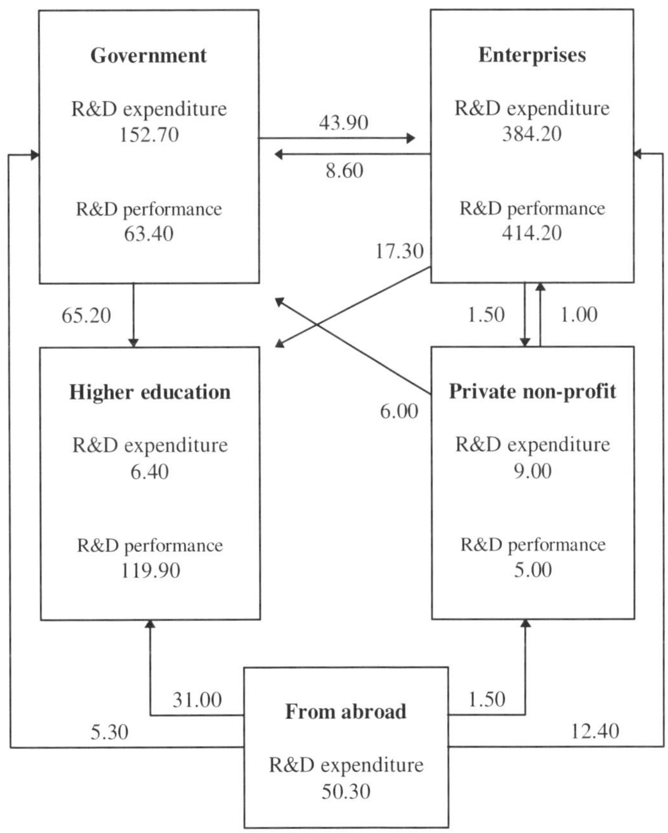

R&D expenditure : All R&D funded by the sector performed in this and other sectors.

R&D performance : R&D performed in this sector.

MEXICO

Table 1. GERD (Gross domestic expenditure on R&D) as a percentage of GDP

	1990	1991	1992	1993	1994
Percentage of GDP	..	..	..	0.32	..

Source: OECD, STIU database.

Table 2. GERD by sector of performance and type of activity

Percentage

	Government	Higher education	Private non-profit	Enterprises	Total	%
Basic research	..	..	..	..	..	..
Applied research	..	..	..	..	..	..
Experimental development	..	..	..	..	..	..
Not specified	..	..	..	..	..	..
Total	..	..	..	..	..	..

Source: OECD, STIU database.

Table 3. Industrial breakdown of BERD (Expenditure on R&D in the business enterprise sector)

Percentage

ISIC	1990	1991	1992	1993	1994
Agriculture	..	..	0.00	0.00	..
Mining	..	..	4.11	1.55	..
Manufacturing	..	..	86.13	86.67	..
Food, beverages & tobacco	..	..	3.16	4.50	..
Textiles, fur & leather	..	..	1.57	0.47	..
Wood, paper, print. & publ.	..	..	7.63	0.88	..
Coke, petrol, nucl. fuel, chem. prod. & plast	..	..	17.53	23.76	..
Non-metallic mineral products	..	..	5.50	3.73	..
Basic metals	..	..	1.11	6.00	..
Fabric. metal products	..	..	0.67	0.65	..
Machin., instruments & transport equip.	..	..	42.49	38.37	..
Furnit. & other manufact., nec	..	..	6.47	8.31	..
Recycling	..	..	0.00	0.00	..
Electricity, gas & water supply	..	..	0.00	3.98	..
Construction	..	..	0.00	0.00	..
Service sector	..	..	9.76	7.79	..
Total	..	..	100.00	100.00	..

Source: OECD, STIU database.

Table 4. R&D personnel by sector of employment, 1992

Percentage

Occupation	Government	Higher education	Private non-profit	Enterprises	Total	%
Scientists and engineers	..	89.91	..	10.09	100.00	66.52
Technicians	..	70.42	..	29.58	100.00	19.18
Other personnel	..	82.02	..	17.98	100.00	14.30
Total	..	85.05	..	14.95	100.00	100.00

Source: OECD, STIU database.

Table 5. Structure of the R&D system (Funding and performance of GERD)

In million US$

1993

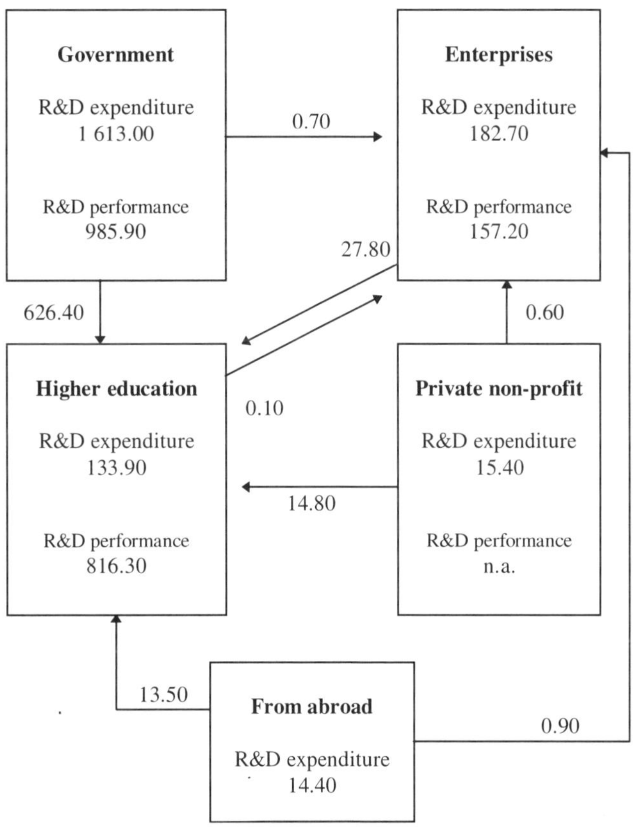

R&D expenditure : All R&D funded by the sector performed in this and other sectors.

R&D performance : R&D performed in this sector.

NETHERLANDS

Table 1. GERD (Gross domestic expenditure on R&D) as a percentage of GDP

	1991	1992	1990	1993	1994
Percentage of GDP	1.91	1.87	2.02	1.89	..

Source: OECD, STIU database.

Table 2. GERD by sector of performance and type of activity, 1991

Percentage

	Government	Higher education	Private non-profit	Enterprises	Total	%
Basic research	46.91	2.58	3.47	47.04	100.00	14.97
Applied research	36.02	1.41	4.43	58.14	100.00	30.04
Experimental development	5.54	0.68	2.09	91.69	100.00	31.27
Not specified	0.00	100.00	0.00	0.00	100.00	23.73
Total	19.57	24.75	2.50	53.17	100.00	100.00

Source: OECD, STIU database.

Table 3. Industrial breakdown of BERD (Expenditure on R&D in the business enterprise sector)

Percentage

ISIC	1990	1991	1992	1993	1994
Agriculture	2.32	2.50	2.58	2.92	..
Mining	..	..	..	..	..
Manufacturing	90.43	89.89	89.61	86.75	..
Food, beverages & tobacco	5.21	5.56	5.57	8.42	..
Textiles, fur & leather	0.41	0.38	0.40	0.21	..
Wood, paper, print. & publ.	0.48	0.53	0.29	0.33	..
Coke, petrol, nucl. fuel, chem. prod. & plast	35.33	37.64	38.49	32.72	..
Non-metallic mineral products	0.27	0.33	0.37	0.42	..
Basic metals	..	..	..	..	..
Fabric. metal products	..	..	..	..	..
Machin., instruments & transport equip.	48.73	45.45	44.49	44.65	..
Furnit. & other manufact., nec	..	..	..	..	..
Recycling	..	..	..	..	..
Electricity, gas & water supply	0.27	0.29	0.24	0.14	..
Construction	0.56	0.60	0.62	0.45	..
Service sector	6.30	6.72	6.94	9.76	..
Total	100.00	100.00	100.00	100.00	..

Source: OECD, STIU database.

Table 4. R&D personnel by sector of employment, 1993

Percentage

Occupation	Government	Higher education	Private non-profit	Enterprises	Total	%
Scientists and engineers	24.10	35.29	2.86	37.75	100.00	43.96
Technicians	..	..	..	..	..	..
Other personnel	..	..	..	..	..	..
Total	22.17	30.10	2.63	45.10	100.00	..

Source: OECD, STIU database.

Table 5. Structure of the R&D system (Funding and performance of GERD)

In million US$

1993

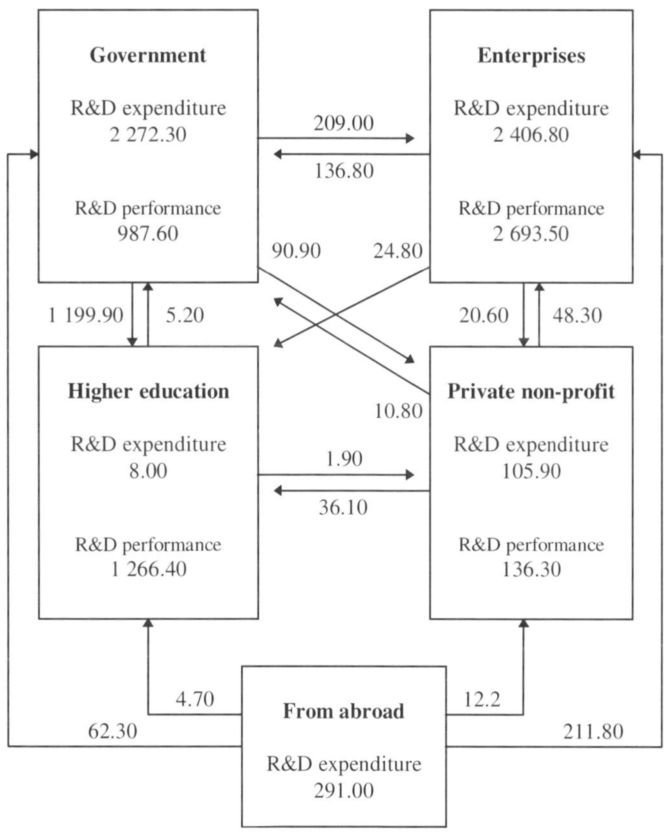

R&D expenditure : All R&D funded by the sector performed in this and other sectors.

R&D performance : R&D performed in this sector.

NEW ZEALAND

Table 1. GERD (Gross domestic expenditure on R&D) as a percentage of GDP

	1990	1991	1992	1993	1994
Percentage of GDP	0.88	0.88	0.99	..	..

Source: OECD, STIU database.

Table 2. GERD by sector of performance and type of activity

Percentage

	Government	Higher education	Private non-profit	Enterprises	Total	%
Basic research	..	..	..	..	..	..
Applied research	..	..	..	..	..	..
Experimental development	..	..	..	..	..	..
Not specified	..	..	..	..	..	..
Total	..	..	..	..	..	..

Source: OECD, STIU database.

Table 3. Industrial breakdown of BERD (Expenditure on R&D in the business enterprise sector)

Percentage

ISIC	1990	1991	1992	1993	1994
Agriculture	1.81	2.20	..	..	..
Mining	..	2.45	..	..	..
Manufacturing	59.69	58.84	..	..	..
Food, beverages & tobacco	20.89	21.46	..	..	..
Textiles, fur & leather	6.75	5.49	..	..	..
Wood, paper, print. & publ.	3.42	2.06	..	..	..
Coke, petrol, nucl. fuel, chem. prod. & plast	9.25	9.31	..	..	..
Non-metallic mineral products	1.91	1.96	..	..	..
Basic metals	0.49	0.73	..	..	..
Fabric. metal products	2.01	1.91	..	..	..
Machin., instruments & transport equip.	14.29	15.34	..	..	..
Furnit. & other manufact., nec	0.64	0.29	..	..	..
Recycling	..	..	..	..	..
Electricity, gas & water supply	1.22	..	..	..	..
Construction	1.57	1.27	..	..	..
Service sector	33.66	35.23	..	..	..
Total	100.00	100.00	..	..	..

Source: OECD, STIU database.

NEW ZEALAND (continued)

Table 4. R&D personnel by sector of employment, 1992

Percentage

Occupation	Government	Higher education	Private non-profit	Enterprises	Total	%
Scientists and engineers	26.26	51.03	..	22.72	100.00	59.27
Technicians	51.23	18.01	..	30.76	100.00	27.59
Other personnel	59.39	16.20	..	24.41	100.00	13.14
Total	37.50	37.34	..	25.16	100.00	100.00

Source: OECD, STIU database.

Table 5. Structure of the R&D system (Funding and performance of GERD)

(In million US $)

1992

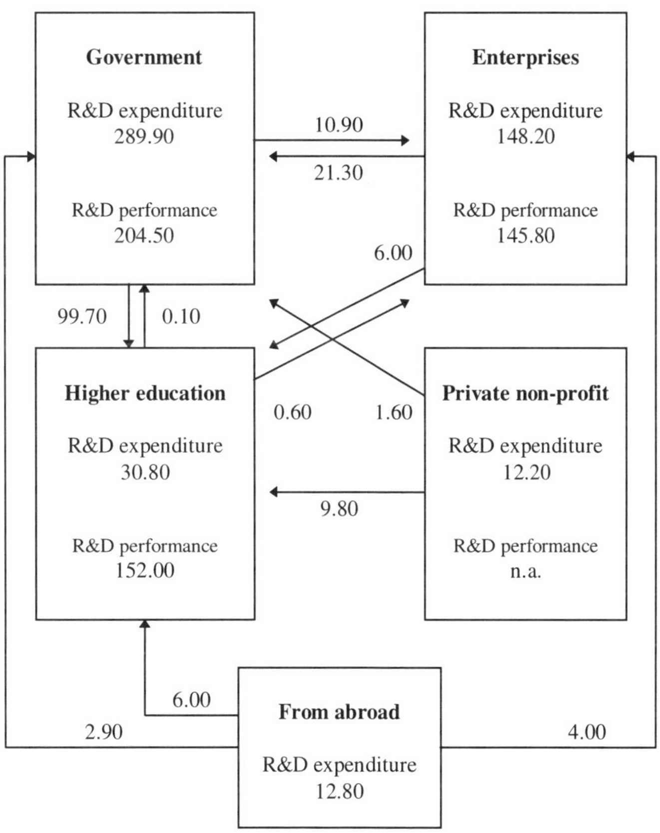

R&D expenditure : All R&D funded by the sector performed in this and other sectors.

R&D performance : R&D performed in this sector.

PORTUGAL

Table 1. GERD (Gross domestic expenditure on R&D) as a percentage of GDP

	1990	1991	1992	1993	1994
Percentage of GDP	0.54	..	0.63	..	..

Source: OECD, STIU database.

Table 2. GERD by sector of performance and type of activity

Percentage

	Government	Higher education	Private non-profit	Enterprises	Total	%
Basic research	..	..	..	..	..	..
Applied research	..	..	..	..	..	..
Experimental development	..	..	..	..	..	..
Not specified	..	..	..	..	..	..
Total	..	..	..	..	..	..

Source: OECD, STIU database.

Table 3. Industrial breakdown of BERD (Expenditure on R&D in the business enterprise sector)

Percentage

ISIC	1990	1991	1992	1993	1994
Agriculture	0.01	..	0.07	..	..
Mining	0.80	..	0.43	..	..
Manufacturing	70.77	..	76.89	..	..
Food, beverages & tobacco	3.48	..	3.99	..	..
Textiles, fur & leather	2.71	..	2.30	..	..
Wood, paper, print. & publ.	11.71	..	5.97	..	..
Coke, petrol, nucl. fuel, chem. prod. & plast	14.77	..	13.64	..	..
Non-metallic mineral products	1.21	..	1.27	..	..
Basic metals	1.20	..	2.84	..	..
Fabric. metal products	1.63	..	3.35	..	..
Machin., instruments & transport equip.	34.06	..	43.37	..	..
Furnit. & other manufact., nec	0.00	..	0.17	..	..
Recycling	..	..	0.00	..	..
Electricity, gas & water supply	1.09	..	1.27	..	..
Construction	0.09	..	0.09	..	..
Service sector	27.24	..	21.25	..	..
Total	100.00	..	100.00	..	..

Source: OECD, STIU database.

Table 4. R&D personnel by sector of employment, 1992

Percentage

Occupation	Government	Higher education	Private non-profit	Enterprises	Total	%
Scientists and engineers	14.04	67.57	12.10	6.29	100.00	56.86
Technicians	45.90	17.21	8.65	28.24	100.00	26.31
Other personnel	55.55	20.90	5.79	17.76	100.00	16.83
Total	29.41	46.47	10.13	13.99	100.00	100.00

Source: OECD, STIU database.

Table 5. Structure of the R&D system (Funding and performance of GERD)

In million US$

1992

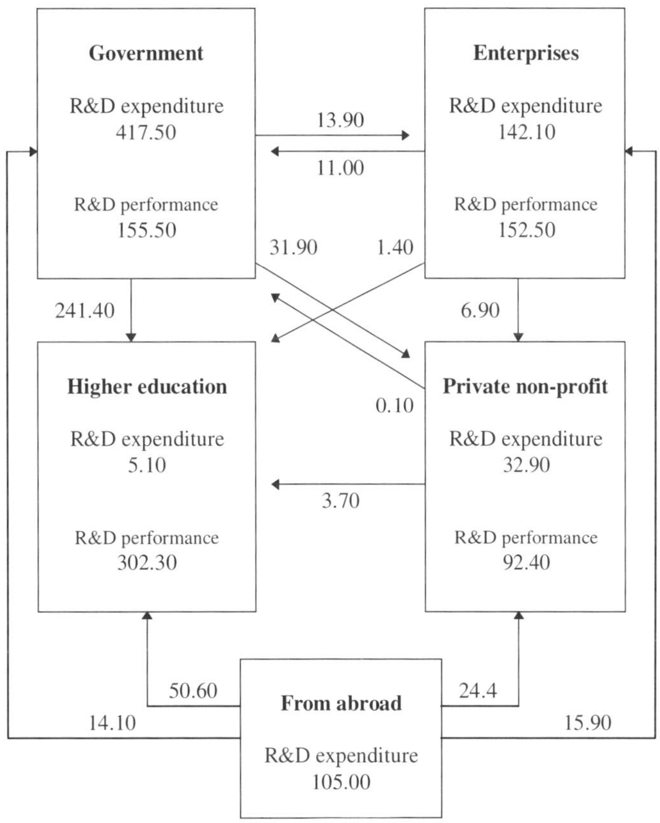

R&D expenditure : All R&D funded by the sector performed in this and other sectors.

R&D performance : R&D performed in this sector.

SPAIN

Table 1. GERD (Gross domestic expenditure on R&D) as a percentage of GDP

	1990	1991	1992	1993	1994
Percentage of GDP	0.85	0.87	0.92	0.88	0.84

Source: OECD, STIU database.

Table 2. GERD by sector of performance and type of activity, 1992

Percentage

	Government	Higher education	Private non-profit	Enterprises	Total	%
Basic research	16.81	69.61	1.02	12.56	100.00	19.91
Applied research	28.18	29.89	0.67	41.26	100.00	37.03
Experimental development	10.89	4.98	0.15	83.97	100.00	42.92
Not specified	0.00	0.00	100.00	0.00	100.00	0.14
Total	18.46	27.06	0.65	53.82	100.00	100.00

Source: OECD, STIU database.

Table 3. Industrial breakdown of BERD (Expenditure on R&D in the business enterprise sector)

Percentage

ISIC	1990	1991	1992	1993	1994
Agriculture	0.72	0.95	1.01	..	..
Mining	1.11	1.15	0.96	..	..
Manufacturing	79.90	78.40	77.26	..	..
Food, beverages & tobacco	2.57	2.42	3.05	..	..
Textiles, fur & leather	0.45	0.54	0.68	..	..
Wood, paper, print. & publ.	0.88	0.78	0.72	..	..
Coke, petrol, nucl. fuel, chem. prod. & plast	18.44	18.37	17.62	..	..
Non-metallic mineral products	1.47	1.25	1.44	..	..
Basic metals	1.31	1.28	1.18	..	..
Fabric. metal products	2.05	1.97	1.04	..	..
Machin., instruments & transport equip.	51.91	51.20	50.98	..	..
Furnit. & other manufact., nec	0.82	0.59	0.55	..	..
Recycling	0.00	0.00	0.00	..	..
Electricity, gas & water supply	2.93	2.53	3.02	..	..
Construction	0.84	0.61	0.67	..	..
Service sector	14.50	16.36	17.08	..	..
Total	100.00	100.00	100.00	..	..

Source: OECD, STIU database.

Table 4. R&D personnel by sector of employment, 1992

Percentage

Occupation	Government	Higher education	Private non-profit	Enterprises	Total	%
Scientists and engineers	18.38	53.18	0.63	27.81	100.00	61.36
Technicians	21.31	..	0.95	77.74	100.00	17.87
Other personnel	45.57	..	0.87	53.56	100.00	20.77
Total	24.55	32.63	0.73	42.08	100.00	100.00

Source: OECD, STIU database.

Table 5. Structure of the R&D system (Funding and performance of GERD)

In million US$

1992

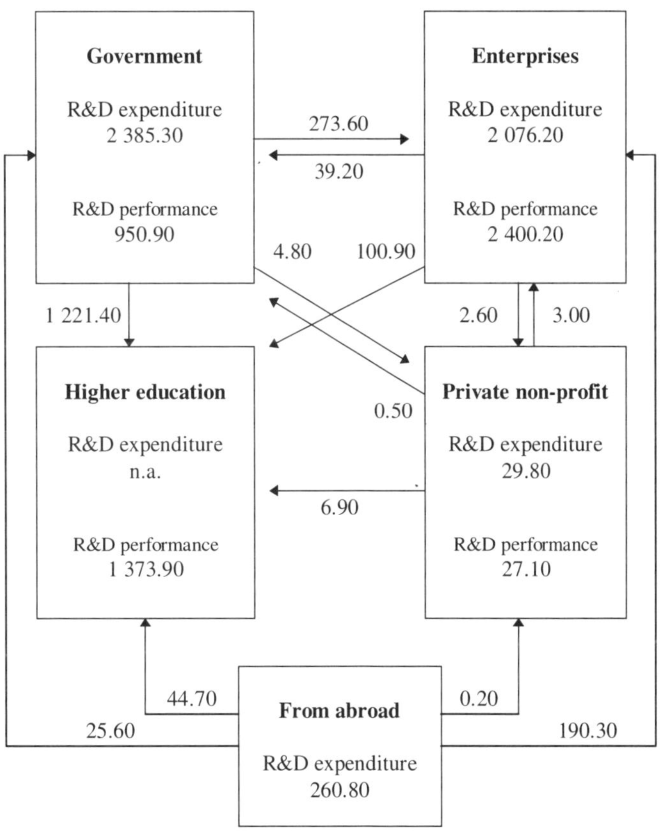

R&D expenditure : All R&D funded by the sector performed in this and other sectors.

R&D performance : R&D performed in this sector.

SWEDEN

Table 1. GERD (Gross domestic expenditure on R&D) as a percentage of GDP

	1990	1991	1992	1993	1994
Percentage of GDP	..	2.86	..	3.26	..

Source: OECD, STIU database.

Table 2. GERD by sector of performance and type of activity, 1991

Percentage

	Government	Higher education	Private non-profit	Enterprises	Total	%
Basic research	2.62	91.95	0.17	5.26	100.00	20.02
Applied research	13.77	34.41	0.22	51.61	100.00	15.29
Experimental development	2.44	5.59	0.04	91.93	100.00	64.69
Not specified	..	..	..	..	..	0.00
Total	4.21	27.29	0.09	68.41	100.00	100.00

Source: OECD, STIU database.

Table 3. Industrial breakdown of BERD (Expenditure on R&D in the business enterprise sector)

Percentage

ISIC	1990	1991	1992	1993	1994
Agriculture	..	0.89	..	1.14	..
Mining	..	0.40	..	0.34	..
Manufacturing	..	92.86	..	92.09	..
Food, beverages & tobacco	..	1.59	..	1.43	..
Textiles, fur & leather	..	0.22	..	0.21	..
Wood, paper, print. & publ.	..	4.57	..	5.60	..
Coke, petrol, nucl. fuel, chem. prod. & plast	..	16.53	..	16.55	..
Non-metallic mineral products	..	0.35	..	0.34	..
Basic metals	..	1.24	..	1.23	..
Fabric. metal products	..	2.72	..	1.60	..
Machin., instruments & transport equip.	..	65.57	..	64.67	..
Furnit. & other manufact., nec	..	0.06	..	0.23	..
Recycling	..	..	..	..	..
Electricity, gas & water supply	..	1.71	..	1.30	..
Construction	..	0.43	..	..	..
Service sector	..	3.72	..	4.44	..
Total	..	100.00	..	100.00	..

Source: OECD, STIU database.

Table 4. R&D personnel by sector of employment, 1993
Percentage

Occupation	Government	Higher education	Private non-profit	Enterprises	Total	%
Scientists and engineers	..	..	..	..	..	..
Technicians	..	..	..	..	..	..
Other personnel	..	..	..	..	..	..
Total	5.23	33.16	0.19	61.42	100.00	..

Source: OECD, STIU database.

Table 5. Structure of the R&D system
(Funding and performance of GERD)
In million US$
1991

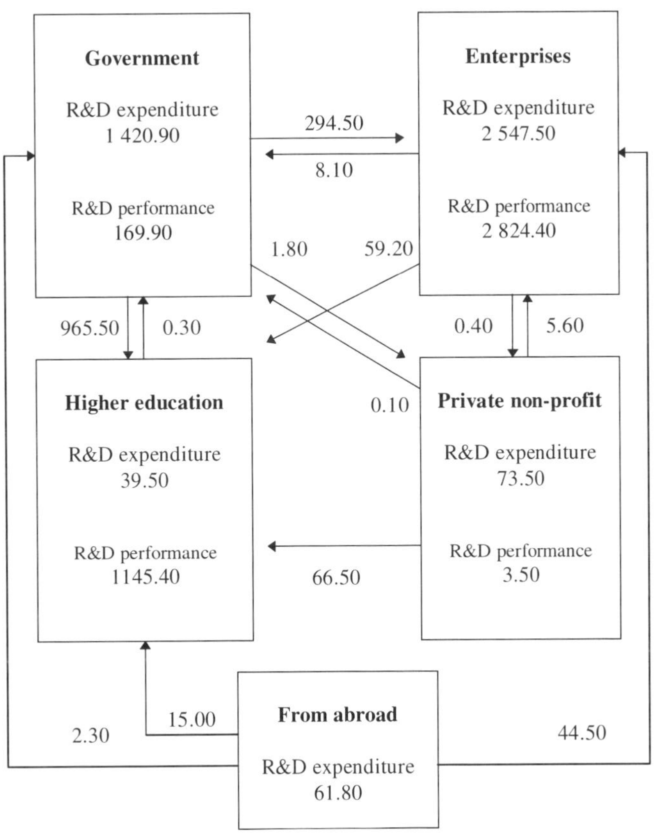

R&D expenditure: All R&D funded by the sector performed in this and other sectors.

R&D performance: R&D performed in this sector.

SWITZERLAND

Table 1. GERD (Gross domestic expenditure on R&D) as a percentage of GDP

	1990	1991	1992	1993	1994
Percentage of GDP	..	..	2.68	..	..

Source: OECD, STIU database.

Table 2. GERD by sector of performance and type of activity, 1992

Percentage

	Government	Higher education	Private non-profit	%	Enterprises	Total
Basic research	1.71	0.00	1.71	5.91	96.59	100.00
Applied research	5.47	27.40	1.22	32.95	65.91	100.00
Experimental development	3.80	2.79	1.52	39.53	91.90	100.00
Not specified	0.00	100.00	0.00	21.62	0.00	100.00
Total	3.40	31.75	1.10	100.00	63.75	100.00

Source: OECD, STIU database.

Table 3. Industrial breakdown of BERD
(Expenditure on R&D in the business enterprise sector)

Percentage

ISIC	1990	1991	1992	1993	1994
Agriculture	..	..	..	..	..
Mining	..	..	..	..	..
Manufacturing	..	..	..	..	..
Food, beverages & tobacco	..	..	..	..	..
Textiles, fur & leather	..	..	..	..	..
Wood, paper, print. & publ.	..	..	..	..	..
Coke, petrol, nucl. fuel, chem. prod. & plast	..	..	..	..	..
Non-metallic mineral products	..	..	..	..	..
Basic metals	..	..	..	..	..
Fabric. metal products	..	..	..	..	..
Machin., instruments & transport equip.	..	..	..	..	..
Furnit. & other manufact., nec	..	..	..	..	..
Recycling	..	..	..	..	..
Electricity, gas & water supply	..	..	..	..	..
Construction	..	..	..	..	..
Service sector	..	..	..	..	..
Total	..	..	..	..	..

Source: OECD, STIU database.

Table 4. R&D personnel by sector of employment, 1992

Percentage

Occupation	Government	Higher education	Private non-profit	Enterprises	Total	%
Scientists and engineers	3.46	42.79	..	53.76	100.00	37.74
Technicians	4.23	18.29	..	77.48	100.00	43.01
Other personnel	2.69	11.29	..	86.02	100.00	19.25
Total	3.64	26.19	..	70.17	100.00	100.00

Source: OECD, STIU database.

Table 5. Structure of the R&D system (Funding and performance of GERD)

In million US$

1992

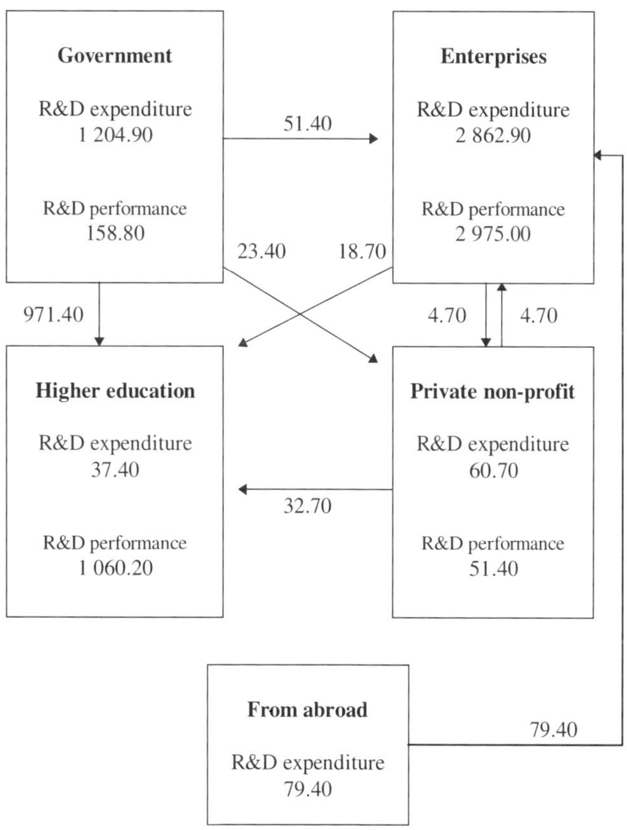

R&D expenditure : All R&D funded by the sector performed in this and other sectors.

R&D performance : R&D performed in this sector.

TURKEY

Table 1. GERD (Gross domestic expenditure on R&D) as a percentage of GDP

	1990	1991	1992	1993	1994
Percentage of GDP	0.32	0.53	0.49	0.46	..

Source: OECD, STIU database.

Table 2. GERD by sector of performance and type of activity

Percentage

	Government	Higher education	Private non-profit	Enterprises	Total	%
Basic research	..	..	..	..	..	..
Applied research	..	..	..	..	..	..
Experimental development	..	..	..	..	..	..
Not specified	..	..	..	..	..	..
Total	..	..	..	..	..	..

Source: OECD, STIU database.

Table 3. Industrial breakdown of BERD (Expenditure on R&D in the business enterprise sector)

Percentage

ISIC	1990	1991	1992	1993	1994
Agriculture	0.19	2.03	1.80	0.48	..
Mining	1.76	0.00	0.00	0.42	..
Manufacturing	95.16	90.64	88.98	88.77	..
Food, beverages & tobacco	6.39	2.87	3.32	4.54	..
Textiles, fur & leather	2.40	8.13	2.76	2.73	..
Wood, paper, print. & publ.	0.94	0.22	0.20	0.29	..
Coke, petrol, nucl. fuel, chem. prod. & plast	13.47	11.88	12.34	9.92	..
Non-metallic mineral products	5.84	4.45	4.20	3.53	..
Basic metals	7.71	5.46	8.59	4.26	..
Fabric. metal products	1.97	0.65	0.95	0.60	..
Machin., instruments & transport equip.	56.15	56.43	55.88	62.09	..
Furnit. & other manufact., nec	0.29	0.54	0.72	0.81	..
Recycling	0.00	0.00	0.00	0.00	..
Electricity, gas & water supply	1.53	2.84	3.00	3.04	..
Construction	0.04	..	0.07	0.00	..
Service sector	1.32	4.50	6.15	7.29	..
Total	100.00	100.00	100.00	100.00	..

Source: OECD, STIU database.

Table 4. R&D personnel by sector of employment, 1993

Percentage

Occupation	Government	Higher education	Private non-profit	Enterprises	Total	%
Scientists and engineers	13.04	75.10	..	11.86	100.00	84.57
Technicians	37.96	..	..	62.04	100.00	8.83
Other personnel	70.53	..	..	29.47	100.00	6.60
Total	19.03	..	..	17.45	100.00	100.00

Source: OECD, STIU database.

Table 5. Structure of the R&D system (Funding and performance of GERD)

In million US$

1993

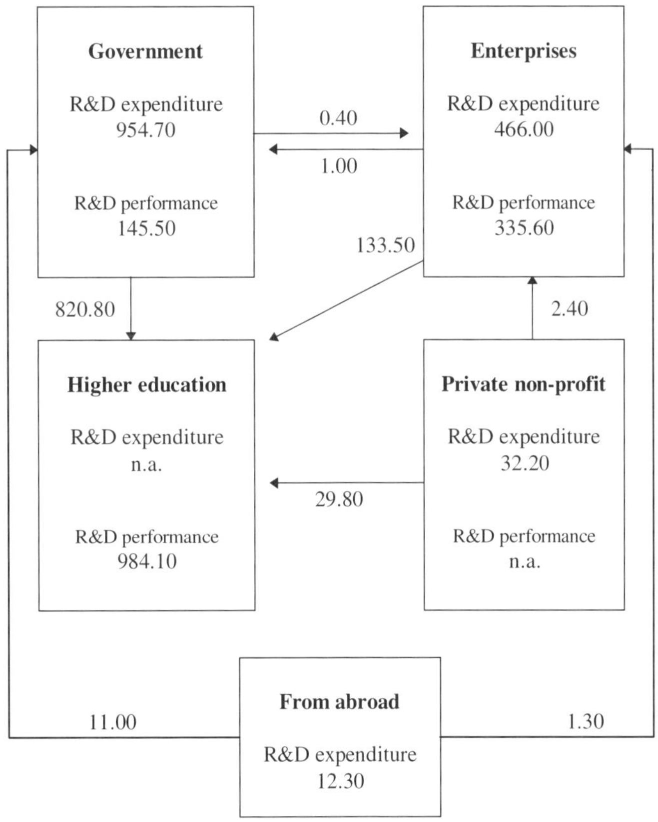

R&D expenditure : All R&D funded by the sector performed in this and other sectors.

R&D performance : R&D performed in this sector.

BACKGROUND NOTES TO COUNTRY TABLES

Data sources

The data reported to OECD have been collected by Member governments to meet national needs, in line with the standard OECD methodology for R&D statistics, as published in OECD (1994), *The Measurement of Scientific and Technological Activities: Proposed Standard Practice for Surveys of Research and Experimental Development – Frascati Manual 1993*. However, a number of differences between national and international practice remain. The main exceptions are shown in Annex 2 of *Main Science and Technology Indicators.* The tables are essentially based on retrospective survey of the units carrying out R&D. National forecasts have been included when available. The underlying data were extracted from the STIU database managed by the EAS Division of DSTI. Most of the data used are published in OECD (1995), *Basic Science and Technology Statistics,* but also include some updates provided in OECD (1996), *Main Science and Technology Indicators 1995/2*.

(1) GERD (Gross domestic expenditure on R&D) as a percentage of GDP

Gross domestic expenditure on R&D (GERD), which covers all R&D carried out on national territory in the year concerned, is presented as a percentage of gross domestic product. The latter is taken from the OECD National Accounts database, updated using the projections in the *OECD Economic Outlook*.

GERD as a percentage of GDP

1993

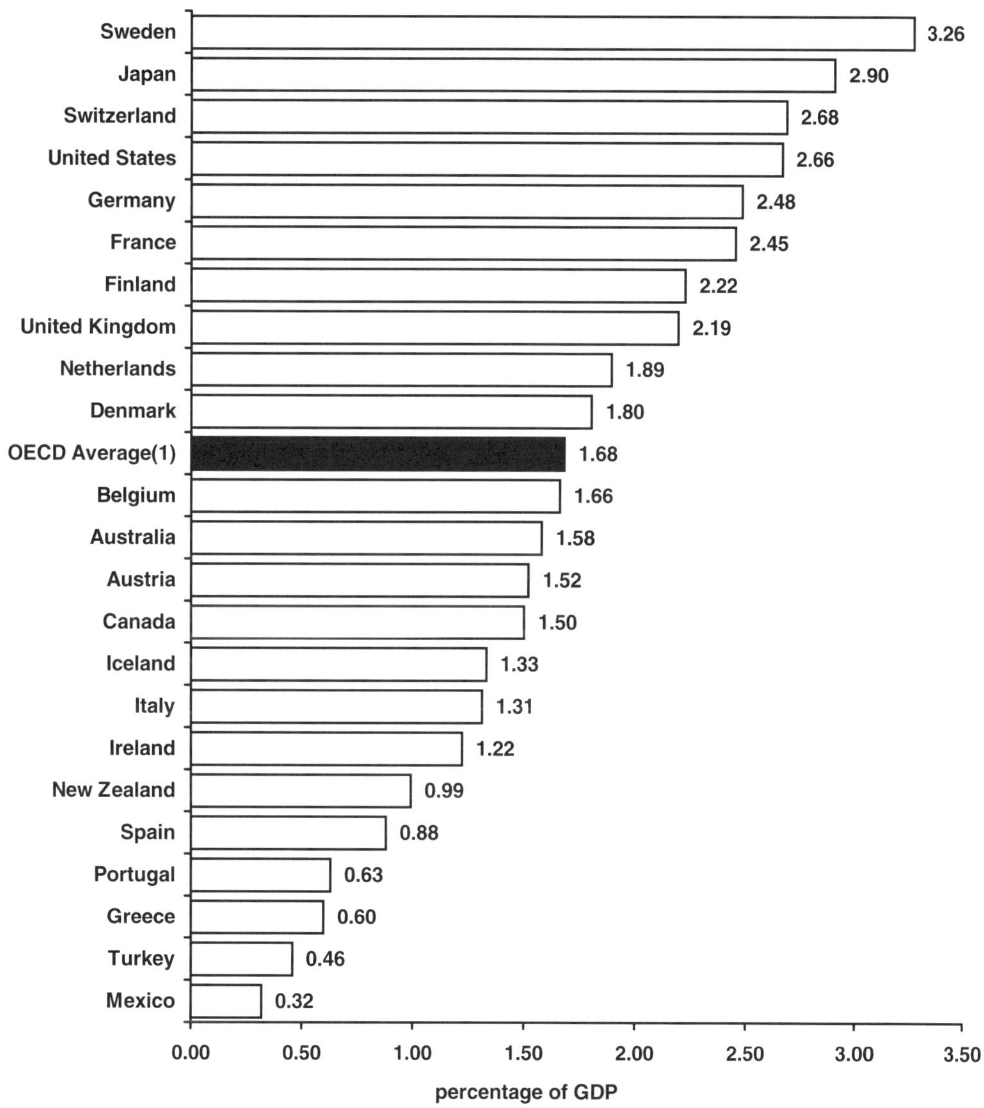

Note: Unweighted average of 23 countries: Australia (1992 data), Canada, Finland, France, Germany, Italy, Japan, Sweden, the United Kingdom, the United States, Spain, the Netherlands, Mexico, Belgium (1991 data), Switzerland (1992 data), Austria, Denmark, Turkey, Portugal (1992 data), Greece, Ireland, New Zealand (1992 data) and Iceland.

(2) National R&D expenditure by type of activity

This breakdown is widely used in the United States but less so in most other Member countries. The breakdown is usually based on current R&D expenditures as capital expenditures cannot readily be allocated to activities. The distribution of the national R&D effort among the three activities is largely a function of each country's economic (industrial) structure and is also affected by the methods used to measure R&D in the higher education sector.

- *Basic research*: Experimental or theoretical work undertaken primarily to acquire new knowledge of the underlying foundations of phenomena and observable facts, without any particular application or use in view.

- *Applied research*: Original investigation undertaken in order to acquire new knowledge. It is, however, directed primarily towards a specific practical aim or objective.

- *Experimental development*: Systematic work, drawing on existing knowledge gained from research and practical experience, that is directed to producing new materials, products and devices; to installing new processes, systems and services; or to improving substantially those already produced or installed.

R&D expenditure by type of activity
(per cent)
1991

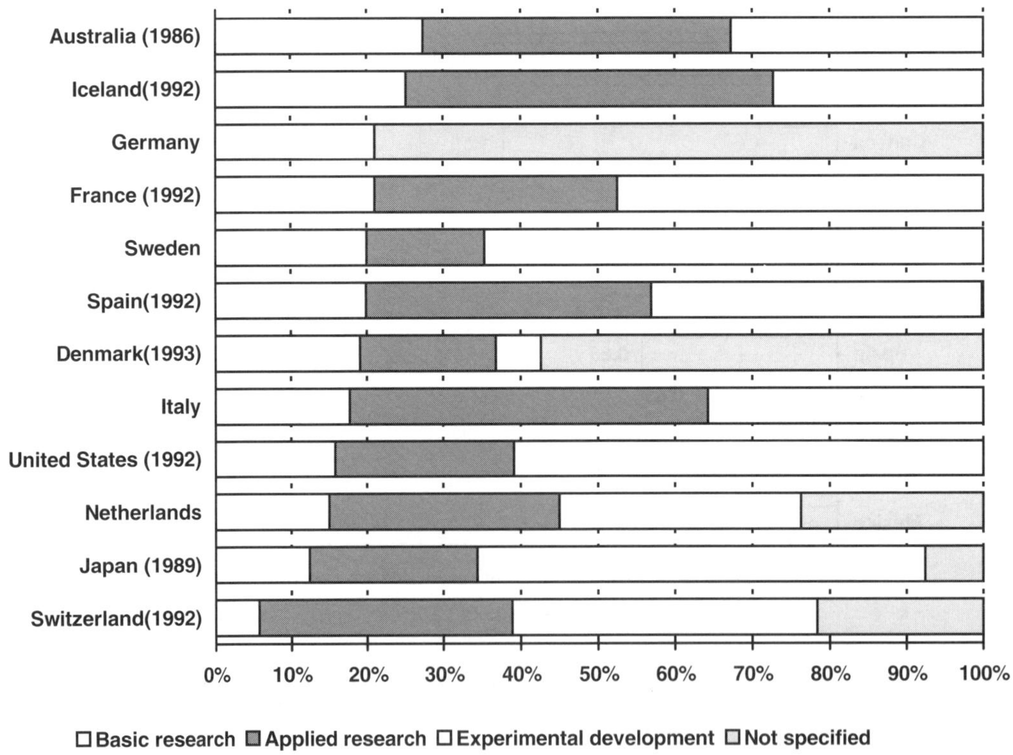

(3) Industrial breakdown of BERD (expenditure on R&D in the business enterprise sector)

The breakdown among industries is, in principle, made at the level of the enterprise, although some countries are able to break down the R&D data for multi-product enterprises among their main lines of business. National statistical regulations prevent publication of results where there are very few firms in the given category; hence the many gaps in the tables, *e.g.* for the United States. Classification follows the International Standard Industrial Classification (for latest years, ISIC Rev. 3) or nearest national classification. Some countries have improved their surveys of R&D in services to match the contribution of the services sector to the economy, while others have still to do so.

Sectoral distribution of BERD

(per cent)

1993

Distribution of R&D expenditure in the manufacturing sector

(per cent)

1993

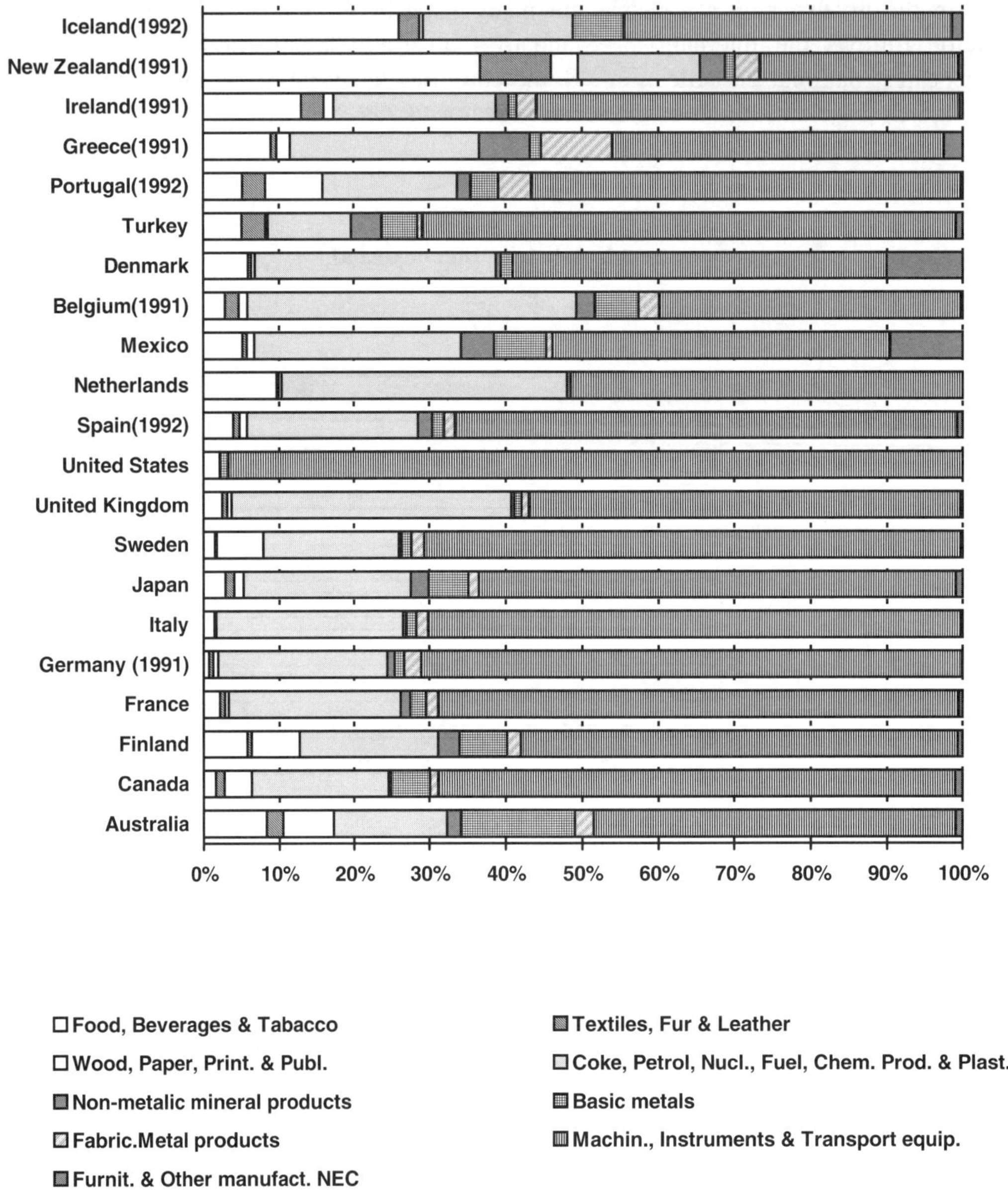

The business enterprise sector covers private and public enterprises and institutes serving such enterprises.

R&D expenditure in the business enterprise sector
(million US$)

1993

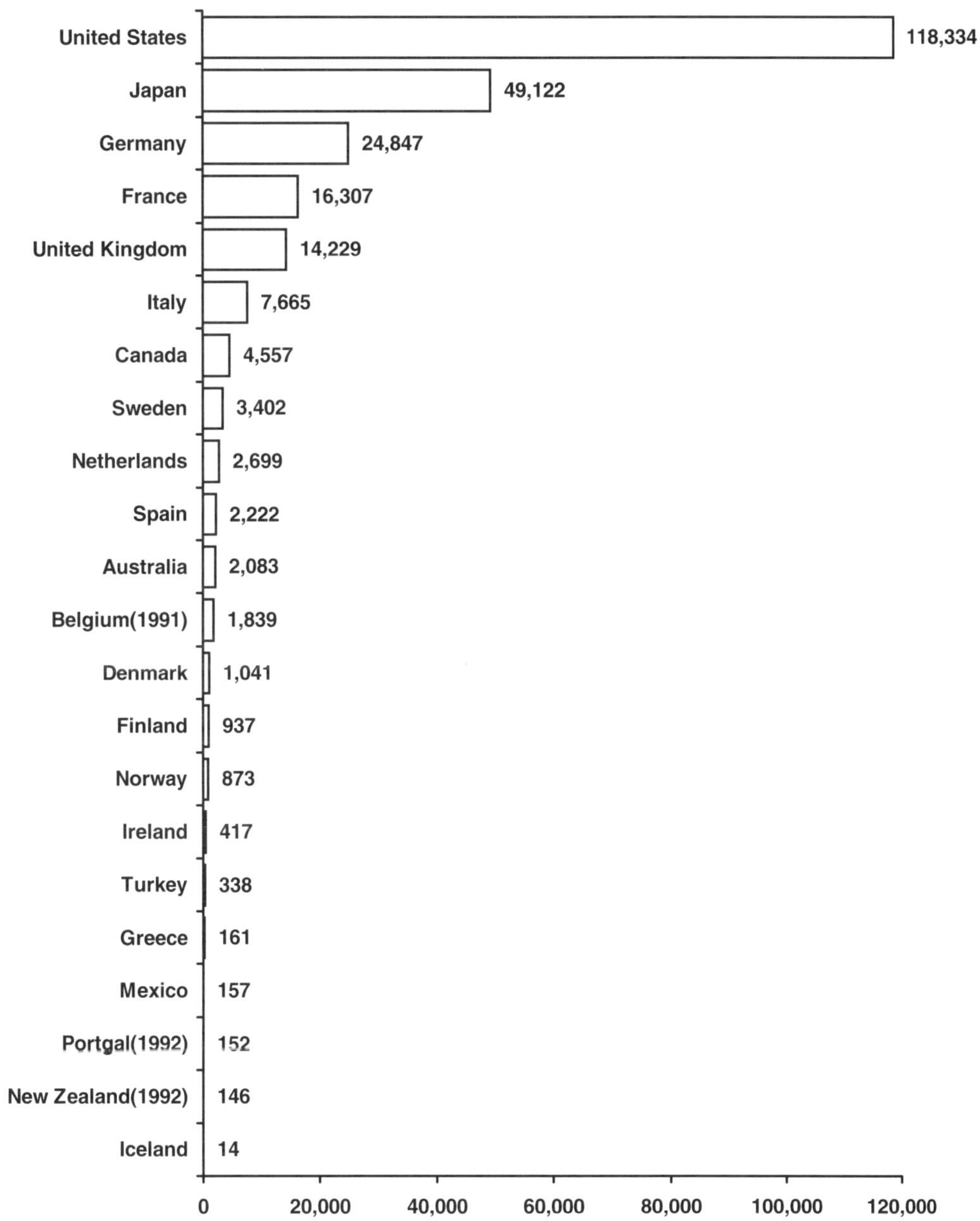

(4) R&D personnel by sector of employment

Resources devoted to R&D can also be measured in labour terms. R&D personnel data should be expressed in full-time equivalent, *e.g.* a person working half-time on R&D is counted as 0.5 years.

R&D personnel (full-time equivalent)
(thousands)
1993

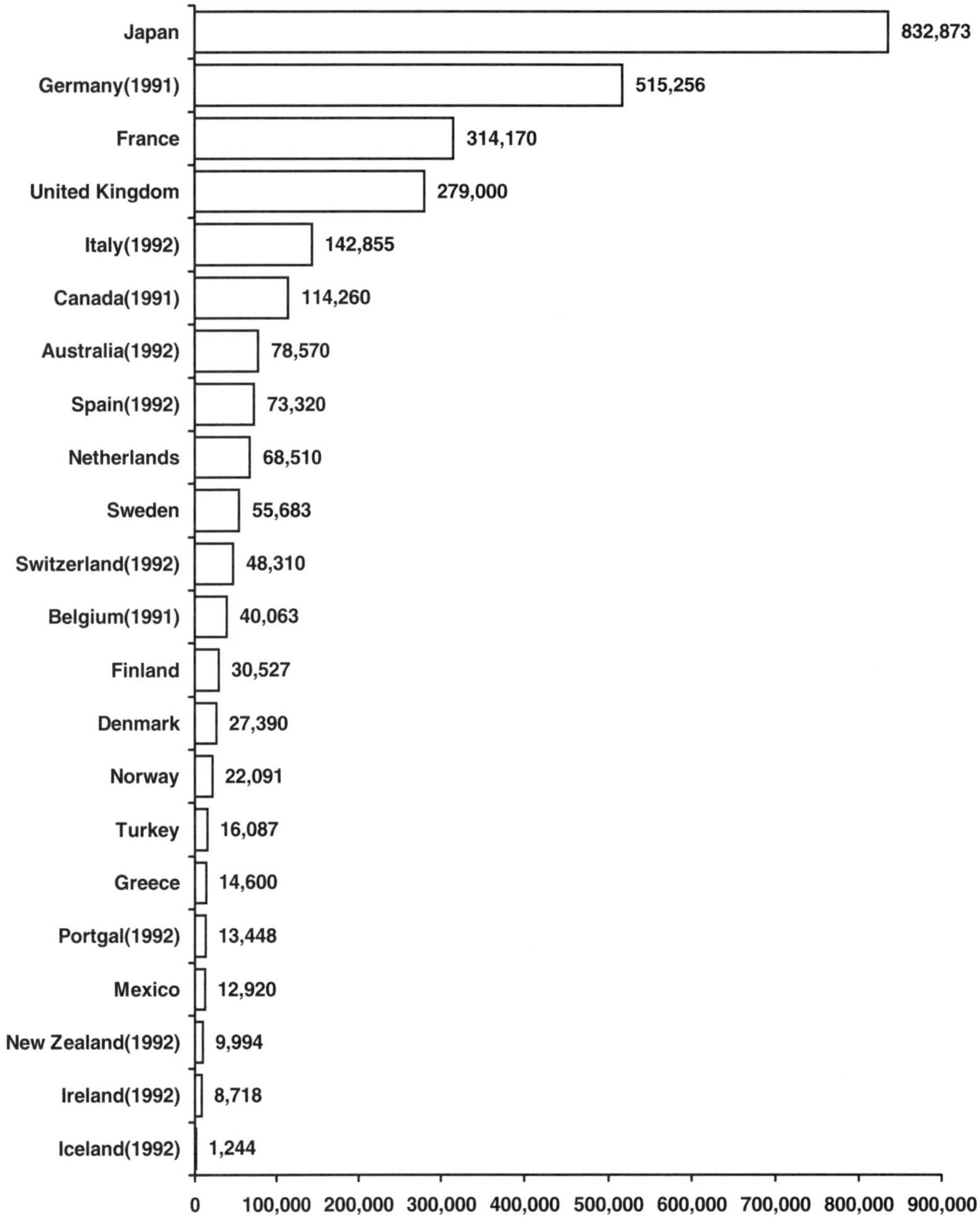

Most countries report R&D personnel by occupation. The United States only supplies data for researchers. Some countries only report data for some or all sectors broken down by the alternative classification – by level of qualification.

Distribution of R&D personnel by sector of employment

(per cent)

1993

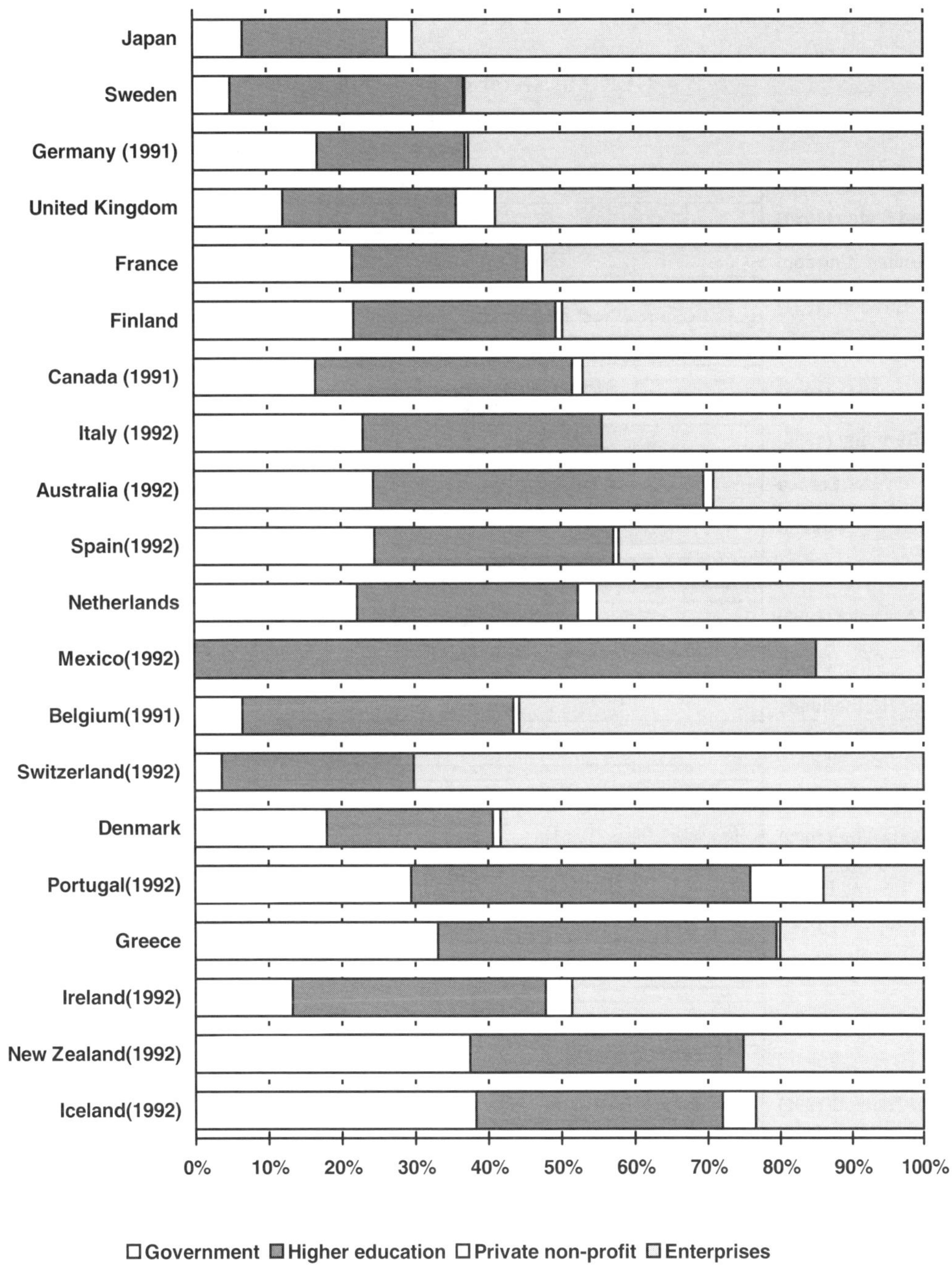

(5) Structure of the R&D system (funding and distribution of GERD)

For statistical purposes domestic R&D efforts (expenditure or personnel) are divided into four sectors of performance: business enterprise (industry), higher education (universities, colleges and attached research units), government and private non-profit institutions (PNP). R&D expenditure is sub-divided into five sources of funds: business enterprises (industry), government (public including the estimated R&D content of government block grants to the higher education sector), higher education, PNPs and abroad. The amounts financed by higher education depend on whether or not there is a significant private component of the higher education sector, as well as on the methods used to measure R&D in the sector. A graph is provided for each of the two breakdowns.

GERD by sector of performance
(per cent)
1993

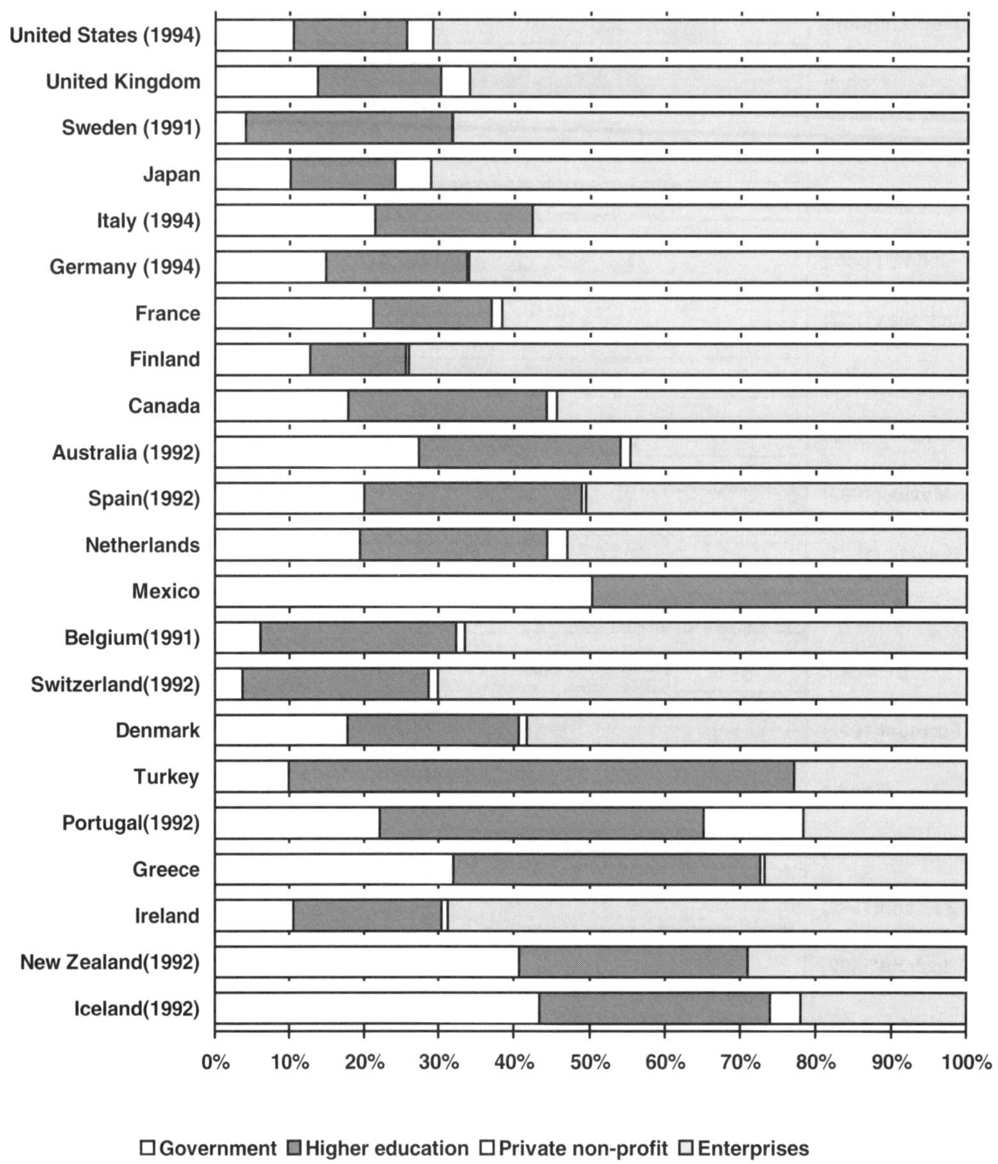

GERD by origin of funds
(per cent)
1993

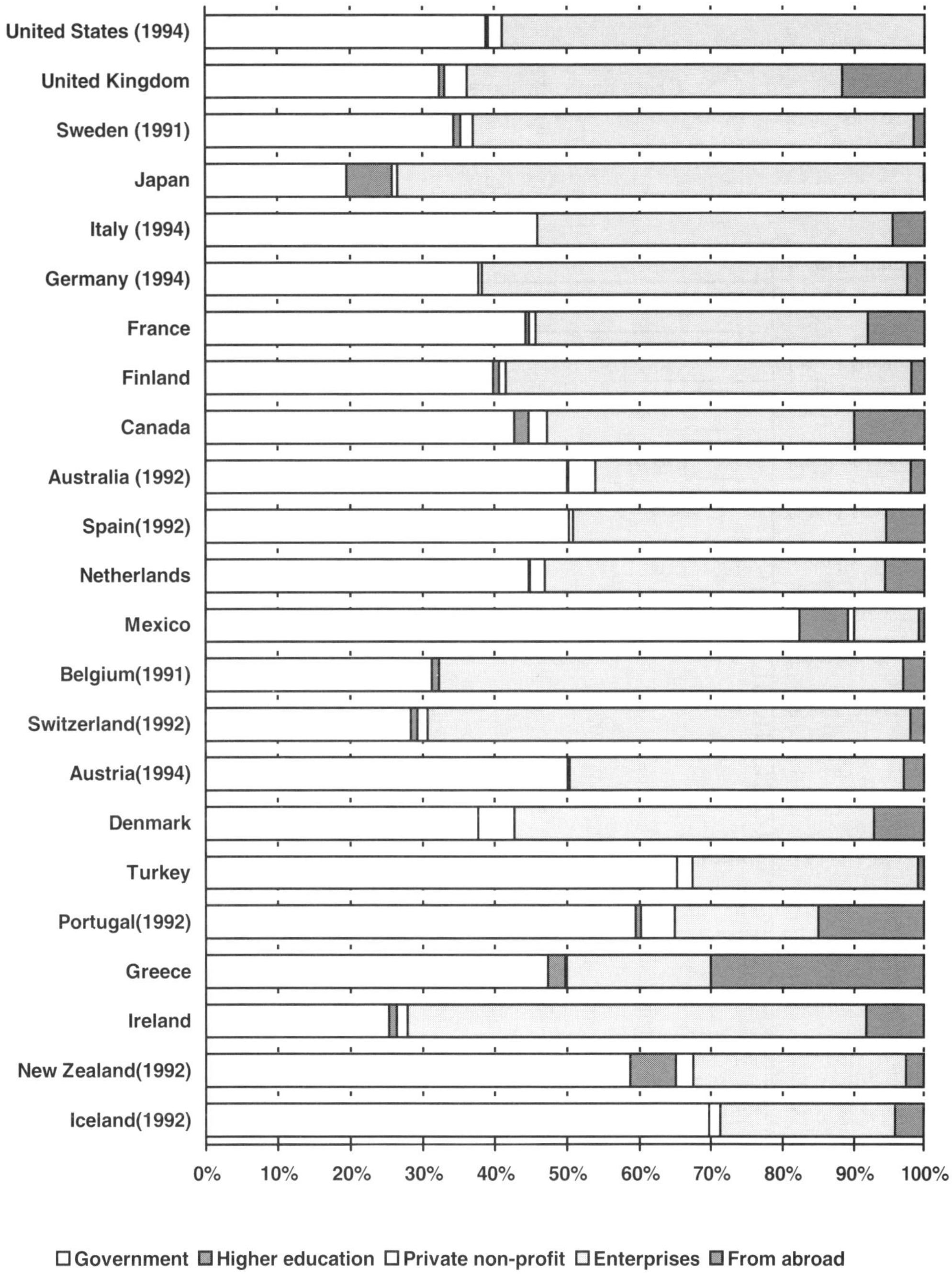

National currency data have been converted to US dollars using purchasing power parities (PPPs). The PPPs used are those developed by the OECD Economic Statistics and National Accounts Division (for further details see Sections VII and VIII of OECD (1995), *National Accounts, Volume I, 1960-1993*), updated for the most recent years by comparing the growth in prices (implicit GDP deflator) in each country with that in the United States.

Gross domestic expenditure on R&D
(million US$)

1993

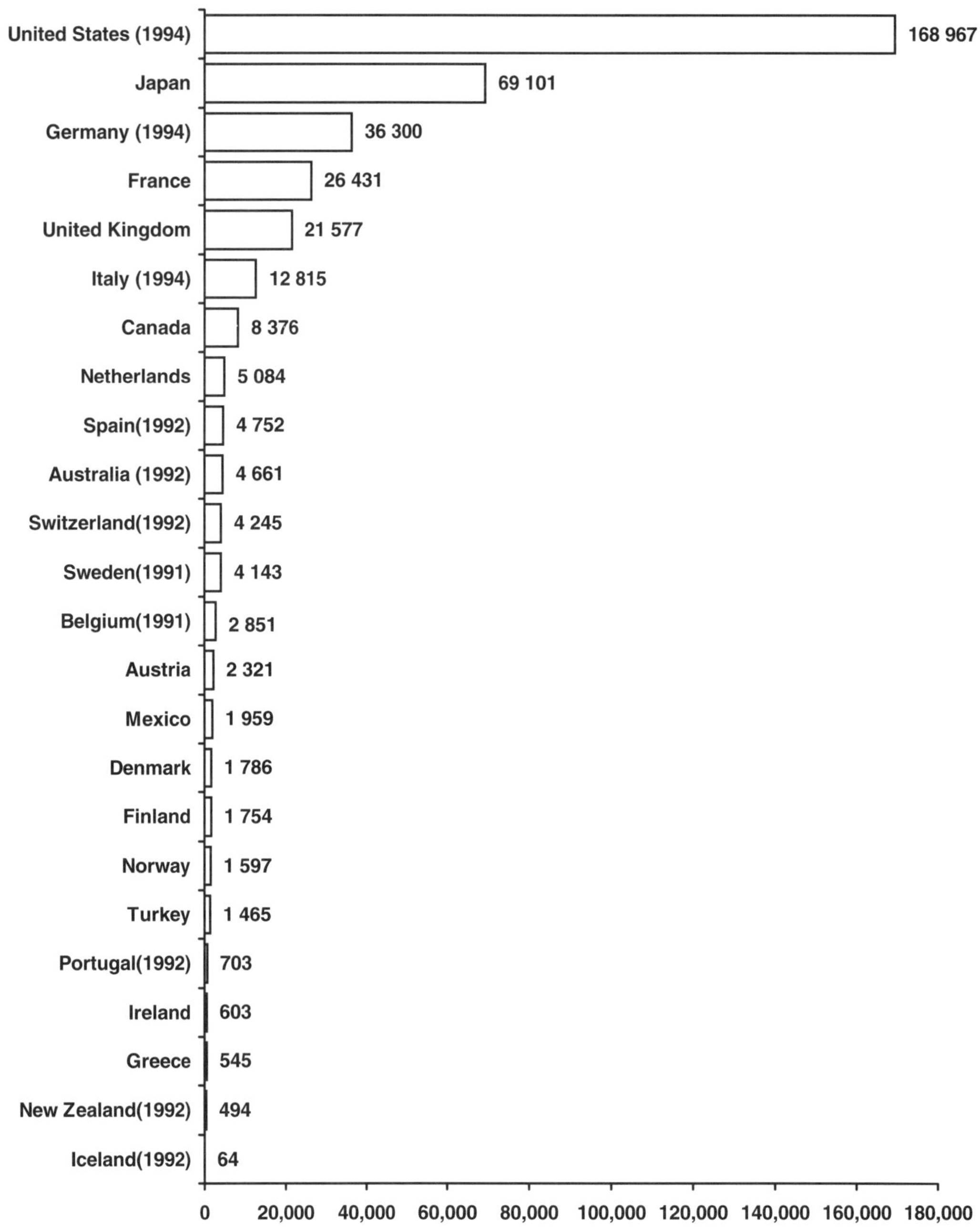

Chapter 3

EDUCATION AND THE LABOUR FORCE

The information provided is drawn in stylised form from extensive work carried out by the Directorate for Education, Employment, Labour and Social Affairs' Centre for Educational Research and Innovation (CERI).

Introduction

The availability of skills – and in particular new skills – has become a major concern for many firms. The issue is to have access to adequate and appropriate skills in order to achieve needed restructuration of industry and services, meet ever higher levels of performance standards, redesign market strategies in line with rapid techno-economic change, and cope with the continuing challenges of technological innovation that affect production processes as well as products. The skills issue has not only prompted increasing efforts by firms themselves to provide complementary training, but has also generated increasing attention to the performance and relevance of the educational systems.

Past and ongoing OECD work has underlined that the quality of the labour force is a significant element in determining business sector performance and competitiveness – and, perhaps, influencing aggregate economic growth – although it is also acknowledged that the instruments through which skills may affect economic performance are complex and diverse, and that there is no such thing as an ideal profile of workforce qualifications relative to better performance. Also to be borne in mind is that skills and skill intensity (*i.e.* competencies) are difficult to define and, given the deficiency of statistical data, hard to measure – especially on an internationally comparable basis.

As regards the issue of skill demand, skill profiles and qualification requirements, and indeed labour demand itself, are affected by a number of changes that ultimately alter the occupational composition within an economy. These are, *inter alia*, related to: the blurring of borderlines between sectors; the growing importance of the services sector *versus* manufacturing in terms of employment growth and GDP generated; the long-term structural trend of the employment system; and the nature of the production process (and type of product) as well as the accompanying work organisation – the latter three factors in themselves affecting the kind of skill structure that is required in a given enterprise

Concerning the data availability issue for this module, attention is drawn to the ongoing work on *Technology, Productivity and Job Creation* carried out jointly by the DSTI and the Directorate for Education, Employment, Labour and Social Affairs [see OECD (1996), *Technology, Productivity and Job Creation*, Volumes 1 and 2]. Within the framework of this complementary activity, the Secretariat is in the process of collecting and analysing data on the skill composition of industries, in order, *inter alia*, to make international comparisons of medium-term trends of industrial employment by industry and by occupation; examine shifts in employment within industries; and investigate the evolution of skilled and unskilled employment over time. Relative to the latter, attention is also drawn to the fact that while occupational profiles and their change over time can only be a proxy for changes in the skill composition of particular industries or of the economy, they do furnish an important element for understanding how employment structures change over time.

Bearing in mind the problems related to measuring skills and the present availability of data mentioned above, occupations and educational attainment are among the stylised proxies used to measure skills and competencies. However, a number of caveats must be kept firmly in mind. First, occupations are not a suitable basis on which to make long-term labour forecasts; nor can occupational projections be used as a criterion for choice of vocational training – *i.e.* how much transfer or retraining is needed in which industries and/or categories of activity. Second, educational attainment, is *not* a good indicator of educational *quality*, neither does it capture experience nor, necessarily, distinguish between such different streams of study as academic or vocational education.

Furthermore, and in view of the fact that educational systems vary widely in terms of their content, sequence and quality, comparing educational attainment levels across countries has inherent limitations. As has been noted, direct comparison of mean attainment levels can only be a very crude universal benchmark. However, this difficulty can be partially redressed by comparing relative distributions (the shape of the attainment profile of the population), rather than mean attainment levels [on which, see OECD (1995), *Jobs Study: Part II – Evidence and Explanations*, p. 114].

This module focuses, in a selective fashion, on educational attainment since it is not only an input to skill formation, but an important domestic parameter affecting business performance. It is argued, for instance, that the commercial competitiveness of a firm is influenced by the education system, in that it is, *inter alia*, the educational system that forms individuals with the skills necessary to perform business tasks. In turn, empirical research indicates that the skills possessed by such individuals are very important to the competitive efforts undertaken by firms – skills that are not easily replicated by on-the-job training.

Also, and despite the above-mentioned inherent limitations, measures of educational attainment correlate well with occupations and earnings, thereby providing a certain picture of a country's "human capital". Furthermore, initial attainment levels are generally accepted as a fairly reliable basis for predicting participation in further education and training.

The data presented in this module are organised into seven tables per country. Taken together, these tables form *summary country matrices*. Background explanatory notes are given in the final section. These provide two types of complementary information on each table: *technical explanations* on the content of each table, and *cross-country graphs* that provide data from the table in cross-country form.

The tables

The source for the tables is OECD (1995), *Education at a Glance: OECD Indicators*. See also the Background Notes.

Table 1. Educational expenditure relative to GDP

Table 1 has been included as the first, perhaps foremost, indicator of human capital investment. Furthermore, an important characteristic of the national education effort is the distribution of resources between the public and private sectors.

Table 2. Educational attainment of the population

Educational attainment may be expressed in terms of years of schooling completed or completion of different stages of education and training. As noted above, educational attainment is closely related to the skills and competencies of the labour force. The table also, albeit indirectly, evokes the need to understand better the processes that affect the relationship between educational expenditures and educational outcomes.

Table 3. Labour force participation by educational level

Table 4. Unemployment by educational level

These tables illustrate that there is, indeed, a close relationship between education and the labour market – *i.e.* that the level of educational attainment is a factor influencing participation rates in the labour force, and that the higher the level of education, the higher the labour force participation. The increased demand for higher skilled workers noted above, suggests that policies to upgrade human capital are a necessary part of any strategy to expand employment and create better jobs.

Table 5. Subject profile of qualified labour force

This table gives a broad picture of the subject profile of university graduates. However, the data do not allow any direct inference to be drawn as to the link between the numbers of graduates holding a degree in a given field and the level of demand for highly qualified labour in that same field.

Table 6. Occupational profile of the labour force

The table shows the occupations and industrial sectors of workers. It is interesting to note that the differences between sectors and occupations in a given country are more significant than the differences for any one sector across countries. The cross-country comparison given in the last section, and which shows the predominance of the "corporate managers category", evokes the notion – brought out by the ongoing OECD work on *Technology, Productivity and Job Creation* – that while advanced technologies do increase productivity, such factors as managerial ability likewise influence productivity and productivity growth.

Table 7. Continuing education and training for adults

This table serves to illustrate the point, made earlier, that initial educational attainment levels provide a basis on which it is possible to forecast participation in further education and training. Table 7 also evokes a general point that is currently receiving a good deal of policy attention; namely, that training – skill formation – is becoming increasingly important to competitiveness, and, subsequently, that education and training systems must be reformed so that they can better address future skill requirements. Not only are enterprises becoming intimately involved in further training, it is often recommended that training should be an integral part of a firm's overall strategy. The reason for this is linked to research findings that indicate that successful firms are not simply those employing advanced technologies, but rather firms that also invest in worker-training – *i.e.* the acquisition and use of new technologies must go hand-in-hand with the acquisition of new skills.

EDUCATION AND THE LABOUR FORCE: COUNTRY TABLES

UNITED STATES

Table 1. Educational expenditure relative to GDP

Educational expenditure as a percentage of GDP by type of institution, 1992

Public institutions	
Primary and secondary	3.9
Tertiary	1.6
Primary, secondary and tertiary	5.6
All levels combined	5.7
Public and private institutions	
Primary and secondary	4.3
Tertiary	2.5
Primary, secondary and tertiary	6.7
All levels combined	7.0

Table 2. Educational attainment of the population

Percentage of the population 25 to 64 years of age that has attained a specific highest level of education, 1992

ISCED	Level	%
0/1/2	Early childhood, primary, lower secondary	16
3	Upper secondary	53
5	Non-university	7
6/7	University	24

Table 3. Labour force participation by educational level

Labour force participation rate by level of educational attainment for men and women 25 to 64 years of age, 1992

ISCED	Level	%
0/1/2	Early childhood, primary, lower secondary	60.3
3	Upper secondary	79.7
5	Non-university	86.7
6/7	University	88.4
Total		79.2

Table 4. Unemployment by educational level

Unemployment rates by level of educational attainment for persons 25 to 64 years of age, 1992

ISCED	Level	%
0/1/2	Early childhood, primary, lower secondary	13.5
3	Upper secondary	7.2
5	Non-university	4.6
6/7	University	2.9
Total		6.6

Table 5. Subject profile of qualified labour force

University degrees as a percentage of total degrees by subject category, 1992

Level	%
Medical science	7.1
Natural and physical science	10.3
Engineering and architecture	8.1
Law and business	27.3
Human sciences	47.3

Table 6. Occupational profile of labour force

Percentage of 35 to 54 year-old employed workers in selected occupations, 1992

ISCO	Occupation	%
12	Corporate managers	4.7
213	Computing professionals	1.3
214	Architects, engineers and related professionals	1.9
31	Physical and engineering science associate professionals	2.5
32	Life science and health associate professionals	6.5
71	Extraction and building trade workers	3.9
73	Precision, handicraft, printing and related trades workers	1.9
80	Plant and machine operators and assemblers	6.3
83	Drivers and mobile-plant operators	4.1

Table 7. Continuing education and training for adults

Participation in job-related continuing education and training as a percentage of the employed population aged 25 to 64, by educational groups, 1991

ISCED	Level	%
0/1/2	Early childhood, primary, lower secondary	10
3	Upper secondary	30
5/6/7	Tertiary education	54
Total		38

JAPAN

Table 1. Educational expenditure relative to GDP

Educational expenditure as a percentage of GDP by type of institution

Public institutions	
Primary and secondary	2.8
Tertiary	0.3
Primary, secondary and tertiary	3.1
All levels combined	3.6
Public and private institutions	
Primary and secondary	3.1
Tertiary	0.8
Primary, secondary and tertiary	3.9
All levels combined	4.8

Table 2. Educational attainment of the population

Percentage of the population 25 to 64 years of age that has attained a specific highest level of education

ISCED	Level	%
0/1/2	Early childhood, primary, lower secondary	..
3	Upper secondary	..
5	Non-university	..
6/7	University	..

Table 3. Labour force participation by educational level

Labour force participation rate by level of educational attainment for men and women 25 to 64 years of age

ISCED	Level	%
0/1/2	Early childhood, primary, lower secondary	..
3	Upper secondary	..
5	Non-university	..
6/7	University	..
Total		..

Table 4. Unemployment by educational level

Unemployment rates by level of educational attainment for persons 25 to 64 years of age

ISCED	Level	%
0/1/2	Early childhood, primary, lower secondary	..
3	Upper secondary	..
5	Non-university	..
6/7	University	..
Total		..

Table 5. Subject profile of qualified labour force

University degrees as a percentage of total degrees by subject category, 1992

Level	%
Medical science	5.3
Natural and physical science	7.3
Engineering and architecture	21.6
Law and business	39.4
Human sciences	26.3

Table 6. Occupational profile of labour force

Percentage of 35 to 54 year-old employed workers in selected occupations, 1992

ISCO	Occupation	%
12	Corporate managers	..
213	Computing professionals	..
214	Architects, engineers and related professionals	..
31	Physical and engineering science associate professionals	..
32	Life science and health associate professionals	..
71	Extraction and building trade workers	..
73	Precision, handicraft, printing and related trades workers	..
80	Plant and machine operators and assemblers	..
83	Drivers and mobile-plant operators	..

Table 7. Continuing education and training for adults

Participation in job-related continuing education and training as a percentage of the employed population aged 25 to 64, by educational groups

ISCED	Level	%
0/1/2	Early childhood, primary, lower secondary	..
3	Upper secondary	..
5/6/7	Tertiary education	..
Total		..

GERMANY

Table 1. Educational expenditure relative to GDP

Educational expenditure as a percentage of GDP by type of institution, 1992

Public institutions	
Primary and secondary	2.4
Tertiary	1.0
Primary, secondary and tertiary	3.4
All levels combined	3.7
Public and private institutions	
Primary and secondary	3.4
Tertiary	1.0
Primary, secondary and tertiary	4.4
All levels combined	4.9

Note: In this table Germany refers to the former territory of the Federal Republic of Germany.

Table 2. Educational attainment of the population

Percentage of the population 25 to 64 years of age that has attained a specific highest level of education, 1992

ISCED	Level	%
0/1/2	Early childhood, primary, lower secondary	18
3	Upper secondary	60
5	Non-university	10
6/7	University	12

Table 3. Labour force participation by educational level

Labour force participation rate by level of educational attainment for men and women 25 to 64 years of age, 1992

ISCED	Level	%
0/1/2	Early childhood, primary, lower secondary	57.0
3	Upper secondary	76.7
5	Non-university	86.5
6/7	University	89.8
Total		75.6

Table 4. Unemployment by educational level

Unemployment rates by level of educational attainment for persons 25 to 64 years of age, 1992

ISCED	Level	%
0/1/2	Early childhood, primary, lower secondary	8.9
3	Upper secondary	6.4
5	Non-University	4.5
6/7	University	3.7
Total		6.2

Table 5. Subject profile of qualified labour force

University degrees as a percentage of total degrees by subject category, 1992

Level	%
Medical science	11.7
Natural and physical science	17.6
Engineering and architecture	22.2
Law and business	24.7
Human sciences	23.7

Note: In this table Germany refers to the former territory of the Federal Republic of Germany.

Table 6. Occupational profile of labour force

Percentage of 35 to 54 year-old employed workers in selected occupations, 1992

ISCO	Occupation	%
12	Corporate managers	3.4
213	Computing professionals	0.3
214	Architects, engineers and related professionals	3.0
31	Physical and engineering science associate professionals	4.7
32	Life science and health associate professionals	2.3
71	Extraction and building trade workers	6.1
73	Precision, handicraft, printing and related trades workers	1.2
80	Plant and machine operators and assemblers	4.4
83	Drivers and mobile-plant operators	4.1

Table 7. Continuing education and training for adults

Participation in job-related continuing education and training as a percentage of the employed population aged 25 to 64, by educational groups, 1991

ISCED	Level	%
0/1/2	Early childhood, primary, lower secondary	11
3	Upper secondary	23
5/6/7	Tertiary education	41
Total		27

FRANCE

Table 1. Educational expenditure relative to GDP

Educational expenditure as a percentage of GDP by type of institution, 1992

Public institutions	
Primary and secondary	3.4
Tertiary	0.9
Primary, secondary and tertiary	4.3
All levels combined	5.1
Public and private institutions	
Primary and secondary	4.0
Tertiary	1.0
Primary, secondary and tertiary	5.0
All levels combined	5.9

Table 2. Educational attainment of the population

Percentage of the population 25 to 64 years of age that has attained a specific highest level of education, 1992

ISCED	Level	%
0/1/2	Early childhood, primary, lower secondary	48
3	Upper secondary	36
5	Non-university	6
6/7	University	10

Table 3. Labour force participation by educational level

Labour force participation rate by level of educational attainment for men and women 25 to 64 years of age, 1992

ISCED	Level	%
0/1/2	Early childhood, primary, lower secondary	64.9
3	Upper secondary	83.5
5	Non-university	89.4
6/7	University	86.9
Total		75.3

Table 4. Unemployment by educational level

Unemployment rates by level of educational attainment for persons 25 to 64 years of age, 1992

ISCED	Level	%
0/1/2	Early childhood, primary, lower secondary	12.1
3	Upper secondary	7.4
5	Non-university	4.6
6/7	University	4.4
Total		8.8

Table 5. Subject profile of qualified labour force

University degrees as a percentage of total degrees by subject category, 1992

Level	%
Medical science	..
Natural and physical science	..
Engineering and architecture	..
Law and business	..
Human sciences	..

Table 6. Occupational profile of labour force

Percentage of 35 to 54 year-old employed workers in selected occupations, 1992

ISCO	Occupation	%
12	Corporate managers	5.3
213	Computing professionals	0.7
214	Architects, engineers and related professionals	2.2
31	Physical and engineering science associate professionals	3.6
32	Life science and health associate professionals	2.5
71	Extraction and building trade workers	6.2
73	Precision, handicraft, printing and related trades workers	0.5
80	Plant and machine operators and assemblers	0.5
83	Drivers and mobile-plant operators	4.0

Table 7. Continuing education and training for adults

Participation in job-related continuing education and training as a percentage of the employed population aged 25 to 64, by educational groups, 1992

ISCED	Level	%
0/1/2	Early childhood, primary, lower secondary	13
3	Upper secondary	31
5/6/7	Tertiary education	46
Total		27

UNITED KINGDOM

Table 1. Educational expenditure relative to GDP

Educational expenditure as a percentage of GDP by type of institution, 1992

Public institutions	
Primary and secondary	4.0
Tertiary	0.1
Primary, secondary and tertiary	4.1
All levels combined	4.1
Public and private institutions	
Primary and secondary	..
Tertiary	0.8
Primary, secondary and tertiary	..
All levels combined	..

Table 2. Educational attainment of the population

Percentage of the population 25 to 64 years of age that has attained a specific highest level of education, 1992

ISCED	**Level**	%
0/1/2	Early childhood, primary, lower secondary	32
3	Upper secondary	49
5	Non-university	8
6/7	University	11

Table 3. Labour force participation by educational level

Labour force participation rate by level of educational attainment for men and women 25 to 64 years of age, 1992

ISCED	**Level**	%
0/1/2	Early childhood, primary, lower secondary	64.5
3	Upper secondary	82.1
5	Non-university	84.0
6/7	University	90.3
Total		77.5

UNITED KINGDOM (continued)

Table 4. Unemployment by educational level

Unemployment rates by level of educational attainment for persons 25 to 64 years of age, 1992

ISCED	Level	%
0/1/2	Early childhood, primary, lower secondary	12.3
3	Upper secondary	8.3
5	Non-University	3.3
6/7	University	3.6
Total		8.4

Table 5. Subject profile of qualified labour force

University degrees as a percentage of total degrees by subject category, 1992

Level	%
Medical science	6.8
Natural and physical science	17.1
Engineering and architecture	15.2
Law and business	21.8
Human sciences	39.1

Table 6. Occupational profile of labour force

Percentage of 35 to 54 year-old employed workers in selected occupations, 1992

ISCO	Occupation	%
12	Corporate managers	17.2
213	Computing professionals	0.8
214	Architects, engineers and related professionals	2.7
31	Physical and engineering science associate professionals	2.0
32	Life science and health associate professionals	1.4
71	Extraction and building trade workers	5.5
73	Precision, handicraft, printing and related trades workers	1.0
80	Plant and machine operators and assemblers	8.6
83	Drivers and mobile-plant operators	4.0

Table 7. Continuing education and training for adults

Participation in job-related continuing education and training as a percentage of the employed population aged 25 to 64, by educational groups, 1992

ISCED	Level	%
0/1/2	Early childhood, primary, lower secondary	4
3	Upper secondary	10
5/6/7	Tertiary education	19
Total		11

CANADA

Table 1. Educational expenditure relative to GDP

Educational expenditure as a percentage of GDP by type of institution, 1992

Public institutions	
Primary and secondary	..
Tertiary	2.4
Primary, secondary and tertiary	..
All levels combined	7.2
Public and private institutions	
Primary and secondary	..
Tertiary	2.4
Primary, secondary and tertiary	..
All levels combined	7.4

Table 2. Educational attainment of the population

Percentage of the population 25 to 64 years of age that has attained a specific highest level of education, 1992

ISCED	Level	%
0/1/2	Early childhood, primary, lower secondary	29
3	Upper secondary	30
5	Non-university	26
6/7	University	15

Table 3. Labour force participation by educational level

Labour force participation rate by level of educational attainment for men and women 25 to 64 years of age, 1992

ISCED	Level	%
0/1/2	Early childhood, primary, lower secondary	62.4
3	Upper secondary	79.9
5	Non-university	85.5
6/7	University	89.6
Total		77.8

Table 4. Unemployment by educational level

Unemployment rates by level of education attainment for persons 25 to 64 years of age, 1992

ISCED	Level	%
0/1/2	Early childhood, primary, lower secondary	15.1
3	Upper secondary	9.7
5	Non-university	9.0
6/7	University	5.2
Total		10.0

Table 5. Subject profile of qualified labour force

University degrees as a percentage of total degrees by subject category, 1992

Level	%
Medical science	6.7
Natural and physical science	12.0
Engineering and architecture	7.0
Law and business	22.6
Human sciences	51.7

Table 6. Occupational profile of labour force

Percentage of 35 to 54 year-old employed workers in selected occupations, 1992

ISCO	Occupation	%
12	Corporate managers	6.2
213	Computing professionals	1.0
214	Architects, engineers and related professionals	1.1
31	Physical and engineering science associate professionals	3.6
32	Life science and health associate professionals	5.4
71	Extraction and building trade workers	4.0
73	Precision, handicraft, printing and related trades workers	3.0
80	Plant and machine operators and assemblers	..
83	Drivers and mobile-plant operators	3.6

Table 7. Continuing education and training for adults

Participation in job-related continuing education and training as a percentage of the employed population aged 25 to 64, by educational groups, 1991

ISCED	Level	%
0/1/2	Early childhood, primary, lower secondary	13
3	Upper secondary	25
5/6/7	Tertiary education	40
Total		30

ITALY

Table 1. Educational expenditure relative to GDP

Educational expenditure as a percentage of GDP by type of institution, 1992

Public institutions	
Primary and secondary	..
Tertiary	..
Primary, secondary and tertiary	..
All levels combined	..
Public and private institutions	
Primary and secondary	..
Tertiary	..
Primary, secondary and tertiary	..
All levels combined	..

Table 2. Educational attainment of the population

Percentage of the population 25 to 64 years of age that has attained a specific highest level of education, 1992

ISCED	Level	%
0/1/2	Early childhood, primary, lower secondary	72
3	Upper secondary	22
5	Non-university	..
6/7	University	6

Table 3. Labour force participation by educational level

Labour force participation rate by level of educational attainment for men and women 25 to 64 years of age, 1992

ISCED	Level	%
0/1/2	Early childhood, primary, lower secondary	58.2
3	Upper secondary	79.8
5	Non-university	..
6/7	University	90.7
Total		65.1

Table 4. Unemployment by educational level

Unemployment rates by level of educational attainment for persons 25 to 64 years of age, 1992

ISCED	Level	%
0/1/2	Early childhood, primary, lower secondary	7.3
3	Upper secondary	8.2
5	Non-university	..
6/7	University	6.0
Total		7.4

Table 5. Subject profile of qualified labour force

University degrees as a percentage of total degrees by subject category, 1992

Level	%
Medical science	25.1
Natural and physical science	12.2
Engineering and architecture	11.4
Law and business	27.1
Human sciences	22.8

Table 6. Occupational profile of labour force

Percentage of 35 to 54 year-old employed workers in selected occupations, 1992

ISCO	Occupation	%
12	Corporate managers	0.2
213	Computing professionals	..
214	Architects, engineers and related professionals	0.8
31	Physical and engineering science associate professionals	2.9
32	Life science and health associate professionals	1.9
71	Extraction and building trade workers	5.9
73	Precision, handicraft, printing and related trades workers	1.2
80	Plant and machine operators and assemblers	..
83	Drivers and mobile-plant operators	4.0

Table 7. Continuing education and training for adults

Participation in job-related continuing education and training as a percentage of the employed population aged 25 to 64, by educational groups

ISCED	Level	%
0/1/2	Early childhood, primary, lower secondary	..
3	Upper secondary	..
5/6/7	Tertiary education	..
Total		..

AUSTRALIA

Table 1. Educational expenditure relative to GDP

Educational expenditure as a percentage of GDP by type of institution, 1992

Public institutions	
Primary and secondary	..
Tertiary	1.8
Primary, secondary and tertiary	..
All levels combined	4.5
Public and private institutions	
Primary and secondary	..
Tertiary	1.9
Primary, secondary and tertiary	..
All levels combined	5.5

Table 2. Educational attainment of the population

Percentage of the population 25 to 64 years of age that has attained a specific highest level of education, 1993

ISCED	Level	%
0/1/2	Early childhood, primary, lower secondary	47
3	Upper secondary	30
5	Non-university	11
6/7	University	12

Table 3. Labour force participation by educational level

Labour force participation rate by level of educational attainment for men and women 25 to 64 years of age, 1992

ISCED	Level	%
0/1/2	Early childhood, primary, lower secondary	65.1
3	Upper secondary	80.2
5	Non-university	83.2
6/7	University	89.2
Total		74.4

Table 4. Unemployment by educational level

Unemployment rates by level of educational attainment for persons 25 to 64 years of age, 1992

ISCED	Level	%
0/1/2	Early childhood, primary, lower secondary	11.2
3	Upper secondary	8.9
5	Non-university	5.7
6/7	University	4.4
Total		8.8

Table 5. Subject profile of qualified labour force

University degrees as a percentage of total degrees by subject category, 1992

Level	%
Medical science	11.5
Natural and physical science	14.9
Engineering and architecture	7.3
Law and business	24.7
Human sciences	41.5

Table 6. Occupational profile of labour force

Percentage of 35 to 54 year-old employed workers in selected occupations, 1992

ISCO	Occupation	%
12	Corporate managers	..
213	Computing professionals	..
214	Architects, engineers and related professionals	..
31	Physical and engineering science associate professionals	..
32	Life science and health associate professionals	..
71	Extraction and building trade workers	..
73	Precision, handicraft, printing and related trades workers	..
80	Plant and machine operators and assemblers	..
83	Drivers and mobile-plant operators	..

Table 7. Continuing education and training for adults

Participation in job-related continuing education and training as a percentage of the employed population aged 25 to 64, by educational groups, 1991

ISCED	Level	%
0/1/2	Early childhood, primary, lower secondary	..
3	Upper secondary	..
5/6/7	Tertiary education	..
Total		..

AUSTRIA

Table 1. Educational expenditure relative to GDP

Educational expenditure as a percentage of GDP by type of institution, 1992

Public institutions	
Primary and secondary	..
Tertiary	..
Primary, secondary and tertiary	..
All levels combined	..
Public and private institutions	
Primary and secondary	..
Tertiary	..
Primary, secondary and tertiary	..
All levels combined	..

Table 2. Educational attainment of the population

Percentage of the population 25 to 64 years of age that has attained a specific highest level of education, 1992

ISCED	Level	%
0/1/2	Early childhood, primary, lower secondary	32
3	Upper secondary	61
5	Non-university	..
6/7	University	7

Table 3. Labour force participation by educational level

Labour force participation rate by level of educational attainment for men and women 25 to 64 years of age, 1992

ISCED	Level	%
0/1/2	Early childhood, primary, lower secondary	52.8
3	Upper secondary	73.9
5	Non-university	..
6/7	University	88.4
Total		68.1

Table 4. Unemployment by educational level

Unemployment rates by level of educational attainment for persons 25 to 64 years of age, 1992

ISCED	Level	%
0/1/2	Early childhood, primary, lower secondary	5.6
3	Upper secondary	3.2
5	Non-university	..
6/7	University	1.3
Total		3.6

Table 5. Subject profile of qualified labour force

University degrees as a percentage of total degrees by subject category, 1992

Level	%
Medical science	..
Natural and physical science	..
Engineering and architecture	..
Law and business	..
Human sciences	..

Table 6. Occupational profile of labour force

Percentage of 35 to 54 year-old employed workers in selected occupations, 1992

ISCO	Occupation	%
12	Corporate managers	..
213	Computing professionals	..
214	Architects, engineers and related professionals	..
31	Physical and engineering science associate professionals	..
32	Life science and health associate professionals	..
71	Extraction and building trade workers	..
73	Precision, handicraft, printing and related trades workers	..
80	Plant and machine operators and assemblers	..
83	Drivers and mobile-plant operators	..

Table 7. Continuing education and training for adults

Participation in job-related continuing education and training as a percentage of the employed population aged 25 to 64, by educational groups, 1991

ISCED	Level	%
0/1/2	Early childhood, primary, lower secondary	..
3	Upper secondary	..
5/6/7	Tertiary education	..
Total		..

BELGIUM

Table 1. Educational expenditure relative to GDP

Educational expenditure as a percentage of GDP by type of institution, 1992

Public institutions	
Primary and secondary	..
Tertiary	..
Primary, secondary and tertiary	..
All levels combined	..
Public and private institutions	
Primary and secondary	..
Tertiary	..
Primary, secondary and tertiary	..
All levels combined	..

Table 2. Educational attainment of the population

Percentage of the population 25 to 64 years of age that has attained a specific highest level of education, 1992

ISCED	Level	%
0/1/2	Early childhood, primary, lower secondary	55
3	Upper secondary	25
5	Non-university	11
6/7	University	9

Table 3. Labour force participation by educational level

Labour force participation rate by level of educational attainment for men and women 25 to 64 years of age, 1992

ISCED	Level	%
0/1/2	Early childhood, primary, lower secondary	56.1
3	Upper secondary	78.8
5	Non-university	85.3
6/7	University	88.9
Total		68.0

Table 4. Unemployment by educational level

Unemployment rates by level of educational attainment for persons 25 to 64 years of age, 1992

ISCED	Level	%
0/1/2	Early childhood, primary, lower secondary	13.0
3	Upper secondary	4.7
5	Non-University	2.3
6/7	University	2.2
Total		7.8

Table 5. Subject profile of qualified labour force

University degrees as a percentage of total degrees by subject category, 1992

Level	%
Medical science	12.8
Natural and physical science	12.1
Engineering and architecture	23.9
Law and business	29.3
Human sciences	21.9

Table 6. Occupational profile of labour force

Percentage of 35 to 54 year-old employed workers in selected occupations, 1992

ISCO	Occupation	%
12	Corporate managers	..
213	Computing professionals	..
214	Architects, engineers and related professionals	..
31	Physical and engineering science associate professionals	..
32	Life science and health associate professionals	..
71	Extraction and building trade workers	..
73	Precision, handicraft, printing and related trades workers	..
80	Plant and machine operators and assemblers	..
83	Drivers and mobile-plant operators	..

Table 7. Continuing education and training for adults

Participation in job-related continuing education and training as a percentage of the employed population aged 25 to 64, by educational groups, 1991

ISCED	Level	%
0/1/2	Early childhood, primary, lower secondary	..
3	Upper secondary	..
5/6/7	Tertiary education	..
Total		..

CZECH REPUBLIC

Table 1. Educational expenditure relative to GDP

Educational expenditure as a percentage of GDP by type of institution, 1992

Public institutions	
Primary and secondary	..
Tertiary	..
Primary, secondary and tertiary	..
All levels combined	..
Public and private institutions	
Primary and secondary	3.8
Tertiary	0.6
Primary, secondary and tertiary	4.4
All levels combined	4.8

Source : Czech statistical office.

Table 2. Educational attainment of the population

Percentage of the population 15 to 64 years of age that has attained a specific highest level of education, 1993

ISCED	Level	%
0/1/2	Early childhood, primary, lower secondary	14
3	Upper secondary	45
5	Non-university	31
6/7	University	10

Source : Statistical Yearbook of the Czech Republic 1994.

Table 3. Labour force participation by educational level

Labour force participation rate by level of educational attainment for men and women 25 to 64 years of age, 1993

ISCED	Level	%
0/1/2	Early childhood, primary, lower secondary	61.9
3	Upper secondary	83.1
5	Non-university	86.0
6/7	University	91.1
Total		80.6

Source: Czech statistical office.

CZECH REPUBLIC (continued)

Table 4. Unemployment by educational level

Unemployment rates by level of educational attainment for persons 25 to 64 years of age, 1993

ISCED	Level	%
0/1/2	Early childhood, primary, lower secondary	4.2
3	Upper secondary	2.8
5	Non-university	2.0
6/7	University	1.4
Total		2.7

Source: Czech statistical office.

Table 5. Subject profile of qualified labour force

University degrees as a percentage of total degrees by subject category, 1991

Level	%
Medical science	10.2
Natural and physical science	14.2
Engineering and architecture	34.5
Law and business	14.3
Human sciences	26.8

Source: Czech 1991 Census.

Table 6. Occupational profile of labour force

Percentage of 35 to 54 year-old employed workers in selected occupations

ISCO	Occupation	%
12	Corporate managers	..
213	Computing professionals	..
214	Architects, engineers and related professionals	..
31	Physical and engineering science associate professionals	..
32	Life science and health associate professionals	..
71	Extraction and building trade workers	..
73	Precision, handicraft, printing and related trades workers	..
80	Plant and machine operators and assemblers	..
83	Drivers and mobile-plant operators	..

Table 7. Continuing education and training for adults

Participation in job-related continuing education and training as a percentage of the employed population aged 25 to 64, by educational groups

ISCED	Level	%
0/1/2	Early childhood, primary, lower secondary	..
3	Upper secondary	..
5/6/7	Tertiary education	..
Total		..

DENMARK

Table 1. Educational expenditure relative to GDP

Educational expenditure as a percentage of GDP by type of institution, 1992

Public institutions	
Primary and secondary	3.9
Tertiary	1.3
Primary, secondary and tertiary	5.2
All levels combined	6.2
Public and private institutions	
Primary and secondary	4.1
Tertiary	1.3
Primary, secondary and tertiary	5.4
All levels combined	6.7

Table 2. Educational attainment of the population

Percentage of the population 25 to 64 years of age that has attained a specific highest level of education, 1992

ISCED	Level	%
0/1/2	Early childhood, primary, lower secondary	41
3	Upper secondary	40
5	Non-university	6
6/7	University	13

Table 3. Labour force participation by educational level

Labour force participation rate by level of educational attainment for men and women 25 to 64 years of age, 1992

ISCED	Level	%
0/1/2	Early childhood, primary, lower secondary	73.0
3	Upper secondary	88.9
5	Non-university	93.4
6/7	University	93.7
Total		83.3

Table 4. Unemployment by educational level

Unemployment rates by level of educational attainment for persons 25 to 64 years of age, 1992

ISCED	Level	%
0/1/2	Early childhood, primary, lower secondary	15.6
3	Upper secondary	9.2
5	Non-university	5.8
6/7	University	4.8
Total		10.6

Table 5. Subject profile of qualified labour force

University degrees as a percentage of total degrees by subject category, 1992

Level	%
Medical science	14.2
Natural and physical science	8.2
Engineering and architecture	16.6
Law and business	20.0
Human sciences	40.9

Table 6. Occupational profile of labour force

Percentage of 35 to 54 year-old employed workers in selected occupations, 1992

ISCO	Occupation	%
12	Corporate managers	3.5
213	Computing professionals	0.4
214	Architects, engineers and related professionals	2.2
31	Physical and engineering science associate professionals	3.8
32	Life science and health associate professionals	3.2
71	Extraction and building trade workers	4.3
73	Precision, handicraft, printing and related trades workers	1.0
80	Plant and machine operators and assemblers	1.1
83	Drivers and mobile-plant operators	3.2

Table 7. Continuing education and training for adults

Participation in job-related continuing education and training as a percentage of the employed population aged 25 to 64, by educational groups, 1991

ISCED	Level	%
0/1/2	Early childhood, primary, lower secondary	6
3	Upper secondary	14
5/6/7	Tertiary education	25
Total		15

FINLAND

Table 1. Educational expenditure relative to GDP

Educational expenditure as a percentage of GDP by type of institution, 1992

Public institutions	
Primary and secondary	4.6
Tertiary	1.8
Primary, secondary and tertiary	6.4
All levels combined	7.3
Public and private institutions	
Primary and secondary	4.9
Tertiary	1.9
Primary, secondary and tertiary	6.8
All levels combined	7.9

Table 2. Educational attainment of the population

Percentage of the population 25 to 64 years of age that has attained a specific highest level of education, 1992

ISCED	Level	%
0/1/2	Early childhood, primary, lower secondary	39
3	Upper secondary	43
5	Non-university	8
6/7	University	10

Table 3. Labour force participation by educational level

Labour force participation rate by level of educational attainment for men and women 25 to 64 years of age, 1992

ISCED	Level	%
0/1/2	Early childhood, primary, lower secondary	69.8
3	Upper secondary	84.7
5	Non-university	85.7
6/7	University	91.8
Total		79.8

Table 4. Unemployment by educational level

Unemployment rates by level of educational attainment for persons 25 to 64 years of age, 1992

ISCED	Level	%
0/1/2	Early childhood, primary, lower secondary	14.9
3	Upper secondary	12.1
5	Non-university	5.7
6/7	University	3.4
Total		11.4

Table 5. Subject profile of qualified labour force

University degrees as a percentage of total degrees by subject category, 1992

Level	%
Medical science	9.5
Natural and physical science	15.6
Engineering and architecture	23.9
Law and business	11.0
Human sciences	40.0

Table 6. Occupational profile of labour force

Percentage of 35 to 54 year-old employed workers in selected occupations, 1992

ISCO	Occupation	%
12	Corporate managers	3.4
213	Computing professionals	0.6
214	Architects, engineers and related professionals	2.3
31	Physical and engineering science associate professionals	5.9
32	Life science and health associate professionals	3.4
71	Extraction and building trade workers	3.6
73	Precision, handicraft, printing and related trades workers	1.2
80	Plant and machine operators and assemblers	8.8
83	Drivers and mobile-plant operators	5.2

Table 7. Continuing education and training for adults

Participation in job-related continuing education and training as a percentage of the employed population aged 25 to 64, by educational groups, 1990

ISCED	Level	%
0/1/2	Early childhood, primary, lower secondary	28
3	Upper secondary	47
5/6/7	Tertiary education	74
Total		46

GREECE

Table 1. Educational expenditure relative to GDP

Educational expenditure as a percentage of GDP by type of institution, 1992

Public institutions	
Primary and secondary	..
Tertiary	..
Primary, secondary and tertiary	..
All levels combined	..
Public and private institutions	
Primary and secondary	..
Tertiary	..
Primary, secondary and tertiary	..
All levels combined	..

Table 2. Educational attainment of the population

Percentage of the population 25 to 64 years of age that has attained a specific highest level of education, 1991

ISCED	Level	%
0/1/2	Early childhood, primary, lower secondary	66
3	Upper secondary	21
5	Non-university	3
6/7	University	10

Table 3. Labour force participation by educational level

Labour force participation rate by level of educational attainment for men and women 25 to 64 years of age, 1992

ISCED	Level	%
0/1/2	Early childhood, primary, lower secondary	..
3	Upper secondary	..
5	Non-university	..
6/7	University	..
Total		..

Table 4. Unemployment by educational level

Unemployment rates by level of educational attainment for persons 25 to 64 years of age, 1992

ISCED	Level	%
0/1/2	Early childhood, primary, lower secondary	..
3	Upper secondary	..
5	Non-university	..
6/7	University	..
Total		..

Table 5. Subject profile of qualified labour force

University degrees as a percentage of total degrees by subject category, 1992

Level	%
Medical science	10.5
Natural and physical science	16.8
Engineering and architecture	13.7
Law and business	12.4
Human sciences	46.6

Table 6. Occupational profile of labour force

Percentage of 35 to 54 year-old employed workers in selected occupations, 1992

ISCO	Occupation	%
12	Corporate managers	..
213	Computing professionals	..
214	Architects, engineers and related professionals	..
31	Physical and engineering science associate professionals	..
32	Life science and health associate professionals	..
71	Extraction and building trade workers	..
73	Precision, handicraft, printing and related trades workers	..
80	Plant and machine operators and assemblers	..
83	Drivers and mobile-plant operators	..

Table 7. Continuing education and training for adults

Participation in job-related continuing education and training as a percentage of the employed population aged 25 to 64, by educational groups, 1991

ISCED	Level	%
0/1/2	Early childhood, primary, lower secondary	..
3	Upper secondary	..
5/6/7	Tertiary education	..
Total		..

HUNGARY

Table 1. Educational expenditure relative to GDP

Educational expenditure as a percentage of GDP by type of institution, 1992

Public institutions	
Primary and secondary	4.4
Tertiary	1.1
Primary, secondary and tertiary	5.5
All levels combined	6.6
Public and private institutions	..
Primary and secondary	..
Tertiary	..
Primary, secondary and tertiary	..
All levels combined	..

Source: Central Statistical Office of Hungary.

Table 2. Educational attainment of the population

Percentage of the population 25 to 64 years of age that has attained a specific highest level of education, 1992

ISCED	Level	%
0/1/2	Early childhood, primary, lower secondary	62.7
3	Upper secondary	25.0
5	Non-university	7.0
6/7	University	5.3

Source: Central Statistical Office of Hungary.

Table 3. Labour force participation by educational level

Labour force participation rate by level of educational attainment for men and women 25 to 64 years of age, 1992

ISCED	Level	%
0/1/2	Early childhood, primary, lower secondary	62.7
3	Upper secondary	81.3
5	Non-university	84.0
6/7	University	86.5
Total		70.0

Source: Central Statistical Office of Hungary.

Table 4. Unemployment by educational level

Unemployment rates by level of educational attainment for persons 25 to 64 years of age, 1992

ISCED	Level	%
0/1/2	Early childhood, primary, lower secondary	11.4
3	Upper secondary	6.2
5	Non-university	2.5
6/7	University	2.3
Total		8.5

Source: Central Statistical Office of Hungary.

Table 5. Subject profile of qualified labour force

University degrees as a percentage of total degrees by subject category, 1992

Level	%
Medical science	..
Natural and physical science	..
Engineering and architecture	..
Law and business	..
Human sciences	..

Table 6. Occupational profile of labour force

Percentage of 35 to 54 year-old employed workers in selected occupations, 1992

ISCO	Occupation	%
12	Corporate managers	..
213	Computing professionals	..
214	Architects, engineers and related professionals	..
31	Physical and engineering science associate professionals	..
32	Life science and health associate professionals	..
71	Extraction and building trade workers	..
73	Precision, handicraft, printing and related trades workers	..
80	Plant and machine operators and assemblers	..
83	Drivers and mobile-plant operators	..

Table 7. Continuing education and training for adults

Participation in job-related continuing education and training as a percentage of the employed population aged 25 to 64, by educational groups, 1992

ISCED	Level	%
0/1/2	Early childhood, primary, lower secondary	..
3	Upper secondary	..
5/6/7	Tertiary education	..
Total		..

IRELAND

Table 1. Educational expenditure relative to GDP

Educational expenditure as a percentage of GDP by type of institution, 1992

Public institutions	
Primary and secondary	3.7
Tertiary	1.4
Primary, secondary and tertiary	5.1
All levels combined	5.7
Public and private institutions	
Primary and secondary	3.7
Tertiary	1.4
Primary, secondary and tertiary	5.1
All levels combined	5.7

Table 2. Educational attainment of the population

Percentage of the population 25 to 64 years of age that has attained a specific highest level of education, 1992

ISCED	Level	%
0/1/2	Early childhood, primary, lower secondary	..
3	Upper secondary	..
5	Non-university	..
6/7	University	..

Table 3. Labour force participation by educational level

Labour force participation rate by level of educational attainment for men and women 25 to 64 years of age, 1992

ISCED	Level	%
0/1/2	Early childhood, primary, lower secondary	57.3
3	Upper secondary	70.7
5	Non-university	81.9
6/7	University	87.9
Total		65.2

Table 4. Unemployment by educational level

Unemployment rates by level of educational attainment for persons 25 to 64 years of age, 1992

ISCED	Level	%
0/1/2	Early childhood, primary, lower secondary	19.8
3	Upper secondary	9.3
5	Non-university	5.8
6/7	University	3.3
Total		13.5

Table 5. Subject profile of qualified labour force

University degrees as a percentage of total degrees by subject category, 1992

Level	%
Medical science	5.8
Natural and physical science	19.2
Engineering and architecture	12.4
Law and business	16.8
Human sciences	45.8

Table 6. Occupational profile of labour force

Percentage of 35 to 54 year-old employed workers in selected occupations, 1992

ISCO	Occupation	%
12	Corporate managers	..
213	Computing professionals	..
214	Architects, engineers and related professionals	..
31	Physical and engineering science associate professionals	..
32	Life science and health associate professionals	..
71	Extraction and building trade workers	..
73	Precision, handicraft, printing and related trades workers	..
80	Plant and machine operators and assemblers	..
83	Drivers and mobile-plant operators	..

Table 7. Continuing education and training for adults

Participation in job-related continuing education and training as a percentage of the employed population aged 25 to 64, by educational groups, 1992

ISCED	Level	%
0/1/2	Early childhood, primary, lower secondary	2
3	Upper secondary	4
5/6/7	Tertiary education	8
Total		4

Table 1. Educational expenditure relative to GDP

Educational expenditure as a percentage of GDP by type of institution, 1992

Public institutions	
Primary and secondary	0.8
Tertiary	0.8
Primary, secondary and tertiary	1.6
All levels combined	1.7
Public and private institutions	
Primary and secondary	3.0
Tertiary	1.4
Primary, secondary and tertiary	4.5
All levels combined	5.0

Table 2. Educational attainment of the population

Percentage of the population 25 to 64 years of age that has attained a specific highest level of education, 1992

ISCED	**Level**	**%**
0/1/2	Early childhood, primary, lower secondary	42
3	Upper secondary	37
5	Non-university	..
6/7	University	21

Table 3. Labour force participation by educational level

Labour force participation rate by level of educational attainment for men and women 25 to 64 years of age, 1992

ISCED	**Level**	**%**
0/1/2	Early childhood, primary, lower secondary	55.4
3	Upper secondary	77.0
5	Non-university	..
6/7	University	85.5
Total		69.7

Table 4. Unemployment by educational level

Unemployment rates by level of educational attainment for persons 25 to 64 years of age, 1992

ISCED	Level	%
0/1/2	Early childhood, primary, lower secondary	8.0
3	Upper secondary	4.7
5	Non-university	..
6/7	University	3.9
Total		5.6

Table 5. Subject profile of qualified labour force

University degrees as a percentage of total degrees by subject category, 1992

Level	%
Medical science	15.6
Natural and physical science	9.7
Engineering and architecture	16.0
Law and business	20.5
Human sciences	38.1

Table 6. Occupational profile of labour force

Percentage of 35 to 54 year-old employed workers in selected occupations, 1992

ISCO	Occupation	%
12	Corporate managers	7.2
213	Computing professionals	1.1
214	Architects, engineers and related professionals	2.3
31	Physical and engineering science associate professionals	3.3
32	Life science and health associate professionals	3.1
71	Extraction and building trade workers	4.4
73	Precision, handicraft, printing and related trades workers	0.8
80	Plant and machine operators and assemblers	7.1
83	Drivers and mobile-plant operators	3.8

Table 7. Continuing education and training for adults

Participation in job-related continuing education and training as a percentage of the employed population aged 25 to 64, by educational groups, 1991

ISCED	Level	%
0/1/2	Early childhood, primary, lower secondary	..
3	Upper secondary	..
5/6/7	Tertiary education	..
Total		..

NEW ZEALAND

Table 1. Educational expenditure relative to GDP

Educational expenditure as a percentage of GDP by type of institution, 1992

Public institutions	
Primary and secondary	..
Tertiary	..
Primary, secondary and tertiary	..
All levels combined	..
Public and private institutions	
Primary and secondary	..
Tertiary	..
Primary, secondary and tertiary	..
All levels combined	..

Table 2. Educational attainment of the population

Percentage of the population 25 to 64 years of age that has attained a specific highest level of education, 1992

ISCED	Level	%
0/1/2	Early childhood, primary, lower secondary	43
3	Upper secondary	33
5	Non-university	13
6/7	University	11

Table 3. Labour force participation by educational level

Labour force participation rate by level of educational attainment for men and women 25 to 64 years of age, 1992

ISCED	Level	%
0/1/2	Early childhood, primary, lower secondary	67.0
3	Upper secondary	79.1
5	Non-university	80.9
6/7	University	89.5
Total		75.2

Table 4. Unemployment by educational level

Unemployment rates by level of educational attainment for persons 25 to 64 years of age, 1992

ISCED	Level	%
0/1/2	Early childhood, primary, lower secondary	11.2
3	Upper secondary	7.5
5	Non-university	4.6
6/7	University	3.7
Total		8.0

Table 5. Subject profile of qualified labour force

University degrees as a percentage of total degrees by subject category, 1992

Level	%
Medical science	6.2
Natural and physical science	11.7
Engineering and architecture	5.1
Law and business	23.4
Human sciences	51.6

Table 6. Occupational profile of labour force

Percentage of 35 to 54 year-old employed workers in selected occupations, 1992

ISCO	Occupation	%
12	Corporate managers	14.5
213	Computing professionals	0.2
214	Architects, engineers and related professionals	1.3
31	Physical and engineering science associate professionals	2.8
32	Life science and health associate professionals	1.0
71	Extraction and building trade workers	4.3
73	Precision, handicraft, printing and related trades workers	1.3
80	Plant and machine operators and assemblers	5.7
83	Drivers and mobile-plant operators	3.2

Table 7. Continuing education and training for adults

Participation in job-related continuing education and training as a percentage of the employed population aged 25 to 64, by educational groups, 1991

ISCED	Level	%
0/1/2	Early childhood, primary, lower secondary	..
3	Upper secondary	..
5/6/7	Tertiary education	..
Total		..

NORWAY

Table 1. Educational expenditure relative to GDP

Educational expenditure as a percentage of GDP by type of institution, 1992

Public institutions	
Primary and secondary	..
Tertiary	..
Primary, secondary and tertiary	..
All levels combined	..
Public and private institutions	
Primary and secondary	..
Tertiary	..
Primary, secondary and tertiary	..
All levels combined	..

Table 2. Educational attainment of the population

Percentage of the population 25 to 64 years of age that has attained a specific highest level of education, 1992

ISCED	Level	%
0/1/2	Early childhood, primary, lower secondary	21
3	Upper secondary	54
5	Non-university	13
6/7	University	12

Table 3. Labour force participation by educational level

Labour force participation rate by level of educational attainment for men and women 25 to 64 years of age, 1992

ISCED	Level	%
0/1/2	Early childhood, primary, lower secondary	65.0
3	Upper secondary	83.2
5	Non-university	88.8
6/7	University	93.3
Total		81.4

Table 4. Unemployment by educational level

Unemployment rates by level of educational attainment for persons 25 to 64 years of age, 1992

ISCED	Level	%
0/1/2	Early childhood, primary, lower secondary	7.1
3	Upper secondary	4.9
5	Non-university	2.8
6/7	University	1.8
Total		4.6

Table 5. Subject profile of qualified labour force

University degrees as a percentage of total degrees by subject category, 1992

Level	%
Medical science	17.2
Natural and physical science	8.7
Engineering and architecture	21.1
Law and business	18.3
Human sciences	31.3

Table 6. Occupational profile of labour force

Percentage of 35 to 54 year-old employed workers in selected occupations, 1992

ISCO	Occupation	%
12	Corporate managers	..
213	Computing professionals	..
214	Architects, engineers and related professionals	..
31	Physical and engineering science associate professionals	..
32	Life science and health associate professionals	..
71	Extraction and building trade workers	..
73	Precision, handicraft, printing and related trades workers	..
80	Plant and machine operators and assemblers	..
83	Drivers and mobile-plant operators	..

Table 7. Continuing education and training for adults

Participation in job-related continuing education and training as a percentage of the employed population aged 25 to 64, by educational groups, 1991

ISCED	Level	%
0/1/2	Early childhood, primary, lower secondary	17
3	Upper secondary	33
5/6/7	Tertiary education	57
Total		37

PORTUGAL

Table 1. Educational expenditure relative to GDP

Educational expenditure as a percentage of GDP by type of institution, 1992

Public institutions	
Primary and secondary	4.0
Tertiary	0.9
Primary, secondary and tertiary	4.9
All levels combined	5.2
Public and private institutions	
Primary and secondary	..
Tertiary	..
Primary, secondary and tertiary	..
All levels combined	..

Table 2. Educational attainment of the population

Percentage of the population 25 to 64 years of age that has attained a specific highest level of education, 1991

ISCED	Level	%
0/1/2	Early childhood, primary, lower secondary	86
3	Upper secondary	7
5	Non-university	2
6/7	University	5

Table 3. Labour force participation by educational level

Labour force participation rate by level of educational attainment for men and women 25 to 64 years of age, 1992

ISCED	Level	%
0/1/2	Early childhood, primary, lower secondary	65.1
3	Upper secondary	88.4
5	Non-university	91.0
6/7	University	95.2
Total		68.8

Table 4. Unemployment by educational level

Unemployment rates by level of educational attainment for persons 25 to 64 years of age, 1991

ISCED	Level	%
0/1/2	Early childhood, primary, lower secondary	5.3
3	Upper secondary	4.5
5	Non-university	1.9
6/7	University	1.8
Total		4.9

Table 5. Subject profile of qualified labour force

University degrees as a percentage of total degrees by subject category, 1992

Level	%
Medical science	..
Natural and physical science	..
Engineering and architecture	..
Law and business	..
Human sciences	..

Table 6. Occupational profile of labour force

Percentage of 35 to 54 year-old employed workers in selected occupations, 1992

ISCO	Occupation	%
12	Corporate managers	..
213	Computing professionals	..
214	Architects, engineers and related professionals	..
31	Physical and engineering science associate professionals	..
32	Life science and health associate professionals	..
71	Extraction and building trade workers	..
73	Precision, handicraft, printing and related trades workers	..
80	Plant and machine operators and assemblers	..
83	Drivers and mobile-plant operators	..

Table 7. Continuing education and training for adults

Participation in job-related continuing education and training as a percentage of the employed population aged 25 to 64, by educational groups, 1991

ISCED	Level	%
0/1/2	Early childhood, primary, lower secondary	..
3	Upper secondary	..
5/6/7	Tertiary education	..
Total		..

SPAIN

Table 1. Educational expenditure relative to GDP

Educational expenditure as a percentage of GDP by type of institution, 1992

Public institutions	
Primary and secondary	2.9
Tertiary	0.9
Primary, secondary and tertiary	3.8
All levels combined	4.2
Public and private institutions	
Primary and secondary	3.7
Tertiary	0.9
Primary, secondary and tertiary	4.7
All levels combined	5.2

Table 2. Educational attainment of the population

Percentage of the population 25 to 64 years of age that has attained a specific highest level of education, 1992

ISCED	Level	%
0/1/2	Early childhood, primary, lower secondary	77
3	Upper secondary	10
5	Non-university	3
6/7	University	10

Table 3. Labour force participation by educational level

Labour force participation rate by level of educational attainment for men and women 25 to 64 years of age, 1992

ISCED	Level	%
0/1/2	Early childhood, primary, lower secondary	57.6
3	Upper secondary	80.2
5	Non-university	89.0
6/7	University	86.4
Total		63.7

Table 4. Unemployment by educational level

Unemployment rates by level of educational attainment for persons 25 to 64 years of age, 1992

ISCED	Level	%
0/1/2	Early childhood, primary, lower secondary	16.0
3	Upper secondary	14.1
5	Non-university	12.5
6/7	University	9.9
Total		14.7

Table 5. Subject profile of qualified labour force

University degrees as a percentage of total degrees by subject category, 1992

Level	%
Medical science	13.4
Natural and physical science	10.4
Engineering and architecture	9.7
Law and business	25.3
Human sciences	41.2

Table 6. Occupational profile of labour force

Percentage of 35 to 54 year-old employed workers in selected occupations, 1992

ISCO	Occupation	%
12	Corporate managers	2.3
213	Computing professionals	0.2
214	Architects, engineers and related professionals	1.3
31	Physical and engineering science associate professionals	1.1
32	Life science and health associate professionals	0.1
71	Extraction and building trade workers	8.4
73	Precision, handicraft, printing and related trades workers	1.1
80	Plant and machine operators and assemblers	12.3
83	Drivers and mobile-plant operators	3.2

Table 7. Continuing education and training for adults

Participation in job-related continuing education and training as a percentage of the employed population aged 25 to 64, by educational groups, 1992

ISCED	Level	%
0/1/2	Early childhood, primary, lower secondary	1
3	Upper secondary	6
5/6/7	Tertiary education	7
Total		3

SWEDEN

Table 1. Educational expenditure relative to GDP

Educational expenditure as a percentage of GDP by type of institution, 1992

Public institutions	
Primary and secondary	4.6
Tertiary	1.0
Primary, secondary and tertiary	5.6
All levels combined	6.7
Public and private institutions	
Primary and secondary	4.6
Tertiary	1.0
Primary, secondary and tertiary	5.6
All levels combined	6.8

Table 2. Educational attainment of the population

Percentage of the population 25 to 64 years of age that has attained a specific highest level of education, 1992

ISCED	**Level**	%
0/1/2	Early childhood, primary, lower secondary	30
3	Upper secondary	46
5	Non-university	12
6/7	University	12

Table 3. Labour force participation by educational level

Labour force participation rate by level of educational attainment for men and women 25 to 64 years of age, 1992

ISCED	**Level**	%
0/1/2	Early childhood, primary, lower secondary	86.2
3	Upper secondary	93.0
5	Non-university	94.3
6/7	University	95.2
Total		91.4

Table 4. Unemployment by educational level

Unemployment rates by level of educational attainment for persons 25 to 64 years of age, 1992

ISCED	Level	%
0/1/2	Early childhood, primary, lower secondary	4.6
3	Upper secondary	4.3
5	Non-university	2.3
6/7	University	2.0
Total		3.8

Table 5. Subject profile of qualified labour force

University degrees as a percentage of total degrees by subject category, 1992

Level	%
Medical science	17.1
Natural and physical science	12.0
Engineering and architecture	16.6
Law and business	23.4
Human sciences	31.0

Table 6. Occupational profile of labour force

Percentage of 35 to 54 year-old employed workers in selected occupations, 1992

ISCO	Occupation	%
12	Corporate managers	1.4
213	Computing professionals	0.1
214	Architects, engineers and related professionals	0.8
31	Physical and engineering science associate professionals	0.1
32	Life science and health associate professionals	1.0
71	Extraction and building trade workers	0.4
73	Precision, handicraft, printing and related trades workers	0.1
80	Plant and machine operators and assemblers	1.5
83	Drivers and mobile-plant operators	0.5

Table 7. Continuing education and training for adults

Participation in job-related continuing education and training as a percentage of the employed population aged 25 to 64, by educational groups, 1993

ISCED	Level	%
0/1/2	Early childhood, primary, lower secondary	21
3	Upper secondary	34
5/6/7	Tertiary education	53
Total		36

SWITZERLAND

Table 1. Educational expenditure relative to GDP

Educational expenditure as a percentage of GDP by type of institution, 1992

Public institutions	
Primary and secondary	..
Tertiary	..
Primary, secondary and tertiary	..
All levels combined	..
Public and private institutions	
Primary and secondary	..
Tertiary	..
Primary, secondary and tertiary	..
All levels combined	..

Table 2. Educational attainment of the population

Percentage of the population 25 to 64 years of age that has attained a specific highest level of education, 1992

ISCED	**Level**	%
0/1/2	Early childhood, primary, lower secondary	19
3	Upper secondary	60
5	Non-university	13
6/7	University	8

Table 3. Labour force participation by educational level

Labour force participation rate by level of educational attainment for men and women 25 to 64 years of age, 1992

ISCED	**Level**	%
0/1/2	Early childhood, primary, lower secondary	71.7
3	Upper secondary	82.2
5	Non-university	91.9
6/7	University	92.7
Total		82.3

Table 4. Unemployment by educational level

Unemployment rates by level of educational attainment for persons 25 to 64 years of age, 1992

ISCED	Level	%
0/1/2	Early childhood, primary, lower secondary	3.5
3	Upper secondary	2.2
5	Non-university	2.3
6/7	University	3.0
Total		2.5

Table 5. Subject profile of qualified labour force

University degrees as a percentage of total degrees by subject category, 1992

Level	%
Medical science	15.2
Natural and physical science	19.1
Engineering and architecture	10.3
Law and business	29.8
Human sciences	24.8

Table 6. Occupational profile of labour force

Percentage of 35 to 54 year-old employed workers in selected occupations, 1992

ISCO	Occupation	%
12	Corporate managers	8.9
213	Computing professionals	1.1
214	Architects, engineers and related professionals	1.7
31	Physical and engineering science associate professionals	3.7
32	Life science and health associate professionals	2.4
71	Extraction and building trade workers	5.3
73	Precision, handicraft, printing and related trades workers	1.1
80	Plant and machine operators and assemblers	4.8
83	Drivers and mobile-plant operators	2.5

Table 7. Continuing education and training for adults

Participation in job-related continuing education and training as a percentage of the employed population aged 25 to 64, by educational groups, 1993

ISCED	Level	%
0/1/2	Early childhood, primary, lower secondary	16
3	Upper secondary	39
5/6/7	Tertiary education	52
Total		38

TURKEY

Table 1. Educational expenditure relative to GDP

Educational expenditure as a percentage of GDP by type of institution, 1992

Public institutions	
Primary and secondary	..
Tertiary	..
Primary, secondary and tertiary	..
All levels combined	..
Public and private institutions	
Primary and secondary	..
Tertiary	..
Primary, secondary and tertiary	..
All levels combined	..

Table 2. Educational attainment of the population

Percentage of the population 25 to 64 years of age that has attained a specific highest level of education, 1992

ISCED	**Level**	**%**
0/1/2	Early childhood, primary, lower secondary	86
3	Upper secondary	9
5	Non-university	..
6/7	University	5

Table 3. Labour force participation by educational level

Labour force participation rate by level of educational attainment for men and women 25 to 64 years of age, 1992

ISCED	**Level**	**%**
0/1/2	Early childhood, primary, lower secondary	58.3
3	Upper secondary	74.7
5	Non-university	..
6/7	University	90.2
Total		61.3

Table 4. Unemployment by educational level

Unemployment rates by level of educational attainment for persons 25 to 64 years of age, 1992

ISCED	Level	%
0/1/2	Early childhood, primary, lower secondary	5.1
3	Upper secondary	6.7
5	Non-university	..
6/7	University	4.1
Total		5.2

Table 5. Subject profile of qualified labour force

University degrees as a percentage of total degrees by subject category, 1992

Level	%
Medical science	10.4
Natural and physical science	5.5
Engineering and architecture	17.2
Law and business	5.6
Human sciences	51.3

Table 6. Occupational profile of labour force

Percentage of 35 to 54 year-old employed workers in selected occupations, 1992

ISCO	Occupation	%
12	Corporate managers	..
213	Computing professionals	..
214	Architects, engineers and related professionals	..
31	Physical and engineering science associate professionals	..
32	Life science and health associate professionals	..
71	Extraction and building trade workers	..
73	Precision, handicraft, printing and related trades workers	..
80	Plant and machine operators and assemblers	..
83	Drivers and mobile-plant operators	..

Table 7. Continuing education and training for adults

Participation in job-related continuing education and training as a percentage of the employed population aged 25 to 64, by educational groups, 1991

ISCED	Level	%
0/1/2	Early childhood, primary, lower secondary	..
3	Upper secondary	..
5/6/7	Tertiary education	..
Total		..

BACKGROUND NOTES TO COUNTRY TABLES

General

- The source of the data presented in the country tables is OECD (1995), *Education at a Glance: OECD Indicators*, *op. cit*.

- ISCED refers to the International Standard Classification of Education. It is used as a means of compiling internationally comparable statistics on education.

- ISCO refers to the International Standard Classification of Occupations.

- The *OECD average* is the simple unweighted average of the indicator values of all countries included. It is sometimes referred to as the value of the "typical country". The OECD *total* is the value of the indicator for the entire OECD area, treated as one country.

- The fiscal years considered for calculating finance indicators are as follows: 1992 for Finland, France, Germany, Italy and Norway; April 1991 to March 1992 for Canada, Japan and the United Kingdom; and July 1991 to June 1992 for Sweden and the United States.

- For country-specific explanatory notes for each table, the original source should be consulted.

- Two symbols are used:

  - X = data included in another category of the question, or in another question. Data not applicable because the question does not apply; and

  - .. = data not available, either because they were not collected in the country, or due to non-response.

Educational expenditure relative to GDP (Table 1)

Reference: Table F01(A), op. cit., p. 73.

The expenditure figures exclude: direct household purchases of educational goods and services; and subsidies for student living expenses.

Expenditures for public institutions and public and private institutions combined, are calculated for: primary and secondary education; tertiary education; the sub-total of primary, secondary and tertiary education; and all levels of education combined. The last includes expenditures for early childhood education and expenditures not allocated by level.

Educational expenditure as a percentage of GDP by type of institution, 1992

Public institutions

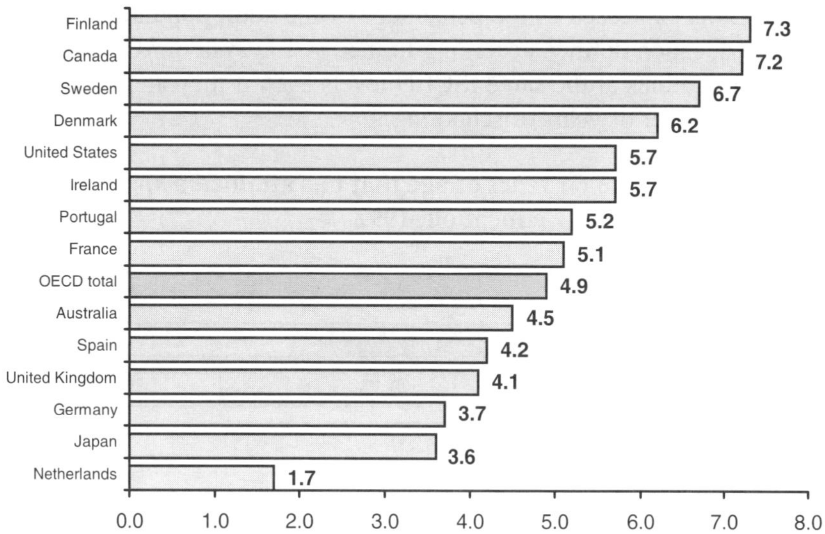

Public and private institutions

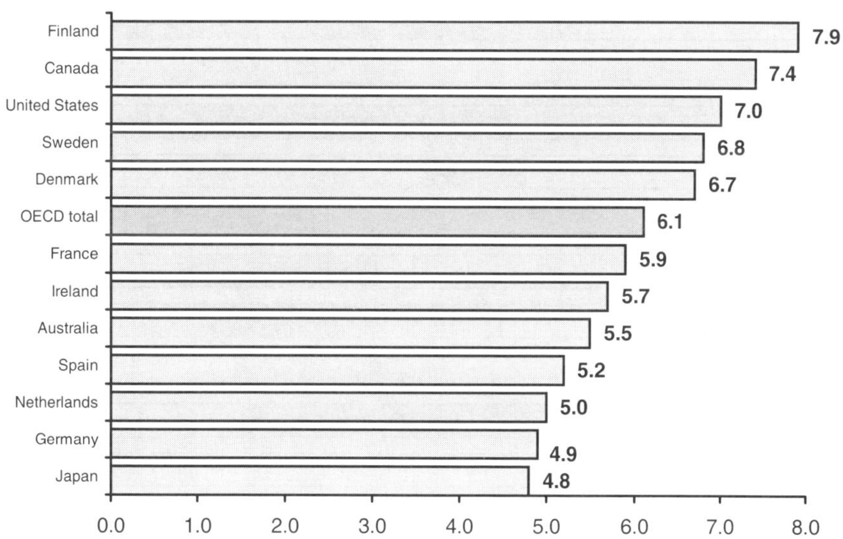

Educational attainment of the population (Table 2)

Reference: Table C01(A), op. cit., p. 20.

Educational attainment is expressed as the percentage of the adult population that has completed a certain highest level of education defined according to the ISCED system. Countries do not always classify diplomas and qualifications at the same ISCED levels even if they are received at roughly the same age or after a similar number of years of schooling.

Percentage of the population 25 to 64 years of age that has attained a specific highest level of education, 1992

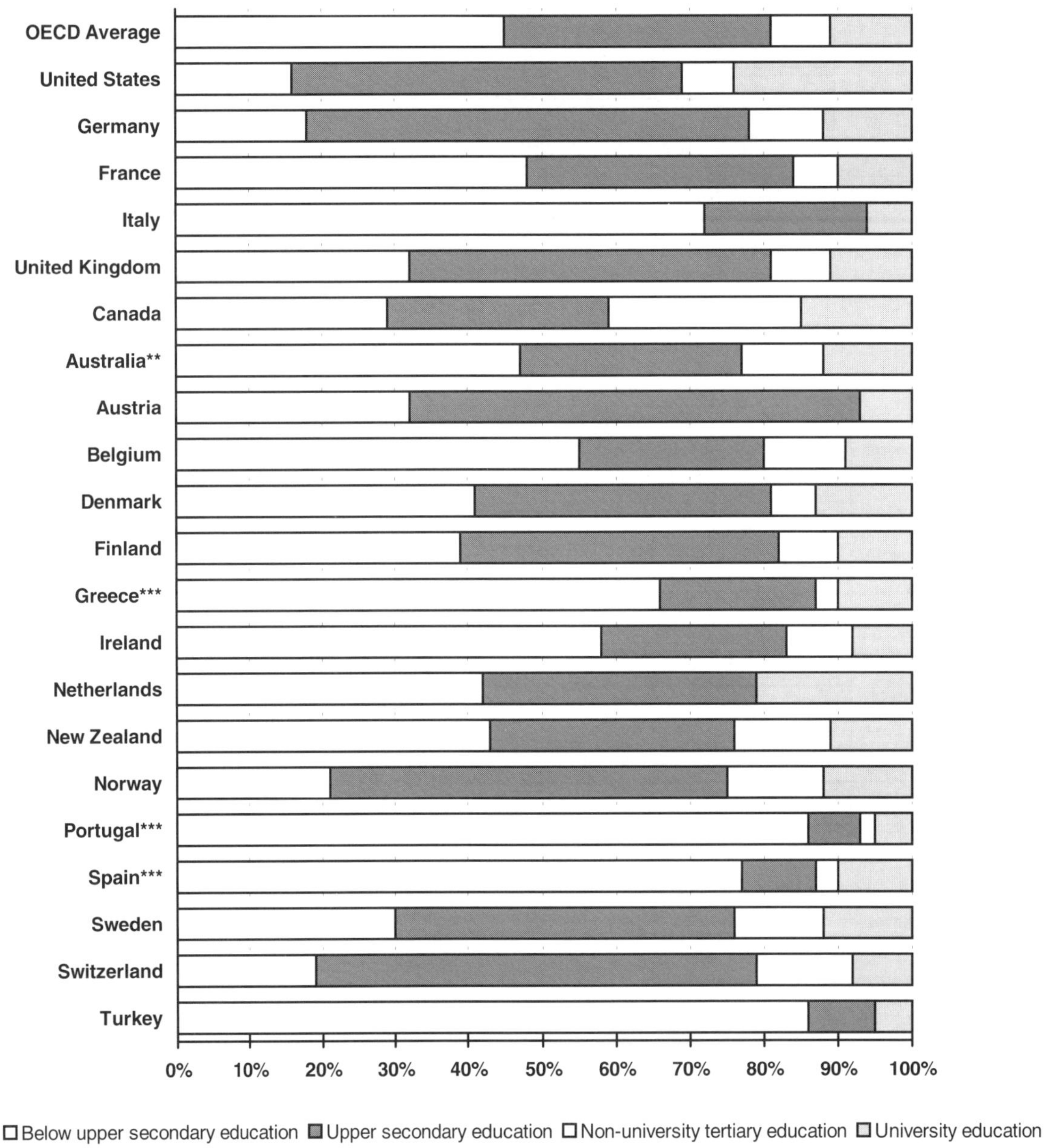

* = OECD unweighted average excluding Japan, Luxembourg, and Iceland; ** = 1993 data; *** = 1991 data.

Labour force participation by educational level (Table 3)

Reference: Table C11(3), op .cit., p. 37.

The labour force participation rate is calculated as the percentage of the population that belongs to the labour force. The labour force is defined in accordance with OECD *Labour Force Statistics*. See also notes to Table 2.

Labour force participation rate by level of education attainment for men and women 25 to 64 years of age, 1992

ISCED Level	**0/1/2 Early childhood, primary and lower secondary education**	**3 Upper secondary education**	**5 Non-university tertiary education**	**6/7 University education**	**Total**
United States	60.3	79.7	86.7	88.4	79.2
Germany	57.0	76.7	86.5	89.8	75.6
France	64.9	83.5	89.4	86.9	75.3
Italy	58.2	79.8	..	85.5	69.7
United Kingdom	64.5	82.1	84.0	90.3	77.5
Canada	62.4	79.9	85.5	89.6	77.8
Australia	65.1	80.2	83.2	89.2	74.4
Austria	52.8	73.9	..	88.4	68.1
Belgium	56.1	78.8	85.3	88.9	68.0
Denmark	73.0	88.9	93.4	93.7	83.3
Finland	69.8	84.7	85.7	91.8	79.8
Ireland	57.3	70.7	81.9	87.9	65.2
Netherlands	55.4	77.0	..	85.5	69.7
New Zealand	67.0	79.1	80.9	89.5	75.2
Norway	65.0	83.2	88.8	93.3	81.4
Portugal	65.1	88.4	91.0	95.2	68.8
Spain	57.6	80.2	89.0	86.4	63.7
Sweden	86.2	93.0	94.3	95.2	91.4
Switzerland	71.7	82.2	91.9	92.7	82.3
Turkey	58.3	74.7	..	90.2	61.3
OECD average[1]	**63.4**	**80.8**	**87.3**	**90.2**	**74.2**

1. OECD unweighted average excluding Japan, Greece, Luxembourg, and Iceland.

Unemployment by educational level (Table 4)

Reference: Table R21(A), op. cit., p. 228.

The unemployed are defined as persons who are without work, seeking work and currently available for work. The unemployment rate is the number of unemployed as a percentage of the labour force. See also notes to Table 2.

Unemployment rates by level of educational attainment for persons 25 to 64 years of age, 1992

ISCED Level	0/1/2 Early childhood, primary and lower secondary education	3 Upper secondary education	5 Non-university tertiary education	6/7 University education	Total
United States	13.5	7.2	4.6	2.9	6.6
Germany	8.9	6.4	4.5	3.7	6.2
France	12.1	7.4	4.6	4.4	8.8
Italy	7.3	8.2	..	6.0	7.4
United Kingdom	12.3	8.3	3.3	3.6	8.4
Canada	15.1	9.7	9.0	5.2	10.0
Australia	11.2	8.9	5.7	4.4	8.8
Austria	5.6	3.2	..	1.3	3.6
Belgium	13.0	4.7	2.3	2.2	7.8
Denmark	15.6	9.2	5.8	4.8	10.6
Finland	14.9	12.1	5.7	3.4	11.4
Ireland	19.8	9.3	5.8	3.3	13.5
Netherlands	8.0	4.7	..	3.9	5.6
New Zealand	11.2	7.5	4.6	3.7	8.0
Norway	7.1	4.9	2.8	1.8	4.6
Portugal[1]	5.3	4.5	1.9	1.8	4.9
Spain	16.0	14.1	12.5	9.9	14.7
Sweden	4.6	4.3	2.3	2.0	3.8
Switzerland	3.5	2.2	2.3	3.0	2.5
Turkey	5.1	6.7	..	4.1	5.2
OECD average[2]	**10.5**	**7.2**	**4.9**	**3.8**	**7.6**

1. 1991 data.
2. OECD unweighted average excluding Japan, Greece, Luxembourg, and Iceland.

Subject profile of qualified labour force (Table 5)

Reference: Table R14, op. cit., p. 222.

The results rely heavily on how far countries have used consistent subject definitions. The inclusion of higher degrees will influence the distribution because the proportions of students pursuing such degrees will vary from subject to subject.

University degrees as a percentage of total degrees by level category, 1992

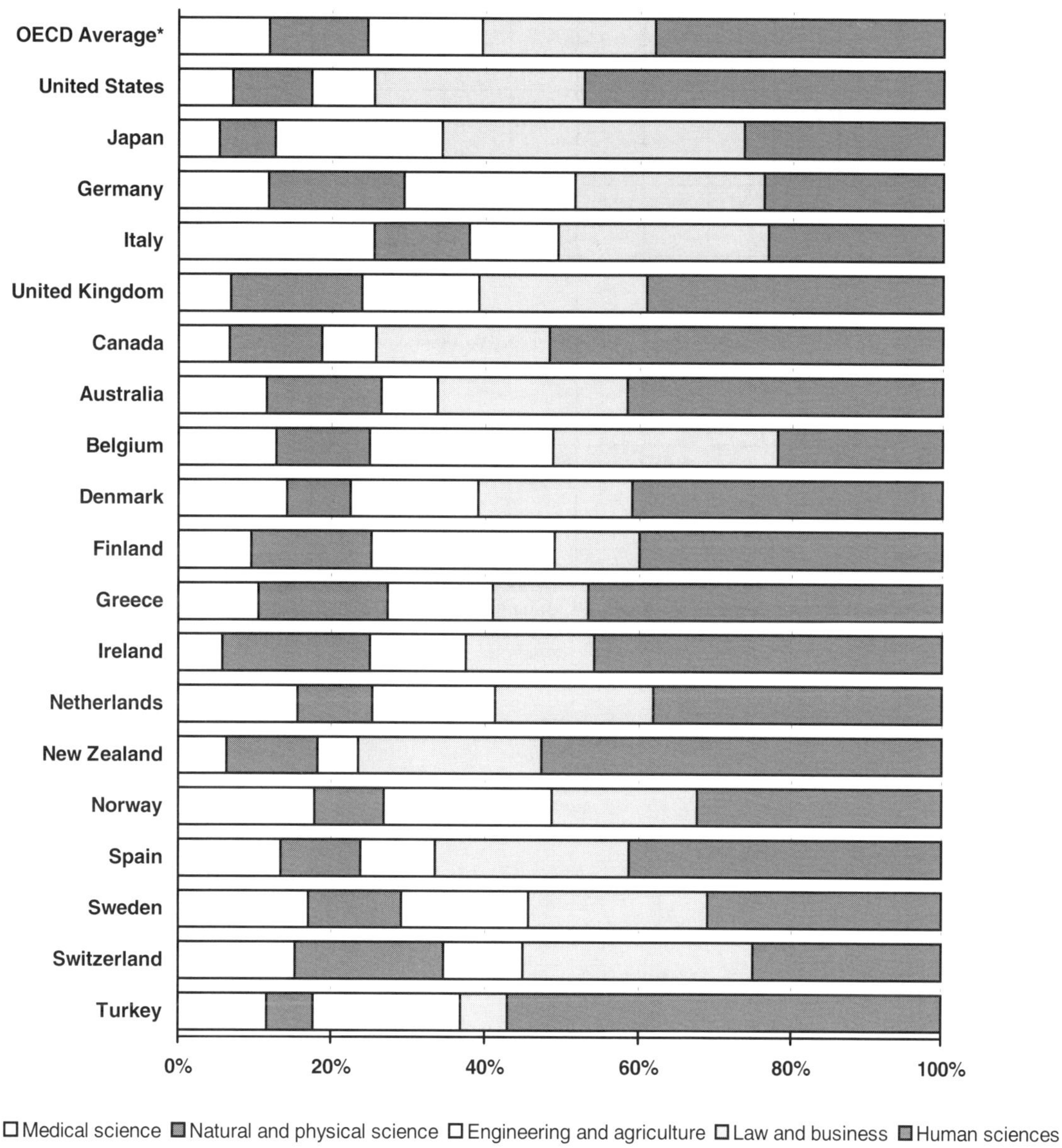

* = OECD unweighted average excluding France, Luxembourg, Portugal, Austria, and Iceland.

Occupational profile of labour force (Table 6)

Reference: Table R23(A2), op. cit., p. 242.

Percentage of 35 to 54 year old employed workers in selected occupations

ISCO	Occupation	US	Ger.	Fr.	Ita.	UK	Can.	Den.	Fin.	Neth	NZ	Spa.	Swe.	Swit.	OECD avg.[1]
12	Corporate managers	4.7	3.4	5.3	0.2	17.2	6.2	3.5	3.4	7.2	14.5	2.3	1.4	8.9	**6.0**
213	Computing professionals	1.3	0.3	0.7	..	0.8	1.0	0.4	0.6	1.1	0.2	0.2	0.1	1.1	**0.7**
214	Architects, engineers and related professionals	1.9	3.0	2.2	0.8	2.7	1.1	2.2	2.3	2.3	1.3	1.3	0.8	1.7	**1.8**
31	Physical and engineering science associate professionals	2.5	4.7	3.6	2.9	2.0	3.6	3.8	5.9	3.3	2.8	1.1	0.1	3.7	**3.1**
32	Life science and health associate professionals	6.5	2.3	2.5	1.9	1.4	5.4	3.2	3.4	3.1	1.0	0.1	1.0	2.4	**2.6**
71	Extraction and building trade workers	3.9	6.1	6.2	5.9	5.5	4.0	4.3	3.6	4.4	4.3	8.4	0.4	5.3	**4.8**
73	Precision, handicraft, printing and related trade workers	1.9	1.2	0.5	1.2	1.0	3.0	1.0	1.2	0.8	1.3	1.1	0.1	1.1	**1.2**
80	Plant and machine operators and assemblers	6.3	4.4	0.5	..	8.6	..	1.1	8.8	7.1	5.7	12.3	1.5	4.8	**5.6**
83	Drivers and mobile-plant operators	4.1	4.1	4.0	4.0	4.0	3.6	3.2	5.2	3.8	3.2	3.2	0.5	2.5	**3.5**

1. OECD unweighted average excluding Australia, Japan, Belgium, Greece, Ireland, Luxembourg, Austria, Iceland, Norway, and Turkey.

Continuing education and training for adults (Table 7)

Reference: Table P08(A), op. cit., p. 158.

Continuing education and training (CET) for adults refers to all kinds of job-related education and training organised, financed or sponsored by authorities, provided by employers or self-financed. Job-related CET covers all organised, systematic education and training activities in which people take part in order to: obtain knowledge and/or new skills for a current or future job; increase earnings; improve job and/or career opportunities in a current or other field; and generally improve their opportunities for advancement and promotion. CET for adults does not include military training or full-time studies at ISCED levels 5, 6 and 7.

Participation in job-related continuing education and training as a percentage of the employed population aged 25 to 64 by educational groups, 1992

ISCED	0/1/2	3	5/6/7	
Level	Early childhood, primary and lower secondary education	Upper secondary education	Tertiary education	Total
During the 12-month period preceding the survey				
United States (1991)	10	30	54	38
Germany (1991)	11	23	41	27
France (1992)	13	31	46	27
Canada (1991)	13	25	40	30
Finland (1990)	28	47	74	46
Norway (1991)	17	33	57	37
Sweden (1993)	21	34	53	36
Switzerland (1993)	16	39	52	38
During the 4-week period preceding the survey				
United Kingdom (1992)	4	10	19	11
Denmark (1991)	6	14	25	15
Ireland (1992)	2	4	8	4
Spain (1992)	1	6	7	3

Chapter 4

CORPORATE GOVERNANCE ENVIRONMENTS

This section includes the information available at the time of finalisation of this report for publication.

Introduction

Corporate governance designates the rules and practices that influence the allocation and monitoring of capital resources in the business sector. It includes the legal and practical procedures which influence the key management decisions of firms and their implementation, especially the involvement of fund suppliers – shareholders and creditors – in these decisions. Corporate governance in a larger sense also includes the processes and factors which affect firms' decisions and behaviour, including their employment relations and relations with public authorities and regulations. Focus will be put here on relations with the suppliers of funds, which are the firms' "principals".

Corporate governance has become a particularly important and topical framework factor for firms' competitiveness, because of the conjunction of two trends. On the one hand, "industry-side" changes in the technical characteristics and competitive environment of firms imply more rapid, larger-size and riskier investments in the business sector. These investments, which are for the most part dedicated to intangible assets (technology-, marketing- and human-capital-related), necessitate particularly sharp decision-making mechanisms to discriminate between good and bad projects, and to implement and monitor desirable projects more rapidly and efficiently. On the other hand, "financial-side" changes generate an unknown level of liberalisation, globalisation and competition in the allocation of savings, requiring from firms which claim capital resources international market level (high and sustained) returns and high management standards. The corporate governance practices of firms, and especially those listed on stock exchanges, need to match the efficiency and profitability performance of their international competitors.

Firms' governance practices and performance depend on their national environment in three main respects: *i) laws and regulations* which enable and constrain firms' governance processes; *ii) standard contract forms* (established routines) available in the national environment, relied upon in establishing contract forms between corporate stakeholders; and *iii) implicit rules* of behaviour in society, shaping tacit expectations and commitments between individuals (and groups) on important corporate governance patterns.

To illustrate this triple origin of rules, the situation of a domestic firm competing, for example, on the world semiconductor market, can be envisioned. The national environment will shape the identity and expectations of its owners, via financial intermediation and investment regulations (insurance companies, pension funds, mutual funds, banks, etc., acting as equity owners), and via existing investment practices. These investors will monitor the company on the basis of information they receive under securities legislation, stock exchange rules and nationally defined information channels and techniques. On this basis, the company will be steered by a board and a management team, nominated, elected and acting under national company law and prevailing organisation patterns. The company will also have to meet commitments *vis-à-vis* its employees, concerning job tenure and human capital building, prescribed by implicit national contracts.

These three sources of rules (laws and regulations, standard contract forms and organisation practices, and implicit social rules) are what the national environment offers to, and enforces on, companies when they design and implement their private governance practices. On this collective (public good) basis, each company's founders, creditors, managers and employees design their company-specific contracting, information-reporting and decision-making procedures, which are highly idiosyncratic and which provide each company with its identity and its corporate culture. This complementarity between national (collective) and idiosyncratic (company-specific) techniques constitutes the corporate governance environment in each nation. This double origin is shown in Graph 1.

Graph 1. National governance environment and company-specific designs

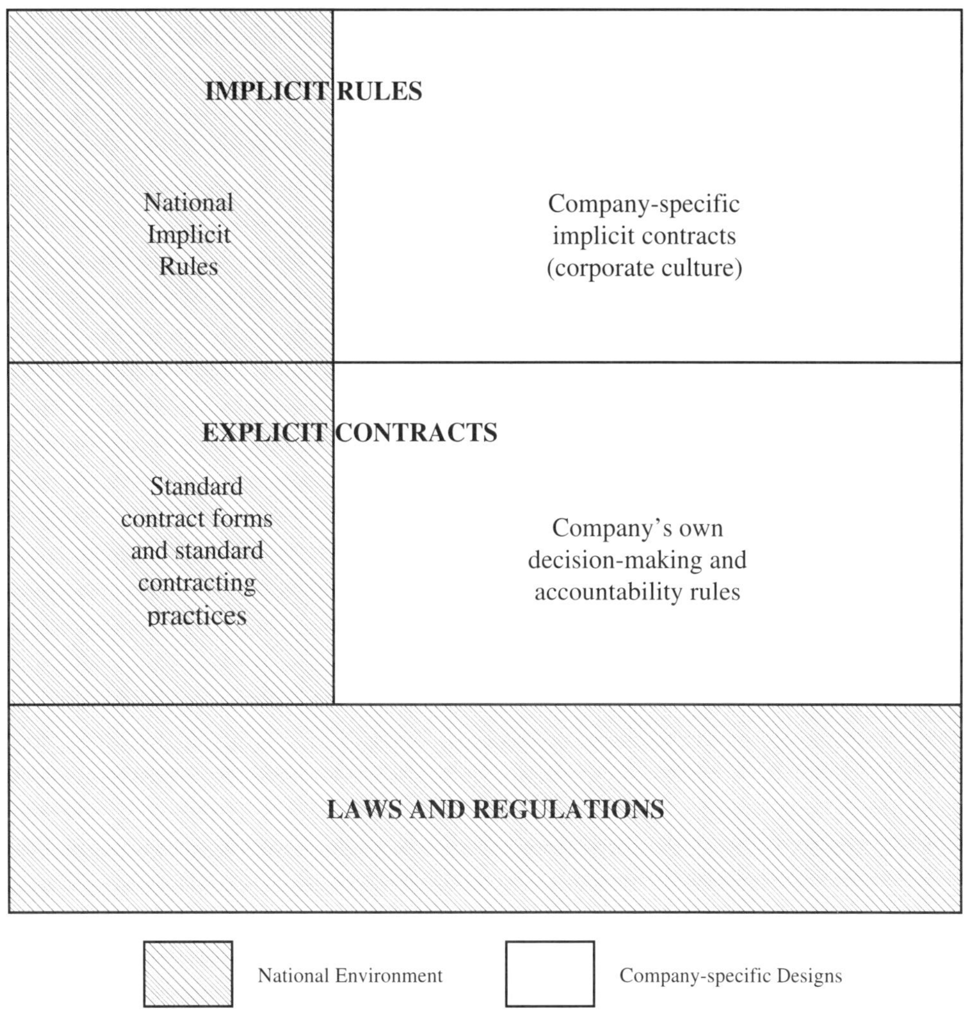

Structure of summary country matrices

This module compiles and presents summary information on each country's national corporate governance environment by describing the impact of the above-mentioned framework factors (laws and regulatory, established routines and implicit social rules) on the main attributes of the corporate governance system. Eight such dimensions can be identified from the recent economic literature as having a particularly important impact on firms' governance practices.

Laws and regulations

Company law, securities legislation and investment regulations (for company investors such as pension funds, life-insurance companies and banks) delineate the legal obligations of companies and investors when they design and implement governance practices. *Company law* prescribes the creation of given types of management bodies and specifies the rights and liabilities of their members.

It can also delineate the types of contracts and benefits which can be offered to company officials and employees. *Securities law* defines information obligations of companies *vis-à-vis* their shareholders and creditors, as well as information and disclosure obligations of different investor categories among themselves. *Investment regulations* delimit the latitude of financial institutions when investing in the industrial sector and codify their use of specific types of financing instruments and monitoring tools (such as banks being allowed or not to develop shareholding positions in their creditors, pension funds required to have widely diversified portfolios, etc.).

Legal rules which have an impact on governance are substantially different across countries, and create country-specific *design bounds* (frames) on financing arrangements, information sources and decision-making procedures between corporate stakeholders: shareowners, creditors, top managers and employees.

Standard contract forms

Standard contract forms are of two sorts and play an important role in Member countries:

- *De facto governance standards* are progressively elaborated, refined and consolidated by influential investor groups in each country, which carry a stock of "goodwill" in implementation know-how, learning economies, legal expertise, information techniques, etc. Japanese main-bank, German house-bank and US venture-capital practices are examples.

- *Voluntary market associations* also promote and enforce governance norms in order to reduce transaction costs among market participants. For example, the use of yearly and quarterly financial statements according to commonly agreed accounting standards is a common case. Beneficiaries of such "user clubs" are both industrial companies and investor institutions, which standardize among themselves the information formats, financing instruments, and rights and liabilities associated to different financing contracts. Major stock exchanges are such market associations: they standardize and enforce, *on a voluntary basis* (nobody is forced to trade in a stock exchange), a range of information and governance-related rules and contract forms.

Both *de facto* governance standards and voluntary market standards are domestic sources of governance patterns. Internationalisation of large shareholders, and internationalisation of national stock exchanges are widening the international use of these standards to some extent, but they remain largely national in practice.

Implicit social rules

Implicit expectations and commitments between individuals and social groups also play an important role, at least in certain countries. These are understandings between market participants concerning their respective rights and liabilities, without written contracts and formal enforcement mechanisms. They are most frequently observed in culturally homogeneous societies (or groups, for example, recent transborder Chinese investment circuits). They can be a more flexible complement to, and in certain instances, a substitute for, formal laws and regulations and explicit contracts. In corporate governance, they intervene particularly in two respects: *i)* implicit commitments between companies and employees concerning job tenure; *ii)* social expectations concerning the education and training role of companies (whatever the microeconomic profitability of these training expenditures).

Implicit contracts exist also at company level – they then constitute the "corporate culture". They include mutual commitments between a company and its employees, and sometimes between a company and its suppliers and the local community it is based in. However, from an internationally comparative perspective, what are important are those commitments which are recognised and enforced across a nation.

Attributes of the corporate governance environment

Analytical studies of corporate governance identify the principal dimensions which build up a governance environment. Since firms' governance practices are partly influenced (inspired and delineated) by their national environment and partly by their own design decisions, each governance environment can be described according to the "impulse" it gives to firms on each of these dimensions. Eight of these attributes are identified in the research literature as being particularly important for the formation of firms' governance practices. Each country's national environment seems to affect these dimensions in particular ways:

- the concentration of company ownership and control;
- constitution and role of corporate boards;
- strategic information of shareholders;
- possibility and role of take-overs;
- concentration of creditors;
- combination of credit and equity positions;
- handling of financial distress and bankruptcy;
- financial return expectations of investors.

Concentration of company owners

Different countries' investment rules and regulations are unevenly permissive to the concentration of company ownership beyond a given threshold. Securities legislation and stock-exchange rules also constrain (unevenly in various countries) legal possibilities for the concentration of ownership in listed companies. Certain countries authorise the build-up of large size and concentrated equity holdings by financial intermediaries, while others promote fragmented and dispersed ownership structures. Also, national company law, standard corporate charters and stock-exchange rules encourage in certain countries, and discourage in others, voting right restrictions and delegations (proxies) which determine the concentration of decision-making power in companies.

Constitution and role of corporate boards

Both company law and standard corporate charters (contracts) prescribe specific rules as to the composition, appointment and responsibilities of corporate boards. The participation of shareholders, creditors and other stakeholders (employees), the rights and liabilities which ensue and, consequently, their legal possibilities and incentives to participate are uneven across countries. Certain countries encourage direct participation of large-size equity holders in company boards, while in others board members are deemed to be independent agents of all shareholders, with fiduciary responsibilities *vis-à-vis* the entire investor community.

Strategic information of shareholders

"Sound and equal" information for shareholders is a commonly recognised principle across the OECD area, but it is interpreted and enforced in different ways in different countries' legislation. Disclosure obligations and the qualification of "insider" information (and related trading possibilities) is the main area of differences: certain countries limit the strategic information of owners to publicly available and greatly detailed financial information, while in others large-size and long-term shareholders have direct access to inside strategic information. The information of investors about the internal context of companies, about the quality of corporate assets (including invisible assets such as likely technological breakthroughs and business alliances), and the competitive prospects of the business in its various market segments, consequently relies on different sources and formats of information in different countries.

Possibility and role of take-overs

Take-overs are a heavily regulated area in all countries. They are controlled, constrained or liberally treated under company law, securities law, and voluntary stock exchange rules (applying only to voluntarily listed companies). Legal authorisation for take-over defences, both *ex-ante* defences (such as poison pills, voting right restrictions, etc.) and *ex-post* defences (green-mails, white knight supports, etc.) differ among countries. Certain countries have take-over legislation which renders these operations difficult and cumbersome, by making them dependant on the consent of various stakeholders. In other countries take-over bids can be decided by unbound and independent decision of shareholders about tendering their stock. Also, countries regulate differently the size and cost of take-over bids: acquirers may be forced to purchase all or part of remaining company shares after reaching certain ownership levels. Take-over rules also vary across different jurisdictions within a country (state company law), and during certain periods within a jurisdiction (take-over legislation reforms).

Concentration of creditors

Creditors of companies can be concentrated or dispersed in different countries, both as a result of financial laws and regulations (the structure and concentration of the banking system) and of prevailing standard financing contracts. Bank-loan financing tends to concentrate creditorships but bond financing by security investors tends to dilute it. The overall concentration of creditors also depends on the structure of national industries – small and medium-sized companies are usually funded by concentrated bilateral financing, while large enterprises issue widely spread securities. Nonetheless, the creditor structures of large companies vary across the OECD area: certain countries' investment rules and banking know-how ("goodwill") nurture a core of concentrated bank funding, while others' securities legislation and investment practices consolidate decentralised bond-holdership and trading.

Combination of credit and equity positions

Investment and securities rules forbid, discourage or allow the combination (accumulation) of credit and equity positions. The emergence of "universal" investors, who can combine equity and debt positions in companies – and use the information and risk-management features of various instruments concurrently – depends on national investment rules. Creditor-owners are allowed in certain countries to use the insider knowledge they gain on their clients' businesses by investing in the latters' equity. Other countries choose to prevent or circumscribe this investment pattern.

Handling of financial distress and bankruptcy

Handling of financial distress and bankruptcy is another fully regulated area. Creditors, shareholders and employees in different countries carry different responsibilities, risks and costs in the face of bankruptcy. Certain countries give priority to the protection of creditors' rights, and prescribe liquidation in case of insolvency. Others target survival of companies, and favour rescue operations under government or judicial authority (possibly delaying creditors' claims). Out-of-court settlements among the various stakeholders (creditors, owners and employees) are also unevenly authorised by regulations: they are encouraged in certain countries and discouraged in others. In addition, nationally established and refined rehabilitation patterns also play an important role: they provide investors with ready-to-use management and re-contracting techniques when facing distress prospects and bankruptcy.

Financial return expectations of investors

Investors in industrial companies in different countries have different return expectations and different alternative investment opportunities. In spite of capital market globalisation, expected rates of return from industrial placements remain internationally uneven. The existing structure and functioning of financial intermediation (regulated banking, life insurance, pension funds, etc.) contribute to these differences. Minimum real return on equity from industrial corporations ranges from 4-5 per cent in yearly averages in certain countries to yearly averages of 14-15 per cent and above in others. Certain capital market segments are quicker to adjust to international prices (*i.e.* international bond markets) than others, but industrial companies still find themselves under different overall return expectations from their investors. This diversity probably constitutes the single most important indicator of remaining corporate governance differences at the international level.

Information on the governance environment of each country is organised into 3 x 8 matrices, presenting the impact of three governance framework sources on the eight governance attributes mentioned above.

These matrices are followed by an Annex, which presents the list of *largest stock market-listed individual companies* in the country surveyed. This list includes companies among the top 1 000 world companies identified each year by *Business Week*. The United States has 379 such companies (100 are listed here), Japan 273 (100 of them listed), the United Kingdom 95 (50 of them listed), France 45 (all listed), Germany 37 (all listed), Canada 22 (all listed) and Sweden 13 (all listed). They are practically all quoted in stock exchanges, and issue large amounts of public securities. The market capitalisation value of each company is indicated for the year 1994 (in current US dollars).

Following these tables, a cross-country comparative graph showing each country's largest companies' return on equity in 1994 is provided, together with a technical explanation on the calculation of this ratio. Other comparative tables summarising the available information on the equity ownership structure of firms in different countries, on the use of mergers and acquisitions, and on the respective roles of debt and equity in the financing structure of firms complete the Annex.

CORPORATE GOVERNANCE ENVIRONMENTS: COUNTRY TABLES

UNITED STATES

	Concentration of ownership and control	Strategic role of boards	Strategic information of owners
Laws and regulations	Securities and investment legislation discourages the concentration of ownership and control.	Regulatory rules discourage shareholders sitting on boards. Board rules and fiduciary duties of directors were recently strengthened.	Company and securities law prescribes widespread public financial information. Strategic and prospective information cannot be selectively divulged to traders of stock.
Standard practices	Private stock exchange rules discourage concentration of ownership. Dispersed owners do not usually exert their proxy rights.	Standard corporate charters and practice do not provide for an independent strategic/operational role for boards.	Detailed quarterly financial information is available. Analysis is provided by securities firms. "Price sensitive" insider information is not diffused.
Implicit rules	Corporations seeking concentrated ownership and control are expected to go "private" (no public issuance of securities).	The board is expected to function as an amicable and advisory body to the CEO. Recent tendency towards a more independent role.	Widespread credibility and use of financial information. Other more strategic information should be made available only if it is equally available to all investors.
Observed outcomes	Dispersed ownership in industry, but some recent consolidation through institutional ownership.	Majority of boards are dominated by managers. Recent cases of exception to this situation.	Excellent diffusion of public information, containment of insider strategic information.

UNITED STATES (continued)

Use of take-overs as restructuring tools	Concentration of creditors	Combination of equity and credit by "universal" investors	Use of bankruptcies as exit tools	Rate of return of investment
Legal recognition of take-overs as governance tool. Recent State anti-take-over legislation.	Banking legislation discourages concentration of credit positions.	Combination of equity and debt is forbidden by law for commercial banks, but permitted for other institutional investors.	Elaborate bankruptcy legislation. In bankruptcy, creditor claims may be subordinated to company survival.	Company law stresses profitability as a key corporate objective.
Corporate charters are designed to permit take-overs. Recent tolerance of anti-take-over devices.	Standard practice is small-size bank loans and dispersed bond ownership.	Equity and debt are distinct instruments. However, there is a recent rise in the use of "hybrid" instruments.	Standard bankruptcy procedures are available. Creditors are incited to use these rather than to negotiate out-of-court rescue arrangements.	Equity is evaluated and ownership is traded according to returns.
Perceived legitimacy and acceptance of take-overs as part of the adjustment process.	Banks and bondholders keep arm's length relations with borrowing companies.	Ownership and creditorship entail basically different rights and responsibilities.	Bankruptcy risks are recognised and accepted.	Companies are recognised as profit maximising organisations.
Large number of take-overs but recent curbs in several States.	Highly dispersed credit positions.	Very few investors having both owner and creditor perspectives through the use of "hybrids".	Large number of exits settled via bankruptcies. Possible excess in the number of bankruptcies.	US BW-1 000 companies' return on equity 1992 = 14.9% 1993 = 18.4% 1994 = 20.8%.

JAPAN

	Concentration of ownership and control	Strategic role of boards	Strategic information of owners
Laws and regulations	Securities legislation allows concentration of ownership, including cross-holdings.	Regulatory rules only lay down general principles concerning the constitution and staffing of boards.	No stringent legal rules regarding the information of shareholders. Some recent new measures in this area.
Standard practices	Standard practice is for concentration and consolidation of ownership within networks of companies.	Boards to do not have a special role as is the standard practice. Management decisions are taken within internal management committees.	Standard practice does not prescribe special information channels for shareholders.
Implicit rules	A company should be accountable to its employees and closed business partners and not to a dispersed group of owners.	Co-opted insiders, including the employees and partners, should be allowed to make decisions, as knowledge and information remain with them.	Shareholders do not need to be informed in great detail. Insiders and partners constituting the core management should be fully informed.
Observed outcomes	Company control is concentrated within a group of co-opted insiders and partners.	Boards are very large and staffed with insider executives who are in daily contact with each other.	Shareholders are not informed about strategy. Strategic information remains with insiders (including bankers).

JAPAN (continued)

Use of take-overs as restructuring tools	Concentration of creditors	Combination of equity and credit by "universal" investors	Use of bankruptcies as exit tools	Rate of return of investment
Take-over rules tend to protect the existing shareholders over the bidder, and discourage hostile take-overs.	Banking and securities legislation allows concentration of credit positions.	Combination of equity and debt beyond a 5 per cent threshold is forbidden by law.	Bankruptcy legislation is available, but to be used as a solution of last resort.	Company law is not focused on the protection of principals' (shareholders') interests.
Corporate charters and standard practice do not recognise hostile take-overs as a management tool.	Concentrated bank contract has long been the standard financing instrument. Bond financing is developing but bond holdings are concentrated.	Equity and debt are strictly separated, but in case of need they can be used interchangeably.	Standard out-of-court bailout procedures are available for private negotiation in facing main sorts of difficulties.	Standard corporate charters stress customers and employees as main constituencies. Shareholders are not privileged in corporate charters, but are beginning to exercise more influence.
Hostile take-over of a company by an external group is inconceivable. In case of financial crisis, it is accepted that the group's bank assumes the overall management and the rescue operation.	Companies are expected to have one main bank which monitors the company as the agent of all investors. The bank should be able and committed to support the company in case of distress.	The main bank should act as a principal shareholder in contingency situations. Cross-holders should extend credit in case of need.	It is not desirable to have companies' going out of business. All available rescue and restructuring alternatives should be tried; costs being shared by all stakeholders.	Profit maximisation should be a secondary objective, to market-share increases and employment preservation.
No hostile take-overs. Amicable mergers conducted by network insiders (including bankers) are very common.	Most companies have their main bank. These banks' overall share in total financing is diminishing even though they retain their "main bank" role.	Debt and equity are *de facto* used as similar instruments by insider/partners in networks.	Very few bankruptcy cases. Practically all insolvency cases are settled out-of-court.	Japanese BW-1 000 companies' return on equity: 1992 = 4.8%; 1993 = 4.8%; 1994 = 4.9%.

GERMANY

	Concentration of ownership and control	Strategic role of boards	Strategic information of owners
Laws and regulations	Legislation allows concentration of ownership, including cross-holdings.	Company law assigns key role to the two-tier board structure (see below). In limited liability companies and in partnerships, the partners assume the key role(s).	Company Law and Act on Trading in Securities requires extensive information of shareholders. The Securities Act stipulates *ad hoc* obligation to register and publish purchases and sales of shares to stock-exchange listed companies.
Standard practices	Company charters and stock exchange rules do not limit concentration of ownership. Proxy rights of owners are exercised by depository banks.	Supervisory boards include shareholder and employee representatives and appoint the management board (*Vorstand*). *Vorstand* members exercise the management authority collectively.	The standard practice is that the main shareholders and proxy holders (banks) are continuously briefed in supervisory boards and through direct contact.
Implicit rules	The concentration of ownership and control is recognised as being efficient. Risks of "excess power" should be contained by law and ethical behaviour on the part of the banks.	In line with the principles of co-management within a social market economy, the role of supervisory boards is a matter of national consensus.	Shareholders are entitled to virtually all information. Pursuant to the Act on Trading in Securities, insider trading is forbidden.
Observed outcomes	Ownership is vested in founding families and is concentrated in enterprises. Proxy rights are concentrated in the hands of banks.	Supervisory boards exercise only an overseeing role. Real managerial functions are exercised by management boards made up of insiders.	Large shareholders and proxy holding banks are kept fully informed with the exception of specific matters of daily management.

GERMANY (continued)

Use of take-overs as restructuring tools	Concentration of creditors	Combination of equity and credit by "universal" investors	Use of bankruptcies as exit tools	Rate of return of investment
Company law and merger law do not encourage (although they do not rule out) take-overs, but render their realisation difficult.	Legislation does not limit the concentration of credit positions.	Legislation authorises debt-equity combinations and "universal" banking.	Bankruptcy legislation protects creditors and in case of insolvency allows liquidation. Nearly all proceedings are based on the Bankruptcy Act; the Act on Composition Proceedings plays only a minor role.	Profit-making is designated in company law as one of three corporate objectives (the others are wealth creation and employment creation).
Company charters make successful completion of take-overs contingent on wide consensus of employees.	Standard practice is *hausbank* relationships, with a main bank monitoring companies and holding proxies.	*Hausbanks* sometimes hold equity and leverage their voting rights with shareholder proxy. However, a company's *hausbank* is not usually the shareholders depository bank. Proxies are held by several banks.	Standard practice is to negotiate out-of-court rescues and non-bankruptcy procedures. However, collateral protection is robust.	Profit-maximisation is not the only decision-making criterion. A minimum level of profit is required for investment growth.
Take-over is not considered to be a desirable restructuring mechanism, because it is difficult to achieve consensus with insiders.	The *hausbank* system has widespread legitimacy and is seen as a main ingredient of German industrial success.	Banks' exerting the monitoring role and voting rights on behalf of shareholders is collectively supported. In order to contain "excess" power, banks are expected to behave in a self-controlling and "ethical" manner.	Bankruptcy is not seen as a socially acceptable outcome due to the loss of jobs and destruction of capital it entails. Banks are expected to lead rescue and rehabilitation.	Profit (return on capital) is considered necessary in a social market economy, but is not recognised as the overwhelming objective of resource allocation.
Very few take-overs and almost no hostile take-overs.	All sizeable companies have one or several *hausbanks*, although the share of *hausbanks* in total financing has recently diminished.	Combination of credit, equity and proxies give prominent role to *hausbanks*. Some supervisory boards are chaired by bankers.	Many insolvencies are registered but bankruptcy is rarely used. Creditors and courts seldom opt for liquidation. Under the new Bankruptcy Ordinance (which will come into effect in 1999), creditors will be offered alternative procedural options.	German BW-1 000 companies' return on equity: 1992 = 11.1%; 1993 = 10.0%; 1994 = 10.4%. (BW list does not include all German banks. Returns are reported according to local accounting standards.)

FRANCE

	Concentration of ownership and control	Strategic role of boards	Strategic information owners
Laws and regulations	Legislation allows concentration of owners and further concentration of voting power of main shareholders.	Company law prescribes various board structures, but PDG (simultaneously chairman of the board and chief executive officer) is confirmed as the dominant authority.	Legislation does not specify that companies should inform all categories of shareholders. Recent measures enlarge the scope of recipients.
Standard practices	Company charters and stock exchange rules authorise voting power concentration.	In standard practice there is no real strategic/ operational role for boards.	Standard practice is to provide in-depth information to leading shareholders.
Implicit rules	Concentrated control in companies seems to be socially accepted. Subsequent to privatisation there is national consensus on "*noyaux durs*".	Direct accountability of PDG to large shareholders seems to be the principle. No special function for boards.	No clear collective consensus on the respective information needs of large and small shareholders.
Observed outcomes	Practically all large-size companies are governed by controlling shareholders.	Boards do not play an independent information, monitoring and decision-making role.	All shareholders may not be informed equally. Leading shareholders act as agents for others. Improvements intended.

FRANCE (continued)

Use of take-overs as restructuring tools	Concentration of creditors	Combination of equity and credit by "universal" investors	Use of bankruptcies as exit tools	Rate of return of investment
Take-overs legally possible but defensive arrangements are also legally permitted.	Credit concentration is legally authorised.	Legislation allows the combination of debt and equity. There are some reservations developing with regard to this situation, due to concentration of risks.	Bankruptcy legislation stresses employment protection and survival of companies. Creditor's claims may be legally subordinated.	Profit maximisation is recognised as a legitimate objective for firms, but investing institutions (often government-owned or influenced) are also expected to consider social and national objectives.
Take-overs are feasible, but to be implemented only if leading shareholder groups agree.	Concentrated or syndicated bank loans are standard practice. Bond emissions are subscribed by institutional investors (*i.e.* life insurance companies).	Combining large credit positions with some equity is standard practice by banks and institutional investors.	Regulated bankruptcy is not favoured as the standard exit procedure by creditors. Insiders tend to prefer reglated bankruptcy to liquidation.	Profit maximisation is not the only stated objective of investors. Banks and institutions may consult with the government on important investment and exit matters.
Reservation about take-overs is the common view. However there is a consensus on their legitimacy as restructuring tools. Government may intervene in the process.	Big national banks are acknowledged as the key source of finance for companies. If necessary, they assume special monitoring and bail-out responsibility.	The collective support by the main bank and the main investor (institutional investor) is seen as desirable, although recently a discomfort with excessive concentration is emerging.	Bankruptcy is considered to be a serious failure for management. For employees, it is considered to be an "external shock" which may justify public support.	Supervision of private investment behaviour in the light of national interest considerations is accepted as legitimate under certain circumstances.
Practically no hostile take-overs in France but friendly take-overs are common (especially after government clearance).	Credit positions are concentrated, but not entirely in main bank relations. Institutional creditors are important.	Many companies have banks and institutional investors as main partners with credit and equity positions.	Bankruptcy proceedings are rare in large-size companies. When they occur, exit costs are often covered with the participation of government.	French BW-1 000 companies' return on equity: 1992 = 8.6%; 1993 = 8.5%; 1994 = 8.9%.

UNITED KINGDOM

	Concentration of ownership and control	Strategic role of boards	Strategic information of owners
Laws and regulations	Prudence discourages most institutional investors from taking large stakes (>5%) in companies.	Directors conduct the business of the company. Although no legal requirements to have a board they exist *de facto* as directors usually meet as a committee.	Company act makes the diffusion of financial information compulsory.
Standard practices	As above.	Recent increase in outside directors and independent audit committees following Cadbury recommendations (on a voluntary basis).	Accounting and financial information is transmitted to investors in formatted and audited form.
Implicit rules	Small shareholders' rights are to be protected against risk of abuse.	Directors are vested with moral authority in the management of the company.	Two ways of understanding the legitimate role of owners co-exist: stable and well informed on company strategy *vs.* those stressing liquidity and capital gains through stock market trading.
Observed outcomes	Most institutional funds are under external fund management which stresses risk diversification, liquidity and short-term performance.	Greatest influence is exercised by executive directors.	Liquidity and capital gains driven fund managers dominate ownership. Emerging experiences of stable ownership.

UNITED KINGDOM (continued)

Use of take-overs as restructuring tools	Concentration of creditors	Combination of equity and credit by "universal" investors	Use of bankruptcies as exit tools	Rate of return of investment
The Take-over Panel, although without statutory power, makes take-over rules to promote "fair" take-overs. Government can intervene to block take-overs if thought anti-competitive.	No legal/regulatory obstacle to the concentration of credit	Prudence discourages large equity holdings by the City banks. Small stakes are allowed. (Laws and regulations weak because this has not been an issue).	Bankruptcy is recognised an adjustment tool. Insolvency Act of 1986 specifies liquidation rules which give priority to creditors.	Joint stock companies are recognised as profit maximising organisations for investors.
Take-overs are accepted practice with monitoring by City's Take-over Panel (non-statutory self-regulating body of market participants).	Companies often have principle bank but multi-banking is common in large companies.	As standard practice banks do not take equity positions in companies.	Standard bankruptcy techniques are used. Banks can convert debt to equity.	Investors generally demand stable dividend payouts. Cuts may be accepted if the need for them is clearly set out to investors.
Take-overs are recognised as a legitimate restructuring tool.		Commercial banking and equity investment are two separate activities. In bankruptcy and bailout situations, debt can be converted to equity.	Bankruptcy is recognised as possible economic occurrence but the managers of the company will cease to have a credit rating. Companies must not trade while insolvent.	Profit maximisation is recognised as a prerequisite of economic efficiency. Some reservations about City financial institutions only pursuing short-term objectives.
A large number of mergers and take-overs in the UK. Contested bids are less common and success depends partly on the form of payment offered by the bidder.	Principal bank not "leader". No central information on borrowers' total exposure.	Long-term credit relations between banks and companies.	Noticeable number of exits via bankruptcies. Few rescues using out-of-court settlements.	UK BW-1 000 companies' return on equity: 1992 = 15.2%; 1993 = 19.1%; 1994 = 21.2%.

CANADA

	Concentration of ownership and control	Strategic role of boards	Strategic information of owners
Laws and regulations	Competition and certain financial and investment legislations regulate the concentration of ownership of control.	Directors are to manage or supervise the management of corporations. Directors must retain ultimate control over the corporation.	Corporate and securities laws ensure widespread information available to the public. Strategic information is protected.
Standard practices	High level of corporate ownership concentration. Approval required for certain mergers and acquisitions.	Directors manage or supervise the management of corporations. Institutional investors are increasing their influence.	Detailed annual/quarterly information of public companies is provided. Analytical information available from securities industry.
Implicit rules	Corporations aiming at concentrated ownership generally go private.	Boards work closely with senior management. They are increasingly independent.	Widespread use of financial information. Aggregate statistical information available.
Observed outcomes	Vast majority of Canadian corporations are privately held. Over 80% of public corporations have dominant shareholders.	Boards are increasing management and supervision of management of corporations to avoid potential liabilities.	Public information widely used. Strategic information generally not available.

CANADA (continued)

Use of take-overs as restructuring tools	Concentration of creditors	Combination of equity and credit by "universal" investors	Use of bankruptcies as exit tools	Rate of return of investment
Take-overs usually allowed as governance tools. Minority shareholders generally protected.	Guidelines with respect to federal deposit-taking institutions (DTIs) discourage concentration of credit positions (*i.e.* limits on single exposures).	DTIs are not restricted in combining debt and equity. Limits are imposed on the amount of equity DTIs provide for non-financial firms.	Comprehensive exit procedures provided for corporations and financial institutions. Procedures aimed at survival.	Corporate law stresses maximisation of shareholder value as key objective.
Corporate and corporation articles generally do not discourage take-overs. Few anti-take-over devices upheld by courts.	Standard practice for larger firms is small-size bank loans and dispersed bond ownership.	Equity and debts are separate instruments. Financial non-DTIs are substantially increasing their equity holdings.	Creditors or debtors may invoke both exit and reorganisation processes.	Equity securities are traded according to returns.
General acceptance of take-overs as part of adjustment process.	DTIs and bondholders keep arms' length relations with borrowing companies.	Ownership and creditorship entail different rights and responsibilities.	Bankruptcy recognised as a risk of business. Process seen as providing an orderly, efficient and fair reallocation of assets.	Corporations recognised as profit maximising organisations.
Increasing number of take-overs. Poison pills often disallowed by courts.	Highly dispersed credit positions with respect to large firms.	Financial non-DTIs have increased their involvement in corporate governance.	Liquidations out-number reorganisations. Recent legislation promotes more reorganisations and survivals of existing entities.	Average return on capital: 1993 = 16.2%; 1992 = 16.0%. Canadian BW-1 000 companies' return on equity: 1993 = 11.4%; 1994 = 13.1%.

ITALY

	Concentration of ownership and control	Strategic role of boards	Strategic information of owners
Laws and regulations	No limit on concentration of ownership, but recent reversal for privatised companies. Delegation of voting power strongly restricted. Corporate law imposes limits on cross-ownership.	Corporate law prescribes a key role for boards. No legislative role concerning composition, but representation of minority shareholders provided for newly privatised companies with limits on concentration.	Corporate law mandates only disclosure of information relevant for balance sheet approval, for mergers and for equity issues.
Standard practices	Corporate by-laws favour concentration of ownership. Hierarchical groups favour concentration of control.	Standard corporate charters and practice do not provide for strategic/operational role for boards.	No further detailed information is provided to minority shareholders before general meetings. No practice exists for a regular flow of information to financial analysts and investors.
Implicit rules	Family links, voting agreements, strategic coalitions play an extremely relevant role in allowing separation of ownership and control.	Direct accountability of CEO and board members to large shareholders.	No consensus on information requirements of majority and minority shareholders. Signs of reversal in recent cases.
Observed outcomes	Very high concentration of ownership in both large and small firms.	Boards are expression of controlling shareholders. No independent monitoring role.	Limited diffusion of information to minority shareholders, especially in subsidiary companies of hierarchical groups.

ITALY (continued)

Use of take-overs as restructuring tools	Concentration of creditors	Combination of equity and credit by "universal" investors	Use of bankruptcies as exit tools	Rate of return of investment
Take-overs are allowed and strictly regulated by a recent law. No anti-take-over legislative provisions. Some co-ordination problems with other corporate roles.	Banking legislation limits the concentration of credit positions. Recent extensions taking into account pyramidal groups.	Under recent banking regulations (June 1993), banks may combine debt and equity positions, without exceeding overall limits.	Bankruptcy law favours creditors over firm restructuring or sale. Financial distress is also taken care of by other laws which protect employment.	Legislation recognises profits to shareholders as main purpose of companies.
Some corporate by-laws help prevent take-overs.	Standard practice is multiple bank loans, but a leader tends to be identified.	No practice exists as yet.	Bankruptcy is considered an extreme solution. Incentives to creditors to use standard bailout procedures rather than negotiate out-of-court rescue arrangements.	Long-term investment project returns rather than high dividend payouts are expected from companies.
Preliminary agreements with leading shareholders usually searched for to implement take-overs. No clear consensus on take-overs as a desirable restructuring mechanism, but signs of reversal.	Arm's length relations between banks and companies.	No implicit rules established as yet.	Bankruptcy is not socially accepted as a restructuring tool.	Preservation of jobs has a relative but diminishing role as an objective for companies.
Rare cases of hostile take-overs but recent cases of reversal. Friendly mergers relatively frequent (mostly among insiders).	Large number of positions with banks. However, most of the debt is concentrated with few of them.	No observable outcome yet.	Large distressed companies have usually been restructured without bankruptcy. Recent cases of creditors appointing new board members to restructure the firm.	Italian BW-1 000 companies' return on equity: 1993 = 9.9%; 1994 = 6.4%.

FINLAND

	Concentration of ownership and control	Strategic role of boards	Strategic information of owners
Laws and regulations	Legislation allows concentration.	Company law accepts the key role of boards.	Legislation prescribes fairly widespread information which has to be delivered equally to all shareholders. The scope of information requirements has recently been widened.
Standard practices	The standard practice is marked concentration with, however, slight trend-like change towards dispersion. The role of banks as major owners is significant.	Board's role is crucial particularly in big and medium-sized companies. In the smallest companies the role of CEO or managing director is often more important.	Companies tend to inform the shareholders widely, however, regarding strategic information, the treatment of large and small shareholders is often unequal. The type of treatment varies by company.
Implicit rules	Concentration is accepted, but small shareholders' rights have been increasingly emphasized.	The major role of boards is commonly accepted, although the CEO is also in charge of results.	Various views on the respective information provided to small and large shareholders. Profound and strategic information is increasingly required.
Observed outcomes	Fairly concentrated ownership stemming largely from the key role of export industries in the economy.	The role of boards is notable.	Shareholders are widely informed, but for the present the role of the profound strategic information has been modest. The role of strategic data is slowly increasing.

FINLAND (continued)

Use of take-overs as restructuring tools	Concentration of creditors	Combination of equity and credit by "universal" investors	Use of bankruptcies as exit tools	Rate of return of investment
The legislation allows (but does not encourage) take-overs. Shareholders' rights to equal treatment are stressed.	The legislation does not essentially limit concentration. However, excessive concentration of bank's credits to one company is not allowed.	Legislation allows the combination of equity and credit, but seeks to keep creditors' risks at a moderate level.	Bankruptcy is recognised as an adjustment tool, but legislation seeks to avoid "unfounded" bankruptcies. Under certain conditions the current legislation allows special credit arrangements to avoid bankruptcy.	Legislation recognises profit maximisation as one of the main corporate targets.
Standard practice is to keep take-overs feasible, but to implement them only in a few, exceptional cases. Companies have increasingly exploited the tools available to prevent hostile take-overs.	Standard practice is the "own bank" or lead bank principle. However, recently, the accelerated competition between major banks, as well as companies' improved balance sheets, have tended to change the "old rules".	Combination of credit and equity is a general solution, but there is a tendency to downsize investors' overall risks.	Bankruptcies belong to standard practice, although arrangements stressing the survival of sound companies have been increasingly exploited.	Long-term profit maximisation is commonly preferred, not necessarily short-term maximisation.
Hostile take-overs are not recognised as an advisable restructuring tool.	The lead bank principle is regarded as socially acceptable.	Combinations have not been considered undesirable, provided that the company-specific risks do not exceed advisable limits.	A large number of bankruptcies is not considered socially advisable.	Profit is accepted as an absolute prerequisite in business life, but the target should not be interpreted too narrowly.
The number of hostile take-overs has been small, whereas the frequency of amicable mergers has recently increased.	Lead bank's role is widespread, but decreasing slightly. Largest companies have made banks compete with one another.	Combination of credit and equity is an essential part of the lead bank principle. Currently, however, banks tend to avoid excessive concentration of risks.	Bankruptcies in large-sized companies are unusual. The amount of small-firm bankruptcies used to be significant at times.	Largest companies' return on equity: 1992 = 4.9% ; 1993 = 5.2% . In BW-1 000 List: Nokia Market value: US$4 65 million, ROE 1993: 11.2%.

SPAIN

	Concentration of ownership and control	Strategic role of boards	Strategic information of owners
Laws and regulations	Legislation allows concentration of owners and further concentration of voting power of main shareholders.	Company law prescribes a board structure which enables a director general (occasionally simultaneously president and CEO) to rule the company in order to plan and implement strategic decisions.	Legislation admits the right to provide to shareholders information on issues included in the agenda of the general meeting (with the exception of information which could cause problems for the company).
Standard practices	Company charters and stock exchange rules authorise voting power concentration.	In standard practice there is no real strategic/ operational role of boards.	In-depth information is provided to leading shareholders.
Implicit rules	Concentrated control in companies seems to be socially accepted. Subsequent to privatisation there is national consensus on "hard cores".	The board celebrates a meeting periodically in order to control the management. The board does not play an executive role.	No clear collective consensus on the respective information needs of large and small shareholders.
Observed outcomes	Practically large-size companies are governed by controlling shareholders.	Boards play an active role of approval and control of decision making, in spite of the dependent information provided by the management. The boards of SMEs with family concentrated ownership is more informal around the coincidence of ownership and management.	Shareholders may not all be equally informed. Leading shareholders act as agents for others. Management information available to the general meeting of shareholders has been enhanced, especially concerning accountability.

SPAIN (continued)

Use of take-overs as restructuring tools	Concentration of creditors	Combination of equity and credit by "universal" investors	Use of bankruptcies as exit tools	Rate of return of investment
Take-overs are legally possible, but certain defensive arrangements are also legally permitted.	Credit concentration is legally authorised.	Legislation allows the combination of debt and equity, with certain reservations due to concentration of risk.	Bankruptcy legislation stresses employment protection. Creditor's claims may be legally subordinated.	Profit maximisation is recognised as legitimate objective for enterprises, but they are expected to include others, such as social, national and technological objectives.
Take-overs are feasible, but to be implemented only if leading shareholding groups agree.	Concentrated or syndicated bank loans are standard practice. Bond emissions are subscribed by institutional investors (*i.e.* insurance companies and banks).	Combining large credit positions with some equity is standard practice by banks.	Regulated bankruptcy is not favoured as the standard exit procedure by creditors, because of the old legislation. Insiders tend to prefer regulated bankruptcy to liquidation.	Profit maximisation is not the only stated objective of investors. In a very few sectors banks and institutions may consult with the government on strategic investment and exit matters only.
Reservation about take-overs is the common view. However, there is a consensus on their legitimacy as restructuring tools. Government may intervene in the process in a very few sectors, such as finance, broadcasting, defence industry.	Main national banks are acknowledged as the key source of finance for companies.	Collective support by the main bank and the main institutional investor is seen as desirable and reliable.	Bankruptcy is considered to be a serious failure for management. For employees, it is regarded as an external shock which may justify public support.	Supervision of private investment behaviour in the light of national interest considerations is accepted as legitimate in exceptional cases.
Practically no hostile take-overs in Spain, due to the fact that friendly take-overs are common.	Credit positions are concentrated, but not entirely in main bank relations.	Many companies have banks and institutional investors as main partners with credit and equity positions.	Bankruptcy proceedings are rare in large-size companies. When they take place, exit costs are frequently covered through public support.	Spanish main companies' return on equity: 1991 = 6.3%; 1992 = 3.8%; 1993 = 1.7%. * *Data from the Central de Balances del Banco de España.*

SWEDEN

	Concentration of ownership and control	Strategic role of boards	Strategic information of owners
Laws and regulations	Legislation allows concentration of ownership in individual firms as well as spheres of owners, including cross-holding. Limits on insurance companies, mutual funds and pension funds.	The board is responsible for the organisation of the company and the management of its affairs. The board appoints a managing director to take charge of day-to-day management. The board is elected by the shareholders. Special rules on employee representation.	Company law, securities law and stock exchange rules prescribe widespread public information on strategic and financial matters. Basically no selective information to large shareholders.
Standard practices	Neither stock exchange rules, nor other kinds of standard practices limit concentration of ownership.	No standard practices affecting strategic role of boards.	Detailed periodic financial information. Additional analytical information by securities firms.
Implicit rules	High concentration of ownership in individual companies and spheres of owners is widely accepted.	Boards are composed of non-outsiders. The managing director is normally the only insider on the board.	Widespread use of financial and other strategic information.
Observed outcomes	Concentrated ownership in individual companies. Dual class voting rights very common. Dominant owners are: investment companies, non-financial listed companies, foundations and families.	Boards take on an active monitoring function: hire and fire management. Boards are composed of owners and executives from other non-related companies.	Good diffusion of public information. At the same time active owners with deep company-specific knowledge.

SWEDEN (continued)

Use of take-overs as restructuring tools	Concentration of creditors	Combination of equity and credit by "universal" investors	Use of bankruptcies as exit tools	Rate of return of investment
Legislation allows for take-overs, but also for extensive defensive measures before a bid is made public.	Banking and securities legislation allows concentration of credit positions. However, concentration of bank's credits to one company is not allowed.	In principle no combination of equity and credit allowed by law. Limited exceptions: insurance companies and companies and commercial banks (mostly equity owners when company or former owner failed.)	Elaborate bankruptcy legislation.	Company law presumes profit-maximisation as corporate objective.
Stock Exchange Code on take-overs prohibits defensive measures once a bid is made public.	Concentrated bank contact has long been the standard financing instrument. Recent increase of multiple domestic and international bank relations. Bond financing minimal.	Equity and debts are stringently separated instruments.	Standard bankruptcy procedures are available. Bankruptcy proceedings may be cancelled if debtor reaches written agreement with all creditors or otherwise satisfies all claims.	Equity securities values and ownership trade according to returns.
Take-overs are widely accepted as part of adjustment process.	Often one main bank, partly monitoring the company. This is increasingly the case as the debt-to-equity ratio rises.	Ownership and creditorship entail basically different rights and responsibilities.	Bankruptcy risks are recognised and accepted.	
Large number of take-overs.	Most companies have main banks, but the share of main banks in total financing is diminishing.	Equity and debt financing are separate worlds. No investor has both an owner and creditor perspective.	Large number of exits settled via bankruptcies or written agreements with creditors.	Largest companies' return on equity: 1993 = 10.4%; 1994 = 18.3%.

ANNEX

100 largest listed US companies

Market value and profitability, 1994

Country composite (396 companies): Market value (US$ million) 3 876 300. Return on equity (%) 20.8 (1994)

		Market US$ mill.	ROE %
1	General Electric	98 245	23.5[c]
2	Exxon	88 648	15.1
3	AT&T	80 299	27.0
4	Coca-Cola	78 629	50.7
5	Philip Morris	61 566	38.1
6	Merck	58 125	27.4
7	Wal-Mart Stores	57 138	21.5
8	International Business Machines	54 002	16.9
9	Procter & Gamble	49 405	35.9
10	Microsoft	49 148	30.4
11	Intel	46 359	29.3
12	Johnson & Johnson	42 662	29.7
13	Mobil	39 402	8.1
14	PepsiCo	38 705	26.1
15	General Motors	36 127	38.9
16	American International group (6)	35 939	13.1
17	Dupont	35 743	24.1
18	Motorola	35 207	17.8
19	Amoco	33 941	13.2
20	Bristol-Myers Squibb	33 671	33.5
21	Hewlett-Packard (6)	33 637	19.7
22	GTE	32 210	22.3
23	Abbott Laboratories	32 120	38.5
24	Chevron	32 017	11.4
25	BellSouth	30 338	14.8
26	Ford Motor	29 962	26.4
27	Walt Disney	29 082	23.0
28	Pfizer	27 879	31.7
29	SBC Communications	27 409	20.4
30	Berkshire Hathaway (6)	26 741	4.1
31	McDonald's	26 247	19.3
32	Fannie Mae	25 304	26.8[c]
33	Minnesota Mining & Mfg.	25 188	20.6
34	Ameritech	24 532	28.6
35	Bell Atlantic	24 208	23.3
36	American Home Products	22 868	35.5
37	Sears, Roebuck	21 910	18.3
38	Eli Lilly	21 786	23.1
39	Citicorp	21 137	22.2
40	Electronic Data Systems (6)	20 502	19.3
41	Eastman Kodak	20 467	16.5
42	Dow Chemical	20 299	16.7
43	Boeing	20.076	7.7
44	BankAmerica	19 492	13.0
45	US West	19 360	19.8
46	Atlantic Richfield	18 696	16.5
47	Home Depot	18 690	21.5[c]
48	Gillette	18 685	37.8
49	Columbia/HCA Healthcare (7)	18 057	14.1
50	Texaco	17 778	10.2
51	Nynex	17 632	14.8
52	American Express	17 603	22.0
53	Viacom	16 769	0.4
54	Hughes Electronics (6)	16 296	12.8
55	Chrysler	16 101	30.4
56	Schlumberger	15 745	12.3
57	NationsBank	15 654	15.7
58	Emerson Electric	15 352	19.5
59	Anheuser-Busch	15 212	23.2
60	Time Warner	15 052	NEG
61	Oracle	14 927	49.3
62	Capital Cities/ABC	14 854	16.4
63	Kellogg	14 835	39.5
64	Schering-Plough	14 650	59.2
65	Southern Co.	14 536	12.9
66	Tele-Communications	13 875	NEG
67	Banc One	13 795	12.9
68	MCI Communications	13 770	11.1
69	Allstate	13 537	21.9
70	WMX Technologies	13 527	16.3
71	Travelers Group	13 455	15.7
72	Sara Lee	13 401	7.5
73	J.P. Morgan	13 303	11.9
74	AirTouch Communications	13 189	3.1[c]
75	Pacific Gas & Electric	12 470	12.1
76	Federal Home Loan Mortage	12 326	18.4
77	Campbell Soup	12 183	34.9
78	Caterpillar	12 077	36.2
79	Xerox	12 017	17.5
80	ITT	11 822	15.1
81	Lockheed Martin	11 793	17.3
82	Cisco Systems	11 754	41.0
83	Sprint	11 669	19.4
84	AlliedSignal	11 431	26.4
85	Union Pacific	11 407	19.1
86	Pacific Telesis Group	11 344	21.7
87	Chemical Banking	11 278	15.4
88	H.J. Heinz	11 269	24.0
89	Warner-Lambert	11 138	38.9
90	Colgate-Palmolive	11 119	39.7
91	General Re	11 083	15.2
92	Texas Instruments	10 741	25.2
93	J.C. Penney	10 697	16.3
94	Computer Associates International	10 680	45.8[c]
95	Compaq Computer	10 256	22.9
96	Rockwell International	9 974	20.0
97	International Paper	9 907	9.3
98	Baxter International	9 864	17.6
99	May Department Stores	9 786	20.9[c]
100	Kimberly-Clark	9 612	21.0

c = Approximation; NEG = Negative return.

Source: Morgan Stanley, Standard & Poor, *Business Week*.

100 largest listed Japanese companies

Market value and profitability, 1994)

Country composite (246 companies): Market value (US$ million) 2 571 054, Return on Equity (%) 4.9 (1994)

		Market US$ mill.	ROE %			Market US $ mill.	ROE %
1	Nippon Telegraph & Telephone	129 009	1.7	51	Canon	13 003	4.0
2	Toyota Motor	72 426	3.6	52	Japan Airlines	12 358	NEG
3	Mitsubishi Bank	68 745	1.4[c]	53	Fuji Photo Film.	12 342	5.7
4	Industrial Bank of Japan	68 339	2.1[c]	54	Kawasaki Steel	12 254	NEG
5	Fuji Bank	66 404	0.2[c]	55	Mitsui & Co	12 220	5.6c
6	Sumitomo Bank	65 311	NEG	56	Kirin Brewery	12 123	7.5c
7	Sanwa Bank	62 031	1.1[c]	57	Tokyo Gas	11 785	3.9*
8	Dai-Ichi Kangyo Bank	58 989	1.4[c]	58	Mitsui Trust & Banking	11 764	1.1c
9	Tokyo Electric Power	42 410	5.7[c]*	59	Takeda Chemical Industries	11 691	8.4
10	Sakura Bank	40 155	1.3[c]	60	Dai Nippon Printing	11 515	7.0c
11	Bank of Tokyo	36 058	4.8	61	Bridgestone	11 455	6.0
12	Nomura Securities	35 250	1.1	62	Shizuoka Bank	11 311	5.3c*
13	Matsushita Electric Industrial	32 458	2.8[c]	63	Tonen	10 999	6.7
14	Hitachi Ltd.	32 158	3.7	64	Bank of Yokohama	10 552	1.3c
15	Asahi Bank	28 802	1.7[c]	65	Mitsubishi Chemical	10 509	NEG*
16	Seven-Eleven Japan	27 954	15.6[c]*	66	Fanuc.	10 377	3.9c
17	Kansai Electric Power	25 527	2.8[c]*	67	Sankyo	10 335	12.2
18	Tokai Bank	25 409	0.4[c]	68	Asahi Chemical Industry	10 122	1.8c
19	Nippon Steel	24 745	NEG	69	Sanyo Electric	10 000	1.6
20	Mitsubishi Heavy Industries	23 125	7.0[c]	70	Kubota	9 659	6.5c
21	Ito-Yokado	21 948	10.5[c]	71	Sumitomo Corp	9 658	1.0c
22	Long-Terme Credit Bank of Japan	21 853	0.6[c]	72	Nippon Credit Bank	9 575	1.4c
23	Mitsubishi Trust & Banking	23 104	NEG	73	Toppan Printing	9 500	2.9c
24	East Japan Railway	20 604	11.2[c]	74	Chugoku Electric Power	9 498	5.7c*
25	Toshiba	20 269	4.0[c]	75	Kajima	9 449	0.3
26	Chubu Electric Power	20 228	4.8[c]*	76	Osaka Gas	9 408	3.9
27	JapanTobacco	18 808	5.7[c]	77	Sumitomo Metal Industries	9 327	NEG
28	Sony	18 023	NEG	78	Murata Mfg.	9 104	9.1c
29	Mitsubishi Corp.	17 920	3.1[c]	79	Mitsui Fudosan	9 087	1.7
30	Tokio Marine & Fire	17 729	4.8[c]*	80	Nippon Express	9 085	11.0c
31	Fujitsu	17 386	4.3[c]	81	Toray Industries	9 073	2.2c
32	Sumitomo Trust & Banking	17 050	0.5[c]	82	NKK	8 867	NEG
33	Seibu Railway	16 688	NEG	83	Daiei	8 853	NEG
34	NEC	16 388	4.5[c]	84	Itochu	8 740	1.7c
35	All Nippon AirWays	16 260	NEG	85	Matsushita Electric Works	8 629	3.6
36	Nissan Motor	16 238	NEG	86	Sekisui House	8 569	6.2c*
37	Sharp	15 781	5.4[c]	87	Nintendo	8 536	9.4c
38	Nippondenso	15 714	4.4	88	Sumitomo Chemical	8 296	NEG
39	Daiwa Bank	14 996	0.3[c]	89	Sumitomo Electric Industries	8 290	5.2c
40	Daiwa Securities	14 898	3.0	90	Yasuda Trust & Banking.	8 172	0.8c
41	Mitsubishi Electric	14 835	5.2[c]	91	Japan Telecom	8 168	9.8c
42	Mitsubishi Estate	14 566	4.5	92	Shimizu	8 011	11.8c
43	Asahi Glass	14 555	1.2	93	Nippon Oil	7 991	3.4c
44	DDI	14 414	23.8[c]	94	Marubeni	7 957	2.4c
45	Honda Motor	14 386	6.4[c]	95	Kobe Steel	7 939	NEG
46	Kyocera	14 202	8.0[c]	96	Mitsubishi Motors	7 939	2.9c
47	Tohoku Electric Power	13 941	8.9[c]*	97	Komatsu	7 816	2.0c
48	Kinki Nippon Railway	13 657	1.9	98	Chiba bank	7 811	2.0c
49	Kyushu Electric Power	13 312	8.0[c]*	99	New Oji Paper	7 733	1.6c
50	Nikko Securities	13 012	1.8	100	Daiwa House Industry	7 464	9.4

* = Based on nonconsolidated results; c = Approximation; NEG = Negative return.

Source: Morgan Stanley, Standard & Poor, *Business Week.*

37 largest listed German companies

Market value and profitability, 1994

Country composite (37 companies): Market value (US$ million)+ 364 599, Return on Equity (%) 10.4 (1994)

		Market Value	ROE			Market Value	ROE
		US$ mill.	%			US$ mill.	%
1	**Allianz Holding**	**37 508**	**6.8**	21	**Bankgesellschaft Berlin**	**6 496**	**n.a.**
2	**Siemens**	**26 585**	**9.8**	22	**Thyssen**	**5 914**	**1.7**
3	**Daimler-Benz**	**24 760**	**5.7**	23	**Henkel**	**5 610**	**14.9**
4	**Deutsche Bank**	**23 192**	**n.a.**	24	**Deutsche Lufthansa**	**5 141**	**NEG**
5	**VEBA**	**18 470**	**10.2**	25	**Linde**	**4 934**	**8.3**
6	**RWE**	**16 497**	**17.0**	26	**Schering**	**4 725**	**10.6**
7	**Bayer**	**16 201**	**8.9**	27	**Preussag**	**4 565**	**9.0**
8	**Münchener Rück**	**14 9265**	**11.0**	28	**Hochtief**	**4 132**	**10.3**
9	**Hoechst**	**12 629**	**11.6**	29	**MAN**	**3 827**	**4.2**
0	**BASF**	**12 493**	**8.3**	30	**Karstadt**	**3 424**	**11.3**
1	**Dresdner Bank**	**12 367**	**n.a.**	31	**Heidelberger Zement**	**3 338**	**13.9**
2	**SAP**	**12 263**	**15.2**	32	**Aachener & Münchener Bet.**	**3 253**	**3.4***
3	**Mannesmann**	**10 667**	**NEG**	33	**Beiersdorf**	**3 148**	**15.0**
4	**BMW**	**10 569**	**11.1**	34	**Kaufhof**	**2 991**	**19.4**
5	**Volkswagen**	**8 950**	**2.9**	35	**Fried. Krupp AG Hoesch-Krupp**	**2 891**	**n.a.**
6	**Commerzbank**	**7 893**	**N.A**	36	**Isar-Amperwerke**	**2 767**	**12.2**
7	**Viag**	**7 757**	**10.6**	37	**Degussa**	**2 683**	**11.5**
8	**Bayerische Vereinsbank**	**7 657**	**n.a.**				
9	**Bayerische Hypotheken- und Wechsel-Bank**	**6 877**	**n.a.**				
0	**Vereinigte Elek. Westfalen**	**6 497**	**17.6**				

* = Based on nonconsolidated results; c = Approximation; NEG = Negative return.

Source: Morgan Stanley, Standard & Poor, *Business Week.*

45 largest listed French companies

Market value and profitability, 1994

Country composite (45 companies): Market value (M. US$) 314 591, Return on Equity (%) 8.9 (1994)

		Market value	ROE			Market value	ROE
		US$ mill.	%			US$ mill.	%
1	**Elf Aquitaine**	**21 325**	**0.0**	24	**Groupe Schneider**	**4 910**	**4.2**
2	**LVMH Moët Hennessy Louis Vuitton**	**16 497**	**12.2**	25	**AGF**	**4 891**	**3.0**
3	**L'Oréal**	**16 147**	**13.6**	26	**Pinault-Printemps—Redoute**	**4 776**	**9.9**
4	**Total**	**14 067**	**6.6**	27	**Legrand**	**4 193**	**16.7**
5	**Alcatel Alsthom**	**13 319**	**6.1**	28	**Promodès Group**	**4 122**	**17.0**
6	**Carrefour**	**12 653**	**16.7**	29	**Havas**	**4 029**	**8.1**
7	**Compagnie Générale Eaux**	**12 490**	**10.1**	30	**Eridania Beghin-Say**	**3 941**	**9.0**
8	**Groupe Danone**	**11 496**	**10.4**	31	**Valeo**	**3 816**	**10.8**
9	**L'Air Liquide**	**10 199**	**12.3**	32	**Pernod Ricard**	**3 642**	**13.4**
10	**Compagnie de Saint-Gobain**	**10 144**	**9.5**	33	**CarnaudMetalbox**	**3 599**	**8.4**
11	**Société Générale**	**9 769**	**7.8**	34	**Alcatel Câble**	**3 587**	**16.2**
12	**Banque nationale de Paris**	**9 363**	**3.4**	35	**Cetelem**	**3 300**	**13.3**
13	**Axa**	**8 495**	**6.9**	36	**Pechiney**	**3 233**	**NEG**
14	**Union des Assurances de Paris**	**8 294**	**4.0**	37	**Accor**	**3 199**	**0.4**
15	**Compagnie de Suez**	**7 940**	**NEG**	38	**Thomson-CSF**	**3 152**	**NEG**
16	**Renault**	**7 775**	**8.6**	39	**Crédit Local de France**	**3 140**	**13.6**
17	**Rhône-Poulenc**	**7 727**	**7.4**	40	**Crédit Commercial de France**	**3 093**	**8.8**
18	**Peugeot**	**7 540**	**5.8**	41	**Compagnie Bancaire**	**3 085**	**6.5**
19	**Paribas**	**7 425**	**3.9**	42	**Compagnie de Navigation Mixte**	**3 001**	**4.6**
20	**Lafarge**	**6 656**	**103**	43	**Crédit Lyonnais**	**2 949**	**NEG**
21	**Lyonnaise des Eaux-Dumez**	**5 803**	**6.8**	44	**Canal Plus**	**2 879**	**10.7**
22	**Sanofi**	**5 227**	**7.9**	45	**Bouygues**	**2 776**	**6.4**
23	**Michelin**	**4 925**	**15.3**				

c = Approximation; NEG = Negative return.
Source: Morgan Stanley, Standard & Poor, *Business Week.*

75 largest listed United Kingdom companies

Market value and profitability, 1994

Country composite (75 companies): Market value (US$ million) 892 331, Return on Equity (%) 21.2 (1994)

		Market value US$ mill.	ROE %			Market value US$ mill.	ROE %
1	**Shell Transport & Trading (1)**	**40 648**	**11.2**	38	**British Sky Broadcasting Group**	**7 460**	**n.a.**
2	**Glaxo Wellcome**	**39 378**	**26.5**	39	**Cadbury Schweppes**	**7 432**	**16.7**
3	**British Telecommunications**	**38 926**	**13.3**[c]	40	**Commercial Union Assurance**	**6 499**	**11.6**
4	**British Petroleum**	**38 880**	**16.1**	41	**TSB Group**	**6 450**	**19.5**
5	**HSBC Holdings**	**33 996**	**19.2**	42	**Rothmans International**	**6 415**	**36.4**
6	**B.A.T. Industries**	**24 058**	**27.1**	43	**British Airways**	**6 240**	**20.5**[c]
7	**SmithKline Beecham**	**21 225**	**160.1**	44	**BOC Group**	**6 037**	**14.6**
8	**British Gas**	**20 847**	**12.2**	45	**Argyll Group**	**5 5977**	**14.5**[c]
9	**BTR**	**19 707**	**33.1**	46	**Peninsular & Oriental Steam Naviguation**	**5 878**	**9.8**
10	**Hanson**	**19 606**	**22.2**	47	**Rank Organisation**	**5 777**	**14.5**
11	**Marks & Spencer**	**18 309**	**18.7**[c]	48	**PowerGen**	**5 772**	**20.3**[c]
12	**Barclays Bank**	**17 528**	**17.5**	49	**Vendome Luxury Group**	**5 625**	**18.8**
13	**Unilever PLC (2)**	**15 768**	**29.9**	50	**British Steel**	**5 610**	**4.8**
14	**Guinness**	**15 278**	**17.1**[c]	51	**Granada Group**	**5 436**	**40.3**
15	**Wellcome**	**14 788**	**22.2**	52	**Standard Chartered**	**5 406**	**25.0**[c]
16	**National Westminster Bank**	**14 689**	**18.1**	53	**Pearson**	**5 322**	**21.6**
17	**Cable & Wireless**	**14 666**	**15.7**[c]	54	**Royal Bank of Scotland Group**	**5 128**	**19.8**
18	**Zeneca Group**	**14 058**	**26.3**	55	**Land Securities**	**5 055**	**5.2**[c]
19	**General Electric Co.**	**13 935**	**16.8**	56	**Kingfischer**	**4 845**	**17.2**
20	**RTZ**	**13 621**	**17.3**	57	**Scottish & Newcastle Breweries**	**4 808**	**12.0**
21	**Lloyds Bank**	**13 509**	**21.9**	58	**Associated British Foods**	**4 559**	**14.2**
22	**Grand Metropolitan**	**13 245**	**18.1**	59	**Tomkins**	**4 544**	**20.8**
23	**J. Sainsbury**	**12 880**	**17.5**[c]	60	**Sun Alliance & London Insurance**	**4 527**	**14.7**
24	**Reuters Holdings**	**12 468**	**50.6**	61	**Whitbreaad**	**4 526**	**8.2**
25	**Prudential**	**10 295**	**55.5**	62	**General Accident Fire & Life Assurance**	**4 453**	**17.6**
26	**Vodafone Group**	**10 057**	**35.5**	63	**Reckit & Colman**	**4 435**	**13.2**
27	**Abbey National**	**9 894**	**16.5**	64	**Rolls-Royce**	**4 332**	**6.0**
28	**Great Universal Stores**	**9 802**	**9.7**	65	**Scottish Power**	**4 326**	**29.1**[c]
29	**Tesco**	**9 645**	**12.7**	66	**Lloyds Abbey Life**	**4 307**	**15.9**
30	**National Power**	**9 491**	**23.2**[c]	67	**Siebe**	**4 088**	**15.4**
31	**Imperial Chemical Industries**	**9 148**	**7.9**	68	**Rentokil Group**	**4 087**	**65.8**
32	**Allied Domecq**	**8 526**	**16.3**[c]	69	**Bank of Scotland**	**3 968**	**23.5**[c]
33	**Thorn EMI**	**8 416**	**35.3**	70	**Legal & General Group**	**3 386**	**33.5**
34	**Bass**	**8 171**	**10.1**	71	**Asda Group**	**3 846**	**NEG**
35	**BAA**	**7 903**	**10.6**	72	**Bowater**	**3 742**	**27.7**
36	**Reed International (4)**	**7 798**	**31.9**	73	**Redland**	**3 567**	**12.6**
37	**Boots**	**7 777**	**22.8**	74	**British Aerospace**	**3 533**	**21.7**
				75	**Blue Circle Industries**	**3 507**	**9.2**

c = Approximation; NEG = Negative return.

Source: Morgan Stanley, Standard & Poor, *Business Week*.

23 largest listed Canadian companies

Market value and profitability, 1994

Country composite (23 companies): Market Value (US$ million) 134 783, Return on Equity (%) 13.1 (1994)

		Market value	ROE
		US$ mill.	%
1	**Seagram**	**11 166**	**14.7**
2	**BCE (Bell Canada Enterprises)**	**9 732**	**9.8**
3	**Northern Telecom**	**9 724**	**8.2**
4	**Barrick Gold**	**8 904**	**10.8**
5	**Thomson**	**8 204**	**13.6**
6	**Imperial Oil**	**7 540**	**6.6**
7	**Alcan Aluminium**	**7 103**	**5.8**
8	**Royal Bank of Canada**	**6 941**	**16.1**
9	**Placer Dome**	**6 032**	**6.9**
10	**Canadian Pacific**	**5 807**	**4.8**
11	**Bank of Montreal**	**5 566**	**14.8**
12	**Canadian Imperial Bank of Commerce**	**5 272**	**11.8**
13	**Bank of Nova Scotia**	**4 804**	**8.0**
14	**Toronto-Dominion Bank**	**4 538**	**13.1**
15	**Pancanadian Petroleum**	**4 448**	**15.5**
16	**Noranda**	**4 423**	**11.0**
17	**Imasco**	**4 262**	**15.4**
18	**Nova Corp**	**4 239**	**20.0**
19	**Shell Canada**	**3 709**	**15.6**[c]
20	**Bombardier**	**3 686**	**17.9**[c]
21	**Inco**	**2 932**	**4.0**
22	**Newbridge Networks**	**2 898**	**38.7**
23	**Falconbridge**	**2 852**	**17.0**

c = Approximation; NEG = Negative return.

Source: Morgan Stanley, Standard & Poor, *Business Week.*

14 largest listed Italian companies

Market value and profitability, 1994

Country composite (14 companies): Market value (US$ million) 112 262, Return on Equity (%) 6.4 (1994)

		Market value	ROE			Market value	ROE
		US$ mill.	%			US$ mill.	%
1	**Telecom Italia**	**20 579**	**7.0**	8	**Istituo Bancario San Paolo di Torino**	**4 197**	**4.7[c]**
2	**Assicurazioni Generali**	**19 386**	**7.4[c]**	9	**Istituto Mobiliare Italiano**	**3 737**	**8.0[c]**
3	**Fiat Group**	**16 941**	**NEG**	10	**RAS**	**3 677**	**5.5[c]**
4	**STET**	**14 325**	**8.2**	11	**Banca Commerciale Italiana**	**3 625**	**4.3**
5	**Alleanza Assicurazioni**	**6 556**	**10.4[c]**	12	**Mediobanco**	**3 597**	**5.8***
6	**Istituo Nazionale Delle Assicurazioni**	**5 509**	**4.7[c]**	13	**Banco di Roma**	**3 128**	**0.4[c]***
7	**Montedison**	**4 243**	**NEG**	14	**Edison**	**2 762**	**10.9**

* = Based on nonconsolidated results; c = Approximation; NEG = Negative return.

Source: Morgan Stanley, Standard & Poor, *Business Week.*

17 largest listed Swedish companies

Market value and profitability, 1994

Country composite (17 companies): Market Value (M. US$) 95 710, Return on Equity (%) 18.3 (1994)

		Market value	ROE			Market Value	ROE
		US$ mill.	%			US$ mill.	%
1	Astra	17 977	34.8	9	Svenska Cellulosa Aktiebolaget	3 515	5.8
2	L.M. Ericsson	15 535	19.4	10	Electrolux	3 382	11.2
3	Volvo	8 156	80.0	11	Svenska Handelsbanken	3 330	10.8
4	ASEA (3)	7 727	20.9	12	Skandinaviska Enskilda Banken	2 922	11.5
5	Investor	5 455	18.4	13	Skanska	2 847	35.4
6	Pharmacia	5 052	19.0	14	AGA	2 808	17.6
7	Sandvik	4 875	19.7	15	Sydkraft	2 780	10.4
8	Stora Kopparbergs Bergslags	4 031	8.7	16	Atlas Copco	2 675	15.6
				17	Assidoman	2 645	21.4

c = Approximation; NEG = Negative return.
Source: Morgan Stanley, Standard & Poor, *Business Week*.

Note: Direct comparison of reported returns on equity raises a host of technical problems. The indicator used here is "the latest twelve months' after tax earnings per share as a percentage of most recent book value per share". This is the closest approximation of the real rate of return on capital earned by industrial companies. Financial analysts estimate that, in spite of accounting and business cycle differences, this indicator reflects relatively accurately the real rate of return differences between countries. Further elaboration and tests on this indicator would imply additional technical elaboration.

Return on equity of top-20 largest firms – 1994

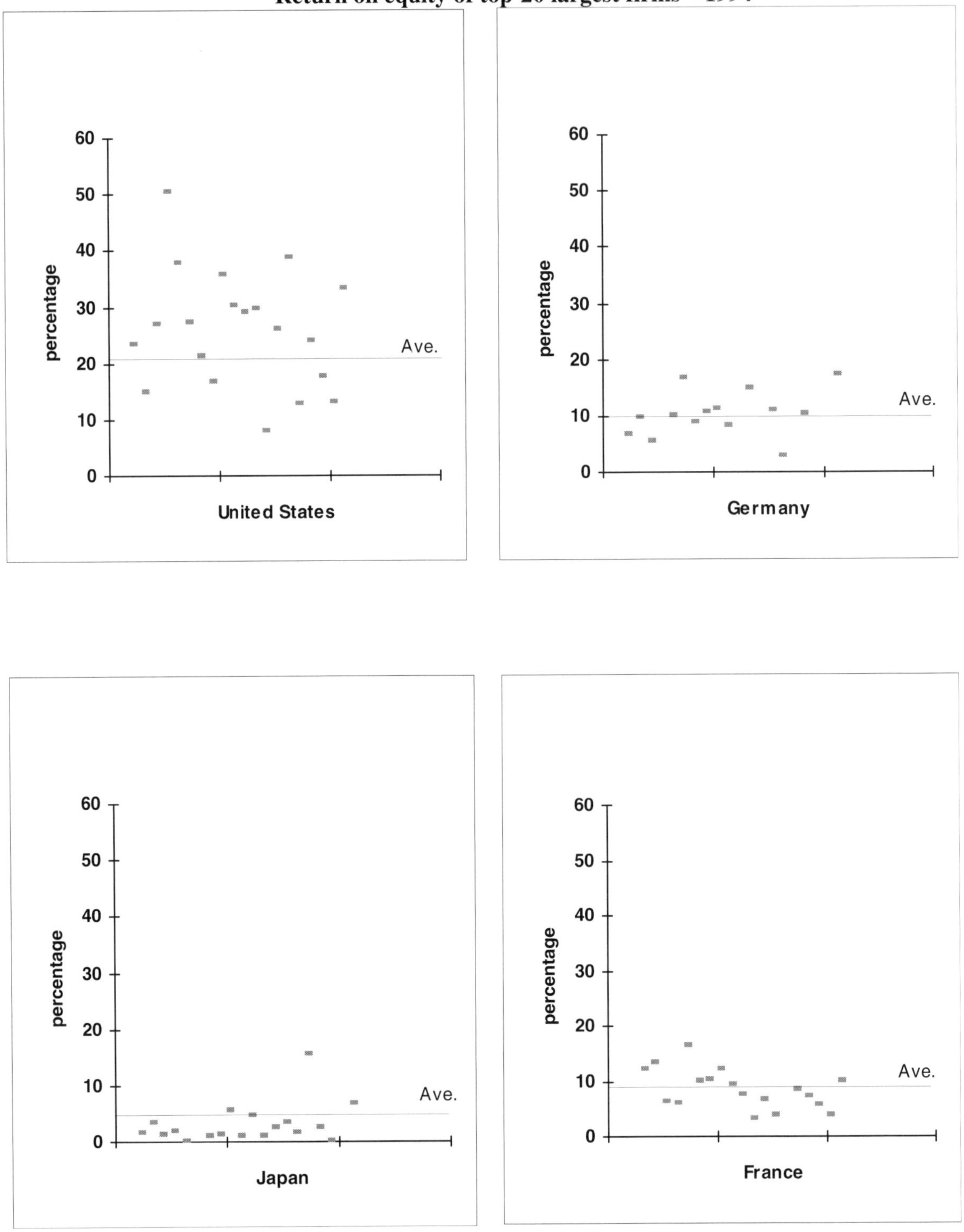

Note: Return on equity = Latest 12 months' after tax earnings per share as percentage of most recent book value per share; Top-20 firms: Ranked by market value.
Ave. = Country composite average.

Return on equity of top 20 largest firms – 1994 *(cont.)*

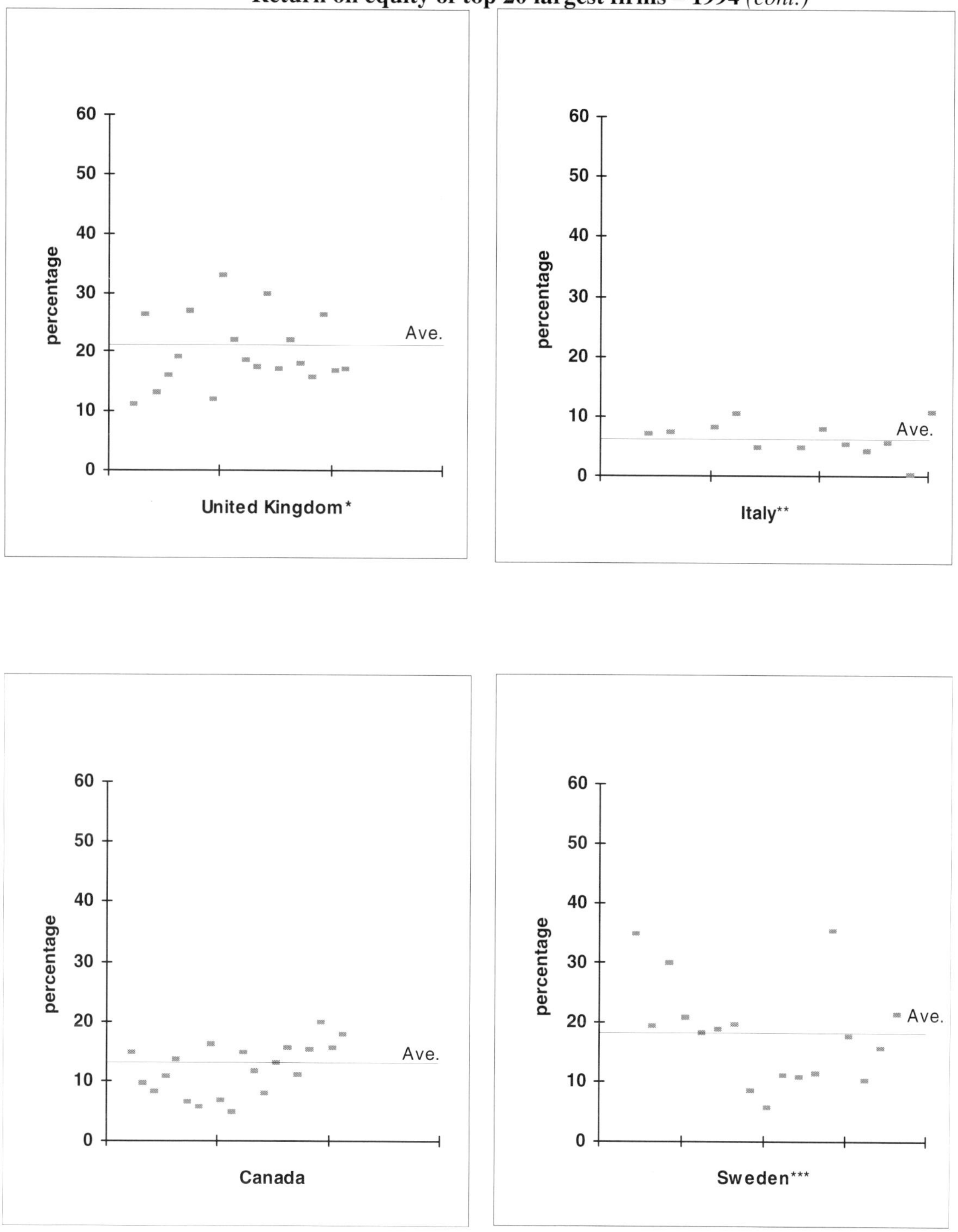

* = Does not include one company which is over 60% of return on equity.
** = Data resource is 14 companies.
*** = Data resource is 17 companies.

Ownership of listed firms

Percentage

	United States	Japan	Germany	France	United Kingdom	Italy
Financial institutions	31.2	48.0	22.0	6.5	58.8	11.3
Banks	0.3	26.7	10.0	4.3	0.9	9.9
Insurance firms	23.9[1]	17.2	12.0[1]	2.2	18.4	0.8
Other	7.0	4.1	--	1.9	39.5	0.6
Non-financial institutions	68.8	52.0	78.0	93.5	41.2	88.7
Households	48.1	22.6	17.0	20.7	21.3	33.9
Non-financial enterprises	14.1	24.8	42.0	54.5	3.6	23.0
Public authorities	--	0.7	5.0	4.5	3.9	27.0
Non-residents	6.6	3.9	14.0	11.9	12.4	4.8

1. Including pension funds.

Source: OECD (1994), various sources.

Ownership concentration in non-financial corporations

Percentage of outstanding shares owned by the largest five shareholders

	United States	Japan	Germany	Italy
Mean	25.4	33.1	41.5	86.9
Median	20.9	29.7	37.0	99.9
Standard deviation	16.0	13.8	14.5	19.7
Minimum	1.3	10.9	15.0	n.a.
Maximum	87.1	85.0	89.6	100.0

Note: United States: 457 non-financial corporations in 1980; Japan: 143 mining and manufacturing corporations in 1984; Germany: 41 non-financial corporations in 1990; Italy: 734 non-financial corporations in 1993.

Source: BIS; Prowse; Banca d'Italia.

Average annual volume of completed domestic mergers and corporate transactions with disclosed values, 1985-89

	United States	United Kingdom	Japan	Germany
Volume(US$ billion)	1 070.0	107.6	61.3	4.2
As a percentage of total market capitalisation	41.1	18.7	3.1	2.3

Source: BIS; Prowse.

Leverage ratios of non-financial firms

Ratio of gross debt to total assets

	United States	United Kingdom	Japan	Germany	Italy
1982	0.32	0.52[1]	0.83[2]	0.59	0.82
1992	0.51	0.56[3]	0.80	0.61	0.76

1. 1983.
2. 1984.
3. 1990.

Source: OECD (1994), *Financial Statistics*.

Chapter 5

EMPLOYMENT REGULATIONS

The changing nature and complexity of employment regulations mean that some information rapidly becomes obsolete and, because of time constraints, it was not possible to validate all the information with national labour market authorities. For complementary references, see publications by DEELSA (Education, Employment, Labour and Social Affairs), for example OECD (1992), *New Directions in Work Organisation – The Industrial Relations Response*, and OECD (1993, 1994, 1996), *OECD Employment Outlook*.

Introduction

The employment regulatory environment appears to be a particularly important and topical framework factor for firms' competitiveness. On the one hand, the social aspect of employment regulations renders it a politically sensitive and delicate factor while, on the other hand, in trying to survive in a challenging economic environment, the competitive edge of firms depends on a workforce that adapts to changes quickly.

Technological innovation and change, and its consequences – organisational change and changing production and management methods – all contribute to the evolution of employment regulatory environments. Such developments bring about shifting training requirements, indispensable upgrading and diffusion of skills, and the subsequent necessity to adapt employment regulations and practices.

In addition to their direct influence on firms' competitiveness, employment regulations may also have an impact on sectoral globalisation patterns through their effect on foreign direct investment patterns. It should also be noted that large multinational firms can be innovative in trying out new labour practices and may have the organisational means to make a significant impact on the institutional process, whereas labour standards imposed by national authorities may be more of a binding constraint on small and medium-sized enterprises.

Employment regulations in the OECD countries have gone through considerable change during the past decade. For example, collective bargaining agreements, which are important factors influencing labour market adjustments, have been changing from union-based to other varieties of collective and individual contracts or in favour of government regulation. Moreover, there is increasing support for works councils and similar employee representative bodies which can contribute to the management decisions of firms.

While, as mentioned above, the transformation of employment regulatory environments is a fact, views diverge as to the direction and optimal configuration of employment regulations in OECD countries. Some support the international harmonization of labour laws, explicit contracts and customary practices, as a prelude to the full economic integration of trading areas, and with the aim of increasing benefits and lessening costs. At the same time, there is support for the subsidiarity principle, whereby national rules are successfully negotiated and resolved at the most decentralised level possible, reflecting the socio-political differences of each country. A third view is that certain labour standards have hampered the ability of labour markets to adapt to shocks, thus necessitating reforms which will allow them to become more flexible.

National regulatory environments regarding employment are complex and distinct due to traditions resulting from diverse social, political, and historical backgrounds in industrialisation. The following sections intend to simplify and standardize the concepts of employment regulatory environments and to guide the interpretation of the country tables which compile and present summary information.

Employment regulatory environments

Sources governing labour relations

Industrial firms operating under market forces face three main sources governing their labour relations: first, there are laws and regulations; second, there are explicit labour contracts, either individual or collective; and third, there are customary practices of regulating trade and the development of industry, which include implicit contracts.

Laws and regulations

Employment may be regulated by statutory legislation alone, by sectoral collective agreement alone, or by both. A variety of statutory laws dominate the employment regulatory environment. In some cases the legislation directly concerns the specific area of employment (*e.g.* Trade Union Law as concerns employee representation or the Hours of Work Act regarding working time). In other cases, legislation concerning one area of employment has an indirect impact on another (*e.g.* Health and Safety Standards as regards working hours). Legislation other than employment regulations may also influence specific areas of employment (*e.g.* the effects on working time of restrictions on weekend shop openings or restrictions on heavy vehicle transport during weekends).

Statutory labour legislation is not always precise as it encompasses such concepts as normal and exceptional circumstances. Neither is it always actively enforced by governments, but rather is applied only through issue judgements when cases are brought before the courts. In addition, some labour legislation leaves to the courts the responsibility for deciding important matters.

Administrative extension of collective agreements also constitutes another form of employment regulation in the sense that collective agreements are extended by government decree to a sector or branch of industry, functioning as a legal provision.

Standard practices

A binding collective agreement between an employer and representatives of his or her employees is regarded as a commercial contract, rather than a form of regulation, on the basis that the employer is free not to sign it. Collective agreements are the most important form of explicit labour contract. They may be signed spontaneously, as needed, between an employer and representatives of his or her employees, or regularly by some form of legal enforcement, between sector employer and employee representatives. The degree of legislative implication in collective agreements as well as the level of industry (*e.g.* firm-level or sectoral) at which these agreements take place, vary. In addition, the degree of centralisation may also alter the coverage of collective agreements (*e.g.* regional as opposed to national).

Labour market institutions – their structure and degree of sophistication – are also determinant in the patterns and functioning of collective agreements and other standard practices regarding employment. This institutional structure is in constant mutation in response to changing economic conditions and increasing competitive pressures: for example, the emphasis on an increased co-decision role by labour at the firm level has brought about a more works-council-type as opposed to a union-based labour organisation.

Implicit rules

In general, public perception of aspects of specific areas of employment relations and, more specifically, employee perceptions of their employee status and employer perceptions of management prerogatives, also plays an important role. These implicit contracts are the outcome of social rules resulting from implicit expectations and commitments among the various economic actors.

These implicit rules, mainly based on values of labour market institutions, are complements to, and in certain instances, substitutes for, formal regulations and standard practices. As a consequence of the above-mentioned institutional transformation, these implicit rules are also changing, although perhaps at a slower pace because their process of formation is lengthy. It can be assumed, for instance, that the formation of common implicit rules represents the biggest challenge to the harmonization of employment rules within international economic areas.

Attributes of the employment regulatory environments

Although a multitude of other regulations exist (*e.g.* equal opportunity legislation, health and safety standards, etc.), five specific areas have been identified as important framework factors forming the basic employment regulatory environment faced by industrial firms and thus covered in this survey: *working time, employment protection, training commitments, employees' representation and wage bargaining.*

Working time

Working time is regulated by way of: *i)* a required minimum of rest hours per day and week; *ii)* a maximum number of daily and weekly work hours; and *iii)* permissible overtime which does not threaten workers' health and safety.

While in most countries, work time issues are covered explicitly by legislation, in others these issues are addressed through health and safety, parental, maternity and child sick leave legislation. Work customs, ethics and family values, to the extent that they affect working time, are often reflected in the legislation and collective agreements of each country.

The governing sources of working time regulations vary between countries. In some countries these regulations are governed by either legislation or collective agreements; in others by both.

As to modernistic working time arrangements and practices, part-time work has increased and flexible working time arrangements are being applied in an experimental manner. Part-time work has increased in some countries spontaneously, *i.e.* without any change in the legislation, while other countries have taken steps to stimulate the growth of part-time employment.

Employment protection

Employment protection basically concerns: *i)* individual dismissals which generally require a case-by-case analysis of employee non-compliance with the established personnel rules of a firm; and *ii)* collective dismissals which can be justified for such reasons as a firm's economic viability (*e.g.* plant closure or bankruptcy or the more recent and significant change in the nature of employment contracts due to technological developments).

As a general rule, collective dismissals generally entail the same severance pay and notice periods as individual dismissals; nonetheless, there exist differences as to the procedures that must be followed by the employers. These procedural differences occur as a result of requirements such as prior approval of government authority, retraining of employees, internal mobility and placement of employees.

Conditions under which collective dismissals may take place rely mainly on law and collective agreement provisions. While laws may address the more general parameters of minimum number of employees to be affected, along with notice requirements and the like, collective agreements tend to establish the particulars of the employer's obligation to retrain or transfer employees to other jobs within the firm.

While the custom of giving prime value to job security in certain countries led to a stronger tendency to legislate the employment protection requirements abided by firms, legal requirements tend to be less strict in countries where the prevailing doctrine is employment "at will" and job-to-job mobility a common practice.

Training commitments

In some countries, no legislation on training exists but customary business practices or employment contract provisions have developed. In other countries, legislation specifies the training responsabilities of employers, particularly in their dealings with apprentices, trainees and redundant status employees in need of training.

There are also institutional and/or legislative schemes such as seniority rights, pension-vesting rules and compensation packages, legal and/or collectively bargained restrictions on layoffs and firings in order to reduce the risks associated with training investments made by firms.

As regards the financing of training, in some countries legislation calls for a national training tax. In others, there is a "levy system" on firms based on annual payroll earnings or on the basis of a minimum amount for training in proportion to the number of employees.

Governments are increasingly recognising the need to play a subsidiary role in employment training within the following configuration: *i)* employers and social partners at inter-firm level; and *ii)* employers and workers' representatives at intra-firm level. This "trend" coincides with efforts that are being made to link training more closely with enterprise needs/demands.

Employee representation

The free right to associate and to establish representation bodies is guaranteed in all OECD countries. Union delegate, works council and board representation is instrumental in establishing working conditions by way of: *i)* accessing information; *ii)* consultation; or *iii)* co-determination procedures.

A union operates as a mobilising force inside the firm, with the effect of obtaining benefits for its members. Moreover, as an outside negotiator, unions sometimes impose constraints that are as, or more, specific than government regulation. Works councils, as compared to unions, encourage active participation of both employers and employees in an effort to produce greater mutual benefits for each in a co-operative relationship.

In some countries, the presence of union delegates in employees' representative bodies is compulsory, in others, works council presence is compulsory, while, in a third group of countries, representation on management boards is mandatory.

Employees' co-decision and co-determination rights vary between countries. As a general rule they cover issues of working conditions, dismissals, restructuring, training and new technology applications. While in some countries these rights remain unregulated (open-ended), they have a limited role in others. In both these cases employees' representative rights are established by collective agreement.

Wage bargaining

A variety of forms of wage bargaining exist across OECD countries. Negotiations essentially occur at three levels: centralised or economy-wide level; industry and sectoral level; and company-level bargaining. In reality a combination of these levels prevails in most countries.

In recent years there has been a shift towards decentralised bargaining. Decentralisation occurs either in organised or in spontaneous forms. In organised decentralisation there is a deliberate delegation of bargaining by the higher-level parties to the lower-level parties, but with overall control being maintained by the delegating parties. Spontaneous decentralisation can be described as a process whereby higher-level bargaining arrangements are dismantled or undergo a certain breakdown. Along with this shift towards more company-based or single-employer bargaining, there has also been a concurrent move towards merit- or performance-related pay.

Governments can "extend" by law the terms of collective agreements to parties not represented in the negotiations. This can be done either by making the terms of the collective agreements legally binding within a given domain and covering employers and workers not affiliated to the negotiating parties, or by enlargement, which is a mechanism by which the influence of the agreement is extended to entire regions or sectors.

EMPLOYMENT REGULATIONS: COUNTRY TABLES

UNITED STATES

	Working time	Employment protection	Training commitments	Employees representation	Wage bargaining
Laws and regulations	Legislation concerning working hours is mainly confined to overtime work. Pay premium for overtime work is 50% of the normal hourly wage. (1)	Legal provisions mainly concentrate on "wrongful discharge". No severance pay is provided by law. 60 days notice is required in plant closures and massive layoffs. (4)	There are no legal provisions directly requiring training. State Council bodies are established under federal act to co-ordinate training at the State level. (7)	Neither the presence of union delegates nor works councils are compulsory. Management board representation is not mandatory. (10)	There is no central system of wage bargaining. Legal provisions do not provide extension procedures. (13)
Standard practices	Collective bargaining agreements do not cover working time issues. (2)	Job-to-job mobility is a common practice. Collective bargaining agreements establish termination procedures. (5)	Collective agreements do not cover training conditions. Training practices vary between sectors. (8)	Employees' representative bodies generally play a limited role. Union representation is concentrated in certain sectors and certain regions. (11)	Company-level collective agreements negotiated between management and the local union are the prevailing practice. (14)
Implicit rules	It is socially agreed that regulating working time may diminish firms' and workers' welfare. (3)	"Employment at will" is the prevailing doctrine. (6)	In-house training may be considered to carry risks with respect to competition. Simultaneously, certain sectors and large firms have high internal training expenditures. (9)	Legislation safeguards many aspects of workplace conditions. Emphasis is placed on furthering enterprises' economic objectives and private employment contracts may obviate the need for active employee involvement. (12)	Free collective bargaining is the dominating doctrine. (15)

JAPAN

	Working time	Employment protection	Training commitments	Employees representation	Wage bargaining
Laws and regulations	Labour Standard Law determines weekly working hours as 40 hours (8 hours a day). Pay premium for overtime work is 25% of the normal hourly wage. (1)	Labour Standard Law provides 30 days notice period or pay in lieu. No severance pay is provided by the legislation. Courts decide on fairness of dismissals. (4)	Human Resources Development Promotion Law indicates the general concepts of vocational training policies. There are no legal provisions directly requiring training. (7)	Neither the presence of union delegates nor works councils are compulsory. Management board representation is not mandatory. (10)	There is no central system of wage bargaining but some co-ordination at national level. Legal provisions provide regional extension but this is not frequently practised. (13)
Standard practices	Firm-level collective agreements set details of working hour conditions. (2)	Collective agreements do not cover dismissals. Almost all corporations have a lump sum severance indemnity plan. (5)	Collective agreements do not cover training conditions. On-the-job training and job rotations are common practices.(8)	A mixture of collective bargaining and joint consultation at the plant level (*i.e.* with company unions) is the general practice.(11)	Wages are negotiated annually: individual enterprise unions simultaneous ly submit their demands under the co-ordination of national labour organisations and industrial federations. (14)
Implicit rules	Despite attempts to reduce working hours, habits of long working days and weeks remain. (3)	Lifetime employment system is the prevailing principle in large-size companies. (6)	Training is an integral part of the lifetime employment system. (9)	Unions behave in a pragmatic manner taking into account the situation of the national economy and of the firm when deciding their positions. (12)	Union demands increasingly concern more general conditions rather than wage increases. (15)

GERMANY

	Working time	Employment protection	Training commitments	Employees representation	Wage bargaining
Laws and regulations	Hours of Work Act stipulates maximum working hours that must be taken into account in collective agreements (*i.e.* working hours must not exceed 8 hours per day). (1)	The Act on the Standardisation of Notice Periods for Dismissals of Workers provides 4 weeks minimum notice period. The law does not provide for severance pay. Mass dismissals are subject to government approval and a special redundancy plan. (4)	In most industries employees have a right to claim one week's paid training time annually. Training for redeployment purposes is obligatory in case of collective dismissals. There is a tax levy system to be activated in case of need. (7)	The Basic Law provides both positive and negative freedom of association. Presence of Works Councils is compulsory, but presence of union delegates is not. Supervisory board representation (1/3 representation if 500 to 2 000 employees and 1/2 representation if more than 2 000 employees) is mandatory. (10)	There is no central system of wage bargaining. Collective bargaining adapts to the special features of individual sectors and regions. Extension can only be applied under specific legal conditions (*e.g.* at least 50% of employees must be represented in negotiations). (13)
Standard practices	Collective agreements mostly stipulate weekly working hours but there is scope for flexibility. In practice it is possible to agree on annual working hours. Pay premium for overtime work set by collective agreement is 25 to 50% of the normal hourly wage. (2)	Collective agreements also govern collective dismissal requirements. For making employees redundant, works councils and employers set "social criteria", and agree on a system of selection. (5)	Besides employer-provided training schemes there is a strong vocational training and apprenticeship system. Works councils and unions identify needs and adapt training through a network. Collective agreements usually cover training issues. (8)	Employees' representative bodies play a significant role through a dual system of statutory Works Councils and free collective bargaining with union representation. (11)	Union bargaining at sectoral and regional level is the prevailing practice. Usually, there are no nation-wide collective agreements. (14)
Implicit rules	Flexible collective agreements increasingly make available to companies more scope for individual rules at company level (*i.e.* experiments with shorter working hours). (3)	Procedures regarding employment protection and the handling of redundancies are settled by consensus. (6)	Firms' training role is considered to be a social function. Employee representatives, firms and government all participate in the management of the training system. (9)	Industrial relations are conducted in a highly consensual manner, including via both supervisory board participation (*i.e.* co-determination) and works councils (*i.e.* co-decision). (12)	Industrial disputes should be used only as a last means in order to reach collective agreement in case of breakdown of negotiations. (15)

FRANCE

	Working time	Employment protection	Training commitments	Employees representation	Wage bargaining
Laws and regulations	The legislation in force, Auroux laws, set weekly working hours at 39 hours. Pay premium for overtime work is 25% of the normal hourly wage. (1)	Legislation passed in 1982 provides employees with severance pay amounting to one-tenth of a month's salary for each year of service and a minimum of one and maximum of two months' notice period. Mass layoffs are subject to special redundancy plans and their causes must be proven. (4)	Legislation enforces various forms of training and the State shares some of the costs. Training for redeployment purposes is obligatory in collective dismissals. A national tax is levied for training. (7)	Presence of both union delegates and works councils are compulsory. Participation as observers on management boards is mandatory in joint stock companies. (10)	There is no central system of wage bargaining. Governments can and do frequently extend collective agreements to whole regions or sectors. (13)
Standard practices	Collective bargaining agreements do not cover working time issues. (2)	Collective agreements determine detailed conditions of collective dismissals. Conditions of special redundancy plans are also set by collective agreement. (5)	Collective agreements at sector level determine individual sectors' specific training conditions. (8)	Employees participate in the elaboration of social plans in case of collective dismissals. Enterprise-level works councils are becoming increasingly important. (11)	Wage bargaining take place at the industry level, negotiated regionally or nationally. The recent trend is towards merit- or performance-related pay and decentralised bargaining. (14)
Implicit rules	Legally determined working time is perceived as a gained social right. (3)	In employment adjustments, the government is expected to play an active legislatory and arbitrary role and monitor "social plans". (6)	The State is expected to play an active role in providing training. (9)	Activist unions with relatively limited membership, and public-sector concentration, represent workers at national level and are socially recognised to play this role. (12)	Unions are the legitimate defenders of "acquired rights" (*i.e.* minimum wage). (15)

UNITED KINGDOM

	Working time	Employment protection	Training commitments	Employees representation	Wage bargaining
Laws and regulations	There are no general legislative provisions on working hours. (1)	Employment Protection (Consolidation) Act provides a one week to 2 months notice period. The Act protects workers employed for a continuous period against unfair dismissal. Industrial Tribunals deal with wrongful dismissal claims. (4)	There are no legal provisions directly requiring training. Training and Enterprise Councils have been set up in order to secure local provision of training opportunities. (7)	Neither the presence of union delegates nor works councils are compulsory. Management board representation is not mandatory. (10)	There is no central system of wage bargaining. Legal provisions do not provide extension procedures. (13)
Standard practices	Collective agreements at the firm level govern working hour arrangements. The basic working week is between 35 and 40 hours. (2)	Collective agreements govern mass layoffs and determine their conditions (*i.e.* last in/first out). (5)	There is a well established apprenticeship system. Industrial Training Boards handle sectoral training issues. Collective agreements do not cover training issues. (8)	The rights of employees' representatives are limited and often established by collective agreement. Collective agreements do not create enforceable obligations. (11)	Enterprise- or company based collective bargaining is the prevailing practice. The recent trend is towards more merit- or performance-related pay and further decentralisation of wage bargaining. (14)
Implicit rules	Free collective agreements is the generally accepted means for settling working time issues. (3)	Traditional flexibility and recent further relaxation of employment protection regulations. (6)	Vocational training is expected to be an integral part of the general education system. (9)	Unions have direct political representation, and thus employee representation is part of the political process. (12)	There is an expressed preference for merit-related pay. (15)

HUNGARY

	Working time	Employment protection	Training commitments	Employees representation	Wage bargaining
Laws and regulations	Regulated by the Labour Code. Main principle: 8 hours daily. Modification possibilities: if agreed otherwise by both parties; in cases of unhealthy, hazardous work; in cases of special, individually regulated jobs	The Labour Code provides detailed regulations regarding the termination of employment, orderly dismissal, final payment, dismissal in special cases, and methods of reducing staff numbers.	The possibility for acquiring the first qualification free of charge is provided by the State for everyone. For the unemployed, the State provides possibilities for acquiring skills for choosing a new job and finding new employment at training institutions for the training of the unemployed.	The national conciliation system is regulated by the Labour Code. Special regulations apply to the rights of unions within places of employment. Regulations regarding the election and operation of factory councils are included in the participation rights of employees.	National level tripartite wage negotiation and agreement on suggested yearly growth rate of average wage and national minimum wage. Use of minimum wage made compulsory by legislation: it is a responsibility regulated by legislation for the employer to initiate annual wage negotiations with the union entitled to conclude collective agreement. There is legislative possibility for extension of the collective agreement.
Standard practices	Based on the daily working time, working time can be defined in a yearly amount as the longest possible term. When defining working time, the collective agreement is the first priority, in the absence of which working time can be set by the employer.	Collective agreements may differ from the specifications in the Labour Code regarding the notice period and the final payment in favour of the employee.	Interest conciliation of strategic issues of national vocational training carried out in Conciliation Council. National Vocational Training Council – incl. employers, employees, economic chambers, school operators and representatives from government – makes proposals on vocational qualifications and training materials.	National tripartite conciliation exists primarily in connection with the minimum wage and the maximum daily working time. The agreements – made within the Conciliation Council – between employers and employees are announced as statutes by the government.	Wage agreements defined in collective agreements can usually be found in larger companies (coverage within the entrepreneurial category is around 30%). There are a few branch-level wage agreements, some with extended scope of authority (coverage about 7%).
Implicit rules	Paid training time is unknown in current Hungarian practice. A related concept is the trial period with different objectives (Labour Code).	In the case of organised mass layoffs, employers use higher final payments and longer notice periods than stipulated by the regulations in order to increase the chance of finding employment for those laid off.	Vocational training is an integral part of the education system.	Distinct from legal regulations, employer and union(s) (may) conclude local agreements (collective) that – based on legislative licences –- may grant different (more favourable) terms than the minimum standard regarding employment, remuneration and working conditions. In the absence of a collective agreement, these terms must be regulated by individual employment contracts.	The government wishes to encourage the extension of the system of collective wage negotiations.

Source: Ministry of Labour, Hungary.

SPAIN

	Working time	Employment protection	Training commitments	Employees representation	Wage bargaining
Laws and regulations	The legislation in force sets weekly working hours at 40 hours. Overtime is limited to a maximum of 80 hours per year, with pay consisting of either money with no premium, or holidays.	Legislation provides workers affected by collective dismissals with severance pay of 20 days for each year of service. Collective redundancies must be approved by labour authorities.	Legislation guarantees a supply for public professional training in favour of the young and the unemployed. Training for the occupied is organised through agreements to which the State provides support.	Double system of employee representation at firm level: *i)* an elective system which corresponds, according to firm size, to personnel delegates or firm committees; *ii)* trade union representation through trade union sections represented by their delegates.	There is no centralised system of wage bargaining with public intervention.
Standard practices	Collective bargaining agreements at the firm level govern working hour arrangements under the regulated maximum, with a mean of 38 hours.	Generally collective agreements exist between the firm and the workers' representatives, establishing a higher severance pay than the legal minimum.	Collective agreements at sector level determine training conditions. Access to training activities is established through training plans at firm- or corporation-level with the economic support of organisations compounded by the social agents.	Elective representation is based on trade union delegates. Personnel delegates and members of the firm committees are elected among candidates presented by trade unions.	Wage bargaining is established through collective agreements at sectoral level and at firm level.
Implicit rules	Collective bargaining agreements cover all working time issues. Overtime is paid in money terms.	The government is expected to play an active legislatory and arbitrary role in employment adjustments and monitor "social plans".	The State plays an active role in providing training for the unemployed, whereas training for the occupied is the responsibility of firms and social agents. Regional agreements will play an active role in vocational training. Ministry of Education is also opening training to workers.	Although membership of trade unions is low among workers, they play a significant role in collective bargaining, which is the usual way of establishing work conditions.	Wage bargaining is beginning to be more linked to the firm situation and to its output.

Source: Ministry of Industry and Energy, Spain.

SWEDEN

	Working time	Employment protection	Training commitments	Employees representation	Wage bargaining
Laws and regulations	The Working Hours Act sets general conditions of working time. The law is non-compulsory, and collective bargaining agreements covering working time issues have been reached for a major part of the labour market, thereby completely replacing the Act or parts thereof. At workplaces where agreements have been reached by collective bargaining, non-unionised workers are also covered by the agreements. The content of the collective bargaining agreements is generally very close to the law. According to the law, weekly working time may not exceed 40 hours. Alternatively, working time may not exceed 40 hours on average over a period of four weeks. Overtime work is limited by law to 50 hours per month, with a maximum of 200 hours per year. Exemptions by collective agreement are possible for an additional 150 hours per year. Exemptions can also be granted by the National Board of Occupational Safety and Health.	Basically, Swedish Act on Security of Employment applies to all employees and same rights apply to part-time and full-time employees. Employment agreements normally valid for an indefinite term. In certain cases contracts for limited periods are allowed, *e.g.* when necessitated by a temporary accumulation of work or related to a probationary period not exceeding 6 months. Dismissals may occur if there is a shortage of work or on grounds related to the employee personally. In principle, employer solely in charge of deciding whether there is a shortage of work. If employer decides to discharge employees, negotiations must start with the union at the firm. According to the law, the system of selection is based on "last in/first out principle". This order of priority can be replaced or supplemented by local collective agreement, provided that provisions for this have been made in central agreements (at industry-level), *e.g.* if there is common understanding that some employees with a very short period of employment have skills necessary for the firm's survival. Whatever the cause, a notice period must be given to discharged employees of between 1 and 6 months, depending on employee's age.	There are no legal provisions requiring the employer to finance training or provide possibilities for training during work hours. However, all employees have the right to study on leave from work without pay.	The Act on Boards, which is applicable at most private companies, states that employees should be represented by 2 representa-tives on the board of directors of companies with at least 25 employees. The Act on Co-determination at Work contains regulations relating to topics such as the right of association, the right of information and the right of negotiation.	There is no central system of wage bargaining.

Source: Ministry of Labour, Sweden.

SWEDEN (continued)

	Working time	Employment protection	Training commitments	Employees representation	Wage bargaining
Standard practices	Through collective bargaining, the full-time work week has been reduced for certain categories of workers. The shortest full-time work week on the labour market is 37 hours. However, no deals have been struck by social partners with the aim to increase employment by reducing working time since "work sharing" is not regarded as an effective means of reducing unemployment. Pay premium for overtime work set by collective agreements at between 50 and 100 per cent.	Some of the provisions in the Swedish Act on Security of Employment, *e.g.* on contracts for limited periods, order of priority, and rules of procedure, can be replaced or supplemented by local collective agreements. These agreements however, require provisions made by collective agreements reached centrally (at industry-level). There is, however, one exception to this rule: summary dismissal, *i.e.* dismissal without a period of notice, may be used if the employee has grossly neglected his or her obligations to the employer.	Collective agreements do not cover training conditions.	Industrial relations are conducted in a highly consensual manner. One of the basic principles underlying the reform of labour legislation has been that employees' powers of co-determination must be framed and elaborated by the social partners, with the statutory provisions as their starting point. One of the aims of the Co-determination Act has been to encourage co-determination agreements. Section 32 calls upon parties concluding collective agreements on pay and general conditions of employment to also conclude collective agreements on co-determination rights for employees in matters relating to the conclusion and termination of contracts of service, the direction and allocation of work and general conduct of activities. The intention has been for the employees to request co-determination agreements at the speed and to the extent they themselves prefer.	Collective bargaining at industry level, negotiated nationally. The recent trend is towards merit- or performance related pay and decentralised bargaining.
Implicit rules	.				Minimum wages set by collective bargaining agreements.

Source: Ministry of Labour, Sweden.

BACKGROUND NOTES TO COUNTRY TABLES

General

The sources of the information presented in country tables are:

- Matindale-Hubbell (1994), *International Law Digest*, Reed Reference Publishing Co., New Providence, New Jersey.
- OECD (1991), *Employment Outlook*, July, Paris.
- OECD (1992), *New Directions in Work Organisation - The Industrial Relations Response*, Paris.
- OECD (1993), *Employment Outlook*, July, Paris.
- OECD (1994), *Employment Outlook*, July, Paris.
- OECD (1996), *Employment Outlook*, July, Paris.
- Price Waterhouse (1995), *Information Guide Series – Doing Business in: France, Germany, Japan, United Kingdom, United States*, Price Waterhouse World Firm Services BV.

Working hours

Laws and regulations

United States

Working time regulations are not stringent and mainly confined to overtime work. The Fair Labour Standards Act (FLSA) 1938 mainly guarantees rights to certain wage and hour considerations. The FLSA also contains a series of laws that require employers to pay overtime for hours worked in excess of 40 in a week. Some States require employers to pay overtime for hours worked in excess of eight in a day. In those cases, employees must be paid according to the law that requires employers to pay the higher amount. Pay premium for overtime work is 50 per cent of pay for normal hour's work. The FLSA also sets limits on the number of hours employees may work in a day or week. In addition, the FLSA regulates hours of work for minors and restricts minors from working in hazardous jobs. Earlier provisions of the legislation on daily working time have now been abolished.

Japan

Every employer with ten or more workers must establish rules of employment in compliance with the minimum standards of the Labour Standards Law of 1989. Such rules must deal with working hours, time off, holidays, paid vacations, etc. The 1993 amendment to the Labour Standards Law determines the maximum working hours at 40 hours per week (eight hours a day). The amendment also sets the pay premium for overtime at a minimum of one-and-a-quarter times the regular base pay rate. Working hours regulated by the law refers to total actual working hours excluding rest periods, etc. The law requires that the employer and the representative of the majority union (representative of the majority of employees in the absence of a union) reach an agreement on and set the number of longer working hours.

Germany

The legislation governing main working hours is the 1938 Law and, according to the Hours of Working Act (*Bundesgesetzblatt*, 1994), daily hours of work may not exceed eight hours. If within 6 calendar months or within 24 weeks an average of eight hours per day is not exceeded, then such hours can be extended to ten hours. The Act also includes the following provisions to be allowed by collective agreement, or in an individual works agreement on the basis of a collective agreement: that working hours may be extended without compensation beyond ten hours daily if on-call work occurs regularly and to a considerable extent within working hours; that a compensatory period be provided; and that working hours be extended without compensation for up to ten hours and not more than 60 days per year. Employers in large establishments are obliged by law to consult employee representatives before introducing part-time work.

France

Working time rules are determined by the legislation in force, *i.e.* the 1983 Auroux Laws. The working week is limited to 39 hours and daily work to ten hours; non-sedentary work is limited to 35 hours per week as of 1983. For certain activities the amount of time spent in business can exceed 39 hours (*e.g.* retail stores, hotels). Prior authorisation of the labour inspector must be obtained for overtime exceeding the statutory or conventional limit. In any case, total work hours cannot exceed 48 hours in a week. According to the 1979 Law, the hourly rate is automatically increased by at least 25 per cent for the first eight hours of overtime and 50 per cent after. In firms with more than ten workers, employees are allowed a compensatory rest period equal to 20 per cent of overtime hours worked in excess of 42 total hours during a week but within a limit of 130 overtime hours per year or statutory limits. Pursuant to the Law of 1986 this limitation on the duration of working hours may be amended by collective bargaining agreement. With regard to flexible time arrangements, the law provides that the period during which average hours actually worked (accounting period) must be equal to "normal" working hours can span from three months to one year. Employers in large establishments are obliged to notify employee representatives before introducing part-time work.

United Kingdom

There are very few regulations regarding working time. The only explicit provisions concern special categories of workers while for the majority working time limits are implicitly laid down by health and safety restrictions. New government regulations give employees working part-time the same statutory employment rights as those working full-time, with the exception that notice periods and redundancy pay following dismissal are explicitly less for part-time workers than for full-time workers.

Standard practices

United States

Collective agreements do not cover working time issues. Part-time work has been increasing in a spontaneous manner without any change in legislation.

Japan

There is no legal provision indicating how to calculate working hours, this is mostly set by collective agreement. In addition, collective agreements also set other conditions of working hours, such as start and finish of ordinary work, rest periods, etc. An employer may request extended hours of work if the average weekly working hours over a four-week period do not exceed 40 hours and provision is made in the employment regulations.

Germany

The collective agreements basically do not prohibit making use of the scope offered in the Hours of Work Act. They mainly stipulate weekly working hours. Pursuant to the stipulations of the collective agreements regarding working hours, these may vary from week to week; there is some scope for flexibility. Working hours do not need to be evenly distributed with regard to days, weeks or seasons. The compensation periods within which average working hours must be carried out generally amount to 12 months; this means that in practice it is possible to agree on annual working hours. Details concerning the implementation of the stipulations regarding working hours (distribution with regard to days, weeks or the whole year) must be agreed at the company level. In the light of the engineering sector (metal) and the Volkswagen company, a 37-hour week was worked, which was reduced to 35 hours as from October 1995. In printing and heavy engineering (iron and steel) the 35-hour week was planned in April 1995. This means that the 35-hour week is agreed for 25 per cent of employees covered by collective bargaining. Overtime is generally payable at rates varying between 125 and 150 per cent of base salary and at double rates if worked on Sundays and bank holidays.

France

Collective bargaining agreements *(accords collectives)* do not cover working time arrangements.

United Kingdom

Collective bargaining agreements determine normal hours of work since there are no general legislative provisions. The basic working week is 35 to 40 hours.

Implicit rules

United States

There appears to be a conception that regulating hours of work diminishes the welfare of workers – consequently there is a strong preference for income over leisure. Regulation is seen as imposing transport and information costs on workers, and imposing real resource costs on society for recruitment, training and record-keeping.

Japan

There is a general tendency to reduce the number of hours worked and a five-day week is becoming more common. The government is trying to promote such labour and management measures as spreading the five-day working week, and encouraging workers to use all annual paid holidays and to take longer consecutive holidays. Despite recent attempts to reduce working hours, entrenched working habits largely remain.

Germany

Perhaps the most important issue that has led to tension between the unions and the employers' federation during the recent period is working time. This situation appears to have calmed down with the adoption by employers of an experimental approach, and due to the fact that collective agreements regarding working hours are reached in a decentralised manner. Conflicting political aims (*e.g.* reducing unemployment or social security costs) have led to a rather disjointed picture of medium-term objectives. Imaginative solutions in a number of "crisis" industries are currently being negotiated, such as the introduction of a four-day working week in conjunction with an overall salary decrease. There is considerable opposition as well as legal restrictions to large amounts of overtime.

France

Working time set by law is considered as one of the acquired rights of workers. However, although not easily compatible with the legal governance environment, flexible time and/or part-time work are increasingly being practised and are becoming more socially accepted as part of new economic rationale. The reduction of working time and the economic feasibility of this reduction is currently being debated.

United Kingdom

Except for certain specific jobs (*e.g.* drivers), free collective agreement is the generally accepted means to settle working time issues.

Employment protection

Laws and regulations

United States

The Civil Rights Act of 1964 prohibits discrimination or discharge on the basis of race, sex, religion, age, martial status, colour, ancestry or national origin. The National Labour Relations Act ensures the right to unionise and protects workers against arbitrary discipline and dismissal when they seek to organise. The Fair Labour Standards Act (FLSA) of 1938 guarantees not only the right to certain wage and hour considerations but also the right to assert them without fear or retaliation in the form of disciplinary measures or outright discharge. The Federal Worker Adjustment Retraining Notification Act (WARN) of 1989 requires employers of one hundred or more workers to give employees 60 days' advance notice of a plant closure or a mass layoff. Under WARN, plant closure occurs when 50 or more full-time workers experience an employment loss during any 30-day period. An employment loss is a termination, a layoff of more than six months, or a cutback in employee's hours of more than 50 per cent. A mass layoff on the other hand, is when 50 or more full-time employees experience an employment loss during any 30-day period. If unconnected events cause separate group layoffs at a single site, and none alone is large enough to reach the minimum requirement, notice still must be given to employees if the total number laid off within a 90-day period reaches the minimum requirement. In addition, a number of States have various notice requirements in cases of plant closure or layoffs.

Japan

According to the Labour Standards Law at least 30 days' notice or pay-in-lieu-of-notice is necessary for discharge. Otherwise employers must pay at least 30 days' wages. The Labour Standards Law except the following employees from this rule: *i)* daily contract employees until they have been employed for more than one month; *ii)* employees employed for a period no longer than two months; and *iii)* employees on probation. Exceptions to the notice provisions of the law are when the continuance of the enterprise becomes impossible due to some natural calamity or other inevitable reason, and when a fault of the employee is the origin of dismissal.

Germany

Legislation for protection of labour include acts to protect employees (Law of 1969) and especially pregnant employees and nursing mothers (Law of 1968) against arbitrary dismissal. There are exact statutory notice periods and discharging without notice is not possible except for cause. In principle contracts of employment can be terminated at any time by the employer or the employee with four weeks' notice. The employer's minimum notice period varies between four weeks and seven months, depending on the length of service. All planned dismissals must first be discussed with the works councils. Mass dismissals are subject to a special redundancy plan (*Sozialplan*) agreed by the works council, the local labour exchange and the trade union. The Act on the Standardisation of Notice Periods for Dismissal of Workers (*Bundesgesetzblatt*, 1993) shortened the period of advance notice of dismissal for employees (previously a minimum of six weeks) and lengthened that of workers (previously a minimum of two weeks) by providing for a basic minimum period of four weeks' advance notice, applicable to everyone. The notice provisions of the Act also apply when the wage-earner resigns. However, during the probation period, which cannot exceed six months, the period for advance notice is two weeks for both dismissal and resignation. Shorter notice periods are also granted for small firms and temporary workers. The Act also brought about more flexible dismissal procedures for white-collar workers.

France

The 1982 laws provide severance pay equal to one-tenth of a month's salary for each year of service after two years and for companies with more than ten employees. For termination of contracts of indefinite duration, except in the case of dismissal for serious offence, all employees having worked more than six months must receive notice varying from one month (for employment duration of six months to two years) to two months (employment duration over two years). Legislative changes in 1986 abolished prior administrative authorisation for collective dismissals and introduced the condition of written information and interview for individual dismissals. The 1989 legislation forces companies to prove cause for dismissals and, in case of collective dismissals, allows labour authorities to make non-binding suggestions for the elaboration of social plans. If the dismissal is based on economic reasons the employer must meet and discuss the terms of the economic layoff with the labour management committee *(Comité d'entreprise)* or personnel representatives *(Délégués du personnel),* depending on size of firm, and inform the local labour authorities of the dismissal. Before discharging an employee for economic reasons, the firm must try to transfer the employee to another position, provided that he has the necessary skills. Firms employing more than 50 employees and which plan to dismiss ten people or more are required to propose social measures for dismissed employees in the form of a report called a "*Plan social*", presented to the labour management committee for discussion. According to the 1993 law, procedures for economic dismissal may be nullified by court if the firm fails to comply with the requirements of the *Plan social*. The 1990 legislation aims at promoting employment stability through adjusting the rules governing precarious contracts (*e.g.* by fixing the termination benefits under fixed-term contracts equivalent to 5 per cent of the gross salary earned). In the case of labour contracts of undefined duration, an employee who has been employed by the same employer for more than two years must, upon discharge, receive a legal minimum separation indemnity. Separation payment cannot be less than a sum equal to either 20 hours of pay (for employees paid by the hour) or 1/10 of a month's salary (for employees paid monthly) multiplied by the number of years of employment plus 1/15 of a month's salary multiplied by the number of years over ten years of seniority.

United Kingdom

Individual rights are principally governed by the Employment Protection (Consolidation) Act 1978, and the Employment Acts of 1980, 1982, 1989 and 1990. Employees whose appointment is terminated are entitled to a minimum period of notice (Employment Protection (Consolidation) Act 1978). Under the same Act, individual employees with a minimum period of service of 104 weeks are entitled to a lump-sum redundancy payment if their job ceases to exist (*i.e.* technological improvements) and if their employers cannot offer alternative work. According to the law passed in 1984, at least one month of service is required for employees to be eligible for a notice period of one week to two months. In 1985 the period of service necessary to claim unfair dismissal was increased from one to two years. The Act protects workers employed for a continuous period of two years against unfair dismissal. Workers gain maternity rights and rights to redundancy payment after continuous employment of two years. Disputes are referred to the Industrial Tribunal which can award compensation or reinstatement where practical if negotiations with the conciliation service (ACAS) provided for under the Act have broken down. The 1989 Employment Act introduced an entitlement to redundancy payment for women over the age of 60. The Act covers the two most important causes of redundancy termination – closing of business or reorganisation for greater efficiency. The legislation passed in 1990 empowered the Industrial Tribunals to deal with wrongful dismissal claims, previously the sole province of civil courts. Individual (as opposed to collective) rights of employees were modified in the Trade Union Reform and Employment Rights Act 1993. The Trade Union Reform and Employment Rights Act of 1993, besides other reforms to industrial relations, further limited the right to claim for unfair dismissal, and detailed coverage of health- and safety-related employment protection. The Transfer of Undertakings (Protection of Employment) Regulations (TUPE) introduced the principle of automatic transfer of employment contracts, collective agreements and trade union recognition in the case of relevant transfers.

Standard practices

United States

Job-to-job mobility is common practice, and as a consequence job security *per se* is not an important preoccupation of employees. Most private employers give an employee two weeks' notice or two weeks' severance pay in the event of an involuntary termination. Labour unions have given their members job security by establishing termination procedures in collective bargaining agreements. These contracts spell out requirements concerning such matters as seniority rights and severance pay.

Japan

Neither individual nor collective dismissals are covered by collective agreements. It is the courts that decide the fairness of dismissals. The courts often take into consideration the employer's efforts to find alternative solutions to dismissal, such as reduction of overtime, retraining within and even outside the company. Almost all corporations have a lump sum severance indemnity plan, although annuity pension contracts are becoming popular. Severance allowances are usually based on current rate of pay and type of severance. Generally, severance allowances are set at one month's basic salary for each year of service based on the current pay rate.

Germany

In making employees redundant, employers ensure that the choice of employee meets a set of "social criteria" and that employees dismissed are those least "socially affected". Works councils and employers agree on a system of selection, taking into account length of service, age and number of dependants, etc.

France

While legislation sets out the principles of employment protection, collective agreements set conditions for details such as retraining, internal replacement. Collective agreements *(Conventions collectives)* also involve, and influence, social plans in case of collective dismissals.

United Kingdom

In collective dismissals the employers provide the unions with detailed information and generally the unions make sure that customary arrangements such as "last in/first out", if in existence, have been followed and that dismissed workers have not been victimised. Failure to consult the unions (if a union complains) leads to the granting of a protective award by an Industrial Tribunal.

Implicit rules

United States

"Employment at will" is the prevailing doctrine. "At will" means that the individual is employed for an indefinite period at the will of his employer or himself. Either party is free to terminate the relationship for any reason or for no reason at all. Unfair practice has led to the concept of "wrongful discharge". Employability represent a superior value compared to job security.

Japan

The labour market structure emphasizes job rotation "employment" over "job" security. Japanese workers attach great importance to employment stability. They are, therefore, sensitive to the performance of their enterprise and co-operative in efforts to increase profitability. Virtual denial of employment termination by the courts is symbolic of the social inclination to condemn unreasonable termination under the lifetime employment system.

Germany

Disciplined and consensual employer and employee representative organisations handle issues concerning employment protection in a consensus and provide stable employment and job security. Recent fine-tuning of provisions regarding dismissals, notice periods, etc., appears to be a reaction to the general economic trend.

France

There is a legislative trend towards lower employment protection. However, the State is expected to protect the rights of employees regarding employment protection – which is considered to be one of their "acquired rights".

United Kingdom

A flexible approach prevails with regard to employment protection.

Training commitments

Laws and regulations

United States

State Council bodies have been established under the federal Job Training Partnership Act to co-ordinate the entire range of workforce preparation programmes operating in a given State. Training is also required of State employment agencies, *e.g.* under the Manpower Training Act of New York. Moreover, working conditions for apprenticeship agreements are also regulated under State laws, *e.g.* the Apprenticeship Labour Standards Act of California. Employers are not reimbursed by the government for training given, but are subsidised to the extent that they may deduct such costs in determining their taxable income.

Japan

The Human Resources Promotion Law of 1969 indicates the general concept of vocational training which is carried out by both the public and private sectors. The law also provides assistance and promotion schemes for human resource development. The law has no provision directly requiring training. Laws were introduced in the early 1970s to cope with the recession after the oil crisis requiring the government to provide subsidies to employers who transfer and retrain employees to avoid redundancy, and allowances to workers who move or accept training.

Germany

In most industries, employees have a legal right to claim one week's paid training time per annum in order to attend such courses and many of these courses are subsidised by government or trade union funds. The Apprenticeship Act of 1971 ended the distinction between apprentices and short-term job trainees. In general, apprenticeship regulations provide for special contract formalities, termination procedures and the right to attend vocational training courses. The Employment Promotion Act of 1985 permits retraining apprentices under fixed-term contracts when a permanent post is otherwise unavailable.

France

A national training tax was established in 1971. An amount must be allocated to staff training on an annual basis; part of the allocation is paid in the form of a tax. In addition to this programme, any employee can claim a year of absence in order to carry out an individual training programme. During this period the employee's salary is paid by an organisation to which a part of the training tax is paid. By law employers also must allow apprentices to attend courses at an outside training centre (to a maximum of 400 hours per year). Collective economic layoffs must be accompanied by social measures proposed by the employer in favour of the employees, such as training courses, financial aid for elderly employees and priority in re-hiring. Redundancy rules provide for redundant workers to be re-hired on temporary retraining contracts of up to six months. Firms are required to propose special training courses (*congés de conversion*) to dismissed employees which are financed partly by employer and partly by governmental bodies. The State also pays all or part of the Social Security payments for certain trainee groups, such as those under 25 years.

United Kingdom

The Employment Act of 1989 dissolved the Training Commission and modified some clauses of the Industrial Training Act of 1982 concerning Industrial Training Boards. Training and Enterprise Councils have recently been set up to secure the provision of local training opportunities, particularly for young people. Apprentices are entitled to wages only if so provided under express regulation. On the other hand, they generally enjoy greater protection against dismissal than other employees. For instance, an employer cannot use redundancy as a defence against a suit for breach of contract unless he has actually gone out of business.

Standard practices

United States

Collective agreements do not cover training conditions. Employers in many industries provide training for their employees, either in-house or through outside consultants and/or vocational and educational programmes offered by various schools. Typically, these employers are not reimbursed by the government but are subsidised to the extent that they may deduct such costs in determining their taxable income. Various labour unions offer training schemes through apprenticeships. Enterprise-based training is also offered to the unemployed on a small scale.

Japan

Collective agreements do not cover training conditions. Employers in many industries provide training for their employees, either in-house or through outside consultants and/or vocational and educational programmes offered by various schools. Typically, these employers are not reimbursed by the government but are subsidised to the extent that they may deduct such costs in determining their taxable income. Regular rotation of assignments is common among white-collar employees to maximise the range of their skills. As a common practice employees receive education and training (on-the-job training) and experience various kinds of jobs (job rotation) within their company or within their group of companies. Blue-collar workers are usually trained in several line positions. Efforts to enhance quality are undertaken in each workshop in a factory, under the responsibility of a team leader.

Germany

Almost all employers in industry provide training schemes for their employees. Training contracts for apprentices are supervised by the relevant sections of the chambers of commerce in conjunction with local educational establishments, which also organise the examinations for basic professional qualifications. Beyond this level, many employers encourage their employees to attend outside courses, or provide their own facilities. Enterprise-based training is also offered on a small scale to the unemployed.

France

Collective agreements *(accords collectives)* determine the conditions for specific training commitments tailored for specific needs at the sectoral level, complementing the prevailing legal provisions on general training conditions.

United Kingdom

Industrial Training Boards, which handle sectoral training issues, are financed by a levy on all employers of the sector. This levy can be offset against the cost of training undertaken by the employer. Training boards continue to exist in certain sectors (construction, hotels and catering, offshore oil), although these are increasingly being replaced by employer-dominated bodies.

Implicit rules

United States

Firms may consider that under high job-turnover training may carry risks with respect to competition. However, there is general acknowledgement that the educational system needs to become more compatible with job-market requirements. Moreover, training expenditures are high by world standards in such sectors as high-technology, and large multinational US firms provide sophisticated training programmes and provide considerable funds for this purpose.

Japan

Training is an integral part of lifetime employment and in this respect is socially expected. The State is expected to give vocational training to the unemployed, the disabled, etc.

Germany

A strong vocational training system exists as part of the educational system and the apprenticeship system is well-established. Active participation of unions, firms and government in training is one component of the "social market" economy.

France

The State has established partnerships with firms for training purposes as well as separate local job-training facilities. It is socially expected to play this active role.

United Kingdom

There is a well-established apprenticeship system and an increasing focus on vocational training which is expected to be an integral part of the general educational system.

Employees' representation

Laws and regulations

United States

The Norris-LaGuardia Act, enacted in 1932, outlawed the anti-union practices. The National Labour Relations Act (NLRA), or Wagner Act, of 1935, went far beyond the earlier act by requiring employers to bargain with unions representing the majority of their employees and by asserting that it was illegal for employers to interfere with their employees' right to organise collectively. The Act ensures the right to unionise, and protects workers against arbitrary discipline and dismissal when workers seek to organise. The Taft-Hartley Act of 1947 restricted some aspects of union activity. Perhaps the most important provision of this Act is its Section 14B, which permits individual States to pass "right-to-work laws". By 1982 some 19 States had passed such laws. The Labour Management Relations Act (Taft-Hartley Act) (LMRA) regulates the activities and outlines the rights of unions, employers and employees, and prohibits certain unfair labour practices. It was enacted after it became apparent that its forerunner, the National Labour Relations Act (Wagner Act), had given too much leverage to the unions, to the detriment of both employers and employees. Thus, the LMRA's basic purpose is to effect a balance of bargaining power between employers and employees by allowing employees to organise and bargain collectively and also to impose certain restrictions on how far unions can go in organising company employees. Closed shops are illegal under the Taft-Hartley Act. A closed shop is an agreement between a union and an employer whereby the employer agrees to hire only union members. Union shops, on the other hand, are legal and oblige employees to join the union within a specific time of hiring (usually 30 days). In an agency shop, an employee does not have to join the union, but has to pay the union dues. Many States have so-called "right-to-work" laws which make union security agreements, such as union shops and agency shops, illegal. These "right-to-work" laws have been given precedence over the Labour Management Relations Act's union security provisions in federal court decisions. Finally, the Landrum-Griffin Act of 1959, designed to protect the rights of union members in relation to their leaders, contained provisions that increased union democracy.

Japan

Article 28 of the Constitution guarantees, and The Trade Union Law of 1949 recognises, that workers have the right to organise, bargain collectively and take other collective actions. The major contents of this law are as follows: *i)* workers have the freedom to organise trade unions without any permission or notification to the administrative officers; *ii)* the following unfair labour practices by employers towards trade unions and workers are prohibited: discriminatory treatment of workers because they are union members, refusal to let a union bargain collectively, control of and/or intervention in union activities by management; *iii)* appropriate acts of trade unions are free from criminal as well as civil liabilities; *iv)* if trade unions and employers reach collective agreements, provisions of individual contracts of employment which contravene the provisions in the collective agreements become void; and *v)* the Labour Relations Commission, with tripartite representation from public interest, labour, and management, has been established by central and local governments. The Labour Relation Commission provides remedy for unfair labour practices and help in settling labour disputes. According to the Labour Union Law labour agreements are made between a company and a lawfully organised union. When labour agreements become applicable to at least three-quarters of regular workers of a given plant, their terms then become applicable to all workers. Labour agreements do not require government approval.

Germany

The right to form and join a trade union is guaranteed under the 1949 Basic Law. Pursuant to article 9, para. 3 of the Basic Law, everyone has the right not only to form an association (trade union or employers' association), to participate in the formation of an association, to become a member of an existing association, to choose among several associations, to stay a member of an association or to leave an association (positive freedom of association), but also not to become a member of an association (negative freedom of association). Within the framework of freedom of activity, associations are entitled to adopt legal rules with a binding affect on their members in collective agreements. Trade unions have representation rights at supervisory board level under the Co-determination Act of 1976, which applies to large public companies (*i.e.* equal representation in companies with more than 2 000 employees, and one-third representation in companies with between 500 and 2 000 employees). Legislation provides works councils with extensive co-decision rights, where workers are heavily involved in the definition of working conditions and hiring/dismissal policy. Extensive rights of co-decision have been affirmed in favour of employees' councils by the Works Council Act of 1972. Within a commercial organisation employees communicate with management through the works council. A works council is voluntary for all places of work employing five or more employees; the employer may not oppose it and there are no sanctions for employees for not organising one. The council's essential function is to represent the workforce; to ensure that employees are correctly and fairly treated within the context of labour law generally and the trade union agreements in particular; and otherwise to represent their interests. Legislation passed in 1988 gives increased information rights to works councils in the case of introduction of new technology.

France

A Labour Union Unit may be created in any firm, whatever number of employees. Nomination of union representatives benefiting from statutory rights is limited to firms of 50 employees or more by the 1982 law. In enterprises where one or more labour union representatives *(délégués syndicaux)* exist, employers must meet annually with labour representatives to negotiate questions relating to wages and hours. Personnel representatives *(délégués du personnel)* are required by law in all enterprises which usually employ more than ten employees. Their function is to represent to management all grievances, both individual and group, relating to salaries, work safety, hygiene, social benefits, etc. Personnel representatives must be received by management at least once a month. A Labour Management Committee *(Comité d'entreprise)* exists by law in all enterprises employing 50 or more employees. In enterprises with several centres of activity management committees are called *"Comités d'établissement"* and are represented by some of their members at the *"Comité central"* which holds meetings at least once every six months. *Comités d'entreprise* or *Comités d'établissement* hold meetings at least once a month. The Committee is not intended to be organ for transmitting grievances but rather for labour and management co-operation. In all commercial firms the Committee is entitled to the same documents as shareholders and, according to the 1986 law, has a right of representation by two members with the right to speak but no vote at all meetings of the board of directors in joint stock companies. In addition, enterprises with more than 300 employees must submit to the Committee a report giving general figures (*Bilan social*). The 1982 Auroux Laws increased the role of the works councils and state that employers have a duty of concertation. As a result of changes in legislation that took place in 1989, works councils must be informed of redundancies and the introduction of new technologies.

United Kingdom

Trade unions and collective labour relations are governed mainly by the Trade Unions and Labour Relations Acts 1974-6, Employment Protection Act 1975, and Employment Acts of 1980 and 1982. The 1980 law practically abolished the closed-shop principle and introduced other curbs to Union power. Furthermore, legislation passed in 1989 introduced restrictions to the right to paid time-off for shop stewards. The Trade Union Reform and Employment Rights Act of 1993, besides other reforms to industrial relations, principally deals with the rights and conduct of unions and their members. The law leaves employers free to decide for themselves whether to bargain collectively with a union, or whether to continue to do so. The union must first obtain support for organising industrial action from a secret postal ballot of the members likely to be called on to take part in the action. Employers of those members must be notified of the ballot and its results. In addition, unions should provide employers with at least seven days notice of their intent to carry out industrial action, and such notice may only be given after the ballot is held.

Standard practices

United States

The structure of US unions rests upon the strength of local unions whose members may all work in the same industry or may all work in the same firm. Unions in some industries are highly organised while there is very little unionism in some other industries. The duties of workers' representatives are limited and often established by decentralised collective agreements.

Japan

Employees' representative bodies are the negotiating parties in collective agreements and the law gives these bodies certain co-decision rights at the plant level, which they freely exercise. This type of co-decision tends to take place in cases of technological change and work rationalisation.

Germany

Employee interests are represented through a dual system of statutory works councils at work-place level and free collective bargaining. Two different types of collective agreements exist in Germany: association collective agreements are concluded between employers' associations and trade unions for individual sectors and regions, while company collective agreements are concluded between trade unions and individual employers. In individual cases, agreements on wages and other conditions apply only if both the employer and the employee are respectively members of the association and trade union that conclude the collective agreement (unless, in the case of a company collective agreement, the employer himself or herself is a contracting party) and if the employment falls within the scope of the collective agreement. The same applies to collective agreements that have been declared legally binding by the government. In addition, the implementation of collective agreement rules may be stipulated in individual contracts between the employer and the employee. The works council system is noteworthy for the formal rights accorded to employee representatives, which include consultation on all hiring and firing, and for the fact that works councils are not mandatory which means that by no means all employers operate within this framework.

France

In practice employees' representative bodies are the negotiating parties in collective agreements. Certain co-decision rights at the plant level are given to these bodies by law, and in practice these bodies exercise their rights such as in the case of collective dismissals where they participate in the drawing up of social plans. The legislative trend is towards an increasing role for enterprise-level works councils. European integration and common social policies reinforce this trend towards more active and significant works councils.

United Kingdom

The duties of workers' representatives are limited and are often established by collective agreement. The law leaves employers free to decide for themselves whether to bargain collectively with a union, or whether to continue to do so. By custom and practice, collective agreements do not create enforceable obligations between the unions and employers who sign them, although their terms can be imported into binding employment contracts between individual employees and their employers.

Implicit rules

United States

The existing legislation largely takes care of many aspects of work-place conditions (*e.g.* Health and Safety regulations, Equal Opportunity Rights, etc.). Emphasis placed on economic objectives and private employment contracts (*i.e.* employment at will) as well as geographic mobility may obviate the need for active employee representation.

Japan

Trade unions, especially the large ones, in deciding the position they are going to take, largely take into account the current situation of the national economy. This pragmatic approach is made possible by the fact that Japanese wage levels have caught up with those of other industrial countries through the large wage increases agreed during high growth periods.

Germany

The trade union movement is a strong, established feature of the German industrial background. Trade unions exercise a strong voice in policy formulation but are far from militant. The main feature of the trade union movement is the principle of democracy within individual trade unions: for example, union members basically decide in democratic elections who shall hold posts in union bodies. In addition, members have the right to participate in decisions regarding aspects of collective bargaining (*e.g.* beginning and end of strikes). Both employer associations and trade unions are strong, representative and disciplined. Despite conflicts over major strategic issues, the day-to-day conduct of industrial relations, especially at the work-place level, remains highly consensual. The works council has an obligation to co-operate with the employer "for the good of the employees and the establishment".

France

As a consequence of the emphasis placed on the creation of an activist leadership rather than mass membership, trade unionism in France has never been strong. Union membership has been steadily declining since the late 1970s. Only around 10 per cent of the workforce is estimated to be unionised, and this is highly concentrated in the public sector. This situation characterises French industrial relations and is socially accepted.

United Kingdom

As one of the first countries to industrialise, industrial relations in the United Kingdom have gone through various phases. Employees' representation in this process has been marked by political preferences. The main characteristics of labour relationships have been sharp swings between measures to promote union power (by Labour governments) and to curb it (by Conservative governments).

Wage bargaining

Laws and regulations

United States

There is no national system of wage bargaining nor does the legislation provide extension procedures.

Japan

Article 28 of the Constitution guarantees the right to bargain and the Labour Standards Law determines the right of employees to wages. There is no central system of wage bargaining. However, as regards wage bargaining, some co-ordination of unions exists at the national level. Collective bargaining power may be executed by the union or by the representatives of the national federations. More than one union may represent employees at a given location. Extension to regional level is authorised but not practised frequently.

Germany

There is no national system of wage bargaining. Collective agreements differ widely throughout the Federal Republic of Germany in accordance with the special features of individual sectors and regions. Once the government declares a collective agreement generally binding, its rules are binding on all employers and employees within the field of application of the agreement – *i.e.* they are also binding on those employers and employees who are not respectively members of the relevant associations and trade unions. Collective agreements may be declared as generally binding only under specific legal conditions (for example, one of the parties to the relevant collective agreement must apply for it). In addition, the employers on whom the collective agreement is binding must employ at least 50 per cent of the employees to whom the agreement applies. Furthermore, there must be a public interest in declaring a collective agreement as generally binding.

France

The 1982 legislation lays an annual obligation to negotiate salary levels at both the sectoral and company levels. Unless provided otherwise in an applicable collective bargaining agreement and provided the salary is at least equal to the minimum legal wage, an employee's remuneration is freely negotiable between the contracting parties. There is no central system of wage bargaining. However, in practice governments can extend collective agreements through legislation. Administrative extension can be applied to a sector where no trade union or no agreement between unions and employers exist (such an extension will typically apply the terms of a collective agreement in a related sector).

United Kingdom

Under the Employment Protection Act of 1975, firms could be obliged to pay salaries which were at least equal to those agreed by collective bargaining. This widely used provision was rescinded in 1980. The 1986 Wages Act makes provisions for payment of wages, implements Wages Councils and alters certain redundancy agreements. The law leaves employers free to decide for themselves whether to bargain collectively with a union, or whether to continue to do so. The Trade Union Reform and Employment Rights Act of 1993, besides other reforms to industrial relations, abolished Wage Councils which had previously set the minimum pay rates for employees in specific sectors. In the past these minimum wages represented a measure against which the average pay for the sector could be determined during salary negotiations.

Standard practices

United States

"Free collective bargaining" as opposed to "co-determination" is the dominating practice and doctrine. Unions tend to bargain with company management over detailed terms of employment including wages. Generally bargaining takes place between local unions and each employer and sets the minimum and maximum terms of employment. Violation of these terms by either party may constitute a breach of contract or unfair labour practice. Grievance arbitration provisions coupled with no strike clauses are very often found in collective agreements.

Japan

Wages are negotiated every spring between labour and management. This negotiation is called *Shunto* and is a bargaining process in which individual enterprise unions simultaneously submit their demands for wage increases, and negotiate with their respective employers under the co-ordination of the national labour organisations and industrial federations. These annual negotiations result in the determination of annual rates of wage increase. The seniority wage system is one of the main elements of Japanese employment practices, together with the lifetime employment practice and the enterprise trade union.

Germany

In general no nation-wide collective agreements exist. Collective agreements differ widely throughout the country. Industrial disputes, *i.e.* strikes or lockouts, may be used by the parties to a collective agreement only as a last resort to reach the conclusion of a collective agreement after the breakdown of negotiations and dispute settlement procedures.

France

Wage bargaining in the form of collective agreements takes place at the industry level and the agreements are negotiated either regionally or nationally. Wages are negotiated by each firm with employees or labour unions, subject to the minimum wage agreed in the collective labour agreement (*Convention collective*) for each employment category. Recent trends indicate a decentralisation of wage bargaining processes. Along with the overall observed shift to more company-based or single-employer bargaining, there has been a concurrent move towards merit- or performance related pay.

United Kingdom

By custom and practice, collective agreements do not create enforceable obligations between the unions and employers who sign them, although their terms can be imported into binding employment contracts between individual employees and their employers. There has been trend towards a shift to lower-level bargaining. As a result of changed labour market conditions and declining union influence, employers are demanding a further shift towards decentralised bargaining. At the same time, major company and plant agreements are taking precedent over annual rounds of wage bargaining.

Implicit rules

United States

There is a traditional preference for merit-related pay, free bargaining and individual competition. "Free collective bargaining" as opposed to "co-determination" is the dominating doctrine.

Japan

In general the unions behave consensually (*i.e.* advance warning for strikes) and abide by annual labour contracts. Recent trade union policy in *Shunto* is to place high priority on securing real wage increases, shorter working hours, child-care leave and a social welfare system. Trade unions also forward to the government various demands, such as price stability, employment security and social security. Thus, more general demands in the direction of improved living standards of workers are being put forward by the unions.

Germany

The general perception of industrial disputes is that they should be used only as last resort in order to reach the conclusion of collective agreements.

France

Unions are considered to be the legitimate defenders of "acquired rights". The minimum wage is considered to be one of these acquired rights.

United Kingdom

There is an expressed preference for merit- or performance-related pay. This principle is increasingly applied to publicly provided services.

Chapter 6

LABOUR COSTS

The data provided are drawn from the Structural Analysis Industrial database (STAN) of the OECD's Directorate for Science, Technology and Industry (DSTI), and the Bureau of Labor Statistics of the United States Department of Labor.

Introduction

Labour costs are among the most studied factors in international competition and trade specialisation. Together with the internationally more mobile and homogeneous capital costs, they constitute the fixed inputs that directly influence absolute and relative competitive advantages.

Basic information on straight labour costs is of prime importance when firms assess and compare their labour environments. Absolute labour costs as projected (including the currency impact) over the medium to long term influence firms' investment and location decisions. However, it is often difficult to isolate this type of data from the multitude of analytical indicators of labour costs.

The competitive performance of countries – technological change, reorganisation, increasing output and rising productivity levels – has impacts on labour costs. Measures of absolute wages or labour costs fail to take account of these productivity differences. This aspect of labour costs is taken up below under *unit labour shares.*

From the employer's point of view, the most useful and simple comparison of labour costs is that which converts hourly rates of compensation (including social security and/or insurance pay, holiday pay, regular bonuses, pension plans, labour taxes, etc.) into a common currency using current exchange rates. However, excessive currency fluctuations may disproportionately accentuate labour cost differences across countries even from this perspective (*e.g.* recent exchange rate movements between the US dollar and the Japanese yen). A method exists to soften the impact of sharp currency fluctuations – applying moving averages of exchange rates. In order to demonstrate the degree of variation, *hourly compensation costs* and *compensation per employee* are converted by three-year moving averages for three countries selected at random from among the countries included in this survey; these are presented in Annex.

As can be observed, important sectoral differences in labour costs exist across and within countries. These differences are even more significant at disaggregated levels of industry. Nevertheless, as the data sets come from different sources and industrial classifications differ across countries, in order to provide maximum comparability only the two-digit level aggregation is considered in this survey.

The purpose of the criteria discussed below is to provide country profiles of labour costs from the business perspective, or from the perspective of the industrial firm. This discussion is also intended to guide the interpretation of the country tables.

Hourly compensation costs

Labour costs, as defined by the International Labour Office (ILO), represent the costs incurred by the employer in the employment of labour, comprising: remuneration of work performed, payments in respect of time paid for but not worked, bonuses and gratuities, the cost of food, drinks and other payments in kind, cost of workers' housing borne by employers, employers' social security expenditures, cost to the employer for vocational training, welfare services and miscellaneous items such as transport of workers, work clothes, recruitment expenses and taxes regarded as labour costs.

Labour cost data are obtained mainly through establishment surveys, *i.e.* labour cost surveys or industrial censuses and surveys, although in some countries estimates may be made on the basis of data obtained from a number of sources. Data furnished by surveys, while necessarily resulting from a sample and therefore not exhaustive, do have the advantage of the bottom-up approach, with the possibility of yielding cost information by industry and by hour which is more meaningful to industry.

One appropriate measure for comparing levels of employer labour costs is the hourly compensation costs published yearly by the United States Department of Labor's Bureau of Labor Statistics (BLS). The Bureau of Labor Statistics develops comparative measures of hourly compensation costs in order to assess international differences in employer labour costs. These statistics should not be considered precise measures of comparative compensation costs as they are partly estimated. Nevertheless, they provide a far better basis for comparing employer labour costs than the average earning statistics published by most countries. National definitions of average earnings differ considerably – most published series of average earnings do not include all items of labour compensation and the omitted items of compensation frequently represent a large proportion of total compensation.

The BLS definition (see Background Notes to Country Tables) of hourly compensation costs is not the same as the ILO definition of total labour costs. Hourly compensation costs do not include all items of labour costs. The costs of recruitment, employee training, and plant facilities and services (*e.g.* cafeterias, medical clinics, etc.) are not included because data is unavailable for most countries. These omissions in labour costs account for no more than 4 per cent of total labour costs in any country for which data is available.

Labour cost composition

The Bureau of Labor Statistics' annual reports also provide supplementary data on the breakdown of the different wage elements constituting hourly compensation costs. Aggregate components of hourly compensation costs (see Background Notes to Country Tables for a detailed breakdown) such as: pay for time worked; bonuses, holiday pay and other payments; and social insurance and other taxes provided for production workers in manufacturing.

In the current highly competitive environment, remuneration systems and, in particular, such non-wage cost elements as social protection costs and/or labour taxes, create increasingly important differences among countries and have a significant impact on overall labour costs.

Wage dispersion

Wage dispersion is dependent on a combination of factors: demographic and economic – age, sex, education and skill levels, occupation – and on the existence of minimum wages and the wage bargaining system in place.

As a consequence of swings in economic cycles and demographic factors during the past decade, there has been a marked increase in earnings dispersion. In addition to the arrival of a large number of young people on labour markets, increases in the earnings of higher skilled workers and an increase in the numbers of those with higher educational attainments, along with persisting mismatches in the skills market yielding shortages in some fields, all contributed to push up the wage ceiling. Non-neutral technological change, which increased the productivity of highly skilled workers resulting in increased demand for such workers, also contributed to upward wage pressures.

Wage dispersion can be analysed across countries, male and female working populations, age groups of the working population (*e.g.* earnings of the young), levels of educational attainment, and industry and industry groups.

The survey focuses on wage dispersion by industry groups and the selected criterion is technology. The *OECD Scoreboard of Indicators* (see Background Notes to Country Tables) uses, besides technology, a number of other aggregation schemes for classifying manufacturing industries into groups; these are orientation (resource-intensive, labour-intensive, scale-intensive and science-based); wages (high-wage, medium-wage and low-wage); and skills (high-skilled, low-skilled). However, technology is the criterion most frequently used to demonstrate wage dispersion, and is considered to be the most appropriate in the context of this survey.

It should be borne in mind that these statistics refer to averages within the industry or branch, and shed no light on intra-industry differentials by function. Moreover, due to differences in data sources and methods, industry and/or country positions may appear different.

Minimum wage

Minimum wages are deemed to be important components of labour costs in a country. They vary between either statutory (legally imposed) or negotiated and effective forms.

Statutory minimum wages aim to provide a minimum wage for sections of the workforce which might not be covered by negotiated agreements. They may be governed by central legislation or local and regional legislation. There are also differences in the application of legislation across countries: while some countries apply a blanket minimum wage across the working population, others apply age (*e.g.* youth exemption), sector (*e.g.* by industry), occupation (*e.g.* skills), and regional (*e.g.* provincial) criteria.

Negotiated and effective minimum wages are set by collective agreement and can be made legally binding on the negotiating parties or, as is often the case, extended to all sectors, occupations or regions. Very often, minimum wages are set at industry level, with the resultant minimum serving as a wage floor for subsequent negotiations at the enterprise level. Companies not included in such agreements may adopt a negotiated minimum wage as being an effective minimum wage.

Compensation per employed person

Compensation of employees as defined in the National Accounts includes all payments by resident producers of wages and salaries to their employees, in kind and in cash, paid or imputed, in respect of their employees to social security schemes and to private pension, family allowance, casualty insurance, life insurance and similar schemes. While this type of statistic has the advantage of being a broad definition comprising many non-wage elements, it suffers from the disadvantage of being an aggregate statistic which can at best give only an indication of labour compensation per employee per year.

Compensation of part-time workers and overtime are subsumed in this ratio and create a potential source of error where a headcount is used in the calculation. It is a measure of average annual nominal wages in an industry; it does not adjust for hours worked.

In comparing the different approaches mentioned so far, one outcome concerning the estimation of labour costs is that the choice of labour cost or compensation measure is critical, and that hard data disaggregated by industry, skill and job type are highly desirable in order to illustrate the inherent range of labour costs by country or by industry. As already mentioned, the choice of exchange rate also has a direct bearing on results.

It should also be noted that the evolution of this ratio through time is determined in large part by wage inflation. Therefore, trends in individual industries can be best observed with respect to the manufacturing industry as a whole.

Unit labour shares

The concept of unit labour cost has recently been widely used to measure net labour costs per unit of output in different sectors and countries. Unit labour cost is a more elaborate concept than straight labour costs as it takes into account the impact of internationally uneven labour productivity levels on total labour costs per unit of output.

However, there are formidable difficulties associated with productivity measurement and its use in international comparisons. First, while production (*i.e.* gross output) data is more readily available than data on value added, the former includes the value of intermediate products, and a rise or a fall in the share of intermediate inputs can be misleading. Second, value added has to be corrected for changes in prices, and as the data necessary for the application of the double-deflation method (deflation of both production and intermediate inputs) are often not available, indices rely solely on price changes in factor inputs, thus underestimating productivity growth. Quality changes also tend to be insufficiently reflected in price series (*e.g.* hedonic price series for the computer industry). Third, and most importantly from the point of view of this survey, market exchange rates are not the appropriate common unit of measure for comparing output levels because they render results sensitive to exchange rate fluctuations. An alternative is to employ economy-wide purchasing power parities which adjust for exchange rate swings. However, these values are derived from the expenditure side of the National Accounts, rather than from the output side and, therefore, do not provide purchasing power parities by industry. Other methods (*e.g.* using proxy purchasing power parities or unit value ratios) have been developed, although these also have significant shortcomings. Fourth, as mentioned earlier, the inclusion or exclusion of part-time and overtime as well as self-employed and unpaid family members creates an accuracy problem for productivity measurement. Finally, different phases of the business cycle have a strong influence on time series of productivity. Thus, in order to make structural comparisons, the underlying output and employment series should be adjusted for cyclical influences.

Because of the above-mentioned problems, unit labour costs are usually limited to international *trend* comparisons (growth rates or indices) as opposed to *level* comparisons. Therefore, a less sophisticated indicator – "unit labour shares" –, which is a simple ratio of labour compensation to value added (both in local currency and current prices), and which reflects the share of the remuneration of the labour factor in total value produced (and therefore also takes into account the productivity of the labour force), is preferred for the purpose of this survey.

A discussion of the technical issues involved in the measurement and interpretation of unit labour costs and the case for a simpler indicator such as the one used here is available in Turner and Van't dack (1993), *Measuring International Price and Cost Competitiveness*, BIS Economic Papers, No. 39, Bank for International Settlements, Basle.

LABOUR COSTS: COUNTRY TABLES

UNITED STATES

Hourly compensation costs

In US$

SIC	1990	1991	1992	1993	1994
Total manufacturing	14.91	15.58	16.09	16.51	16.86
Food, beverages & tobacco	13.58	14.14	14.76	15.12	15.48
Textile, wearing apparel & leather	9.23	9.56	10.07	10.26	10.60
Lumber, wood products & furniture	11.67	11.98	12.38	12.66	12.85
Paper, printing and publishing	15.68	16.23	16.78	17.17	17.41
Chemicals, petroleum, rubber & plastic	16.66	17.44	18.03	18.35	18.55
Stone, clay & glass	15.30	15.85	16.27	16.67	16.97
Primary metal manufacturing	19.72	20.73	21.54	22.29	22.80
Fabricated metal, machinery & equipment	16.59	17.46	17.97	18.51	19.74
Miscellaneous manufacturing	11.30	11.70	12.25	12.62	12.91

Note: Total manufacturing 1995 = 17.20
Source: US Department of Labor.

Labour cost composition, 1995

Percentage

Pay for time worked:	71.8
Social insurance and other labour taxes:	21.9
Bonuses, holiday pay and other payments:	6.3

Source: US Department of Labor.

Wage dispersion by industry group, 1993

Total manufacturing = 100

High-technology industries:	123
Medium-technology industries:	110
Low-technology industries:	86

Source: OECD, STAN database.

Minimum wage, 1993

Statutory wage:	US$4.25 hourly
Governing source:	Federal and state legislation

Source: Various sources.

UNITED STATES (continued)

	Compensation per employed person (US$)					Unit labour shares (per cent)				
ISIC	**1989**	**1990**	**1991**	**1992**	**1993**	**1989**	**1990**	**1991**	**1992**	**1993**
Total manufacturing	32 954	34 729	37 070	38 188	40 747	0.67	0.66	0.67	0.67	0.67
Food, beverages & tobacco	30 143	30 966	32 256	34 126	34 470	0.52	0.51	0.48	0.47	0.47
Textiles, wearing apparel & leather	19 523	20 928	21 864	22 207	22 570	0.79	0.77	0.76	0.76	0.76
Wood, cork & furniture	23 304	24 256	26 400	24 936	30 188	0.67	0.65	0.69	0.68	0.68
Paper, printing & publishing	31 689	32 708	35 254	36 764	37 955	0.65	0.63	0.66	0.68	0.67
Chemicals	38 259	39 726	42 735	44 420	45 642	0.48	0.49	0.50	0.50	0.50
Non-metallic mineral products	31 789	33 517	36 204	35 870	37 612	0.76	0.75	0.77	0.79	0.79
Basic metal industries	40 224	42 336	45 104	46 386	49 107	0.71	0.70	0.74	0.74	0.74
Fabricated metal products & machinery	37 115	39 500	42 163	43 797	47 785	0.76	0.76	0.77	0.78	0.78
Other manufacturing	22 998	24 553	26 036	26 271	27 757	0.59	0.57	0.57	0.58	0.57

Source: OECD, STAN database.

Hourly compensation costs
In US$

SIC	1990	1991	1992	1993	1994
Total manufacturing	12.80	14.66	16.28	19.01	21.07
Food, beverages & tobacco	10.18	11.48	12.71	15.05	16.79
Textile, wearing apparel & leather	8.07	9.27	10.27	11.62	12.76
Lumber, wood products & furniture	10.48	11.92	13.15	15.47	16.81
Paper, printing and publishing	13.52	15.50	17.35	20.38	22.43
Chemicals, petroleum, rubber & plastic	15.80	18.73	20.65	23.45	26.03
Stone, clay & glass	13.26	15.48	17.10	19.95	22.26
Primary metal manufacturing	19.04	21.44	24.03	28.02	30.60
Fabricated metal, machinery & equipment	13.46	15.45	17.17	20.06	22.33
Miscellaneous manufacturing	11.26	13.09	14.77	17.55	19.59

Note: Total manufacturing 1995 = 23.66
Source: US Department of Labor.

Labour cost composition, 1995
Percentage

Pay for time worked:	59.0
Social insurance and other labour taxes:	14.4
Bonuses, holiday pay and other payments:	26.7

Source: US Department of Labor.

Wage dispersion by industry group, 1993
Total manufacturing = 100

High-technology industries:	97
Medium-technology industries:	114
Low-technology industries:	93

Source: OECD, STAN database.

Minimum wage, 1993

Statutory wage:	None
Governing source:	Local wage councils

Source: Various sources.

JAPAN (continued)

	Compensation per employed person (US$)					Unit labour shares (per cent)				
ISIC	**1989**	**1990**	**1991**	**1992**	**1993**	**1989**	**1990**	**1991**	**1992**	**1993**
Total manufacturing	27 290	27 807	31 089	33 718	37 062	0.50	0.50	0.50	0.53	0.53
Food, beverages & tobacco	20 119	20 394	22 590	24 715	27 719	0.38	0.38	0.38	0.38	0.38
Textiles, wearing apparel & leather	16 633	17 117	19 161	21 007	21 884	0.83	0.82	0.73	0.74	0.74
Wood, cork & furniture	20 907	21 745	24 445	26 724	35 377	0.68	0.62	0.62	0.67	0.68
Paper, printing & publishing	31 484	31 820	35 414	38 702	42 732	0.58	0.58	0.57	0.62	0.62
Chemicals	30 798	31 266	34 623	37 675	39 976	0.39	0.41	0.42	0.42	0.42
Non-metallic mineral products	27 559	27 973	31 207	35 667	42 009	0.52	0.53	0.56	0.61	0.61
Basic metal industries	39 393	39 235	43 442	46 473	50 229	0.36	0.37	0.38	0.42	0.42
Fabricated metal products & machinery	29 863	30 431	34 117	36 517	39 757	0.57	0.56	0.56	0.60	0.60

Source: OECD, STAN database.

GERMANY

Hourly compensation costs

In US$

SIC	1990	1991	1992	1993	1994
Total manufacturing	21.96	22.69	25.40	25.36	26.90
Food, beverages & tobacco	18.60	19.15	21.58	21.42	22.77
Textile, wearing apparel & leather	15.84	16.34	18.40	18.12	19.30
Lumber, wood products & furniture	19.42	20.16	24.97	23.27	23.44
Paper, printing and publishing	21.94	22.73	25.41	25.10	26.48
Chemicals, petroleum, rubber & plastic	23.06	23.77	..	26.16	27.57
Stone, clay & glass	20.34	21.02	23.55	23.26	24.62
Primary metal manufacturing	23.90	24.57	27.59	27.34	28.99
Fabricated metal, machinery & equipment	23.08	23.89	26.66	26.79	27.92
Miscellaneous manufacturing	17.72	18.36	20.62	20.39	21.66

Note: Total manufacturing 1995 = 31.88
Source: US Department of Labor.

Labour cost composition, 1995

Percentage

Pay for time worked:	55.7
Social insurance and other labour taxes:	23.6
Bonuses, holiday pay and other payments:	20.6

Source: US Department of Labor.

Wage dispersion by industry group, 1993

Total manufacturing = 100

High-technology industries:	111
Medium-technology industries:	115
Low-technology industries:	84

Source: OECD, STAN database.

Minimum wage, 1993

Statutory wage:	None
Governing source:	Collective agreements

Source: Various sources.

GERMANY (continued)

	Compensation per employed person (US$)					Unit labour shares (per cent)				
ISIC	1989	1990	1991	1992	1993	1989	1990	1991	1992	1993
Total manufacturing	28 252	34 627	35 563	39 931	34 698	0.67	0.67	0.68	0.71	0.71
Food, beverages & tobacco	19 353	23 676	24 650	27 734	23 910	0.43	0.41	0.43	0.44	0.44
Textiles, wearing apparel & leather	18 501	22 512	23 398	26 233	23 391	0.71	0.70	0.70	0.75	0.75
Wood, cork & furniture	20 727	25 369	26 574	29 888	26 598	0.75	0.73	0.70	0.74	0.74
Paper, printing & publishing	25 512	31 219	32 650	36 278	32 955	0.69	0.67	0.68	0.74	0.74
Chemicals	34 801	41 947	42 547	47 918	43 674	0.55	0.57	0.57	0.60	0.60
Non-metallic mineral products	27 955	33 952	34 897	39 469	32 586	0.62	0.62	0.61	0.61	0.62
Basic metal industries	28 265	34 614	35 642	40 102	33 637	0.69	0.71	0.73	0.80	0.81
Fabricated metal products & machinery	30 669	37 727	38 623	43 286	37 399	0.76	0.77	0.77	0.80	0.81
Other manufacturing	18 652	22 456	23 469	26 206	22 897	0.55	0.55	0.55	0.56	0.56

Source: OECD, STAN database.

FRANCE

Hourly compensation costs

In US$

SIC	1990	1991	1992	1993	1994
Total manufacturing	15.23	15.26	16.89	16.23	17.04
Food, beverages & tobacco	15.06	15.14	16.82	16.21	17.00
Textile, wearing apparel & leather	11.98	12.09	13.37	12.91	13.54
Lumber, wood products & furniture	13.15	13.21	14.66	14.09	14.77
Paper, printing and publishing	18.32	18.33	20.16	19.41	20.41
Chemicals, petroleum, rubber & plastic	16.15	16.14	17.64	17.15	17.96
Stone, clay & glass	16.32	16.30	18.08	17.41	18.22
Primary metal manufacturing	17.94	18.04	19.99	19.16	20.17
Fabricated metal, machinery & equipment	15.58	15.58	17.24	16.54	17.36
Miscellaneous manufacturing	13.85	13.87	15.36	14.76	15.50

Note: Total manufacturing 1995 = 19.34

Source: US Department of Labor.

Labour cost composition, 1995

Percentage

Pay for time worked:	54.3
Social insurance and other labour taxes:	29.0
Bonuses, holiday pay and other payments:	16.7

Source: US Department of Labor.

Wage dispersion by industry group, 1993

Total manufacturing = 100

High-technology industries:	123
Medium-technology industries:	101
Low-technology industries:	91

Source: OECD, STAN database.

Minimum wage, 1993

Statutory wage:	US$1 062 monthly
Governing source:	Collective agreements

Source: Various sources.

FRANCE (continued)

	Compensation per employed person (US$)					Unit labour shares (per cent)				
ISIC	1989	1990	1991	1992	1993	1989	1990	1991	1992	1993
Total manufacturing	27 097	33 620	34 637	38 094	..	0.59	0.60	0.63	0.61	..
Food, beverages & tobacco	23 740	29 879	30 834	34 767	32 514	0.52	0.54	0.54	0.52	0.52
Textiles, wearing apparel & leather	20 914	26 912	28 822	31 702	29 411	0.73	0.75	0.82	0.79	0.79
Wood, cork & furniture	18 619	23 048	23 975	25 695	23 994	0.62	0.59	0.59	0.57	0.57
Paper, printing & publishing	28 500	35 152	36 068	39 537	32 186	0.67	0.66	0.65	0.63	0.63
Chemicals	31 910	39 343	40 131	45 262	43 449	0.43	0.44	0.45	0.46	0.46
Non-metallic mineral products	35 258	43 881	45 198	47 432	43 789	0.61	0.62	0.64	0.64	0.64
Basic metal industries	25 686	32 304	33 617	37 240	31 676	0.51	0.56	0.66	0.68	0.68
Fabricated metal products & machinery	28 953	35 518	36 282	39 416	..	0.66	0.66	0.70	0.69	..
Other manufacturing	18 761	23 095	24 046	27 532	..	0.62	0.62	0.69	0.68	..

Source: OECD, STAN database.

UNITED KINGDOM

Hourly compensation costs

In US$

SIC	1990	1991	1992	1993	1994
Total manufacturing	12.71	13.77	14.44	12.47	12.86
Food, beverages & tobacco	12.23	13.34	13.92	12.08	12.24
Textile, wearing apparel & leather	9.06	9.70	10.26	8.91	8.69
Lumber, wood products & furniture	10.88	11.53	11.95	10.16	10.30
Paper, printing and publishing	14.90	15.92	16.65	14.32	14.91
Chemicals, petroleum, rubber & plastic	13.55	14.59	15.38	13.14	13.73
Stone, clay & glass	12.05	13.08	13.46	11.53	12.05
Primary metal manufacturing	13.75	14.85	15.63	13.37	13.91
Fabricated metal, machinery & equipment	13.12	14.30	14.97	12.90	13.36
Miscellaneous manufacturing	10.78	11.36	12.27	10.43	10.67

Note: Total manufacturing 1995 = 13.77

Source: US Department of Labor.

Labour cost composition, 1995

Percentage

Pay for time worked:	74.7
Social insurance and other labour taxes:	13.2
Bonuses, holiday pay and other payments:	12.1

Source: US Department of Labor.

Wage dispersion by industry group, 1993

Total manufacturing = 100

High-technology industries:	111
Medium-technology industries:	108
Low-technology industries:	91

Source: OECD, STAN database.

Minimum wage, 1993

Statutory wage:	None
Governing source:	Industrial relations legislation

Source: Various sources.

UNITED KINGDOM (continued)

	Compensation per employed person (US$)					Unit labour shares (per cent)				
ISIC	1989	1990	1991	1992	1993	1989	1990	1991	1992	1993
Total manufacturing	23 604	26 192	28 127	29 039	27 212	0.73	0.71	0.73	0.73	0.73
Food, beverages & tobacco	22 658	25 082	27 114	28 546	27 172	0.40	0.39	0.39	0.39	0.39
Textiles, wearing apparel & leather	15 245	17 018	18 288	18 790	16 651	0.94	0.90	0.90	0.90	0.91
Wood, cork & furniture	16 123	17 346	18 171	18 646	17 629	0.64	0.62	0.62	0.63	0.63
Paper, printing & publishing	26 778	28 728	30 362	31 542	29 084	0.84	0.78	0.76	0.77	0.77
Chemicals	24 929	28 184	30 658	32 022	30 686	0.67	0.68	0.72	0.73	0.73
Non-metallic mineral products	27 928	32 643	34 230	34 673	33 838	0.69	0.72	0.76	0.78	0.78
Basic metal industries	19 281	23 225	24 326	25 089	23 818	0.67	0.77	0.81	0.82	0.82
Fabricated metal products & machinery	23 659	25 773	27 832	28 497	26 836	0.86	0.73	0.87	0.87	0.88
Other manufacturing	97 130	119 497	127 729	131 611	115 867	0.89	0.91	0.90	0.91	0.91

Source: OECD, STAN database.

CANADA

Hourly compensation costs
In US$

SIC	1990	1991	1992	1993	1994
Total manufacturing	15.83	17.16	17.03	16.43	15.87
Food, beverages & tobacco	14.42	15.40	14.89	14.79	14.18
Textile, wearing apparel & leather	9.77	10.58	10.56	9.81	9.59
Lumber, wood products & furniture	14.33	14.98	14.74	14.39	14.00
Paper, printing and publishing	18.04	20.02	19.89	18.91	17.76
Chemicals, petroleum, rubber & plastic	15.70	16.68	16.64	15.86	15.34
Stone, clay & glass	16.22	17.79	17.90	17.02	16.08
Primary metal manufacturing	21.08	22.84	23.05	22.59	21.40
Fabricated metal, machinery & equipment	16.85	18.38	18.42	17.71	17.30
Miscellaneous manufacturing	13.47	13.77	12.58	12.64	12.31

Note: Total manufacturing 1995 = 16.03
Source: US Department of Labor.

Labour cost composition, 1995
Percentage

Pay for time worked:	73.5
Social insurance and other labour taxes:	17.0
Bonuses, holiday pay and other payments:	9.5

Source: US Department of Labor.

Wage dispersion by industry group, 1993
Total manufacturing = 100

High-technology industries:	107
Medium-technology industries:	107
Low-technology industries:	95

Source: OECD, STAN database.

Minimum wage, 1993

Statutory wage:	Varies between provinces.
Governing source:	Provincial legislation.

Source: Various sources.

CANADA (continued)

	Compensation per employed person (US$)					Unit labour shares (per cent)				
ISIC	**1989**	**1990**	**1991**	**1992**	**1993**	**1989**	**1990**	**1991**	**1992**	**1993**
Total manufacturing	29 782	31 934	34 001	33 266	33 532	0.63	0.65	0.65	0.65	0.65
Food, beverages & tobacco	27 790	29 700	30 776	29 876	30 360	0.54	0.51	0.51	0.51	0.51
Textiles, wearing apparel & leather	18 955	20 348	22 970	22 597	20 800	0.72	0.73	0.73	0.73	0.73
Wood, cork & furniture	25 996	27 824	31 015	30 588	34 697	0.77	0.83	0.83	0.83	0.83
Paper, printing & publishing	33 611	35 692	36 909	35 729	33 848	0.60	0.64	0.64	0.64	0.63
Chemicals	33 090	35 491	39 328	39 669	38 817	0.54	0.53	0.53	0.53	0.52
Non-metallic mineral products	30 889	32 576	34 659	33 382	32 722	0.57	0.61	0.62	0.63	0.63
Basic metal industries	41 531	44 199	47 526	46 368	47 073	0.66	0.80	0.79	0.79	0.78
Fabricated metal products & machinery	30 812	33 310	34 912	34 383	35 063	0.67	0.69	0.69	0.70	0.69
Other manufacturing	23 617	24 832	23 888	21 605	23 168	0.77	0.74	0.75	0.75	0.74

Source: OECD, STAN database.

ITALY

Hourly compensation costs

In US$

SIC	1990	1991	1992	1993	1994
Total manufacturing	17.74	18.60	19.60	16.00	16.10
Food, beverages & tobacco	18.34	18.89	20.11	16.59	17.00
Textile, wearing apparel & leather	14.32	14.81	15.72	12.77	12.90
Lumber, wood products & furniture	15.21	16.06	17.03	13.92	14.03
Paper, printing and publishing	20.31	20.91	21.85	17.84	17.92
Chemicals, petroleum, rubber & plastic	19.71	20.13	21.18	17.32	17.49
Stone, clay & glass	17.27	18.28	19.46	15.86	15.77
Primary metal manufacturing	20.49	21.79	22.85	18.60	18.62
Fabricated metal, machinery & equipment	18.17	19.34	20.28	16.52	16.56
Miscellaneous manufacturing	15.05	15.80	16.64	13.60	13.74

Note: Total manufacturing 1995 = 16.48
Source: US Department of Labor.

Labour cost composition, 1995

Percentage

Pay for time worked:	50.2
Social insurance and other labour taxes:	30.7
Bonuses, holiday pay and other payments:	19.2

Source: US Department of Labor.

Wage dispersion by industry group, 1993

Total manufacturing = 100

High-technology industries:	131
Medium-technology industries:	135
Low-technology industries:	84

Source: OECD, STAN database.

Minimum wage, 1993

Statutory wage:	None
Governing source:	Collective agreements.

Source: Various sources.

ITALY (continued)

	Compensation per employed person (US$)					Unit labour shares (per cent)				
ISIC	**1989**	**1990**	**1991**	**1992**	**1993**	**1989**	**1990**	**1991**	**1992**	**1993**
Total manufacturing	21 293	26 516	27 938	29 894	24 243	0.53	0.55	0.58	0.58	0.56
Food, beverages & tobacco	20 934	25 931	27 333	29 245	24 002	0.39	0.39	0.40	0.39	0.36
Textiles, wearing apparel & leather	13 915	17 304	18 045	18 965	15 180	0.51	0.53	0.54	0.53	0.50
Wood, cork & furniture	12 417	15 538	16 451	17 241	13 696	0.44	0.45	0.46	0.45	0.42
Paper, printing & publishing	25 447	32 123	33 370	36 183	29 964	0.54	0.55	0.58	0.58	0.55
Chemicals	29 699	37 314	39 426	43 295	34 514	0.54	0.58	0.61	0.63	0.63
Non-metallic mineral products	21 959	27 344	28 698	31 054	25 892	0.55	0.55	0.56	0.56	0.62
Basic metal industries	29 832	36 514	38 613	41 170	33 708	0.51	0.56	0.64	0.68	0.64
Fabricated metal products & machinery	24 618	30 512	32 441	34 682	28 263	0.59	0.62	0.65	0.66	0.64
Other manufacturing	14 664	18 470	19 037	20 017	15 968	0.49	0.51	0.53	0.52	0.49

Source: OECD, STAN database.

AUSTRALIA

Hourly compensation costs

In US$

SIC	1990	1991	1992	1993	1994
Total manufacturing	13.07	13.53	13.02	12.49	14.02
Food, beverages & tobacco	12.57	13.29	13.03	12.64	13.89
Textile, wearing apparel & leather	11.09	11.65	11.28	10.73	12.16
Lumber, wood products & furniture	..	..	..	..	..
Paper, printing and publishing	14.32	14.90	14.26	13.95	15.19
Chemicals, petroleum, rubber & plastic	..	..	..	..	..
Stone, clay & glass	..	..	..	..	..
Primary metal manufacturing	15.27	15.98	15.18	14.48	17.16
Fabricated metal, machinery & equipment	..	..	..	..	..
Miscellaneous manufacturing	..	..	..	..	..

Note: Total manufacturing 1995 = 14.40
Source: US Department of Labor.

Labour cost composition, 1995

Percentage

Pay for time worked	73.5
Social insurance and other labour taxes:	16.5
Bonuses, holiday pay and other payments:	9.9

Source: US Department of Labor.

Wage dispersion by industry group, 1993

Total manufacturing = 100

High-technology industries:	107
Medium-technology industries:	107
Low-technology industries:	95

Source: OECD, STAN database.

Minimum wage, 1993

Statutory wage:	None
Governing source:	Job classifications

Source: Various sources.

AUSTRALIA (continued)

	Compensation per employed person (US$)					Unit labour shares (per cent)				
ISIC	1989	1990	1991	1992	1993	1989	1990	1991	1992	1993
Total manufacturing	21 726	22 910	23 458	23 553	..	0.59	0.62	0.62	0.61	0.61
Food, beverages & tobacco	22 056	23 308	22 254	23 051	..	0.51	0.53	0.52	0.51	0.52
Textiles, wearing apparel & leather	18 215	19 624	18 187	19 499	..	0.70	0.77	0.76	0.75	0.75
Wood, cork & furniture	15 203	18 891	16 101	15 834	..	0.69	0.79	0.78	0.77	0.77
Paper, printing & publishing	23 366	22 190	25 702	24 767	..	0.61	0.68	0.67	0.68	0.68
Chemicals	25 492	28 112	29 398	28 815	..	0.48	0.53	0.53	0.54	0.54
Non-metallic mineral products	22 655	23 529	23 238	23 206	..	0.51	0.54	0.56	0.55	0.55
Basic metal industries	30 279	31 141	33 786	35 249	..	0.48	0.46	0.47	0.50	0.50
Fabricated metal products & machinery	22 156	22 792	24 320	23 868	..	0.67	0.70	0.70	0.68	0.69
Other manufacturing	8 657	9 402	10 625	11 111	..	0.70	0.75	0.74	0.70	0.70

Source: OECD, STAN database.

AUSTRIA

Hourly compensation costs

In US$

SIC	1990	1991	1992	1993	1994
Total manufacturing	17.75	18.09	20.29	20.16	21.51
Food, beverages & tobacco	18.08	18.43	20.51	20.24	21.65
Textile, wearing apparel & leather	12.20	12.39	13.96	13.76	14.73
Lumber, wood products & furniture	14.94	15.23	17.23	17.13	18.62
Paper, printing and publishing	..	..	..	..	..
Chemicals, petroleum, rubber & plastic	20.37	20.77	23.38	23.33	24.74
Stone, clay & glass	18.63	19.00	21.31	21.14	22.38
Primary metal manufacturing	21.24	21.59	24.03	23.95	25.32
Fabricated metal, machinery & equipment	18.18	18.54	20.73	20.60	21.88
Miscellaneous manufacturing	..	..	..	..	..

Note: Total manufacturing 1995 = 25.38
Source: US Department of Labor.

Labour cost composition, 1995

Percentage

Pay for time worked	50.6
Social insurance and other labour taxes:	27.7
Bonuses, holiday pay and other payments:	21.7

Source: US Department of Labor.

Wage dispersion by industry group, 1993

Total manufacturing = 100

High-technology industries:	112
Medium-technology industries:	101
Low-technology industries:	96

Source: OECD, STAN database.

Minimum wage, 1993

Statutory wage:	None
Governing source:	Collective agreements

Source: Various sources.

AUSTRIA (continued)

	Compensation per employed person (US$)					Unit labour shares (per cent)				
ISIC	1989	1990	1991	1992	1993	1989	1990	1991	1992	1993
Total manufacturing	21 067	26 385	27 180	30 515	..	0.51	0.52	0.52	0.52	..
Food, beverages & tobacco	17 453	22 284	23 515	26 811	..	0.39	0.39	0.40	0.40	..
Textiles, wearing apparel & leather	15 608	19 652	19 972	22 649	..	0.66	0.67	0.65	0.64	..
Wood, cork & furniture	10 900	13 832	15 128	17 015	..	0.40	0.41	0.45	0.46	..
Paper, printing & publishing	24 009	29 426	30 891	35 833	..	0.57	0.57	0.59	0.63	..
Chemicals	27 956	34 609	34 813	39 154	..	0.40	0.41	0.40	0.39	..
Non-metallic mineral products	25 960	31 234	33 021	36 804	..	0.58	0.58	0.58	0.58	..
Basic metal industries	30 436	37 170	35 432	40 994	..	0.63	0.70	0.79	0.78	..
Fabricated metal products & machinery	21 599	27 470	28 342	31 271	..	0.54	0.54	0.53	0.52	..
Other manufacturing	..	..	..	..	..	..	..	..	..	..

Source: OECD, STAN database.

BELGIUM

Hourly compensation costs

In US$

SIC	1990	1991	1992	1993	1994
Total manufacturing	19.22	19.83	22.23	21.62	23.25
Food, beverages & tobacco	17.65	18.22	20.51	19.88	21.29
Textile, wearing apparel & leather	14.35	14.88	16.69	16.27	17.37
Lumber, wood products & furniture	16.87	17.36	19.39	18.71	19.93
Paper, printing and publishing	20.45	20.91	23.62	22.98	24.31
Chemicals, petroleum, rubber & plastic	23.79	24.77	27.67	27.51	30.05
Stone, clay & glass	19.73	20.34	22.69	22.12	23.52
Primary metal manufacturing	23.69	24.44	27.34	26.83	28.94
Fabricated metal, machinery & equipment	19.79	20.52	22.88	22.16	23.91
Miscellaneous manufacturing	13.48	14.14	15.92	15.21	16.52

Note: Total manufacturing 1995 = 26.88
Source: US Department of Labor.

Labour cost composition, 1995

Percentage

Pay for time worked	52.3
Social insurance and other labour taxes:	27.4
Bonuses, holiday pay and other payments:	20.3

Source: US Department of Labor.

Wage dispersion by industry group, 1993

Total manufacturing = 100

High-technology industries:	..
Medium-technology industries:	..
Low-technology industries:	..

Source: OECD, STAN database.

Minimum wage, 1992

Statutory wage:	BF 38 857
Governing source:	Joint industry committees

Source: Various sources.

BELGIUM (continued)

	Compensation per employed person (US$)					Unit labour shares (per cent)				
ISIC	1989	1990	1991	1992	1993	1989	1990	1991	1992	1993
Total manufacturing	26 324	32 778	34 247	37 638	..	0.59	0.60	0.66	0.67	0.67
Food, beverages & tobacco	23 533	29 747	31 857	35 720	..	0.44	0.44	0.46	0.48	0.48
Textiles, wearing apparel & leather	16 461	20 609	21 333	23 192	..	0.76	0.72	0.75	0.74	0.74
Wood, cork & furniture	16 844	21 008	22 309	23 533	..	0.43	0.45	0.45	0.48	0.49
Paper, printing & publishing	25 050	31 317	32 663	36 260	..	0.67	0.66	0.71	0.72	0.72
Chemicals	34 310	42 824	45 552	51 688	..	0.64	0.70	0.75	0.72	0.72
Non-metallic mineral products	29 704	36 414	37 935	42 926	..	0.76	0.78	0.87	0.86	0.86
Basic metal industries	33 999	42 482	45 753	52 346	..	0.53	0.61	0.85	0.82	0.83
Fabricated metal products & machinery	28 390	34 895	35 595	38 087	..	0.72	0.73	0.84	0.87	0.87
Other manufacturing	14 982	19 503	18 886	21 195	..	0.08	0.07	0.06	0.07	0.07

Source: OECD, STAN database.

CZECH REPUBLIC

Hourly compensation costs

In US$

SIC	1990	1991	1992	1993	1994
Total manufacturing	..	..	..	2.01	2.32
Food, beverages & tobacco	..	..	..	1.90	2.17
Textile, wearing apparel & leather	..	..	..	1.63	1.83
Lumber, wood products & furniture	..	..	..	1.72	2.02
Paper, printing and publishing	..	..	..	2.03	2.50
Chemicals, petroleum, rubber & plastic	..	..	..	2.34	2.61
Stone, clay & glass	..	..	..	2.08	2.42
Primary metal manufacturing	..	..	..	2.42	2.79
Fabricated metal, machinery & equipment	..	..	..	2.05	2.38
Miscellaneous manufacturing	..	..	..	1.79	2.10

Source: Ministry of Industry and Trade of the Czech Republic.

Labour cost composition, 1993

Percentage

Pay for time worked	68.4
Social insurance and other labour taxes:	26.8
Bonuses, holiday pay and other payments:	4.8

Source: Ministry of Industry and Trade of the Czech Republic.

Wage dispersion by industry group, 1993

Total manufacturing = 100

High-technology industries:	..
Medium-technology industries:	..
Low-technology industries:	..

Source: OECD, STAN database.

Minimum wage, 1993

Statutory wage:	US$0.41/hour
Governing source:	State legislation

Source: Various sources.

CZECH REPUBLIC (continued)

ISIC	Compensation per employed person (US$)					Unit labour shares (per cent)				
	1989	1990	1991	1992	1993	1989	1990	1991	1992	1993
Total manufacturing	..	..	1 568	1 955	2 385	..	..	..	..	..
Food, beverages & tobacco	..	..	..	..	..	..	..	..	..	..
Textiles, wearing apparel & leather	..	..	..	..	..	..	..	..	..	..
Wood, cork & furniture	..	..	..	..	..	..	..	..	..	..
Paper, printing & publishing	..	..	..	..	..	..	..	..	..	..
Chemicals	..	..	..	..	..	..	..	..	..	..
Non-metallic mineral products	..	..	..	..	..	..	..	..	..	..
Basic metal industries	..	..	..	..	..	..	..	..	..	..
Fabricated metal products & machinery	..	..	..	..	..	..	..	..	..	..
Other manufacturing	..	..	..	..	..	..	..	..	..	..

Source: OECD, STAN database.

DENMARK

Hourly compensation costs

In US$

SIC	1990	1991	1992	1993	1994
Total manufacturing	17.96	18.26	20.02	19.11	20.40
Food, beverages & tobacco	19.13	19.34	21.18	20.46	..
Textile, wearing apparel & leather	15.37	15.62	17.03	16.32	..
Lumber, wood products & furniture	16.41	16.66	18.10	17.07	..
Paper, printing and publishing	21.60	22.52	24.47	23.53	..
Chemicals, petroleum, rubber & plastic	18.61	18.84	20.59	19.64	..
Stone, clay & glass	18.78	18.86	20.66	19.56	..
Primary metal manufacturing	17.27	17.53	19.18	18.58	..
Fabricated metal, machinery & equipment	17.31	17.53	19.39	18.42	..
Miscellaneous manufacturing	17.13	17.38	18.80	17.64	..

Note: Total manufacturing 1995 = 24.19

Source: US Department of Labor.

Labour cost composition, 1995

Percentage

Pay for time worked:	81.6
Social insurance and other labour taxes:	5.8
Bonuses, holiday pay and other payments:	12.6

Source: US Department of Labor.

Wage dispersion by industry group, 1993

Total manufacturing = 100

High-technology industries:	112
Medium-technology industries:	101
Low-technology industries:	97

Source: OECD, STAN database.

Minimum wage, 1993

Statutory wage:	None
Governing source:	Collective agreements

Source: Various sources.

DENMARK (continued)

	Compensation per employed person (US$)					Unit labour shares (per cent)				
ISIC	**1989**	**1990**	**1991**	**1992**	**1993**	**1989**	**1990**	**1991**	**1992**	**1993**
Total manufacturing	23 105	28 713	28 900	31 678	30 088	0.71	0.71	0.70	0.68	0.68
Food, beverages & tobacco	23 283	28 670	29 040	31 926	28 943	0.61	0.60	0.60	0.58	0.58
Textiles, wearing apparel & leather	17 192	21 176	21 193	23 247	20 708	0.74	0.73	0.69	0.69	0.69
Wood, cork & furniture	19 021	23 578	23 128	25 099	23 625	0.75	0.75	0.74	0.68	0.68
Paper, printing & publishing	28 019	35 164	35 573	38 684	36 199	0.79	0.80	0.80	0.74	0.74
Chemicals	26 220	32 736	33 405	36 809	34 336	0.57	0.56	0.56	0.54	0.54
Non-metallic mineral products	23 609	30 000	30 461	33 882	30 939	0.67	0.67	0.67	0.66	0.66
Basic metal industries	24 818	30 024	30 226	33 150	28 156	0.70	0.68	0.71	0.72	0.72
Fabricated metal products & machinery	22 975	28 556	28 577	31 322	30 842	0.79	0.80	0.80	0.79	0.79
Other manufacturing	18 133	22 498	22 904	25 228	26 347	0.52	0.54	0.53	0.47	0.47

Source: OECD, STAN database.

Hourly compensation costs
In US$

SIC	1990	1991	1992	1993	1994
Total manufacturing	21.03	21.25	19.92	16.56	19.19
Food, beverages & tobacco	18.80	18.78	17.35	14.37	16.99
Textile, wearing apparel & leather	15.16	15.63	14.67	12.26	13.61
Lumber, wood products & furniture	18.59	18.69	17.68	14.77	16.25
Paper, printing and publishing	24.93	25.22	23.80	20.07	22.89
Chemicals, petroleum, rubber & plastic	20.56	20.48	19.05	15.73	19.00
Stone, clay & glass	20.40	19.99	18.56	15.11	16.85
Primary metal manufacturing	24.18	25.80	21.96	18.52	21.51
Fabricated metal, machinery & equipment	20.25	20.37	18.90	15.67	17.86
Miscellaneous manufacturing	..	..	..	..	..

Note: Total manufacturing 1995 = 24.78
Source: US Department of Labor.

Labour cost composition, 1995
Percentage

Pay for time worked:	55.5
Social insurance and other labour taxes:	25.4
Bonuses, holiday pay and other payments:	19.1

Source: US Department of Labor.

Wage dispersion by industry group, 1993
Total manufacturing = 100

High-technology industries:	109
Medium-technology industries:	102
Low-technology industries:	98

Source: OECD, STAN database.

Minimum wage, 1993

Statutory wage:	None
Governing source:	Collective agreements

Source: Various sources.

FINLAND (continued)

	Compensation per employed person (US$)					Unit labour shares (per cent)				
ISIC	1989	1990	1991	1992	1993	1989	1990	1991	1992	1993
Total manufacturing	28 732	35 690	34 356	32 060	29 451	0.58	0.63	0.70	0.64	0.64
Food, beverages & tobacco	27 607	33 735	33 267	31 099	26 858	0.59	0.61	0.59	0.57	0.57
Textiles, wearing apparel & leather	19 259	23 047	22 325	20 653	20 667	0.74	0.79	0.80	0.73	0.73
Wood, cork & furniture	23 455	29 069	26 481	23 967	22 818	0.62	0.63	0.79	0.64	0.64
Paper, printing & publishing	33 721	41 672	40 876	37 814	32 981	0.54	0.64	0.76	0.68	0.68
Chemicals	31 683	38 848	37 551	34 790	30 263	0.46	0.49	0.53	0.54	0.54
Non-metallic mineral products	28 275	35 505	33 291	31 842	28 528	0.49	0.56	0.63	0.63	0.63
Basic metal industries	33 173	41 296	39 731	37 784	33 013	0.41	0.58	0.68	0.54	0.54
Fabricated metal products & machinery	29 527	36 798	34 850	32 513	31 337	0.64	0.66	0.75	0.67	0.67
Other manufacturing	20 460	25 936	25 212	25 389	21 506	0.56	0.62	0.66	0.67	0.67

Source: OECD, STAN database.

HUNGARY

Hourly compensation costs

In US$

SIC	1989	1990	1991	1992	1993
Total manufacturing	..	..	..	..	..
Food, beverages & tobacco	..	..	..	..	..
Textile, wearing apparel & leather	..	..	..	..	..
Lumber, wood products & furniture	..	..	..	..	..
Paper, printing and publishing	..	..	..	..	..
Chemicals, petroleum, rubber & plastic	..	..	..	..	..
Stone, clay & glass	..	..	..	..	..
Primary metal manufacturing	..	..	..	..	..
Fabricated metal, machinery & equipment	..	..	..	..	..
Miscellaneous manufacturing	..	..	..	..	..

Source: Central Statistical Office of Hungary.

Labour cost composition, 1993

Percentage

Pay for time worked:	..
Social insurance and other labour taxes:	30.4
Bonuses, holiday pay and other payments:	25.1

Source: Central Statistical Office of Hungary.

Wage dispersion by industry group, 1993

Total manufacturing = 100

High-technology industries:	..
Medium-technology industries:	..
Low-technology industries:	..

Minimum wage, 1992

Statutory wage:	Ft 9000 monthly
Governing source:	..

Source: Central Statistical Office of Hungary.

HUNGARY (continued)

	Compensation per employed person (US$)					Unit labour shares (per cent)				
ISIC	1989	1990	1991	1992	1993	1989	1990	1991	1992	1993
Total manufacturing	..	..	..	486.9	500.0	..	..	..	..	..
Food, beverages & tobacco	..	..	..	485.8	511.3	..	..	..	..	..
Textiles, wearing apparel & leather	..	..	..	361.5	318.5	..	..	..	..	..
Wood, cork & furniture	..	..	..	..	..	..	..	..	..	..
Paper, printing & publishing	..	..	..	..	..	..	..	..	..	..
Chemicals	..	..	..	..	..	..	..	..	..	..
Non-metallic mineral products	..	..	..	474.6	513.9	..	..	..	..	..
Basic metal industries	..	..	..	529.6	508.1	..	..	..	..	..
Fabricated metal products & machinery	..	..	..	475.4	532.7	..	..	..	..	..
Other manufacturing	..	..	..	..	..	..	..	..	..	..

Source: Central Statistical Office of Hungary.

MEXICO

Hourly compensation costs

In US$

SIC	1990	1991	1992	1993	1994
Total manufacturing	1.58	1.84	2.17	2.40	2.47
Food, beverages & tobacco	1.35	1.61	1.83	2.04	2.21
Textile, wearing apparel & leather	1.32	1.52	1.81	1.96	1.98
Lumber, wood products & furniture	0.98	1.14	1.33	1.54	1.49
Paper, printing and publishing	1.57	1.88	2.28	2.51	2.50
Chemicals, petroleum, rubber & plastic	2.29	2.66	3.18	3.58	3.67
Stone, clay & glass	1.54	1.79	2.12	2.46	2.52
Primary metal manufacturing	2.63	2.76	3.44	3.66	3.79
Fabricated metal, machinery & equipment	1.61	1.89	2.26	2.50	2.52
Miscellaneous manufacturing	1.15	1.36	1.59	1.86	1.76

Note: Total manufacturing 1995 = 1.51
Source: US Department of Labor.

Labour cost composition, 1995

Percentage

Pay for time worked	..
Social insurance and other labour taxes:	11.9
Bonuses, holiday pay and other payments:	..

Source: US Department of Labor.

Wage dispersion by industry group, 1993

Total manufacturing = 100

High-technology industries:	133
Medium-technology industries:	139
Low-technology industries:	82

Source: OECD, STAN database.

Minimum wage, 1993

Statutory wage:	..
Governing source:	..

Source: Various sources.

MEXICO (continued)

ISIC	Compensation per employed person (US$)					Unit labour shares (per cent)				
	1989	1990	1991	1992	1993	1989	1990	1991	1992	1993
Total manufacturing	4 530	5 199	6 258	7 647	..	0.22	0.24	0.25	0.27	..
Food, beverages & tobacco	3 083	3 603	4 447	5 443	..	0.16	0.17	0.18	0.20	..
Textiles, wearing apparel & leather	3 366	3 786	4 560	5 459	..	0.27	0.28	0.30	0.34	..
Wood, cork & furniture	2 517	2 833	3 295	3 860	..	0.16	0.18	0.19	0.21	..
Paper, printing & publishing	4 495	4 978	6 006	7 315	..	0.17	0.18	0.19	0.22	..
Chemicals	7 106	7 992	9 565	12 054	..	0.25	0.27	0.28	0.31	..
Non-metallic mineral products	4 070	4 774	5 959	7 349	..	0.20	0.21	0.21	0.22	..
Basic metal industries	8 182	9 492	10 893	14 195	..	0.22	0.23	0.25	0.30	..
Fabricated metal products & machinery	5 675	6 544	7 890	9 723	..	0.29	0.31	0.30	0.34	..
Other manufacturing	3 497	3 777	4 318	4 326	..	0.19	0.19	0.20	0.17	..

Source: OECD, STAN database.

NETHERLANDS

Hourly compensation costs

In US$

SIC	1990	1991	1992	1993	1994
Total manufacturing	18.29	18.30	20.34	20.05	20.92
Food, beverages & tobacco	18.94	19.05	21.09	20.82	..
Textile, wearing apparel & leather	14.86	14.75	16.56	16.49	..
Lumber, wood products & furniture	15.54	15.39	17.10	17.35	..
Paper, printing and publishing	20.17	19.92	22.17	21.90	..
Chemicals, petroleum, rubber & plastic	..	..	..	..	..
Stone, clay & glass	18.03	18.15	20.36	20.09	..
Primary metal manufacturing	21.86	22.32	24.92	24.18	..
Fabricated metal, machinery & equipment	17.18	17.27	19.27	18.90	..
Miscellaneous manufacturing	..	..	..	..	..

Note: Total manufacturing 1995 = 24.18

Source: US Department of Labor.

Labour cost composition, 1995

Percentage

Pay for time worked:	57.0
Social insurance and other labour taxes:	23.2
Bonuses, holiday pay and other payments:	19.7

Source: US Department of Labor.

Wage dispersion by industry group, 1993

Total manufacturing = 100

High-technology industries:	111
Medium-technology industries:	111
Low-technology industries:	92

Source: OECD, STAN database.

Minimum wage, 1992

Statutory wage:	FL 2 133.3 monthly
Governing source:	Ministry of Labour

Source: Various sources.

NETHERLANDS (continued)

	Compensation per employed person (US$)					Unit labour shares (per cent)				
ISIC	1989	1990	1991	1992	1993	1989	1990	1991	1992	1993
Total manufacturing	27 148	33 054	33 510	37 453	34 744	0.57	0.57	0.58	0.58	0.58
Food, beverages & tobacco	24 316	29 551	30 254	33 655	30 739	0.58	0.57	0.57	0.52	0.52
Textiles, wearing apparel & leather	20 728	25 308	25 015	27 594	27 975	0.68	0.67	0.69	0.72	0.72
Wood, cork & furniture	20 258	23 764	24 691	28 190	26 261	0.73	0.71	0.71	0.73	0.72
Paper, printing & publishing	27 050	33 106	33 747	37 386	34 860	0.64	0.63	0.64	0.66	0.66
Chemicals	33 088	41 685	42 366	47 029	42 620	0.41	0.41	0.42	0.43	0.43
Non-metallic mineral products	26 986	32 455	33 445	37 298	35 337	0.52	0.53	0.57	0.57	0.56
Basic metal industries	34 766	40 671	42 465	46 942	47 545	0.45	0.46	0.50	0.52	0.52
Fabricated metal products & machinery	27 274	33 065	33 166	37 367	34 508	0.65	0.66	0.66	0.67	0.67
Other manufacturing	21 649	25 741	26 424	29 577	28 720	0.61	0.63	0.60	0.60	0.60

Source: OECD, STAN database.

NEW ZEALAND

Hourly compensation costs

In US$

SIC	1990	1991	1992	1993	1994
Total manufacturing	8.33	8.36	7.91	8.01	8.93
Food, beverages & tobacco	..	..	..	..	..
Textile, wearing apparel & leather	..	..	..	..	..
Lumber, wood products & furniture	..	..	..	..	..
Paper, printing and publishing	..	..	..	..	..
Chemicals, petroleum, rubber & plastic	..	..	..	..	..
Stone, clay & glass	..	..	..	..	..
Primary metal manufacturing	..	..	..	..	..
Fabricated metal, machinery & equipment	..	..	..	..	..
Miscellaneous manufacturing	..	..	..	..	..

Note: Total manufacturing 1995 = 10.11

Source: US Department of Labor.

Labour cost composition, 1995

Percentage

Pay for time worked:	81.6
Social insurance and other labour taxes:	6.0
Bonuses, holiday pay and other payments:	12.4

Source: US Department of Labor.

Wage dispersion by industry group, 1993

Total manufacturing = 100

High-technology industries:	91
Medium-technology industries:	104
Low-technology industries:	100

Source: OECD, STAN database.

Minimum wage, 1992

Statutory wage:	44% of average wage
Governing source:	State legislation

Source: Various sources.

NEW ZEALAND (continued)

	Compensation per employed person (US$)					Unit labour shares (per cent)				
ISIC	1989	1990	1991	1992	1993	1989	1990	1991	1992	1993
Total manufacturing	15 420	17 119	17 910	18 241	19 673	0.56	0.53	0.55	0.55	0.54
Food, beverages & tobacco	16 204	16 255	18 123	17 018	19 427	0.46	0.45	0.45	0.44	0.44
Textiles, wearing apparel & leather	10 130	11 750	10 642	12 415	13 345	0.75	0.69	0.65	0.66	0.65
Wood, cork & furniture	13 511	15 801	15 604	16 000	17 899	0.68	0.67	0.70	0.70	0.69
Paper, printing & publishing	20 438	22 252	25 349	23 109	26 194	0.60	0.56	0.56	0.57	0.57
Chemicals	17 360	20 307	21 679	22 595	25 442	0.43	0.42	0.50	0.47	0.46
Non-metallic mineral products	17 050	19 816	23 087	23 938	25 421	0.56	0.55	0.54	0.55	0.54
Basic metal industries	26 326	29 491	31 413	34 645	34 148	0.97	0.68	0.79	0.75	0.75
Fabricated metal products & machinery	14 247	16 399	15 999	17 507	17 218	0.63	0.60	0.63	0.62	0.62
Other manufacturing	10 681	12 488	11 052	11 393	11 806	0.49	0.52	0.50	0.51	0.51

Source: OECD, STAN database.

NORWAY

Hourly compensation costs

In US$

SIC	1990	1991	1992	1993	1994
Total manufacturing	21.47	21.63	23.03	20.21	20.97
Food, beverages & tobacco	19.97	20.24	21.66	18.99	19.66
Textile, wearing apparel & leather	..	..	..	..	..
Lumber, wood products & furniture	18.42	18.44	19.15	16.90	17.67
Paper, printing and publishing	..	..	..	..	..
Chemicals, petroleum, rubber & plastic	22.29	22.94	24.40	21.57	21.93
Stone, clay & glass	21.32	21.27	22.60	19.45	20.33
Primary metal manufacturing	22.85	23.28	24.84	21.64	22.73
Fabricated metal, machinery & equipment	21.45	20.46	23.02	20.34	21.12
Miscellaneous manufacturing	..	..	..	..	..

Note: Total manufacturing 1995 = 24.38
Source: US Department of Labor.

Labour cost composition, 1995

Percentage

Pay for time worked:	70.8
Social insurance and other labour taxes:	16.9
Bonuses, holiday pay and other payments:	12.3

Source: US Department of Labor.

Wage dispersion by industry group, 1993

Total manufacturing = 100

High-technology industries:	120
Medium-technology industries:	120
Low-technology industries:	94

Source: OECD, STAN database.

Minimum wage, 1993

Statutory wage:	None
Governing source:	Collective agreements

Source: Various sources.

NORWAY (continued)

	Compensation per employed person (US$)					Unit labour shares (per cent)				
ISIC	1989	1990	1991	1992	1993	1989	1990	1991	1992	1993
Total manufacturing	30 323	35 453	36 036	38 849	35 020	0.66	0.69	0.69	0.69	0.69
Food, beverages & tobacco	27 303	32 183	32 656	35 256	28 899	0.57	0.55	0.50	0.50	0.50
Textiles, wearing apparel & leather	20 442	24 356	24 705	26 677	21 000	0.85	0.83	0.79	0.79	0.78
Wood, cork & furniture	23 821	27 936	28 171	30 051	26 421	0.77	0.74	0.80	0.80	0.80
Paper, printing & publishing	33 377	38 789	39 112	41 546	38 962	0.69	0.70	0.72	0.72	0.72
Chemicals	33 089	38 961	39 635	42 273	37 850	0.53	0.51	0.55	0.57	0.56
Non-metallic mineral products	29 315	34 831	35 081	37 247	33 202	0.66	0.67	0.74	0.74	0.74
Basic metal industries	33 643	39 526	40 563	43 224	38 170	0.40	0.62	0.72	0.72	0.71
Fabricated metal products & machinery	32 050	37 115	37 807	41 231	38 988	0.83	0.85	0.81	0.82	0.81
Other manufacturing	27 264	32 501	32 315	34 645	31 038	0.80	0.83	0.63	0.63	0.63

Source: OECD, STAN database.

PORTUGAL

Hourly compensation costs
In US$

SIC	1989	1990	1991	1992	1993
Total manufacturing	2.97	3.77	4.24	5.17	4.50
Food, beverages & tobacco	2.78	..	..	..	..
Textile, wearing apparel & leather	2.31	..	..	..	..
Lumber, wood products & furniture	2.19	..	..	..	..
Paper, printing and publishing	3.64	..	..	..	..
Chemicals, petroleum, rubber & plastic	4.12	..	..	..	..
Stone, clay & glass	3.21	..	..	..	..
Primary metal manufacturing	3.94	..	..	..	..
Fabricated metal, machinery & equipment	3.90	..	..	..	..
Miscellaneous manufacturing	2.16	..	..	..	..

Note: Total manufacturing 1994 = 4.60; 1995 = 5.35
Source: US Department of Labour.

Labour cost composition, 1995
Percentage

Pay for time worked	..
Social insurance and other labour taxes:	23.4
Bonuses, holiday pay and other payments:	..

Source: US Department of Labor.

Wage dispersion by industry group, 1993
Total manufacturing = 100

High-technology industries:	144
Medium-technology industries:	104
Low-technology industries:	96

Source: OECD, STAN database.

Minimum wage, 1992

Statutory wage:	ESC 44 500 monthly
Governing source:	Permanent Council of Social Consultation

Source: Various sources.

PORTUGAL (continued)

ISIC	Compensation per employed person (US$)					Unit labour shares (per cent)				
	1989	1990	1991	1992	1993	1989	1990	1991	1992	1993
Total manufacturing	6 287	8 108	..	..	..	0.42	0.43	..	..	..
Food, beverages & tobacco	5 459	7 149	8 392	10 187	..	0.26	0.24	0.25	0.25	..
Textiles, wearing apparel & leather	5 259	6 711	8 505	10 999	..	0.46	0.48	0.47	0.46	..
Wood, cork & furniture	3 920	4 714	6 172	8 215	..	0.40	0.39	0.40	0.40	..
Paper, printing & publishing	9 337	11 846	..	..	..	0.31	0.39	..	..	..
Chemicals	9 914	12 630	..	..	..	0.43	0.57	..	..	..
Non-metallic mineral products	6 890	9 219	10 554	13 537	..	0.44	0.50	0.50	0.50	..
Basic metal industries	10 349	12 432	13 371	19 549	..	0.40	0.33	0.34	0.34	..
Fabricated metal products & machinery	8 009	10 494	..	..	..	0.56	0.52	..	..	..
Other manufacturing	4 907	6 550	..	..	..	0.55	0.54	..	..	..

Source: OECD, STAN database.

SPAIN

Hourly compensation costs
In US$

SIC	1990	1991	1992	1993	1994
Total manufacturing	11.33	12.20	13.37	11.50	11.39
Food, beverages & tobacco	10.91	11.77	12.91	10.87	10.72
Textile, wearing apparel & leather	8.34	8.84	9.68	8.20	7.97
Lumber, wood products & furniture	7.99	8.77	9.62	8.27	7.96
Paper, printing and publishing	11.73	12.45	13.47	11.91	11.85
Chemicals, petroleum, rubber & plastic	13.52	14.53	15.94	13.31	13.32
Stone, clay & glass	11.05	12.04	13.28	11.41	11.38
Primary metal manufacturing	14.73	16.12	18.08	15.45	15.37
Fabricated metal, machinery & equipment	12.28	13.23	14.50	12.66	12.60
Miscellaneous manufacturing	10.15	10.85	11.74	10.05	9.61

Note: Total manufacturing 1995 = 12.70
Source: US Department of Labor.

Labour cost composition, 1995
Percentage

Pay for time worked:	..
Social insurance and other labour taxes:	25.0
Bonuses, holiday pay and other payments:	..

Source: US Department of Labor.

Wage dispersion by industry group, 1993
Total manufacturing = 100

High-technology industries:	137
Medium-technology industries:	190
Low-technology industries:	89

Source: OECD, STAN database.

Minimum wage, 1992

Statutory wage:	Pta 56 280 monthly
Governing source:	Government decree

Source: Various sources.

SPAIN (continued)

	Compensation per employed person (US$)					Unit labour shares (per cent)				
ISIC	1989	1990	1991	1992	1993	1989	1990	1991	1992	1993
Total manufacturing	15 983	19 951	20 873	22 511	..	0.48	0.51	0.58	0.60	0.58
Food, beverages & tobacco	14 107	17 455	18 401	..	..	0.35	0.36	0.41	0.43	0.41
Textiles, wearing apparel & leather	10 933	13 710	13 581	..	..	0.59	0.64	0.66	0.69	0.67
Wood, cork & furniture	8 108	10 109	10 396	..	..	0.65	0.68	0.77	0.80	0.78
Paper, printing & publishing	17 156	21 282	23 398	..	..	0.56	0.59	0.67	0.70	0.68
Chemicals	22 914	28 774	30 353	..	..	0.31	0.32	0.35	0.37	0.36
Non-metallic mineral products	16 975	21 252	22 092	..	..	0.45	0.46	0.52	0.55	0.53
Basic metal industries	25 543	31 704	33 416	..	..	0.44	0.56	0.63	0.66	0.64
Fabricated metal products & machinery	18 361	22 918	23 956	..	..	0.65	0.68	0.80	0.83	0.81
Other manufacturing	12 276	15 680	17 813	..	..	0.58	0.58	0.60	0.62	0.61

Source: OECD, STAN database.

Hourly compensation costs

In US$

SIC	1990	1991	1992	1993	1994
Total manufacturing	20.93	22.15	24.59	17.70	18.86
Food, beverages & tobacco	19.93	20.95	23.59	16.95	18.07
Textile, wearing apparel & leather	17.86	18.88	21.12	15.24	16.12
Lumber, wood products & furniture	19.69	20.77	23.24	16.72	17.67
Paper, printing and publishing	23.82	25.07	28.13	20.18	21.37
Chemicals, petroleum, rubber & plastic	21.19	22.18	24.27	17.87	19.14
Stone, clay & glass	21.44	22.32	24.43	17.41	18.54
Primary metal manufacturing	22.79	23.42	25.25	18.70	20.06
Fabricated metal, machinery & equipment	20.49	21.82	24.17	17.32	18.50
Miscellaneous manufacturing	19.08	19.43	21.45	15.47	16.50

Note: Total manufacturing 1995 = 21.36
Source: US Department of Labor.

Labour cost composition, 1995

Percentage

Pay for time worked:	59.7
Social insurance and other labour taxes:	28.3
Bonuses, holiday pay and other payments:	11.9

Source: US Department of Labor.

Wage dispersion by industry group, 1993

Total manufacturing = 100

High-technology industries:	118
Medium-technology industries:	106
Low-technology industries:	91

Source: OECD, STAN database.

Minimum wage, 1993

Statutory wage:	None
Governing source:	Collective agreements

Source: Various sources.

SWEDEN (continued)

	Compensation per employed person (US$)					Unit labour shares (per cent)				
ISIC	**1989**	**1990**	**1991**	**1992**	**1993**	**1989**	**1990**	**1991**	**1992**	**1993**
Total manufacturing	28 576	34 248	36 309	39 563	35 772	0.70	0.72	0.76	0.75	0.75
Food, beverages & tobacco	26 325	30 715	33 459	36 679	30 658	0.58	0.56	0.56	0.51	0.51
Textiles, wearing apparel & leather	20 876	25 377	26 260	24 232	19 758	0.78	0.76	0.74	0.69	0.69
Wood, cork & furniture	25 259	30 111	31 368	33 831	29 389	0.62	0.62	0.72	0.71	0.71
Paper, printing & publishing	31 982	38 462	39 696	42 106	34 677	0.65	0.71	0.74	0.71	0.71
Chemicals	32 280	36 476	40 038	44 246	40 340	0.52	0.52	0.50	0.49	0.49
Non-metallic mineral products	28 910	35 337	36 593	40 446	35 039	0.64	0.66	0.69	0.69	0.69
Basic metal industries	31 597	37 071	39 053	43 844	41 636	0.70	0.78	0.91	1.11	1.10
Fabricated metal products & machinery	29 046	35 364	37 527	41 955	39 633	0.76	0.79	0.86	0.85	0.85
Other manufacturing	18 041	21 687	23 619	22 879	20 622	3.00	2.89	2.87	2.66	2.66

Source: OECD, STAN database.

BACKGROUND NOTES TO COUNTRY TABLES

General

The sources of the data presented in country tables are:

- US Department of Labor (1996), *Bureau of Labour Statistics Report 909*, June. Hourly compensation costs and labour cost composition (1994 data).
- OECD (1995), *Industry and Technology: Scoreboard of Indicators 1995.* Wage dispersion by industry group (1993 data).
- OECD (1995), *The OECD STAN Database for Industrial Analysis.* Compensation per employee and unit labour costs.
- OECD (1994), *Employment Outlook,* and Institute of Personnel Management (1993). *Pay and Benefits*, London. Minimum wage (1993 data).

Hourly compensation costs

Hourly compensation is defined as: *i)* all payments made directly to the worker – pay for time worked (basic time and piece rates plus overtime premiums, regularly paid premiums and bonuses, and cost of living adjustments), pay for time not worked (vacations, holidays, and other leave except sick leave), irregular bonuses, and selected social allowances – before payroll deductions of any kind; and *ii)* employer expenditures for legally required insurance programmes and contractual and private benefit plans. In addition, for some countries compensation is adjusted for other taxes on payrolls or employment, even if they do not finance programmes that directly benefit workers, because such taxes are regarded as labour costs.

The data concern production workers, which generally include those employees who are engaged in: fabricating, assembly and related activities; material handling, warehousing, and shipping; maintenance and repair; janitorial and guard services; auxiliary production (*e.g.* power plants); and other services closely related to the above activities.

The industrial classification is according to the 1987 US Standard Industrial Classification (SIC). The following are the major differences in industrial classification systems, in worker coverage, and other variations from the survey coverage (exclusions for comparability).

United States

(i) Lumber, wood products & furniture includes metal furniture, while in other countries metal furniture is classified under fabricated metal products.

Japan

(i) Lumber, wood products & furniture includes metal furniture, while in other countries metal furniture is classified under fabricated metal products;

(ii) Miscellaneous manufacturing includes ordnance.

Germany

(i) Refers to former West Germany;

(ii) Excludes workers in establishments considered handicraft manufacturers.

France

(i) Chemicals, petroleum, rubber & plastic excludes petroleum refining.

Canada

(i) Lumber, wood products & furniture includes metal furniture, while in other countries metal furniture is classified under fabricated metal products;

(ii) Fabricated metal , machinery and equipment excludes instruments and related products;

(iii) Miscellaneous manufacturing includes instruments and related products.

Australia

(i) Compensation relates to production workers and non-production workers other than those in managerial, executive, professional, and higher supervisory positions;

(ii) Textile, apparel, and leather products exclude leather products except footwear.

Austria

(i) Excludes workers in establishments considered handicraft manufacturers (all printing and miscellaneous manufacturing establishments are classified in handicrafts);

(ii) Fabricated metal products includes instruments.

Finland

(i) Includes workers in mining and electrical power plants;

(ii) Compensation excludes some obligatory training and plant facilities costs.

Netherlands

(i) Textile, apparel, and leather products excludes leather and leather products.

New Zealand

(i) Hourly earnings are the mid-point of an estimated production worker earnings range.

Norway

(i) Pay for time worked includes irregular bonuses;

(ii) Compensation excludes some obligatory training and plant facilities costs.

Portugal

(i) Direct pay excludes profit-sharing bonuses but includes social allowances;

(ii) Profit-sharing bonuses are included in social insurance expenditures.

Spain

(i) Leather and leather products includes rubber and plastic footwear;

(ii) Primary metal manufacturing excludes foundries.

Hourly compensation costs for production workers in manufacturing
1989

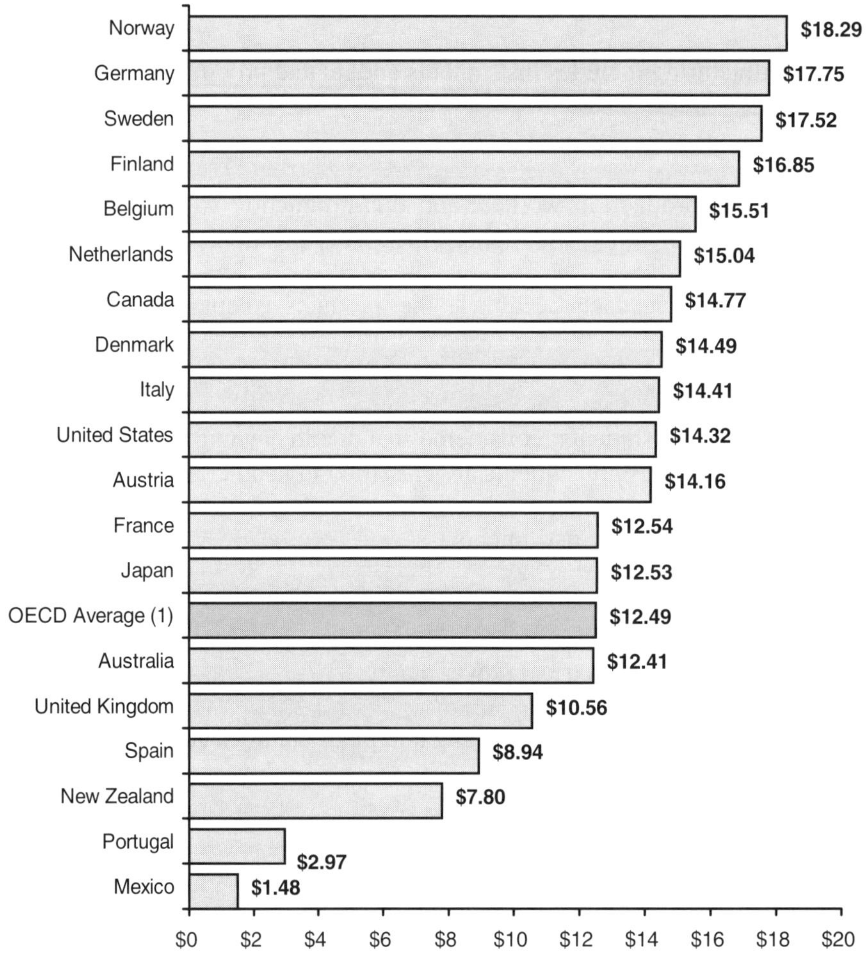

1995

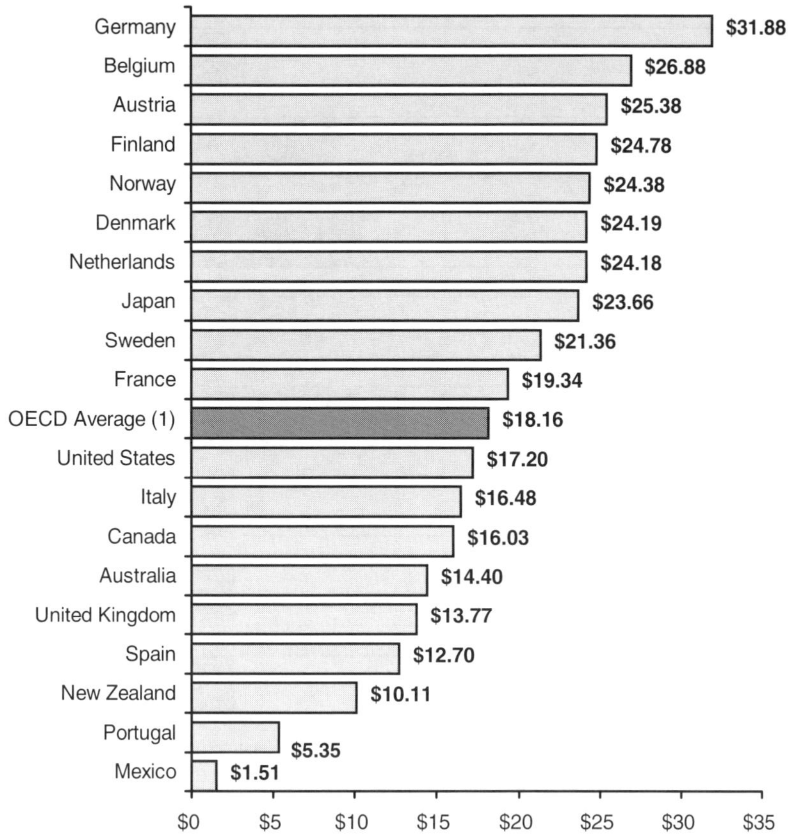

Note: Trade-weighted average of OECD including: Canada, Mexico, Australia, Japan, New Zealand and all European countries. Trade weights used are the sum of US imports of manufactured products for consumption (customs value) and US exports of domestic manufactured products (free along side value) in 1992.

Source: US Department of Labor.

Labour cost composition

Hourly compensation costs consist of pay for time worked; bonuses, holiday pay and other payments; and social insurance and other labour taxes. *i)* Pay for time worked is composed of basic time and piece rates plus overtime premiums; shift differentials; other premia and bonuses paid regularly each pay period; cost of living adjustments; and other direct pay *ii)* Bonuses, holiday pay, and other payments include pay for time not worked (vacations, holidays and other leave except sick leave); seasonal and irregular bonuses and other special payments; selected social allowances; and the cost of payments in kind. *iii)* Social insurance and other labour taxes include employer expenditures for legally required insurance programmes; contractual and private benefit plans; and other taxes on payrolls or employment.

Components of hourly compensation costs for production workers in manufacturing

1995

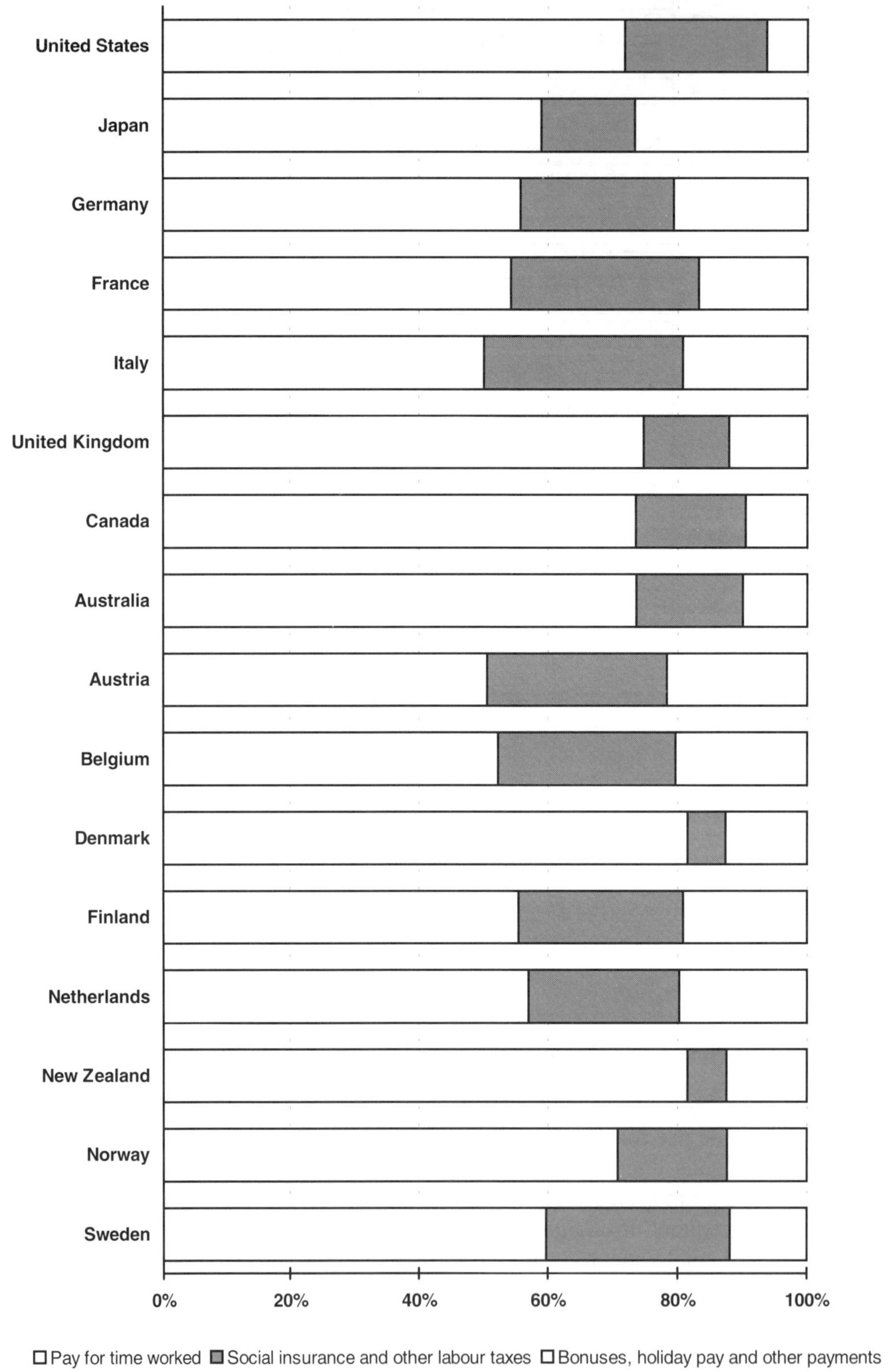

Source: US Department of Labor.

Wage dispersion by industry group

The wage dispersion indicator used here is based on compensation per employee values by industry group relative to total manufacturing. The aggregation scheme for classifying manufacturing industries into groups selected here, in order to demonstrate wage dispersion, is based on technology. Industries are grouped on the basis of their R&D intensity in the OECD area as a whole, defined as the ratio of business-enterprise R&D to production. On this basis the following industry groups (International Standard Industrial Classification, ISIC) emerge:

- *High-technology:* Aerospace (ISIC 3845), computers and office equipment (ISIC 3825), communication equipment and semiconductors (ISIC 3832), electrical machinery (ISIC 383-3832), pharmaceuticals (ISIC 3522), scientific instruments (ISIC 385).
- *Medium-technology:* Chemicals excluding drugs (ISIC 351+352-3522), rubber and plastic products (ISIC 355+356), non-ferrous metals (ISIC 372), non-electrical machinery (ISIC 382-3825), motor vehicles (ISIC 3843), other transport equipment (ISIC 3842+3844+3849), other manufacturing (ISIC 39).
- *Low-technology:* Food, beverages, tobacco (ISIC 31), textiles, apparel and leather (ISIC 32), wood products (ISIC 33), paper and printing (ISIC 34), petroleum refining (ISIC 353+354), non-metallic mineral products (ISIC 36), iron and steel (ISIC 371), metal products (ISIC 381), shipbuilding (ISIC 3841).

Wage dispersion by industry group

Total manufacturing = 100, 1993

Country	High-technology industries	Medium-technology industries	Low-technology industries
United States	123	110	86
Japan	97	114	93
Germany	111	115	84
France	123	101	91
Italy	131	135	84
United Kingdom	111	108	91
Canada	107	107	95
Australia	107	107	95
Austria	112	101	96
Denmark	112	101	97
Finland	109	102	98
Mexico	133	139	82
Netherlands	111	111	92
New Zealand	91	104	100
Norway	120	120	94
Portugal	144	104	96
Spain	137	190	89
Sweden	118	106	91

Source: OECD, STAN database (DSTI, EAS Division), March 1995.

Minimum wage

Minimum wages are a feature of many OECD countries. They take a variety of forms: either statutory (legally imposed) or negotiated and effective. Statutory minimum wages are applied in order to provide coverage for sections of the workforce who might not be covered by negotiated agreements. There are differences in application of legislation across countries. While some countries apply a blanket minimum wage across the working population, others apply age, sector, occupational or regional criteria. Below is the situation in the countries covered in this survey in the early 1990s:

- *United States:* The federally established minimum wage in the United States serve as a nation-wide floor with individual States setting their own minimum wage in excess of the Federal minimum (*e.g.* highest State level minimum in 1989 represented 130 per cent of the Federal level). Despite recent increases the minimum wage is less than 40 per cent of the average wage. In 1993 the minimum wage stood at US$4.25 (US$3.1 in 1980 and US$4.14 in 1991). However, it is estimated that approximately 4 per cent of workers earned less than the minimum at the end of the 1980s. There is neither a statutory minimum wage nor there is evidence of an effective wage floor. However, minimum wages are decided regionally through local wage councils in each Prefecture and are adapted each year in accordance with local wage and price movements.

- *Germany:* There is no statutory minimum wage in Germany. However, the system of wage determination in operation yields minimum wages on an industry or regional basis and are legally binding on the signatory parties. The differential between minimum rates and actual pay can be high and is estimated to be 25 to 30 per cent of pay in the chemical and metalworking industries.

- *France:* The statutory minimum wage – *Salaire minimum interprofessionnel de croissance* (SMIC) – exists since the mid-1970s and applies to all employees aged 18 and over in the private sector. The SMIC is estimated to be earned by 11 per cent of employees, while the wages of a much higher percentage of workers are in fact tied to it. It is revised annually by decree after consultation among the social partners and is linked to the consumer price index. The minimum rate stood at FF 33.31 (FF 13.18 in 1980) per hour , and FF 5629.39 per month (for 169 hours worked) in March 1992.

- *Italy:* There is no statutory minimum wage in Italy. However, minimum wages by industry are set through negotiations between the employers' confederation and the main unions . These industry minima, once set, are legally binding throughout the entire sector.

- *United Kingdom:* Minimum wages were abolished in 1993 when the Wage Councils were disbanded.

- *Canada:* Statutory minimum wages are determined at the Provincial level. Regional differentials between the highest rate, for Ontario, and the lowest, for Newfoundland, are estimated to be almost 30 per cent. Overall, the ratio of the minimum wage to the average wage is low in relation to European levels. It is estimated that about 5 per cent of full-time workers were earning less than the minimum in 1987.

- *Australia:* While there is no statutory minimum wage, a relatively high effective minimum wage exists for workers belonging to particular job classifications, which is valid across all firms, irrespective of local conditions.

- *Austria:* No statutory minimum wage exists.

- *Belgium:* A statutory minimum wage is enforced for all full-time workers in the private sector. This minimum applies to those workers not covered by negotiated collective agreements. The statutory minimum wage exists in two forms: one for 21-year olds and over; and a second rate applying to the under-21s having at least six months' service. On 1 January 1992 the respective rates were BF 39 940 and BF 38 857 per month.

- *Denmark*: There is no statutory minimum wage, but collective agreements reached at the industry level set industry minima or "standard pay" for new starters. Actual pay is considered to be around 125 per cent of industry minima.

- *Finland:* In the absence of a statutory minimum wage, negotiated agreements provide for minimum wages. A tripartite system decides the minimum wage and the agreed minima is often extended to the entire economy by government decision, thereby substituting for legal minimum wages.

- *Netherlands*: A statutory minimum wage exists, applying to all those over 23 years' old, and is reviewed twice-yearly. The link between the minimum wage and prevailing wages has been on occasions broken and reinstated in recent years. In January 1992 the minimum wage stood at FL 2133.3 per month, with youth rates calculated in the 30 to 85 per cent range for 15- to 22-year olds. It is estimated that the percentage of those earning the minimum wage has fallen from 6 to 3 per cent over the last decade.

- *New Zealand*: A statutory minimum wage applies for workers over 20 years' of age. It corresponds to approximately 44 per cent of the average wage. In 1994 the government decided to implement a youth (16-19 years) minimum wage of 60 per cent of the adult minimum, at a yet unconfirmed future date.

- *Norway:* There is no statutory minimum wage in force. A minimum wage is set by bi- or tripartite system. The legislation passed in 1994 gives to a committee appointed by the government the authority to extend the provisions of national collective agreements to plant level.

- *Portugal*: A statutory minimum wage exists for all workers over 18 years' of age. Younger employees, apprentices and trainees are paid at a reduced rate. The rate is revised annually in a tripartite consultation. It is estimated that 6.5 per cent of employees earn the minimum rate. The minimum wage is not perceived to be an effective wage floor. The rate in 1992 was ESC 44 500 per month, compared with average monthly earnings of ESC 83 300.

- *Spain*: A statutory minimum wage exists at two rates – an adult rate (Ptas 56 280 monthly, 1992) and an under-18 rate (Ptas 37 170) – these rates are revised annually by decree. Changes in legislation in 1993 permit wages below the minimum rate for apprentices. It is estimated that 250 000 workers earn the minimum wage.

- *Sweden:* There is no statutory minimum wage in force. A minimum wage is set by centralised bargaining which in turn is supplemented by company arrangements. Administrative extension of agreements is possible.

Compensation per employed person

Compensation of employees is a National Accounts based definition. Relative labour compensation per employee in manufacturing is presented here through a compensation per employed person indicator.

This indicator is defined as yearly labour compensation in a particular industry or industry grouping (covering wages and salaries as well as social costs such as pensions, medical payments, etc.) in current prices divided by the number engaged, which includes the number of employees as well as self-employed, owner-proprietors, and unpaid family workers.

Industrial classification in country tables is according to the International Standard Industrial Classification (ISIC), Revision 2.

Compensation per employed person in manufacturing
1989

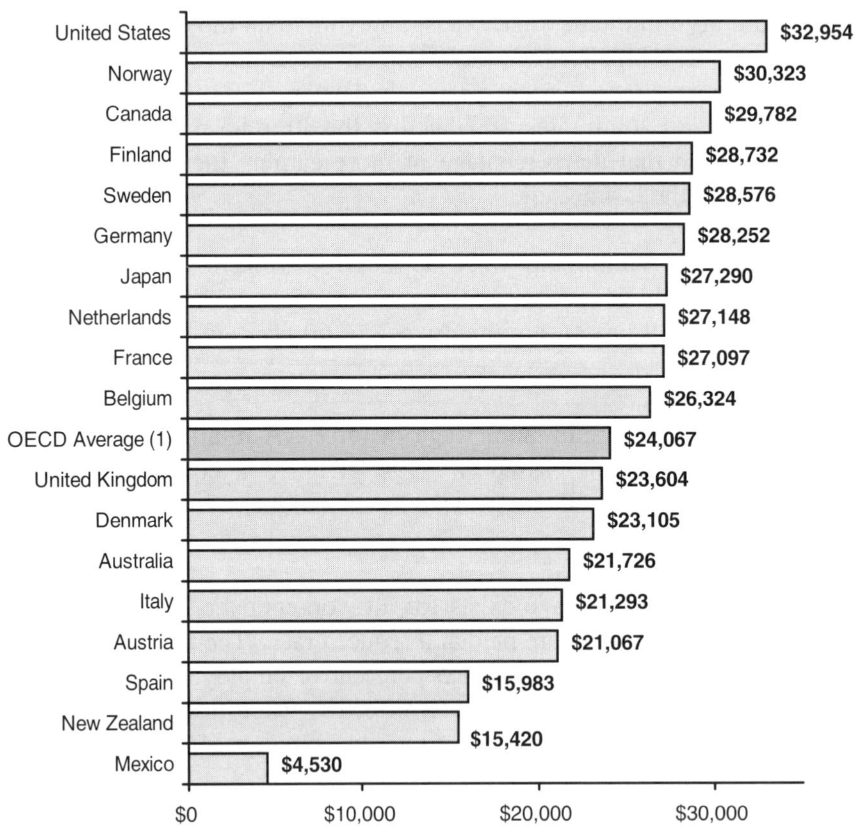

1993

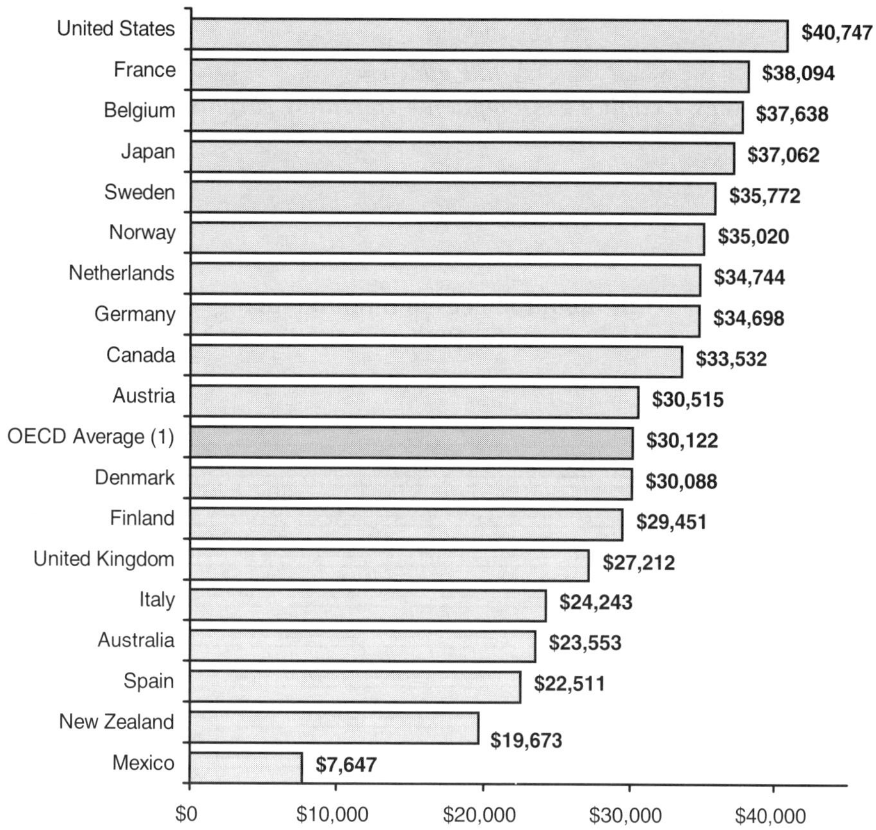

Note: Unweighted average of 18 OECD countries: Australia (1992 data), Austria (1992 data), Belgium (1992 data), Canada, Denmark, Finland, France (1992 data), Germany, Italy, Japan, Mexico (1992 data), the Netherlands, New Zealand, Norway, Spain, Sweden, the United Kingdom and the United States.
Source: OECD, STAN database (DSTI, EAS Division), August 1995.

Unit labour shares

The unit labour shares is the ratio of labour compensation to value-added. It is actually an output indicator measuring wages and salaries per unit of output. It is calculated by dividing labour compensation in current prices by current price value added and thus corresponds to the share of labour remuneration in output.

Both labour compensation and value added are National Accounts based definitions. Labour compensation includes wages and salaries as well as social costs (*e.g.* pensions, medical payments, etc.), and value-added is the gross output in an industry or an industry group less the intermediate products.

Industrial classification in the country tables is according to the International Standard Industrial Classification (ISIC), Revision 2.

For some countries, ratios for miscellaneous manufacturing (ISIC 3900) are equal to or greater than one. This results from a rather general technical problem related to the National Accounts calculation of value added. For example value added might be recorded at "producer prices" as opposed to its expression at "factor costs", which means that compensation can exceed value added if large subsidies are involved.

Value added =
compensation of employees + capital consumption + operating surplus + indirect taxes - subsidies

Unit labour shares in manufacturing
1989

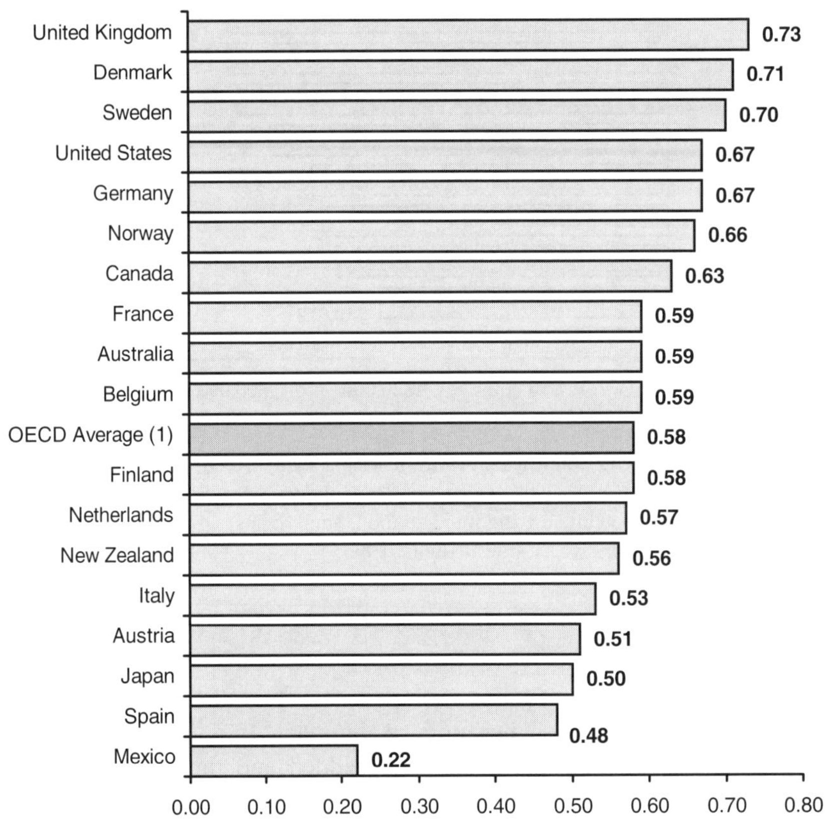

1993

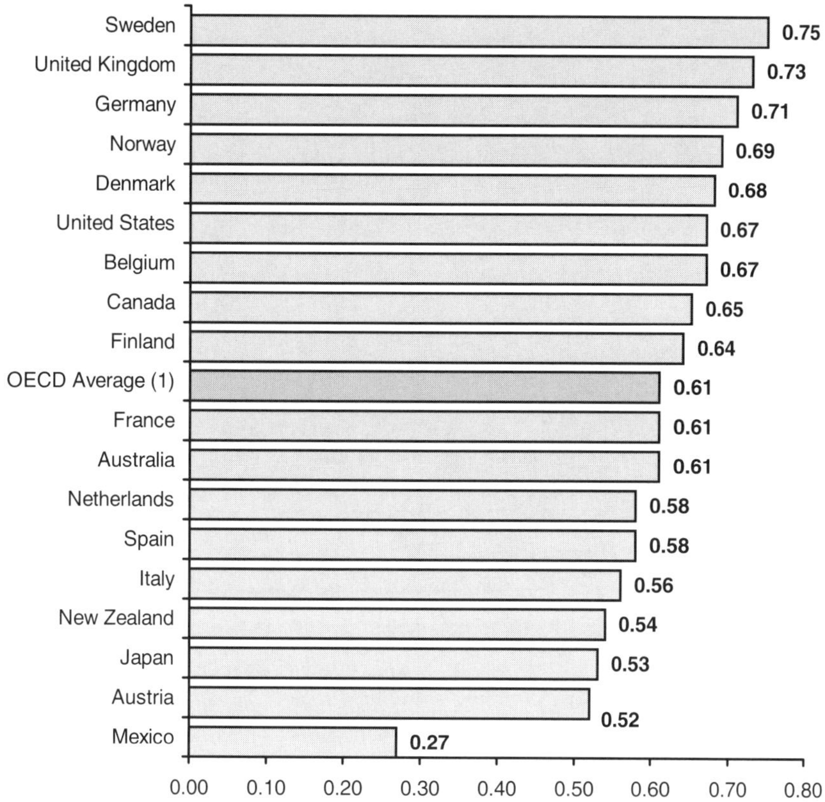

Note: Unweighted average of 18 OECD countries: Australia, Austria (1992 data), Belgium, Canada, Denmark, Finland, France (1992 data), Germany, Italy, Japan, Mexico (1992 data), the Netherlands, New Zealand, Norway, Spain, Sweden, the United Kingdom and the United States.

Source: OECD, STAN database (DSTI, EAS Division), September 1995.

ANNEX

HOURLY COMPENSATION COSTS

In US$ by three-year moving average exchange rates

JAPAN

SIC	1989	1990	1991	1992	1993
Total manufacturing	12.6	13.3	14.5	16.6	18.6
Food, beverages & tobacco	9.8	10.6	11.4	12.9	14.7
Textile, wearing apparel & leather	7.9	8.4	9.2	10.4	11.3
Lumber, wood products & furniture	10.3	10.9	11.8	13.4	15.1
Paper, printing & publishing	13.6	14.0	15.4	17.7	19.9
Chemicals, petroleum, rubber & plastic	15.4	16.4	18.6	21.0	22.9
Stone, clay & glass	13.1	13.8	15.3	17.4	19.5
Primary metal manufacturing	18.8	19.8	21.3	24.5	27.4
Fabricated metal manufacturing	13.2	14.0	15.3	17.5	19.6
Miscellaneous manufacturing	11.0	11.7	13.0	15.0	17.1

ITALY

SIC	1989	1990	1991	1992	1993
Total manufacturing	15.3	16.7	18.8	17.9	17.1
Food, beverages & tobacco	15.7	17.2	19.1	18.3	17.7
Textile, wearing apparel & leather	12.2	13.5	15.0	14.3	13.6
Lumber, wood products & furniture	13.1	14.3	16.2	15.5	14.8
Paper, printing & publishing	17.2	19.1	21.2	19.9	19.0
Chemicals, petroleum, rubber & plastic	16.7	18.5	20.4	19.3	18.5
Stone, clay & glass	14.9	16.2	18.5	17.7	16.9
Primary metal manufacturing	17.8	19.3	22.0	20.8	19.8
Fabricated metal manufacturing	15.7	17.1	19.6	18.5	17.6
Miscellaneous manufacturing	12.9	14.1	16.0	15.2	14.5

FINLAND

SIC	1989	1990	1991	1992	1993
Total manufacturing	17.6	19.8	20.8	18.8	18.4
Food, beverages & tobacco	15.7	17.7	18.4	16.3	15.9
Textile, wearing apparel & leather	12.8	14.3	15.3	13.8	13.6
Lumber, wood products & furniture	15.4	17.5	18.3	16.6	16.4
Paper, printing & publishing	20.4	23.5	24.7	22.4	22.3
Chemicals, petroleum, rubber & plastic	17.2	19.3	20.1	17.9	17.4
Stone, clay & glass	16.9	19.2	19.6	17.5	16.8
Primary metal manufacturing	19.2	22.8	25.3	20.7	20.5
Fabricated metal manufacturing	16.8	19.1	20.0	17.8	17.2
Miscellaneous manufacturing	..	..	..	..	..

Source: US Department of Labor, April 1995.

COMPENSATION PER EMPLOYED PERSON
In US$ by three-year moving average exchange rates

JAPAN

ISIC	1989	1990	1991	1992	1993
Total manufacturing	27 462	28 917	30 915	34 393	36 354
Food, beverages & tobacco	20 245	21 208	22 464	25 209	27 190
Textile, wearing apparel & leather	16 737	17 800	19 054	21 427	21 466
Wood, cork & furniture	21 038	22 613	24 309	27 259	34 701
Paper, printing & publishing	31 681	33 090	35 217	39 477	41 915
Chemicals	30 991	32 514	34 429	38 429	39 212
Non-metallic mineral products	27 732	29 089	31 033	36 380	41 206
Basic metal industries	39 641	40 801	43 199	47 403	49 270
Fabricated metal products & machinery	30 050	31 646	33 926	37 248	38 997
Other manufacturing	23 507	24 737	26 987	31 975	33 706

ITALY

ISIC	1989	1990	1991	1992	1993
Total manufacturing	22 636	25 009	28 325	27 318	25 917
Food, beverages & tobacco	22 255	24 457	27 711	26 724	25 660
Textile, wearing apparel & leather	14 793	16 320	18 295	17 331	16 229
Wood, cork & furniture	13 201	14 655	16 679	15 755	14 642
Paper, printing & publishing	27 053	30 296	33 382	33 064	32 033
Chemicals	31 573	35 192	39 972	39 563	36 898
Non-metallic mineral products	23 345	25 789	29 096	28 377	27 680
Basic metal industries	31 714	34 437	39 147	37 621	36 036
Fabricated metal products & machinery	26 172	28 777	32 890	31 693	30 215
Other manufacturing	15 589	17 419	19 300	18 292	17 071

FINLAND

ISIC	1989	1990	1991	1992	1993
Total manufacturing	30 028	33 620	33 698	30 208	32 679
Food, beverages & tobacco	28 852	31 778	32 629	29 303	29 802
Textile, wearing apparel & leather	20 127	21 710	21 897	19 460	22 933
Wood, cork & furniture	24 513	27 383	26 039	22 583	25 319
Paper, printing & publishing	35 242	39 254	40 092	35 630	36 596
Chemicals	33 112	36 593	36 831	32 781	33 580
Non-metallic mineral products	29 550	33 445	32 653	30 003	31 656
Basic metal industries	34 670	38 900	38 969	35 602	36 632
Fabricated metal products & machinery	30 859	34 663	34 182	30 636	34 772
Other manufacturing	21 283	24 431	24 729	23 923	23 863

Source: OECD, STAN database (DSTI, EAS Division), August 1995.

Chapter 7

CORPORATE TAXATION

The information provided is drawn in stylised form from extensive work by the OECD's Directorate for Financial, Fiscal and Enterprise Affairs and Price Waterhouse. It includes the information available at the time of finalisation of this report for publication.

The reader should note that the extreme complexity of corporate taxation, including international aspects and special regimes, cannot be given full justice in a compact review, and makes it difficult to evaluate individual indicators in isolation and to make fully accurate comparisons across countries. For an in-depth analysis of corporate taxation the reader is referred to publications by the OECD's Directorate for Financial, Fiscal and Enterprise Affairs (DAFFE), in particular, OECD (1991), *Taxing Profits in the Global Economy – Domestic and International Issues* and OECD (1994), *Taxation and Household Saving*. A relevant non-OECD publication is: Price Waterhouse (1995), *Information Guide: Corporate Taxes – A Worldwide Summary*, Price Waterhouse World Firm Services BV.

Introduction

Taxation is one of the important determinants of investment and financing decisions and appears to be an important framework factor for firms' competitiveness.

By adding a wedge to factor costs (capital, labour, fixed assets and inventory) the corporation tax creates an additional charge to industrial firms. By altering the cost of finance, the minimum required rate of return and the effective price of the investment, the corporation tax has an impact on firms' investment behaviour. Therefore, regarding the frame of business behaviour and performance, tax systems have both cost and decision implications.

Taxation of profits often has a considerable impact on marginal investments and their financing as well as their location both within a country and across borders. Other taxes, such as those on business properties and assets or on corporate wealth, also affect costs and thus the location of investment.

The liberalisation of international capital movements and the globalisation of business activities make international capital flows more sensitive to differences in tax regimes. At the same time, the increased interaction of these already complex systems renders their intricacies more apparent.

There is always a trade-off between other determinants of investment and the taxes involved. It is the aggregate tax liability that an investor will consider against the potential market size, the pre-tax profitability of the investment, and the strategic importance of the investment. On the other hand, this tax liability will be considered in comparison to what it would have been in other locations and how it shapes up according to the particular activity. Moreover, these questions will also be influenced by the way the investment is structured and financed.

In sum, the business decision-making process involves the answering of complex questions. Nevertheless, some of the variables that bear on investment decisions and the most important insights regarding corporate taxes can be identified.

In addition to the level of the statutory corporate income tax rates, the existence of incentives (reliefs, credits, allowances) is the most obvious criterion involved in such decisions.

The generosity of the depreciation system, the way capital gains and losses are treated, the methods used to evaluate the inventory stock, the specified provisions for R&D, conditions regarding the deductibility of expenses, restrictions on the deductibility of interest expenses, constitute the criteria regarding the provisions determining the corporate income tax base.

The possibility of creating tax-free reserves and provisions regarding carry back and forward of trading losses are additional criteria that exist in certain systems.

The degree of relief from economic double taxation and the methods used to achieve this alleviation, in addition to the withholding tax rates, constitute the criteria regarding the tax treatment of distribution of profits.

The criteria regarding international taxation considerations consist of how profits, interest and royalties paid out are treated in the home country, and the extent and nature of tax treaties and international provisions (*e.g.* withholding taxes, deferral arrangements, sourcing rules, etc.).

Other non-profit-related taxation, such as net wealth taxes, taxes on labour, taxes on property, which can adversely effect returns on investment also constitute further important criteria regarding international investment decisions.

In this context, the vast variation of tax provisions across countries is a striking feature.

The following country tables and accompanying background notes aim to provide a description of the main features of the corporate tax regimes in OECD countries. Given the wide variety of company circumstances and asset structures, quantitative averaging of tax liabilities has not been included in the scope at this stage. Moreover, for the sake of simplicity, detailed information in some important tax policy areas is excluded: these include international arrangements (*i.e.* the impact of tax treaties and the international provisions); special regimes (*i.e.* the impact on tax competition); and differential tax treatment (*i.e.* tax treatment of the corporation and its owners as determinants of the cost of capital).

The Directorate for Financial, Fiscal and Enterprise Affairs has ongoing and published work in the above-mentioned areas. Some examples include the ongoing work of the Working Party No. 8 on Tax Avoidance and Evasion of the Committee on Fiscal Affairs on Fiscal Degradation; the ongoing work of the Working Party No. 2 on Tax Policy Analysis and Tax Statistics; the publication *Taxing Profits in a Global Economy - Domestic and International Issues*; and the publication by the Centre for Co-operation with the Economies in Transition, *Taxation and Foreign Direct Investment - The Experience of the Economies in Transition.*

Corporate tax systems

The purpose of the following sections are to simplify and standardize the concepts of corporate tax systems, and to serve as a guide to interpreting the country tables.

Corporate income tax

Corporate income tax is the main tax imposed on corporations. Both statutory tax rates and the tax base influence the effective burden imposed by the corporate income tax.

Corporate income tax base

The standard corporate income tax base is the definition, adopted by central governments, of income subject to tax, *i.e.* taxable income. Taxable income is, as a rule, computed on the ordinary principles of “sound commercial accounting practice”. Income originating from all sources is normally included in the corporate income tax base. However, a number of issues arise in defining the concept of income, and in measuring the corporate tax base.

Different tax provisions have an impact on the intermediate levels of the income statement, and thus, taxable income. Some of the items typically considered in measuring the tax base and the most typical examples of the impacts of corporate income tax provisions on the income statement are listed below.

- Mandatory inventory methods or methods allowed by provisions have an impact on the cost of goods sold.
- Provisions regarding the carry forward or back of trading losses concern the gross income.

- Mandatory depreciation methods and rates or those allowed by provisions, allowances for R&D and certain other expenses (*e.g.* patents, royalties, etc.), and the deductibility of interest payments, all have an impact on operating expenses.

- Provisions regarding the exemption or deduction of domestic and foreign dividend incomes and those regarding the deduction of foreign interest (portfolio) income have an impact on investment income.

- Provisions regarding exemption or deferral of, application of a special rate on, and inflation adjustments to capital gains as well as those regarding the carry forward or back of capital losses and how these losses are offset concern extraordinary items.

- Provisions allowing the deduction of certain investments or transfers to reserves and those applying lower rates on, or deduction of, distributed dividends all result in deductions from taxable income.

Corporate income tax rate

Corporate income tax is also levied at the intermediate and local government levels. The rates applied at these levels differ from central rates and vary throughout countries. Statutory corporate income tax rates are thus a combination of these various rates. Intermediate and local level income taxes are either deductible or non-deductible from the national corporate income tax, depending on the country.

Tax credits

Tax credits are usually granted after having calculated (by applying the nominal rates to the taxable income) the corporate income tax liability. In order to determine the corporate income tax due, tax credits are subtracted from the corporate income tax liability.

Tax credits are accorded for various reasons. The most typical are: credits accorded in order to compensate for double taxation resulting from intercorporate dividends; credits accorded to compensate for the double taxation resulting from foreign source income; and, credits accorded for certain types of investment (*e.g.* environmental protection related investments, investments in certain priority regions, etc.).

Other business taxes

Other partially income related or non-income-related taxes, such as the net wealth tax, immovable property tax and labour tax, as well as social insurance charges (considered as taxes due to their compulsory nature), constitute an additional tax burden.

Final tax obligation of corporations

In this framework, the final tax obligation of a corporation (*i.e.* the total tax burden on a corporation) is the sum of the corporate income tax and other business taxes and social charges due.

CORPORATE TAXATION: COUNTRY TABLES

UNITED STATES

Corporate income tax

Corporate income tax base	Provision	Adjustment and/or exception
Cost of goods sold	Both FIFO and LIFO methods are allowed. (1)	(2)
Gross income	Trading losses can be carried back for three years and forward for 15 years. Several States do not permit carry back or forward of trading losses. (3)	A limit is placed on the amount of future income that can be offset by losses carried forward in case of change of ownership. (4)
Operating expenses	Shorter-lived equipment is entitled to depreciation using the double-declining balance method, with an optimal switch to straight-line. Longer-lived equipment, and public utility property, is depreciated using a 150% declining balance method, also with an optimal switch to straight-line. Taxpayers also may elect to use less generous straight-line method for depreciating equipment. Structures are depreciated using the straight-line method. (5)	Accelerated depreciation of automobiles and certain other property is subject to some limitations. Pollution control facilities may be entitled to rapid amortisation. (6)
Investment income	70-80 per cent deduction of domestic dividend receipts if 20-80 per cent ownership, and 100 per cent deduction in case of affiliates (over 80 per cent ownership). (7)	For foreign dividends received a deduction of foreign taxes paid may be claimed as an alternative to credit. (8)
Extraordinary items	Capital gains are taxed as ordinary income, not adjusted for inflation nor deferred if reinvested. Capital losses are offset against capital gains, carried back for three and forward for five years. (9)	Losses on depreciable business property generally are not subject to the capital loss restriction, they may offset ordinary income. (10)
Deductions from income	No deduction of distributed dividends is allowed for double taxation purposes. There are no reserve options nor investment deductions. (11)	(12)
Corporate income tax rate	The top central government rate is 35 per cent. Local and intermediate government rates vary between 4 and 17 per cent. Local taxes are deductible. The overall top rate is 41.5 per cent. (13)	Lower rates apply for small businesses and to companies with low profits. (14)
Tax credits	Tax credit is granted for foreign income taxes paid. Tax credits are given for incremental R&D expenditures. Other tax credits are granted for energy investment, real estate rehabilitation etc. (15)	(16)
Corporate income tax collection lags	Corporate income tax is collected on an annual basis in four equal instalments. (17)	Failure to pay at least 100 per cent on dates due may result in penalty. (18)

Other business taxes

Labour taxes and social charges	Social insurance and other labour taxes account for 23.1 per cent of total wage costs. (19)
Tax on immovable property	Taxes on immovable property vary throughout the country. These state and municipal taxes are deductible for federal income tax purposes. (20)
Net wealth tax	There is no net wealth tax on corporations. (21)
Other non-income taxes	There is a penalty tax on accumulated earnings. There is also an environment tax. Most States and some cities impose sale, use, and franchise taxes. (22)

JAPAN

Corporate income tax

Corporate income tax base	Provision	Adjustment and/or exception
Cost of goods sold	FIFO, LIFO, weighted average, moving average, straight average, most recent purchase, retail, and lower cost of market methods allowed. (1)	(2)
Gross income	Trading losses can be carried back for one year and forward for five years. No carry back of losses is allowed for either enterprise or inhabitants taxes. (3)	Losses incurred during the initial three-year period after establishment may be carried forward seven to ten years. (4)
Operating expenses	Methods of straight line (10%) and declining balance (3xSL) allowed for machinery and buildings (2.2% to 4.3% straight line and 3xSL declining balance). Switch over is permitted for both types of assets. (5)	On approval accelerated depreciation is available for some assets for up to five years. Accelerated depreciation is also available for inward investments and as a consequence of import incentives. (6)
Investment income	Domestic dividend receipts are exempt if the ownership is more than 25% of shares. If the ownership is less, 80 per cent of dividends received is excluded. (7)	For foreign dividends received a deduction of foreign taxes paid may be claimed as an alternative to credit. (8)
Extraordinary items	Capital gains are taxed as ordinary income, are not adjusted for inflation but may be deferred if reinvested in designated assets. Capital losses are offset against capital gains. No carry forward or back allowed. (9)	Special capital gains tax charged if the asset is held less than two and/or five years. (10)
Deductions from income	No deduction of distributed dividends is allowed for double taxation purposes. Tax-free reserves are allowed for bad debts, bonuses and retirement allowances, and for certain qualified investments. (11)	The deductibility of interest charges paid is limited in the case of thinly capitalised companies. (12)
Corporate income tax rate	Central government rate is 37.5 per cent. There are no taxes at intermediate level. The two types of local tax rates are (17.3 to 20.7%) non deductible and (12 to 13.2%) deductible. The overall top rate is 52.5 per cent. (13)	Low rates apply to small businesses. (14)
Tax credits	Tax credit corresponding to the tax on the total foreign income is granted against corporation and inhabitants taxes, but not against enterprise tax. Tax credit is allowed for incremental R&D expenditure and for total R&D expenditures of SMEs. Other credits are granted for: inward investments, energy-saving equipment, and designated equipment for SMEs. (15)	(16)
Corporate income tax collection lags	Corporate income tax is collected on an annual basis. (17)	In cases where an extension is granted, 7.3% par annum interest is charged. (18)

Other business taxes

Labour taxes and social charges	Social insurance and other labour taxes account for 13.6 per cent of total wage costs. (19)
Tax on immovable property	Real property and depreciable fixed assets are taxed at 1.4 per cent of their taxable value. There is also a land value tax of 0.3 per cent of taxable value on high value land. (20)
Net wealth tax	There is no wealth tax on corporations. (21)
Other non-income taxes	In certain designated cities companies are liable to a tax based on space and gross payroll. (22)

GERMANY

Corporate income tax

Corporate income tax base	Provision	Adjustment and/or exception
Cost of goods sold	LIFO method is allowed but FIFO method is not. (1)	Standard or average cost methods are acceptable if identification of inventories is not possible. In practice companies usually fulfil the conditions to apply FIFO. (2)
Gross income	Trading losses up to DM 10 million can be carried back for two years. Remaining losses can be carried forward to the five years following occurrence. (3)	(4)
Operating expenses	Both straight line (10%) and declining balance (3xSL) allowed for machinery. Switch over is permitted. Buildings are depreciated with straight line (2.5 to 10%) method. (5)	R&D capital expenditure is depreciated with higher rate. The rate depends on the degree of R&D relevance of the asset. Accelerated depreciation is allowed for SMEs. Certain investment incentives take the form of accelerated depreciation. (6)
Investment income	Domestic dividends receipts are taxed as ordinary income. Foreign dividend receipts from non treaty countries are taxed as ordinary income but from treaty countries are exempt. (7)	For foreign dividends received a deduction of foreign taxes paid may be claimed as an alternative to tax credit. (8)
Extraordinary items	Capital gains are taxed as ordinary income and are not adjusted for inflation but may be deferred if reinvested. Capital losses are offset against capital gains. No carry forward nor back allowed. (9)	(10)
Deductions from income	Reduction for double taxation purposes is done through using lower rate on distributed profits. There are several investment incentives for regional areas which may take the form of reserves. There are no reserve options for inventories. (11)	Limited deductibility of interest charges based on debt/equity ratios. (12)
Corporate income tax rate	Central government rate is 45 per cent on retained profits and 30 per cent on distributed profits. A 7.5 per cent surcharge is applied. There are no intermediate level taxes. Local taxes vary between 12 and 20.5 per cent. Local taxes are deductible. The overall top rate is 59 per cent. (13)	(14)
Tax credits	Tax credit is granted for, full 30% imputation tax and 25% withholding tax, domestic intercompany dividends. Tax credit for foreign taxes paid is given for foreign source income from non-treaty countries. (15)	(16)
Corporate income tax collection lags	Corporate income tax is collected on a quarterly basis. (17)	(18)

Other business taxes

Labour taxes and social charges	Social insurance and other labour taxes account for 24.2 per cent of total wage costs. (19)
Tax on immovable property	Net asset tax is levied at 0.45 per cent of taxable business assets. This tax is not deductible for corporation tax purposes. (20)
Net wealth tax	The base for this tax is world-wide net wealth and is valued according to the Valuation Act. 10 per cent of the world-wide net wealth is considered as "substantial interest" and is exempt from this tax. (21)
Other non-income taxes	Municipal tax authorities levy a tax on capital (*Gewerbesteuer)* which varies between 0.5 and 0.96 per cent. This tax is deductible for corporation tax purposes. (22)

FRANCE

Corporate income tax

Corporate income tax base	Provision	Adjustment and/or exception
Cost of goods sold	Both FIFO and average cost methods are allowed. LIFO method is prohibited. (1)	Temporary inventory relief available where inventory cost/unit increases more than 10% over 2 consecutive years. (2)
Gross income	Trading losses can be carried back for 3 years and forward 5 years. (3)	Portion of operating losses resulting from depreciation can be carried forward indefinitely. (4)
Operating expenses	Both straight line (10-20%) and declining balance (1.5 to 2.5xSL) allowed for machinery. The switch over is permitted. Buildings are depreciated with straight line (5%) method. All R&D expenses other than depreciable assets deductible first year. R&D-related buildings may be depreciated up to 50% first year. (5)	Special accelerated depreciation rates applicable to energy-saving and environment-related installations, and buildings in depressed areas. Accelerated depreciation offered to inward investments and declining balance to capital investments. (6)
Investment income	If the holding interest is more than 10%, both domestic and international dividends received are 95% tax exempt and remaining 5% is taxable. If holding interest is less than 10%, dividend revenues (domestic and international) are taxed on net dividends. (7)	Profits made by subsidiaries owned more than 10% and established in countries with privileged tax regimes are included in taxable income. (8)
Extraordinary items	Long-term capital gains are taxed at a special rate. Short-term capital gains are taxable as ordinary income. Short-term capital losses are offset against short-term capital gains and long-term capital losses against long-term capital gains. Capital gains are not adjusted for inflation nor deferred if reinvested. No carry forward or back allowed. (9)	(10)
Deductions from income	No reduction of distributed dividends is allowed for double taxation purposes. Reserves are allowed for investments abroad, commodity fluctuations, and as part of the temporary inventory relief. (11)	(12)
Corporate income tax rate	Central government rate is 33.33%. A surcharge of 10% is applied. There are no income taxes at intermediate and local level government. Companies are liable to lump sum tax if no profit is realised. Overall top rate is 36.66%. (13)	Tax holiday of three years for the lump sum tax may be allowed for new companies. Reduced tax treaty rate at 25% is applied to branches of foreign companies. (14)
Tax credits	Tax credit for the foreign income taxes paid is granted. Tax credits given for incremental R&D expenditures. Temporary inventory relief also provides a tax credit. (15)	(16)
Corporate income tax collection lags	Corporate income tax is collected yearly in four instalments. (17)	(18)

Other business taxes

Labour taxes and social charges	Social insurance and total labour taxes account for 29.2 per cent of total wage costs. (19)
Tax on immovable property	The taxes on immovable property vary throughout the country. (20)
Net wealth tax	There are no net wealth taxes on corporations. (21)
Other non-income taxes	Business tax (*Taxe professionnelle*) based on rental value and salaries and wages is levied at local level. (22)

UNITED KINGDOM

Corporate income tax

Corporate income tax base	Provision	Adjustment and/or exception
Cost of goods sold	FIFO method is allowed but LIFO method is not. (1)	(2)
Gross income	Trading losses can be carried back for three years and forward without time limit. (3)	(4)
Operating expenses	Declining balance (25%) method is applied for machinery and straight line (4%) method for buildings. (5)	100% depreciation is allowed for R&D capital expenditure. Patents can be depreciated 25% on declining balance. In "enterprise zones" 100% depreciation is allowed for buildings. (6)
Investment income	Domestic dividend receipts are exempt. (7)	For foreign dividends received a deduction of foreign taxes paid may be claimed as an alternative to credit. (8)
Extraordinary items	Capital gains are taxed as ordinary income, they are adjusted for inflation and deferred if reinvested. Capital losses are offset against capital gains. No carry forward or back allowed. (9)	(10)
Deductions from income	No deduction of distributed dividends is allowed for double taxation purposes. There are no reserve options nor investment deductions. (11)	The deductibility of interest charges paid is limited in the case of thinly capitalised companies. (12)
Corporate income tax rate	The central government rate is 33 per cent. There are no income taxes at intermediate and local level government. The overall top rate is 33 per cent. (13)	Low rates apply to small businesses. (14)
Tax credits	Tax credit is available for foreign direct taxes paid and if the ownership is more than 10% then also for the underlying taxes on profits. A credit on relevant UK tax is also given for income from non-treaty countries. Incentives for "enterprise zones" may also take the form of credits for investments. (15)	(16)
Corporate income tax collection lags	Corporate income tax is collected on an annual basis. (17)	(18)

Other business taxes

Labour taxes and social charges	Social insurance and other labour taxes account for 15.5 per cent of total wage costs. (19)
Tax on immovable property	Local municipal tax is based on a system of uniform business rates and levied on the base of estimated rental value of immovable property. (20)
Net wealth tax	There is no net wealth tax on corporations. (21)
Other non-income taxes	There are no other business taxes. (22)

SPAIN

Corporate income tax

Corporate income tax base	Provision	Adjustment and/or exception
Cost of goods sold	FIFO, average cost and LIFO methods are allowed by legislation.	
Gross income	Trading losses can be carried back or forward seven years.	New firms can carry losses forward until the first year of operating profit.
Operating expenses	Most common scheme is straight line depreciation. Other depreciation schemes are also allowed.	Free depreciation can be applied to co-operative corporations, mining and other companies with special features, such as micro-enterprises.
Investment income	If the holding interest is more than 5 per cent, both domestic and international dividends received are 100 per cent tax exempt. If the holding interest is less than 5 per cent, dividend revenues are 50 per cent tax exempt.	The 5 or more per cent holding affiliates must belong to the firm since the previous year.
Extraordinary items	Capital gains indexed before being evaluated and then taxed as ordinary income. Capital losses are offset against capital gains.	For SMEs and in the case of investments of less than 50 million pesetas, there is a deferral scheme for up to seven years for reinvested capital gains.
Deductions from income	No deduction of distributed dividends is allowed for double taxation purposes. Reserves are allowed for liquidation risks from debts, commodity fluctuations, doubtful payable client accounts, risks and expenditures linked to court cases, and high repairing costs.	
Corporate income tax rate	The central government rate is 35 per cent. There are no income taxes at sub-central and local level governments. (If no profits are realised a maximum rate of 0.75% based on earlier profits is paid to the Chamber of Commerce.)	A special reduced rate of 30% is applied to small and medium-sized enterprises for their profits ranging from 0 to 50 million pesetas.
Tax credits	Tax credits for R&D expenditures, export activities (investment abroad, advertising and product launching), training activities costs and investment on cultural goods and film production.	Tax credits do not cover legal services of industrial property, engineering, monitoring and process development control. Tax credit cannot exceed 35 per cent of the total tax quota.
Corporate income tax collection lags	Corporate income tax is paid during the current year in three installments. Total tax due is paid at the end of the tax period once these installments have been deducted.	

Source: Ministry of Industry and Energy, Ministry of Economy and Housing, Spain.

Other business taxes

Labour taxes and social charges	Social security and total labour taxes account for 28.66 per cent of total wage costs.
Tax on immovable property	The taxes on immovable property vary throughout the country.
Net wealth tax	There is no net wealth tax on corporations.
Other non-income taxes	Business tax (*Impuesto sobre actividades economicas* – IAE) is applied to professionals based on rental value and salaries and is levied at local level. There is a tax of 1 per cent on company start-ups and similar operations in accordance with the EU Directives on so-called "droit d'apport".

Source: Ministry of Industry and Energy, Ministry of Economy and Housing, Spain.

HUNGARY

Corporate income tax

Corporate income tax base	Provision	Adjustment and/or exception
Cost of goods sold		
Gross income	Negative tax base can be carried forward for five years.	For newly established taxpayers first 2 years' losses can be carried for an unlimited period. For taxpayers belonging to agricultural sector losses can be carried back for 2 years.
Operating expenses	Straight line method is allowed for machinery (14.5%), vehicles (20%) and buildings (2%).	Relatively lower depreciation norms allowed for assets capitalised before 1 Jan. 1992 (build. 1%, mach. 9-12-15%). In "enterprise zones" 100% depreciation for new machinery, 10% for buildings. Machinery put into operation after 31 Dec. 1995 can be depreciated 30% on straight line.
Investment income	Tax base can be reduced by the amount of dividends and profit share.	
Extraordinary items	Capital gains are taxed as ordinary income, they are not adjusted for inflation. Capital losses are offset against capital gains.	
Deductions from income	Tax base can be reduced by the social insurance contribution paid by corporation for an employee who had been unemployed earlier and by the amount of contribution given to public foundations. No reserve options for investment deductions.	
Corporate income tax rate	Central government rate = 18%. No income taxes at intermediate and local level government. Supplementary tax (cent. gov., 23%) payable on the paid dividend and on distributed shares and other liquid assets.	Lower supplementary tax rates apply to foreign shareholders.
Tax credits	Tax credit available for firms where foreign ownership is at least 30% (eligibility may be obtained until 31 Dec. 1993). Tax benefit may be claimed according to rates of interest on loans and credits. Incentives for "enterprise zones" may take form of credits for investment. Tax credit available for corporations making investment of great value.	
Corporate income tax collection lags	Basis of tax payment is tax declaration for previous year. Corporations must supplement the tax advance to the sum of the expected annual tax payable.	

Source: Ministry of Finance, Hungary.

Other business taxes

Labour taxes and social charges	Social insurance accounts for 42.5 per cent of total wage costs. Employers pay 4.2% of the gross earnings paid to employees as employer's contribution. Tax on staff employed by the corporation is HUF 2 000 per person at local government level.
Tax on immovable property	There are taxes on buildings (HUF 900/sq-m, 3% of the adjusted market value) at local government level.
Net wealth tax	There is no net wealth tax on corporations.
Other non-income taxes	Local industrial tax according to the net sales revenues of products sold or services provided (1.2 per cent). Gambling organiser must pay game tax.

Source: Ministry of Finance, Hungary.

BACKGROUND NOTES TO COUNTRY TABLES

General

The sources of the information presented in the country tables are:

- OECD (1991), *Taxing Profits in a Global Economy - Domestic and International Issues*, Paris.
- Price Waterhouse (1995), *Information Guide: Corporate Taxes - A Worldwide Summary*, Price Waterhouse World Firm Services BV.
- Price Waterhouse (1995), Information Guide Series - *Doing Business in: France, Germany, Japan, United Kingdom, United States*, Price Waterhouse World Firm Services BV.

Corporate income tax

Corporate income tax base

(1) Treatment of inventory stock

	First in/First out (FIFO)	*Last in/First out (LIFO)*
United States	Yes	Yes
Japan	Yes	Yes
Germany	No	Yes
France	Yes	No
United Kingdom	Yes	No

In the LIFO method, when the cost of sales from inventories is evaluated, the items last acquired are assumed to be disposed of first. Under the FIFO method, when the cost of sales from inventories is evaluated, the first items purchased are assumed to be disposed of first.

United States

Inventories are generally stated at the lower of cost or market on a FIFO basis. LIFO, on a cost basis only, can be elected for tax purposes, with book and tax conformity generally required.

Japan

Inventory valuation methods allowable upon election by the taxpayer include actual individual cost, FIFO, LIFO, weighted average, moving average, straight average, most recent purchase, retail and lower cost of market. Conformity between statutory accounting and tax reporting is required.

Germany

Inventories are normally valued at the lowest actual cost, replacement cost or net realisable value. The LIFO method is usually acceptable for tax purposes, provided it is also applied in the legal accounts. Theoretically, FIFO is unacceptable unless its assumption accords with the facts.

France

Inventories must be valued at the lower cost of the market. Costs must be determined in accordance with the FIFO or average cost method. The LIFO method is prohibited.

United Kingdom

Inventories are generally stated at the lower of cost or market value. In practice, inventories are generally valued for tax purposes at the lower of cost or net realisable value. A FIFO basis of determining cost where items cannot be identified is acceptable, but not the base-stock or the LIFO method.

(2) Germany

If specific identification of the inventories is not possible, valuation at either standard or average cost is acceptable. Although theoretically FIFO is unacceptable unless its assumption accords with the facts, in practice this condition is often fulfilled.

France

Temporary inventory relief is available where inventory cost per unit increases by more than 10 per cent over two consecutive years. Any excess increase over 10 percentage points may be reserved. The amount reserved is added back to taxable income after six years.

(3) Treatment of trading losses

	Carry forward	*Carry back*
United States	15 years	3 years
Japan	5 years	1 year
Germany	Indefinitely	2 years
France	5 years	3 years
United Kingdom	Indefinitely	3 years

United States

Generally, a three-year carry back is allowed for federal income tax purposes. If the loss is not fully utilised, it may be carried forward 15 years. An irrevocable election to forgo the carry back period is permitted. For State tax purposes, carry back and carry forward provisions are often similar to the federal provisions, except that several States do not permit any carry backs or carry forwards.

Japan

For corporate income tax purposes and enterprise tax purposes (and indirectly, inhabitants tax purposes), tax loss can be carried forward for offsetting income for future income for a five-year period. Carry back of tax loss can be made for one year only for national tax purposes. No carry back of losses is allowed for either enterprise or inhabitants tax purposes.

Germany

Trading losses which cannot be offset against other positive receipts in the year they occur are first carried back for two preceding years. This is, however, only allowed up to a total amount of DM 10 million. As far as losses are not offset by this procedure they are carried forward to the five years following the year of occurrence.

France

For tax purposes, net operating losses may be carried forward for five years. Businesses may also elect a form of carry back. Losses of a given fiscal year may be offset against undistributed taxable profits of the three preceding years.

United Kingdom

Losses may be carried forward indefinitely. Loss carry back is available against total profits of (normally) the three previous years (provided the same trade was being carried out in those years) for a trading loss of a company.

(4) *United States*

Complex rules may limit the utilisation of net operating losses after a reorganisation or other change in ownership. Generally, if the ownership of more than 50 per cent in value of the shares of the corporation changes, a limit is placed on the amount of future income that may be offset by losses carried forward.

Japan

Losses incurred during taxable periods ending 31 March 1991 and prior to 1 April 1996 cannot in general be carried back. Losses incurred during the initial three-year period following the establishment of the designated inward investment business may be carried forward for a period of seven to ten years if certain requirements are met.

France

The portion of operating losses resulting from depreciation can be carried forward indefinitely provided that the depreciation was properly disclosed.

(5) *United States*

In general cost recovery periods are 3, 5, 7, 10, 15, 20, 27.5 and 39 years. Property placed in the 3, 5, 7 and 10-year class is depreciated by using the 200 per cent declining balance method. Switching to straight line is mandatory but there is no switching from straight-line to double or 150 per cent declining balance Property in the 15 or 20-year class is depreciated by using the 150 per cent declining balance method with a later switch to the straight line method. Machinery can be depreciated both with straight line and declining balance methods and switch over is allowed. Research expenditure incurred by a taxpayer is either currently deductible or deferred and amortised over a period of not less than five years.

Japan

Depreciation of tangible fixed assets is computed by using either straight line or declining balance at the taxpayer's election. The declining balance does not apply to intangible fixed assets. Machinery can be depreciated with both straight line and declining balance methods and the switch over between these methods is allowed. The straight line rate is 10 per cent and the declining balance rate is three times the straight line rate. Buildings can also depreciated with both methods and switch over between these methods is allowed. The straight line rate is between 2.2 and 4.3 per cent and the declining balance rate is three times the straight line rate.

Germany

Depreciation is normally calculated by either the straight line or declining balance method over the anticipated useful life. Machinery can be depreciated both with straight line and declining balance methods and the switch over between these methods is allowed. The straight line rate is 10 per cent and the declining balance rate is three times the straight line rate. Buildings are depreciated by the straight line method; the rate varies between 2.5 and 10 per cent.

France

In general, the straight line method should be used over the useful life method for all depreciable assets. The basis of depreciation is the cost of fixed assets. Machinery and qualified equipment having a useful life of three years or more can be depreciated both with straight line and declining balance methods and the switch over between these methods is allowed. The straight line rate varies between 10 and 20 per cent and the declining balance rate is 1.5 and/or 2.5 times the straight line rate. The basis of depreciation for the declining balance method is net book value. Buildings are depreciated with the straight line method at the rate of 5 per cent. Interest payments are deductible. All R&D expenses other than depreciable assets are deductible the first year. R&D-related buildings may be depreciated up to 50 per cent first year.

United Kingdom

In the period expenditure depreciation is available at 25 per cent of the cost of machinery and equipment acquired for use in trade; thereafter; depreciation is 25 per cent on the remaining balance. Industrial buildings are depreciated with the straight line method at the rate of 4 per cent on cost.

(6) United States

Business use rules apply to automobiles and certain other property with obviously personal, as opposed to business, uses. These rules restrict the declining balance method to such property that is used more than 50% in a qualified business use. Property that does not meet the business use test is depreciated using a less generous straight-line method. Automobiles also face an additional limitation on the amount of annual depreciation that may be claimed, regardless of whether the automobile meets the business use test.

Japan

On approval of the authorities accelerated depreciation is available. First year depreciation ranges between 8 to 30 per cent depending on the area, type of business and assets. For some assets accelerated depreciation can be taken over a period of five years. Additional depreciation is available for corporations that are permitted to use a blue form tax return. It applies to fixed assets for creating designated inward investments acquired within a specified period. Additional depreciation can be claimed for five years from acquisition at an amount equal to 20 per cent of the ordinary depreciation deduction. Accelerated depreciation also applies, as a consequence of certain import incentives, to machinery acquired in the accounting year or the two preceding years.

Germany

Special depreciation allowance for R&D capital expenditure is available. If the asset is wholly used for R&D – 40 per cent; if more than two-thirds used in R&D – 15 per cent; and if between one-third and two-thirds used for R&D – 10 per cent special depreciation rate is applicable. Accelerated depreciation is allowed for small enterprises with a taxable value of less than DM 240 000 and stock in trade of no more than DM 500 000. This accelerated depreciation is up to 20 per cent of the cost of acquisition of new movable assets during five years in addition to normal depreciation. Investment incentives in the former GDR may take the form of accelerated depreciation. These grant schemes correspond to 8 to 10 per cent of the qualifying capital investment.

France

Special accelerated depreciation rates are applicable to investments in fixed assets such as installations aimed at saving energy, installations used for purification of water or air, and industrial and commercial buildings located in depressed areas. Inward investments are encouraged through accelerated depreciation of industrial and commercial buildings, and capital investments through the declining balance method of depreciation for capital expenditure.

United Kingdom

Accelerated depreciation can be used for plants and buildings employed in scientific research. 100 per cent depreciation is available for this kind of expenditure, and patents can be depreciated at 25 per cent per annum on a declining balance. In certain areas (enterprise zones) depreciation at 100 per cent is available for all kinds of commercial buildings.

(7) *United States*

A US corporation can generally deduct 70 per cent of dividends received from other US corporations. The dividends received deduction is increased from 70 to 80 per cent if the recipient of the dividend distribution owns 20 per cent or more but less than 80 per cent of the distributing corporation. 100 per cent of dividends received from US corporations in which there is 80 per cent or more ownership is deductible.

Japan

Domestic intercorporate dividends are normally excluded from gross income, provided that the ownership is 25 per cent or more of the shares in the dividend-paying corporation. If the ownership is less than 25 per cent, 80 per cent of the dividends received is excluded from the taxable income. However, interest allocable to the investment cost of the shares that generate dividend income effectively reduce the amount of non-taxable dividend income.

Germany

Dividends received from other resident companies are included in the corporate taxable income. For trade tax purposes, dividends are tax exempt if ownership is at least 10 per cent of the distributing company's shares. Foreign dividend income received is included in the taxable income unless the tax treaty provides for exemption. Irrespective of any tax treaty, taxable income for trade tax purposes is deductible if the shareholding is at least 10 per cent in the foreign company.

France

If the holding is more than 10 per cent, received domestic dividends are deductible after the definition for a share fixed at 5 per cent of gross dividends. If dividends are distributed the company is liable for an equalisation tax and the "avoir fiscal" can be offset against this tax. Under certain conditions holdings of foreign companies are exempt from equalisation tax. If the foreign dividend income is from a non-treaty country foreign withholding taxes are deductible, if this income is from a treaty country and the holding is more than 10 per cent, like domestic dividend income they are 95 per cent tax exempt and the remaining 5 per cent is subject to domestic tax on gross dividend (including foreign taxes paid). If the holding is less than 10 per cent, in case of domestic dividend revenues, companies are taxed on net dividends plus the "avoir fiscal", and in case of foreign dividend income they are taxed on net dividends.

United Kingdom

All dividends from UK companies are excluded from the taxable income of the recipient company.

(8) *United States*

For foreign dividends received a deduction for actual foreign taxes may be claimed as an alternative to a credit.

Japan

Foreign income taxes may also be deductible if a Japanese corporation does not elect to claim a foreign tax credit.

Germany

Generally, for foreign dividends received a deduction for actual foreign taxes may be claimed as an alternative to a credit. Dividends received by a German corporation on a holding of 10 per cent or more in a foreign corporation in a treaty country are tax exempt.

France

French corporations are required to include in their taxable income profits made by their more than 10 per cent owned subsidiaries and branches established in a country where they are subject to privileged tax regime.

United Kingdom

For foreign dividends received a deduction for actual foreign taxes may be claimed as an alternative to a credit.

(9) United States

Net capital gain (*i.e.* gain less loss) is the sum of the separately calculated net gain on short-term assets (held less than 12 months) plus the net gain on long-term assets (held more than 12 months). Corporations may not use a net capital loss to offset ordinary income, but may carry the loss back three years and forward five years.

Japan

Capital gains or losses are taxed as ordinary income at corporation income tax rates. If the proceeds of a sale of real property are reinvested in specified fixed assets, taxes on capital gains may be deferred under certain limited conditions.

Germany

Capital gains and losses are taxed as part of ordinary business income or losses. It is possible to postpone the taxation of a part or all of the gains on certain fixed assets where the gain is offset against the cost of certain replacement items.

France

Short-term (assets held less than two years) capital gains are taxable as ordinary income (option to spread over three years). Long-term gains are taxed at 19 per cent (plus 10 per cent surcharge since mid-1995) if their net amount (81 per cent) is booked in the special reserve for investment – if they are distributed the effective rate of taxation is reached with a supplement. Short-term capital losses can be offset against short-term capital gains (balance added to taxable income base) and long-term capital losses against long-term capital gains (for a maximum of ten years).

United Kingdom

Capital gains are taxed at corporation tax rates and are subject to indexation. Tax on business assets can be deferred if a new asset is acquired or unconditionally ordered within 12 months before or three years after the disposal of an asset. Capital losses are computed as for gains; they can be set against gains and unused balances can be carried forward without limitation but cannot be carried back.

(10) United States

There is a recapture provision that treats future gains on depreciable business property as ordinary income to the extent that losses on such property were recognised during the previous five years.

Japan

A special capital gains tax on land and land rights is levied if held less than two years (standard corporation tax rate plus additional tax rate of 30 per cent), less than five years (normal corporation tax plus additional tax rate of 20 per cent), and more than five years (normal corporation tax plus additional tax rate of 10 per cent).

(11) United States

A US corporation can generally claim a deduction for royalties, management service fees and interest charges paid to foreign affiliates to the extent that the amounts are actually paid and are at arm's length. Deductions for allowable charitable contributions may not exceed 10 per cent of taxable income and, subject to this limit annually, can be carried over to the five succeeding years. The deduction for business meal and entertainment expenses is 50 per cent of the expenses incurred. As regards double taxation of distributed dividends, there is no reduction at the corporate level. No investment or inventory provisions allowing for reserves exist. There are no investment tax allowances and/or relieves.

Japan

As regards double taxation of distributed dividends, there is no reduction at the corporate level. Qualified investments in a designated country or designated business to promote the production of certain designated natural resources allow the establishment of a tax deductible reserve to the extent of 15 to 100 per cent of the invested amount. This reserve must be restored from the sixth to tenth year after a five-year grace period. A Japanese corporation can generally claim a deduction for royalties, management service fees and interest charges paid to foreign affiliates to the extent that the amounts are actually paid and are at arm's length. A management fee to foreign affiliates may be deductible to the extent considered reasonable for the specific benefits received. Certain reserves, such as those for doubtful receivables and employee's severance indemnities, may be tax deductible at statutory percentages. Deduction for charitable contributions is limited to the sum of 1.25 per cent of taxable income and 0.125 per cent of paid-in capital.

Germany

The split rate system is effective where personal and corporate income taxes are fully integrated and the reduction of the impact of double taxation is carried out through applying lower rate on distributed dividends. A variety of investment incentives are available for capital investments. Investment incentives in the former GDR may take the form of non-taxable reserves. These grant schemes correspond to 8 to 10 per cent of the qualifying capital investment A German corporation can claim a deduction for royalties, management service fees and interest charges paid to foreign affiliates provided such amounts are at arm's length. Subject to appearing reasonable, 80 per cent of entertainment expenses are deductible. Charitable donations are allowable subject to certain limits. These limits are either 5 per cent of taxable income or 0.2 per cent of the total sales revenue plus employee remuneration.

France

As regards double taxation, there is no reduction at the corporate level. Deduction of payments to foreign affiliates is generally allowed as long as they are at arm's length. Royalties or payments for use of intangibles are tax deductible if reasonable and *bona fide*. Gifts and charitable donations to recognised organisations are tax deductible up to two to three per thousand of turnover. A reserve for investment abroad is allowed. This reserve must be added back to taxable income in annual instalments as of the sixth year. In addition a reserve for commodity fluctuations is allowed to businesses who process listed raw materials. Temporary inventory relief is available where inventory cost per unit increases more than 10 per cent over two consecutive years. Any excess increase over 10 percentage points may be reserved. The amount reserved is added back to taxable income after six years. Losses in a given fiscal year may be offset against undistributed taxable profits of the three preceding years.

United Kingdom

As regards double taxation, there is no reduction at the corporate level. Generally, deductions can be claimed for royalties, management service fees and interest charges paid to foreign affiliates provided the amounts do not exceed what would be paid to unrelated entities. Charitable donations can be claimed as a charge on income if income tax at the basic rate has been withheld from the payment. No deduction of entertainment costs allowed, other than those relating to staff. No investment or inventory provisions allowing for reserves exist.

(12) Japan

In the case of thinly capitalised companies, the deductibility of interest paid on related party debt of a Japanese corporation has been restricted for business years beginning 1 April 1992. Entertainment expenses are not deductible for tax purposes. However, corporations whose paid-in capital does not exceed ¥ 50 million may take tax deduction to the extent of ¥ 3 million or ¥ 4 million.

Germany

Detailed provisions define the limits of deductibility of interest charges paid to foreign affiliates. These are basically debt/equity ratios (3:1 on fixed interest loans and 1:2 on finance provided for a consideration based on profits or similar criteria).

France

Tax incentives – notably a ten year corporate income tax holiday – is available in listed depressed areas. Interest payment deductions are limited to the average yield on private bonds during the same year, and any interest paid on the portion of a loan that exceeds 1.5 times the share capital of the paying company is disallowed when paid to a foreign company who owns 50 per cent of the paying company.

United Kingdom

Deduction of interest charges paid to foreign affiliates may be limited where the paying company is thinly capitalised.

(13) Corporate income tax rate

In considering overall corporate tax rates in the survey, where countries have additional levies at intermediate or local government level these are included by taking up the top rates. On the other hand, the deductibility of these taxes from the tax base is considered when the national tax rate is calculated. Also, rates on non-distributed profits and average rates of progressive schedules are taken up for the sake of simplicity.

Central government corporate income tax rates, 1995

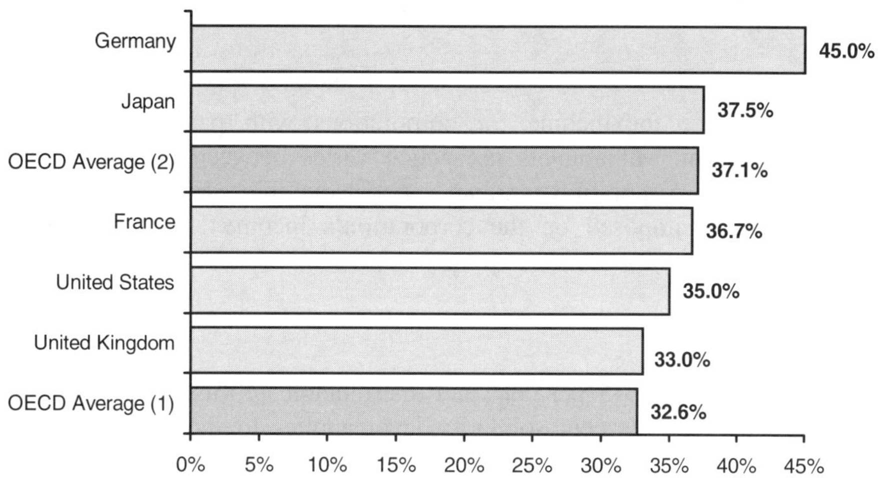

Overall top corporate income tax rates, 1995

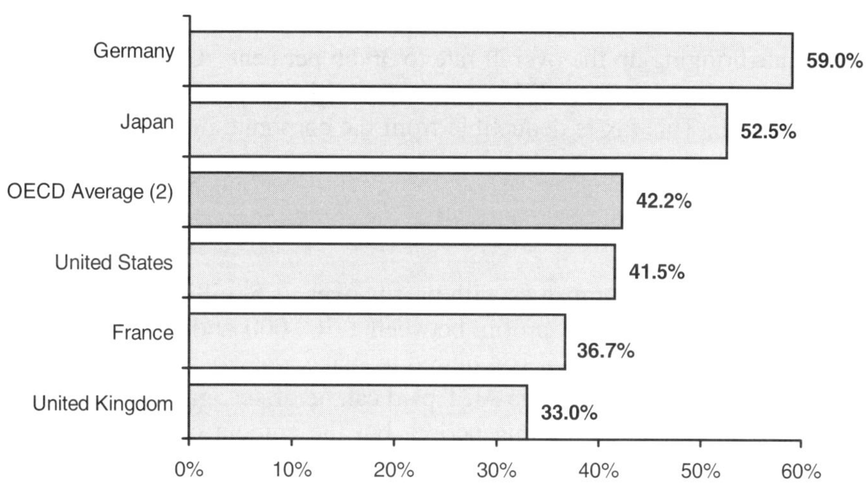

1. Average of 24 OECD countries. Including Mexico and excluding Luxembourg.
2. Average of 11 OECD countries. These are: Belgium, France, Germany, Italy, Ireland, the Netherlands, Portugal, Spain, the United Kingdom, the United States, and Japan.

Source: OECD, DAFFE ; Price Waterhouse.

United States

The 35 per cent rate applies where taxable income exceeds US$18 333 000. Marginal rates to income below range from 15 to 39 per cent. State and local taxes are deductible from the Federal Corporate income tax. They vary mostly between 4 and 17 per cent, but can be higher in some States. The 41.5 per cent top overall statutory rate is obtained by taking a typical 10 per cent state/local rate (35%*(1-10%)+10%°). Companies with a commercial profit but a fiscal loss are taxed on their income by means of minimum tax. An alternative minimum tax must be paid if it is higher than the corporate income tax and the Alternative Minimum Tax (AMT) rate is 20 per cent. The tax is levied over AMT income of over US$40 000. In addition to normal taxable income, the AMT includes accelerated depreciation, 75% of the excess of a statutorily provided alternative measure of corporate earnings (*i.e.* ACE) over taxable income, as well as the benefits of certain other tax preferences.

Japan

Basic corporate tax rate for income for corporations with paid-in capital of more than ¥ 100 million is 37.5 per cent. Inhabitants tax which varies between 17.3 and 20.7 per cent is computed as a percentage of corporation tax and is not deductible. Enterprise tax varies between 12 and 13.2 per cent and is imposed on the corporation's income allocated to each prefecture. Enterprise tax is deductible for corporation tax purposes.

Germany

Retained profits are taxed at 45 per cent and distributable profits at 30 per cent. Surcharge applied to basic rate: the 7.5 per cent solidarity level applies to the tax charge, as reduced (if applicable). Municipal trade tax on income (*Gewerbeertragsteuer*) rates vary from 12 to 20.5 per cent (around 20 per cent in most larger cities) but is deductible for federal tax purposes.

France

The basic corporate income tax is 33.33 per cent. Since mid-1995 a surcharge of 10 per cent is applied to this basic rate bringing up the overall rate to 36.66 per cent. Companies that are subject to corporate income tax are liable to an annual lump sum tax which depends on the company's turnover even if no profit is realised. This tax is deductible from the corporate income tax in the tax year and two subsequent years if the company is profitable.

United Kingdom

Corporate income tax rate for companies with profits over £1.5 million is 33 per cent. However, the maximum effective marginal rate on profits between £ 300 000 and £1.5 million is 35 per cent. When a corporation makes a distribution it is required to make a payment of advance corporation tax (ACT) equal to 20/80 of the distribution. The ACT paid can be offset against the ultimate corporation tax liability on profits of the same accounting period, but the amount cannot exceed 20 per cent of taxable profits.

(14) United States

Lower rates apply to lower profits. The rate is 15 per cent for taxable income up to US$50 000, and 25 per cent for taxable income between US$50 000 and US$75 000. The 34 per cent rate applies to taxable income over US$75 000 and not exceeding US$100 000.

Japan

For companies with paid-in capital of ¥ 100 million or less the small business rate applies. For these companies the corporate income tax rate for the first ¥ 8 million of income is 28 per cent.

France

Newly created companies are exempt from lump sum tax during their first three years provided that cash contributions represent at least 50 per cent of their capital. A distribution tax is levied on

French branches of foreign corporations at the rate of 25 per cent or a reduced tax treaty rate on net profits.

United Kingdom

Small company tax rates apply to companies with profits up to £300 000. A lower rate of 25 per cent is imposed where company profits do not exceed this amount.

Tax credits

(15) United States

A tax credit for the foreign (both treaty and non-treaty countries) income taxes paid is granted against the domestic tax up to the amount of US tax on that income and subject to a variety of special limitations. A credit against the federal tax equal to 20 per cent of the sum of qualified R&D expenses in excess of the base amount and basic R&D payments may be obtained each year. The base amount cannot be less than 50 per cent of the current year's qualified R&D expenditures. Unused credits can be carried back three years and carried forward 15 years. An energy investment credit is allowed for 10 per cent of investments in qualified energy property. A credit is also available in connection with the rehabilitation of older business real estate. The allowable credit is either 10 or 20 per cent of qualifying expenditures for buildings. Certain other credits are also available.

Japan

Japanese corporations are allowed to claim a tax credit against corporation and inhabitants taxes for foreign income taxes paid. A foreign tax credit is not available for enterprise tax purposes, although foreign branch income is exempt from the enterprise tax. As an alternative to accelerated depreciation offered for import incentives related to inward investment, a corporation may claim a tax credit. A corporation tax credit of 3.5 or 7 per cent of the adjusted of acquisition cost of energy-saving equipment and 7 per cent of the acquisition cost of designated electronic equipment for SMEs is available. The maximum credit, however, is limited to 20 per cent of the corporation tax otherwise payable. A tax credit is allowed for an increase in research expenditures; this credit corresponds to 20 per cent of the increase (limited to 10 per cent of corporation tax). Also a tax credit at 6 per cent for total R&D expenditures is available to SMEs (limited to 15 per cent of corporation tax). In addition, an investment credit of 7 per cent of the acquisition costs of R&D assets is available. The combined maximum claim is not to exceed 15 per cent of corporation tax in any one year.

Germany

For domestic intercompany dividends tax credit is granted for the full underlying (30 per cent) imputation tax and the 25 per cent withholding tax. Dividend income from foreign (non-treaty countries) sources is segregated and the tax credit for taxes paid abroad is granted for the domestic taxes due on that particular income. Dividend income from foreign (treaty countries) sources is tax exempt if the ownership is more than 10 per cent. If the ownership is less than 10 per cent, the foreign source income (treaty countries) is treated in the same way as for non-treaty countries.

France

If the holding is less than 10 per cent, dividend income from foreign (both treaty and non-treaty countries) sources (portfolio income) is taxed and a credit is given for foreign taxes paid. Interest from foreign sources (both treaty and non-treaty countries) is segregated and a tax credit is given for foreign taxes paid against the domestic tax due.

Qualifying R&D expenses may give rise to a tax credit that can be offset against corporate income tax. The standard tax credit is equal to 50 per cent of the excess of expenses incurred during a given year over the average of those of the two preceding years, with a maximum of FF 40 million per year. Temporary inventory relief is available where inventory cost per unit increases more than 10 per cent over two consecutive years. Any excess increase over 10 percentage points may be reserved. The amount reserved is added back to taxable income after six years. Losses of a given fiscal year may be offset against undistributed taxable profits of the three preceding years. The lower of the tax paid on these or the potential tax savings represented by the tax loss of the fiscal year is a tax credit. Such credit may be offset against corporate income tax of the following five fiscal years, and thereafter any excess credit may be reimbursed in cash.

United Kingdom

Income from foreign (both treaty and non-treaty countries) sources is segregated. Credit is available for foreign direct taxes; if the ownership is more than 10 per cent credit is also available for the underlying taxes on the profits. Credits can be offset only against the domestic tax which is due on that particular investment or source. A credit on relevant UK tax "spared" in the overseas territory is also given for foreign income from treaty countries. Special incentives are given to investments in certain areas known as "enterprise zones". These incentives also include tax credits for such investments.

Corporate income tax collection lags

(17) *United States*

Generally a corporation is required to repay its estimated tax liability for the year in four equal instalments. Taxpayer's liability is generally required to be fully paid by the earlier of the filing of the return or the fifteenth day of the third month following the close of the tax year.

Japan

Corporate income taxes payable with the final corporate income tax return should be paid on or before the filing due date of the final returns, which is usually two months after the end of the accounting period.

Germany

Taxes are payable in quarterly instalments during the year, with a final settlement when the assessment is issued. The quarterly instalments are based on the estimated ultimate liability.

France

Payment of tax is made during the fiscal year by way of four instalments totalling the corporate income tax rate of the taxable income of the preceding year. The balance, if any, is due three and one-half months after the year end.

United Kingdom

For most companies, corporation tax is strictly payable annually, nine months after the end of the accounting period to which it relates. Companies are assessed by reference to accounting periods. Normally, the accounting period is the period for which the company makes up its accounts. Where the accounting period does not coincide with the financial year ending March 31, taxable profits are apportioned to the financial years into which the accounting period falls.

(18) United States

Failure to pay at least 100 per cent of the corporate income tax on dates due can result in a penalty.

Japan

In case an extension is accorded, a 7.3 per cent interest rate is charged per annum for the period from the day following the original due date.

Other business taxes

Labour taxes

(19) Social charges and other labour taxes, 1994 (1)(2)

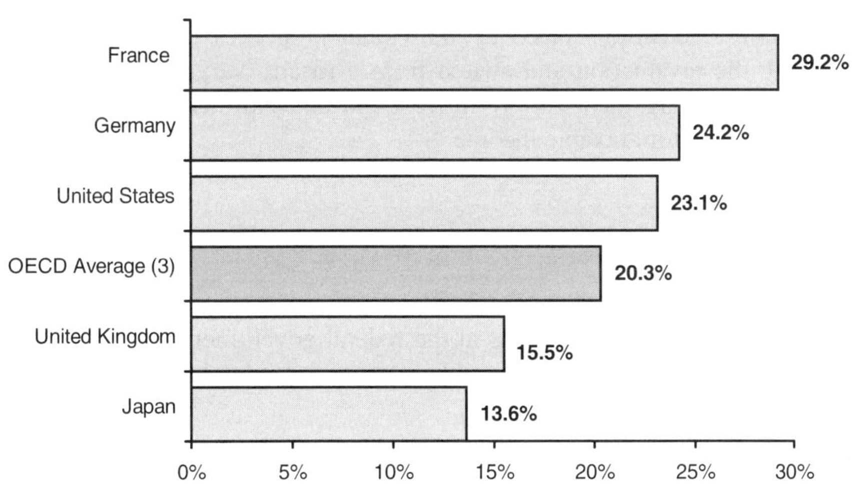

1. As a percentage of hourly compensation costs.
2. For production workers in manufacturing.
3. OECD average excluding Greece, Iceland, Ireland, Luxembourg and Turkey.

Source: US Department of Labor.

Tax on immovable property

(20) *United States*

States impose taxes on immovable property which vary throughout the country. State and municipal taxes are deductible expenses for federal income tax purposes.

Japan

Real property and tangible depreciable fixed assets are subject to a 1.4 per cent fixed assets tax (1.7 per cent in certain large cities). There is also a land value tax at the rate of 0.3 per cent of the aggregate value of the land imposed on corporations that own high-value land.

Germany

Net assets tax is levied at 0.45 per cent of taxable business assets amounting to more than DM 500 000 per annum. This tax is not deductible as an expense for corporation tax purposes.

France

The taxes on immovable property vary throughout the country.

United Kingdom

For local municipal taxes there is a system of uniform business rates which are levied on the base of estimated rental values. National non-domestic rating multipliers are applied to these rateable values. In order to limit fluctuations faced by individual properties in a single year, transitional arrangements following the revaluation and switch from a locally varying business rate apply each year. Somewhat different arrangements apply in Scotland and Northern Ireland. Local municipal taxes (rates) may be deducted from taxable income.

Net wealth tax

(21) *United States*

There is no net wealth tax on corporations at the federal government level. States impose taxes on the capital of a corporation which are a deductible expense for federal income tax purposes.

Japan

There is no net wealth tax on corporations.

Germany

The base for the net wealth tax on corporations is the world-wide net wealth of the corporation valued according to the Valuation Act. The value of a "substantial interest" (10 per cent) is exempt from the net wealth tax. The first DM 125 000 is exempt from tax; any value above this amount is valued at 75 per cent and the rate is 0.6 per cent.

France

There is no net wealth tax on corporations.

United Kingdom

There is no net wealth tax on corporations.

Other non-income taxes

(22) *United States*

Corporations accumulating earnings and profits for the purpose of avoiding shareholder personal income tax are subject to accumulated earnings tax in addition to any other tax that may be applicable. This penalty tax is equal to 39.6 per cent of accumulated taxable income. The environmental tax is 0.12 per cent of modified alternative minimum taxable income in excess of US$2 million. It is payable regardless of whether the corporation is subject to regular tax or the alternative minimum tax. Most States and some cities impose sale or use taxes. Many also impose franchise taxes, which are either supplemental or in lieu of income taxes.

Japan

A company that use premises in excess of 1 000 square meters and/or has 1 010 or more employees in designated cities is liable to a tax based on space and gross payroll.

Germany

Municipal tax authorities impose a trade tax on capital (*Gewerbekapitalsteuer*) which varies from 0.5 to 0.96 per cent. This tax is deductible as an expense for corporation tax purposes.

France

Business tax *(Taxe professionnelle)* is levied at local level and its rate varies. This tax is based on the rental value of the corporate fixed assets and on salaries and wages.

United Kingdom

There are no other non-profit-related or partially related business taxes.

Chapter 8

ENERGY COSTS

The information provided is drawn, in summary form, from extensive data compiled by the OECD's International Energy Agency. More detailed information, including on measurement methodologies employed, is published regularly in OECD/IEA, *Energy Prices and Taxes*.

Introduction

Energy infrastructure is a principal component of the basic infrastructure for industry. For a number of manufacturing industries which are heavy users of energy – steel, aluminium, petrochemical, chemical, pulp and paper, industries, etc. – energy inputs have traditionally constituted a major cost component. For such activities, the availability of a high-capacity and low-price energy supply has always been a core framework factor and a significant parameter in localisation and investment decisions, including at the international level. With increased global components in product markets, the impact of the supply-responsiveness and cost-efficiency of energy sources on the competitiveness of energy-intensive enterprises is attracting increased attention.

The role of energy supply is also significant in certain rapidly growing service industries such as transportation, waste processing and housing. Overall, even when it does not constitute a key cost component quantitatively, the quality, regularity and reliability of energy supply is, nevertheless, an important framework factor for most economic activities, including in high-technology manufacturing and services. For OECD economies, maintaining an energy infrastructure that meets international quality and cost standards has always been an important objective of economic policy.

In the 1990s, three new developments are generating renewed policy interest for energy infrastructure: *i)* increased environmental awareness is placing national energy production under closer scrutiny in many countries, raising additional cost constraints on energy production under higher environmental standards; *ii)* new energy technologies alter the economics of energy production, creating new opportunities for cost-efficient energy supply and distribution in wider geographical areas – technological choices made, as well as the age (vintage) of the infrastructure, increase potential disparities between different locations as regards energy availability and its cost; and *iii)* geopolitical and other risks on energy provision are not dissipated in the world economy, encouraging governments to adopt national energy policies which may cause differentiation of energy sources, safety, capacity and costs across countries.

Against this background, OECD governments' energy policies also contribute to the differentiation of national infrastructures in terms of regulation of supply, and the taxation of energy production and consumption. Several governments have been pursuing a mix of regulatory reforms in production and distribution over the past decade, opening wider opportunities for new entries by competing companies and technologies in the different segments of energy provision. Also, national governments implement different energy taxation policies – the tax component of energy costs is becoming significant or even predominant for certain energy sources. User cost impacts on business are, therefore, becoming extremely important due to these tax policies.

This section provides a summary picture of key national specificities and international differences, in the energy infrastructure of OECD economies. Extensive and detailed information produced by International Energy Agency is compiled and summarised from the viewpoint of the business sector. The following indicators and parameters are included in descriptive country matrices:

Table 1. Electricity end-use prices for industry

Table 2. Natural gas end-use prices for industry and electric generation

Table 3. Steam coal gas end-use prices for industry and electric generation

Table 4. Coking coal gas end-use prices for industry

Table 5. Automotive fuels end-use prices

Table 6. Light fuel oil end-use prices for industry

Table 7. Heavy fuel oil end-use prices for industry and electric generation

Table 8. Total primary energy supply in 1993

Table 9. Regulation in public utilities (electricity and gas) in 1990

Detailed technical information on each indicator is provided in the Background notes to the country tables.

ENERGY COSTS: COUNTRY TABLES

UNITED STATES

Table 1. Electricity end-use prices for industry

US$/kWh

	1991	1992	1993	1994	1995
Industry	0.049	0.048	0.049	0.047	0.051

Source: IEA, *Energy Prices and Taxes, 2nd Quarter 1995.*

Table 2. Natural gas end-use prices for industry and electric generation

US$/$10^7$ kcal

	1991	1992	1993	1994	1995
Industry	101.0	106.3	114.3	116.2	103.5
Electric generation	84.9	91.4	99.2	86.4	74.5

Source: IEA, *Energy Prices and Taxes, 2nd Quarter 1995.*

Table 3. Steam coal gas end-use prices for industry and electric generation

US$/metric tonne

	1991	1992	1993	1994	1995
Industry	36.9	36.2	35.8	35.9	36.4
Electric generation	33.4	32.5	31.7	31.0	31.1

Source: IEA, *Energy Prices and Taxes, 2nd Quarter 1995.*

Table 4. Coking coal gas end-use prices for industry

US$/metric tonne

	1991	1992	1993	1994	1995
Industry	53.8	52.8	52.3	51.3	51.6

Source: IEA, *Energy Prices and Taxes, 2nd Quarter 1995.*

Table 5. Automotive fuels end-use prices

US$/litre

	1991	1992	1993	1994	1995
Premium leaded gasoline	..	..	..	..	..
Premium unleaded gasoline (98 RON)	..	..	..	..	..
Premium unleaded gasoline (95 RON)	0.349	0.348	0.344	0.345	0.360
Regular unleaded gasoline	0.301	0.298	0.293	0.294	0.311
Automotive diesel oil	0.299	0.295	0.294	0.294	0.296

Source: IEA, *Energy Prices and Taxes, 2nd Quarter 1995.*

Table 6. Light fuel oil end-use prices for industry for industry

US$/1 000 litres

	1991	1992	1993	1994	1995
Industry	185.7	175.7	143.9	133.7	130.7

Source: IEA, *Energy Prices and Taxes, 2nd Quarter 1995.*

Table 7. Heavy fuel oil end-use prices for industry and electric generation

US$/metric tonne

	1991	1992	1993	1994	1995
Industry	83.8	85.8	93.2	98.5	116.1
Electric generation	103.2	104.5	98.9	100.5	123.4

Source: IEA, *Energy Prices and Taxes, 2nd Quarter 1995.*

Table 8. Total primary energy supply in 1993

Million tonnes oil equivalent

	Indigenous production	Imports	Exports	Intl. marine bunker	Stock changes	Total
Coal	482.90	5.30	-47.20	0.00	28.25	469.24
Crude oil	404.27	400.91	-1.68	0.00	-2.85	800.65
Petroleum products	0.00	49.03	-46.66	-32.11	-1.30	-31.04
Gas	431.67	54.35	-3.23	0.00	6.58	489.37
Nuclear	168.61	0.00	0.00	0.00	0.00	168.61
Hydro	24.23	0.00	0.00	0.00	0.00	24.23
Geothermal solar, etc.	15.63	0.00	0.00	0.00	0.00	15.63
Combustible renewable & waste	89.39	0.02	0.00	0.00	0.03	89.44
Electricity	0.00	3.17	-0.70	0.00	0.00	2.47
Heat	0.00	0.00	0.00	0.00	0.00	0.00
Total	1 616.70	512.78	-99.47	-32.11	30.37	2 028.60

Source: IEA, *Energy Balances of OECD Countries 1992-93.*

Table 9. Regulation in public utilities (electricity and gas) in 1990

		Ownership	Entry	Price
	Generation	Mixed	Partially regulated	Partially regulated
Electricity	Transmission	Mixed	Regulated	Regulated
	Distribution	Mixed	Regulated	Regulated
	Production	Private	Unregulated	Unregulated
Gas	Transmission	Private	Partially regulated	Partially regulated
	Distribution	Private	Regulated	Regulated

Source: OECD, DAFFE.

JAPAN

Table 1. Electricity end-use prices for industry

US$/kWh

	1991	1992	1993	1994	1995
Industry	0.132	0.142	0.163	0.173	..

Source: IEA, *Energy Prices and Taxes, 2nd Quarter 1995.*

Table 2. Natural gas end-use prices for industry and electric generation

US$/$10^7$ kcal

	1991	1992	1993	1994	1995
Industry	424.7	436.1	464.9	466.1	..
Electric generation	167.9	158.4	153.6	145.6	..

Source: IEA, *Energy Prices and Taxes, 2nd Quarter 1995.*

Table 3. Steam coal gas end-use prices for industry and electric generation

US$/metric tonne

	1991	1992	1993	1994	1995
Industry	57.7	52.4	49.2	47.2	..
Electric generation	87.0	86.6	86.0	87.8	..

Source: IEA, *Energy Prices and Taxes, 2nd Quarter 1995.*

Table 4. Coking coal gas end-use prices for industry

US$/metric tonne

	1991	1992	1993	1994	1995
Industry	62.6	60.1	58.0	54.3	..

Source: IEA, *Energy Prices and Taxes, 2nd Quarter 1995.*

Table 5. Automotive fuels end-use prices

US$/litre

	1991	1992	1993	1994	1995
Premium leaded gasoline	..	..	..	..	..
Premium unleaded gasoline (98 RON)	..	..	..	..	..
Premium unleaded gasoline (95 RON)	..	..	..	..	..
Regular unleaded gasoline	0.914	0.945	1.063	1.154	1.326
Automotive diesel oil	0.558	0.578	0.647	0.760	0.817

Source: IEA, *Energy Prices and Taxes, 2nd Quarter 1995.*

Table 6. Light fuel oil end-use prices for industry for industry

US$/1 000 litres

	1991	1992	1993	1994	1995
Industry	268.9	273.4	297.3	287.1	310.2

Source: IEA, *Energy Prices and Taxes, 2nd Quarter 1995.*

Table 7. Heavy fuel oil end-use prices for industry and electric generation

US$/metric tonne

	1991	1992	1993	1994	1995
Industry	240.5	210.3	216.9	179.8	205.4
Electric generation	219.6	197.1	199.7	197.3	..

Source: IEA, *Energy Prices and Taxes, 2nd Quarter 1995.*

Table 8. Total primary energy supply in 1993

Million tonnes oil equivalent

	Indigenous production	Imports	Exports	Intl. marine bunker	Stock changes	Total
Coal	3.98	74.26	-1.97	0.00	0.56	76.83
Crude oil	0.87	221.44	0.00	0.00	-2.08	220.23
Petroleum products	0.00	48.58	-6.32	-6.55	-0.07	35.64
Gas	1.94	45.88	0.00	0.00	-0.16	47.66
Nuclear	64.96	0.00	0.00	0.00	0.00	64.96
Hydro	8.41	0.00	0.00	0.00	0.00	8.41
Geothermal, solar, etc.	1.53	0.00	0.00	0.00	0.00	1.53
Combustible, renewable & waste	2.18	0.00	0.00	0.00	0.00	2.18
Electricity	0.00	0.00	0.00	0.00	0.00	0.00
Heat	0.00	0.00	0.00	0.00	0.00	0.00
Total	83.87	390.15	-8.28	-6.55	-1.75	457.44

Source: IEA, *Energy Balances of OECD Countries, 1992-93.*

Table 9. Regulation in public utilities (electricity and gas) in 1990

		Ownership	Entry	Price
	Generation	Private	..	Regulated
Electricity	Transmission	Private	..	Regulated
	Distribution	Private	..	Regulated
	Production	Private	..	Regulated
Gas	Transmission	Private	..	Regulated
	Distribution	Private	..	Regulated

Source: OECD, DAFFE.

GERMANY

Table 1. Electricity end-use prices for industry
US$/kWh

	1991	1992	1993	1994	1995
Industry	0.088	0.093	0.089	0.092	0.107

Source: IEA, *Energy Prices and Taxes, 2nd Quarter 1995.*

Table 2. Natural gas end-use prices for industry and electric generation
US$/$10^7$ kcal

	1991	1992	1993	1994	1995
Industry	201.1	200.5	187.3	184.8	..
Electric generation	165.7	169.3	152.3	146.0	..

Source: IEA, *Energy Prices and Taxes, 2nd Quarter 1995.*

Table 3. Steam coal gas end-use prices for industry and electric generation
US$/metric tonne

	1991	1992	1993	1994	1995
Industry	182.5	206.2	195.7	200.3	232.8
Electric generation	134.9	149.1	138.8	141.6	166.1

Source: IEA, *Energy Prices and Taxes, 2nd Quarter 1995.*

Table 4. Coking coal gas end-use prices for industry
US$/metric tonne

	1991	1992	1993	1994	1995
Industry	62.3	61.8	58.2	56.3	..

Source: IEA, *Energy Prices and Taxes, 2nd Quarter 1995.*

Table 5. Automotive fuels end-use prices
US$/litre

	1991	1992	1993	1994	1995
Premium leaded gasoline	0.867	0.980	0.920	1.042	1.231
Premium unleaded gasoline (98 RON)	..	..	..	..	..
Premium unleaded gasoline (95 RON)	0.797	0.896	0.842	0.960	1.130
Regular unleaded gasoline	0.767	0.864	0.812	0.929	1.095
Automotive diesel oil	0.574	0.601	0.564	0.612	0.712

Source: IEA, *Energy Prices and Taxes, 2nd Quarter 1995.*

Table 6. Light fuel oil end-use prices for industry for industry
US$/1 000 litres

	1991	1992	1993	1994	1995
Industry	270.9	252.3	240.2	226.7	254.1

Source: IEA, *Energy Prices and Taxes, 2nd Quarter 1995.*

Table 7. Heavy fuel oil end-use prices for industry and electric generation

US$/metric tonne

	1991	1992	1993	1994	1995
Industry	137.6	133.8	118.5	125.6	163.9
Electric generation	146.2	140.6	127.4	126.4	158.9

Source: IEA, *Energy Prices and Taxes, 2nd Quarter 1995.*

Table 8. Total primary energy supply in 1993

Million tonnes oil equivalent

	Indigenous production	Imports	Exports	Intl. marine bunker	Stock changes	Total
Coal	87.78	10.81	-1.72	0.00	1.02	97.89
Crude oil	3.83	101.68	-0.11	0.00	0.40	105.80
Petroleum products	0.00	47.46	-15.05	-2.22	-0.45	29.75
Gas	13.75	48.68	-1.31	0.00	-1.39	59.72
Nuclear	40.00	0.00	0.00	0.00	0.00	40.00
Hydro	1.52	0.00	0.00	0.00	0.00	1.52
Geothermal, solar, etc.	0.01	0.00	0.00	0.00	0.00	0.01
Combustible, renewable & waste	2.48	0.00	0.00	0.00	0.00	2.48
Electricity	0.00	2.89	-2.82	0.00	0.00	0.07
Heat	0.00	0.00	0.00	0.00	0.00	0.00
Total	149.36	211.53	-21.02	-2.22	-0.41	337.23

Source: IEA, *Energy Balances of OECD Countries, 1992-93.*

Table 9. Regulation in public utilities (electricity and gas) in 1990

		Ownership	Entry	Price
	Generation	Mixed	Mixed	Unregulated
Electricity	Transmission	Mixed	Partially regulated	Unregulated
	Distribution	Mixed	Partially regulated	Partially regulated
	Production	Private	Unregulated	Unregulated
Gas	Transmission	Private	Unregulated	Unregulated
	Distribution	Private	Unregulated	Unregulated

Source: OECD, DAFFE.

FRANCE

Table 1. Electricity end-use prices for industry

US$/kWh

	1991	1992	1993	1994	1995
Industry	0.054	0.057	0.055	0.053	..

Source: IEA, *Energy Prices and Taxes, 2nd Quarter 1995.*

Table 2. Natural gas end-use prices for industry and electric generation

US$/$10^7$ kcal

	1991	1992	1993	1994	1995
Industry	151.3	152.8	143.0	141.8	..
Electric generation	..	..	..	..	..

Source: IEA, *Energy Prices and Taxes, 2nd Quarter 1995.*

Table 3. Steam coal gas end-use prices for industry and electric generation

US$/metric tonne

	1991	1992	1993	1994	1995
Industry	101.2	108.8	102.6	104.7	..
Electric generation	46.1	45.7	40.7	..	..

Source: IEA, *Energy Prices and Taxes, 2nd Quarter 1995.*

Table 4. Coking coal gas end-use prices for industry

US$/metric tonne

	1991	1992	1993	1994	1995
Industry	64.3	65.3	56.4	..	..

Source: IEA, *Energy Prices and Taxes, 2nd Quarter 1995.*

Table 5. Automotive fuels end-use prices

US$/litre

	1991	1992	1993	1994	1995
Premium leaded gasoline	0.948	0.991	0.959	1.011	1.191
Premium unleaded gasoline (98 RON)	0.920	0.958	0.924	0.967	1.153
Premium unleaded gasoline (95 RON)	0.910	0.942	0.901	0.949	1.145
Regular unleaded gasoline	..	..	..	..	..
Automotive diesel oil	0.536	0.551	0.546	0.586	0.657

Source: IEA, *Energy Prices and Taxes, 2nd Quarter 1995.*

Table 6. Light fuel oil end-use prices for industry for industry

US$/1 000 litres

	1991	1992	1993	1994	1995
Industry	296.1	272.0	261.3	255.4	279.1

Source: IEA, *Energy Prices and Taxes, 2nd Quarter 1995.*

Table 7. Heavy fuel oil end-use prices for industry and electric generation

US$/metric tonne

	1991	1992	1993	1994	1995
Industry	116.3	120.2	105.0	143.8	174.4
Electric generation	..	..	..	..	..

Source: IEA, *Energy Prices and Taxes, 2nd Quarter 1995.*

Table 8. Total primary energy supply in 1993

Million tonnes oil equivalent

	Indigenous production	Imports	Exports	Intl. marine bunker	Stock changes	Total
Coal	6.52	10.03	-0.75	0.00	-0.85	14.95
Crude oil	3.46	80.14	-1.33	0.00	0.58	82.85
Petroleum products	0.00	24.49	-15.56	-2.41	0.10	6.62
Gas	2.88	25.80	-0.50	0.00	0.77	28.95
Nuclear	95.95	0.00	0.00	0.00	0.00	95.95
Hydro	5.48	0.00	0.00	0.00	0.00	5.48
Geothermal, solar, etc.	0.05	0.00	0.00	0.00	0.00	0.05
Combustible, renewable & waste	4.19	0.00	0.00	0.00	0.00	4.19
Electricity	0.00	0.32	-5.60	0.00	0.00	-5.28
Heat	0.00	0.00	0.00	0.00	0.00	0.00
Total	118.54	140.78	-23.74	-2.41	0.60	233.77

Source: IEA, *Energy Balances of OECD Countries, 1992-93.*

Table 9. Regulation in public utilities (electricity and gas) in 1990

		Ownership	Entry	Price
	Generation	..	..	..
Electricity	Transmission	..	..	..
	Distribution	..	..	..
	Production	..	..	..
Gas	Transmission	..	..	..
	Distribution	..	..	..

Source: OECD, DAFFE.

UNITED KINGDOM

Table 1. Electricity end-use prices for industry

US$/kWh

	1991	1992	1993	1994	1995
Industry	0.071	0.076	0.068	0.068	..

Source: IEA, *Energy Prices and Taxes, 2nd Quarter 1995.*

Table 2. Natural gas end-use prices for industry and electric generation

US$/$10^7$ kcal

	1991	1992	1993	1994	1995
Industry	162.0	157.6	129.1	126.3	..
Electric generation	..	..	122.8	118.8	..

Source: IEA, *Energy Prices and Taxes, 2nd Quarter 1995.*

Table 3. Steam coal gas end-use prices for industry and electric generation

US$/metric tonne

	1991	1992	1993	1994	1995
Industry	77.4	76.3	61.0	61.5	..
Electric generation	76.7	80.4	63.7	..	..

Source: IEA, *Energy Prices and Taxes, 2nd Quarter 1995.*

Table 4. Coking coal gas end-use prices for industry

US$/metric tonne

	1991	1992	1993	1994	1995
Industry	..	..	..	..	..

Source: IEA, *Energy Prices and Taxes, 2nd Quarter 1995.*

Table 5. Automotive fuels end-use prices

US$/litre

	1991	1992	1993	1994	1995
Premium leaded gasoline	0.856	0.882	0.812	0.871	0.968
Premium unleaded gasoline (98 RON)	0.834	0.849	0.794	0.858	0.952
Premium unleaded gasoline (95 RON)	0.795	0.809	0.742	0.790	0.875
Regular unleaded gasoline	..	..	..	..	..
Automotive diesel oil	0.661	0.672	0.629	0.672	0.746

Source: IEA, *Energy Prices and Taxes, 2nd Quarter 1995.*

Table 6. Light fuel oil end-use prices for industry for industry

US$/1 000 litres

	1991	1992	1993	1994	1995
Industry	222.9	198.0	181.8	171.5	..

Source: IEA, *Energy Prices and Taxes, 2nd Quarter 1995.*

Table 7. Heavy fuel oil end-use prices for industry and electric generation

US$/metric tonne

	1991	1992	1993	1994	1995
Industry	123.2	114.4	99.2	116.7	147.6
Electric generation	..	..	..	..	..

Source: IEA, *Energy Prices and Taxes, 2nd Quarter 1995.*

Table 8. Total primary energy supply in 1993

Million tonnes oil equivalent

	Indigenous production	Imports	Exports	Intl. marine bunker	Stock changes	Total
Coal	37.49	12.33	-0.84	0.00	0.93	49.90
Crude oil	103.07	63.96	-65.90	0.00	-0.34	100.79
Petroleum products	0.00	8.82	-23.65	-2.47	-0.27	-17.58
Gas	54.51	3.75	-0.53	0.00	0.12	57.85
Nuclear	23.29	0.00	0.00	0.00	0.00	23.29
Hydro	0.37	0.00	0.00	0.00	0.00	0.37
Geothermal, solar, etc.	0.02	0.00	0.00	0.00	0.00	0.02
Combustible, renewable & waste	0.92	0.00	0.00	0.00	0.00	0.92
Electricity	0.00	1.44	0.00	0.00	0.00	1.44
Heat	0.00	0.00	0.00	0.00	0.00	0.00
Total	219.65	90.30	-90.92	-2.47	0.43	216.99

Source: IEA, *Energy Balances of OECD Countries, 1992-93.*

Table 9. Regulation in public utilities (electricity and gas) in 1990

		Ownership	Entry	Price
	Generation	Mixed	Partially regulated	Partially regulated
Electricity	Transmission	Public	Regulated	Regulated
	Distribution	Public	Regulated	Regulated
	Production	Private	Unregulated	Unregulated
Gas	Transmission	Private	Partially regulated	Partially regulated
	Distribution	Private	Partially regulated	Partially regulated

Source: OECD, DAFFE.

CANADA

Table 1. Electricity end-use prices for industry

US$/kWh

	1991	1992	1993	1994	1995
Industry	0.039	0.040	0.039	0.038	..

Source: IEA, *Energy Prices and Taxes, 2nd Quarter 1995.*

Table 2. Natural gas end-use prices for industry and electric generation

US$/$10^7$ kcal

	1991	1992	1993	1994	1995
Industry	87.0	83.7	74.7	78.5	..
Electric generation	68.3	56.6	..	..	..

Source: IEA, *Energy Prices and Taxes, 2nd Quarter 1995.*

Table 3. Steam coal gas end-use prices for industry and electric generation

US$/metric tonne

	1991	1992	1993	1994	1995
Industry	..	..	..	..	..
Electric generation	54.4	52.2	..	..	..

Source: IEA, *Energy Prices and Taxes, 2nd Quarter 1995.*

Table 4. Coking coal gas end-use prices for industry

US$/metric tonne

	1991	1992	1993	1994	1995
Industry	..	..	..	..	..

Source: IEA, *Energy Prices and Taxes, 2nd Quarter 1995.*

Table 5. Automotive fuels end-use prices

US$/litre

	1991	1992	1993	1994	1995
Premium leaded gasoline	..	..	..	..	..
Premium unleaded gasoline (98 RON)	0.557	0.513	0.480	0.450	..
Premium unleaded gasoline (95 RON)	0.525	0.484	0.449	0.420	..
Regular unleaded gasoline	0.507	0.456	0.415	0.385	..
Automotive diesel oil	0.492	0.439	0.403	0.375	..

Source: IEA, *Energy Prices and Taxes, 2nd Quarter 1995.*

Table 6. Light fuel oil end-use prices for industry for industry

US$/1 000 litres

	1991	1992	1993	1994	1995
Industry	192.0	175.4	157.4	144.9	..

Source: IEA, *Energy Prices and Taxes, 2nd Quarter 1995.*

Table 7. Heavy fuel oil end-use prices for industry and electric generation

US$/metric tonne

	1991	1992	1993	1994	1995
Industry	104.0	102.9	104.4	106.6	..
Electric generation	..	..	..	..	..

Source: IEA, *Energy Prices and Taxes, 2nd Quarter 1995.*

Table 8. Total primary energy supply in 1993

Million tonnes oil equivalent

	Indigenous production	Imports	Exports	Intl. marine bunker	Stock changes	Total
Coal	37.52	5.82	-19.62	0.00	0.35	24.08
Crude oil	103.61	29.99	-51.47	0.00	-0.14	81.99
Petroleum products	0.00	7.31	-12.58	-0.56	0.20	-5.64
Gas	112.49	0.66	-51.47	0.00	-0.50	61.18
Nuclear	24.87	0.00	0.00	0.00	0.00	24.87
Hydro	27.83	0.00	0.00	0.00	0.00	27.83
Geothermal, solar, etc.	0.01	0.00	0.00	0.00	0.00	0.01
Combustible, renewable & waste	8.76	0.00	0.00	0.00	0.00	8.76
Electricity	0.00	0.65	-3.01	0.00	0.00	-2.36
Heat	0.00	0.00	0.00	0.00	0.00	0.00
Total	315.09	44.43	-138.15	-0.56	-0.09	220.73

Source: IEA, *Energy Balances of OECD Countries, 1992-93.*

Table 9. Regulation in public utilities (electricity and gas) in 1990

		Ownership	Entry	Price
	Generation	Public	Unregulated	Partially regulated
Electricity	Transmission	Public	Partially regulated	Partially regulated
	Distribution	Public	Unregulated	Unregulated
	Production	Private	Unregulated	Regulated
Gas	Transmission	Private	Regulated	Regulated
	Distribution	Private	Unregulated	Unregulated

Source: OECD, DAFFE.

ITALY

Table 1. Electricity end-use prices for industry

US$/kWh

	1991	1992	1993	1994	1995
Industry	0.105	0.113	0.092	0.094	0.088

Source: IEA, *Energy Prices and Taxes, 2nd Quarter 1995.*

Table 2. Natural gas end-use prices for industry and electric generation

US\$/10^7 kcal

	1991	1992	1993	1994	1995
Industry	170.6	177.2	150.0	157.5	167.1
Electric generation	120.0	120.2	100.6	118.3	..

Source: IEA, *Energy Prices and Taxes, 2nd Quarter 1995.*

Table 3. Steam coal gas end-use prices for industry and electric generation

US$/metric tonne

	1991	1992	1993	1994	1995
Industry	50.9	46.3	46.8	..	..
Electric generation	58.9	63.9	59.2	56.8	..

Source: IEA, *Energy Prices and Taxes, 2nd Quarter 1995.*

Table 4. Coking coal gas end-use prices for industry

US$/metric tonne

	1991	1992	1993	1994	1995
Industry	60.9	58.6	54.9	..	..

Source: IEA, *Energy Prices and Taxes, 2nd Quarter 1995.*

Table 5. Automotive fuels end-use prices

US$/litre

	1991	1992	1993	1994	1995
Premium leaded gasoline	1.233	1.236	1.027	1.050	1.126
Premium unleaded gasoline (98 RON)	..	..	..	..	..
Premium unleaded gasoline (95 RON)	1.189	1.196	0.973	0.979	1.054
Regular unleaded gasoline	..	..	..	..	..
Automotive diesel oil	0.761	0.767	0.658	0.644	0.686

Source: IEA, *Energy Prices and Taxes, 2nd Quarter 1995.*

Table 6. Light fuel oil end-use prices for industry for industry

US$/1 000 litres

	1991	1992	1993	1994	1995
Industry	746.8	768.6	650.2	639.2	..

Source: IEA, *Energy Prices and Taxes, 2nd Quarter 1995.*

Table 7. Heavy fuel oil end-use prices for industry and electric generation

US$/metric tonne

	1991	1992	1993	1994	1995
Industry	184.0	189.2	152.1	158.8	173.2
Electric generation	140.4	136.9	124.6	119.8	..

Source: IEA, *Energy Prices and Taxes, 2nd Quarter 1995.*

Table 8. Total primary energy supply in 1993

Million tonnes oil equivalent

	Indigenous production	Imports	Exports	Intl. marine bunker	Stock changes	Total
Coal	0.16	9.96	-0.12	0.00	0.65	10.66
Crude oil	5.01	88.54	-0.43	0.00	0.07	93.19
Petroleum products	0.00	23.85	-23.03	-2.44	1.09	-0.53
Gas	15.68	26.77	-0.03	0.00	-0.48	41.94
Nuclear	0.00	0.00	0.00	0.00	0.00	0.00
Hydro	3.56	0.00	0.00	0.00	0.00	3.56
Geothermal, solar, etc.	3.18	0.00	0.00	0.00	0.00	3.18
Combustible, renewable & waste	0.96	0.12	0.00	0.00	0.00	1.08
Electricity	0.00	3.45	-0.06	0.00	0.00	3.39
Heat	0.00	0.00	0.00	0.00	0.00	0.00
Total	28.55	152.69	-23.66	-2.44	1.33	156.48

Source: IEA, *Energy Balances of OECD Countries, 1992-93.*

Table 9. Regulation in public utilities (electricity and gas) in 1990

		Ownership	Entry	Price
	Generation	..	..	..
Electricity	Transmission	..	..	..
	Distribution	..	..	..
	Production	..	..	..
Gas	Transmission	..	..	..
	Distribution	..	..	..

Source: OECD, DAFFE.

AUSTRALIA

Table 1. Electricity end-use prices for industry

US$/kWh

	1991	1992	1993	1994	1995
Industry	0.047	0.046	0.042	..	..

Source: IEA, *Energy Prices and Taxes, 2nd Quarter 1995.*

Table 2. Natural gas end-use prices for industry and electric generation

US$/$10^7$ kcal

	1991	1992	1993	1994	1995
Industry	136.0	127.0	121.4	..	..
Electric generation	..	..	..	..	..

Source: IEA, *Energy Prices and Taxes, 2nd Quarter 1995.*

Table 3. Steam coal gas end-use prices for industry and electric generation

US$/metric tonne

	1991	1992	1993	1994	1995
Industry	..	..	..	..	..
Electric generation	28.6	..	..	..	..

Source: IEA, *Energy Prices and Taxes, 2nd Quarter 1995.*

Table 4. Coking coal end-use prices for industry

US$/metric tonne

	1991	1992	1993	1994	1995
Industry	..	..	..	..	..

Source: IEA, *Energy Prices and Taxes, 2nd Quarter 1995.*

Table 5. Automotive fuels end-use prices

US$/litre

	1991	1992	1993	1994	1995
Premium leaded gasoline	0.518	0.499	0.458	0.497	..
Premium unleaded gasoline (98 RON)	..	..	..	..	..
Premium unleaded gasoline (95 RON)	..	0.535	0.491	0.515	..
Regular unleaded gasoline	0.518	0.499	0.458	0.487	..
Automotive diesel oil	0.503	0.482	0.455	0.498	..

Source: IEA, *Energy Prices and Taxes, 2nd Quarter 1995.*

Table 6. Light fuel oil end-use prices for industry for industry

US$/1 000 litres

	1991	1992	1993	1994	1995
Industry	..	..	..	..	..

Source: IEA, *Energy Prices and Taxes, 2nd Quarter 1995.*

Table 7. Heavy fuel oil end-use prices for industry and electric generation

US$/metric tonne

	1991	1992	1993	1994	1995
Industry	..	..	..	..	..
Electric generation	..	..	..	..	..

Source: IEA, *Energy Prices and Taxes, 2nd Quarter 1995.*

Table 8. Total primary energy supply in 1993

Million tonnes oil equivalent

	Indigenous production	Imports	Exports	Intl. marine bunker	Stock changes	Total
Coal	118.93	0.00	-83.51	0.00	2.28	37.70
Crude oil	27.61	17.03	-8.35	0.00	-0.09	36.21
Petroleum products	0.00	2.93	-4.08	-0.67	-0.21	-2.04
Gas	20.86	0.00	-5.94	0.00	0.00	14.92
Nuclear	0.00	0.00	0.00	0.00	0.00	0.00
Hydro	1.39	0.00	0.00	0.00	0.00	1.39
Geothermal, solar, etc.	0.06	0.00	0.00	0.00	0.00	0.06
Combustible, renewable & waste	4.35	0.00	0.00	0.00	0.00	4.35
Electricity	0.00	0.00	0.00	0.00	0.00	0.00
Heat	0.00	0.00	0.00	0.00	0.00	0.00
Total	173.20	19.96	-101.89	-0.67	1.98	92.58

Source: IEA, *Energy Balances of OECD Countries, 1992-93.*

Table 9. Regulation in public utilities (electricity and gas) in 1990

		Ownership	Entry	Price
	Generation	Public	Unregulated	Unregulated
Electricity	Transmission	Public	Unregulated	Unregulated
	Distribution	Public	Unregulated	Unregulated
	Production	Private	..	..
Gas	Transmission	..	..	..
	Distribution	..	..	..

Source: OECD, DAFFE.

AUSTRIA

Table 1. Electricity end-use prices for industry

US$/kWh

	1991	1992	1993	1994	1995
Industry	0.067	0.070	0.071	0.072	..

Source: IEA, *Energy Prices and Taxes, 2nd Quarter 1995.*

Table 2. Natural gas end-use prices for industry and electric generation

US$/$10^7$ kcal

	1991	1992	1993	1994	1995
Industry	188.7	183.8	169.4	172.0	..
Electric generation	162.7	157.2	154.0	..	..

Source: IEA, *Energy Prices and Taxes, 2nd Quarter 1995.*

Table 3. Steam coal gas end-use prices for industry and electric generation

US$/metric tonne

	1991	1992	1993	1994	1995
Industry	77.4	84.2	70.5	69.4	..
Electric generation	79.7	86.6	80.1	..	..

Source: IEA, *Energy Prices and Taxes, 2nd Quarter 1995.*

Table 4. Coking coal gas end-use prices for industry

US$/metric tonne

	1991	1992	1993	1994	1995
Industry	..	..	..	..	..

Source: IEA, *Energy Prices and Taxes, 2nd Quarter 1995.*

Table 5. Automotive fuels end-use prices

US$/litre

	1991	1992	1993	1994	1995
Premium leaded gasoline	0.842	0.970	..	..	..
Premium unleaded gasoline (98 RON)	..	..	..	..	..
Premium unleaded gasoline (95 RON)	0.808	0.889	0.838	0.894	1.056
Regular unleaded gasoline	0.782	0.873	0.820	0.870	1.141
Automotive diesel oil	0.609	0.607	0.579	0.578	0.760

Source: IEA, *Energy Prices and Taxes, 2nd Quarter 1995.*

Table 6. Light fuel oil end-use prices for industry for industry

US$/1 000 litres

	1991	1992	1993	1994	1995
Industry	260.1	254.0	224.3	229.5	..

Source: IEA, *Energy Prices and Taxes, 2nd Quarter 1995.*

Table 7. Heavy fuel oil end-use prices for industry and electric generation
US$/metric tonne

	1991	1992	1993	1994	1995
Industry	124.5	130.1	119.2	101.00	..
Electric generation	127.0	142.0	125.2	..	..

Source: IEA, *Energy Prices and Taxes, 2nd Quarter 1995.*

Table 8. Total primary energy supply in 1993
Million tonnes oil equivalent

	Indigenous production	Imports	Exports	Intl. marine bunker	Stock changes	Total
Coal	0.44	2.64	0.00	0.00	-0.16	2.92
Crude oil	1.22	8.32	0.00	0.00	0.04	9.59
Petroleum products	0.00	2.51	-0.68	0.00	0.04	1.87
Gas	1.26	4.57	0.00	0.00	-0.17	5.66
Nuclear	0.00	0.00	0.00	0.00	0.00	0.00
Hydro	3.16	0.00	0.00	0.00	0.00	3.16
Geothermal, solar, etc.	0.00	0.00	0.00	0.00	0.00	0.00
Combustible, renewable & waste	3.02	0.06	0.00	0.00	0.00	3.08
Electricity	0.00	0.69	-0.76	0.00	0.00	-0.06
Heat	0.00	0.00	0.00	0.00	0.00	0.00
Total	9.10	18.80	-1.44	0.00	-0.24	26.21

Source: IEA, *Energy Balances of OECD Countries, 1992-93.*

Table 9. Regulation in public utilities (electricity and gas) in 1990

		Ownership	Entry	Price
	Generation	Public	Partially regulated	Partially regulated
Electricity	Transmission	Public	..	..
	Distribution	Public	Regulated	Partially regulated
	Production	Mixed	Regulated	Regulated
Gas	Transmission	Mixed	Regulated	Partially regulated
	Distribution	Mixed	Regulated	Partially regulated

Source: OECD, DAFFE.

BELGIUM

Table 1. Electricity end-use prices for industry

US$/kWh

	1991	1992	1993	1994	1995
Industry	0.061	0.064	0.059	0.059	..

Source: IEA, *Energy Prices and Taxes, 2nd Quarter 1995.*

Table 2. Natural gas end-use prices for industry and electric generation

US$/$10^7$ kcal

	1991	1992	1993	1994	1995
Industry	159.2	144.5	129.3	124.3	146.0
Electric generation	137.4	121.6	114.8	105.7	108.4

Source: IEA, *Energy Prices and Taxes, 2nd Quarter 1995.*

Table 3. Steam coal gas end-use prices for industry and electric generation

US$/metric tonne

	1991	1992	1993	1994	1995
Industry	41.0	..	..	..	..
Electric generation	44.9	46.8	41.5	40.1	..

Source: IEA, *Energy Prices and Taxes, 2nd Quarter 1995.*

Table 4. Coking coal gas end-use prices for industry

US$/metric tonne

	1991	1992	1993	1994	1995
Industry	61.0	57.7	56.1	54.2	58.0

Source: IEA, *Energy Prices and Taxes, 2nd Quarter 1995.*

Table 5. Automotive fuels end-use prices

US$/litre

	1991	1992	1993	1994	1995
Premium leaded gasoline	0.918	0.987	0.962	1.020	1.189
Premium unleaded gasoline (98 RON)	0.880	0.923	0.879	0.945	1.096
Premium unleaded gasoline (95 RON)	0.846	0.894	0.855	0.917	1.071
Regular unleaded gasoline	..	..	..	..	..
Automotive diesel oil	0.554	0.622	0.597	0.610	0.699

Source: IEA, *Energy Prices and Taxes, 2nd Quarter 1995.*

Table 6. Light fuel oil end-use prices for industry for industry

US$/1 000 litres

	1991	1992	1993	1994	1995
Industry	215.73	195.33	193.58	185.62	202.35

Source: IEA, *Energy Prices and Taxes, 2nd Quarter 1995.*

Table 7. Heavy fuel oil end-use prices for industry and electric generation

US$/metric tonne

	1991	1992	1993	1994	1995
Industry	96.4	100.0	104.2	116.9	141.8
Electric generation	96.4	100.0	104.2	116.9	141.8

Source: IEA, *Energy Prices and Taxes, 2nd Quarter 1995.*

Table 8. Total primary energy supply in 1993

Million tonnes oil equivalent

	Indigenous production	Imports	Exports	Intl. marine bunker	Stock changes	Total
Coal	0.46	8.90	-1.02	0.00	0.55	8.89
Crude oil	0.00	31.56	-2.66	0.00	0.24	29.15
Petroleum products	0.00	12.91	-16.79	-4.30	-0.08	-8.25
Gas	0.00	9.47	0.00	0.00	-0.06	9.40
Nuclear	10.93	0.00	0.00	0.00	0.00	10.93
Hydro	0.02	0.00	0.00	0.00	0.00	0.02
Geothermal, solar, etc.	0.00	0.00	0.00	0.00	0.00	0.00
Combustible, renewable & waste	0.32	0.00	0.00	0.00	0.00	0.00
Electricity	0.00	0.65	-0.46	0.00	0.00	0.19
Heat	0.00	0.00	0.00	0.00	0.00	0.00
Total	11.74	63.49	-20.92	-4.30	0.65	50.65

Source: IEA, *Energy Balances of OECD Countries, 1992-93.*

Table 9. Regulation in public utilities (electricity and gas) in 1990

		Ownership	Entry	Price
	Generation	..	Unregulated	Partially regulated
Electricity	Transmission	..	Unregulated	Partially regulated
	Distribution	..	Unregulated	Partially regulated
	Production	Public	Regulated	Regulated
Gas	Transmission	Public	Regulated	Regulated
	Distribution	Public	Regulated	Regulated

Source: OECD, DAFFE.

CZECH REPUBLIC

Table 1. Electricity end-use prices for industry

US$/kWh

	1991	1992	1993	1994	1995
Industry	0.056	0.057	0.059	0.061	0.062

Source: Ministry of Finance of the Czech Republic.

Table 2. Natural gas end-use prices for industry and electric generation

US$/$10^7$ kcal

	1991	1992	1993	1994	1995
Industry	158.5	134.2	146.3	146.3	158.5
Electric generation	158.5	134.2	146.3	146.3	158.5

Source: Ministry of Finance of the Czech Republic.

Table 3. Steam coal gas end-use prices for industry and electric generation

US$/metric tonne

	1991	1992	1993	1994	1995
Industry	13.45	14.36	18.18	20.00	..
Electric generation	..	..	..	..	..

Source: Ministry of Industry and Trade of the Czech Republic.

Table 4. Coking coal gas end-use prices for industry

US$/metric tonne

	1991	1992	1993	1994	1995
Industry	53.8	53.8	50.9	50.9	..

Source: Ministry of Industry and Trade of the Czech Republic.

Table 5. Automotive fuels end-use prices

US$/litre

	1991	1992	1993	1994	1995
Premium leaded gasoline	0.611	0.672	0.679	0.681-0.702	0.738-0.765
Premium unleaded gasoline (98 RON)	..	..	..	0.764-0.796	0.829-0.863
Premium unleaded gasoline (95 RON)	..	0.679	0.659	0.657-0.671	0.708-0.761
Regular unleaded gasoline	0.611	0.676	..	..	..
Automotive diesel oil	0.509	0.513	0.539	0.528-0.542	0.573-0.610

Source: Ministry of Industry and Trade of the Czech Republic.

Table 6. Light fuel oil end-use prices for industry for industry

US$/metric tonne

	1991	1992	1993	1994	1995
Industry	..	..	174.9	191.1	291.9

Source: Ministry of Industry and Trade of the Czech Republic.

Table 7. Heavy fuel oil end-use prices for industry and electric generation

US$/metric tonne

	1991	1992	1993	1994	1995
Industry	101.8	98.4	82.0	107.7	109.2
Electric generation	..	..	..	..	..

Source: Ministry of Industry and Trade of the Czech Republic.

Table 8. Total primary energy supply in 1993

Million tonnes oil equivalent

	Indigenous production	Imports	Exports	Intl. marine bunker	Stock changes	Total
Coal	31.10	1.10	-7.20	..	-23.6	24.70
Crude oil	0.10	6.10	-0.07	..	0.07	6.20
Petroleum products	0.00	1.60	..	..	0.20	1.10
Gas	0.20	5.70	0.00	..	0.01	6.00
Nuclear	3.30	..	..	..	..	3.30
Hydro	0.10	..	..	..	..	0.10
Geothermal, solar, etc.	..	..	..	..	..	..
Combustible, renewable & waste	..	..	..	..	..	..
Electricity	0.00	0.08	-0.26	..	..	-0.20
Heat	..	..	..	..	..	..
Total	35.30	..	..	..	..	..

Source: Ministry of Industry and Trade of the Czech Republic.

Table 9. Regulation in Public Utilities (electricity and gas) in 1995

		Ownership	Entry	Price
	Generation	Private	Unregulated	Unregulated
Electricity	Transmission	Private	Unregulated	Unregulated
	Distribution	Private	Unregulated	Regulated
	Production	Private	Unregulated	Unregulated
Gas	Transmission	State	Unregulated	Mixed
	Distribution	Private	Unregulated	Regulated

Source: Ministry of Industry and Trade of the Czech Republic.

DENMARK

Table 1. Electricity end-use prices for industry

US$/kWh

	1991	1992	1993	1994	1995
Industry	0.065	0.067	0.070	0.063	0.071

Source: IEA, *Energy Prices and Taxes, 2nd Quarter 1995.*

Table 2. Natural gas end-use prices for industry and electric generation

US$/$10^7$ kcal

	1991	1992	1993	1994	1995
Industry	87.0	83.7	74.7	78.5	..
Electric generation	..	..	..	..	..

Source: IEA, *Energy Prices and Taxes, 2nd Quarter 1995.*

Table 3. Steam coal gas end-use prices for industry and electric generation

US$/metric tonne

	1991	1992	1993	1994	1995
Industry	115.0	115.9	75.9	74.2	92.9
Electric generation	..	..	..	..	..

Source: IEA, *Energy Prices and Taxes, 2nd Quarter 1995.*

Table 4. Coking coal gas end-use prices for industry

US$/metric tonne

	1991	1992	1993	1994	1995
Industry	..	..	..	..	..

Source: IEA, *Energy Prices and Taxes, 2nd Quarter 1995.*

Table 5. Automotive fuels end-use prices

US$/litre

	1991	1992	1993	1994	1995
Premium leaded gasoline	0.947	0.961	0.873	0.888	1.131
Premium unleaded gasoline (98 RON)	0.875	0.895	0.859	0.883	1.126
Premium unleaded gasoline (95 RON)	..	..	..	..	..
Regular unleaded gasoline	0.819	0.835	0.804	0.846	1.085
Automotive diesel oil	0.415	0.478	0.491	0.485	0.595

Source: IEA, *Energy Prices and Taxes, 2nd Quarter 1995.*

Table 6. Light fuel oil end-use prices for industry

US$/1 000 litres

	1991	1992	1993	1994	1995
Industry	288.6	251.5	265.8	256.0	287.2

Source: IEA, *Energy Prices and Taxes, 2nd Quarter 1995.*

Table 7. Heavy fuel oil end-use prices for industry and electric generation

US$/metric tonne

	1991	1992	1993	1994	1995
Industry	134.2	126.0	140.7	140.1	166.5
Electric generation	..	..	..	..	..

Source: IEA, *Energy Prices and Taxes, 2nd Quarter 1995.*

Table 8. Total primary energy supply in 1993

Million tonnes oil equivalent

	Indigenous production	Imports	Exports	Intl. marine bunker	Stock changes	Total
Coal	0.00	6.36	-0.02	0.00	0.00	7.22
Crude oil	8.43	5.52	-5.28	0.00	0.13	8.79
Petroleum products	0.00	4.97	-4.03	-1.35	0.31	-0.11
Gas	3.95	0.00	-1.43	0.00	-0.11	2.41
Nuclear	0.00	0.00	0.00	0.00	0.00	0.00
Hydro	0.00	0.00	0.00	0.00	0.00	0.00
Geothermal, solar, etc.	0.09	0.00	0.00	0.00	0.00	0.09
Combustible, renewable & waste	1.26	0.00	0.00	0.00	0.00	1.26
Electricity	0.00	0.54	-0.44	0.00	0.00	0.10
Heat	0.00	0.00	0.00	0.00	0.00	0.00
Total	13.74	17.38	-11.20	-1.35	1.21	19.78

Source: IEA, *Energy Balances of OECD Countries, 1992-93.*

Table 9. Regulation in public utilities (electricity and gas) in 1990

		Ownership	Entry	Price
	Generation	Public	Regulated	Regulated
Electricity	Transmission	Public	Regulated	Regulated
	Distribution	Public	Regulated	Regulated
	Production	Public	Regulated	Regulated
Gas	Transmission	Public	Regulated	Regulated
	Distribution	Public	Regulated	Regulated

Source: OECD, DAFFE.

FINLAND

Table 1. Electricity end-use prices for industry

US$/kWh

	1991	1992	1993	1994	1995
Industry	0.062	0.057	0.048	0.052	0.064

Source: IEA, *Energy Prices and Taxes, 2nd Quarter 1995.*

Table 2. Natural gas end-use prices for industry and electric generation

US$/$10^7$ kcal

	1991	1992	1993	1994	1995
Industry	140.2	129.5	105.4	120.2	161.2
Electric generation	..	..	..	..	..

Source: IEA, *Energy Prices and Taxes, 2nd Quarter 1995.*

Table 3. Steam coal gas end-use prices for industry and electric generation

US$/metric tonne

	1991	1992	1993	1994	1995
Industry	59.9	57.6	46.6	56.9	..
Electric generation	59.9	57.6	46.6	56.9	..

Source: IEA, *Energy Prices and Taxes, 2nd Quarter 1995.*

Table 4. Coking coal gas end-use prices for industry

US$/metric tonne

	1991	1992	1993	1994	1995
Industry	..	..	..	..	..

Source: IEA, *Energy Prices and Taxes, 2nd Quarter 1995.*

Table 5. Automotive fuels end-use prices

US$/litre

	1991	1992	1993	1994	1995
Premium leaded gasoline	1.093	1.014	0.932	..	..
Premium unleaded gasoline (98 RON)	..	..	..	0.905	1.155
Premium unleaded gasoline (95 RON)	1.004	0.878	0.818	0.868	1.127
Regular unleaded gasoline	..	..	..	..	..
Automotive diesel oil	0.774	0.665	0.549	0.639	0.824

Source: IEA, *Energy Prices and Taxes, 2nd Quarter 1995.*

Table 6. Light fuel oil end-use prices for industry

US$/1 000 litres

	1991	1992	1993	1994	1995
Industry	269.4	248.1	235.8	233.9	273.0

Source: IEA, *Energy Prices and Taxes, 2nd Quarter 1995.*

Table 7. Heavy fuel oil end-use prices for industry and electric generation
US$/metric tonne

	1991	1992	1993	1994	1995
Industry	157.2	144.2	140.2	167.8	215.4
Electric generation	157.2	144.2	139.8	167.8	226.9

Source: IEA, *Energy Prices and Taxes, 2nd Quarter 1995.*

Table 8. Total primary energy supply in 1993
Million tonnes oil equivalent

	Indigenous production	Imports	Exports	Intl. marine bunker	Stock changes	Total
Coal	1.40	4.24	-0.02	0.00	0.12	5.74
Crude oil	0.00	8.53	0.00	0.00	0.40	8.92
Petroleum products	0.00	4.25	-3.50	-0.53	0.23	0.45
Gas	0.00	2.57	0.00	0.00	0.00	2.57
Nuclear	5.18	0.00	0.00	0.00	0.00	5.18
Hydro	1.17	0.00	0.00	0.00	0.00	1.17
Geothermal, solar, etc.	0.00	0.00	0.00	0.00	0.00	0.00
Combustible, renewable & waste	4.21	0.00	0.00	0.00	0.03	4.24
Electricity	0.00	0.69	-0.04	0.00	0.00	0.65
Heat	0.00	0.00	0.00	0.00	0.00	0.00
Total	11.96	20.28	-3.56	-0.53	0.78	28.93

Source: IEA, *Energy Balances of OECD Countries, 1992-93.*

Table 9. Regulation in public utilities (electricity and gas) in 1990

		Ownership	Entry	Price
	Generation	Mixed	Regulated	Unregulated
Electricity	Transmission	Mixed	Regulated	Unregulated
	Distribution	Private	Regulated	Unregulated
	Production	Public	Unregulated	Unregulated
Gas	Transmission	Public	Unregulated	Unregulated
	Distribution	Public	Partially regulated	Unregulated

Source: OECD, DAFFE.

GREECE

Table 1. Electricity end-use prices for industry

US$/kWh

	1991	1992	1993	1994	1995
Industry	0.065	0.070	0.059	..	..

Source: IEA, *Energy Prices and Taxes, 2nd Quarter 1995.*

Table 2. Natural gas end-use prices for industry and electric generation

US$/107 kcal

	1991	1992	1993	1994	1995
Industry	..	..	..	..	..
Electric generation	..	..	..	..	..

Source: IEA, *Energy Prices and Taxes, 2nd Quarter 1995.*

Table 3. Steam coal gas end-use prices for industry and electric generation

US$/metric tonne

	1991	1992	1993	1994	1995
Industry	..	..	..	..	..
Electric generation	..	..	..	..	..

Source: IEA, *Energy Prices and Taxes, 2nd Quarter 1995.*

Table 4. Coking coal gas end-use prices for industry

US$/metric tonne

	1991	1992	1993	1994	1995
Industry	..	..	..	..	..

Source: IEA, *Energy Prices and Taxes, 2nd Quarter 1995.*

Table 5. Automotive fuels end-use prices

US$/litre

	1991	1992	1993	1994	1995
Premium leaded gasoline	0.755	0.820	0.880	0.827	0.911
Premium unleaded gasoline(98 RON)	..	..	..	..	..
Premium unleaded gasoline(95 RON)	0.700	0.747	0.822	0.771	0.850
Regular unleaded gasoline	..	..	..	..	..
Automotive diesel oil	0.397	0.521	0.495	0.453	0.522

Source: IEA, *Energy Prices and Taxes, 2nd Quarter 1995.*

Table 6. Light fuel oil end-use prices for industry

US$/1 000 litres

	1991	1992	1993	1994	1995
Industry	396.7	421.9	359.3	357.9	447.8

Source: IEA, *Energy Prices and Taxes, 2nd Quarter 1995.*

Table 7. Heavy fuel oil end-use prices for industry and electric generation

US$/metric tonne

	1991	1992	1993	1994	1995
Industry	157.7	162.8	134.7	168.2	208.5
Electric generation	157.7	162.8	134.7	168.2	208.5

Source: IEA, *Energy Prices and Taxes, 2nd Quarter 1995.*

Table 8. Total primary energy supply in 1993

Million tonnes oil equivalent

	Indigenous production	Imports	Exports	Intl. marine bunker	Stock changes	Total
Coal	7.16	0.88	0.00	0.00	0.12	8.17
Crude oil	0.58	14.55	-0.76	0.00	-0.50	13.87
Petroleum products	0.00	5.81	-3.03	-3.13	0.06	-0.30
Gas	0.09	0.00	0.00	0.00	0.00	0.09
Nuclear	0.00	0.00	0.00	0.00	0.00	0.00
Hydro	0.20	0.00	0.00	0.00	0.00	0.20
Geothermal, solar, etc.	0.00	0.00	0.00	0.00	0.00	0.00
Combustible, renewable & waste	0.58	0.00	0.00	0.00	0.00	0.58
Electricity	0.00	0.09	-0.02	0.00	0.00	0.07
Heat	0.00	0.00	0.00	0.00	0.00	0.00
Total	8.61	21.33	-3.81	-3.13	-0.32	22.68

Source: IEA, *Energy Balances of OECD Countries, 1992-93.*

Table 9. Regulation in public utilities (electricity and gas) in 1990

		Ownership	Entry	Price
	Generation	..	..	..
Electricity	Transmission	..	..	..
	Distribution	..	..	..
	Production	..	..	..
Gas	Transmission	..	..	..
	Distribution	..	..	..

Source: OECD, DAFFE.

IRELAND

Table 1. Electricity end-use prices for industry

US$/kWh

	1991	1992	1993	1994	1995
Industry	0.066	0.070	0.060	0.061	..

Source: IEA, *Energy Prices and Taxes, 2nd Quarter 1995.*

Table 2. Natural gas end-use prices for industry and electric generation

US$/$10^7$ kcal

	1991	1992	1993	1994	1995
Industry	321.9	340.5	291.9	296.4	..
Electric generation	90.4	101.1	90.5	104.6	..

Source: IEA, *Energy Prices and Taxes, 2nd Quarter 1995.*

Table 3. Steam coal gas end-use prices for industry and electric generation

US$/metric tonne

	1991	1992	1993	1994	1995
Industry	..	..	..	..	..
Electric generation	51.2	50.1	40.8	40.9	..

Source: IEA, *Energy Prices and Taxes, 2nd Quarter 1995.*

Table 4. Coking coal gas end-use prices for industry

US$/metric tonne

	1991	1992	1993	1994	1995
Industry	..	..	..	..	..

Source: IEA, *Energy Prices and Taxes, 2nd Quarter 1995.*

Table 5. Automotive fuels end-use prices

US$/litre

	1991	1992	1993	1994	1995
Premium leaded gasoline	1.002	1.004	0.870	0.891	..
Premium unleaded gasoline (98 RON)	..	0.989	..	0.876	..
Premium unleaded gasoline (95 RON)	0.971	..	0.830	0.835	..
Regular unleaded gasoline	..	..	..	..	..
Automotive diesel oil	0.717	0.736	0.782	0.794	..

Source: IEA, *Energy Prices and Taxes, 2nd Quarter 1995.*

Table 6. Light fuel oil end-use prices for industry

US$/1 000 litres

	1991	1992	1993	1994	1995
Industry	308.3	285.7	271.5	269.9	..

Source: IEA, *Energy Prices and Taxes, 2nd Quarter 1995.*

Table 7. Heavy fuel oil end-use prices for industry and electric generation
US$/metric tonne

	1991	1992	1993	1994	1995
Industry	139.8	142.7	137.0	147.3	..
Electric generation	103.0	110.5	89.0	95.0	..

Source: IEA, *Energy Prices and Taxes, 2nd Quarter 1995.*

Table 8. Total primary energy supply in 1993
Million tonnes oil equivalent

	Indigenous production	Imports	Exports	Intl. marine bunker	Stock changes	Total
Coal	1.13	2.12	-0.02	0.00	0.10	3.34
Crude oil	0.00	1.93	0.00	0.00	0.01	1.94
Petroleum products	0.00	4.09	-0.77	-0.05	-0.07	3.19
Gas	2.16	0.00	0.00	0.00	0.00	2.16
Nuclear	0.00	0.00	0.00	0.00	0.00	0.00
Hydro	0.07	0.00	0.00	0.00	0.00	0.07
Geothermal, solar, etc.	0.00	0.00	0.00	0.00	0.00	0.00
Combustible, renewable & waste	0.01	0.00	0.00	0.00	0.00	0.01
Electricity	0.00	0.00	0.00	0.00	0.00	0.00
Heat	0.00	0.00	0.00	0.00	0.00	0.00
Total	3.37	8.15	-0.79	-0.05	0.03	10.70

Source: IEA, *Energy Balances of OECD Countries, 1992-93.*

Table 9. Regulation in public utilities (electricity and gas) in 1990

		Ownership	Entry	Price
	Generation	Public	Regulated	Partially regulated
Electricity	Transmission	Public	Regulated	Partially regulated
	Distribution	Public	Regulated	Partially regulated
	Production	Public	Regulated	..
Gas	Transmission	Public	Regulated	Regulated
	Distribution	Public	Regulated	Regulated

Source: OECD, DAFFE.

Table 1. Electricity end-use prices for industry

US$/kWh

	1991	1992	1993	1994	1995
Industry	..	..	..	..	..

Source: IEA, *Energy Prices and Taxes, 2nd Quarter 1995.*

Table 2. Natural gas end-use prices for industry and electric generation

US$/$10^7$ kcal

	1991	1992	1993	1994	1995
Industry	..	..	..	..	..
Electric generation	..	..	..	..	..

Source: IEA, *Energy Prices and Taxes, 2nd Quarter 1995.*

Table 3. Steam coal gas end-use prices for industry and electric generation

US$/metric tonne

	1991	1992	1993	1994	1995
Industry	..	..	..	..	..
Electric generation	..	..	..	..	..

Source: IEA, *Energy Prices and Taxes, 2nd Quarter 1995.*

Table 4. Coking coal gas end-use prices for industry

US$/metric tonne

	1991	1992	1993	1994	1995
Industry	..	..	..	..	..

Source: IEA, *Energy Prices and Taxes, 2nd Quarter 1995.*

Table 5. Automotive fuels end-use prices

US$/litre

	1991	1992	1993	1994	1995
Premium leaded gasoline	0.660	0.746	0.759	0.807	0.976
Premium unleaded gasoline (98 RON)	..	..	..	..	..
Premium unleaded gasoline (95 RON)	0.595	0.640	0.657	0.711	0.865
Regular unleaded gasoline	..	..	..	..	..
Automotive diesel oil	0.179	0.213	0.249	0.257	..

Source: IEA, *Energy Prices and Taxes, 2nd Quarter 1995.*

Table 6. Light fuel oil end-use prices for industry

US$/1 000 litres

	1991	1992	1993	1994	1995
Industry	245.2	230.1	221.8	212.9	234.5

Source: IEA, *Energy Prices and Taxes, 2nd Quarter 1995.*

Table 7. Heavy fuel oil end-use prices for industry and electric generation

US$/metric tonne

	1991	1992	1993	1994	1995
Industry	121.8	136.9	117.1	128.1	159.1
Electric generation	..	..	..	..	..

Source: IEA, *Energy Prices and Taxes, 2nd Quarter 1995.*

Table 8. Total primary energy supply in 1993

Million tonnes oil equivalent

	Indigenous production	Imports	Exports	Intl. marine bunker	Stock changes	Total
Coal	0.00	1.04	0.00	0.00	0.00	1.04
Crude oil	0.00	0.00	0.00	0.00	0.00	0.00
Petroleum products	0.00	1.95	0.00	0.00	0.02	1.96
Gas	..	0.48	0.00	0.00	0.00	0.48
Nuclear	0.00	0.00	0.00	0.00	0.00	0.00
Hydro	0.01	0.00	0.00	0.00	0.00	0.01
Geothermal, solar, etc.	0.00	0.00	0.00	0.00	0.00	0.00
Combustible, renewable & waste	0.02	0.00	0.00	0.00	0.00	0.02
Electricity	0.00	0.38	-0.03	0.00	0.00	0.35
Heat	0.00	0.00	0.00	0.00	0.00	0.00
Total	0.03	3.85	-0.04	0.00	0.02	3.87

Source: IEA, *Energy Balances of OECD Countries, 1992-93.*

Table 9. Regulation in public utilities (electricity and gas) in 1990

		Ownership	Entry	Price
	Generation	..	..	..
Electricity	Transmission	..	..	..
	Distribution	..	..	..
	Production	..	..	..
Gas	Transmission	..	..	..
	Distribution	..	..	..

Source: OECD, DAFFE.

MEXICO

Table 1. Electricity end-use prices for industry

US$/kWh

	1991	1992	1993	1994	1995
Industry	0.048	0.050	0.049	0.042	0.030

Source: IEA, *Energy Prices and Taxes, 2nd Quarter 1995.*

Table 2. Natural gas end-use prices for industry and electric generation

US$/$10^7$ kcal

	1991	1992	1993	1994	1995
Industry	70.7	76.2	91.3	80.5	65.5
Electric generation	70.7	76.2	91.3	80.5	65.5

Source: IEA, *Energy Prices and Taxes, 2nd Quarter 1995.*

Table 3. Steam coal gas end-use prices for industry and electric generation

US$/metric tonne

	1991	1992	1993	1994	1995
Industry	..	..	..	..	..
Electric generation	31.7	30.5	28.7	28.8	23.6

Source: IEA, *Energy Prices and Taxes, 2nd Quarter 1995.*

Table 4. Coking coal gas end-use prices for industry

US$/metric tonne

	1991	1992	1993	1994	1995
Industry	..	..	..	..	..

Source: IEA, *Energy Prices and Taxes, 2nd Quarter 1995.*

Table 5. Automotive fuels end-use prices

US$/litre

	1991	1992	1993	1994	1995
Premium leaded gasoline	0.255	0.356	0.381	0.376	..
Premium unleaded gasoline (98 RON)	..	..	..	..	..
Premium unleaded gasoline (95 RON)	..	..	..	..	..
Regular unleaded gasoline	0.345	0.396	0.413	0.394	..
Automotive diesel oil	0.179	0.213	0.249	0.257	..

Source: IEA, *Energy Prices and Taxes, 2nd Quarter 1995.*

Table 6. Light fuel oil end-use prices for industry

US$/1 000 litres

	1991	1992	1993	1994	1995
Industry	165.5	200.3	243.2	257.2	..

Source: IEA, *Energy Prices and Taxes, 2nd Quarter 1995.*

Table 7. Heavy fuel oil end-use prices for industry and electric generation

US$/metric tonne

	1991	1992	1993	1994	1995
Industry	60.5	62.9	62.6	63.4	..
Electric generation	60.5	62.9	62.6	63.4	..

Source: IEA, *Energy Prices and Taxes, 2nd Quarter 1995.*

Table 8. Total primary energy supply in 1993

Million tonnes oil equivalent

	Indigenous production	Imports	Exports	Intl. marine bunker	Stock changes	Total
Coal	3.09	0.40	0.00	0.00	0.61	4.10
Crude oil	158.65	0.00	-71.90	0.00	-0.13	86.61
Petroleum products	0.00	8.16	-7.29	-0.38	0.48	0.96
Gas	24.15	0.93	-0.05	0.00	0.19	25.23
Nuclear	1.29	0.00	0.00	0.00	0.00	1.29
Hydro	2.26	0.00	0.00	0.00	0.00	2.26
Geothermal, solar, etc.	5.05	0.00	0.00	0.00	0.00	5.05
Combustible, renewable & waste	9.15	0.00	0.00	0.00	0.00	9.15
Electricity	0.00	0.08	-0.17	0.00	0.00	-0.10
Heat	0.00	0.00	0.00	0.00	0.00	0.00
Total	203.63	9.57	-79.42	-0.38	1.15	134.55

Source: IEA, *Energy Balances of OECD Countries, 1992-93.*

Table 9. Regulation in public utilities (electricity and gas) in 1990

		Ownership	Entry	Price
	Generation	..	..	..
Electricity	Transmission	..	..	..
	Distribution	..	..	..
	Production	..	..	..
Gas	Transmission	..	..	..
	Distribution	..	..	..

Source: OECD, DAFFE.

NETHERLANDS

Table 1. Electricity end-use prices for industry

US$/kWh

	1991	1992	1993	1994	1995
Industry	0.053	0.051	0.056	0.057	..

Source: IEA, *Energy Prices and Taxes, 2nd Quarter 1995.*

Table 2. Natural gas end-use prices for industry and electric generation

US$/$10^7$ kcal

	1991	1992	1993	1994	1995
Industry	126.0	122.1	120.2	118.6	158.3
Electric generation	126.6	123.9	120.5	119.7	148.5

Source: IEA, *Energy Prices and Taxes, 2nd Quarter 1995.*

Table 3. Steam coal gas end-use prices for industry and electric generation

US$/metric tonne

	1991	1992	1993	1994	1995
Industry	58.8	..	..	..	..
Electric generation	72.5	76.4	68.7	..	..

Source: IEA, *Energy Prices and Taxes, 2nd Quarter 1995.*

Table 4. Coking coal gas end-use prices for industry

US$/metric tonne

	1991	1992	1993	1994	1995
Industry	136.4	..	..	..	..

Source: IEA, *Energy Prices and Taxes, 2nd Quarter 1995.*

Table 5. Automotive fuels end-use prices

US$/litre

	1991	1992	1993	1994	1995
Premium leaded gasoline	1.032	1.143	1.070	1.132	..
Premium unleaded gasoline (98 RON)	0.993	1.075	1.001	1.071	..
Premium unleaded gasoline (95 RON)	0.972	1.052	0.980	1.038	..
Regular unleaded gasoline	..	..	..	..	..
Automotive diesel oil	0.522	0.552	0.590	0.621	..

Source: IEA, *Energy Prices and Taxes, 2nd Quarter 1995.*

Table 6. Light fuel oil end-use prices for industry

US$/1 000 litres

	1991	1992	1993	1994	1995
Industry	291.4	..	..	..	..

Source: IEA, *Energy Prices and Taxes, 2nd Quarter 1995.*

Table 7. Heavy fuel oil end-use prices for industry and electric generation

US$/metric tonne

	1991	1992	1993	1994	1995
Industry	165.0	178.5	169.3	172.9	216.1
Electric generation	..	..	..	..	..

Source: IEA, *Energy Prices and Taxes, 2nd Quarter 1995.*

Table 8. Total primary energy supply in 1993

Million tonnes oil equivalent

	Indigenous production	Imports	Exports	Intl. marine bunker	Stock changes	Total
Coal	0.00	9.66	-1.99	0.00	0.20	7.86
Crude oil	3.35	56.61	-0.88	0.00	0.88	59.96
Petroleum products	0.00	32.99	-55.73	-11.67	-0.33	-34.73
Gas	63.10	2.64	-31.47	0.00	-0.01	34.26
Nuclear	1.03	0.00	0.00	0.00	0.00	1.03
Hydro	0.01	0.00	0.00	0.00	0.00	0.01
Geothermal, solar, etc.	0.02	0.00	0.00	0.00	0.00	0.02
Combustible, renewable & waste	0.38	0.00	0.00	0.00	0.00	0.38
Electricity	0.00	0.91	-0.02	0.00	0.00	0.89
Heat	0.00	0.00	0.00	0.00	0.00	0.00
Total	67.88	102.81	-90.09	-11.67	0.74	69.67

Source: IEA, *Energy Balances of OECD Countries, 1992-93.*

Table 9. Regulation in public utilities (electricity and gas) in 1990

		Ownership	Entry	Price
	Generation	..	..	..
Electricity	Transmission	..	..	..
	Distribution	..	..	..
	Production	..	..	..
Gas	Transmission	..	..	..
	Distribution	..	..	..

Source: OECD, DAFFE.

NEW ZEALAND

Table 1. Electricity end-use prices for industry

US$/kWh

	1991	1992	1993	1994	1995
Industry	0.032	0.029	0.033	0.036	0.042

Source: IEA, *Energy Prices and Taxes, 2nd Quarter 1995.*

Table 2. Natural gas end-use prices for industry and electric generation

US$/$10^7$ kcal

	1991	1992	1993	1994	1995
Industry	198.7	184.9	184.0	203.0	232.5
Electric generation	..	..	..	..	..

Source: IEA, *Energy Prices and Taxes, 2nd Quarter 1995.*

Table 3. Steam coal gas end-use prices for industry and electric generation

US$/metric tonne

	1991	1992	1993	1994	1995
Industry	..	..	..	..	..
Electric generation	..	..	..	..	..

Source: IEA, *Energy Prices and Taxes, 2nd Quarter 1995.*

Table 4. Coking coal gas end-use prices for industry

US$/metric tonne

	1991	1992	1993	1994	1995
Industry	..	..	..	..	..

Source: IEA, *Energy Prices and Taxes, 2nd Quarter 1995.*

Table 5. Automotive fuels end-use prices

US$/litre

	1991	1992	1993	1994	1995
Premium leaded gasoline	0.577	0.541	0.540	0.563	0.641
Premium unleaded gasoline (98 RON)	..	..	..	..	..
Premium unleaded gasoline (95 RON)	..	..	..	..	..
Regular unleaded gasoline	0.548	0.519	0.515	0.533	0.608
Automotive diesel oil	0.287	0.270	0.265	0.274	0.320

Source: IEA, *Energy Prices and Taxes, 2nd Quarter 1995.*

Table 6. Light fuel oil end-use prices for industry

US$/1 000 litres

	1991	1992	1993	1994	1995
Industry	257.0	226.2	217.0	226.4	255.8

Source: IEA, *Energy Prices and Taxes, 2nd Quarter 1995.*

Table 7. Heavy fuel oil end-use prices for industry and electric generation

US$/metric tonne

	1991	1992	1993	1994	1995
Industry	263.0	217.0	195.8	226.8	229.6
Electric generation	..	..	..	..	..

Source: IEA, *Energy Prices and Taxes, 2nd Quarter 1995.*

Table 8. Total primary energy supply in 1993

Million tonnes oil equivalent

	Indigenous production	Imports	Exports	Intl. marine bunker	Stock changes	Total
Coal	1.78	0.00	-0.56	0.00	-0.09	1.14
Crude oil	2.10	3.68	-1.08	0.00	-0.07	4.63
Petroleum products	0.00	0.52	-0.45	-0.28	0.07	-0.15
Gas	4.39	0.00	0.00	0.00	0.00	4.39
Nuclear	0.00	0.00	0.00	0.00	0.00	0.00
Hydro	2.01	0.00	0.00	0.00	0.00	2.01
Geothermal, solar, etc.	1.86	0.00	0.00	0.00	0.00	1.86
Combustible, renewable & waste	1.02	0.00	0.00	0.00	0.00	1.02
Electricity	0.00	0.00	0.00	0.00	0.00	0.00
Heat	0.00	0.00	0.00	0.00	0.00	0.00
Total	13.16	4.20	-2.09	-0.28	-0.09	14.90

Source: IEA, *Energy Balances of OECD Countries, 1992-93.*

Table 9. Regulation in public utilities (electricity and gas) in 1990

		Ownership	Entry	Price
	Generation	Mixed	Unregulated	Unregulated
Electricity	Transmission	Public	Unregulated	Unregulated
	Distribution	Public	Regulated	Unregulated
	Production	Mixed	Unregulated	Unregulated
Gas	Transmission	Private	Regulated	Regulated
	Distribution	Mixed	Regulated	Regulated

Source: OECD, DAFFE.

NORWAY

Table 1. Electricity end-use prices for industry

US$/kWh

	1991	1992	1993	1994	1995
Industry	0.035	..	..	..	..

Source: IEA, *Energy Prices and Taxes, 2nd Quarter 1995.*

Table 2. Natural gas end-use prices for industry and electric generation

US$/$10^7$ kcal

	1991	1992	1993	1994	1995
Industry	..	..	..	..	..
Electric generation	..	..	..	..	..

Source: IEA, *Energy Prices and Taxes, 2nd Quarter 1995.*

Table 3. Steam coal gas end-use prices for industry and electric generation

US$/metric tonne

	1991	1992	1993	1994	1995
Industry	48.0	40.8	31.9	43.6	56.1
Electric generation	..	..	..	..	..

Source: IEA, *Energy Prices and Taxes, 2nd Quarter 1995.*

Table 4. Coking coal gas end-use prices for industry

US$/metric tonne

	1991	1992	1993	1994	1995
Industry	86.4	90.1	76.6	77.2	87.3

Source: IEA, *Energy Prices and Taxes, 2nd Quarter 1995.*

Table 5. Automotive fuels end-use prices

US$/litre

	1991	1992	1993	1994	1995
Premium leaded gasoline	1.143	1.279	1.180	1.170	1.413
Premium unleaded gasoline (98 RON)	1.088	1.203	1.111	1.129	1.365
Premium unleaded gasoline (95 RON)	1.044	1.154	1.065	1.085	1.316
Regular unleaded gasoline	..	..	..	..	..
Automotive diesel oil	0.438	0.439	0.469	0.755	0.910

Source: IEA, *Energy Prices and Taxes, 2nd Quarter 1995.*

Table 6. Light fuel oil end-use prices for industry

US$/1 000 litres

	1991	1992	1993	1994	1995
Industry	388.1	386.8	343.6	343.2	369.1

Source: IEA, *Energy Prices and Taxes, 2nd Quarter 1995.*

Table 7. Heavy fuel oil end-use prices for industry and electric generation

US$/metric tonne

	1991	1992	1993	1994	1995
Industry	376.0	404.5	349.3	330.2	335.7
Electric generation	..	..	..	..	..

Source: IEA, *Energy Prices and Taxes, 2nd Quarter 1995.*

Table 8. Total primary energy supply in 1993

Million tonnes oil equivalent

	Indigenous production	Imports	Exports	Intl. marine bunker	Stock changes	Total
Coal	0.18	0.80	-0.15	0.00	0.03	0.85
Crude oil	117.59	1.37	-103.02	0.00	-1.13	14.80
Petroleum products	0.00	2.97	-8.92	-0.52	-0.03	-6.51
Gas	24.21	0.00	-21.70	0.00	0.00	2.51
Nuclear	0.00	0.00	0.00	0.00	0.00	0.00
Hydro	10.24	0.00	0.00	0.00	0.00	10.24
Geothermal, solar, etc.	0.00	0.00	0.00	0.00	0.00	0.00
Combustible, renewable & waste	1.02	0.00	0.00	0.00	0.00	1.02
Electricity	0.00	0.05	-0.72	0.00	0.00	-0.67
Heat	0.00	0.00	0.00	0.00	0.00	0.00
Total	153.24	5.18	-134.52	-0.52	-1.13	22.25

Source: IEA, *Energy Balances of OECD Countries, 1992-93.*

Table 9. Regulation in public utilities (electricity and gas) in 1990

		Ownership	Entry	Price
	Generation	Mixed	Regulated	Unregulated
Electricity	Transmission	Public	Regulated	Regulated
	Distribution	Public	Regulated	Unregulated
	Production	..	..	..
Gas	Transmission	..	..	..
	Distribution	..	..	..

Source: OECD, DAFFE.

PORTUGAL

Table 1. Electricity end-use prices for industry

US$/kWh

	1991	1992	1993	1994	1995
Industry	0.128	0.145	0.121	0.116	0.124

Source: IEA, *Energy Prices and Taxes, 2nd Quarter 1995.*

Table 2. Natural gas end-use prices for industry and electric generation

US\$/10^7 kcal

	1991	1992	1993	1994	1995
Industry	..	..	..	..	..
Electric generation	..	..	..	..	..

Source: IEA, *Energy Prices and Taxes, 2nd Quarter 1995.*

Table 3. Steam coal gas end-use prices for industry and electric generation

US$/metric tonne

	1991	1992	1993	1994	1995
Industry	..	..	..	..	..
Electric generation	52.5	47.1	39.4	38.9	43.8

Source: IEA, *Energy Prices and Taxes, 2nd Quarter 1995.*

Table 4. Coking coal gas end-use prices for industry

US$/metric tonne

	1991	1992	1993	1994	1995
Industry	51.6	46.2	38.5	37.6	42.7

Source: IEA, *Energy Prices and Taxes, 2nd Quarter 1995.*

Table 5. Automotive fuels end-use prices

US$/litre

	1991	1992	1993	1994	1995
Premium leaded gasoline	1.018	1.083	0.941	0.931	1.060
Premium unleaded gasoline (98 RON)	..	..	..	0.931	1.066
Premium unleaded gasoline (95 RON)	0.949	1.009	0.879	0.907	1.046
Regular unleaded gasoline	..	..	..	..	..
Automotive diesel oil	0.646	0.702	0.610	0.593	0.674

Source: IEA, *Energy Prices and Taxes, 2nd Quarter 1995.*

Table 6. Light fuel oil end-use prices for industry

US$/1 000 litres

	1991	1992	1993	1994	1995
Industry	646.3	701.5	610.1	579.3	673.6

Source: IEA, *Energy Prices and Taxes, 2nd Quarter 1995.*

Table 7. Heavy fuel oil end-use prices for industry and electric generation

US$/metric tonne

	1991	1992	1993	1994	1995
Industry	182.8	196.4	166.0	157.0	179.1
Electric generation	81.7	83.8	70.1	84.8	103.1

Source: IEA, *Energy Prices and Taxes, 2nd Quarter 1995.*

Table 8. Total primary energy supply in 1993

Million tonnes oil equivalent

	Indigenous production	Imports	Exports	Intl. marine bunker	Stock changes	Total
Coal	0.08	3.06	-0.01	0.00	0.03	3.16
Crude oil	0.00	11.74	0.00	0.00	-0.16	11.58
Petroleum products	0.00	4.60	-3.22	-0.51	0.10	0.97
Gas	0.00	0.00	0.00	0.00	0.00	0.00
Nuclear	0.00	0.00	0.00	0.00	0.00	0.00
Hydro	0.73	0.00	0.00	0.00	0.00	0.73
Geothermal, solar, etc.	0.00	0.00	0.00	0.00	0.00	0.00
Combustible, renewable & waste	1.09	0.00	0.00	0.00	0.00	1.09
Electricity	0.00	0.18	-0.16	0.00	0.00	0.02
Heat	0.00	0.00	0.00	0.00	0.00	0.00
Total	1.91	19.58	-3.40	-0.51	-0.03	17.55

Source: IEA, *Energy Balances of OECD Countries, 1992-93.*

Table 9. Regulation in public utilities (electricity and gas) in 1990

		Ownership	Entry	Price
	Generation	..	..	..
Electricity	Transmission	..	..	..
	Distribution	..	..	..
	Production	..	..	..
Gas	Transmission	..	..	..
	Distribution	..	..	..

Source: OECD, DAFFE.

SPAIN

Table 1. Electricity end-use prices for industry

US$/kWh

	1991	1992	1993	1994	1995
Industry	0.103	0.105	0.085	0.080	..

Source: IEA, *Energy Prices and Taxes, 2nd Quarter 1995.*

Table 2. Natural gas end-use prices for industry and electric generation

US$/$10^7$ kcal

	1991	1992	1993	1994	1995
Industry	152.1	152.4	129.0	137.6	168.8
Electric generation	141.4	142.7	..	146.2	..

Source: IEA, *Energy Prices and Taxes, 2nd Quarter 1995.*

Table 3. Steam coal gas end-use prices for industry and electric generation

US$/metric tonne

	1991	1992	1993	1994	1995
Industry	..	..	..	..	..
Electric generation	..	..	..	..	..

Source: IEA, *Energy Prices and Taxes, 2nd Quarter 1995.*

Table 4. Coking coal gas end-use prices for industry

US$/metric tonne

	1991	1992	1993	1994	1995
Industry	..	..	..	..	..

Source: IEA, *Energy Prices and Taxes, 2nd Quarter 1995.*

Table 5. Automotive fuels end-use prices

US$/litre

	1991	1992	1993	1994	1995
Premium leaded gasoline	0.854	0.943	0.821	0.813	0.930
Premium unleaded gasoline (98 RON)	..	..	..	..	..
Premium unleaded gasoline (95 RON)	..	0.923	0.797	0.789	0.882
Regular unleaded gasoline	..	..	..	..	..
Automotive diesel oil	0.608	0.634	0.555	0.529	0.575

Source: IEA, *Energy Prices and Taxes, 2nd Quarter 1995.*

Table 6. Light fuel oil end-use prices for industry

US$/1 000 litres

	1991	1992	1993	1994	1995
Industry	360.6	356.2	325.0	275.4	292.4

Source: IEA, *Energy Prices and Taxes, 2nd Quarter 1995.*

Table 7. Heavy fuel oil end-use prices for industry and electric generation

US$/metric tonne

	1991	1992	1993	1994	1995
Industry	138.0	129.6	118.2	136.0	186.1
Electric generation	138.0	130.1	118.2	134.5	186.1

Source: IEA, *Energy Prices and Taxes, 2nd Quarter 1995.*

Table 8. Total primary energy supply in 1993

Million tonnes oil equivalent

	Indigenous production	Imports	Exports	Intl. marine bunker	Stock changes	Total
Coal	10.95	8.20	-0.06	0.00	-0.04	19.04
Crude oil	1.14	53.50	0.00	0.00	-0.16	54.47
Petroleum products	0.00	10.20	-12.46	-3.41	-0.18	-5.85
Gas	0.60	5.09	0.00	0.00	0.06	5.74
Nuclear	14.61	0.00	0.00	0.00	0.00	14.61
Hydro	2.10	0.00	0.00	0.00	0.00	2.10
Geothermal, solar, etc.	0.00	0.00	0.00	0.00	0.00	0.00
Combustible, renewable & waste	0.76	0.00	0.00	0.00	0.00	0.76
Electricity	0.00	0.40	-0.29	0.00	0.00	0.11
Heat	0.00	0.00	0.00	0.00	0.00	0.00
Total	30.14	77.38	-12.81	-3.41	-0.33	90.98

Source: IEA, *Energy Balances of OECD Countries, 1992-93.*

Table 9. Regulation in public utilities (electricity and gas) in 1990

		Ownership	Entry	Price
	Generation	Mixed	Regulated	Regulated
Electricity	Transmission	Public	Regulated	Regulated
	Distribution	Mixed	Regulated	Regulated
	Production	Public	Regulated	Regulated
Gas	Transmission	Public	Regulated	Regulated
	Distribution	Public	Regulated	Regulated

Source: OECD, DAFFE.

SWEDEN

Table 1. Electricity end-use prices for industry

US$/kWh

	1991	1992	1993	1994	1995
Industry	0.053	0.055	0.035	0.037	0.041

Source: IEA, *Energy Prices and Taxes, 2nd Quarter 1995.*

Table 2. Natural gas end-use prices for industry and electric generation

US$/$10^7$ kcal

	1991	1992	1993	1994	1995
Industry	..	..	..	..	..
Electric generation	..	..	..	..	..

Source: IEA, *Energy Prices and Taxes, 2nd Quarter 1995.*

Table 3. Steam coal gas end-use prices for industry and electric generation

US$/metric tonne

	1991	1992	1993	1994	1995
Industry	104.3	..	..	..	..
Electric generation	..	..	..	..	..

Source: IEA, *Energy Prices and Taxes, 2nd Quarter 1995.*

Table 4. Coking coal gas end-use prices for industry

US$/metric tonne

	1991	1992	1993	1994	1995
Industry	..	..	..	..	..

Source: IEA, *Energy Prices and Taxes, 2nd Quarter 1995.*

Table 5. Automotive fuels end-use prices

US$/litre

	1991	1992	1993	1994	1995
Premium leaded gasoline	1.124	1.136	1.031	1.017	1.096
Premium unleaded gasoline (98 RON)	..	..	1.024	1.017	1.076
Premium unleaded gasoline (95 RON)	..	..	0.985	0.972	1.035
Regular unleaded gasoline	..	..	..	..	..
Automotive diesel oil	0.687	0.669	0.545	0.649	0.689

Source: IEA, *Energy Prices and Taxes, 2nd Quarter 1995.*

Table 6. Light fuel oil end-use prices for industry

US$/1 000 litres

	1991	1992	1993	1994	1995
Industry	433.3	411.6	218.1	208.3	201.8

Source: IEA, *Energy Prices and Taxes, 2nd Quarter 1995.*

Table 7. Heavy fuel oil end-use prices for industry and electric generation
US$/metric tonne

	1991	1992	1993	1994	1995
Industry	372.3	366.3	178.7	165.1	189.3
Electric generation	130.2	148.2	120.1	..	..

Source: IEA, *Energy Prices and Taxes, 2nd Quarter 1995.*

Table 8. Total primary energy supply in 1993
Million tonnes oil equivalent

	Indigenous production	Imports	Exports	Intl. marine bunker	Stock changes	Total
Coal	0.29	2.32	-0.09	0.00	0.20	2.72
Crude oil	0.00	18.66	-0.46	0.00	0.13	18.34
Petroleum products	0.00	7.19	-9.72	-0.90	-0.12	-3.55
Gas	0.00	0.70	0.00	0.00	0.00	0.70
Nuclear	16.00	0.00	0.00	0.00	0.00	16.00
Hydro	6.42	0.00	0.00	0.00	0.00	6.42
Geothermal, solar, etc.	0.00	0.00	0.00	0.00	0.00	0.00
Combustible, renewable & waste	6.21	0.00	0.00	0.00	0.00	6.21
Electricity	0.00	0.69	-0.74	0.00	0.00	-0.05
Heat	0.34	0.00	0.00	0.00	0.00	0.34
Total	29.27	29.56	-11.00	-0.90	0.21	47.13

Source: IEA, *Energy Balances of OECD Countries, 1992-93.*

Table 9. Regulation in public utilities (electricity and gas) in 1990

		Ownership	Entry	Price
	Generation	Mixed	Unregulated	Partially regulated
Electricity	Transmission	Public	..	..
	Distribution	Mixed	Regulated	Partially regulated
	Production	Private	Unregulated	Partially regulated
Gas	Transmission	Public	Regulated	Unregulated
	Distribution	Private	Regulated	Partially regulated

Source: OECD, DAFFE.

SWITZERLAND

Table 1. Electricity end-use prices for industry

US$/kWh

	1991	1992	1993	1994	1995
Industry	0.090	0.097	0.096	0.106	0.128

Source: IEA, *Energy Prices and Taxes, 2nd Quarter 1995.*

Table 2. Natural gas end-use prices for industry and electric generation

US$/$10^7$ kcal

	1991	1992	1993	1994	1995
Industry	262.3	276.5	265.3	267.7	305.3
Electric generation	..	..	..	..	..

Source: IEA, *Energy Prices and Taxes, 2nd Quarter 1995.*

Table 3. Steam coal gas end-use prices for industry and electric generation

US$/metric tonne

	1991	1992	1993	1994	1995
Industry	60.0	54.1	45.9	47.7	60.7
Electric generation	..	..	..	..	..

Source: IEA, *Energy Prices and Taxes, 2nd Quarter 1995.*

Table 4. Coking coal gas end-use prices for industry

US$/metric tonne

	1991	1992	1993	1994	1995
Industry	..	..	..	..	..

Source: IEA, *Energy Prices and Taxes, 2nd Quarter 1995.*

Table 5. Automotive fuels end-use prices

US$/litre

	1991	1992	1993	1994	1995
Premium leaded gasoline	0.769	0.761	0.827	0.911	1.077
Premium unleaded gasoline (98 RON)	..	..	..	0.879	1.037
Premium unleaded gasoline (95 RON)	0.713	0.702	0.766	0.844	0.999
Regular unleaded gasoline	..	..	..	..	..
Automotive diesel oil	0.760	0.731	0.805	0.774	0.841

Source: IEA, *Energy Prices and Taxes, 2nd Quarter 1995.*

Table 6. Light fuel oil end-use prices for industry

US$/1 000 litres

	1991	1992	1993	1994	1995
Industry	241.5	207.5	190.4	164.3	174.6

Source: IEA, *Energy Prices and Taxes, 2nd Quarter 1995.*

Table 7. Heavy fuel oil end-use prices for industry and electric generation

US$/metric tonne

	1991	1992	1993	1994	1995
Industry	142.2	137.3	138.5	142.1	..
Electric generation	..	..	..	..	..

Source: IEA, *Energy Prices and Taxes, 2nd Quarter 1995.*

Table 8. Total primary energy supply in 1993

Million tonnes oil equivalent

	Indigenous production	Imports	Exports	Intl. marine bunker	Stock changes	Total
Coal	0.00	0.11	0.00	0.00	0.07	0.18
Crude oil	0.00	4.86	0.00	0.00	0.02	4.88
Petroleum products	0.00	7.96	-0.60	-0.02	0.73	8.07
Gas	0.00	2.02	0.00	0.00	0.00	2.02
Nuclear	6.10	0.00	0.00	0.00	0.00	6.10
Hydro	3.08	0.00	0.00	0.00	0.00	3.08
Geothermal, solar, etc.	0.00	0.00	0.00	0.00	0.00	0.00
Combustible, renewable & waste	0.99	0.01	0.00	0.00	0.00	1.00
Electricity	0.00	1.68	-2.30	0.00	0.00	-0.62
Heat	0.00	0.00	0.00	0.00	0.00	0.00
Total	10.17	16.64	-2.90	-0.02	0.82	24.72

Source: IEA, *Energy Balances of OECD Countries, 1992-93.*

Table 9. Regulation in public utilities (electricity and gas) in 1990

		Ownership	Entry	Price
	Generation	Mixed	Regulated	Unregulated
Electricity	Transmission	Mixed	Regulated	Unregulated
	Distribution	Mixed	Regulated	Unregulated
	Production	Mixed	Regulated	Unregulated
Gas	Transmission	Mixed	Regulated	Unregulated
	Distribution	Mixed	Regulated	Unregulated

Source: OECD, DAFFE.

TURKEY

Table 1. Electricity end-use prices for industry

US$/kWh

	1991	1992	1993	1994	1995
Industry	0.084	0.093	0.095	0.077	0.075

Source: IEA, *Energy Prices and Taxes, 2nd Quarter 1995.*

Table 2. Natural gas end-use prices for industry and electric generation

US$/$10^7$ kcal

	1991	1992	1993	1994	1995
Industry	136.7	134.3	156.4	140.7	167.3
Electric generation	139.3	137.0	160.2	144.2	169.0

Source: IEA, *Energy Prices and Taxes, 2nd Quarter 1995.*

Table 3. Steam coal gas end-use prices for industry and electric generation

US$/metric tonne

	1991	1992	1993	1994	1995
Industry	50.0	53.1	42.8	31.5	33.5
Electric generation	11.5	13.4	16.2	13.2	16.2

Source: IEA, *Energy Prices and Taxes, 2nd Quarter 1995.*

Table 4. Coking coal gas end-use prices for industry

US$/metric tonne

	1991	1992	1993	1994	1995
Industry	56.7	46.5	49.8	43.2	..

Source: IEA, *Energy Prices and Taxes, 2nd Quarter 1995.*

Table 5. Automotive fuels end-use prices

US$/litre

	1991	1992	1993	1994	1995
Premium leaded gasoline	0.730	0.745	0.648	0.547	0.668
Premium unleaded gasoline (98 RON)	..	..	..	..	..
Premium unleaded gasoline (95 RON)	0.825	0.826	0.649	0.542	0.668
Regular unleaded gasoline	..	..	..	..	..
Automotive diesel oil	0.519	0.536	0.457	0.350	0.433

Source: IEA, *Energy Prices and Taxes, 2nd Quarter 1995.*

Table 6. Light fuel oil end-use prices for industry

US$/1 000 litres

	1991	1992	1993	1994	1995
Industry	..	..	..	..	..

Source: IEA, *Energy Prices and Taxes, 2nd Quarter 1995.*

Table 7. Heavy fuel oil end-use prices for industry and electric generation
US$/metric tonne

	1991	1992	1993	1994	1995
Industry	179.3	164.6	153.1	120.8	183.6
Electric generation	179.3	164.6	153.1	120.8	183.6

Source: IEA, *Energy Prices and Taxes, 2nd Quarter 1995.*

Table 8. Total primary energy supply in 1993
Million tonnes oil equivalent

	Indigenous production	Imports	Exports	Intl. marine bunker	Stock changes	Total
Coal	11.59	4.11	0.00	0.00	0.57	16.27
Crude oil	3.98	22.46	0.00	0.00	-0.30	26.13
Petroleum products	0.00	3.97	-2.05	-0.10	-0.24	1.59
Gas	0.16	4.08	0.00	0.00	0.00	4.24
Nuclear	0.00	0.00	0.00	0.00	0.00	0.00
Hydro	2.92	0.00	0.00	0.00	0.00	2.92
Geothermal, solar, etc.	0.10	0.00	0.00	0.00	0.00	0.10
Combustible, renewable & waste	7.94	0.00	0.00	0.00	0.00	7.94
Electricity	0.00	0.02	-0.05	0.00	0.00	-0.03
Heat	0.00	0.00	0.00	0.00	0.00	0.00
Total	26.70	34.63	-2.10	-0.10	0.02	59.16

Source: IEA, *Energy Balances of OECD Countries, 1992-93.*

Table 9. Regulation in public utilities (electricity and gas) in 1990

		Ownership	Entry	Price
	Generation	Mixed	Unregulated	Regulated
Electricity	Transmission	Mixed	Partially regulated	Regulated
	Distribution	Mixed	Partially regulated	Regulated
	Production	Public	Unregulated	Unregulated
Gas	Transmission	Public	Regulated	Regulated
	Distribution	Public	Regulated	Regulated

Source: OECD, DAFFE.

BACKGROUND NOTES TO COUNTRY TABLES

General

The sources of the data presented in country tables are:

- OECD/International Energy Agency, *Energy Prices and Taxes, 2nd Quarter 1995*;
- OECD/International Energy Agency, *Energy Balances of OECD Countries 1992-1993*;
- Ongoing work on Competition, Regulation and Performance in the Directorate for Financial, Fiscal and Enterprise Affairs, Committee on Competition Law and Policy.

The data have been derived from *Energy Prices and Taxes, 2nd Quarter 1995*. The methodology for calculating cost for end-users is as follows:

- include transport costs to the consumer;
- prices are the prices actually paid, *i.e.* net of rebates;
- include taxes which have to be paid by the consumer as part of the transaction and which are not refundable. This excludes value-added tax paid in many European countries by industry (including electric power stations) and commercial end-users for all goods and services (including energy). In these cases value-added tax is refunded to the customer, usually in the form of a tax credit. Therefore it is not shown as part of prices and taxes in the respective columns. This also applies to the data on automotive diesel fuel oil shown for the EU countries (70-80 per cent of total automotive diesel oil is sold to industry and commerce).

Quarterly data are used for 1995 and are in US dollars, using quarterly and yearly average of exchange rates as published by the IMF. The difference between world market prices and national end-use prices in US dollars quantifies the sum of the remaining pricing parameters, such as transformation and distribution costs, non-internationally tradeable energy sources (mainly hydro-power, but also, to a certain extent, natural gas), market structures (for instance, mix of large and small purchase lots), and pricing policies of central and local authorities including tax policies.

Further methodological information on the indicators presented can be found in OECD/IEA, *Energy Prices and Taxes, 2nd Quarter 1995*.

(1) Electricity end-use prices for industry

Most of these data exist only on an annual basis and may be published long after the period to which they relate.

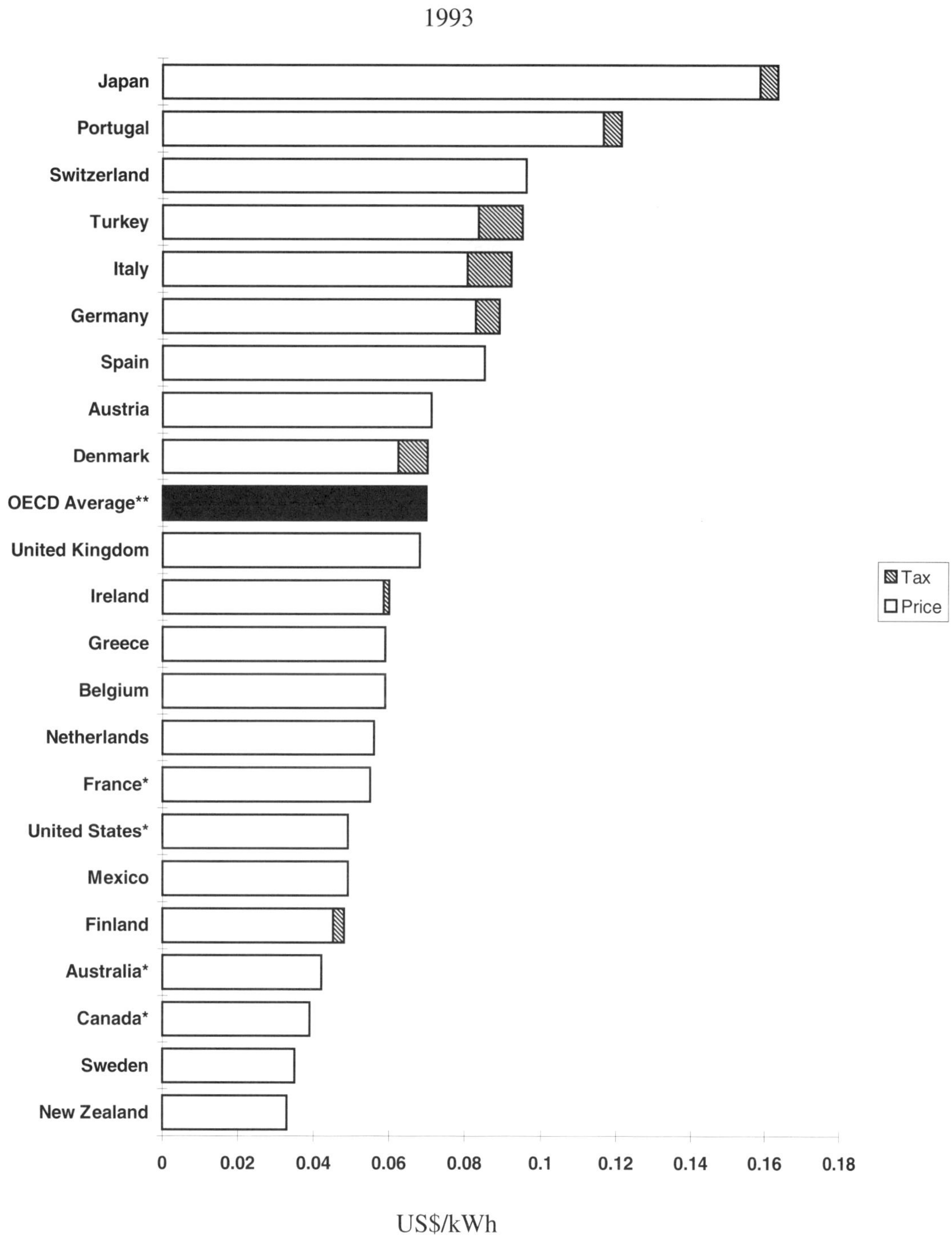

* Tax data is not available.

** Unweighted average of 22 countries: Australia, Austria, Belgium, Canada, Denmark, Finland, France, Germany, Greece, Ireland, Italy, Japan, Mexico, the Netherlands, New Zealand, Portugal, Spain, Sweden, Switzerland, Turkey, the United Kingdom and the United States.

(2) Natural gas end-use prices for industry and electricity generation

The prices for natural gas refer to 10^7 kcal using the gross calorific value of the gas. Prices for 10^7 kcal using the net calorific value would be approximately 11 per cent higher.

For industry
1993

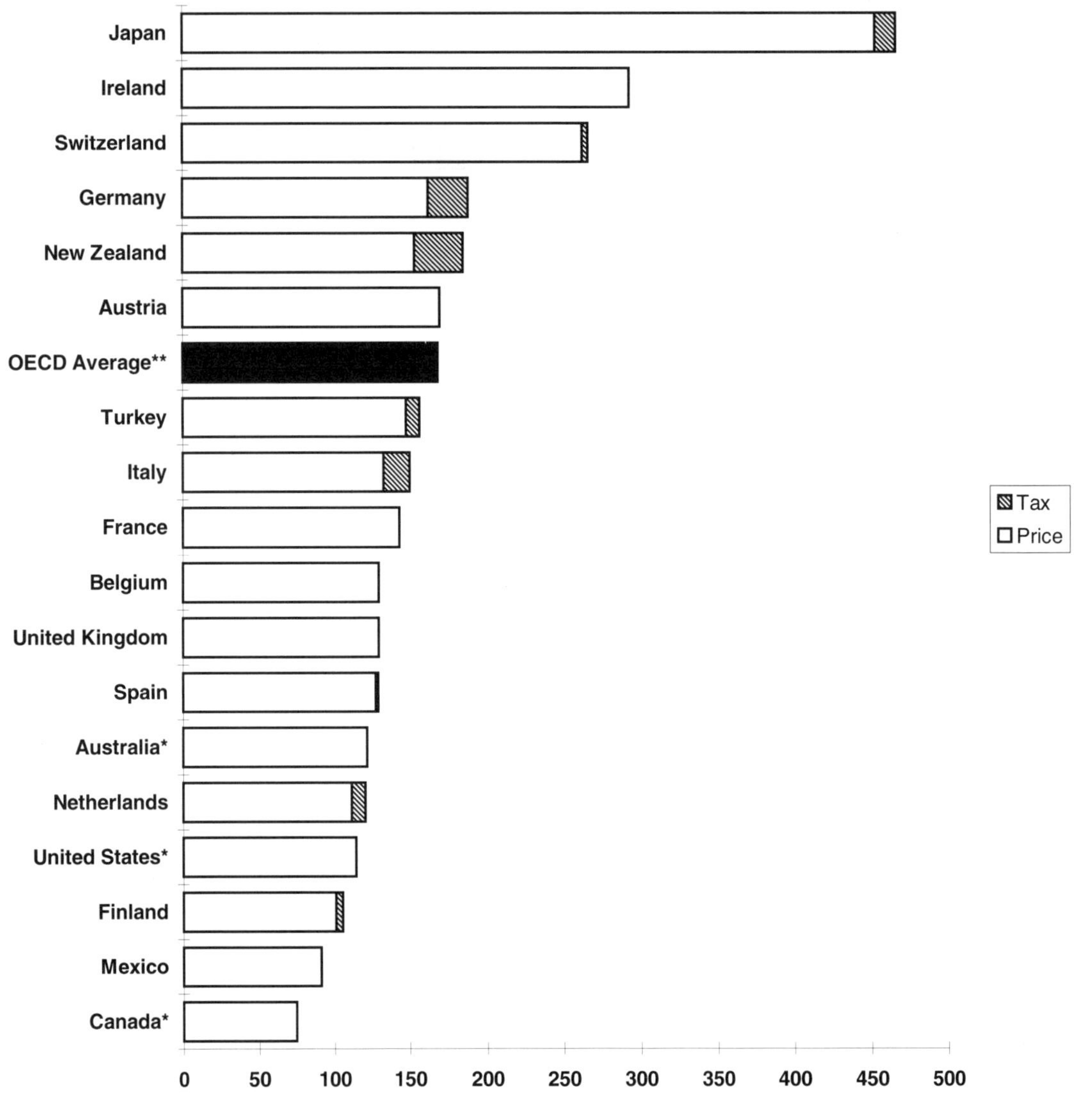

US$/$10^7$ kcal

* Tax data is not available.

** Unweighted average of 18 countries: Australia, Austria, Belgium, Canada, Finland, France, Germany, Ireland, Italy, Japan, Mexico, the Netherlands, New Zealand, Spain, Switzerland, Turkey, the United Kingdom and the United States.

For electricity generation
1993

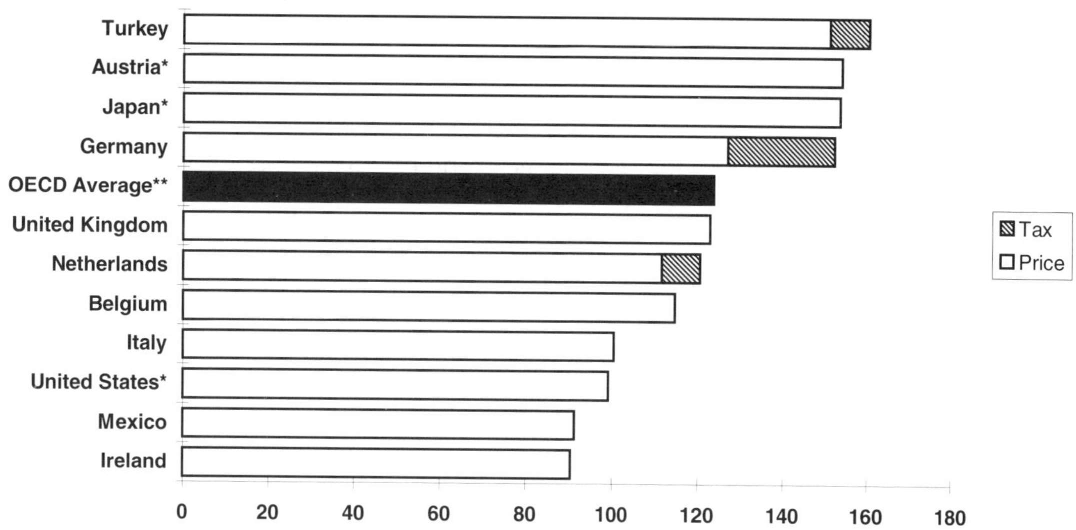

US$/$10^7$ kcal

* Tax data is not available.

** Unweighted average of 11 countries: Austria, Belgium, Germany, Ireland, Italy, Japan, Mexico, the Netherlands, Turkey, the United Kingdom and the United States.

(3) Steam coal end-use prices for industry and electricity generation

Given the great variety of coal qualities in domestic and international coal trade, selection of a standard coal quality for international comparisons of end-use prices is not possible. Therefore, prices refer instead to the most common qualities in each country and are not necessarily comparable across countries with respect to coal quality.

Steam coal is mainly used for electric generation. In addition, it is used for industrial manufacturing, such as the paper, ceramic industries, etc.

For industry
1994

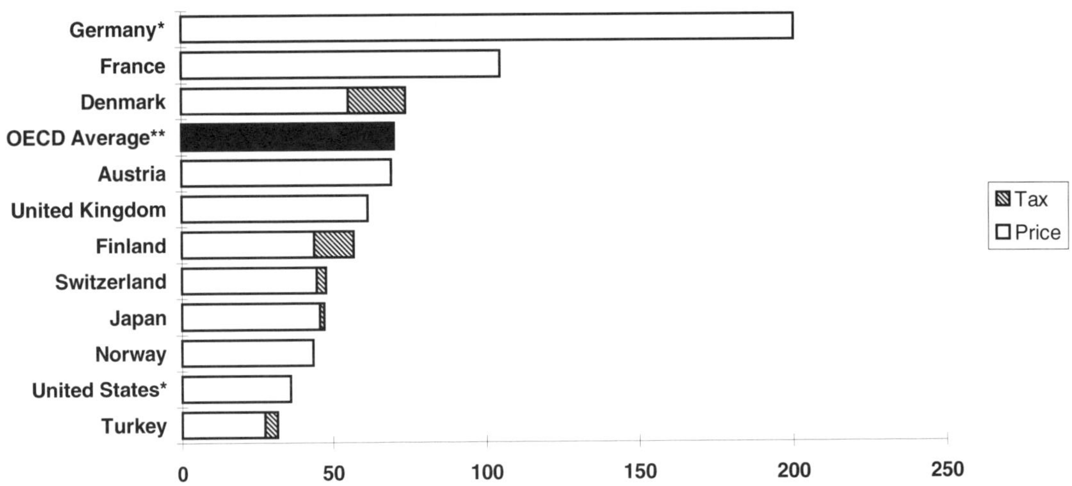

US$/metric tonne

* Tax data is not available.
** Unweighted average of 11 countries: Austria, Denmark, Finland, France, Germany, Japan, Norway, Switzerland, Turkey, the United Kingdom and the United States.

For electricity generation
1993

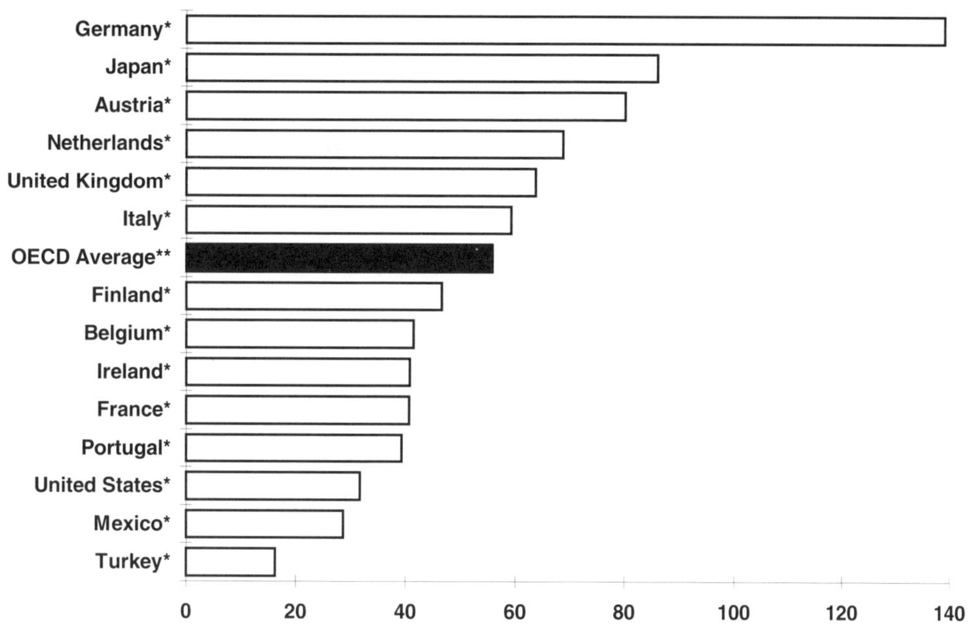

US$/metric tonne

* Tax data is not available.

** Unweighted average of 14 countries: Austria, Belgium, Finland, France, Germany, Ireland, Italy, Japan, Mexico, the Netherlands, Portugal, Turkey, the United Kingdom and the United States.

(4) Coking coal gas end-use prices for industry

Coking coal is used for making a coke or briquette that is utilised for industrial manufacturing material in several industries, such as steel, etc.

1993

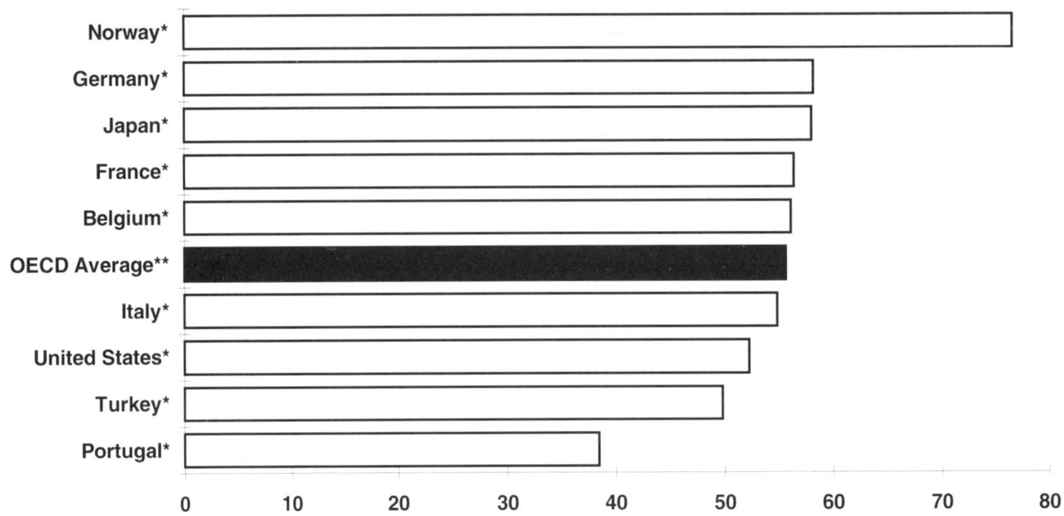

US$/metric tonne

* Tax data is not available.

** Unweighted average of 9 countries: Belgium, France, Germany, Italy, Japan, Norway, Portugal, Turkey and the United States.

(5) Automotive fuels end-use prices

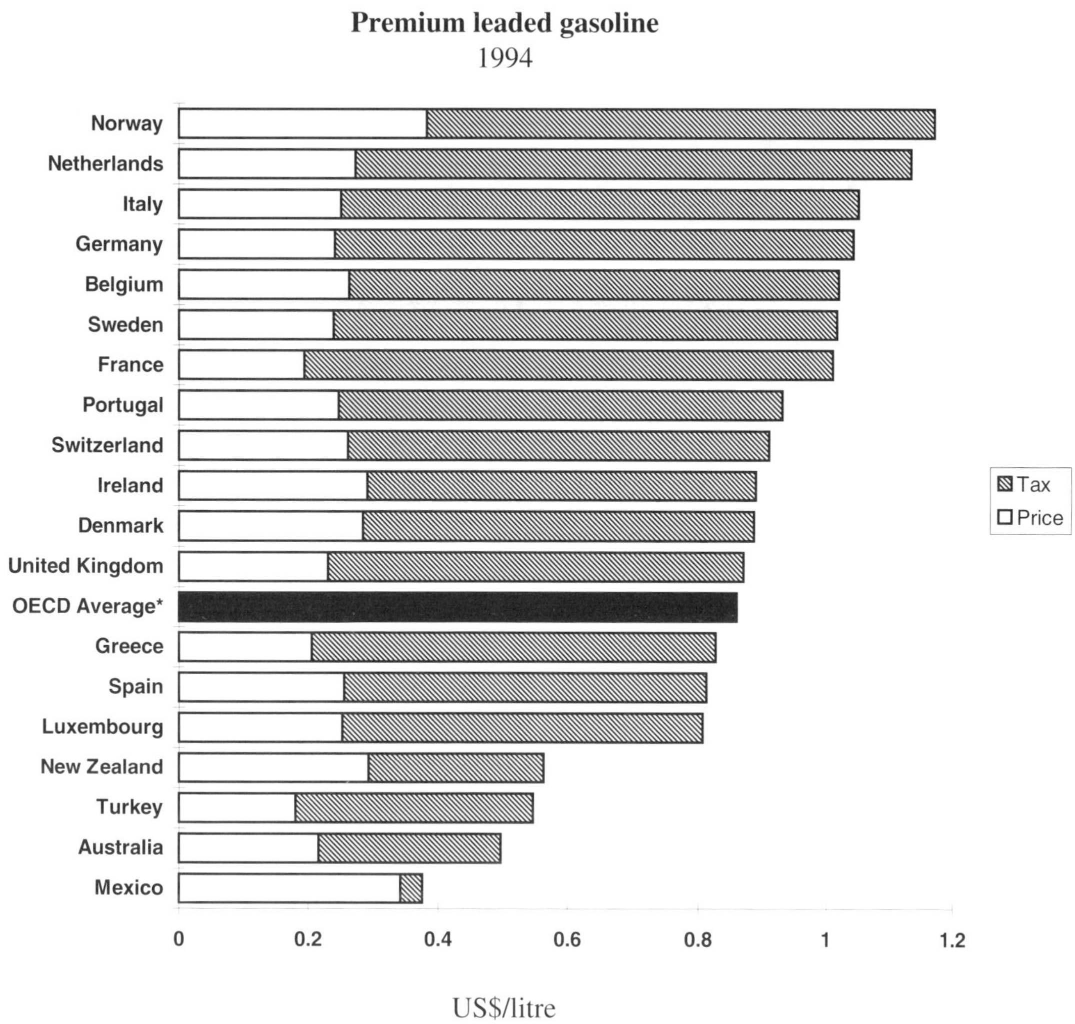

* Unweighted average of 19 countries: Australia, Belgium, Denmark, France, Germany, Greece, Ireland, Italy, Luxembourg, Mexico, the Netherlands, New Zealand, Norway, Portugal, Spain, Sweden, Switzerland, Turkey and the United Kingdom.

Premium unleaded gasoline (98 RON)
1994

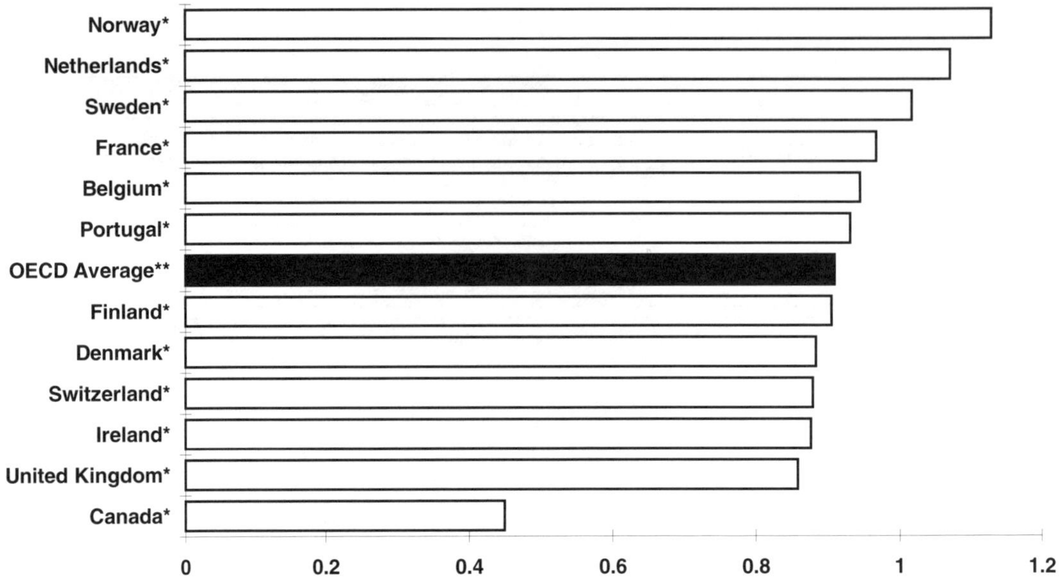

US$/litre

* Tax data is not available.

** Unweighted average of 12 countries: Belgium, Canada, Denmark, Finland, France, Ireland, the Netherlands, Norway, Portugal, Sweden, Switzerland and the United Kingdom.

Premium unleaded gasoline (95 RON)

1994

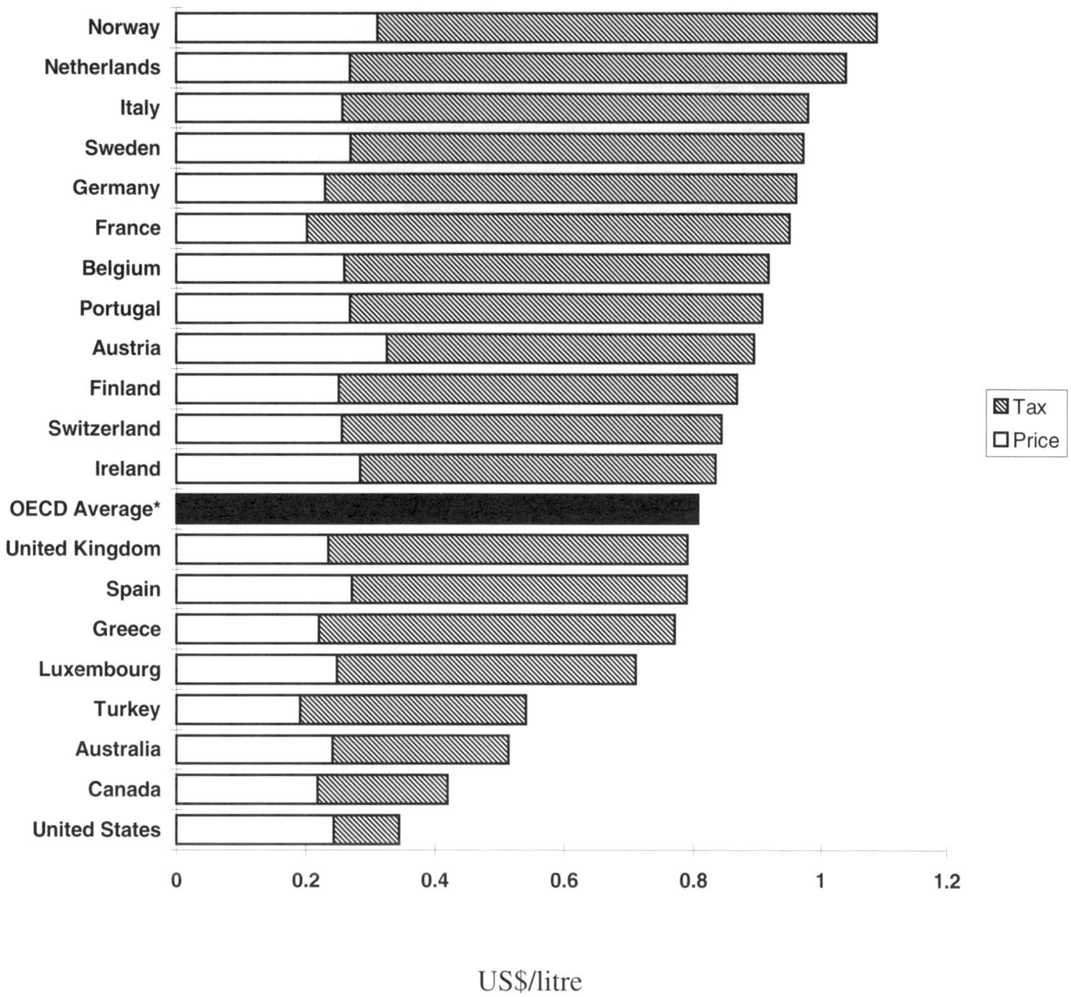

* Unweighted average of 20 countries: Australia, Austria, Belgium, Canada, Finland, France, Germany, Greece, Ireland, Italy, Luxembourg, the Netherlands, Norway, Portugal, Spain, Sweden, Switzerland, Turkey, the United Kingdom and the United States.

Regular unleaded gasoline

1994

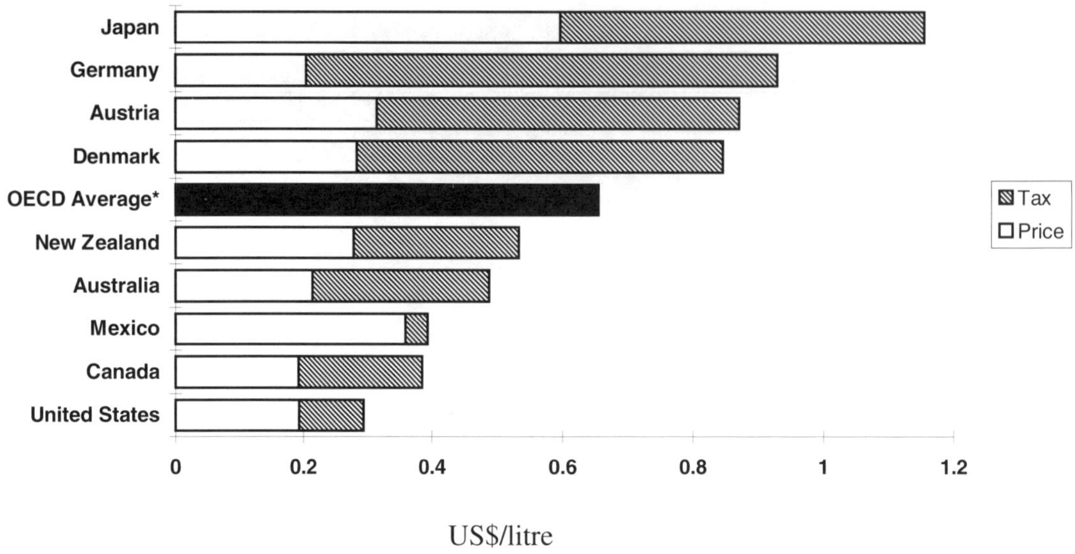

* Unweighted average of 9 countries: Australia, Austria, Canada, Denmark, Germany, Japan, Mexico, New Zealand and the United States.

Automotive diesel oil
1994

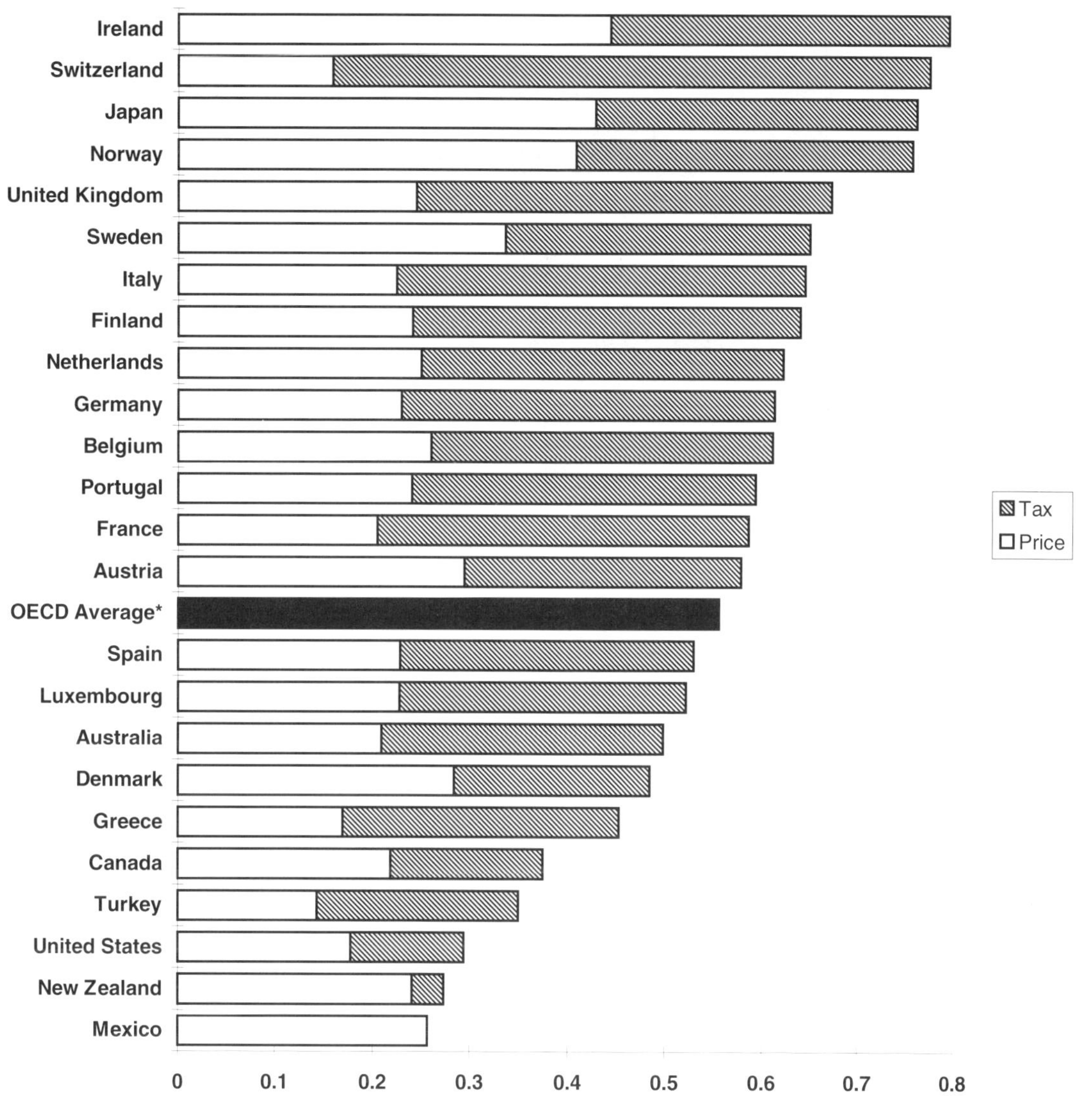

US$/litre

* Unweighted average of 24 countries: Australia, Austria, Belgium, Canada, Denmark, Finland, France, Germany, Greece, Ireland, Italy, Japan, Luxembourg, Mexico, the Netherlands, New Zealand, Norway, Portugal, Spain, Sweden, Switzerland, Turkey, the United Kingdom and the United States.

(6) Light fuel oil end-use prices for industry

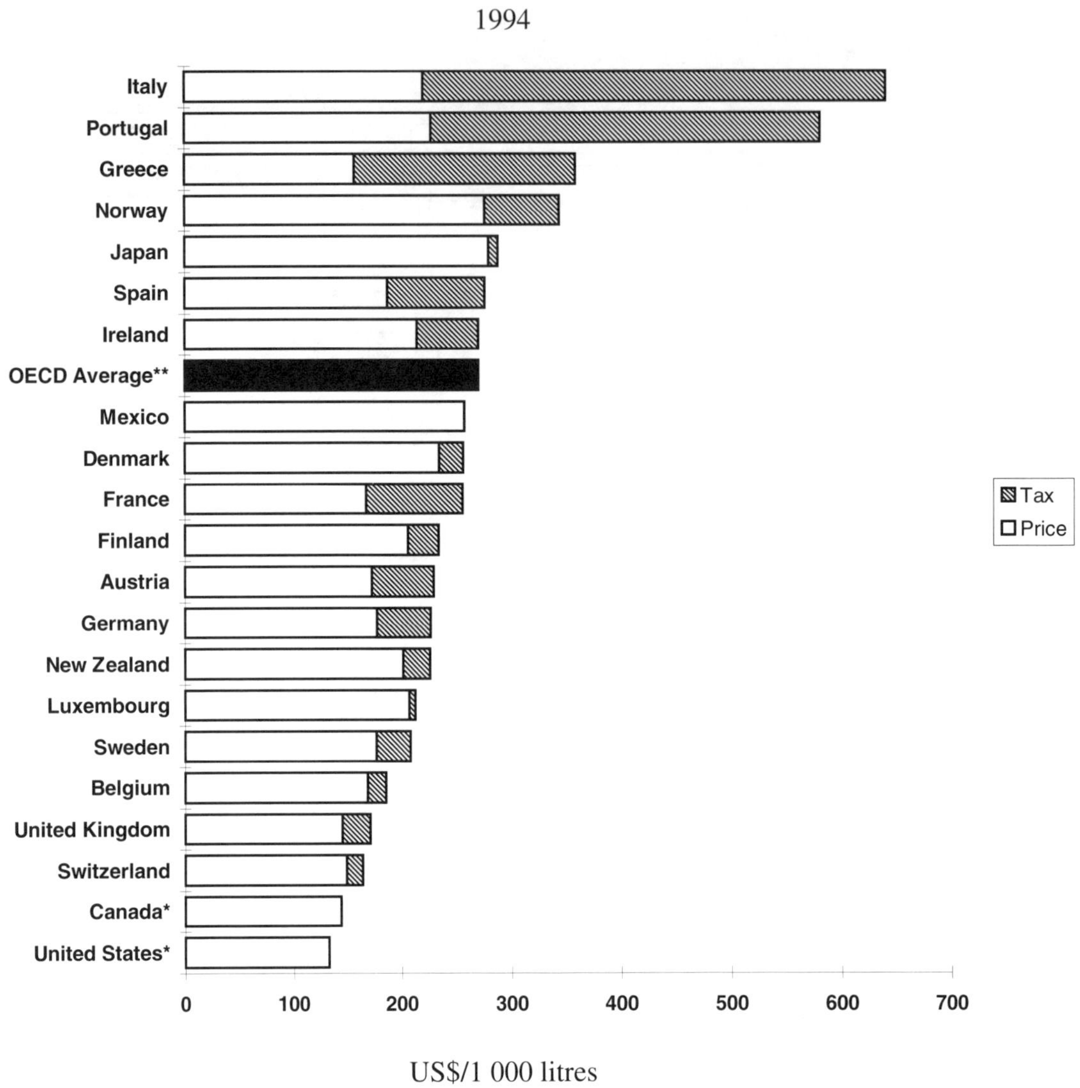

* Tax data is not available.

** Unweighted average of 21 countries: Austria, Belgium, Canada, Denmark, Finland, France, Germany, Greece, Ireland, Italy, Japan, Luxembourg, Mexico, New Zealand, Norway, Portugal, Spain, Sweden, Switzerland, the United Kingdom and the United States.

(7) Heavy fuel oil end-use prices for industry and electricity generation

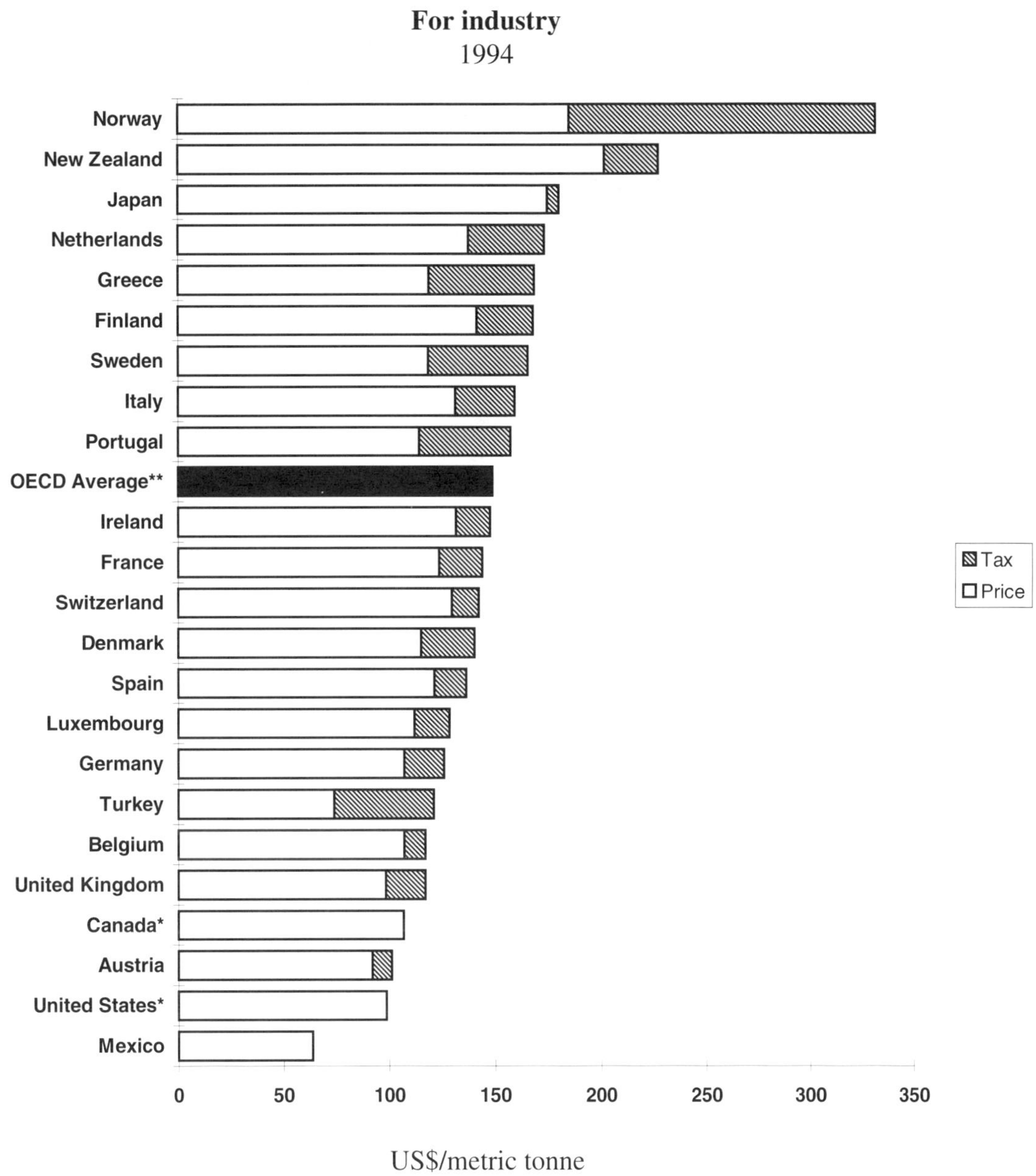

* Tax data is not available.

** Unweighted average of 23 countries: Austria, Belgium, Canada, Denmark, Finland, France, Germany, Greece, Ireland, Italy, Japan, Luxembourg, Mexico, the Netherlands, New Zealand, Norway, Portugal, Spain, Sweden, Switzerland, Turkey, the United Kingdom, and the United States.

For electricity generation

1994

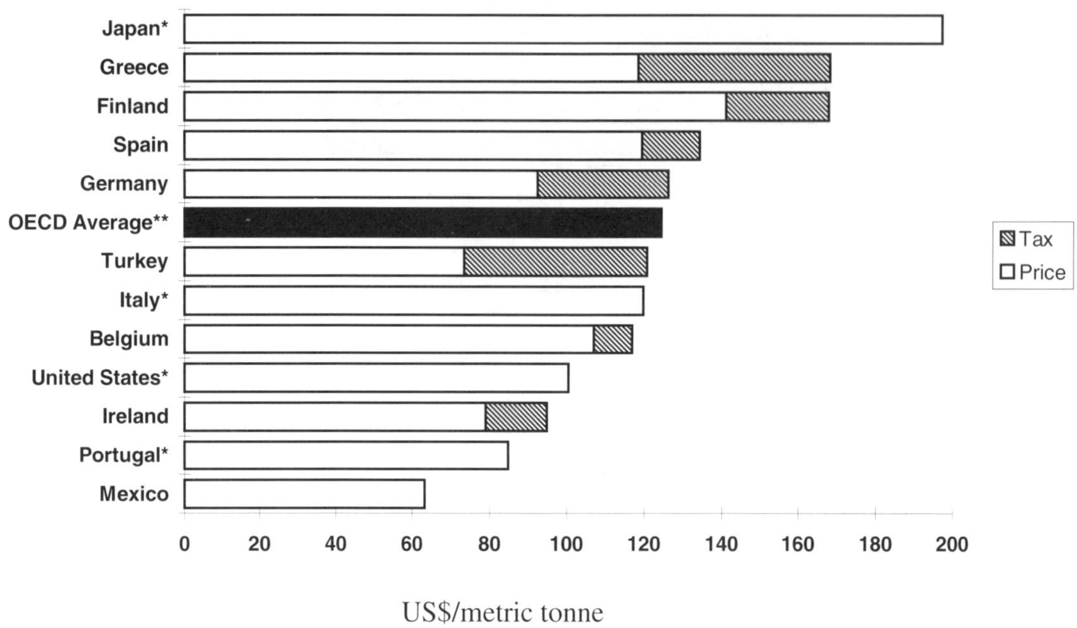

* Tax data is not available.

** Unweighted average of 12 countries: Belgium, Finland, Germany, Greece, Ireland, Italy, Japan, Mexico, Portugal, Spain, Turkey, and the United States.

(8) Total primary energy supply

Total primary energy supply comprises:

Indigenous production + imports - exports - international marine bunkers ± stock changes.

The rows and columns in the table are as follows:

- *Coal*: Includes all coal, both primary (including hard coal and lignite) and derived fuels (including patent fuel, coke oven coke, gas coke, coke oven gas, etc.). Peat is also included in this category.
- *Crude oil*: Comprises crude oil, natural gas liquids, refinery feed stocks and additives, as well as other hydrocarbons.
- *Petroleum products*: Comprised of refinery gas, ethane, LPG, aviation gasoline, motor gasoline, jet fuels, kerosene, gas/diesel oil, heavy fuel oil, naphtha, white spirit, lubricants, bitumen, paraffin waxes, petroleum coke and other petroleum products.
- *Gas*: Includes natural gas (excluding natural gas liquids) and gas works gas.
- *Nuclear*: Shows the primary heat equivalent of the electricity produced by a nuclear power plant.
- *Hydro*: Shows the energy content of the electricity produced in hydro power plants. Hydro output excludes output from pumped storage plants.
- *Geothermal, solar, etc.*: Indigenous production of geothermal, solar, wind, tide and wave energy and the use of these energy forms for electricity generation.
- *Combustible, renewable & waste*: Comprises solid biomass and animal products, gas/liquids from biomass, industrial waste and municipal waste. Biomass is defined as any plant matter used directly as fuel or converted into fuels or electricity and/or heat.
- *Electricity*: Shows final consumption and trade in electricity.
- *Heat*: Shows the disposition of heat produced for sale. The large majority of the heat included in this column results from the combustion of fuels, although some small amounts are produced from electrically powered heat pumps and boilers.
- *Indigenous production*: Production of primary energy, *i.e.* hard coal, lignite, peat crude oil, natural gas, nuclear, etc.
- *Imports and exports*: Comprises amounts having crossed the national territorial boundaries of the country, whether or not customs clearance has taken place.
- *International marine bunkers*: Covers those quantities delivered to sea-going ships of all flags, including warships. Consumption by ships engaged in transport in inland and coastal waters is not included.

- *Stock changes*: Reflects the difference between opening stock levels at the first day of the year and closing levels on the last day of the year of stocks on national territory held by producers, importers, energy transformation industries and large consumers.

Total primary energy supply by each resource

Million tonnes oil equivalent, 1993

	Coal	Crude oil	Petroleum products	Gas	Nuclear	Hydro	Geotherm. solar, etc.	Combust., renew & waste	Elect.	Heat	Total
Australia	37.70	36.21	-2.04	14.92	-	1.39	0.06	4.35	-	-	92.58
Austria	2.92	9.59	1.87	5.66	-	3.16	-	3.08	-0.06	-	26.21
Belgium	8.89	29.15	-8.25	9.40	10.93	0.02	-	0.32	0.19	-	50.65
Canada	24.08	81.99	-5.64	61.18	24.87	27.83	0.01	8.76	-2.36	-	220.73
Denmark	7.22	8.79	-0.11	2.41	-	-	0.09	1.26	0.10	-	19.78
Finland	5.74	8.92	0.45	2.57	5.18	1.17	-	4.24	0.65	-	28.93
France	18.60	80.29	8.24	28.06	88.20	5.84	0.05	4.20	-4.63	-	233.77
Germany	97.89	105.80	29.75	59.72	40.00	1.52	0.10	2.48	0.07	-	337.23
Greece	8.17	13.87	-0.30	0.09	-	0.20	-	0.58	0.07	-	22.68
Ireland	3.34	1.94	3.19	2.16	-	0.07	-	0.01	-	-	10.70
Italy	10.66	93.19	-0.53	41.94	-	3.56	3.18	1.08	3.39	-	156.48
Japan	76.83	220.23	35.64	47.66	64.96	8.41	1.53	2.18	-	-	457.44
Luxembourg	1.04	-	1.96	0.48	-	0.01	-	0.02	0.35	-	3.87
Mexico	4.10	86.61	0.96	25.23	1.29	2.26	5.05	9.15	-0.10	-	134.55
Netherlands	7.86	59.96	-34.73	34.26	1.03	0.01	0.02	0.38	0.89	-	69.67
New Zealand	1.14	4.63	-0.15	4.39	-	2.01	1.86	1.02	-	-	14.90
Norway	0.85	14.80	-6.51	2.51	-	10.24	-	1.02	-0.67	-	22.25
Portugal	3.16	11.58	0.97	-	-	0.73	-	1.09	0.02	-	17.55
Spain	19.04	54.47	-5.85	5.74	14.61	2.10	-	0.76	0.11	-	90.98
Sweden	2.72	18.34	-3.55	0.70	16.00	6.42	-	6.21	-0.05	0.34	47.13
Switzerland	0.18	4.88	8.07	2.02	6.10	3.08	-	1.00	-0.62	-	24.72
Turkey	16.27	26.13	1.59	4.24	-	2.92	0.10	7.94	-0.03	-	59.16
United Kingdom	49.90	100.79	-17.58	57.85	23.29	0.37	0.02	0.92	1.44	-	216.99
United States	469.24	800.65	-31.04	489.37	168.61	24.23	15.63	89.44	2.47	-	2 028.60

Total primary energy supply

1993

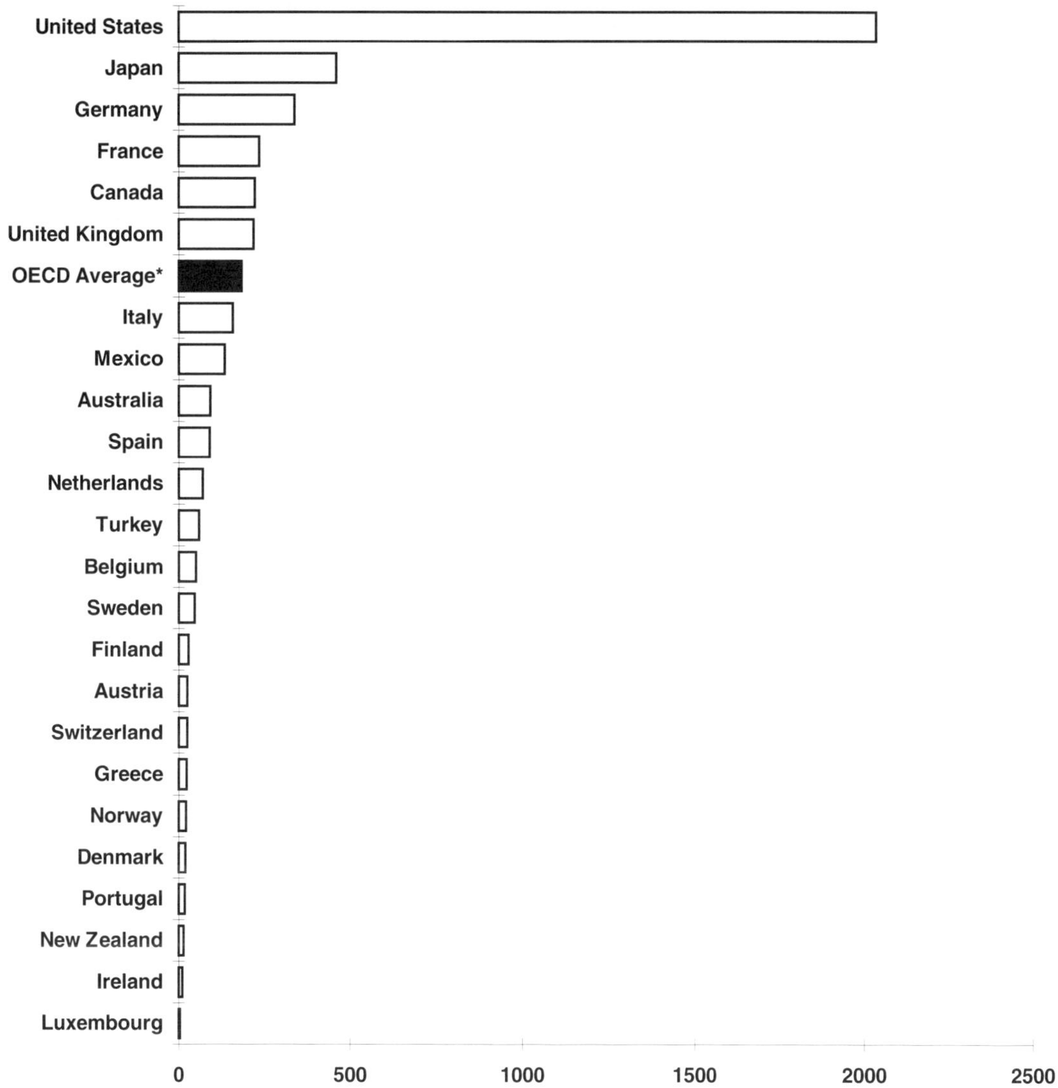

Million tonnes of oil equivalent

* Unweighted average of 24 countries: Australia, Austria, Belgium, Canada, Denmark, Finland, France, Germany, Greece, Ireland, Italy, Japan, Luxembourg, Mexico, the Netherlands, New Zealand, Norway, Portugal, Spain, Sweden, Switzerland, Turkey, the United Kingdom, and the United States.

Indigenous production by each resource

Million tonnes oil equivalent ,1993

	Coal	Crude oil	Petroleum products	Gas	Nucear	Hydro	Geotherm., solar , etc.	Combust., renew. & waste	Elect.	Heat	Total
Australia	118.93	27.61	-	20.86	-	1.39	0.06	4.35	-	-	173.20
Austria	0.44	1.22	-	1.26	-	3.16	-	3.02	-	-	9.10
Belgium	0.46	-	-	-	10.93	0.02	-	0.32	-	-	11.74
Canada	37.52	103.61	-	112.49	24.87	27.83	0.01	8.76	-	-	315.09
Denmark	-	8.43	-	3.95	-	-	0.09	1.26	-	-	13.74
Finland	1.40	-	-	-	5.18	1.17	-	4.21	-	-	11.96
France	6.52	3.46	-	2.88	95.95	5.48	0.05	4.19	-	-	118.54
Germany	87.78	3.83	-	13.75	40.00	1.52	0.01	2.48	-	-	149.36
Greece	7.16	0.58	-	0.09	-	0.20	-	0.58	-	-	8.61
Ireland	1.13	-	-	2.16	-	0.07	-	0.01	-	-	3.37
Italy	0.16	5.01	-	15.68	-	3.56	3.18	0.96	-	-	28.55
Japan	3.98	0.87	-	1.94	64.96	8.41	1.53	2.18	-	-	83.87
Luxembourg	-	-	-	-	-	0.01	-	0.02	-	-	0.03
Mexico	3.09	158.65	-	24.15	1.29	2.26	5.05	9.15	-	-	203.63
Netherlands	-	3.35	-	63.10	1.03	0.01	0.02	0.38	-	-	67.88
New Zealand	1.78	2.10	-	4.39	-	2.01	1.86	1.02	-	-	13.16
Norway	0.18	117.59	-	24.21	-	10.24	-	1.02	-	-	153.24
Portugal	0.08	-	-	-	-	0.73	-	1.09	-	-	1.91
Spain	10.95	1.14	-	0.60	14.61	2.10	-	0.76	-	-	30.14
Sweden	0.29	-	-	-	16.00	6.42	-	6.21	-	0.34	29.27
Switzerland	-	-	-	-	6.10	3.08	-	0.99	-	-	10.17
Turkey	11.59	3.98	-	0.16	-	2.92	0.10	7.94	-	-	26.70
United Kingdom	37.49	103.07	-	54.51	23.29	0.37	0.02	92.00	-	-	219.65
United States	482.90	404.27	-	431.67	168.61	24.23	15.63	89.39	-	-	1 616.70

Share of indigenous production in total primary energy supply
Percentage, 1993

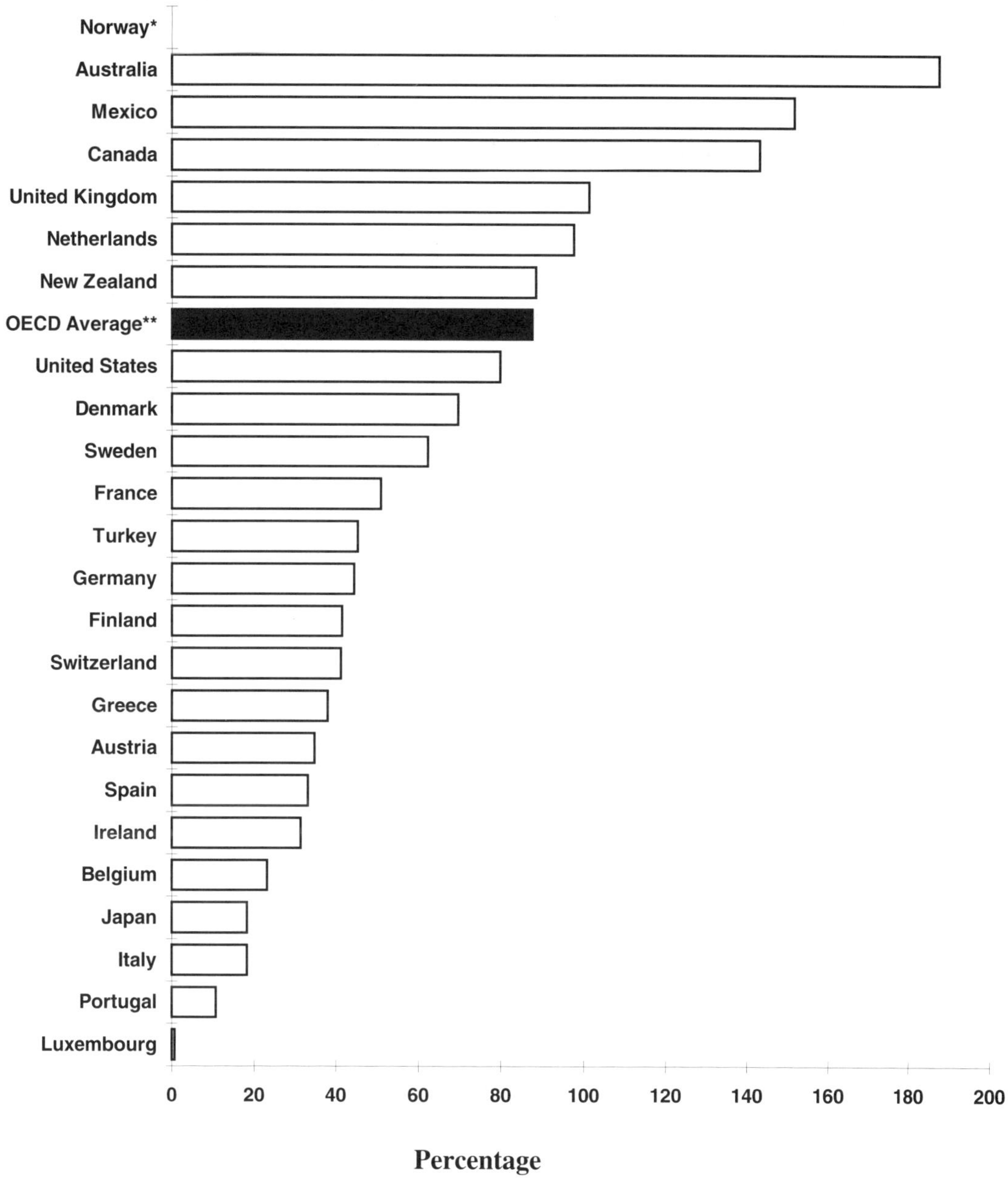

* Norway is up to 650%.

** Unweighted average of 24 countries: Australia, Austria, Belgium, Canada, Denmark, Finland, France, Germany, Greece, Ireland, Italy, Japan, Luxembourg, Mexico, the Netherlands, New Zealand, Norway, Portugal, Spain, Sweden, Switzerland, Turkey, the United Kingdom, and the United States.

(9) Regulation in public utilities (electricity and gas) in 1990

The table shows the diversity of regulatory arrangements in the electric power and gas sector. The following arrangements are distinguished :

Ownership: PUB = Public; MIX = Mixed: PRI = Private.

Entry/Price: REG = Regulated; PAR = Partially regulated; UNR = Unregulated.

Electricity

	Generation			Transmission			Distribution		
	Ownership	Entry	Price	Ownership	Entry	Price	Ownership	Entry	Price
Australia	PUB	UNR	UNR	PUB	UNR	UNR	PUB	UNR	UNR
Austria	PUB	PAR	PAR	PUB	..	..	PUB	REG	PAR
Belgium	..	UNR	PAR	..	UNR	PAR	..	UNR	PAR
Canada	PUB	UNR	PAR	PUB	PAR	PAR	PUB	UNR	UNR
Denmark	PUB	REG	REG	PUB	REG	REG	PUB	REG	REG
Finland	MIX	REG	UNR	MIX	REG	UNR	PRI	REG	UNR
Germany	MIX	PAR	UNR	MIX	PAR	UNR	MIX	PAR	PAR
Ireland	PUB	REG	PAR	PUB	REG	PAR	PUB	REG	PAR
Japan	PRI	..	REG	PRI	..	REG	PRI	..	REG
New Zealand	MIX	UNR	UNR	PUB	UNR	UNR	PUB	REG	UNR
Norway	MIX	REG	UNR	PUB	REG	REG	PUB	REG	UNR
Spain	MIX	REG	REG	PUB	REG	REG	MIX	REG	REG
Sweden	MIX	UNR	PAR	PUB	..	..	MIX	REG	PAR
Switzerland	MIX	REG	UNR	MIX	REG	UNR	MIX	REG	UNR
Turkey	MIX	UNR	REG	MIX	PAR	REG	MIX	PAR	REG
United Kingdom	MIX	PAR	PAR	PUB	REG	REG	PUB	REG	REG
United States	MIX	PAR	PAR	MIX	REG	REG	MIX	REG	REG

Gas

	Production			Transmission			Distribution		
	Ownership	Entry	Price	Ownership	Entry	Price	Ownership	Entry	Price
Australia	PRI	..	..	..	..	..	..	..	..
Austria	MIX	REG	REG	MIX	REG	PAR	MIX	REG	PAR
Belgium	..	..	..	..	REG	PAR	..	REG	PAR
Canada	PRI	UNR	REG	PRI	REG	REG	PRI	UNR	UNR
Denmark	PUB	REG	REG	PUB	REG	REG	PUB	REG	REG
Finland	PUB	UNR	UNR	PUB	UNR	UNR	PUB	PAR	UNR
Germany	PRI	UNR	UNR	PRI	UNR	UNR	PRI	UNR	UNR
Ireland	PUB	REG	..	PUB	REG	REG	PUB	REG	REG
Japan	PRI	..	REG	PRI	..	REG	PRI	..	REG
New Zealand	MIX	UNR	UNR	PRI	REG	REG	MIX	REG	REG
Spain	PUB	REG	REG	PUB	REG	REG	PUB	REG	REG
Sweden	PRI	UNR	PAR	PUB	REG	UNR	PRI	REG	PAR
Switzerland	MIX	REG	UNR	MIX	REG	UNR	MIX	REG	UNR
Turkey	PUB	UNR	UNR	PUB	REG	REG	PUB	REG	REG
United Kingdom	PRI	UNR	UNR	PRI	PAR	PAR	PRI	PAR	PAR
United States	PRI	UNR	UNR	PRI	PAR	PAR	PRI	REG	REG

ANNEX

US DOLLAR EXCHANGE RATES IN NATIONAL CURRENCIES

	1991	1992	1993	1994	1995
Australia	1.28	1.36	1.47	1.37	1.38
Austria	11.67	10.99	11.63	11.42	9.82
Belgium	34.16	32.15	34.56	33.46	28.73
Canada	1.15	1.21	1.29	1.37	1.37
Denmark	6.40	6.04	6.48	6.36	5.47
Finland	4.04	4.49	5.72	5.22	4.30
France	5.64	5.29	5.66	5.55	4.92
Germany	1.66	1.56	1.65	1.62	1.40
Greece	182.06	190.47	229.14	242.24	226.34
Ireland	0.62	0.59	0.68	0.67	0.62
Italy	1 241.00	1 232.00	1 572.00	1 612.83	1 668.00
Japan	134.50	126.70	111.20	102.24	84.47
Luxembourg	34.16	32.15	34.56	33.46	28.73
Mexico	3.00	3.10	3.10	3.38	6.13
Netherlands	1.87	1.76	1.86	1.82	1.56
New Zealand	1.73	1.86	1.85	1.69	1.50
Norway	6.48	6.21	7.09	7.06	6.24
Portugal	144.35	134.82	160.65	166.04	147.14
Spain	103.93	102.40	127.24	133.96	123.06
Sweden	6.05	5.82	7.79	7.72	7.30
Switzerland	1.43	1.41	1.48	1.37	1.15
Turkey	4 168.90	6 860.60	10 965.60	29 778.17	42 962.73
United Kingdom	0.57	0.57	0.67	0.65	0.63
United States	1.00	1.00	1.00	1.00	1.00

Chapter 9

TELECOMMUNICATION COSTS AND INFRASTRUCTURE

Two main complementary sources were used in the collection and compilation of the following information: the OECD*'s Communications Outlook* published by the Information, Computer, Communications Policy Division of the Directorate for Science, Technology and Industry; and the *Communication Indicators for Major Economics*, jointly published by the OECD, the Statistical Office of European Communities (Eurostat) and the International Telecommunications Union (ITU). The OECD's Directorate for Fiscal and Financial Affairs' work on regulatory review for the Competition Law and Policy Committee has also been used for regulatory information. The Information, Computer and Communications Policy (ICCP) Division also provided technical assistance in the design of the following matrices.

Introduction

Telecommunications infrastructure is becoming an increasingly important framework factor for OECD economies. As the role of information in the management of business organisations and the conduct of business transactions increases, the quality of the infrastructure available for the transmission and distribution of such information is gaining in importance.

Telecommunications infrastructure provides the basis for companies' information systems at both the domestic and the international levels. The range and quality of the telecommunication services available, and their prices, influence and in certain instances shape companies' technical choices and operation costs, both within firms and in their transactions with customers and business partners. Telecommunications infrastructure is, indeed, becoming a central framework factor of the information economy.

This role of telecommunications can, for instance, be measured by the increasing use of telecommunication services by business corporations. It has been calculated that the number of telecommunication mainlines per 100 employees in the business sectors of OECD economies doubled from 15 to 27 between 1985 and 1995. When compounded with a quantum increase in the intensity of mainline use by business users, thanks to private networks, multiplexing and PBX technologies, these figures reflect an explosion in telecom use. The information-intensive industries and services, especially those interacting with their customers through telecommunications – such as banking, financial services, computer services, etc., – play a special role in this trend.

National environments offer different ranges, conditions, quality and costs of telecommunication services to business users. Specificities are due to uneven capital investment in the telecommunications sector, different institutional and regulatory arrangements which shape the extent, innovativeness, investment capability and pricing choices of service providers, and a host of other national factors. More active deregulation and competition policies in the telecommunications sector have promoted very dynamic and cost-effective environments in several countries in recent years.

This module aims to document and illustrate differences across countries. It shows that international differences remain, and are indeed, significant, in service range, service use, service costs and organisational settings for service provision. In spite of widespread perceptions of increasing homogeneity in telecom infrastructures, it remains an area where national industries definitely operate in different framework conditions.

The information used to produce the following module was provided by the OECD's Information, Computer and Communications Policy Division. ICCP also helped the Industry Division to take stock of their findings from a user industries' perspective. The structure of the summary country matrices, and their constituent parameters, has been selected as follows:

Physical indicators

Table 1: Main telephone lines per inhabitant in operation

A mainline is a telephone line connecting the subscriber's terminal equipment (*e.g.* telephone set, facsimile machine) to the public switched network and which has a dedicated port in the telephone exchange. This is a way to measure the number of residential mainlines and the number of telecommunication mainlines per 100 people.

Table 2. Percentage of digitalisation

The number of mainlines connected to digital telephone exchanges. Calculated by dividing the number of mainlines connected to digital exchanges by the total number of mainlines.

Table 3. Cellular mobile telephone subscribers

Subscribers to an automatic public mobile telephone service which provides access to the Public Switched Telephone Network (PSTN) using cellular technology. The number of mobile telecommunications subscribers in the OECD area is growing very rapidly.

Table 4. Percentage of cellular mobile telephone subscribers in total telecom services

The number of cellular mobile telephones and the digitalisation of mainlines are growing rapidly.

Table 5. Estimated number of facsimile machines

The number of facsimile machines is also growing rapidly. This rapid growth in the utilisation of fax machines has been driven by consumer demand and built using the existing public switched telephone network (PSTN).

Telecommunication tariffs

These data (Tables 5, 6, 7, 8 and 9) were presented to the OECD Working Party on Telecommunications and Information Services Policy.

Table 6. Basket of business telephone charges in January 1994 (local)

Table 7. Basket of business telephone charges in January 1994 (international)

In liberalising telecommunication markets, analysis of tariff structure is increasingly important for service providers, users and policy makers. Comparisons are undertaken using a basket approach, rather than a methodology of direct comparison, to avoid as far as possible conditions specific to one country.

Table 8. Basket of mobile telecommunication tariffs in January 1994

Mobile telecommunications are one of the most dynamic areas of the telecommunications sector and this is reflected in the change in prices over recent years.

Table 9. Basket of leased line charges in January 1994

Leased lines provide important facilities for business telecommunications users. They allow large users to take advantage of volume discounts and to have control over their own telecommunications facilities and traffic.

Table 10. Basket of packet switched data communication charges in January 1994

Packet switched data communication is one of the most common non-PSTN services used by business users.

Regulation indicators

Table 11. Status of facilities competition in 1994

There are important differences in the regulatory and market structures in place across OECD countries. While a number of countries have been liberalising their telecommunications markets and putting into place frameworks for equal access and interconnection for competitors in a range of telecommunications services, a number of countries have preferred to maintain existing market structures based on the concept of public provision of basic services and infrastructures.

TELECOMMUNICATION COSTS AND INFRASTRUCTURE : COUNTRY TABLES

UNITED STATES

Table 1. Main telephone lines per inhabitant in operation

Thousands

	1990	1991	1992	1993	1994
Total number of mainlines	136 337.00	139 658.30	144 056.71	148 084.38	154 953.00
Mainlines per 100 inhabitants	54.55	55.27	56.49	57.38	59.48

Source: Communications Indicators for Major Economies, 1995, OECD/ITU/Eurostat.

Table 2. Percentage of digitalisation in mainlines

Percentage

	1990	1991	1992	1993	1994
Digitalisation	47.0	53.0	58.0	65.0	..

Source: Communications Indicators for Major Economies, 1995, OECD/ITU/Eurostat.

Table 3. Cellular mobile telephone subscribers

Thousands

	1990	1991	1992	1993	1994
Total number of subscribers	5 283.06	7 557.15	11 032.75	16 009.46	24 134.42
Subscribers per 100 inhabitants	2.11	2.99	4.33	6.20	9.26

Source: Communications Indicators for Major Economies, 1995, OECD/ITU/Eurostat.

Table 4. Percentage of cellular mobile telephone subscribers in total telecom services

Percentage

		1990	1991	1992	1993	1994
Main lines	Analog	51.0	44.6	39.0	31.6	..
	Digital	45.2	50.3	53.9	58.7	..
Cellular		3.7	5.1	7.1	9.8	13.5
Total		100.0	100.0	100.0	100.0	100.0

Source: Communications Indicators for Major Economies, 1995, OECD/ITU/Eurostat.

Table 5. Estimated number of facsimile machines

Thousands

	1990	1991	1992	1993	1994
Number of fax machines	5 084.0	7 210.0	9 056.0	11 304.0	14 052.0
Number of fax machines per 100 inhabitants	2.03	2.85	3.55	4.38	5.39

Source: Communications Indicators for Major Economies, 1995, OECD/ITU/Eurostat.

Table 6. Basket of business telephone charges in January 1994 (local)

Values express the average annual spending by a business user, in 1993 US$ based on PPPs, excluding tax

	Fixed charge	Usage charge	Total
Annual spending charge	219.77	740.42	960.19

Source: OECD (1995), *Communications Outlook.*

Table 7. Basket of business telephone charges in January 1994 (international)

1993 US$ based on PPPs, excluding tax

	Call pair methodology	Zone distribution methodology
Business telephone charge	113.19	94.09

Source: OECD (1995),, *Communications Outlook.*

Table 8. Basket of mobile telecommunication tariffs in January 1994

1993 US$ based on PPPs, excluding tax

	Fixed charge	Usage charge	Total
Mobile telecom. tariffs	496.07	1 263.68	1 759.74

Source: OECD (1995), *Communications Outlook.*

Table 9. Basket of leased line charges in January 1994

1993 US$ based on PPPs, excluding tax

	9.6 kbit/s	64 kbit/s	1.5/2.0 Mbit/s
Leased line charge	45 542	76 565	423 233

Source: OECD (1995), *Communications Outlook.*

Table 10. Basket of packet switched data communication charges in January 1994

1993 US$ based on PPPs, excluding tax

	Fixed charge	Usage charge	Total
Packet switched data communication charge	6 347.73	2 419.23	8 766.96

Source: OECD (1995), *Communications Outlook.*

Table 11. Status of facilities competition in 1994

Equipment	PSTN competition			Data comms. and leased lines		Mobile communication		
CPE	Local	Trunk	Intl.	X25	LLs	Anal.	Digl.	Paging
FC	PC	FC	FC	FC	FC	RD	FC	FC

Note: FC: Full Competition; PC: Partial Competition; D: Duopoly; M: Monopoly; RD: Regional Duopoly;
B: Competition allowed at border of concessions.
199X: Competition expected to be introduced this year.

Source: OECD (1995), *Communications Outlook.*

JAPAN

Table 1. Main telephone lines per inhabitant in operation

Thousands

	1990	1991	1992	1993	1994
Total number of mainlines	54 527.95	56 259.92	57 652.33	58 830.00	59 600.00
Mainlines per 100 inhabitants	44.14	45.40	46.37	47.13	47.76

Source: Communications Indicators for Major Economies, 1995, OECD/ITU/Eurostat.

Table 2. Percentage of digitalisation in mainlines

Percentage

	1990	1991	1992	1993	1994
Digitalisation	39.0	50.0	60.0	72.0	..

Source: Communications Indicators for Major Economies, 1995, OECD/ITU/Eurostat.

Table 3. Cellular mobile telephone subscribers

Thousands

	1990	1991	1992	1993	1994
Total number of subscribers	868.08	1 378.11	1 712.55	2 131.37	2 891.29
Subscribers per 100 inhabitants	0.70	1.11	1.38	1.71	2.32

Source: Communications Indicators for Major Economies, 1995, OECD/ITU/Eurostat.

Table 4. Percentage of cellular mobile telephone subscribers in total telecom services

Percentage

		1990	1991	1992	1993	1994
Mainlines	Analog	60.0	48.8	38.8	27.0	..
	Digital	38.4	48.8	58.8	69.5	..
Cellular		1.6	2.4	2.9	3.5	4.6
Total		100.0	100.0	100.0	100.0	100.0

Source: Communications Indicators for Major Economies, 1995, OECD/ITU/Eurostat.

Table 5. Estimated number of facsimile machines

Thousands

	1990	1991	1992	1993	1994
Number of fax machines	4 000.0	5 000.0	5 500.0	5 750.0	6 000.0
Number of fax machines per 100 inhabitants	3.24	4.03	4.42	4.61	4.81

Source: Communications Indicators for Major Economies, 1995, OECD/ITU/Eurostat.

Table 6. Basket of business telephone charges in January 1994 (local)

Values express the average annual spending by a business user, in 1993 US$ based on PPPs, excluding tax

	Fixed charge	Usage charge	Total
Annual spending charge	170.00	669.18	839.18

Source: OECD (1995), *Communications Outlook.*

Table 7. Basket of business telephone charges in January 1994 (international)

1993 US$ based on PPPs, excluding tax

	Call pair methodology	Zone distribution methodology
Business telephone charge	91.76	108.52

Source: OECD (1995), *Communications Outlook.*

Table 8. Basket of mobile telecommunication tariffs in January 1994

1993 US$ based on PPPs, excluding tax

	Fixed charge	Usage charge	Total
Mobile telecom. tariffs	910.99	947.95	1 858.94

Source: OECD (1995), *Communications Outlook.*

Table 9. Basket of leased line charges in January 1994

1993 US$ based on PPPs, excluding tax

	9.6 kbit/s	64 kbit/s	1.5/2.0 Mbit/s
Leased line charge	38 910	70 771	558 271

Source: OECD (1995), *Communications Outlook.*

Table 10. Basket of packet switched data communication charges in January 1994

1993 US$ based on PPPs, excluding tax

	Fixed charge	Usage charge	Total
Packet switched data communication charge	1 855.11	10 546.66	12 401.76

Source: OECD (1995), *Communications Outlook.*

Table 11. Status of facilities competition in 1994

Equipment	PSTN competition			Data comms. and leased lines		Mobile communication		
CPE	Local	Trunk	Intl.	X25	LLs	Anal.	Digl.	Paging
FC	FC	FC	FC	FC	FC	RD	FC	FC

Note: FC: Full Competition; PC: Partial Competition; D: Duopoly; M: Monopoly; RD: Regional Duopoly;
B: Competition allowed at border of concessions.
199X: Competition expected to be introduced this year.

Source: OECD (1995), *Communications Outlook.*

GERMANY

Table 1. Main telephone lines per inhabitant in operation

Thousands

	1990	1991	1992	1993	1994
Total number of mainlines	31 887.00	33 559.72	35 420.84	36 899.78	38 800[1]
Mainlines per 100 inhabitants	40.13	41.97	43.96	45.68	48.31

1. Data provided by the Federal Ministry of Economics of Germany

Source: Communications Indicators for Major Economies, 1995, OECD/ITU/Eurostat.

Table 2. Percentage of digitalisation in mainlines

Percentage

	1990	1991	1992	1993	1994
Digitalisation	12.0	16.0	25.0	37.0	45.0

Source: Communications Indicators for Major Economies, 1995, OECD/ITU/Eurostat.

Table 3. Cellular mobile telephone subscribers

Thousands

	1990	1991	1992	1993	1994
Total number of subscribers	272.61	532.25	974.9	1 767.98	2 501.40
Subscribers per 100 inhabitants	0.34	0.67	1.21	2.19	3.08

Source: Communications Indicators for Major Economies, 1995, OECD/ITU/Eurostat.

Table 4. Percentage of cellular mobile telephone subscribers in total telecom services

Percentage

		1990	1991	1992	1993	1994
Main lines	Analog	87.3	82.7	73.0	60.1	51.7
	Digital	11.9	15.8	24.3	35.3	42.3
Cellular		0.8	1.6	2.7	4.6	6.0
Total		100.0	100.0	100.0	100.0	100.0

Source: Communications Indicators for Major Economies, 1995, OECD/ITU/Eurostat.

Table 5. Estimated number of facsimile machines

Thousands

	1990	1991	1992	1993	1994
Number of fax machines	696.2	946.2	1 172.7	1 296.0	1 446.6
Number of fax machines per 100 inhabitants	0.88	1.18	1.46	1.60	1.78

Source: Communications Indicators for Major Economies, 1995, OECD/ITU/Eurostat.

Table 6. Basket of business telephone charges in January 1994 (local)

Values express the average annual spending by a business user, in 1993 US$ based on PPPs, excluding tax

	Fixed charge	Usage charge	Total
Annual spending charge	131.12	855.66	986.78

Source: OECD (1995), *Communications Outlook.*

Table 7. Basket of business telephone charges in January 1994 (international)

In 1993 US$ based on PPPs, excluding tax

	Call pair methodology	Zone distribution methodology
Business telephone charge	96.74	81.13

Source: OECD (1995), *Communications Outlook.*

Table 8. Basket of mobile telecommunication tariffs in January 1994

In 1993 US$ based on PPPs, excluding tax

	Fixed charge	Usage charge	Total
Mobile telecom. tariffs	380.22	1 108.65	1 488.87

Source: OECD (1995), *Communications Outlook.*

Table 9. Basket of leased line charges in January 1994

1993 US$ based on PPPs, excluding tax

	9.6 kbit/s	64 kbit/s	1.5/2.0 Mbit/s
Leased line charge	68 582	78 075	414 346

Source: OECD (1995), *Communications Outlook.*

Table 10. Basket of packet switched data communication charges in January 1994

1993 US$ based on PPPs, excluding tax

	Fixed charge	Usage charge	Total
Packet switched data communication charge	2 440.81	11 782.50	14 223.31

Source: OECD (1995), *Communications Outlook.*

Table 11. Status of facilities competition in 1994

Equipment	PSTN competition			Data comms. and leased lines		Mobile communication		
CPE	Local	Trunk	Intl.	X25	LLs	Anal.	Digl.	Paging
FC	M	M	M	FC	M	FC*	FC*	FC*

Note: FC: Full Competition; PC: Partial Competition; D: Duopoly; M: Monopoly; RD: Regional Duopoly;
B: Competition allowed at border of concessions.
199X: Competition expected to be introduced this year.
* Data provided by the Federal Ministry of Economics of Germany

Source: OECD (1995), *Communications Outlook.*

FRANCE

Table 1. Main telephone lines per inhabitant in operation

Thousands

	1990	1991	1992	1993	1994
Total number of mainlines	28 084.92	29 100.00	30 100.00	30 900.00	31 600.00
Mainlines per 100 inhabitants	49.50	51.01	52.46	53.60	54.74

Source: Communications Indicators for Major Economies, 1995, OECD/ITU/Eurostat.

Table 2. Percentage of digitalisation in mainlines

Percentage

	1990	1991	1992	1993	1994
Digitalisation	75.0	79.0	83.2	86.4	89.0

Source: Communications Indicators for Major Economies, 1995, OECD/ITU/Eurostat.

Table 3. Cellular mobile telephone subscribers

Thousands

	1990	1991	1992	1993	1994
Total number of subscribers	283.20	375.00	436.70	572.00	803.90
Subscribers per 100 inhabitants	0.50	0.66	0.76	0.99	1.39

Source: Communications Indicators for Major Economies, 1995, OECD/ITU/Eurostat.

Table 4. Percentage of cellular mobile telephone subscribers in total telecom services

Percentage

		1990	1991	1992	1993	1994
Main lines	Analog	24.8	20.7	16.6	13.4	10.7
	Digital	74.3	78.0	82.0	84.8	86.8
Cellular		1.0	1.3	1.4	1.8	2.5
Total		100.0	100.0	100.0	100.0	100.0

Source: Communications Indicators for Major Economies, 1995, OECD/ITU/Eurostat.

Table 5. Estimated number of facsimile machines

Thousands

	1990	1991	1992	1993	1994
Number of fax machines	580.0	650.0	750.0	1 000.0	..
Number of fax machines per 100 inhabitants	1.02	1.14	1.31	1.73	..

Source: Communications Indicators for Major Economies, 1995, OECD/ITU/Eurostat.

Table 6. Basket of business telephone charges in January 1994 (local)

Values express the average annual spending by a business user, in 1993 US$ based on PPPs, excluding tax

	Fixed charge	Usage charge	Total
Annual spending charge	154.92	809.53	964.45

Source: OECD (1995), *Communications Outlook.*

Table 7. Basket of business telephone charges in January 1994 (international)
1993 US$ based on PPPs, excluding tax

	Call pair methodology	Zone distribution methodology
Business telephone charge	94.67	80.94

Source: OECD (1995), *Communications Outlook.*

Table 8. Basket of mobile telecommunication tariffs in January 1994
1993 US$ based on PPPs, excluding tax

	Fixed charge	Usage charge	Total
Mobile telecom. tariffs	928.13	1 009.63	1 937.76

Source: OECD (1995), *Communications Outlook.*

Table 9. Basket of leased line charges in January 1994
1993 US$ based on PPPs, excluding tax

	9.6 kbit/s	64 kbit/s	1.5/2.0 Mbit/s
Leased line charge	47 622	71 705	435 291

Source: OECD (1995), *Communications Outlook.*

Table 10. Basket of packet switched data communication charges in January 1994
1993 US$ based on PPPs, excluding tax

	Fixed charge	Usage charge	Total
Packet switched data communication charge	3 337.41	4 508.69	7 846.10

Source: OECD (1995), *Communications Outlook.*

Table 11. Status of facilities competition in 1994

Equipment	PSTN competition			Data comms. and leased lines		Mobile communication		
CPE	Local	Trunk	Intl.	X25	LLs	Anal.	Digl.	Paging
FC	M	M	M	1993	M	D	D	D

Note: FC: Full Competition; PC: Partial Competition; D: Duopoly; M: Monopoly; RD: Regional Duopoly;
B: Competition allowed at border of concessions.
199X: Competition expected to be introduced this year.
Source: OECD (1995), *Communications Outlook.*

UNITED KINGDOM

Table 1. Main telephone lines per inhabitant in operation

Thousands

	1990	1991	1992	1993	1994
Total number of mainlines	25 817.00	25 920.00	26 560.00	27 380.00	28 388.56
Mainlines per 100 inhabitants	44.97	44.96	45.91	47.17	48.87

Source: Communications Indicators for Major Economies, 1995, OECD/ITU/Eurostat.

Table 2. Percentage of digitalisation in mainlines

Percentage

	1990	1991	1992	1993	1994
Digitalisation	46.9	54.6	64.0	74.9	82.7

Source: Communications Indicators for Major Economies, 1995, OECD/ITU/Eurostat.

Table 3. Cellular mobile telephone subscribers

Thousands

	1990	1991	1992	1993	1994
Total number of subscribers	1 114.00	1 260.00	1 507.00	2 266.00	3 757.00
Subscribers per 100 inhabitants	1.94	2.19	2.61	3.90	6.47

Source: Communications Indicators for Major Economies, 1995, OECD/ITU/Eurostat.

Table 4. Percentage of cellular mobile telephone subscribers in total telecom services

Percentage

		1990	1991	1992	1993	1994
Main lines	Analog	50.9	43.3	34.1	23.2	15.3
	Digital	45.0	52.1	60.6	69.2	73.0
Cellular		4.1	4.6	5.4	7.6	11.7
Total		100.0	100.0	100.0	100.0	100.0

Source: Communications Indicators for Major Economies, 1995, OECD/ITU/Eurostat.

Table 5. Estimated number of facsimile machines

Thousands

	1990	1991	1992	1993	1994
Number of fax machines	750.0	900.0	1 005.0	1 300.0	..
Number of fax machines per 100 inhabitants	1.31	1.56	1.74	2.24	..

Source: Communications Indicators for Major Economies, 1995, OECD/ITU/Eurostat.

Table 6. Basket of business telephone charges in January 1994 (local)

Values express the average annual spending by a business user, in 1993 US$ based on PPPs, excluding tax

	Fixed charge	Usage charge	Total
Annual spending charge	239.62	570.06	809.67

Source: OECD (1995), *Communications Outlook.*

Table 7. Basket of business telephone charges in January 1994 (international)
1993 US$ based on PPPs, excluding tax

	Call pair methodology	Zone distribution methodology
Business telephone charge	96.13	68.61

Source: OECD (1995), *Communications Outlook.*

Table 8. Basket of mobile telecommunication tariffs in January 1994
1993 US$ based on PPPs, excluding tax

	Fixed charge	Usage charge	Total
Mobile telecom. tariffs	504.25	839.63	1 343.88

Source: OECD (1995), *Communications Outlook.*

Table 9. Basket of leased line charges in January 1994
1993 US$ based on PPPs, excluding tax

	9.6 kbit/s	64 kbit/s	1.5/2.0 Mbit/s
Leased line charge	39 514	43 229	211 233

Source: OECD (1995), *Communications Outlook.*

Table 10. Basket of packet switched data communication charges in January 1994
1993 US$ based on PPPs, excluding tax

	Fixed charge	Usage charge	Total
Packet switched data communication charge	7 803.61	6 243.06	14 046.67

Source: OECD (1995), *Communications Outlook.*

Table 11. Status of facilities competition in 1994

Equipment	PSTN competition			Data comms. and leased lines		Mobile communication		
CPE	Local	Trunk	Intl.	X25	LLs	Anal.	Digl.	Paging
FC	FC	FC	D	FC	FC	D	FC	FC

Note: FC: Full Competition; PC: Partial Competition; D: Duopoly; M: Monopoly; RD: Regional Duopoly;
B: Competition allowed at border of concessions.
199X: Competition expected to be introduced this year.

Source: OECD (1995), *Communications Outlook.*

CANADA

Table 1. Main telephone lines per inhabitant in operation

Thousands

	1990	1991	1992	1993	1994
Total number of mainlines	15 295.82	15 814.93	16 246.59	16 470.88	16 756.44
Mainlines per 100 inhabitants	57.48	58.57	59.20	59.22	57.54

Source: Communications Indicators for Major Economies, 1995, OECD/ITU/Eurostat.

Table 2. Percentage of digitalisation in mainlines

Percentage

	1990	1991	1992	1993	1994
Digitalisation	60.2	69.0	80.0	88.0	..

Source: Communications Indicators for Major Economies, 1995, OECD/ITU/Eurostat.

Table 3. Cellular mobile telephone subscribers

Thousands

	1990	1991	1992	1993	1994
Total number of subscribers	583.00	786.00	1 022.75	1 326.39	..
Subscribers per 100 inhabitants	2.19	2.91	3.73	4.77	..

Source: Communications Indicators for Major Economies, 1995, OECD/ITU/Eurostat.

Table 4. Percentage of cellular mobile telephone subscribers in total telecom services

Percentage

		1990	1991	1992	1993	1994
Main lines	Analog	38.3	29.5	18.8	11.1	..
	Digital	58.0	65.7	75.3	81.4	..
Cellular		3.7	4.7	5.9	7.5	..
Total		100.0	100.0	100.0	100.0	..

Source: Communications Indicators for Major Economies, 1995, OECD/ITU/Eurostat.

Table 5. Estimated number of facsimile machines

Thousands

	1990	1991	1992	1993	1994
Number of fax machines	300.0	450.0	500.0	525.0	..
Number of fax machines per 100 inhabitants	1.13	1.67	1.82	1.89	..

Source: Communications Indicators for Major Economies, 1995, OECD/ITU/Eurostat.

Table 6. Basket of business telephone charges in January 1994 (local)

Values express the average annual spending by a business user, in 1993 US$ based on PPPs, excluding tax

	Fixed charge	Usage charge	Total
Annual spending charge	349.24	597.69	946.93

Source: OECD (1995), *Communications Outlook.*

Table 7. Basket of business telephone charges in January 1994 (international)

1993 US$ based on PPPs, excluding tax

	Call pair methodology	Zone distribution methodology
Business telephone charge	95.93	64.78

Source: OECD (1995), *Communications Outlook.*

Table 8. Basket of mobile telecommunication tariffs in January 1994

1993 US$ based on PPPs, excluding tax

	Fixed charge	Usage charge	Total
Mobile telecom. tariffs	389.92	617.80	1 007.72

Source: OECD (1995), *Communications Outlook.*

Table 9. Basket of leased line charges in January 1994

1993 US$ based on PPPs, excluding tax

	9.6 kbit/s	64 kbit/s	1.5/2.0 Mbit/s
Leased line charge	55 476	87 344	454 944

Source: OECD (1995), *Communications Outlook.*

Table 10. Basket of packet switched data communication charges in January 1994

1993 US$ based on PPPs, excluding tax

	Fixed charge	Usage charge	Total
Packet switched data communication charge	4 597.33	4 059.18	8 656.51

Source: OECD (1995), *Communications Outlook.*

Table 11. Status of facilities competition in 1994

Equipment	PSTN competition			Data comms. and leased lines		Mobile communication		
CPE	Local	Trunk	Intl.	X25	LLs	Anal.	Digl.	Paging
FC	M	C	M[1]	FC	FC	RD	D	FC

Note: FC: Full Competition; PC: Partial Competition; D: Duopoly; M: Monopoly; RD: Regional Duopoly;
B: Competition allowed at border of concessions.
199X: Competition expected to be introduced this year.

1. See Background Note

Source: OECD (1995), *Communications Outlook.*

ITALY

Table 1. Main telephone lines per inhabitant in operation

Thousands

	1990	1991	1992	1993	1994
Total number of mainlines	22 350.00	23 071.00	23 709.00	24 167.00	24 542.00
Mainlines per 100 inhabitants	38.77	39.93	40.95	41.74	42.94

Source: Communications Indicators for Major Economies, 1995, OECD/ITU/Eurostat.

Table 2. Percentage of digitalisation in mainlines

Percentage

	1990	1991	1992	1993	1994
Digitalisation	33.0	41.0	48.4	56.6	67.4

Source: Communications Indicators for Major Economies, 1995, OECD/ITU/Eurostat.

Table 3. Cellular mobile telephone subscribers

Thousands

	1990	1991	1992	1993	1994
Total number of subscribers	266.00	568.00	783.00	1 206.95	2 239.74
Subscribers per 100 inhabitants	0.46	0.98	1.35	2.08	3.92

Source: Communications Indicators for Major Economies, 1995, OECD/ITU/Eurostat.

Table 4. Percentage of cellular mobile telephone subscribers in total telecom services

Percentage

		1990	1991	1992	1993	1994
Main lines	Analog	66.2	57.6	50.0	41.3	29.9
	Digital	32.6	40.0	46.9	53.9	61.8
Cellular		1.2	2.4	3.2	4.8	8.4
Total		100.0	100.0	100.0	100.0	100.0

Source: Communications Indicators for Major Economies, 1995, OECD/ITU/Eurostat.

Table 5. Estimated number of facsimile machines

Thousands

	1990	1991	1992	1993	1994
Number of fax machines	170.45	190.99	201.00	202.00	..
Number of fax machines per 100 inhabitants	0.30	0.33	0.35	0.35	..

Source: Communications Indicators for Major Economies, 1995, OECD/ITU/Eurostat.

Table 6. Basket of business telephone charges in January 1994 (local)

Values express the average annual spending by a business user, in 1993 US$ based on PPPs, excluding tax

	Fixed charge	Usage charge	Total
Annual spending charge	164.27	1 081.89	1 258.18

Source: OECD (1995), *Communications Outlook.*

Table 7. Basket of business telephone charges in January 1994 (international)

1993 US$ based on PPPs, excluding tax

	Call pair methodology	Zone distribution methodology
Business telephone charge	109.65	109.28

Source: OECD (1995), *Communications Outlook.*

Table 8. Basket of mobile telecommunication tariffs in January 1994

1993 US$ based on PPPs, excluding tax

	Fixed charge	Usage charge	Total
Mobile telecom. tariffs	449.44	754.00	1 203.45

Source: OECD (1995), *Communications Outlook.*

Table 9. Basket of leased line charges in January 1994

1993 US$ based on PPPs, excluding tax

	9.6 kbit/s	64 kbit/s	1.5/2.0 Mbit/s
Leased line charge	50 566	113 251	988 267

Source: OECD (1995), *Communications Outlook.*

Table 10. Basket of packet switched data communication charges in January 1994

1993 US$ based on PPPs, excluding tax

	Fixed charge	Usage charge	Total
Packet switched data communication charge	2 668.44	6 620.51	9 288.95

Source: OECD (1995), *Communications Outlook.*

Table 11. Status of facilities competition in 1994

Equipment	PSTN competition			Data comms. and leased lines		Mobile communication		
CPE	Local	Trunk	Intl.	X25	LLs	Anal.	Digl.	Paging
FC	M	M	M	1993	M	M	D(1994)	M

Note: FC: Full Competition; PC: Partial Competition; D: Duopoly; M: Monopoly; RD: Regional Duopoly;
B: Competition allowed at border of concessions.
199X: Competition expected to be introduced this year.

Source: OECD (1995), *Communications Outlook.*

AUSTRALIA

Table 1. Main telephone lines per inhabitant in operation

Thousands

	1990	1991	1992	1993	1994
Total number of mainlines	7 786.89	8 046.03	8 257.00	8 540.00	8 850.00
Mainlines per 100 inhabitants	45.68	46.53	47.10	48.23	49.60

Source: Communications Indicators for Major Economies, 1995, OECD/ITU/Eurostat.

Table 2. Percentage of digitalisation in mainlines

Percentage

	1990	1991	1992	1993	1994
Digitalisation	..	26.0	..	50.0	51.0

Source: Communications Indicators for Major Economies, 1995, OECD/ITU/Eurostat.

Table 3. Cellular mobile telephone subscribers

Thousands

	1990	1991	1992	1993	1994
Total number of subscribers	184.94	291.46	497.00	760.00	1 250.00
Subscribers per 100 inhabitants	1.09	1.69	2.84	4.29	7.01

Source: Communications Indicators for Major Economies, 1995, OECD/ITU/Eurostat.

Table 4. Percentage of cellular mobile telephone subscribers in total telecom services

Percentage

		1990	1991	1992	1993	1994
Main lines	Analog	..	71.4	..	45.9	42.9
	Digital	..	25.1	..	45.9	44.7
Cellular		2.3	3.5	5.7	8.2	12.4
Total		100.0	100.0	100.0	100.0	100.0

Source: Communications Indicators for Major Economies, 1995, OECD/ITU/Eurostat.

Table 5. Estimated number of facsimile machines

Thousands

	1990	1991	1992	1993	1994
Number of fax machines	280.0	350.0	400.0	425.0	450.0
Number of fax machines per 100 inhabitants	1.64	2.02	2.28	2.40	2.52

Source: Communications Indicators for Major Economies, 1995, OECD/ITU/Eurostat.

Table 6. Basket of business telephone charges in January 1994 (local)

Values express the average annual spending by a business user, in 1993 US$ based on PPPs, excluding tax

	Fixed charge	Usage charge	Total
Annual spending charge	232.63	888.39	1 121.02

Source: OECD (1995), *Communications Outlook.*

Table 7. Basket of business telephone charges in January 1994 (international)

1993 US$ based on PPPs, excluding tax

	Call pair methodology	Zone distribution methodology
Business telephone charge	87.45	86.40

Source: OECD (1995), *Communications Outlook.*

Table 8. Basket of mobile telecommunication tariffs in January 1994

1993 US$ based on PPPs, excluding tax

	Fixed charge	Usage charge	Total
Mobile telecom. tariffs	385.96	632.70	1 018.67

Source: OECD (1995), *Communications Outlook.*

Table 9. Basket of leased line charges in January 1994

1993 US$ based on PPPs, excluding tax

	9.6 kbit/s	64 kbit/s	1.5/2.0 Mbit/s
Leased line charge	47 805	86 278	344 113

Source: OECD (1995), *Communications Outlook.*

Table 10. Basket of packet switched data communication charges in January 1994

1993 US$ based on PPPs, excluding tax

	Fixed charge	Usage charge	Total
Packet switched data communication charge	3 823.20	6 994.90	10 818.11

Source: OECD (1995), *Communications Outlook.*

Table 11. Status of facilities competition in 1994

Equipment	PSTN competition			Data comms. and leased lines		Mobile communication		
CPE	Local	Trunk	Intl.	X25	LLs	Anal.	Digl.	Paging
FC	D	D	D	D	D	D	FC	FC

Note: FC: Full Competition; PC: Partial Competition; D: Duopoly; M: Monopoly; RD: Regional Duopoly;
B: Competition allowed at border of concessions.
199X: Competition expected to be introduced this year.

Source: OECD (1995), *Communications Outlook.*

AUSTRIA

Table 1. Main telephone lines per inhabitant in operation

Thousands

	1990	1991	1992	1993	1994
Total number of mainlines	3 223.16	3 344.18	3 466.49	3 579.24	3 681.37
Mainlines per 100 inhabitants	41.76	42.75	43.97	45.10	46.51

Source: Communications Indicators for Major Economies, 1995, OECD/ITU/Eurostat.

Table 2. Percentage of digitalisation in mainlines

Percentage

	1990	1991	1992	1993	1994
Digitalisation	11.0	18.1	27.0	35.1	46.3

Source: Communications Indicators for Major Economies, 1995, OECD/ITU/Eurostat.

Table 3. Cellular mobile telephone subscribers

Thousands

	1990	1991	1992	1993	1994
Total number of subscribers	73.70	115.40	172.45	220.86	278.20
Subscribers per 100 inhabitants	0.95	1.48	2.19	2.78	3.51

Source: Communications Indicators for Major Economies, 1995, OECD/ITU/Eurostat.

Table 4. Percentage of cellular mobile telephone subscribers in total telecom services

Percentage

		1990	1991	1992	1993	1994
Main lines	Analog	87.0	79.2	69.5	61.2	49.9
	Digital	10.8	17.5	25.7	33.0	43.1
Cellular		2.2	3.3	4.7	5.8	7.0
Total		100.0	100.0	100.0	100.0	100.0

Source: Communications Indicators for Major Economies, 1995, OECD/ITU/Eurostat.

Table 5. Estimated number of facsimile machines

Thousands

	1990	1991	1992	1993	1994
Number of fax machines	85.0	160.0	190.0	210.0	..
Number of fax machines per 100 inhabitants	1.10	2.04	2.41	2.65	..

Source: Communications Indicators for Major Economies, 1995, OECD/ITU/Eurostat.

Table 6. Basket of business telephone charges in January 1994 (local)

Values express the average annual spending by a business user, in 1993 US$ based on PPPs, excluding tax

	Fixed charge	Usage charge	Total
Annual spending charge	148.97	1 103.82	1 252.79

Source: OECD (1995), *Communications Outlook.*

Table 7. Basket of business telephone charges in January 1994 (international)

1993 US$ based on PPPs, excluding tax

	Call pair methodology	Zone distribution methodology
Business telephone charge	103.56	100.42

Source: OECD (1995), *Communications Outlook.*

Table 8. Basket of mobile telecommunication tariffs in January 1994

1993 US$ based on PPPs, excluding tax

	Fixed charge	Usage charge	Total
Mobile telecom. tariffs	372.41	788.34	1 160.75

Source: OECD (1995), *Communications Outlook.*

Table 9. Basket of leased line charges in January 1994

1993 US$ based on PPPs, excluding tax

	9.6 kbit/s	64 kbit/s	1.5/2.0 Mbit/s
Leased line charge	37 638	124.379	685.517

Source: OECD (1995), *Communications Outlook.*

Table 10. Basket of packet switched data communication charges in January 1994

1993 US$ based on PPPs, excluding tax

	Fixed charge	Usage charge	Total
Packet switched data communication charge	2 462.07	8 449.77	10 911.84

Source: OECD (1995), *Communications Outlook.*

Table 11. Status of facilities competition in 1994

Equipment	PSTN competition			Data comms. and leased lines		Mobile communication		
CPE	Local	Trunk	Intl.	X25	LLs	Anal.	Digl.	Paging
FC	M	M	M	M	M	M	M	FC

Note: FC: Full Competition; PC: Partial Competition; D: Duopoly; M: Monopoly; RD: Regional Duopoly;
B: Competition allowed at border of concessions.
199X: Competition expected to be introduced this year.

Source: OECD (1995), *Communications Outlook.*

BELGIUM

Table 1. Main telephone lines per inhabitant in operation

Thousands

	1990	1991	1992	1993	1994
Total number of mainlines	3 912.63	4 096.07	4 264.34	4 395.70	4 526.31
Mainlines per 100 inhabitants	39.26	40.94	42.53	43.66	42.22

Source: Communications Indicators for Major Economies, 1995, OECD/ITU/Eurostat.

Table 2. Percentage of digitalisation in mainlines

Percentage

	1990	1991	1992	1993	1994
Digitalisation	37.2	44.8	48.2	54.0	60.0

Source: Communications Indicators for Major Economies, 1995, OECD/ITU/Eurostat.

Table 3. Cellular mobile telephone subscribers

Thousands

	1990	1991	1992	1993	1994
Total number of subscribers	42.88	51.42	61.46	66.93	126.94
Subscribers per 100 inhabitants	0.43	0.51	0.61	0.66	1.26

Source: Communications Indicators for Major Economies, 1995, OECD/ITU/Eurostat.

Table 4. Percentage of cellular mobile telephone subscribers in total telecom services

Percentage

		1990	1991	1992	1993	1994
Main lines	Analog	62.1	54.5	51.1	45.3	38.8
	Digital	36.8	44.2	47.5	53.2	58.3
Cellular		1.1	1.2	1.4	1.5	2.9
Total		100.0	100.0	100.0	100.0	100.0

Source: Communications Indicators for Major Economies, 1995, OECD/ITU/Eurostat.

Table 5. Estimated number of facsimile machines

Thousands

	1990	1991	1992	1993	1994
Number of fax machines	67.0	93.3	150.0	165.0	..
Number of fax machines per 100 inhabitants	0.67	0.93	1.50	1.64	..

Source: Communications Indicators for Major Economies, 1995, OECD/ITU/Eurostat.

Table 6. Basket of business telephone charges in January 1994 (local)

Values express the average annual spending by a business user, in 1993 US$ based on PPPs, excluding tax

	Fixed charge	Usage charge	Total
Annual spending charge	123.51	590.38	713.89

Source: OECD (1995), *Communications Outlook.*

Table 7. Basket of business telephone charges in January 1994 (international)

1993 US$ based on PPPs, excluding tax

	Call pair methodology	Zone distribution methodology
Business telephone charge	91.76	70.69

Source: OECD (1995), *Communications Outlook.*

Table 8. Basket of mobile telecommunication tariffs in January 1994

1993 US$ based on PPPs, excluding tax

	Fixed charge	Usage charge	Total
Mobile telecom. tariffs	389.32	777.14	1 166.46

Source: OECD (1995), *Communications Outlook.*

Table 9. Basket of leased line charges in January 1994

1993 US$ based on PPPs, excluding tax

	9.6 kbit/s	64 kbit/s	1.5/2.0 Mbit/s
Leased line charge	16 504	140 651	511 411

Source: OECD (1995), *Communications Outlook.*

Table 10. Basket of packet switched data communication charges in January 1994

1993 US$ based on PPPs, excluding tax

	Fixed charge	Usage charge	Total
Packet switched data communication charge	2 749.35	4 047.66	6 797.02

Source: OECD (1995), *Communications Outlook.*

Table 11. Status of facilities competition in 1994

Equipment	PSTN competition			Data comms. and leased lines		Mobile communication		
CPE	Local	Trunk	Intl.	X25	LLs	Anal.	Digl.	Paging
FC	M	M	M	1993	M	M	M	M

Note: FC: Full Competition; PC: Partial Competition; D: Duopoly; M: Monopoly; RD: Regional Duopoly;
B: Competition allowed at border of concessions.
199X: Competition expected to be introduced this year.

Source: OECD (1995), *Communications Outlook.*

CZECH REPUBLIC

Table 1. Main telephone lines per inhabitant in operation

Thousands

	1990	1991	1992	1993	1994
Total number of mainlines	..	..	..	1961.6	2150.6
Mainlines per 100 inhabitants	..	..	..	19.2	21.1

Source: Ministry of Economy of the Czech Republic.

Table 2. Percentage of digitalisation in mainlines

Percentage

	1990	1991	1992	1993	1994
Digitalisation	..	..	..	10.5	14.7

Source: Ministry of Economy of the Czech Republic.

Table 3. Cellular mobile telephone subscribers

Thousands

	1990	1991	1992	1993	1994
Total number of subscribers	..	..	..	11.2	30.4
Subscribers per 100 inhabitants	..	..	..	0.11	0.3

Source: Ministry of Economy of the Czech Republic.

Table 4. Percentage of cellular mobile telephone subscribers in total telecom services

Percentage

		1990	1991	1992	1993	1994
Main lines	Analog	..	..	..	89.0	84.1
	Digital	..	..	..	10.4	14.5
Cellular		..	..	..	0.6	1.4
Total		..	..	..	100.0	100.0

Source: Ministry of Economy of the Czech Republic.

Table 5. Estimated number of facsimile machines

Thousands

	1990	1991	1992	1993	1994
Number of fax machines	..	..	..	45.6	58.5
Number of fax machines per 100 inhabitants	..	..	..	0.44	0.57

Source: Ministry of Economy of the Czech Republic.

Table 6. Basket of business telephone charges in January 1994 (local)

Values express the average annual spending by a business user, in 1993 US$ based on PPPs, excluding tax

	Fixed charge	Usage charge	Total
Annual spending charge	62.13	566.96	629.09

Source: Ministry of Economy of the Czech Republic.

Table 7. Basket of business telephone charges in January 1994 (international)

1993 US$ based on PPPs, excluding tax

	Call pair methodology	Zone distribution methodology
Business telephone charge	..	..

Source: Ministry of Economy of the Czech Republic.

Table 8. Basket of mobile telecommunication tariffs in January 1994

1993 US$ based on PPPs, excluding tax

	Fixed charge	Usage charge	Total
Mobile telecom. tariffs	778.26	936.89	1 715.15

Source: Ministry of Economy of the Czech Republic.

Table 9. Basket of leased line charges in January 1994

1993 US$ based on PPPs, excluding tax

	9.6 kbit/s	64 kbit/s	1.5/2.0 Mbit/s
Leased line charge	23 846	38 154	381 538

Source: Ministry of Economy of the Czech Republic.

Table 10. Basket of packet switched data communication charges in January 1994

1993 US$ based on PPPs, excluding tax

	Fixed charge	Usage charge	Total
Packet switched data communication charge	..	..	..

Source: Ministry of Economy of the Czech Republic.

Table 11. Status of facilities competition in 1994

Equipment	PSTN competition			Data comms. and leased lines		Mobile communication		
CPE	Local	Trunk	Intl.	X25	LLs	Anal.	Digl.	Paging
FC	RD	2000	2000	FC	FC	M	D	B

Note: FC: Full Competition; PC: Partial Competition; D: Duopoly; M: Monopoly; RD: Regional Duopoly;
B: Competition allowed at border of concessions.
199X: Competition expected to be introduced this year.

Source: Ministry of Economy of the Czech Republic.

DENMARK

Table 1. Main telephone lines per inhabitant in operation

Thousands

	1990	1991	1992	1993	1994
Total number of mainlines	2 911.20	2 950.76	3 004.94	3 059.81	3 123.03
Mainlines per 100 inhabitants	56.63	57.25	58.12	58.88	60.37

Source: Communications Indicators for Major Economies, 1995, OECD/ITU/Eurostat.

Table 2. Percentage of digitalisation in mainlines

Percentage

	1990	1991	1992	1993	1994
Digitalisation	28.0	33.4	39.2	46.0	53.3

Source: Communications Indicators for Major Economies, 1995, OECD/ITU/Eurostat.

Table 3. Cellular mobile telephone subscribers

Thousands

	1990	1991	1992	1993	1994
Total number of subscribers	148.22	175.94	211.06	357.59	503.50
Subscribers per 100 inhabitants	2.88	3.41	4.08	6.88	9.73

Source: Communications Indicators for Major Economies, 1995, OECD/ITU/Eurostat.

Table 4. Percentage of cellular mobile telephone subscribers in total telecom services

Percentage

		1990	1991	1992	1993	1994
Main lines	Analog	68.5	62.9	56.8	48.3	40.2
	Digital	26.6	31.5	36.6	41.2	45.9
Cellular		4.8	5.6	6.6	10.5	13.9
Total		100.0	100.0	100.0	100.0	100.0

Source: Communications Indicators for Major Economies, 1995, OECD/ITU/Eurostat.

Table 5. Estimated number of facsimile machines

Thousands

	1990	1991	1992	1993	1994
Number of fax machines	100.0	150.0	170.0	185.0	..
Number of fax machines per 100 inhabitants	1.95	2.91	3.29	3.56	..

Source: Communications Indicators for Major Economies, 1995, OECD/ITU/Eurostat.

Table 6. Basket of business telephone charges in January 1994 (local)

Values express the average annual spending by a business user, in 1993 US$ based on PPPs, excluding tax

	Fixed charge	Usage charge	Total
Annual spending charge	125.98	269.43	395.41

Source: OECD (1995), *Communications Outlook.*

DENMARK (continued)

Table 7. Basket of business telephone charges in January 1994 (international)

1993 US$ based on PPPs, excluding tax

	Call pair methodology	Zone distribution methodology
Business telephone charge	85.85	72.85

Source: OECD (1995), *Communications Outlook.*

Table 8. Basket of mobile telecommunication tariffs in January 1994

1993 US$ based on PPPs, excluding tax

	Fixed charge	Usage charge	Total
Mobile telecom. tariffs	103.54	502.05	605.59

Source: OECD (1995), *Communications Outlook.*

Table 9. Basket of leased line charges in January 1994

1993 US$ based on PPPs, excluding tax

	9.6 kbit/s	64 kbit/s	1.5/2.0 Mbit/s
Leased line charge	24 226	42 198	318 533

Source: OECD (1995), *Communications Outlook.*

Table 10. Basket of packet switched data communication charges in January 1994

1993 US$ based on PPPs, excluding tax

	Fixed charge	Usage charge	Total
Packet switched data communication charge	1 617.93	3 340.76	4 958.69

Source: OECD (1995), *Communications Outlook.*

Table 11. Status of facilities competition in 1994

Equipment	PSTN competition			Data comms. and leased lines		Mobile communication		
CPE	Local	Trunk	Intl.	X25	LLs	Anal.	Digl.	Paging
FC	M	M	M	1993	M	D	FC	M

Note: FC: Full Competition; PC: Partial Competition; D: Duopoly; M: Monopoly; RD: Regional Duopoly;
B: Competition allowed at border of concessions.
199X: Competition expected to be introduced this year.

Source: OECD (1995), *Communications Outlook.*

FINLAND

Table 1. Main telephone lines per inhabitant in operation

Thousands

	1990	1991	1992	1993	1994
Total number of mainlines	2 670.00	2 717.60	2 742.05	2 760.66	2 780.00
Mainlines per 100 inhabitants	53.55	54.04	54.38	54.37	54.70

Source: Communications Indicators for Major Economies, 1995, OECD/ITU/Eurostat.

Table 2. Percentage of digitalisation in mainlines

Percentage

	1990	1991	1992	1993	1994
Digitalisation	35.1	42.4	50.5	62.1	68.0

Source: Communications Indicators for Major Economies, 1995, OECD/ITU/Eurostat.

Table 3. Cellular mobile telephone subscribers

Thousands

	1990	1991	1992	1993	1994
Total number of subscribers	225.98	283.05	354.22	459.07	600.00
Subscribers per 100 inhabitants	4.53	5.63	7.03	9.04	11.80

Source: Communications Indicators for Major Economies, 1995, OECD/ITU/Eurostat.

Table 4. Percentage of cellular mobile telephone subscribers in total telecom services

Percentage

		1990	1991	1992	1993	1994
Main lines	Analog	59.8	52.2	43.8	32.5	26.3
	Digital	32.4	38.4	44.7	53.2	55.9
Cellular		7.8	9.4	11.4	14.3	17.8
Total		100.0	100.0	100.0	100.0	100.0

Source: Communications Indicators for Major Economies, 1995, OECD/ITU/Eurostat.

Table 5. Estimated number of facsimile machines

Thousands

	1990	1991	1992	1993	1994
Number of fax machines	75.0	92.0	105.0	115.0	..
Number of fax machines per 100 inhabitants	1.50	1.83	2.08	2.26	..

Source: Communications Indicators for Major Economies, 1995, OECD/ITU/Eurostat.

Table 6. Basket of business telephone charges in January 1994 (local)

Values express the average annual spending by a business user, in 1993 US$ based on PPPs, excluding tax

	Fixed charge	Usage charge	Total
Annual spending charge	154.61	235.02	389.62

Source: OECD (1995), *Communications Outlook.*

Table 7. Basket of business telephone charges in January 1994 (international)

1993 US$ based on PPPs, excluding tax

	Call pair methodology	Zone distribution methodology
Business telephone charge	81.24	60.86

Source: OECD (1995), *Communications Outlook.*

Table 8. Basket of mobile telecommunication tariffs in January 1994

1993 US$ based on PPPs, excluding tax

	Fixed charge	Usage charge	Total
Mobile telecom. tariffs	99.91	457.63	557.54

Source: OECD (1995), *Communications Outlook.*

Table 9. Basket of leased line charges in January 1994

1993 US$ based on PPPs, excluding tax

	9.6 kbit/s	64 kbit/s	1.5/2.0 Mbit/s
Leased line charge	40 420	53 335	..

Source: OECD (1995), *Communications Outlook.*

Table 10. Basket of packet switched data communication charges in January 1994

1993 US$ based on PPPs, excluding tax

	Fixed charge	Usage charge	Total
Packet switched data communication charge	633.01	2 016.03	2 649.09

Source: OECD (1995), *Communications Outlook.*

Table 11. Status of facilities competition in 1994

Equipment	PSTN competition			Data comms. and leased lines		Mobile communication		
CPE	Local	Trunk	Intl.	X25	LLs	Anal.	Digl.	Paging
FC	FC	FC	FC	FC	FC	D	D	D

Note: FC: Full Competition; PC: Partial Competition; D: Duopoly; M: Monopoly; RD: Regional Duopoly;
B: Competition allowed at border of concessions.
199X: Competition expected to be introduced this year.

Source: OECD (1995), *Communications Outlook.*

GREECE

Table 1. Main telephone lines per inhabitant in operation

Thousands

	1990	1991	1992	1993	1994
Total number of mainlines	3 948.65	4 190.09	4 496.54	4 744.02	4 976.21
Mainlines per 100 inhabitants	38.94	40.80	43.66	45.72	47.81

Source: Communications Indicators for Major Economies, 1995, OECD/ITU/Eurostat.

Table 2. Percentage of digitalisation in mainlines

Percentage

	1990	1991	1992	1993	1994
Digitalisation	0.5	6.4	11.5	21.8	31.4

Source: Communications Indicators for Major Economies, 1995, OECD/ITU/Eurostat.

Table 3. Cellular mobile telephone subscribers

Thousands

	1990	1991	1992	1993	1994
Total number of subscribers	..	..	..	48.00	167.00
Subscribers per 100 inhabitants	..	..	..	0.46	1.60

Source: Communications Indicators for Major Economies, 1995, OECD/ITU/Eurostat.

Table 4. Percentage of cellular mobile telephone subscribers in total telecom services

Percentage

		1990	1991	1992	1993	1994
Main lines	Analog	..	..	..	77.4	66.4
	Digital	..	..	..	21.6	30.4
Cellular		..	..	..	1.0	3.2
Total		..	..	..	100.0	100.0

Source: Communications Indicators for Major Economies, 1995, OECD/ITU/Eurostat.

Table 5. Estimated number of facsimile machines

Thousands

	1990	1991	1992	1993	1994
Number of fax machines	9.2	12.1	13.3	15.3	..
Number of fax machines per 100 inhabitants	0.09	0.12	0.13	0.15	..

Source: Communications Indicators for Major Economies, 1995, OECD/ITU/Eurostat.

Table 6. Basket of business telephone charges in January 1994 (local)

Values express the average annual spending by a business user, in 1993 US$ based on PPPs, excluding tax

	Fixed charge	Usage charge	Total
Annual spending charge	142.19	885.73	1 027.91

Source: OECD (1995), *Communications Outlook.*

Table 7. Basket of business telephone charges in January 1994 (international)

1993 US$ based on PPPs, excluding tax

	Call pair methodology	Zone distribution methodology
Business telephone charge	107.48	112.30

Source: OECD (1995), *Communications Outlook.*

Table 8. Basket of mobile telecommunication tariffs in January 1994

1993 US$ based on PPPs, excluding tax

	Fixed charge	Usage charge	Total
Mobile telecom. tariffs	..	..	..

Source: OECD (1995), *Communications Outlook.*

Table 9. Basket of leased line charges in January 1994

1993 US$ based on PPPs, excluding tax

	9.6 kbit/s	64 kbit/s	1.5/2.0 Mbit/s
Leased line charge	35 513	90 260	358 802

Source: OECD (1995), *Communications Outlook.*

Table 10. Basket of packet switched data communication charges in January 1994

1993 US$ based on PPPs, excluding tax

	Fixed charge	Usage charge	Total
Packet switched data communication charge	1 918.40	10 461.35	12 379.75

Source: OECD (1995), *Communications Outlook.*

Table 11. Status of facilities competition in 1994

Equipment	PSTN competition			Data comms. and leased lines		Mobile communication		
CPE	Local	Trunk	Intl.	X25	LLs	Anal.	Digl.	Paging
FC	M	M	M	1997	M	..	D	M

Note: FC: Full Competition; PC: Partial Competition; D: Duopoly; M: Monopoly; RD: Regional Duopoly;
B: Competition allowed at border of concessions.
199X: Competition expected to be introduced this year.

Source: OECD (1995), *Communications Outlook.*

ICELAND

Table 1. Main telephone lines per inhabitant in operation

Thousands

	1990	1991	1992	1993	1994
Total number of mainlines	130.50	135.56	140.03	143.60	150.00
Mainlines per 100 inhabitants	51.18	52.54	53.65	54.39	56.36

Source: Communications Indicators for Major Economies, 1995, OECD/ITU/Eurostat.

Table 2. Percentage of digitalisation in mainlines

Percentage

	1990	1991	1992	1993	1994
Digitalisation	41.0	42.0	49.0	66.0	85.0

Source: Communications Indicators for Major Economies, 1995, OECD/ITU/Eurostat.

Table 3. Cellular mobile telephone subscribers

Thousands

	1990	1991	1992	1993	1994
Total number of subscribers	10.01	12.89	15.25	17.41	..
Subscribers per 100 inhabitants	3.93	5.00	5.84	6.59	..

Source: Communications Indicators for Major Economies, 1995, OECD/ITU/Eurostat.

Table 4. Percentage of cellular mobile telephone subscribers in total telecom services

Percentage

		1990	1991	1992	1993	1994
Main lines	Analog	54.8	53.0	46.0	30.3	..
	Digital	38.1	38.4	44.2	58.9	..
Cellular		7.1	8.7	9.8	10.8	..
Total		100.0	100.0	100.0	100.0	..

Source: Communications Indicators for Major Economies, 1995, OECD/ITU/Eurostat.

Table 5. Estimated number of facsimile machines

Thousands

	1990	1991	1992	1993	1994
Number of fax machines	1.3	..	4.0	4.1	..
Number of fax machines per 100 inhabitants	0.53	..	1.53	1.55	..

Source: Communications Indicators for Major Economies, 1995, OECD/ITU/Eurostat.

Table 6. Basket of business telephone charges in January 1994 (local)

Values express the average annual spending by a business user, in 1993 US$ based on PPPs, excluding tax

	Fixed charge	Usage charge	Total
Annual spending charge	99.57	212.21	314.13

Source: OECD (1995), *Communications Outlook.*

Table 7. Basket of business telephone charges in January 1994 (international)

1993 US$ based on PPPs, excluding tax

	Call pair methodology	Zone distribution methodology
Business telephone charge	90.43	84.99

Source: OECD (1995), *Communications Outlook.*

Table 8. Basket of mobile telecommunication tariffs in January 1994

1993 US$ based on PPPs, excluding tax

	Fixed charge	Usage charge	Total
Mobile telecom. tariffs	94.50	339.41	433.91

Source: OECD (1995), *Communications Outlook.*

Table 9. Basket of leased line charges in January 1994

1993 US$ based on PPPs, excluding tax

	9.6 kbit/s	64 kbit/s	1.5/2.0 Mbit/s
Leased line charge	77 370	103.174	425 792

Source: OECD (1995), *Communications Outlook.*

Table 10. Basket of packet switched data communication charges in January 1994

1993 US$ based on PPPs, excluding tax

	Fixed charge	Usage charge	Total
Packet switched data communication charge	3 342.28	2 105.95	5 448.22

Source: OECD (1995), *Communications Outlook.*

Table 11. Status of facilities competition in 1994

Equipment	PSTN competition			Data comms. and leased lines		Mobile communication		
CPE	Local	Trunk	Intl.	X25	LLs	Anal.	Digl.	Paging
FC	M	M	M	M	M	M	M	M

Note: FC: Full Competition; PC: Partial Competition; D: Duopoly; M: Monopoly; RD: Regional Duopoly;
B: Competition allowed at border of concessions.
199X: Competition expected to be introduced this year.

Source: OECD (1995), *Communications Outlook.*

IRELAND

Table 1. Main telephone lines per inhabitant in operation

Thousands

	1990	1991	1992	1993	1994
Total number of mainlines	983.00	1 048.00	1 113.00	1 170.00	1 240.00
Mainlines per 100 inhabitants	28.06	29.74	31.38	32.78	35.00

Source: Communications Indicators for Major Economies, 1995, OECD/ITU/Eurostat.

Table 2. Percentage of digitalisation in mainlines

Percentage

	1990	1991	1992	1993	1994
Digitalisation	n.a.	58.0	68.0	n.a.	..

Source: Communications Indicators for Major Economies, 1995, OECD/ITU/Eurostat.

Table 3. Cellular mobile telephone subscribers

Thousands

	1990	1991	1992	1993	1994
Total number of subscribers	25.00	32.00	44.00	61.10	88.00
Subscribers per 100 inhabitants	0.71	0.91	1.24	1.71	2.48

Source: Communications Indicators for Major Economies, 1995, OECD/ITU/Eurostat.

Table 4. Percentage of cellular mobile telephone subscribers in total telecom services

Percentage

		1990	1991	1992	1993	1994
Main lines	Analog	..	40.8	30.8	..	..
	Digital	..	56.3	65.4	..	..
Cellular		2.5	3.0	3.8	5.0	6.6
Total		100.0	100.0	100.0	100.0	100.0

Source: Communications Indicators for Major Economies, 1995, OECD/ITU/Eurostat.

Table 5. Estimated number of facsimile machines

Thousands

	1990	1991	1992	1993	1994
Number of fax machines	53.0	60.0	75.0	80.0	..
Number of fax machines per 100 inhabitants	1.51	1.70	2.11	2.24	..

Source: Communications Indicators for Major Economies, 1995, OECD/ITU/Eurostat.

Table 6. Basket of business telephone charges in January 1994 (local)

Values express the average annual spending by a business user, in 1993 US$ based on PPPs, excluding tax

	Fixed charge	Usage charge	Total
Annual spending charge	219.85	959.26	1 189.77

Source: OECD (1995), *Communications Outlook.*

Table 7. Basket of business telephone charges in January 1994 (international)

1993 US$ based on PPPs, excluding tax

	Call pair methodology	Zone distribution methodology
Business telephone charge	102.71	85.64

Source: OECD (1995), *Communications Outlook.*

Table 8. Basket of mobile telecommunication tariffs in January 1994

1993 US$ based on PPPs, excluding tax

	Fixed charge	Usage charge	Total
Mobile telecom. tariffs	391.86	690.34	1 082.20

Source: OECD (1995), *Communications Outlook.*

Table 9. Basket of leased line charges in January 1994

1993 US$ based on PPPs, excluding tax

	9.6 kbit/s	64 kbit/s	1.5/2.0 Mbit/s
Leased line charge	32 122	46 237	280 527

Source: OECD (1995), *Communications Outlook.*

Table 10. Basket of packet switched data communication charges in January 1994

1993 US$ based on PPPs, excluding tax

	Fixed charge	Usage charge	Total
Packet switched data communication charge	3 479.90	4 118.23	7 598.13

Source: OECD (1995), *Communications Outlook.*

Table 11. Status of facilities competition in 1994

Equipment	PSTN competition			Data comms. and leased lines		Mobile communication		
CPE	Local	Trunk	Intl.	X25	LLs	Anal.	Digl.	Paging
FC	M	M	M	1993	M	M	M	M

Note: FC: Full Competition; PC: Partial Competition; D: Duopoly; M: Monopoly; RD: Regional Duopoly;
B: Competition allowed at border of concessions.
199X: Competition expected to be introduced this year.

Source: OECD (1995), *Communications Outlook.*

LUXEMBOURG

Table 1. Main telephone lines per inhabitant in operation

Thousands

	1990	1991	1992	1993	1994
Total number of mainlines	183.70	191.76	206.21	214.82	221.90
Mainlines per 100 inhabitants	48.34	49.68	52.87	54.11	55.35

Source: Communications Indicators for Major Economies, 1995, OECD/ITU/Eurostat.

Table 2. Percentage of digitalisation in mainlines

Percentage

	1990	1991	1992	1993	1994
Digitalisation	33.0	50.0	70.0	82.0	..

Source: Communications Indicators for Major Economies, 1995, OECD/ITU/Eurostat.

Table 3. Cellular mobile telephone subscribers

Thousands

	1990	1991	1992	1993	1994
Total number of subscribers	0.82	1.13	1.14	5.08	13.77
Subscribers per 100 inhabitants	0.22	0.29	0.29	1.28	3.43

Source: Communications Indicators for Major Economies, 1995, OECD/ITU/Eurostat.

Table 4. Percentage of cellular mobile telephone subscribers in total telecom services

Percentage

		1990	1991	1992	1993	1994
Main lines	Analog	66.7	49.7	29.8	17.6	..
	Digital	32.9	49.7	69.6	80.1	..
Cellular		0.4	0.6	0.5	2.3	5.8
Total		100.0	100.0	100.0	100.0	100.0

Source: Communications Indicators for Major Economies, 1995, OECD/ITU/Eurostat.

Table 5. Estimated number of facsimile machines

Thousands

	1990	1991	1992	1993	1994
Number of fax machines	3.5	4.0	5.0	5.5	..
Number of fax machines per 100 inhabitants	0.92	1.04	1.28	1.39	..

Source: Communications Indicators for Major Economies, 1995, OECD/ITU/Eurostat.

Table 6. Basket of business telephone charges in January 1994 (local)

Values express the average annual spending by a business user, in 1993 US$ based on PPPs, excluding tax

	Fixed charge	Usage charge	Total
Annual spending charge	..	..	..

Source: OECD (1995), *Communications Outlook.*

Table 7. Basket of business telephone charges in January 1994 (international)

1993 US$ based on PPPs, excluding tax

	Call pair methodology	Zone distribution methodology
Business telephone charge	99.47	102.44

Source: OECD (1995), *Communications Outlook.*

Table 8. Basket of mobile telecommunication tariffs in January 1994

1993 US$ based on PPPs, excluding tax

	Fixed charge	Usage charge	Total
Mobile telecom. tariffs	542.12	701.27	1 243.39

Source: OECD (1995), *Communications Outlook.*

Table 9. Basket of leased line charges in January 1994

1993 US$ based on PPPs, excluding tax

	9.6 kbit/s	64 kbit/s	1.5/2.0 Mbit/s
Leased line charge	26 739	49 609	496 086

Source: OECD (1995), *Communications Outlook.*

Table 10. Basket of packet switched data communication charges in January 1994

1993 US$ based on PPPs, excluding tax

	Fixed charge	Usage charge	Total
Packet switched data communication charge	2 656.40	4 846.67	7 503.07

Source: OECD (1995), *Communications Outlook.*

Table 11. Status of facilities competition in 1994

Equipment	PSTN competition			Data comms. and leased lines		Mobile communication		
CPE	Local	Trunk	Intl.	X25	LLs	Anal.	Digl.	Paging
FC	M	M	M	1993	M	M	M	M

Note: FC: Full Competition; PC: Partial Competition; D: Duopoly; M: Monopoly; RD: Regional Duopoly;

B: Competition allowed at border of concessions.

199X: Competition expected to be introduced this year.

Source: OECD (1995), *Communications Outlook.*

MEXICO

Table 1. Main telephone lines per inhabitant in operation

Thousands

	1990	1991	1992	1993	1994
Total number of mainlines	5 354.50	6 024.80	6 753.65	7 620.88	8 492.52
Mainlines per 100 inhabitants	6.55	7.23	7.95	8.79	9.25

Source: Communications Indicators for Major Economies, 1995, OECD/ITU/Eurostat.

Table 2. Percentage of digitalisation in mainlines

Percentage

	1990	1991	1992	1993	1994
Digitalisation	28.7	38.6	52.0	68.0	82.7

Source: Communications Indicators for Major Economies, 1995, OECD/ITU/Eurostat.

Table 3. Cellular mobile telephone subscribers

Thousands

	1990	1991	1992	1993	1994
Total number of subscribers	34.94	170.08	311.51	385.34	..
Subscribers per 100 inhabitants	0.04	0.20	0.37	0.44	..

Source: Communications Indicators for Major Economies, 1995, OECD/ITU/Eurostat.

Table 4. Percentage of cellular mobile telephone subscribers in total telecom services

Percentage

		1990	1991	1992	1993	1994
Main lines	Analog	70.8	59.7	45.9	30.5	..
	Digital	28.5	37.5	49.7	64.7	..
Cellular		0.6	2.7	4.4	4.8	..
Total		100.0	100.0	100.0	100.0	..

Source: Communications Indicators for Major Economies, 1995, OECD/ITU/Eurostat.

Table 5. Estimated number of facsimile machines

Thousands

	1990	1991	1992	1993	1994
Number of fax machines	..	..	150.0	180.0	..
Number of fax machines per 100 inhabitants	..	..	0.18	0.21	..

Source: Communications Indicators for Major Economies, 1995, OECD/ITU/Eurostat.

Table 6. Basket of business telephone charges in January 1994 (local)

Values express the average annual spending by a business user, in 1993 US$ based on PPPs, excluding tax

	Fixed charge	Usage charge	Total
Annual spending charge	..	..	..

Source: OECD (1995), *Communications Outlook.*

Table 7. Basket of business telephone charges in January 1994 (international)
1993 US$ based on PPPs, excluding tax

	Call pair methodology	Zone distribution methodology
Business telephone charge	..	..

Source: OECD (1995), *Communications Outlook.*

Table 8. Basket of mobile telecommunication tariffs in January 1994
1993 US$ based on PPPs, excluding tax

	Fixed charge	Usage charge	Total
Mobile telecom. tariffs	..	..	..

Source: OECD (1995), *Communications Outlook.*

Table 9. Basket of leased line charges in January 1994
1993 US$ based on PPPs, excluding tax

	9.6 kbit/s	64 kbit/s	1.5/2.0 Mbit/s
Leased line charge	..	..	..

Source: OECD (1995), *Communications Outlook.*

Table 10. Basket of packet switched data communication charges in January 1994
1993 US$ based on PPPs, excluding tax

	Fixed charge	Usage charge	Total
Packet switched data communication charge	..	..	..

Source: OECD (1995), *Communications Outlook.*

Table 11. Status of facilities competition in 1994

Equipment	PSTN competition			Data comms. and leased lines		Mobile communication		
CPE	Local	Trunk	Intl.	X25	LLs	Anal.	Digl.	Paging
..	..	..	..	..	..	..	..	..

Note: FC: Full Competition; PC: Partial Competition; D: Duopoly; M: Monopoly; RD: Regional Duopoly;
B: Competition allowed at border of concessions.
199X: Competition expected to be introduced this year.
Source: OECD (1995), *Communications Outlook.*

NETHERLANDS

Table 1. Main telephone lines per inhabitant in operation

Thousands

	1990	1991	1992	1993	1994
Total number of mainlines	6 940.00	7 175.00	7 395.00	7 630.00	7 830.00
Mainlines per 100 inhabitants	46.42	47.61	48.72	49.94	50.87

Source: Communications Indicators for Major Economies, 1995, OECD/ITU/Eurostat.

Table 2. Percentage of digitalisation in mainlines

Percentage

	1990	1991	1992	1993	1994
Digitalisation	69.0	79.0	83.0	93.0	100.0

Source: Communications Indicators for Major Economies, 1995, OECD/ITU/Eurostat.

Table 3. Cellular mobile telephone subscribers

Thousands

	1990	1991	1992	1993	1994
Total number of subscribers	79.00	115.00	166.00	216.00	321.00
Subscribers per 100 inhabitants	0.53	0.76	1.09	1.41	2.09

Source: Communications Indicators for Major Economies, 1995, OECD/ITU/Eurostat.

Table 4. Percentage of cellular mobile telephone subscribers in total telecom services

Percentage

		1990	1991	1992	1993	1994
Main lines	Analog	30.7	20.7	16.6	6.8	0.0
	Digital	68.2	77.8	81.2	90.4	96.1
Cellular		1.1	1.6	2.2	2.8	3.9
Total		100.0	100.0	100.0	100.0	100.0

Source: Communications Indicators for Major Economies, 1995, OECD/ITU/Eurostat.

Table 5. Estimated number of facsimile machines

Thousands

	1990	1991	1992	1993	1994
Number of fax machines	180.0	325.0	372.8	400.0	..
Number of fax machines per 100 inhabitants	1.20	2.16	2.46	2.62	..

Source: Communications Indicators for Major Economies, 1995, OECD/ITU/Eurostat.

Table 6. Basket of business telephone charges in January 1994 (local)

Values express the average annual spending by a business user, in 1993 US$ based on PPPs, excluding tax

	Fixed charge	Usage charge	Total
Annual spending charge	156.22	337.77	493.99

Source: OECD (1995), *Communications Outlook.*

Table 7. Basket of business telephone charges in January 1994 (international)

1993 US$ based on PPPs, excluding tax

	Call pair methodology	Zone distribution methodology
Business telephone charge	98.44	82.78

Source: OECD (1995), *Communications Outlook.*

Table 8. Basket of mobile telecommunication tariffs in January 1994

1993 US$ based on PPPs, excluding tax

	Fixed charge	Usage charge	Total
Mobile telecom. tariffs	402.46	831.57	1 234.03

Source: OECD (1995), *Communications Outlook.*

Table 9. Basket of leased line charges in January 1994

1993 US$ based on PPPs, excluding tax

	9.6 kbit/s	64 kbit/s	1.5/2.0 Mbit/s
Leased line charge	34 065	64 865	340 051

Source: OECD (1995), *Communications Outlook.*

Table 10. Basket of packet switched data communication charges in January 1994

1993 US$ based on PPPs, excluding tax

	Fixed charge	Usage charge	Total
Packet switched data communication charge	3 394.78	6 997.37	10 392.15

Source: OECD (1995), *Communications Outlook.*

Table 11. Status of facilities competition in 1994

Equipment	PSTN competition			Data comms. and leased lines		Mobile communication		
CPE	Local	Trunk	Intl.	X25	LLs	Anal.	Digl.	Paging
FC	M	M	M	1993	M	M	D(1994)	1993

Note: FC: Full Competition; PC: Partial Competition; D: Duopoly; M: Monopoly; RD: Regional Duopoly;
B: Competition allowed at border of concessions.
199X: Competition expected to be introduced this year.

Source: OECD (1995), *Communications Outlook.*

NEW ZEALAND

Table 1. Main telephone lines per inhabitant in operation

Thousands

	1990	1991	1992	1993	1994
Total number of mainlines	1 469.00	1 493.00	1 534.00	1 593.00	1 658.00
Mainlines per 100 inhabitants	43.68	43.83	44.93	46.01	46.96

Source: Communications Indicators for Major Economies, 1995, OECD/ITU/Eurostat.

Table 2. Percentage of digitalisation in mainlines

Percentage

	1990	1991	1992	1993	1994
Digitalisation	..	92.4	95.0	97.0	98.0

Source: Communications Indicators for Major Economies, 1995, OECD/ITU/Eurostat.

Table 3. Cellular mobile telephone subscribers

Thousands

	1990	1991	1992	1993	1994
Total number of subscribers	54.10	72.30	100.20	143.80	229.20
Subscribers per 100 inhabitants	1.61	2.12	2.93	4.15	6.49

Source: Communications Indicators for Major Economies, 1995, OECD/ITU/Eurostat.

Table 4. Percentage of cellular mobile telephone subscribers in total telecom services

Percentage

		1990	1991	1992	1993	1994
Main lines	Analog	..	7.2	4.7	2.8	1.8
	Digital	..	88.1	89.2	89.0	86.1
Cellular		3.6	4.6	6.1	8.3	12.1
Total		100.0	100.0	100.0	100.0	100.0

Source: Communications Indicators for Major Economies, 1995, OECD/ITU/Eurostat.

Table 5. Estimated number of facsimile machines

Thousands

	1990	1991	1992	1993	1994
Number of fax machines	28.0	35.0	40.0	45.0	50.0
Number of fax machines per 100 inhabitants	0.83	1.03	1.17	1.30	1.42

Source: Communications Indicators for Major Economies, 1995, OECD/ITU/Eurostat.

Table 6. Basket of business telephone charges in January 1994 (local)

Values express the average annual spending by a business user, in 1993 US$ based on PPPs, excluding tax

	Fixed charge	Usage charge	Total
Annual spending charge	472.26	463.80	936.06

Source: OECD (1995), *Communications Outlook.*

Table 7. Basket of business telephone charges in January 1994 (international)

1993 US$ based on PPPs, excluding tax

	Call pair methodology	Zone distribution methodology
Business telephone charge	94.46	100.02

Source: OECD (1995), *Communications Outlook.*

Table 8. Basket of mobile telecommunication tariffs in January 1994

1993 US$ based on PPPs, excluding tax

	Fixed charge	Usage charge	Total
Mobile telecom. tariffs	520.35	876.37	1 396.72

Source: OECD (1995), *Communications Outlook.*

Table 9. Basket of leased line charges in January 1994

1993 US$ based on PPPs, excluding tax

	9.6 kbit/s	64 kbit/s	1.5/2.0 Mbit/s
Leased line charge	29 205	103 994	400 487

Source: OECD (1995), *Communications Outlook.*

Table 10. Basket of packet switched data communication charges in January 1994

1993 US$ based on PPPs, excluding tax

	Fixed charge	Usage charge	Total
Packet switched data communication charge	2 110.39	2 666.44	4 776.83

Source: OECD (1995), *Communications Outlook.*

Table 11. Status of facilities competition in 1994

Equipment	PSTN competition			Data comms. and leased lines		Mobile communication		
CPE	Local	Trunk	Intl.	X25	LLs	Anal.	Digl.	Paging
FC	FC	FC	FC	FC	FC	FC	FC	FC

Note: FC: Full Competition; PC: Partial Competition; D: Duopoly; M: Monopoly; RD: Regional Duopoly;
B: Competition allowed at border of concessions.
199X: Competition expected to be introduced this year.

Source: OECD (1995), *Communications Outlook.*

NORWAY

Table 1. Main telephone lines per inhabitant in operation

Thousands

	1990	1991	1992	1993	1994
Total number of mainlines	2 132.29	2 198.24	2 268.49	2 334.84	2 392.04
Mainlines per 100 inhabitants	50.28	51.58	52.93	54.17	55.40

Source: Communications Indicators for Major Economies, 1995, OECD/ITU/Eurostat.

Table 2. Percentage of digitalisation in mainlines

Percentage

	1990	1991	1992	1993	1994
Digitalisation	38.0	45.0	50.0	59.0	71.0

Source: Communications Indicators for Major Economies, 1995, OECD/ITU/Eurostat.

Table 3. Cellular mobile telephone subscribers

Thousands

	1990	1991	1992	1993	1994
Total number of subscribers	196.83	227.73	280.00	379.50	588.80
Subscribers per 100 inhabitants	4.64	5.34	6.53	8.81	13.64

Source: Communications Indicators for Major Economies, 1995, OECD/ITU/Eurostat.

Table 4. Percentage of cellular mobile telephone subscribers in total telecom services

Percentage

		1990	1991	1992	1993	1994
Main lines	Analog	56.8	49.8	44.5	35.3	23.3
	Digital	34.8	40.8	44.5	50.8	57.0
Cellular		8.5	9.4	11.0	14.0	19.8
Total		100.0	100.0	100.0	100.0	100.0

Source: Communications Indicators for Major Economies, 1995, OECD/ITU/Eurostat.

Table 5. Estimated number of facsimile machines

Thousands

	1990	1991	1992	1993	1994
Number of fax machines	85.0	107.0	120.0	130.0	..
Number of fax machines per 100 inhabitants	2.00	2.51	2.80	3.02	..

Source: Communications Indicators for Major Economies, 1995, OECD/ITU/Eurostat.

Table 6. Basket of business telephone charges in January 1994 (local)

Values express the average annual spending by a business user, in 1993 US$ based on PPPs, excluding tax

	Fixed charge	Usage charge	Total
Annual spending charge	138.45	307.63	446.08

Source: OECD (1995), *Communications Outlook.*

Table 7. Basket of business telephone charges in January 1994 (international)

1993 US$ based on PPPs, excluding tax

	Call pair methodology	Zone distribution methodology
Business telephone charge	71.97	47.32

Source: OECD (1995), *Communications Outlook.*

Table 8. Basket of mobile telecommunication tariffs in January 1994

1993 US$ based on PPPs, excluding tax

	Fixed charge	Usage charge	Total
Mobile telecom. tariffs	166.01	685.73	851.75

Source: OECD (1995), *Communications Outlook.*

Table 9. Basket of leased line charges in January 1994

1993 US$ based on PPPs, excluding tax

	9.6 kbit/s	64 kbit/s	1.5/2.0 Mbit/s
Leased line charge	43 277	84 916	505 014

Source: OECD (1995), *Communications Outlook.*

Table 10. Basket of packet switched data communication charges in January 1994

1993 US$ based on PPPs, excluding tax

	Fixed charge	Usage charge	Total
Packet switched data communication charge	1 975.83	4 988.49	6 964.32

Source: OECD (1995), *Communications Outlook.*

Table 11. Status of facilities competition in 1994

Equipment	PSTN competition			Data comms. and leased lines		Mobile communication		
CPE	Local	Trunk	Intl.	X25	LLs	Anal.	Digl.	Paging
FC	M	M	M	1993	M	M	D	1993

Note: FC: Full Competition; PC: Partial Competition; D: Duopoly; M: Monopoly; RD: Regional Duopoly;
B: Competition allowed at border of concessions.
199X: Competition expected to be introduced this year.

Source: OECD (1995), *Communications Outlook.*

PORTUGAL

Table 1. Main telephone lines per inhabitant in operation

Thousands

	1990	1991	1992	1993	1994
Total number of mainlines	2 379.27	2 694.14	3 014.17	3 260.32	3 444.27
Mainlines per 100 inhabitants	24.26	27.45	30.61	31.13	35.03

Source: Communications Indicators for Major Economies, 1995, OECD/ITU/Eurostat.

Table 2. Percentage of digitalisation in mainlines

Percentage

	1990	1991	1992	1993	1994
Digitalisation	30.0	45.0	54.0	59.0	62.0

Source: Communications Indicators for Major Economies, 1995, OECD/ITU/Eurostat.

Table 3. Cellular mobile telephone subscribers

Thousands

	1990	1991	1992	1993	1994
Total number of subscribers	6.50	12.60	37.26	101.23	173.51
Subscribers per 100 inhabitants	0.07	0.13	0.38	0.97	1.76

Source: Communications Indicators for Major Economies, 1995, OECD/ITU/Eurostat.

Table 4. Percentage of cellular mobile telephone subscribers in total telecom services

Percentage

		1990	1991	1992	1993	1994
Main lines	Analog	69.8	54.7	45.4	39.8	36.2
	Digital	29.9	44.8	53.3	57.2	59.0
Cellular		0.3	0.5	1.2	3.0	4.8
Total		100.0	100.0	100.0	100.0	100.0

Source: Communications Indicators for Major Economies, 1995, OECD/ITU/Eurostat.

Table 5. Estimated number of facsimile machines

Thousands

	1990	1991	1992	1993	1994
Number of fax machines	10.5	17.7	26.76	35.34	..
Number of fax machines per 100 inhabitants	0.11	0.18	0.27	0.34	..

Source: Communications Indicators for Major Economies, 1995, OECD/ITU/Eurostat.

Table 6. Basket of business telephone charges in January 1994 (local)

Values express the average annual spending by a business user, in 1993 US$ based on PPPs, excluding tax

	Fixed charge	Usage charge	Total
Annual spending charge	161.43	1 309.32	1 470.75

Source: OECD (1995), *Communications Outlook.*

Table 7. Basket of business telephone charges in January 1994 (international)

1993 US$ based on PPPs, excluding tax

	Call pair methodology	Zone distribution methodology
Business telephone charge	131.87	163.01

Source: OECD (1995), *Communications Outlook.*

Table 8. Basket of mobile telecommunication tariffs in January 1994

1993 US$ based on PPPs, excluding tax

	Fixed charge	Usage charge	Total
Mobile telecom. tariffs	586.56	1 083.02	1 669.58

Source: OECD (1995), *Communications Outlook.*

Table 9. Basket of leased line charges in January 1994

1993 US$ based on PPPs, excluding tax

	9.6 kbit/s	64 kbit/s	1.5/2.0 Mbit/s
Leased line charge	49 815	53 033	330 742

Source: OECD (1995), *Communications Outlook.*

Table 10. Basket of packet switched data communication charges in January 1994

1993 US$ based on PPPs, excluding tax

	Fixed charge	Usage charge	Total
Packet switched data communication charge	4 277.21	6 682.32	10 959.53

Source: OECD (1995), *Communications Outlook.*

Table 11. Status of facilities competition in 1994

Equipment	PSTN competition			Data comms. and leased lines		Mobile communication		
CPE	Local	Trunk	Intl.	X25	LLs	Anal.	Digl.	Paging
FC	M[1]	M	M[1]	FC	M[1]	M	D	FC

Note: FC: Full Competition; PC: Partial Competition; D: Duopoly; M: Monopoly; RD: Regional Duopoly;
B: Competition allowed at border of concessions.
199X: Competition expected to be introduced this year.

1. See Background Notes.

Source: OECD (1995), *Communications Outlook.*

SPAIN

Table 1. Main telephone lines per inhabitant in operation

Thousands

	1990	1991	1992	1993	1994
Total number of mainlines	12 602.60	13 264.36	13 792.16	14 253.47	14 685.41
Mainlines per 100 inhabitants	32.35	33.99	35.29	36.43	37.13

Source: Communications Indicators for Major Economies, 1995, OECD/ITU/Eurostat.

Table 2. Percentage of digitalisation in mainlines

Percentage

	1990	1991	1992	1993	1994
Digitalisation	28.0	33.6	36.4	41.4	47.8

Source: Communications Indicators for Major Economies, 1995, OECD/ITU/Eurostat.

Table 3. Cellular mobile telephone subscribers

Thousands

	1990	1991	1992	1993	1994
Total number of subscribers	54.7	108.45	180.30	257.25	411.93
Subscribers per 100 inhabitants	0.14	0.28	0.46	0.66	1.04

Source: Communications Indicators for Major Economies, 1995, OECD/ITU/Eurostat.

Table 4. Percentage of cellular mobile telephone subscribers in total telecom services

Percentage

		1990	1991	1992	1993	1994
Main lines	Analog	71.7	65.9	62.8	57.6	50.8
	Digital	27.9	33.3	35.9	40.7	46.5
Cellular		0.4	0.8	1.3	1.8	2.7
Total		100.0	100.0	100.0	100.0	100.0

Source: Communications Indicators for Major Economies, 1995, OECD/ITU/Eurostat.

Table 5. Estimated number of facsimile machines

Thousands

	1990	1991	1992	1993	1994
Number of fax machines	144.3	176.1	195.0	215.0	..
Number of fax machines per 100 inhabitants	0.37	0.45	0.50	0.55	..

Source: Communications Indicators for Major Economies, 1995, OECD/ITU/Eurostat.

Table 6. Basket of business telephone charges in January 1994 (local)

Values express the average annual spending by a business user, in 1993 US$ based on PPPs, excluding tax

	Fixed charge	Usage charge	Total
Annual spending charge	161.67	1 060.82	1 222.49

Source: OECD (1995), *Communications Outlook.*

Table 7. Basket of business telephone charges in January 1994 (international)

1993 US$ based on PPPs, excluding tax

	Call pair methodology	Zone distribution methodology
Business telephone charge	119.31	146.10

Source: OECD (1995), *Communications Outlook.*

Table 8. Basket of mobile telecommunication tariffs in January 1994

1993 US$ based on PPPs, excluding tax

	Fixed charge	Usage charge	Total
Mobile telecom. tariffs	519.44	925.89	1 445.33

Source: OECD (1995), *Communications Outlook.*

Table 9. Basket of leased line charges in January 1994

1993 US$ based on PPPs, excluding tax

	9.6 kbit/s	64 kbit/s	1.5/2.0 Mbit/s
Leased line charge	96 083	194 100	1 274 546

Source: OECD (1995), *Communications Outlook.*

Table 10. Basket of packet switched data communication charges in January 1994

1993 US$ based on PPPs, excluding tax

	Fixed charge	Usage charge	Total
Packet switched data communication charge	5 200.90	13 041.86	18 242.76

Source: OECD (1995), *Communications Outlook.*

Table 11. Status of facilities competition in 1994

Equipment	PSTN competition			Data comms. and leased lines		Mobile communication		
CPE	Local	Trunk	Intl.	X25	LLs	Anal.	Digl.	Paging
FC	M	M	M	FC	M	M	M	FC

Note: FC: Full Competition; PC: Partial Competition; D: Duopoly; M: Monopoly; RD: Regional Duopoly;
B: Competition allowed at border of concessions.
199X: Competition expected to be introduced this year.

Source: OECD (1995), *Communications Outlook.*

SWEDEN

Table 1. Main telephone lines per inhabitant in operation

Thousands

	1990	1991	1992	1993	1994
Total number of mainlines	5 848.70	5 957.00	5 929.00	5 910.00	5 967.00
Mainlines per 100 inhabitants	68.33	69.13	68.32	67.84	68.31

Source: Communications Indicators for Major Economies, 1995, OECD/ITU/Eurostat.

Table 2. Percentage of digitalisation in mainlines

Percentage

	1990	1991	1992	1993	1994
Digitalisation	38.0	47.0	53.9	67.0	..

Source: Communications Indicators for Major Economies, 1995, OECD/ITU/Eurostat.

Table 3. Cellular mobile telephone subscribers

Thousands

	1990	1991	1992	1993	1994
Total number of subscribers	461.20	568.20	656.00	811.60	1 380.00
Subscribers per 100 inhabitants	5.39	6.59	7.56	9.32	15.80

Source: Communications Indicators for Major Economies, 1995, OECD/ITU/Eurostat.

Table 4. Percentage of cellular mobile telephone subscribers in total telecom services

Percentage

		1990	1991	1992	1993	1994
Main lines	Analog	57.5	48.4	41.5	29.0	..
	Digital	35.2	42.9	48.5	58.9	..
Cellular		7.3	8.7	10.0	12.1	18.8
Total		100.0	100.0	100.0	100.0	100.0

Source: Communications Indicators for Major Economies, 1995, OECD/ITU/Eurostat.

Table 5. Estimated number of facsimile machines

Thousands

	1990	1991	1992	1993	1994
Number of fax machines	170.0	230.0	300.0	325.0	..
Number of fax machines per 100 inhabitants	1.99	2.67	3.46	3.73	..

Source: Communications Indicators for Major Economies, 1995, OECD/ITU/Eurostat.

Table 6. Basket of business telephone charges in January 1994 (local)

Values express the average annual spending by a business user, in 1993 US$ based on PPPs, excluding tax

	Fixed charge	Usage charge	Total
Annual spending charge	187.39	218.61	406.00

Source: OECD (1995), *Communications Outlook.*

Table 7. Basket of business telephone charges in January 1994 (international)
1993 US$ based on PPPs, excluding tax

	Call pair methodology	Zone distribution methodology
Business telephone charge	86.95	69.88

Source: OECD (1995), *Communications Outlook.*

Table 8. Basket of mobile telecommunication tariffs in January 1994
1993 US$ based on PPPs, excluding tax

	Fixed charge	Usage charge	Total
Mobile telecom. tariffs	150.19	707.82	858.01

Source: OECD (1995), *Communications Outlook.*

Table 9. Basket of leased line charges in January 1994
1993 US$ based on PPPs, excluding tax

	9.6 kbit/s	64 kbit/s	1.5/2.0 Mbit/s
Leased line charge	36 026	48 686	..

Source: OECD (1995), *Communications Outlook.*

Table 10. Basket of packet switched data communication charges in January 1994
1993 US$ based on PPPs, excluding tax

	Fixed charge	Usage charge	Total
Packet switched data communication charge	2 485.42	3 597.33	6 082.75

Source: OECD (1995), *Communications Outlook.*

Table 11. Status of facilities competition in 1994

Equipment	PSTN competition			Data comms. and leased lines		Mobile communication		
CPE	Local	Trunk	Intl.	X25	LLs	Anal.	Digl.	Paging
FC	FC	FC	FC	FC	FC	FC	FC	FC

Note: FC: Full Competition; PC: Partial Competition; D: Duopoly; M: Monopoly; RD: Regional Duopoly;
B: Competition allowed at border of concessions.
199X: Competition expected to be introduced this year.
Source: OECD (1995), *Communications Outlook.*

SWITZERLAND

Table 1. Main telephone lines per inhabitant in operation

Thousands

	1990	1991	1992	1993	1994
Total number of mainlines	3 942.70	4 080.65	4 184.84	4 265.82	4 257.60
Mainlines per 100 inhabitants	58.74	60.08	60.61	61.14	59.74

Source: Communications Indicators for Major Economies, 1995, OECD/ITU/Eurostat.

Table 2. Percentage of digitalisation in mainlines

Percentage

	1990	1991	1992	1993	1994
Digitalisation	29.0	33.1	42.0	48.0	57.0

Source: Communications Indicators for Major Economies, 1995, OECD/ITU/Eurostat.

Table 3. Cellular mobile telephone subscribers

Thousands

	1990	1991	1992	1993	1994
Total number of subscribers	125.05	174.56	215.06	257.70	332.17
Subscribers per 100 inhabitants	1.86	2.57	3.11	3.69	4.66

Source: Communications Indicators for Major Economies, 1995, OECD/ITU/Eurostat.

Table 4. Percentage of cellular mobile telephone subscribers in total telecom services

Percentage

		1990	1991	1992	1993	1994
Main lines	Analog	68.8	64.2	55.2	49.0	39.9
	Digital	28.1	31.7	39.9	45.3	52.9
Cellular		3.1	4.1	4.9	5.7	7.2
Total		100.0	100.0	100.0	100.0	100.0

Source: Communications Indicators for Major Economies, 1995, OECD/ITU/Eurostat.

Table 5. Estimated number of facsimile machines

Thousands

	1990	1991	1992	1993	1994
Number of fax machines	83.0	118.0	135.0	169.0	175.0
Number of fax machines per 100 inhabitants	1.24	1.74	1.96	2.42	2.46

Source: Communications Indicators for Major Economies, 1995, OECD/ITU/Eurostat.

Table 6. Basket of business telephone charges in January 1994 (local)

Values express the average annual spending by a business user, in 1993 US$ based on PPPs, excluding tax

	Fixed charge	Usage charge	Total
Annual spending charge	160.00	711.59	871.59

Source: OECD (1995), *Communications Outlook.*

Table 7. Basket of business telephone charges in January 1994 (international)

1993 US$ based on PPPs, excluding tax

	Call pair methodology	Zone distribution methodology
Business telephone charge	84.17	62.13

Source: OECD (1995), *Communications Outlook.*

Table 8. Basket of mobile telecommunication tariffs in January 1994

1993 US$ based on PPPs, excluding tax

	Fixed charge	Usage charge	Total
Mobile telecom. tariffs	360.61	496.94	857.55

Source: OECD (1995), *Communications Outlook.*

Table 9. Basket of leased line charges in January 1994

1993 US$ based on PPPs, excluding tax

	9.6 kbit/s	64 kbit/s	1.5/2.0 Mbit/s
Leased line charge	29 864	37 273	361 593

Source: OECD (1995), *Communications Outlook.*

Table 10. Basket of packet switched data communication charges in January 1994

1993 US$ based on PPPs, excluding tax

	Fixed charge	Usage charge	Total
Packet switched data communication charge	1 321.97	4 571.49	5 893.46

Source: OECD (1995), *Communications Outlook.*

Table 11. Status of facilities competition in 1994

Equipment	PSTN competition			Data comms. and leased lines		Mobile communication		
CPE	Local	Trunk	Intl.	X25	LLs	Anal.	Digl.	Paging
FC	M	M	M	M	M	M	M	FC

Note: FC: Full Competition; PC: Partial Competition; D: Duopoly; M: Monopoly; RD: Regional Duopoly;
B: Competition allowed at border of concessions.
199X: Competition expected to be introduced this year.

Source: OECD (1995), *Communications Outlook.*

TURKEY

Table 1. Main telephone lines per inhabitant in operation

Thousands

	1990	1991	1992	1993	1994
Total number of mainlines	6 861.46	8 151.74	9 410.49	10 935.52	12 212.26
Mainlines per 100 inhabitants	12.15	14.13	16.01	18.39	20.10

Source: Communications Indicators for Major Economies, 1995, OECD/ITU/Eurostat.

Table 2. Percentage of digitalisation in mainlines

Percentage

	1990	1991	1992	1993	1994
Digitalisation	48.0	51.0	56.3	57.5	55.6

Source: Communications Indicators for Major Economies, 1995, OECD/ITU/Eurostat.

Table 3. Cellular mobile telephone subscribers

Thousands

	1990	1991	1992	1993	1994
Total number of subscribers	31.81	47.83	61.40	84.19	93.50
Subscribers per 100 inhabitants	0.06	0.08	0.10	0.14	0.15

Source: Communications Indicators for Major Economies, 1995, OECD/ITU/Eurostat.

Table 4. Percentage of cellular mobile telephone subscribers in total telecom services

Percentage

		1990	1991	1992	1993	1994
Main lines	Analog	51.8	48.7	43.5	42.2	44.1
	Digital	47.8	50.7	55.9	57.1	55.1
Cellular		0.5	0.6	0.6	0.8	0.8
Total		100.0	100.0	100.0	100.0	100.0

Source: Communications Indicators for Major Economies, 1995, OECD/ITU/Eurostat.

Table 5. Estimated number of facsimile machines

Thousands

	1990	1991	1992	1993	1994
Number of fax machines	32.9	48.3	62.9	77.2	..
Number of fax machines per 100 inhabitants	0.06	0.08	0.11	0.13	..

Source: Communications Indicators for Major Economies, 1995, OECD/ITU/Eurostat.

Table 6. Basket of business telephone charges in January 1994 (local)

Values express the average annual spending by a business user, in 1993 US$ based on PPPs, excluding tax

	Fixed charge	Usage charge	Total
Annual spending charge	60.01	1 791.44	1 851.45

Source: OECD (1995), *Communications Outlook.*

Table 7. Basket of business telephone charges in January 1994 (international)

1993 US$ based on PPPs, excluding tax

	Call pair methodology	Zone distribution methodology
Business telephone charge	164.82	344.83

Source: OECD (1995), *Communications Outlook.*

Table 8. Basket of mobile telecommunication tariffs in January 1994

1993 US$ based on PPPs, excluding tax

	Fixed charge	Usage charge	Total
Mobile telecom. tariffs	294.44	1 827.06	2 121.50

Source: OECD (1995), *Communications Outlook.*

Table 9. Basket of leased line charges in January 1994

1993 US$ based on PPPs, excluding tax

	9.6 kbit/s	64 kbit/s	1.5/2.0 Mbit/s
Leased line charge	129 784	389 353	1 945 601

Source: OECD (1995), *Communications Outlook.*

Table 10. Basket of packet switched data communication charges in January 1994

1993 US$ based on PPPs, excluding tax

	Fixed charge	Usage charge	Total
Packet switched data communication charge	789.45	11 471.41	12 260.86

Source: OECD (1995), *Communications Outlook.*

Table 11. Status of facilities competition in 1994

Equipment	PSTN competition			Data comms. and leased lines		Mobile communication		
CPE	Local	Trunk	Intl.	X25	LLs	Anal.	Digl.	Paging
FC	M	M	M	M	M	M	M	M

Note: FC: Full Competition; PC: Partial Competition; D: Duopoly; M: Monopoly; RD: Regional Duopoly;
B: Competition allowed at border of concessions.
199X: Competition expected to be introduced this year.

Source: OECD (1995), OECD (1995), *Communications Outlook.*

BACKGROUND NOTES TO COUNTRY TABLES

General

The sources of the information presented in country tables are:

- OECD/ITU/Eurostat (1995), *Communications Indicators for Major Economies,* OECD/International Telecommunication Union/Eurostat (Statistical Office of the European Communities).

- OECD (1995), *Communications Outlook*, OECD/Directorate for Science, Technology and Industry, Information and Communications Policy Division.

The telecommunication tariff indicator (Tables 5, 6, 7, 8, and 9) uses PPPs. The OECD generally prefers to undertake tariff comparisons in terms of PPPs.

(1) Main telephone lines

The data show the number of telecommunication mainlines and number of mainlines per 100 people.

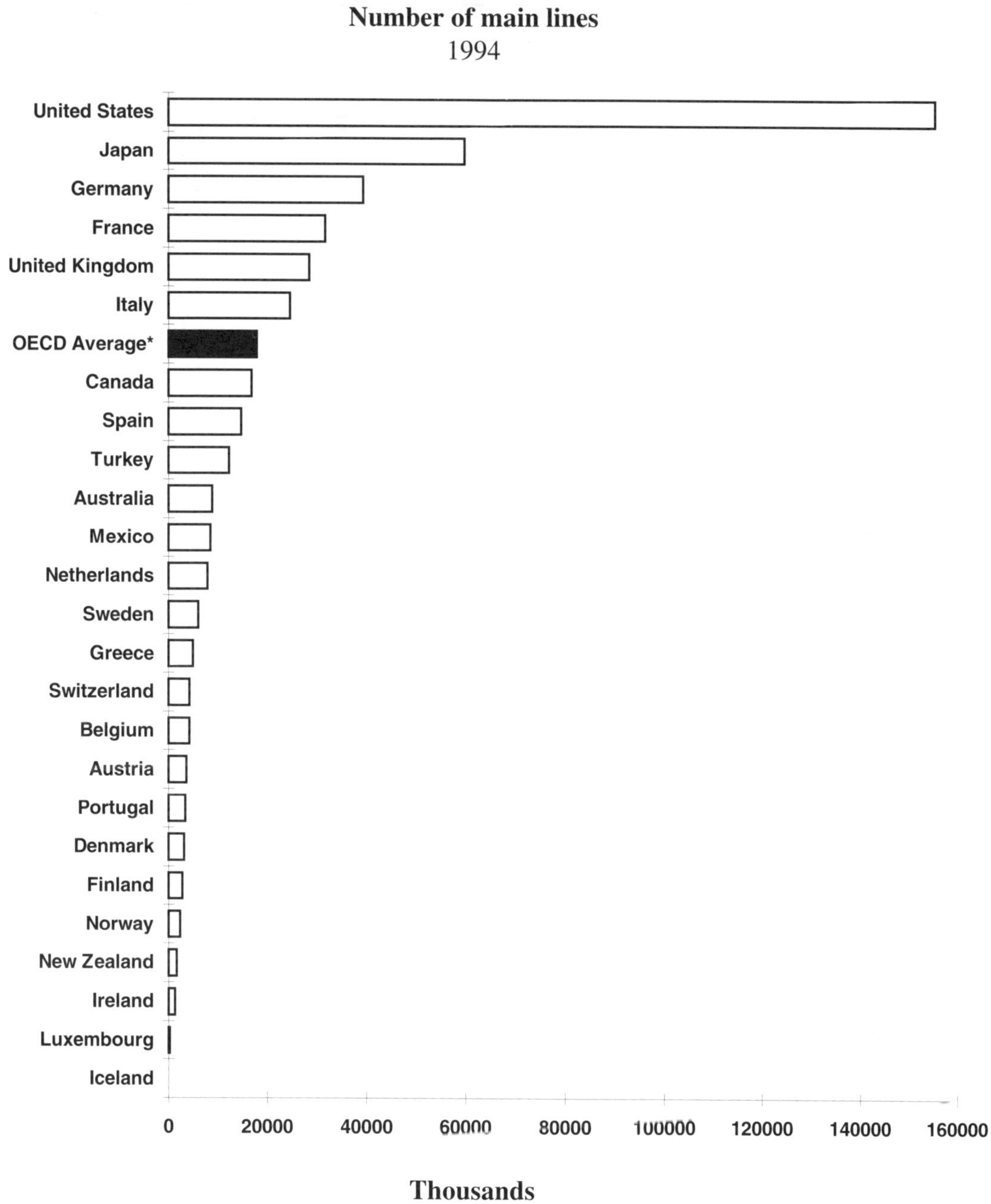

* Unweighted average of 25 countries: Australia, Austria, Belgium, Canada, Denmark, Finland, France, Germany, Greece, Iceland, Ireland, Italy, Japan, Luxembourg, Mexico, the Netherlands, New Zealand, Norway, Portugal, Spain, Sweden, Switzerland, Turkey, the United Kingdom and the United States.

Main telephone lines per 100 inhabitants
1994

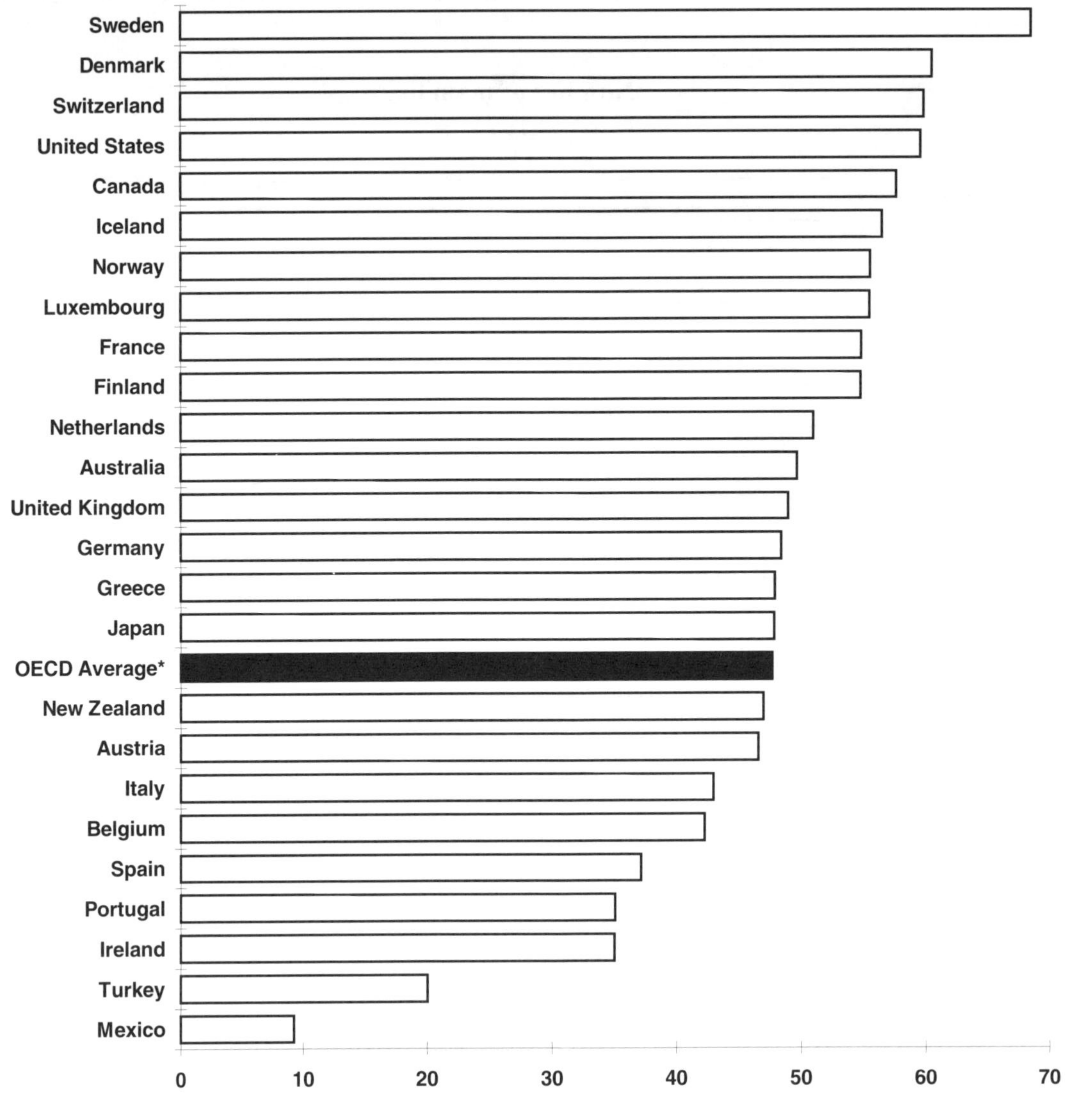

* Unweighted average of 25 countries: Australia, Austria, Belgium, Canada, Denmark, Finland, France, Germany, Greece, Iceland, Ireland, Italy, Japan, Luxembourg, Mexico, the Netherlands, New Zealand, Norway, Portugal, Spain, Sweden, Switzerland, Turkey, the United Kingdom and the United States.

(2) Percentage of digitalisation in mainlines

This table indicates the modernisation of the telecommunications networks. It should be made clear that this indicator does not measure exchanges which are digital, inter-exchange lines which are digital or digital network termination points.

1993

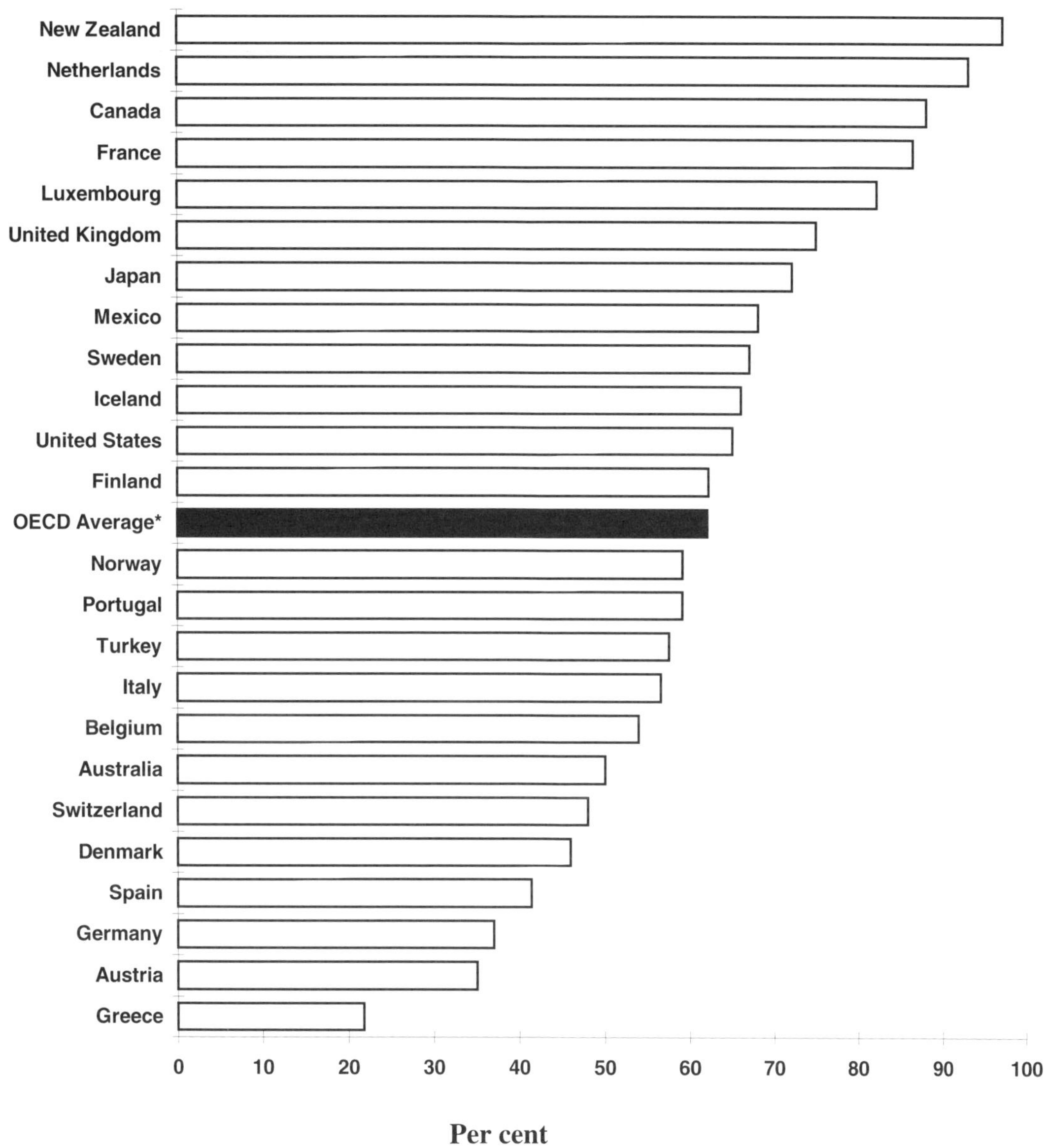

* Unweighted average of 24 countries: Australia, Austria, Belgium, Canada, Denmark, Finland, France, Germany, Greece, Iceland, Italy, Japan, Luxembourg, Mexico, the Netherlands, New Zealand, Norway, Portugal, Spain, Sweden, Switzerland, Turkey, United Kingdom and United States.

(3) Cellular mobile telephone subscribers

The data cover both analog and digital systems and Personal Communication Services (PCS). Data do not include subscribers to public mobile data services, private trunked mobile radio, telepoint, non-cellular mobile, fixed cellular, or radio paging services.

Number of subscribers

1993

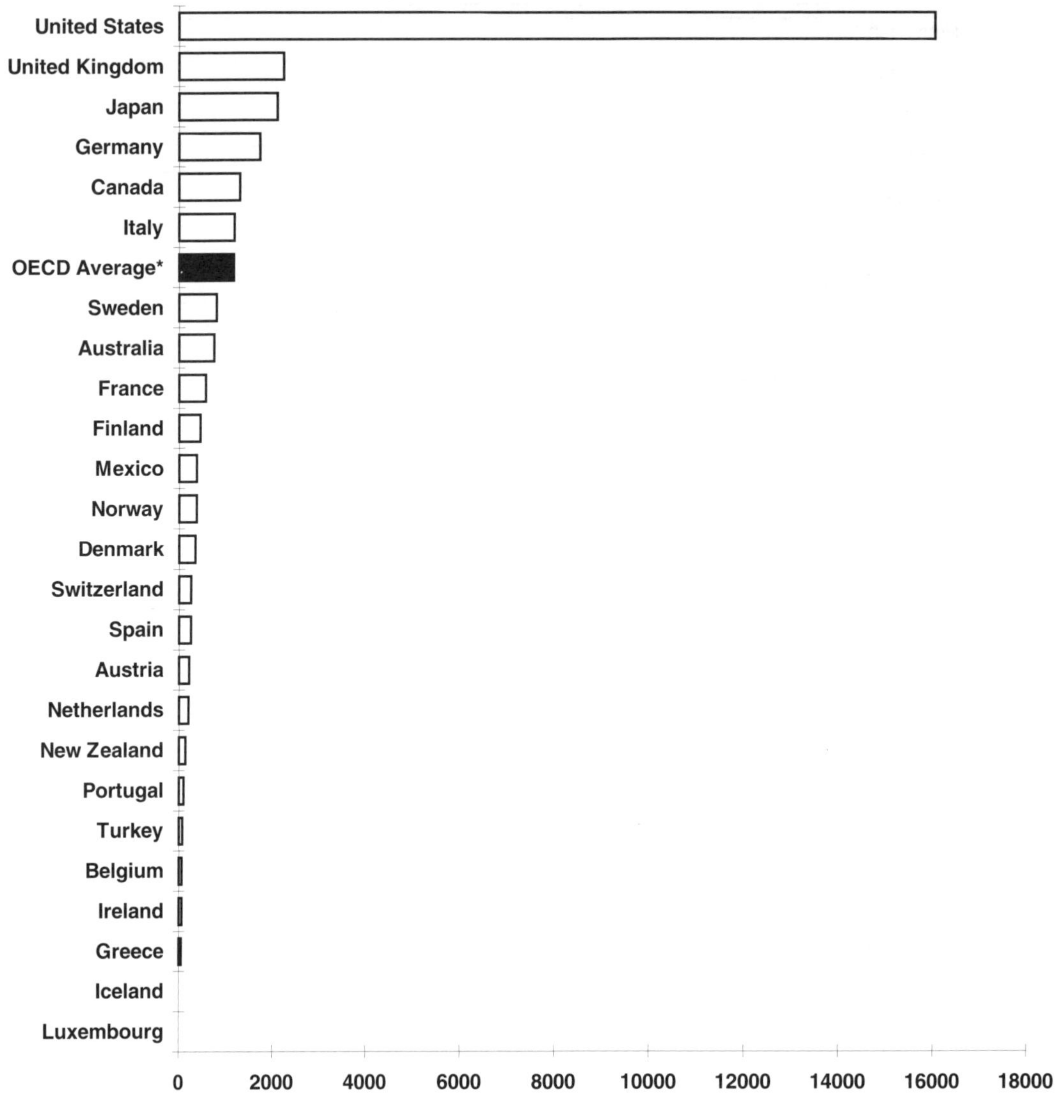

Thousands

* Unweighted average of 25 countries: Australia, Austria, Belgium, Canada, Denmark, Finland, France, Germany, Greece, Iceland, Ireland, Italy, Japan, Luxembourg, Mexico, the Netherlands, New Zealand, Norway, Portugal, Spain, Sweden, Switzerland, Turkey, the United Kingdom and the United States.

Per 100 inhabitants
1993

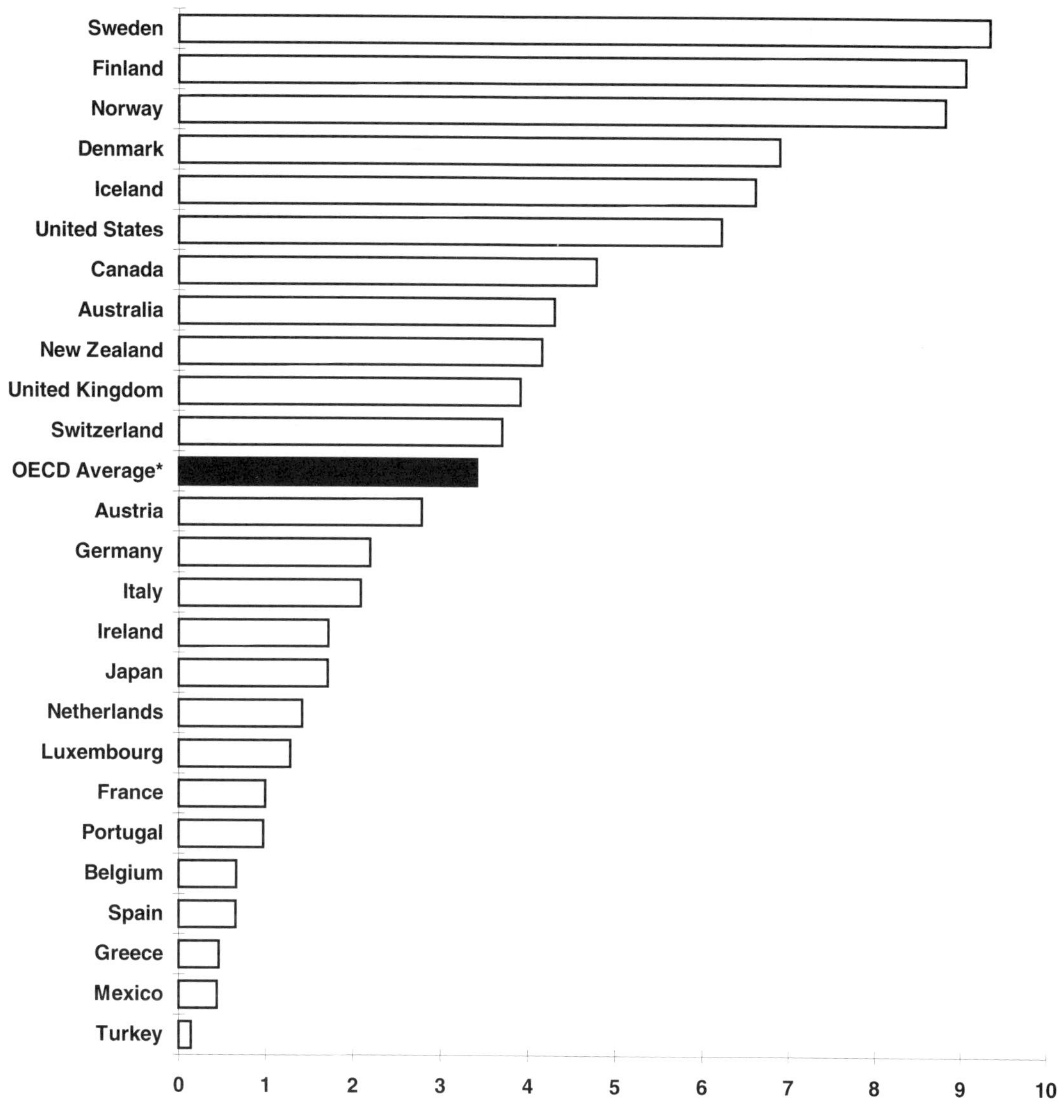

* Unweighted average of 25 countries: Australia, Austria, Belgium, Canada, Denmark, Finland, France, Germany, Greece, Iceland, Ireland, Italy, Japan, Luxembourg, Mexico, the Netherlands, New Zealand, Norway, Portugal, Spain, Sweden, Switzerland, Turkey, the United Kingdom and the United States.

(4) Percentage of cellular mobile telephone subscribers in total telecom services

This table is based on the total amount of "Total number of mainlines" (Table 1) and "Total number of cellular mobile telephone subscribers" (Table 3).

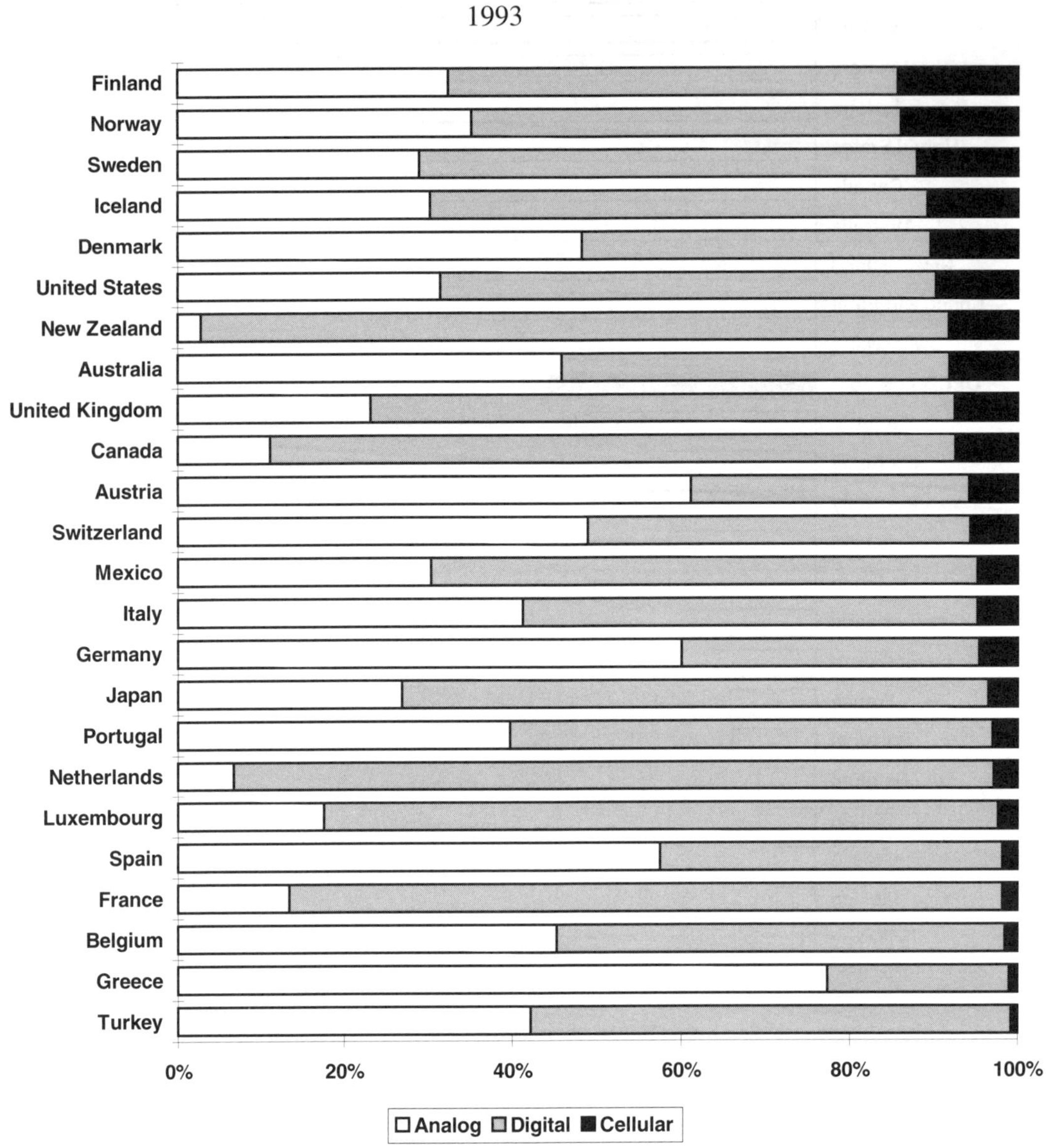

Per cent

(5) Estimated number of facsimile machines

Estimated number of facsimile machines. Estimates are obtained from Telefax directories.

Number of facsimile machines
1993

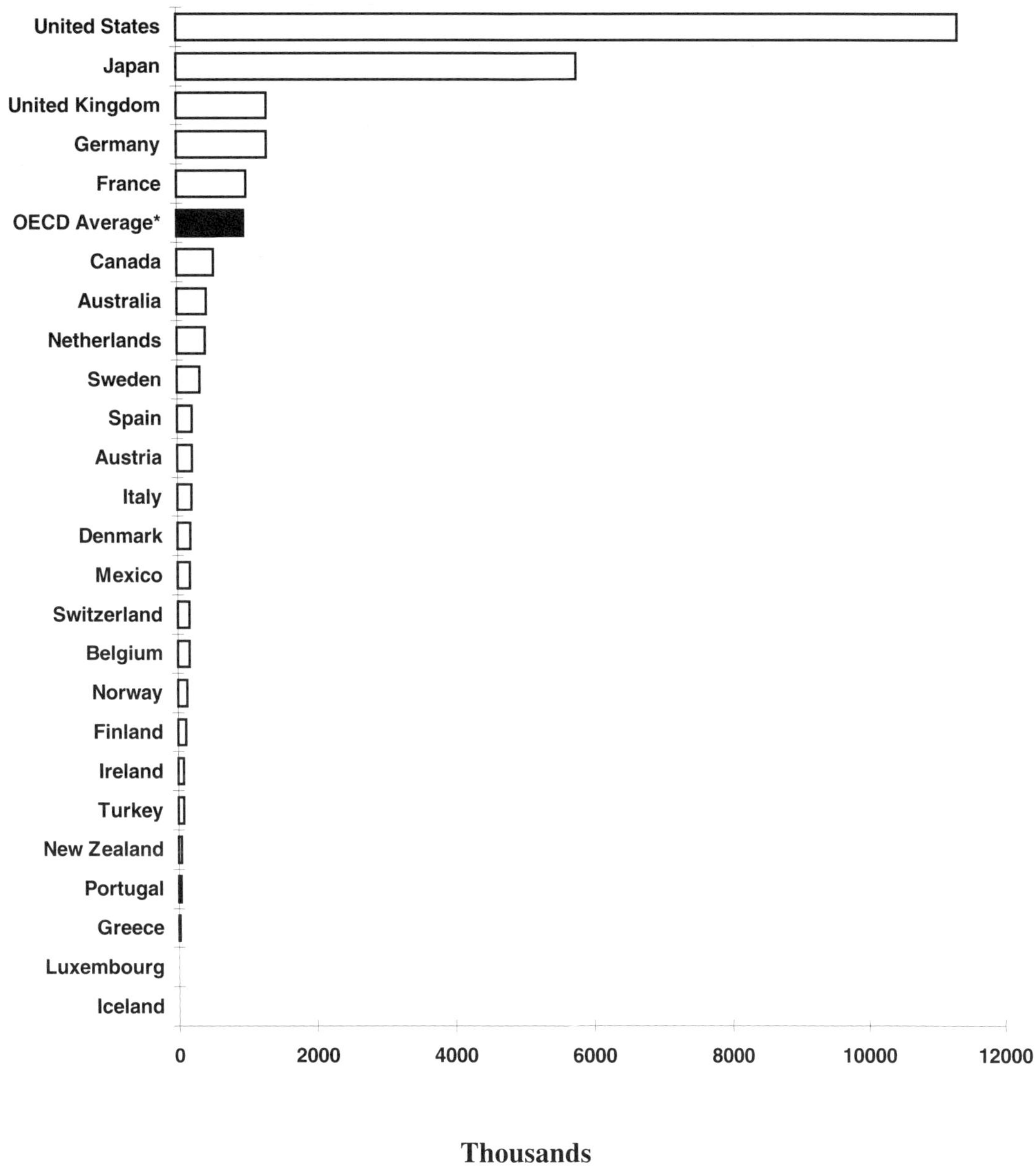

* Unweighted average of 25 countries: Australia, Austria, Belgium, Canada, Denmark, Finland, France, Germany, Greece, Iceland, Ireland, Italy, Japan, Luxembourg, Mexico, the Netherlands, New Zealand, Norway, Portugal, Spain, Sweden, Switzerland, Turkey, the United Kingdom and the United States.

Per 100 inhabitants
1993

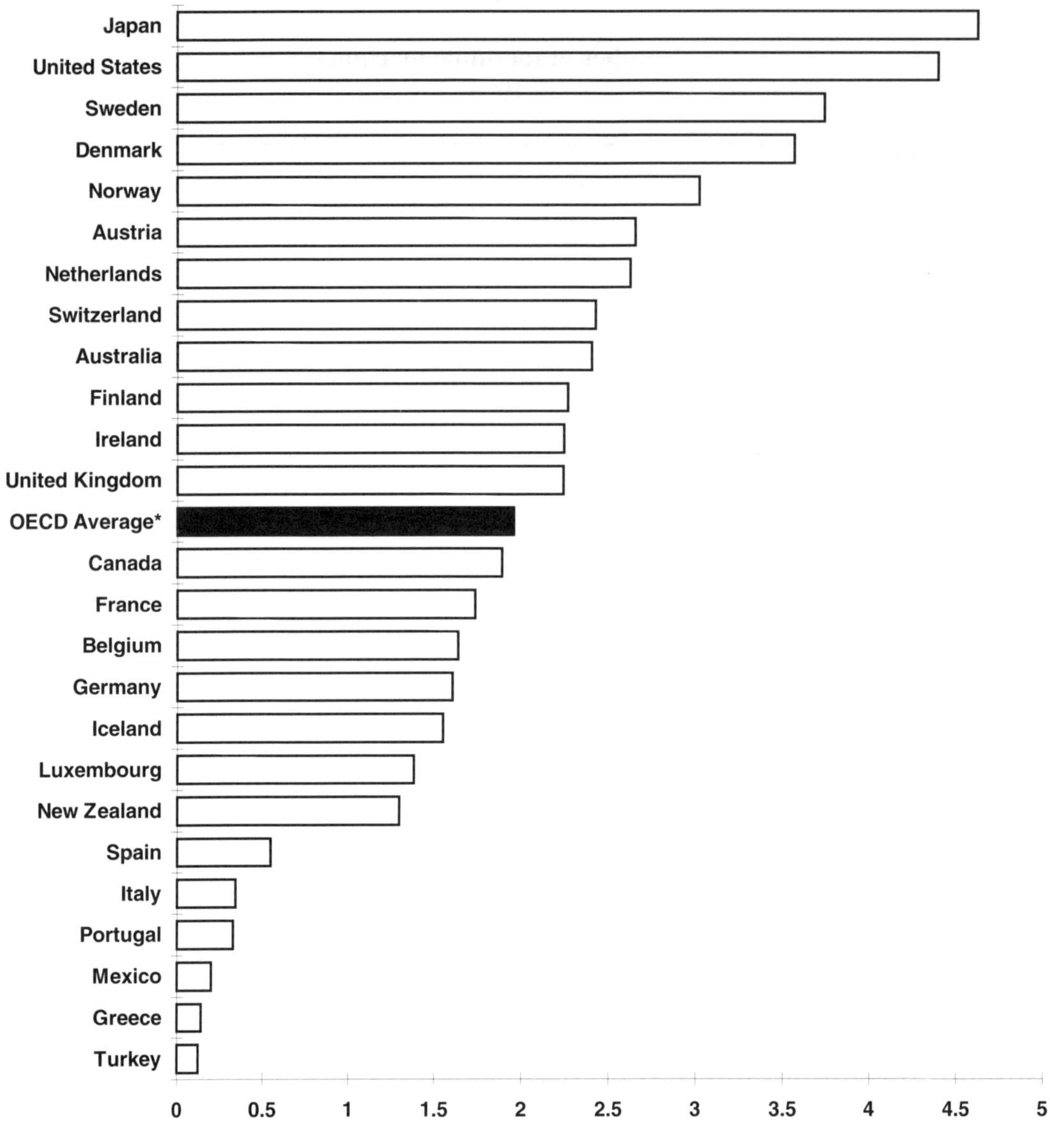

* Unweighted average of 25 countries: Australia, Austria, Belgium, Canada, Denmark, Finland, France, Germany, Greece, Iceland, Ireland, Italy, Japan, Luxembourg, Mexico, the Netherlands, New Zealand, Norway, Portugal, Spain, Sweden, Switzerland, Turkey, the United Kingdom and the United States.

(6) Basket of business telephone charges in January 1994 (local)

Comparisons are undertaken using a basket approach, rather than a methodology of direct comparison, to avoid, as far as possible, conditions specific to one country. Purchasing power parity exchange rates are used. Ten countries are used representative telecommunication operator's data, as follows: Australia (Telstra), Canada (Bell Canada), Denmark (KTAS), Finland (HTC), Japan (NTT), New Zealand (TCNZ), Portugal (TP/TLP), Sweden (Telia), the United Kingdom (BT), the United States (Nynex).

1994

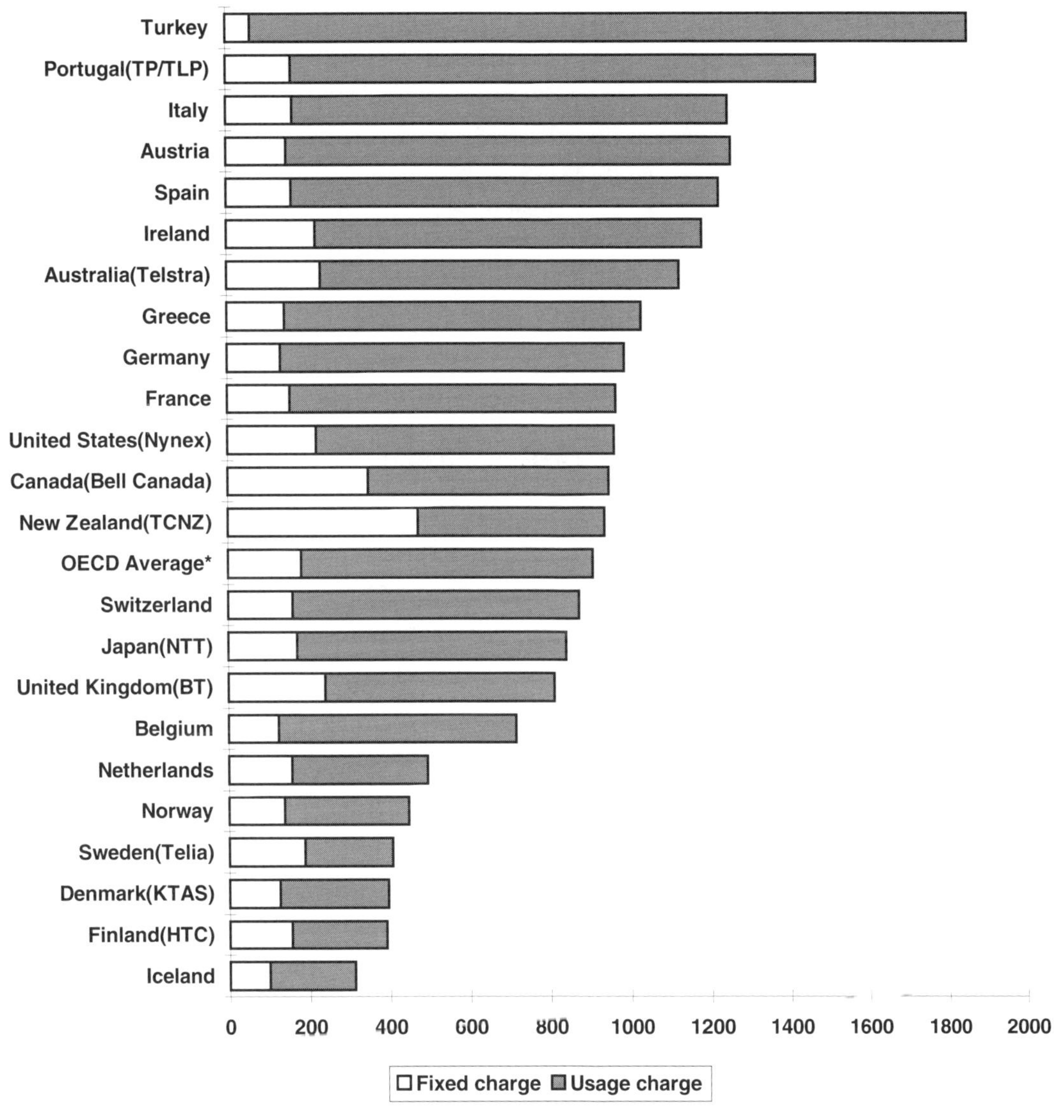

PPPs US$

* Average of 23 countries: Australia, Austria, Belgium, Canada, Denmark, Finland, France, Germany, Greece, Iceland, Ireland, Italy, Japan, the Netherlands, New Zealand, Norway, Portugal, Spain, Sweden, Switzerland, Turkey, the United Kingdom and the United States.

(7) Basket of business telephone charges in January 1994 (international)

Call pairs represent the relative cost to users of making international calls from one country to another. The advantage of this methodology is that it neutralises the geographical proximity of countries as a factor in the cost of a basket. The disadvantage of this methodology is that, because the methodology expresses relative relationships, some countries may have expensive or inexpensive international tariffs but this is not fully reflected in the outcome. This is because the call prices of corresponding countries may be higher or lower for that particular destination. Six countries are used for representative telecommunication operator's data, as follows: Australia (Telstra), Canada (Bell Canada), Japan (KDD), New Zealand (TCNZ), the United Kingdom (BT), the United States (AT&T).

Call pair methodology
1994

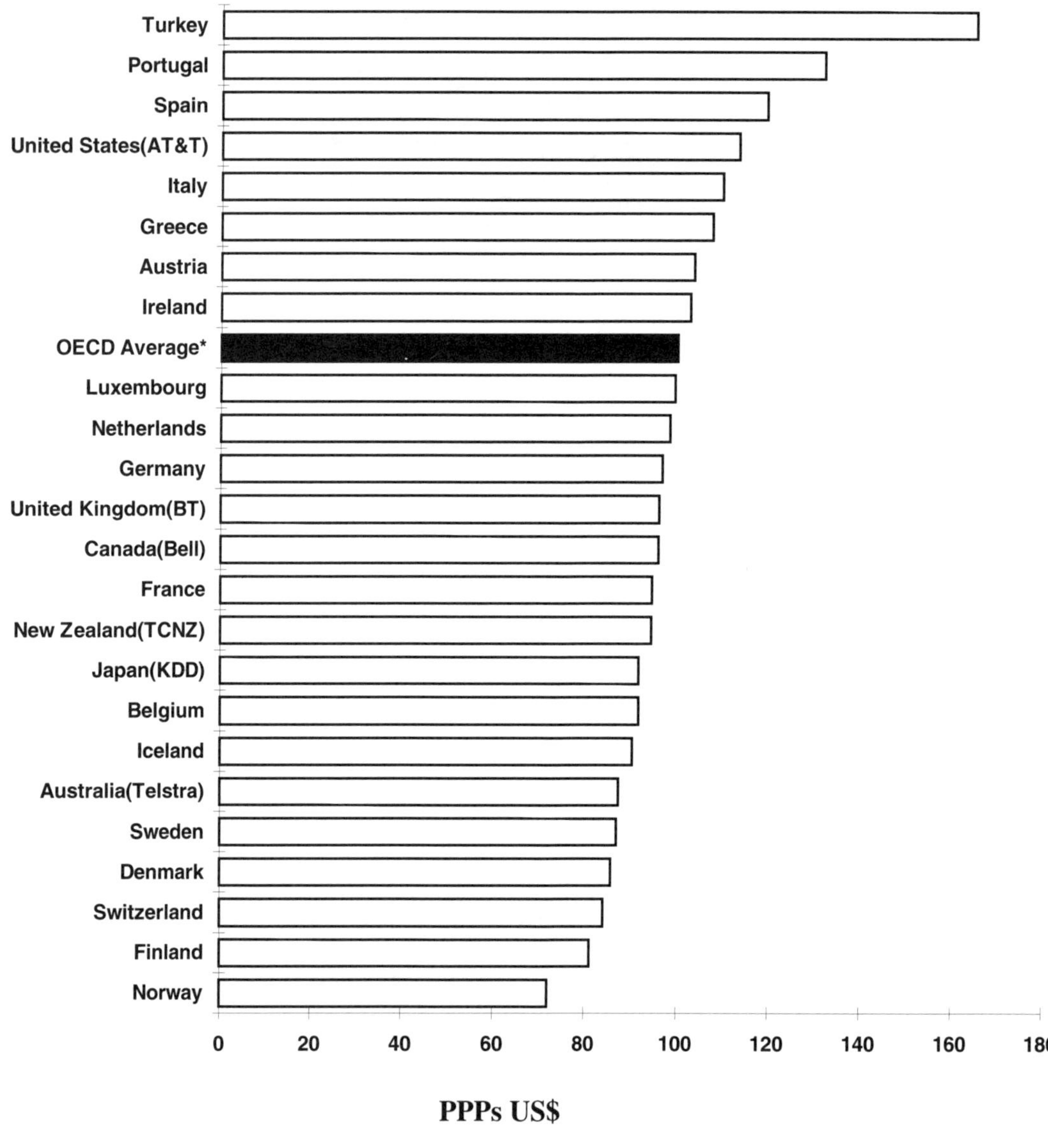

* Unweighted average of 24 countries: Australia, Austria, Belgium, Canada, Denmark, Finland, France, Germany, Greece, Iceland, Ireland, Italy, Japan, Luxembourg, the Netherlands, New Zealand, Norway, Portugal, Spain, Sweden, Switzerland, Turkey, the United Kingdom and the United States.

Zone distribution methodology

1994

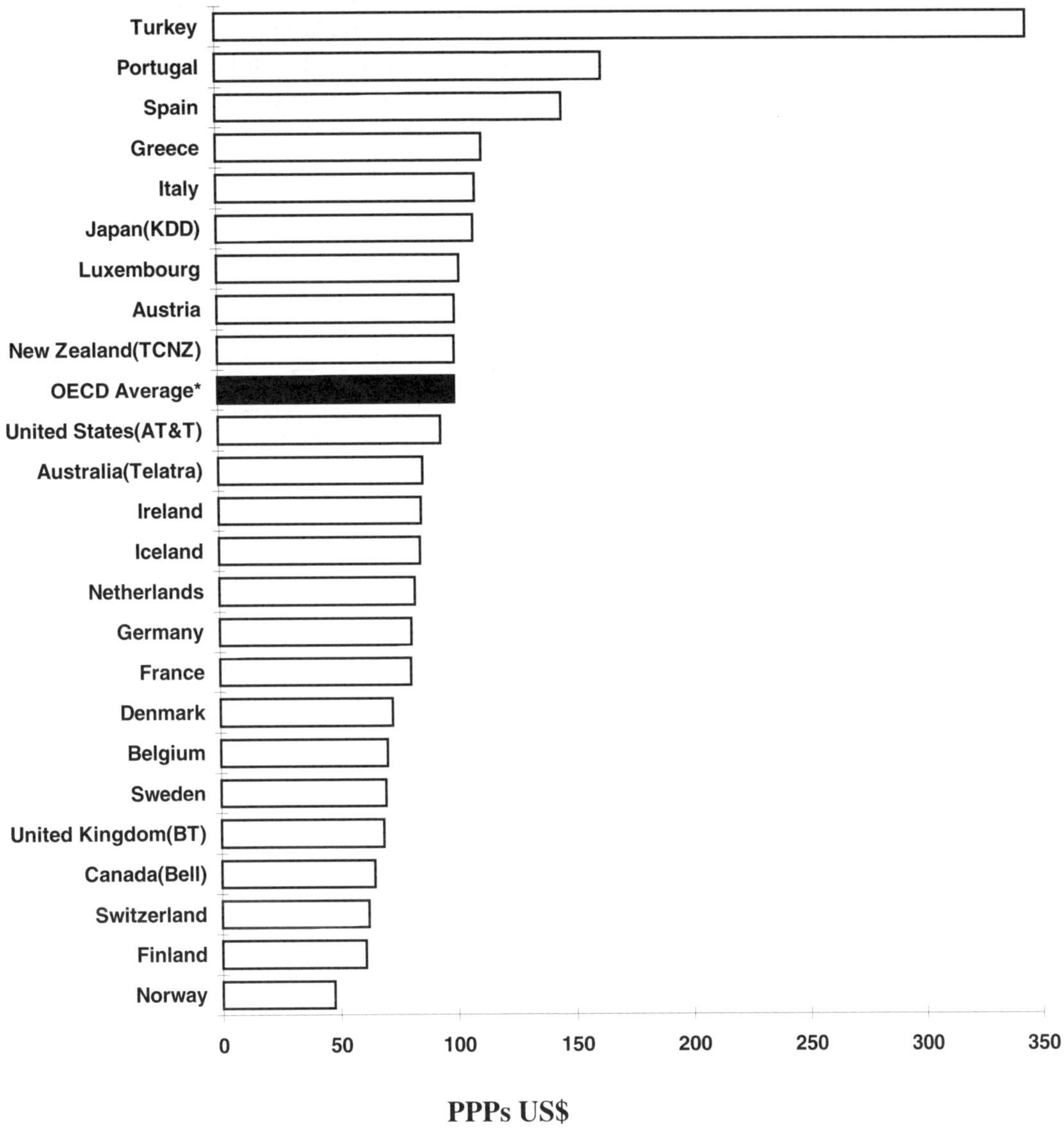

* Unweighted average of 24 countries: Australia, Austria, Belgium, Canada, Denmark, Finland, France, Germany, Greece, Iceland, Ireland, Italy, Japan, Luxembourg, the Netherlands, New Zealand, Norway, Portugal, Spain, Sweden, Switzerland, Turkey, the United Kingdom and the United States.

(8) Basket of mobile telecommunication tariffs in January 1994

Baskets of mobile telecommunication tariffs are collected from major operators in each OECD country and are compared. Eleven countries are used for representative telecommunication operator's data, as follows: Australia (Telstra), Canada (Bell Canada), Denmark (KTAS), Finland (HTC), Germany (DBP), Japan (NTT Mobile), New Zealand (TCNZ), Sweden (Telia), the United Kingdom (Cellnet), the United Kingdom (Vodafone), the United States (Nynex).

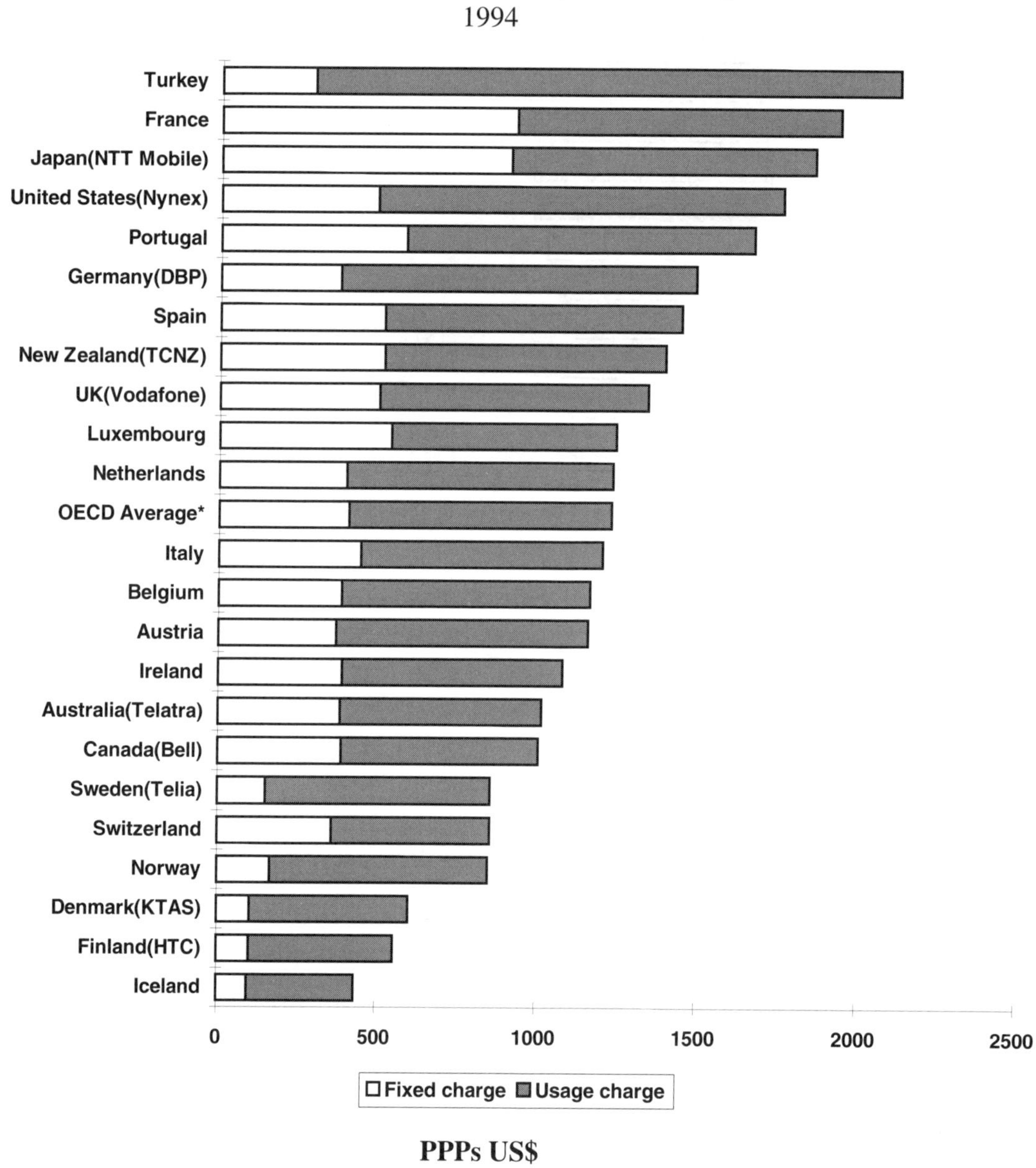

* Average of 23 countries: Australia, Austria, Belgium, Canada, Denmark, Finland, France, Germany, Iceland, Ireland, Italy, Japan, Luxembourg, the Netherlands, New Zealand, Norway, Portugal, Spain, Sweden, Switzerland, Turkey, the United Kingdom and the United States.

(9) Basket of leased line charges in January 1994

Leased lines, that offer "exclusive" two-way links, are particularly important in that they provide a platform to user companies in developing internal telecommunications services, and to third parties to offer a range of value-added services to customers. The table provides data for different speeds and distances. Ten countries are used for representative telecommunication operator's data, as follows: Australia (Telstra), Canada (Bell Canada), Denmark (KTAS), Finland (Telecom Fin.), Japan (NTT), New Zealand (TCNZ), Portugal (TP/TLP), Spain (Telefonica), the United Kingdom (BT), the United States (Nynex).

9.6 kbit/s
1994

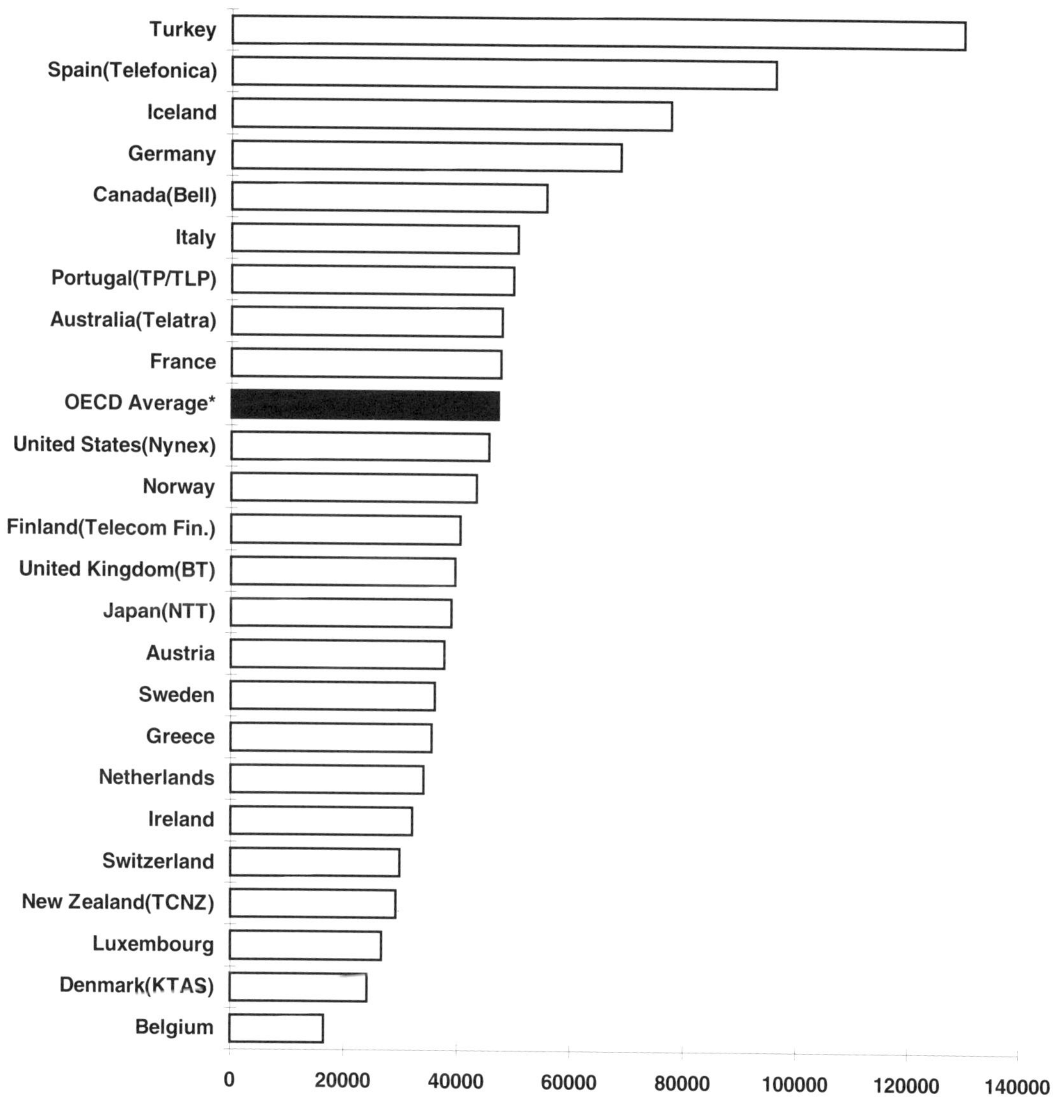

PPPs US$

* Unweighted average of 24 countries: Australia, Austria, Belgium, Canada, Denmark, Finland, France, Germany, Greece, Iceland, Ireland, Italy, Japan, Luxembourg, the Netherlands, New Zealand, Norway, Portugal, Spain, Sweden, Switzerland, Turkey, the United Kingdom and the United States.

64 kbit/s
1994

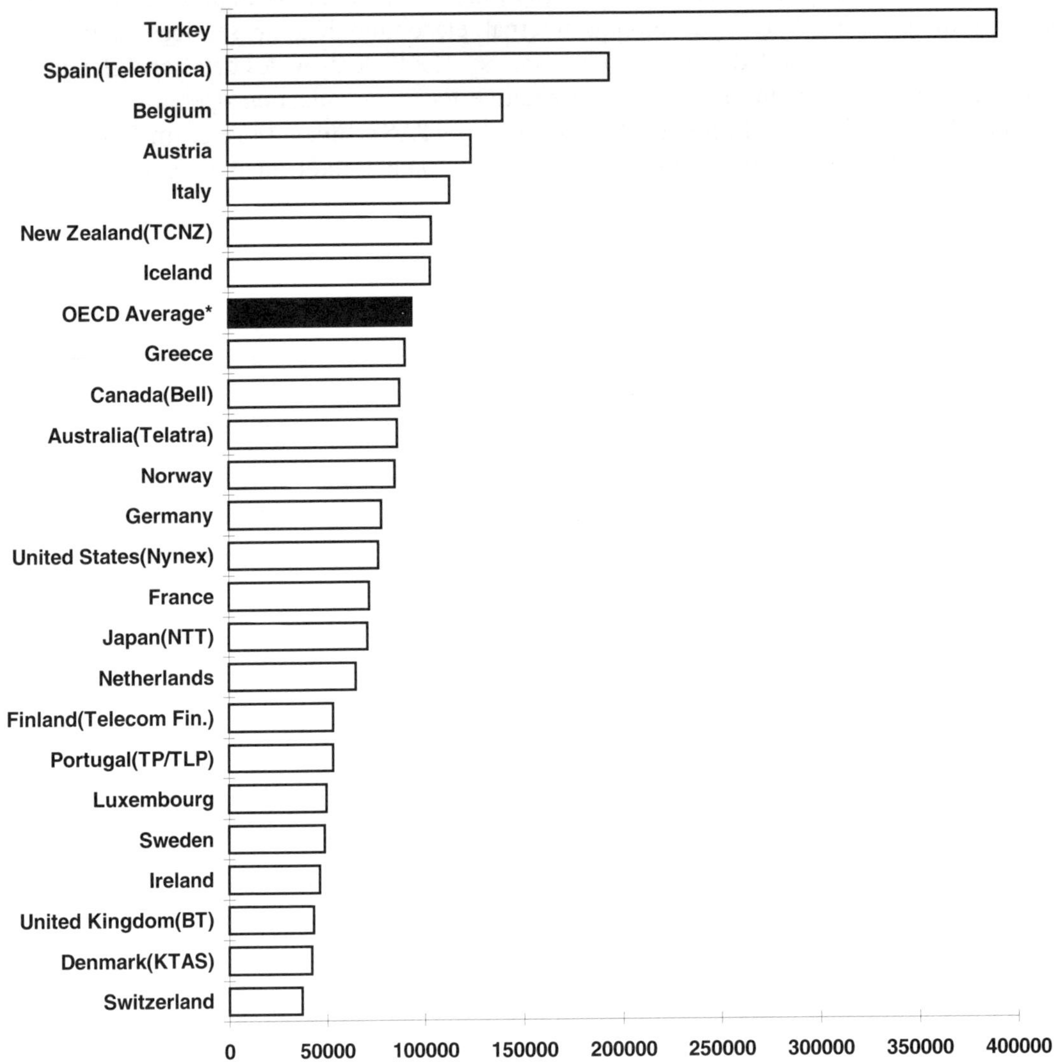

PPPs US$

* Unweighted average of 24 countries: Australia, Austria, Belgium, Canada, Denmark, Finland, France, Germany, Greece, Iceland, Ireland, Italy, Japan, Luxembourg, the Netherlands, New Zealand, Norway, Portugal, Spain, Sweden, Switzerland, Turkey, the United Kingdom and the United States.

1.5/2.0 Mbit/s
1994

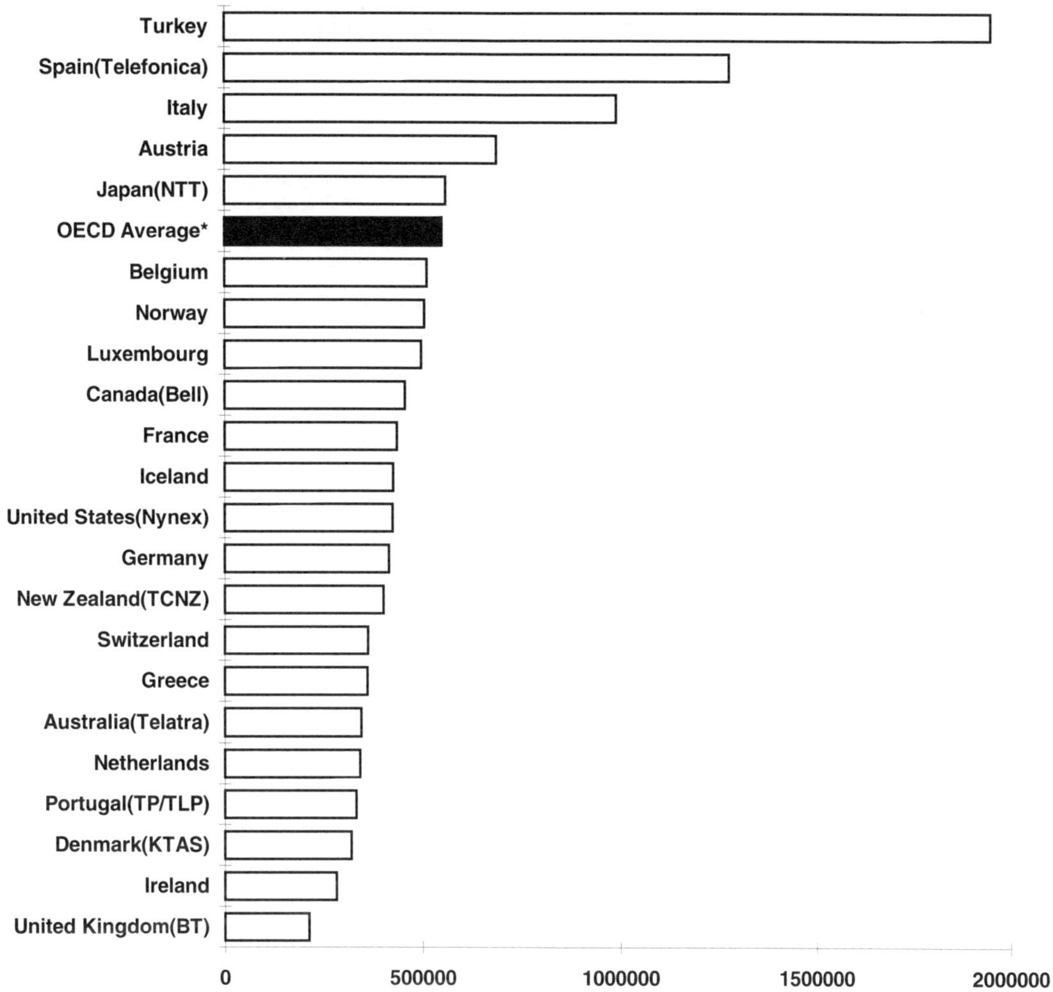

PPPs US$

* Unweighted average of 22 countries: Australia, Austria, Belgium, Canada, Denmark, France, Germany, Greece, Iceland, Ireland, Italy, Japan, Luxembourg, the Netherlands, New Zealand, Norway, Portugal, Spain, Switzerland, Turkey, the United Kingdom and the United States.

(10) Basket of packet switched data communication charges in January 1994

Packet-switched data communications is a technology on which today's computer communication networks are based and is suitable for PC communications, database search, home banking, etc.

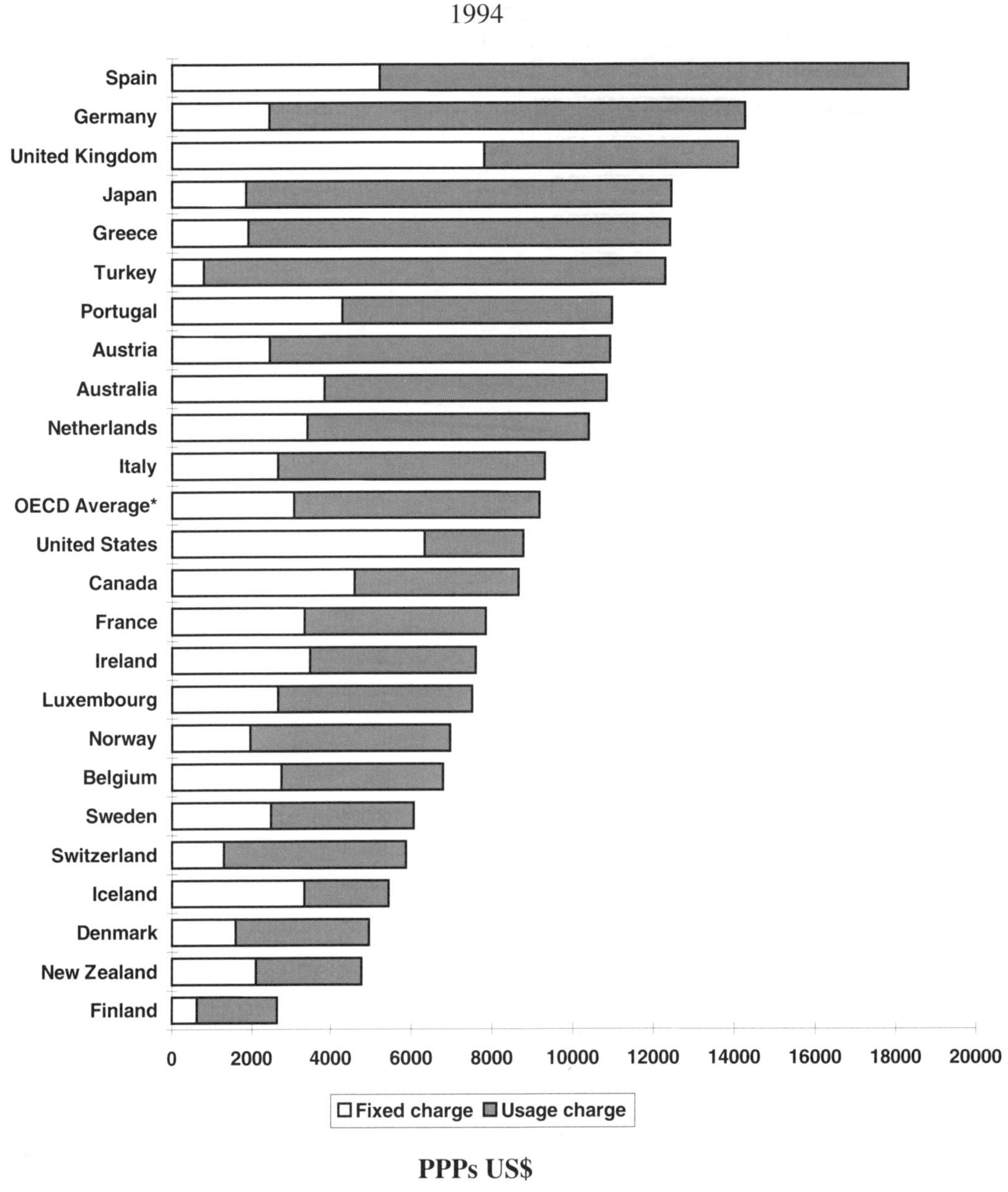

* Average of 24 countries: Australia, Austria, Belgium, Canada, Denmark, Finland, France, Germany, Greece, Iceland, Ireland, Italy, Japan, Luxembourg, the Netherlands, New Zealand, Norway, Portugal, Spain, Sweden, Switzerland, Turkey, the United Kingdom and the United States.

(11) Status of facilities competition in 1994

The data indicate the status of competition in each of the categories: PSTN, Data communication and leased lines, Mobile communication and Equipment. The following symbols are used in the table:

- CPE: Customer premise equipment (*e.g.* LAN, telephone set, etc.).
- Local: Local communication service.
- Trunk: Inter exchange communication service.
- Intl.: International communication service.
- X25: X25 Packet Switched networks. Allows remote devices to communicate with each other across high-speed digital links without the expense of individual leased lines.
- Lls: Leased lines.
- Anal.: Analog.
- Digl: Digital.

1994

	Equipment	**PSTN competition**			**Data comms. and leased lines**		**Mobile communication**		
	CPE	Local	Trunk	Intl.	X25	LLs	Anal.	Digl.	Paging
United States	FC	PC	FC	FC	FC	FC	RD	FC	FC
Japan	FC	FC	FC	FC	FC	FC	RD	FC	FC
Germany	FC	M	M	M	FC	M	M	D	1994
France	FC	M	M	M	1993	M	D	D	D
United Kingdom	FC	FC	FC	D	FC	FC	D	FC	FC
Italy	FC	M	M	M	1993	M	M	D(1994)	M
Canada	FC	M	C	M[1]	FC	FC	RD	D	FC
Australia	FC	D	D	D	D	D	D	FC	FC
Austria	FC	M	M	M	M	M	M	M	FC
Belgium	FC	M	M	M	1993	M	M	M	M
Denmark	FC	M	M	M	1993	M	D	FC	M
Finland	FC	FC	FC	FC	FC	FC	D	D	D
Greece	FC	M	M	M	1997	M	n.a.	D	M
Iceland	FC	M	M	M	M	M	M	M	M
Ireland	FC	M	M	M	1993	M	M	M	M
Luxembourg	FC	M	M	M	1993	M	M	M	M
Netherlands	FC	M	M	M	1993	M	M	D(1994)	1993
New Zealand	FC	FC	FC	FC	FC	FC	FC	FC	FC
Norway	FC	M	M	M	1993	M	M	D	1993
Portugal	FC	M[2]	M	M[2]	FC	M[2]	M	D	FC
Spain	FC	M	M	M	FC	M	M	M	FC
Sweden	FC	FC	FC	FC	FC	FC	FC	FC	FC
Switzerland	FC	M	M	M	M	M	M	M	FC
Turkey	FC	M	M	M	M	M	M	M	M

Note: FC: Full Competition; PC: Partial Competition; D: Duopoly; M: Monopoly; RD: Regional Duopoly;
B: Competition allowed at border of concessions.
199X: Competition expected to be introduced this year.

1. Intercontinental. Canada-US traffic, which constitutes 70% of Canada-originated international traffic is handled by Stentor regional telcos, Unitel and resellers on a competitive basis. International (non-Canada-US) facilities-based traffic is carried by Teleglobe; international resale has been allowed in Canada since 1991.
2. Exclusive rights of PTOs according to their respective concessions. For local regional service, Telecom Portugal and Telefones de Lisboa. For international, Telecom Portugal and Comphania Portuguesa Radio Marconi.

MAIN SALES OUTLETS OF OECD PUBLICATIONS
PRINCIPAUX POINTS DE VENTE DES PUBLICATIONS DE L'OCDE

AUSTRALIA – AUSTRALIE
D.A. Information Services
648 Whitehorse Road, P.O.B 163
Mitcham, Victoria 3132 Tel. (03) 9210.7777
Fax: (03) 9210.7788

AUSTRIA – AUTRICHE
Gerold & Co.
Graben 31
Wien I Tel. (0222) 533.50.14
Fax: (0222) 512.47.31.29

BELGIUM – BELGIQUE
Jean De Lannoy
Avenue du Roi, Koningslaan 202
B-1060 Bruxelles Tel. (02) 538.51.69/538.08.41
Fax: (02) 538.08.41

CANADA
Renouf Publishing Company Ltd.
5369 Canotek Road
Unit 1
Ottawa, Ont. K1J 9J3 Tel. (613) 745.2665
Fax: (613) 745.7660

Stores:
71 1/2 Sparks Street
Ottawa, Ont. K1P 5R1 Tel. (613) 238.8985
Fax: (613) 238.6041

12 Adelaide Street West
Toronto, QN M5H 1L6 Tel. (416) 363.3171
Fax: (416) 363.5963

Les Éditions La Liberté Inc.
3020 Chemin Sainte-Foy
Sainte-Foy, PQ G1X 3V6 Tel. (418) 658.3763
Fax: (418) 658.3763

Federal Publications Inc.
165 University Avenue, Suite 701
Toronto, ON M5H 3B8 Tel. (416) 860.1611
Fax: (416) 860.1608

Les Publications Fédérales
1185 Université
Montréal, QC H3B 3A7 Tel. (514) 954.1633
Fax: (514) 954.1635

CHINA – CHINE
Book Dept., China Natinal Publiations
Import and Export Corporation (CNPIEC)
16 Gongti E. Road, Chaoyang District
Beijing 100020 Tel. (10) 6506-6688 Ext. 8402
(10) 6506-3101

CHINESE TAIPEI – TAIPEI CHINOIS
Good Faith Worldwide Int'l. Co. Ltd.
9th Floor, No. 118, Sec. 2
Chung Hsiao E. Road
Taipei Tel. (02) 391.7396/391.7397
Fax: (02) 394.9176

CZECH REPUBLIC – RÉPUBLIQUE TCHÈQUE
National Information Centre
NIS – prodejna
Konviktská 5
Praha 1 113 57 Tel. (02) 24.23.09.07
Fax: (02) 24.22.94.33
E-mail: nkposp@dec.niz.cz
Internet: http://www.nis.cz

DENMARK – DANEMARK
Munksgaard Book and Subscription Service
35, Nørre Søgade, P.O. Box 2148
DK-1016 København K Tel. (33) 12.85.70
Fax: (33) 12.93.87

J. H. Schultz Information A/S,
Herstedvang 12,
DK – 2620 Albertslung Tel. 43 63 23 00
Fax: 43 63 19 69
Internet: s-info@inet.uni-c.dk

EGYPT – ÉGYPTE
The Middle East Observer
41 Sherif Street
Cairo Tel. (2) 392.6919
Fax: (2) 360.6804

FINLAND – FINLANDE
Akateeminen Kirjakauppa
Keskuskatu 1, P.O. Box 128
00100 Helsinki

Subscription Services/Agence d'abonnements :
P.O. Box 23
00100 Helsinki Tel. (358) 9.121.4403
Fax: (358) 9.121.4450

***FRANCE**
OECD/OCDE
Mail Orders/Commandes par correspondance :
2, rue André-Pascal
75775 Paris Cedex 16 Tel. 33 (0)1.45.24.82.00
Fax: 33 (0)1.49.10.42.76
Telex: 640048 OCDE
Internet: Compte.PUBSINQ@oecd.org

Orders via Minitel, France only/
Commandes par Minitel, France exclusivement :
36 15 OCDE

OECD Bookshop/Librairie de l'OCDE :
33, rue Octave-Feuillet
75016 Paris Tel. 33 (0)1.45.24.81.81
33 (0)1.45.24.81.67

Dawson
B.P. 40
91121 Palaiseau Cedex Tel. 01.89.10.47.00
Fax: 01.64.54.83.26

Documentation Française
29, quai Voltaire
75007 Paris Tel. 01.40.15.70.00

Economica
49, rue Héricart
75015 Paris Tel. 01.45.78.12.92
Fax: 01.45.75.05.67

Gibert Jeune (Droit-Économie)
6, place Saint-Michel
75006 Paris Tel. 01.43.25.91.19

Librairie du Commerce International
10, avenue d'Iéna
75016 Paris Tel. 01.40.73.34.60

Librairie Dunod
Université Paris-Dauphine
Place du Maréchal-de-Lattre-de-Tassigny
75016 Paris Tel. 01.44.05.40.13

Librairie Lavoisier
11, rue Lavoisier
75008 Paris Tel. 01.42.65.39.95

Librairie des Sciences Politiques
30, rue Saint-Guillaume
75007 Paris Tel. 01.45.48.36.02

P.U.F.
49, boulevard Saint-Michel
75005 Paris Tel. 01.43.25.83.40

Librairie de l'Université
12*a*, rue Nazareth
13100 Aix-en-Provence Tel. 04.42.26.18.08

Documentation Française
165, rue Garibaldi
69003 Lyon Tel. 04.78.63.32.23

Librairie Decitre
29, place Bellecour
69002 Lyon Tel. 04.72.40.54.54

Librairie Sauramps
Le Triangle
34967 Montpellier Cedex 2 Tel. 04.67.58.85.15
Fax: 04.67.58.27.36

A la Sorbonne Actual
23, rue de l'Hôtel-des-Postes
06000 Nice Tel. 04.93.13.77.75
Fax: 04.93.80.75.69

GERMANY – ALLEMAGNE
OECD Bonn Centre
August-Bebel-Allee 6
D-53175 Bonn Tel. (0228) 959.120
Fax: (0228) 959.12.17

GREECE – GRÈCE
Librairie Kauffmann
Stadiou 28
10564 Athens Tel. (01) 32.55.321
Fax: (01) 32.30.320

HONG-KONG
Swindon Book Co. Ltd.
Astoria Bldg. 3F
34 Ashley Road, Tsimshatsui
Kowloon, Hong Kong Tel. 2376.2062
Fax: 2376.0685

HUNGARY – HONGRIE
Euro Info Service
Margitsziget, Európa Ház
1138 Budapest Tel. (1) 111.60.61
Fax: (1) 302.50.35
E-mail: euroinfo@mail.matav.hu
Internet: http://www.euroinfo.hu//index.html

ICELAND – ISLANDE
Mál og Menning
Laugavegi 18, Pósthólf 392
121 Reykjavik Tel. (1) 552.4240
Fax: (1) 562.3523

INDIA – INDE
Oxford Book and Stationery Co.
Scindia House
New Delhi 110001 Tel. (11) 331.5896/5308
Fax: (11) 332.2639
E-mail: oxford.publ@axcess.net.in

17 Park Street
Calcutta 700016 Tel. 240832

INDONESIA – INDONÉSIE
Pdii-Lipi
P.O. Box 4298
Jakarta 12042 Tel. (21) 573.34.67
Fax: (21) 573.34.67

IRELAND – IRLANDE
Government Supplies Agency
Publications Section
4/5 Harcourt Road
Dublin 2 Tel. 661.31.11
Fax: 475.27.60

ISRAEL – ISRAËL
Praedicta
5 Shatner Street
P.O. Box 34030
Jerusalem 91430 Tel. (2) 652.84.90/1/2
Fax: (2) 652.84.93

R.O.Y. International
P.O. Box 13056
Tel Aviv 61130 Tel. (3) 546 1423
Fax: (3) 546 1442
E-mail: royil@netvision.net.il

Palestinian Authority/Middle East:
INDEX Information Services
P.O.B. 19502
Jerusalem Tel. (2) 627.16.34
Fax: (2) 627.12.19

ITALY – ITALIE
Libreria Commissionaria Sansoni
Via Duca di Calabria, 1/1
50125 Firenze Tel. (055) 64.54.15
Fax: (055) 64.12.57
E-mail: licosa@ftbcc.it

Via Bartolini 29
20155 Milano Tel. (02) 36.50.83

Editrice e Libreria Herder
Piazza Montecitorio 120
00186 Roma Tel. 679.46.28
Fax: 678.47.51

Libreria Hoepli
Via Hoepli 5
20121 Milano Tel. (02) 86.54.46
Fax: (02) 805.28.86

Libreria Scientifica
Dott. Lucio de Biasio 'Aeiou'
Via Coronelli, 6
20146 Milano Tel. (02) 48.95.45.52
Fax: (02) 48.95.45.48

JAPAN – JAPON
OECD Tokyo Centre
Landic Akasaka Building
2-3-4 Akasaka, Minato-ku
Tokyo 107 Tel. (81.3) 3586.2016
Fax: (81.3) 3584.7929

KOREA – CORÉE
Kyobo Book Centre Co. Ltd.
P.O. Box 1658, Kwang Hwa Moon
Seoul Tel. 730.78.91
Fax: 735.00.30

MALAYSIA – MALAISIE
University of Malaya Bookshop
University of Malaya
P.O. Box 1127, Jalan Pantai Baru
59700 Kuala Lumpur
Malaysia Tel. 756.5000/756.5425
Fax: 756.3246

MEXICO – MEXIQUE
OECD Mexico Centre
Edificio INFOTEC
Av. San Fernando no. 37
Col. Toriello Guerra
Tlalpan C.P. 14050
Mexico D.F. Tel. (525) 528.10.38
Fax: (525) 606.13.07
E-mail: ocde@rtn.net.mx

NETHERLANDS – PAYS-BAS
SDU Uitgeverij Plantijnstraat
Externe Fondsen
Postbus 20014
2500 EA's-Gravenhage Tel. (070) 37.89.880
Voor bestellingen: Fax: (070) 34.75.778

Subscription Agency/ Agence d'abonnements :
SWETS & ZEITLINGER BV
Heereweg 347B
P.O. Box 830
2160 SZ Lisse Tel. 252.435.111
Fax: 252.415.888

NEW ZEALAND – NOUVELLE-ZÉLANDE
GPLegislation Services
P.O. Box 12418
Thorndon, Wellington Tel. (04) 496.5655
Fax: (04) 496.5698

NORWAY – NORVÈGE
NIC INFO A/S
Ostensjoveien 18
P.O. Box 6512 Etterstad
0606 Oslo Tel. (22) 97.45.00
Fax: (22) 97.45.45

PAKISTAN
Mirza Book Agency
65 Shahrah Quaid-E-Azam
Lahore 54000 Tel. (42) 735.36.01
Fax: (42) 576.37.14

PHILIPPINE – PHILIPPINES
International Booksource Center Inc.
Rm 179/920 Cityland 10 Condo Tower 2
HV dela Costa Ext cor Valero St.
Makati Metro Manila Tel. (632) 817 9676
Fax: (632) 817 1741

POLAND – POLOGNE
Ars Polona
00-950 Warszawa
Krakowskie Prezdmiescie 7 Tel. (22) 264760
Fax: (22) 265334

PORTUGAL
Livraria Portugal
Rua do Carmo 70-74
Apart. 2681
1200 Lisboa Tel. (01) 347.49.82/5
Fax: (01) 347.02.64

SINGAPORE – SINGAPOUR
Ashgate Publishing
Asia Pacific Pte. Ltd
Golden Wheel Building, 04-03
41, Kallang Pudding Road
Singapore 349316 Tel. 741.5166
Fax: 742.9356

SPAIN – ESPAGNE
Mundi-Prensa Libros S.A.
Castelló 37, Apartado 1223
Madrid 28001 Tel. (91) 431.33.99
Fax: (91) 575.39.98
E-mail: mundiprensa@tsai.es
Internet: http://www.mundiprensa.es

Mundi-Prensa Barcelona
Consell de Cent No. 391
08009 – Barcelona Tel. (93) 488.34.92
Fax: (93) 487.76.59

Libreria de la Generalitat
Palau Moja
Rambla dels Estudis, 118
08002 – Barcelona
(Suscripciones) Tel. (93) 318.80.12
(Publicaciones) Tel. (93) 302.67.23
Fax: (93) 412.18.54

SRI LANKA
Centre for Policy Research
c/o Colombo Agencies Ltd.
No. 300-304, Galle Road
Colombo 3 Tel. (1) 574240, 573551-2
Fax: (1) 575394, 510711

SWEDEN – SUÈDE
CE Fritzes AB
S–106 47 Stockholm Tel. (08) 690.90.90
Fax: (08) 20.50.21

For electronic publications only/
Publications électroniques seulement
STATISTICS SWEDEN
Informationsservice
S-115 81 Stockholm Tel. 8 783 5066
Fax: 8 783 4045

Subscription Agency/Agence d'abonnements :
Wennergren-Williams Info AB
P.O. Box 1305
171 25 Solna Tel. (08) 705.97.50
Fax: (08) 27.00.71

Liber distribution
Internatinal organizations
Fagerstagatan 21
S-163 52 Spanga

SWITZERLAND – SUISSE
Maditec S.A. (Books and Periodicals/Livres et périodiques)
Chemin des Palettes 4
Case postale 266
1020 Renens VD 1 Tel. (021) 635.08.65
Fax: (021) 635.07.80

Librairie Payot S.A.
4, place Pépinet
CP 3212
1002 Lausanne Tel. (021) 320.25.11
Fax: (021) 320.25.14

Librairie Unilivres
6, rue de Candolle
1205 Genève Tel. (022) 320.26.23
Fax: (022) 329.73.18

Subscription Agency/Agence d'abonnements :
Dynapresse Marketing S.A.
38, avenue Vibert
1227 Carouge Tel. (022) 308.08.70
Fax: (022) 308.07.99

See also – Voir aussi :
OECD Bonn Centre
August-Bebel-Allee 6
D-53175 Bonn (Germany) Tel. (0228) 959.120
Fax: (0228) 959.12.17

THAILAND – THAÏLANDE
Suksit Siam Co. Ltd.
113, 115 Fuang Nakhon Rd.
Opp. Wat Rajbopith
Bangkok 10200 Tel. (662) 225.9531/2
Fax: (662) 222.5188

TRINIDAD & TOBAGO, CARIBBEAN TRINITÉ-ET-TOBAGO, CARAÏBES
Systematics Studies Limited
9 Watts Street
Curepe
Trinadad & Tobago, W.I. Tel. (1809) 645.3475
Fax: (1809) 662.5654
E-mail: tobe@trinidad.net

TUNISIA – TUNISIE
Grande Librairie Spécialisée
Fendri Ali
Avenue Haffouz Imm El-Intilaka
Bloc B 1 Sfax 3000 Tel. (216-4) 296 855
Fax: (216-4) 298.270

TURKEY – TURQUIE
Kültür Yayinlari Is-Türk Ltd.
Atatürk Bulvari No. 191/Kat 13
06684 Kavaklidere/Ankara
Tel. (312) 428.11.40 Ext. 2458
Fax : (312) 417.24.90

Dolmabahce Cad. No. 29
Besiktas/Istanbul Tel. (212) 260 7188

UNITED KINGDOM – ROYAUME-UNI
The Stationery Office Ltd.
Postal orders only:
P.O. Box 276, London SW8 5DT
Gen. enquiries Tel. (171) 873 0011
Fax: (171) 873 8463

The Stationery Office Ltd.
Postal orders only:
49 High Holborn, London WC1V 6HB

Branches at: Belfast, Birmingham, Bristol, Edinburgh, Manchester

UNITED STATES – ÉTATS-UNIS
OECD Washington Center
2001 L Street N.W., Suite 650
Washington, D.C. 20036-4922 Tel. (202) 785.6323
Fax: (202) 785.0350
Internet: washcont@oecd.org

Subscriptions to OECD periodicals may also be placed through main subscription agencies.

Les abonnements aux publications périodiques de l'OCDE peuvent être souscrits auprès des principales agences d'abonnement.

Orders and inquiries from countries where Distributors have not yet been appointed should be sent to: OECD Publications, 2, rue André-Pascal, 75775 Paris Cedex 16, France.

Les commandes provenant de pays où l'OCDE n'a pas encore désigné de distributeur peuvent être adressées aux Éditions de l'OCDE, 2, rue André-Pascal, 75775 Paris Cedex 16, France.

12-1996

OECD PUBLICATIONS, 2, rue André-Pascal, 75775 PARIS CEDEX 16
PRINTED IN FRANCE
(70 96 08 1) ISBN 92-64-15344-6 – No. 49133 1997